THE COMPLETE
Ultimate
Spanish

Ronni L. Gordon, PhD
and David M. Stillman, PhD

New York Chicago San Francisco Athens London Madrid
Mexico City Milan New Delhi Singapore Sydney Toronto

1 2 3 4 5 6 7 8 9   LWI   26 25 24 23 22 21

ISBN   978-1-264-25910-6
MHID   1-264-25910-7

e-ISBN   978-1-264-25911-3
e-MHID   1-264-25911-5

McGraw Hill books are available at special quantity discounts to use as premiums and sales promotions, or for use in corporate training programs. To contact a representative, please visit the Contact Us page at www.mhprofessional.com.

McGraw Hill Language Lab App

Audio recordings, review exercises, and flashcards that supplement this book can be found in the McGraw Hill Language Lab app. Go to mhlanguagelab.com to access the online version of this application, or download the free mobile version from the Apple App store (for iPhone and iPad), or the Google Play store (for Android devices). Note: Internet connection required for audio content.

By the same authors

The Ultimate Spanish 101
The Ultimate Spanish Review and Practice, Fourth Edition
The Ultimate Spanish Verb Review and Practice, Second Edition
The Big Red Book of Spanish Verbs, Second Edition
The Red Pocket Book of Spanish Verbs
Spanish Vocabulary Drills

The Ultimate French Review and Practice, Fourth Edition
The Ultimate French Verb Review and Practice, Second Edition
The Big Blue Book of French Verbs, Second Edition
The Blue Pocket Book of French Verbs
French Vocabulary Drills

Note

The first part of this book was published in *The Ultimate Spanish 101,* McGraw Hill. The preliminary chapter, "Pronunciation and Spelling," first appeared in *Comunicando: A First Course in Spanish,* Second Edition, D.C. Heath and Company. Both titles are by Ronni L. Gordon, PhD and David M. Stillman, PhD.

For Alex and Mimi, our wondrous children,
whose brilliance, talents, and love
illuminate and inspire every word we write

RLG and DMS

Preface

Almost seventy years later, I remember clearly how the magic of translating the words in books into images enriched my life, breaking the barriers of time and space.
  —Mario Vargas Llosa, 2010 Nobel Prize in Literature

Knowledge of languages is the doorway to wisdom.
  —Roger Bacon

The Complete Ultimate Spanish is a uniquely comprehensive, user-friendly, and engaging first- and second-year program designed for beginning through advanced learners of Spanish who want to develop the proficiency to communicate effectively with native speakers of Spanish on a wide variety of topics. Learners using the program will master the fundamental structures of Spanish sentences and acquire a broad, authentic, and current vocabulary. Complete with textbook and app, the program provides abundant practice in all language skills—listening, speaking, reading, and writing.

The Complete Ultimate Spanish includes the very successful *The Ultimate Spanish 101* and continues its signature conceptual features of varied practice and modularity in *The Ultimate Spanish 201*. *The Ultimate Spanish 201*, the second-year course, presents Spanish compound and complex sentences, thereby preparing you to use the language for personal and professional purposes. The more than 200 *Diálogos* and more than 400 oral and written exercises in *The Complete Ultimate Spanish* reflect authentic language usage and touch on all areas of modern life. A wealth of practice exercises will enable you to read all types of Spanish prose and write short pieces on familiar topics.

"How do you get to Carnegie Hall? Practice, practice, practice!" How do you get to fluency in Spanish? Practice, practice, practice! *The Complete Ultimate Spanish* audio component on the Language Lab app includes more than 200 *Diálogos* and their *Variantes*, all recorded by native speakers of Spanish, with pauses for repetition. *The Ultimate Spanish 101* chapters also contain an audio component for the *Prácticas* (oral exercises), as well as flashcards for building vocabulary. The modular organization enables you to adapt your practice time to your schedule, making it ideal for people working on their own. *The Complete Ultimate Spanish* is also an excellent ancillary for students using a textbook in a classroom setting. The easy-to-use, innovative Language Lab app makes it possible for you to progress at your own pace using a computer, tablet, or cell phone.

Structure and Components of *The Complete Ultimate Spanish*

The Complete Ultimate Spanish includes a preliminary chapter, **Pronunciation and Spelling**, that describes the sounds of Spanish. Using the app, you will be able to listen to and repeat, in the pauses provided, the sounds of Spanish. Mastering the sound system of Spanish will enable you to pronounce and understand better, an achievement that will result in enhanced communication skills.

The Complete Ultimate Spanish is comprised of 21 chapters, all but the final one structured in the same way. Chapters 1 through 20 open with **Communication Goals**, a statement of the chapter's objectives for learner achievement, and **Grammar Topics**, an outline of grammar points to be presented and practiced.

The **Diálogo** is the nucleus of Chapters 1 through 20. Each chapter has a series of *Diálogos* that present grammatical structures and vocabulary targeted in the chapter. These *Diálogos*, some appearing in two parts, present engaging conversations on a variety of topics. Some topics presented in *The Ultimate Spanish 101* are revisited in *The Ultimate Spanish 201* with greater depth and sophistication. For example, on the subject of health, Chapter 11 deals with a medical check-up and a pediatrician treating a child's earache, while Chapter 18 treats the pros and cons of vaccination and life in the time of Covid-19. Environmental pollution is dealt with as a cause for itchy eyes in Chapter 12; in Chapter 20, it is responsible for the erosion of the granite stones in the Roman aqueduct of Segovia (Spain). Each *Diálogo* has an audio icon, indicating that it is available for listening on the app. You will study the *Diálogo*, listen to the recording, and repeat each speech after the speaker. Listening to and repeating the *Diálogo* should be rehearsed until you are satisfied with your progress; memorization of the *Diálogo* is beneficial.

The **Análisis** section, immediately following the *Diálogo*, provides a linguistic breakdown, that is, an analysis of the sentence structures and vocabulary presented in the *Diálogo*. Each element is presented with a translation in English.

The **Variantes** section following the *Análisis* expands on the grammatical structures presented in the *Diálogo* and presents new structures and vocabulary based on the Spanish language material of the *Diálogo*. Each *Variantes* section has an audio icon, indicating that the material is also available on the app.

The Complete Ultimate Spanish presents all Spanish tenses and all the necessary grammatical structures of Spanish for optimum use of the language. The **Estructura y Práctica** section presents clear, concise explanations of the grammatical topics deriving from the *Diálogo*, followed by exercises for practice. The grammatical explanations are based on a contrastive approach, comparing Spanish to English usage. In the *Práctica* that follows each grammatical point, structural, writing, translation, and free expression exercises, some contextual or thematic, reinforce the grammar and review the vocabulary presented in the lesson.

Un paso más *(A Step Further)*, the culminating section of each chapter, encourages you to use what you have learned through activities designed to enhance your knowledge of the Spanish language and the Spanish-speaking world. You are encouraged to express yourself freely in Spanish by answering *Preguntas personales* (personal questions) and writing compositions on topics related to the content of each chapter—all in Spanish. For example, you will write about family relationships, the university and freedom of speech, teleworking, shopping online, the pyramids of Mexico, a political demonstration, outer space, the aqueduct of Segovia, charter schools, a sweet fifteen party (*una quinceañera*), and effects of the Covid-19 pandemic; you will also read quotations by eminent men and women from all walks of life, translate them from Spanish to English, and explain their meaning in Spanish.

Language boxes, placed judiciously throughout the chapters, include current idiomatic usage that will increase your mastery of authentic Spanish exponentially.

Chapter 21, **Building Spanish Vocabulary**, is the culminating chapter of *The Complete Ultimate Spanish*. It deals with **Word Formation**, and ends with *"La higuera"* ("The Fig Tree"), a beautiful and inspiring poem by Juana de Ibarbourou, one of the most important and innovative women poets of Uruguayan and Spanish American literature of the 20th century. You will be guided in your reading of this poem in Spanish by a vocabulary list, a translation in English, and a series of *Preguntas* that will help you analyze the poem to find its meaning. You will also be able to listen to a recitation of the poem on the app.

The Complete Ultimate Spanish provides **Verb Charts** you can consult when in doubt about a verb form or tense; an **Answer Key** so that you can check your answers to the exercises; and a **Glossary** of the words and expressions used throughout the book, each entry indicating in which chapter it appears for the first time.

The Complete Ultimate Spanish is a powerful tool that will lead you to mastery of the Spanish language, empowering you to communicate with accuracy, confidence, and enjoyment. As language is the verbal expression of culture, you will, at the same time, increase your understanding and appreciation of the culture of Spanish-speaking peoples.

We wish to thank the following people for their part in bringing this book to fruition.

Christopher Brown, our peerless publisher at McGraw-Hill, esteemed colleague, and dear friend—our heartfelt gratitude for his complete ultimate vision, wisdom, and guidance through our latest (and longest) publication.

Terry Yokota and **Daniel Franklin**, principals of Village Bookworks—our deepest appreciation for their impressive expertise, knowledge, and consistently valuable assistance in all aspects of the production of this book.

Ignacio Martínez, Presidente del Consejo de Derechos de Autor, Ministerio de Educación y Cultura, Biblioteca Nacional de Uruguay—nuestro más sincero agradecimiento por el apoyo que nos brindó en facilitar el permiso de publicar "La higuera" de Juana de Ibarbourou en *The Complete Ultimate Spanish*.

Ronni L. Gordon, PhD
David M. Stillman, PhD

About the Authors

Ronni L. Gordon, PhD, is a prominent author of foreign language textbooks and materials for multimedia, including more than 30 titles in Spanish and other languages. She has taught and coordinated Spanish language programs and taught Spanish American literature at Harvard University, Boston University, Cornell University, and Drexel University. A foreign language consultant, she has read for the National Endowment for the Humanities, presented at the United States Department of Education, and consulted on states' K–12 academic standards for world languages. She has presented at conferences on foreign language pedagogy and Spanish American literature as one of the first scholars to give a college course on Spanish American women writers.

David M. Stillman, PhD, is a well-known author of foreign language textbooks and materials for multimedia, with a bibliography that includes titles in four languages. He taught languages and linguistics at The College of New Jersey, where he also coordinated an innovative program of student-led oral proficiency classes. He has taught and coordinated foreign language programs at Boston University, Harvard University, and Cornell University. He has consulted on states' K–12 academic standards for world languages and presented at national and regional conventions of language educators, being appointed to national committees devoted to the improvement of teacher training.

Contents

THE ULTIMATE SPANISH 101

THE ULTIMATE SPANISH 201

The
Ultimate Spanish
101

Pronunciation and Spelling

PRONUNCIATION

Learning to speak a foreign language requires changing many of the pronunciation habits formed in learning your own language. Because these habits are so ingrained, acquiring acceptable pronunciation of a foreign language requires not only intensive practice, but also analysis of the individual sounds—how they are produced and how they compare to those of your own language. This introduction serves to aid your perception and production of the sounds of Spanish. The use of technical terms has been limited to allow you to concentrate on producing the sounds accurately.

To present Spanish sounds and their representation in Spanish spelling, certain symbols are used: Basic sounds of the language are written between slashes; variants of a sound in certain positions are written between square brackets; and letters used in spelling are in bold. Note that the symbol chosen to transcribe a sound may or may not be the letter that represents it in the Spanish spelling system.

This initial presentation will limit itself to "Standard Spanish" as spoken in Hispanic America, a set of pronunciation features devoid of regional peculiarities. Important dialect variations will be mentioned in individual chapters.

Vowels

Spanish has five vowel sounds, represented by the letters **a, e, i, o, u**. Listen to the speaker pronounce the following syllables. Notice that the Spanish vowels are shorter and tenser than their stressed counterparts in English.

ba	ka	fa	sa	ma
be	ke	fe	se	me
bi	ki	fi	si	mi
bo	ko	fo	so	mo
bu	ku	fu	su	mu

Now repeat each of the above syllables after the speaker. If you compare English *see* and Spanish **si** you will observe that the vowel sound in *see* really consists of two vowels pronounced as one syllable—the vowel of *sit* plus a glide similar to the *y* in *you*: /iy/. Diphthong is the technical term for two vowels pronounced together as a single syllable. The English vowels of the words *bay, bow, boo* are also diphthongs: /ey/, /ow/, /uw/, respectively. The similarity between Spanish and English diphthongs is limited, however. Diphthongs are far less frequent in Spanish than in English, where they are the norm in stressed syllables.

Repeat the following words and syllables after the speaker, taking care to produce a short, tense vowel and not a diphthong.

i si mi li pi bi bis mis fin sin
e se me le be pe fe mes les bes pes fes
o lo so fo mo los sos bos pos kos fos pon kon son
u bu ku tu lu nu mu su mus tus sus pus bun mun

English speakers should avoid pronouncing the letter **a** in Spanish like the English sound represented by the letter *a* in *class, cab, bag.*

a la pa ma sa ba ga bas las pas sas

In English, most unstressed vowels are reduced to a neutral vowel called "schwa" that is transcribed as /ə/. This is not reflected in English spelling, and many pairs of words that are pronounced alike, such as *affect/effect* and *accept/except*, are spelled differently. Any of the five written vowels may represent /ə/ in an unstressed syllable in English spelling. For example, the vowel of the first syllable of each of the following words is pronounced /ə/:

machine semantic mirage corrode supply

In Spanish, the sound /ə/ does not exist. All unstressed syllables have one of the five vowels **a, e, i, o, u**. Differences in unstressed vowels in Spanish not only distinguish countless pairs of words, but also signal some of the most fundamental grammatical functions of the language.

Correlated with the reduction of unstressed vowels to /ə/ in English is the shortening of unstressed syllables. In other words, stressed syllables in English take longer to say than unstressed syllables. In Spanish, however, stressed and unstressed syllables are the same length.

The following Spanish two-syllable words are all stressed on the first syllable. They have the vowel /a/ in both syllables. Repeat each one after the speaker, making sure to pronounce /a/ the same way in both syllables and to make the two syllables of equal length.

mala sala saca sana fama mapa matas
latas lana vana chata sacan sanan laman

The following Spanish two-syllable words have /e/ in both syllables and are stressed on the first syllable. To pronounce them correctly, concentrate on the following points:

1 · Avoid the diphthong /ey/, as in English *pay.*

2 · Pronounce the /e/ the same way in both syllables.

3 · Make the two syllables of equal length.

Repeat the following words after the speaker:

nene mece queme pele seque cheque
meten temen quemen peles seques meces

The following Spanish two-syllable words have /o/ in both syllables and are stressed on the first syllable. To pronounce them correctly, concentrate on the following points:

1 · Avoid the diphthong /ow/, as in English *toe*.

2 · Pronounce the /o/ the same way in both syllables.

3 · Make the two syllables of equal length.

Repeat the following words after the speaker:

> como loco polo foso coso soso
> cocos pocos somos lomos monos bonos

The following words are three syllables long, and they are all stressed on the middle syllable. Each word has the same vowel in all three syllables. Repeat each word after the speaker, concentrating on pronouncing the vowels of all three syllables in the same way and making all syllables of equal length.

/a/	batata macana canasta hamaca alpaca
/e/	demente pelele clemente deseque deseche
/o/	mocoso doloso conozco goloso coloco

The following pairs of words are distinguished solely by differences in the unstressed vowels. Repeat each pair of words after the speaker:

a / o	e / i	i / o
coma / como	pesó / pisó	mirar / morar
meta / meto	case / casi	pisando / posando
famosas / famosos	teces / tesis	misión / moción
calor / color	delatan / dilatan	timaron / tomaron
molina / molino	cemento / cimento	trincar / troncar

a / e	e / u
toma / tome	lechón / luchón
caminas / camines	regir / rugir
alemanas / alemanes	pechito / puchito
patinan / patinen	besito / busito
señoras / señores	hendir / hundir

e / o	o / u
pesó / posó	dorado / durado
velaron / volaron	fondita / fundita
tomes / tomos	goloso / guloso
quesito / cosito	mostela / mustela
velita / bolita	osamos / usamos

Consonants

b/v, d, g   The Spanish letters **b** and **v** (which represent the same sound in Spanish), **d**, and **g** have more than one sound, depending on the letter's position in a word or sentence. After a pause and after **m** or **n**, Spanish **b/v**, **d**, and **g** represent sounds similar to those corresponding to English *b, d,* and *g* in *boy, does,* and *go.* Spanish /d/ is produced with the tip of the tongue touching the back of the upper front teeth rather than the gum ridge above them as in English. Spanish /g/ is spelled **gu** before **e** and **i**.

Repeat the following words after the speaker:

> base donde goza vaso conde goma betún
> dote hongo bomba dime tango invita demás
> gasto bote anda gala voy lindo gusano
> ambos dones ganga envase doy manga vino

These versions of Spanish /b/, /d/, and /g/ are called the hard variants of the sounds; they are transcribed in square brackets as [b], [d], and [g].

In all other positions, **b/v, d,** and **g** represent the soft variants of [b], [d], and [g], transcribed as [ƀ], [đ], and [ǥ].

[ƀ] is produced by forcing air through slightly parted lips, drawn back and not puckered.

> coba cavamos tubo sabes lavas levantar

[đ] is pronounced similarly to the *th* in *rather, father,* and *other,* but with much less friction.

> lodo desde podemos comida pierde guardan

Note that [d], not [đ], is used after /l/:

> falda molde balde caldo peldaño celda

[ǥ] is produced similarly to [g], except that air is forced through a very narrow opening between the back of the tongue and the soft palate (back of the roof of the mouth).

> pago digo agosto sigamos sagrado algo

The soft variants [ƀ], [đ], and [ǥ] are used between vowels, even when the vowels are in two different words.

> yo bato   yo doy   yo gasto
> tú vas   tú dices   tú gozas
> la boca   la danza   la gota

r   The sound represented by **r** in Spanish spelling is completely different from the one represented by *r* in English spelling. It consists of a single flap made by a rapid tap of the tongue against the gum ridge above the upper teeth. A similar sound exists in American English and is represented in English spelling by *t, d, tt, dd* between vowels (where the first vowel is stressed).

> *later spider batter ladder*

Repeat the following words after the speaker, being careful to use a flap similar to the one appearing in the English words above.

> cara cero poro toro cura lira

The flap occurring after an unstressed vowel is harder for English speakers to produce.

pirata parece morimos directo

The single flap /r/ is also used after consonants (written **r**).

preso traste cromo grande bravo drama frota

Spanish also has a trilled consonant /rr/ represented at the beginning of words by **r** and between vowels as **rr**. This sound consists of two or more flaps of the tongue against the upper gum ridge; it does not exist in American English. Repeat the following words after the speaker:

carro forro perro burrito ferrocarril amarramos
rato ropa reto rico ruso raqueta

Before another consonant or at the end of a word, the letter **r** may be pronounced either /r/ or /rr/, depending on the speaker and the degree of emphasis. Repeat the following words after the speaker:

puerta corto carpa tomar meter ser

j   In Spanish spelling, the letter **j** and the letter **g** before **e** and **i** (but not before **a**, **o**, **u** or a consonant) represent a sound that does not exist in English and that we transcribe as /x/. The sound /x/ differs from /k/ in the same way that [g] differs from [g]: It is produced by forcing air through a narrow opening between the arched back of the tongue and the soft palate. For many Spanish speakers, especially those from the Caribbean, /x/ is usually replaced by /h/, as in English *hope*. Repeat the following words after the speaker:

jota jefe gente gime jale
lijo moja ajo teje caja
lijar mojar ají tejer cajera

ll/y   Both **ll** and **y** represent the sound /y/. This sound is considerably tenser than the initial sound in English *yes*. English speakers must pay special attention to /y/, especially when it occurs between vowels. Repeat the following words after the speaker:

llamo hallo arroyo bello rayo yerno yodo

l   Spanish **l** is pronounced very much like the /l/ sound in English *leak* and *less*. The tip of the tongue touches the gum ridge above the upper teeth, and air is forced out on the sides of the tongue. For final /l/ in English (as in *sell*, *tall*, *cool*, *full*), the tip of the tongue is lowered and the tongue is arched. In Spanish, final /l/ is pronounced exactly like initial /l/. Repeat the following words after the speaker:

lata lema liso losa luna
cal hiel gila col tul

p, t, k   The sounds /p/, /t/, and /k/ before stressed vowels differ from their closest English counterparts by being unaspirated. The term "unaspirated" refers to the absence of the puff of air that follows these sounds in English. If you say English *pale*, *tale*, or *kale* while holding a lighted match at your mouth, the puff of air following /p/, /t/, or /k/ will extinguish the flame, because /p/, /t/, and /k/ are aspirated in English. However, when a Spanish speaker holds a lighted match at his mouth and says **pon**, **ten**, or **con**, the match does not go out, because /p/, /t/, and /k/ are unaspirated in Spanish.

While English /t/ is made by touching the gum ridge above the upper teeth, for Spanish /t/, the tip of the tongue touches the back of the upper teeth.

In Spanish, /k/ is spelled **qu** before **e** and **i**, but **c** is used elsewhere. Repeat the following words after the speaker:

> panes pozo plano pica prado rompió toparon
> tapa teme tripas tiza tope quitó votamos
> cama queso quise clase creo coloqué cubre

s For all Spanish Americans and many Spaniards in southern Spain, the letters **s**, **z**, and **c** (when it appears before **e** and **i**) represent a sound similar to the one represented by *s* in English *sale, so,* and *see.* Repeat the following words after the speaker:

> sala posa rosas comes cinco cacería
> mozo luz luces haces zapato zurdo

f, m, n, ch These letters and combination of letters in Spanish represent sounds similar to their English counterparts. Repeat the following words after the speaker:

> feo rifa mono lima nariz zona chato techo

h In Spanish spelling, **h** represents no sound—it is a silent letter, as in English *honor.* Repeat the following words after the speaker:

> hablo haber han historia hombre humano

ñ The mark above the **n** is called a **tilde**. This letter represents a sound similar to the one written as *ni* in English *onion.* However, in English, the /n/ and the /y/ are pronounced in different syllables; in Spanish, the /ny/ goes with the following vowel. This sound is rare at the beginning of a word.

> año piña uña mañas riñen ñame

c/z A major geographical variation in Spanish revolves around the pronunciation of the letter **c** before **e** and **i**, and the letter **z**. In Spanish America, these letters represent the sound /s/. However, in central and northern Spain, and in the speech of many speakers in southern Spain as well, these letters represent a sound similar to English *th* in *think, thank, cloth.* The phonetic symbol for this sound is the Greek letter theta, /θ/.

Dialects that distinguish the two sounds are described as having *distinción.* Dialects that do not have *distinción* pronounce **casa** and **caza** the same. Thus, in Spain, these pairs of words are pronounced differently, whereas in Spanish America, they are pronounced alike.

		SPAIN		SPANISH AMERICA	
casa *house*	caza *hunt*	/kasa/	/kaθa/	/kasa/	/kasa/
coser *sew*	cocer *cook*	/koser/	/koθer/	/koser/	/koser/
caso *case*	cazo *ladle*	/kaso/	/kaθo/	/kaso/	/kaso/

SPELLING

The Spanish Alphabet

a	a	**j**	jota	**r**	erre
b	be	**k**	ka	**s**	ese
c	ce	**l**	ele	**t**	te
d	de	**m**	eme	**u**	u
e	e	**n**	ene	**v**	uve
f	efe	**ñ**	eñe	**w**	doble uve
g	ge	**o**	o	**x**	equis
h	hache	**p**	pe	**y**	ye
i	i	**q**	cu	**z**	zeta

THE SPANISH ALPHABET

The Real Academia Española is Spain's official institution for overseeing the Spanish language. In 2010, it instituted a series of spelling reforms designed to standardize orthography. The Spanish alphabet was reduced to 27 letters, omitting the digraphs **ch** (**che** or **ce hache**) and **ll** (**doble ele**), which had been officially recognized letters. Today, the Spanish alphabet has the same letters as the English alphabet, plus **ñ**. In speech, many Spanish speakers disambiguate certain pairs of letters as follows: **b** = **be de burro, be grande, be larga** and **v** = **ve de vaca, ve chica, ve corta; i** = **i latina** and **y** = **i griega.** The digraph **rr** (**doble erre**) is not a letter of the alphabet.

Syllabification

A syllable in Spanish may consist of a single vowel, a diphthong, or a vowel or diphthong together with its preceding and following consonants. The following rules guide syllabification in Spanish.

1 · A single consonant between vowels goes with the following vowel.

   rei-na a-mo ma-tan cau-sas te-mi-do

2 · Groups of two consonants that can begin a word (**p, t, c, b, d, g, f** + **l** or **r**) go with the following vowel.

   co-pla ha-blo sue-gra pa-dre co-fre

3 · Other groups of two consonants are divided as follows:

   him-no es-ta mun-do fal-ta sor-do

4 · Groups of three consonants are divided according to Rules 2 and 3. When the last two consonants of the three form one of the groups mentioned in Rule 2, they both go with the following vowel.

   ram-bla ham-bre con-tra san-gre as-tro

If the last two consonants of a three-consonant cluster do not form one of the groups in Rule 2, only the third consonant goes with the following vowel.

> ist-mo trans-ferir trans-porte

5 · Groups of four consonants are divided after the second consonant.

> mons-truo ins-trumento ins-crito trans-plante

▶ Accentuation

1 · Spanish words ending in a vowel or the letters -n or -s are stressed on the next-to-last syllable.

> triste hablan escriben señoritas provincias

2 · Spanish words ending in a consonant other than -n or -s (usually -d, -l, -z, -r) are stressed on the last syllable.

> azul hotel Brasil vejez terminar señor usted

3 · When **i** or **u** precedes or follows **a**, **e**, or **o**, the two vowels are pronounced as one syllable.

> estud**io** s**ie**te c**ie**ncia limp**io** s**ei**s c**ua**ndo esc**ue**la resta**u**rante

Combinations of **a, e,** and **o** form two syllables, not one.

> tar**ea** mus**eo** m**ae**stro pr**eo**cupado des**ea**

4 · A written accent mark is required in Spanish when the stress of a word does not occur as presented above.

> alemán inglés Canadá está cafés también
> sábado jóvenes miércoles exámenes médico química
> lápiz fácil Pérez rápido tránsito pantalón

In the following words, the combination of **i** or **u** + vowel forms two syllables, not one as in Rule 3, because here the /i/ and the /u/ are stressed. A written accent is therefore placed over the **i** or the **u**.

> día tío economía biología reúne baúl actúa

5 · Words that are spelled the same but have different meanings are distinguished in writing by a written accent mark.

él *he, him*	el *the*
tú *you* (familiar)	tu *your*
más *more*	mas *but*
mí *me*	mi *my*
sí *yes*	si *if*
sólo *only*	solo *alone*

Punctuation and Capitalization

1 · Spanish questions are written with an inverted question mark (¿) at the beginning and a regular question mark (?) at the end.

> ¿Habla usted español?   *Do you speak Spanish?*

2 · Exclamations in Spanish begin with an inverted exclamation point (¡) and end with a regular exclamation point (!).

> ¡Qué va!   *You're kidding!*

3 · Interrogative words in Spanish are written with an accent mark.

> ¿Quién?   *Who?*
> ¿Qué?   *What?*
> ¿Cuándo?   *When?*
> ¿Dónde?   *Where?*

4 · Languages, nationalities, days of the week, and months of the year are written with an initial lowercase letter in Spanish, rather than with a capital letter as in English.

> mexicano   *Mexican*
> americano   *American*
> viernes   *Friday*
> marzo   *March*

5 · Subject pronouns in Spanish follow a different capitalization pattern than subject pronouns in English. **Yo** (*I*) is written with an initial lowercase letter when it is not the first word in a sentence. Likewise, **usted** (*you,* formal singular) and **ustedes** (*you,* formal plural; also informal plural in Spanish America) are written with an initial lowercase letter when they are not the first word in a sentence. However, they are often abbreviated in writing as **Ud.** and **Uds.**; when abbreviated, they begin with a capital **U**.

Getting Around Town— Where Is It?

Communication Goals
- Talking about gift-giving
- Asking for directions in a Spanish-speaking city
- Talking about shopping
- Getting attention to ask for information
- Vocabulary: everyday items, numbers 1 to 20

Grammar Topics
- **Hay** *there is, there are*
- **Ser** *to be* (third person singular)
- Articles and Gender of Nouns
- Question Formation
- Negative Sentences
- Plural Nouns
- Compound Nouns
- Numbers 1 to 20
- Noun Phrases

DIÁLOGO 1 · ¿Qué hay en la caja?

Study the dialogue, then listen to the recording and repeat each line.

ALEJANDRA	¿Qué hay en la caja?
BENJAMÍN	Una cámara.
ALEJANDRA	¿Es un regalo?
BENJAMÍN	Sí, es un regalo para Paula.

Análisis

Check that you understand the linguistic breakdown of each speech from *Diálogo 1*.

¿Qué hay en la caja?	*What is (there) in the box?*
¿Qué?	*What?*
hay	*is there*
en	*in*
la	*the* (feminine definite article)
caja	*box* (feminine noun)
en la caja	*in the box*
Una cámara.	*A camera.*
una	*a, an* (feminine indefinite article)
cámara	*camera* (feminine noun)
una cámara	*a camera*
¿Es un regalo?	*Is it a gift?*
es	*it is, he is, she is, you* (formal singular) *are* (**ser**)
un	*a, an* (masculine indefinite article)
un regalo	*a gift*
Sí, es un regalo para Paula.	*Yes, it's a gift for Paula.*
sí	*yes*
para	*for*
para Paula	*for Paula*

▶ Variantes

Listen, and repeat the same structures from *Diálogo 1*, now with new vocabulary.

¿Qué hay en la caja ?	*What is **in the box**?*
en la bolsa	*in the bag*
en la carpeta	*in the folder*
en la maleta	*in the suitcase*
en la gaveta	*in the drawer*
en la mochila	*in the backpack*
en el paquete	*in the package*
en el cartapacio	*in the briefcase*
en el armario	*in the closet*
en el maletín	*in the attaché case*
en el estante	*on the shelf*
Hay una cámara en la caja.	*There's **a camera** in the box.*
una computadora	*a computer*
una agenda electrónica	*an electronic appointment book*
un libro	*a book*
un CD (cedé)	*a CD*
un iPod	*an iPod*
un teléfono	*a telephone*
un (teléfono) celular	*a cell phone*

Hay una cámara en la caja.	There's **a camera** in the box.
un móvil	a cell phone (Spain)
una cartera	a wallet (for some speakers, handbag)
un bolso	a handbag
un billetero	a wallet

¿Qué hay en la caja? ¿Un regalo?	What's in the box? A gift?
No, no es un regalo.	No, it's not a gift.

¿Qué hay en la caja? ¿Un reloj?	What's in the box? A wristwatch?
No, es una pulsera.	No, it's a bracelet.

¿Es un regalo?	Is it a gift?
No, no es un regalo.	No, it's not a gift.

¿Es un regalo para Gabriela?	Is it a gift for Gabriela?
No, no es para Gabriela.	No, it's not for Gabriela.

Estructura y Práctica

Hay *there is, there are*

The word **hay** is an irregular verb form meaning *there is, there are*. It can be followed by either a singular or a plural noun.

Hay un regalo en la caja.	***There's a gift*** *in the box.*
Hay regalos en la caja.	***There are gifts*** *in the box.*

The noun that follows **hay** is considered to be the direct object of the verb. The direct object is a noun or pronoun that completes the thought of a verb by serving as the goal of the action.

¿Hay **regalos** en la caja?	*Are there **gifts** in the box?*
(*direct object noun*)	
Sí, **los** hay. (*direct object pronoun*)	*Yes, there are.*
¿Hay **carpetas** en la gaveta?	*Are there **folders** in the drawer?*
(*direct object noun*)	
Sí, **las** hay. (*direct object pronoun*)	*Yes, there are.*

Ser *to be* (third person singular)

The verb form **es** means *you are* (formal singular), as well as *he/she/it is*. It is a form of the irregular verb **ser** (*to be*). (See also Chapters 2, 3, and 4.)

¿Qué hay en el paquete?	*What is (there) in the package?*
Es un regalo.	***It's*** *a gift.*

A ***¿Qué hay?*** Express each dialogue exchange in Spanish.

1. *What's in the briefcase?*
   There's a cell phone in the briefcase.

2. *Are there folders in the drawer?*
   Yes, there are.

3. *What's on the shelf?*
   There are books on the shelf.

4. *Are there CDs in the package?*
   Yes, there are.

5. *Is there a computer in the backpack?*
   No, there's a camera.

B *¿Qué hay en la caja?* Write a sentence to tell what gift is in each box, using **es** and the noun provided. Include the corresponding indefinite article (**un, una**). Follow the *modelo*.

MODELO   libro
        → Es un libro.

1. billetero	5. bolso
2. cartera	6. cámara
3. reloj	7. iPod
4. agenda electrónica	8. cartapacio

C *¿Para quién es el regalo?* **(Whom is the gift for?)** Write sentences stating that the gift mentioned is not for the person named in the first cue, but rather for the person named in the second cue. Follow the *modelo*.

MODELO   libro: Ricardo / Tomás
        → El libro no es para Ricardo. Es para Tomás.

1. billetero: José / Juan	5. bolso: Rosa / Margarita
2. cartera: Matilde / Julia	6. cámara: Luz / Daniel
3. reloj: Jorge / Alberto	7. iPod: Susana / Guillermo
4. agenda electrónica: Lorenzo / Nora	8. cartapacio: Carlos / Roberto

---

SPELLING

After **g** and **q** and before the vowels **e** and **i**, the letter **u** does not represent a vowel, but is merely a spelling convention. The combinations of letters **gue** and **gui** represent the spoken syllables /ge/ and /gi/ (with the **g** pronounced as in English *go*), respectively: **jug̲u̲ete**, **g̲u̲itarra**. The combinations of letters **que** and **qui** represent the spoken syllables /ke/ and /ki/, respectively: **paq̲u̲ete**, **embarq̲u̲e**, **aq̲u̲í**.

Articles and Gender of Nouns

Articles

Like English, Spanish has a definite article equivalent to *the* and an indefinite article equivalent to *a, an*. The Spanish articles agree in gender and number with the noun they are associated with.

Here are the forms of the definite article in Spanish.

	MASCULINE	FEMININE
SINGULAR	**el** carro (*car*)	**la** caja
PLURAL	**los** carros	**las** cajas

Here are the forms of the indefinite article in Spanish.

	MASCULINE	FEMININE
SINGULAR	**un** carro	**una** caja
PLURAL	**unos** carros	**unas** cajas

The plural forms of the indefinite article in Spanish are sometimes not translated, and sometimes they are the equivalent of English *some*. They are also used before nouns that usually come in pairs, such as *eyes*, *ears*, or nouns that have no singular, such as *scissors*.

Gender of Nouns

Spanish nouns are divided into two broad classes, traditionally called masculine and feminine. Most (but not all) nouns referring to males are masculine, and most (but not all) nouns referring to females are feminine. Inanimate nouns such as **regalo** and **caja** are assigned to one of the two classes, usually (but not always) on the basis of their endings.

1 · Most nouns ending in **-o** are masculine, while most nouns ending in **-a** are feminine.

2 · Nouns ending in **-e** or a consonant typically give no clue as to gender (unless they refer to people), so their gender must be learned as you learn the noun.

The following nouns are all masculine.

el aceite *oil*	el hospital *hospital*
el aire *air*	el hotel *hotel*
el análisis *analysis*	el informe *report*
el animal *animal*	el juguete *toy*
el arete *earring*	el lápiz *pencil*
el automóvil *car*	el lugar *place*
el bar *bar*	el maletín *attaché case*
el billete *ticket, bill* (currency)	el mes *month*
el café *café*	el papel *paper*
el cibercafé *internet café*	el paquete *package*
el cine *movie theater*	el pez *fish*
el coche *car*	el plan *plan*
el estante *shelf*	el reloj *wristwatch*
el examen *exam*	el tren *train*

The following nouns are all feminine.

la base *base*	la paz *peace*
la calle *street*	la piel *skin*
la catedral *cathedral*	la pirámide *pyramid*
la ciudad *city*	la red *web, internet*
la clase *class*	la sed *thirst*
la crisis *crisis*	la suerte *luck*
la flor *flower*	la torre *tower*
la gente *people*	la tos *cough*
la llave *key*	la verdad *truth*
la luz *light*	la vez *time* (*occasion*)
la nariz *nose*	la voz *voice*

3 · The following suffixes indicate feminine nouns.

-ción, -ión	la nación, la religión, la unión
-tad, -dad	la libertad, la nacionalidad, la felicidad (*happiness*)
-tud	la gratitud, la virtud, la juventud (*youth*)
-ie	la serie (*series*), la superficie (*surface*)

4 · Some nouns have anomalous genders.

la mano *hand*	el día *day*
la moto (la motocicleta) *motorcycle*	el mapa *map*
la foto (la fotografía) *photograph*	el tranvía *trolley*

5 · Many nouns ending in **-ma** (usually international words borrowed from Greek) are masculine.

el clima *climate*	el programa *program*
el drama *drama*	el sistema *system*
el idioma *language*	el tema *subject*
el poema *poem*	el trauma *trauma*
el problema *problem*	

D **Nouns and articles.** Write the correct definite and indefinite articles for each noun. Follow the *modelo*.

MODELO   libro
         → el libro   un libro

1. maleta
2. coche
3. reloj
4. clase
5. hotel
6. oficina
7. cosa (*thing*)
8. mano
9. cámara
10. paquete
11. teléfono
12. flor
13. problema
14. ciudad
15. maletín
16. tema

E   Unscramble the letters in each item to form a Spanish noun. Write the noun and the definite article for each noun.

1. e m s   6. t a m a l e

2. n e e g t   7. s l a e c

3. h o a m i l c   8. a o p r c a d m u t o

4. r a c o r   9. b o l r i

5. g e a o r l   10. j e o l r

F   **Sentence completion.**   Select the correct word or phrase that completes each sentence. Write the word or phrase that you have selected.

1. Es un _____ celular.
   a. teléfono   b. computadora

2. ¿Qué hay en la _____?
   a. paquete   b. cartera

3. No hay gente en _____.
   a. la gaveta   b. el cibercafé

4. ¿Qué libros _____ en el estante?
   a. hay   b. es

5. —¿Hay documentos? —Sí, _____ la carpeta.
   a. para   b. en

6. Hay una _____ en la caja.
   a. pulsera   b. juguete

7. —¿Hay maletas en el armario? —Sí, _____ hay.
   a. las   b. los

8. Es un _____.
   a. clase   b. cartapacio

Question Formation: Information Questions, Yes/No Questions

There are two types of questions in Spanish: yes/no questions and information questions. In Spanish, all questions are written with an inverted question mark at the beginning of the sentence and a regular question mark at the end. Information questions begin with a question word. They expect a piece of information as an answer. (See also Chapters 2 and 3.)

¿**Qué** hay en la maleta?	*What is in the suitcase?*
¿**Qué** es?	*What is it?*
¿**Para quién** es el regalo?	*Whom is the gift for?*

Questions not beginning with a question word are called yes/no questions, that is, they ask for either *yes* or *no* as an answer.

¿Hay libros en la mochila?	*Are there books in the backpack?*
Sí, los hay.	*Yes, there are.*
No, no los hay.	*No, there aren't.*

The most common way to ask a yes/no question is to change the intonation from statement intonation to rising question intonation. This is shown in writing by enclosing the sentence in question marks.

El bolso es para Raquel.	*The handbag is for Raquel.*
¿El bolso es para Raquel?	*Is the handbag for Raquel?*

The subject can also be placed after the verb.

Antonio trabaja por aquí.	*Antonio works around here.*
¿Trabaja Antonio por aquí?	*Does Antonio work around here?*
(**trabajar** (*to work*))	

When a question includes a form of the verb **ser** + an adjective, the subject is placed at the end of the sentence. The pattern of the question is thus verb + adjective + subject.

El hotel es cómodo.	*The hotel is comfortable.*
¿Es cómodo el hotel?	*Is the hotel comfortable?*

G   *Preguntas* (**Questions**). Write a yes/no question or an information question from each string of elements. Follow the *modelo*.

> MODELO   una / es / bolsa
>   → ¿Es una bolsa?

1. hay / en el armario / qué
2. regalo / es / un
3. cómodo / el hotel / es
4. flores / hay / qué
5. en / cafés / hay / la ciudad / qué
6. papeles / en / unos / hay / la mochila
7. hay / los estantes / qué / en / libros
8. para / el juguete / es / Juanito

Negative Sentences

Spanish sentences are made negative by placing **no** before the verb.

> **No** hay restaurantes por aquí.   *There are **no** restaurants around here.*

To form negative questions (*isn't, aren't, doesn't,* etc.), the negative statement is spoken with rising intonation.

> ¿No hay un hotel por aquí?   *Isn't there a hotel around here?*

No is the equivalent of both the English response *no* and a marker of negation. Therefore, many negative responses to questions have two occurrences of **no**.

¿Hay unos bancos por aquí?	*Are there any banks around here?*
No, no hay.	*No, there aren't.*

H   Restate each sentence in the negative.

1. La cámara es un regalo.

2. Hay una computadora en el armario.

3. Es un iPod.

4. El paquete es para Miguel.

5. Hay un cibercafé por aquí.

6. Hay maletas en el carro.

7. Es una oficina cómoda.

8. Hay dinero (*money*) en el billetero.

I   *¡No!* Answer each question in the negative. Follow the *modelo*.

> MODELO   ¿Hay un banco por aquí?
> → No, no hay banco por aquí.

1. ¿Es una agenda electrónica?

2. ¿Hay libros en el estante?

3. ¿El reloj es para Carlos?

4. ¿Hay un supermercado por aquí?

5. ¿Es un regalo para Julieta?

6. ¿Hay ropa (*clothing*) en la maleta?

7. ¿Hay un cartapacio en la oficina?

8. ¿Es un problema?

DIÁLOGO 2 · Hay dos farmacias.

Study the dialogue, then listen to the recording and repeat each line.

BENJAMÍN	¿Hay una farmacia por aquí?
ALEJANDRA	Hay dos farmacias.
BENJAMÍN	¿Dónde?
ALEJANDRA	Hay una en la esquina y otra en frente.

Análisis

Check that you understand the linguistic breakdown of each speech from *Diálogo 2*.

¿Hay una farmacia por aquí?	*Is there a drugstore around here?*
una farmacia	*a drugstore, a pharmacy*
por	*around, in the area of*
aquí	*here*
por aquí	*around here*
Hay dos farmacias.	*There are two drugstores.*
dos	*two*
farmacias	*drugstores*
¿Dónde?	*Where?*
Hay una en la esquina y otra en frente.	*There's one on the corner and another one across the street.*
una	*one (feminine indefinite article)*
la esquina	*street corner*
en la esquina	*on/at the corner*

y	*and*
otra	*another one* (feminine)
en frente	*across the street, opposite*
y otra en frente	*and another one across the street*

▶ Variantes

Listen, and repeat the same structures from *Diálogo 2*, now with new vocabulary.

¿Hay una farmacia por aquí?	*Is there **a drugstore** around here?*
una oficina de turismo	*a tourist office*
un supermercado	*a supermarket*
una peluquería	*a hair salon, a barber shop*
un café	*a café*
un bar	*a bar*
un restaurante	*a restaurant*
una librería	*a bookstore*
un cine	*a movie theater*
un teatro	*a theater*
un hotel	*a hotel*
una heladería	*an ice cream shop*
un hospital	*a hospital*

Hay dos farmacias por aquí.	*There are **two drugstores** around here.*
dos oficinas de turismo	*two tourist offices*
tres hoteles	*three hotels*
cuatro supermercados	*four supermarkets*
cinco peluquerías	*five hair salons, five barber shops*
seis cafés	*six cafés*
siete teatros	*seven theaters*
ocho bares	*eight bars*
nueve restaurantes	*nine restaurants*
diez librerías	*ten bookstores*

| ¿Hay un supermercado por aquí? | *Is there a supermarket around here?* |
| No, no hay. | *No, there isn't.* |

| ¿No hay un restaurante por aquí? | *Isn't there a restaurant around here?* |
| No, no hay. | *No, there isn't.* |

| ¿Hay farmacias por aquí? | *Are there any drugstores around here?* |
| No, no hay. | *No, there aren't.* |

| ¿No hay librerías por aquí? | *Aren't there any bookstores around here?* |
| No, no hay. | *No, there aren't.* |

Estructura y Práctica

Plural Nouns

Spanish forms the plural of nouns by adding -s to nouns ending in a vowel and -es to nouns ending in a consonant. The **s** of the plural is always pronounced /s/, never /z/.

SINGULAR	PLURAL
cuarto (*room*)	cuartos
persona	personas
estante	estantes
cibercafé	cibercafés
señor	señores
catedral	catedrales

When the last syllable of a noun ending in a consonant has an accent mark, that accent mark is eliminated when the -**es** plural ending is added.

SINGULAR	PLURAL
maletín	maletines
nación (*nation*)	naciones
inglés (*Englishman*)	ingleses
alemán (*German*)	alemanes

El país (*country*) is an exception: **los países**.

A singular noun that ends in a consonant and is stressed on the next-to-last syllable adds a written accent on the vowel of that stressed syllable when the -**es** plural ending is added. These apparent irregularities follow the rules for the placement of accent marks in Spanish.

SINGULAR	PLURAL
joven	jóvenes
examen	exámenes
origen	orígenes

SPELLING

Nouns ending in -**z** change -**z** to -**c** when the plural ending -**es** is added.

el pez (*fish*) → los peces
la voz (*voice*) → las voces
el lápiz → los lápices (*retains the written accent*)

J **Nouns and articles in the plural.** Write the plural form of each noun with its corresponding definite and indefinite articles. Follow the *modelo*.

MODELO   libro
          → los libros   unos libros

1. maleta
2. cine
3. reloj
4. librería
5. problema
6. oficina
7. teatro
8. restaurante
9. papel
10. ciudad
11. teléfono
12. flor
13. mes
14. calle
15. maletín
16. luz

K Write the singular form of each noun with its corresponding definite and indefinite articles.

1. libros
2. bolsas
3. clases
4. lugares
5. hoteles
6. llaves
7. trenes
8. animales
9. cosas
10. veces
11. pulseras
12. cámaras
13. mapas
14. temas
15. cafés
16. hospitales

▶ DIÁLOGO 3 · ¿Hay un cibercafé por aquí?

Study the dialogue, then listen to the recording and repeat each line.

BENJAMÍN   Perdón, ¿hay un cibercafé por aquí?
ALEJANDRA   Sí, hay uno en la esquina.
BENJAMÍN   Muchas gracias, señorita.
ALEJANDRA   De nada, señor. Adiós.

Análisis

Check that you understand the linguistic breakdown of each speech from *Diálogo 3*.

Perdón, ¿hay un cibercafé por aquí?	*Excuse me. Is there an internet café around here?*
Perdón	*Excuse me, Pardon me*
un cibercafé	*an internet café*

Sí, hay uno en la esquina.	*Yes, there's one on the corner.*
uno	*one* (masculine)
Muchas gracias, señorita.	*Thank you very much, miss.*
gracias	*thank you*
muchas gracias	*thank you very much*
señorita	*miss*
De nada, señor. Adiós.	*You're welcome, sir. Goodbye.*
de nada	*you're welcome*
señor	*sir*
adiós	*goodbye*

▶ Variantes

Listen, and repeat the same structure from *Diálogo 3*, now with new vocabulary.

Perdón , señorita.	***Excuse me**, miss.*
Oiga	*Say* (literally, *Hear, Listen*)
Por favor	*Please*

Estructura y Práctica

GETTING ATTENTION TO ASK FOR INFORMATION

Words such as **Perdón** (*Excuse me*) and **Oiga** (*Say, Hey* (literally, *Hear, Listen*)) can be used to get someone's attention when you want to ask a question. They are often followed by the appropriate form of address.

Perdón/Oiga, señor (*sir*), **señora** (*ma'am*), **señorita** (*miss*).

These expressions can often be used when stopping someone on the street to ask directions, as illustrated in the dialogues of this chapter.

Perdón, señorita. ¿Hay una oficina de turismo por aquí?	*Excuse me, miss. Is there a tourist office around here?*

L **Asking for and getting directions.** Express each dialogue in Spanish.

1. *Excuse me, sir. Is there a bank around here?*
   Yes, miss, there's one on the corner.
   Thank you, sir.
   You're welcome. Goodbye.

2. *Please, miss. Where (¿Dónde?) is there a hair salon?*
   There's one on the corner, ma'am.
   Thank you very much, miss.
   You're welcome, ma'am.

▶ DIÁLOGO 4 · El centro comercial

Study the dialogue, then listen to the recording and repeat each line.

ALEJANDRA	Hay veinte tiendas en el centro comercial.
BENJAMÍN	¿Qué tiendas hay?
ALEJANDRA	Hay zapaterías, tiendas de ropa, jugueterías, una heladería, una tienda de deportes, una tienda por departamentos.
BENJAMÍN	¿Hay una tienda de electrodomésticos también?
ALEJANDRA	Claro que sí. Y una tienda de cómputo.

Análisis

Check that you understand the linguistic breakdown of each speech from *Diálogo 4*.

Hay veinte tiendas en el centro comercial.	*There are 20 stores in the shopping center.*
veinte	*20*
la tienda	*store*
veinte tiendas	*20 stores*
el centro comercial	*shopping center*
¿Qué tiendas hay?	*What stores are there?*
Hay zapaterías, tiendas de ropa, jugueterías, una heladería, una tienda de deportes, una tienda por departamentos.	*There are shoe stores, clothing stores, toy stores, an ice cream shop, a sporting goods store, a department store.*
el zapato	*shoe*
la zapatería	*shoe store*
la ropa	*clothing*
la tienda de ropa	*clothing store*
el juguete	*toy*
la juguetería	*toy store*
el helado	*ice cream*
la heladería	*ice cream shop*
el deporte	*sport*
la tienda de deportes	*sporting goods store*
el departamento	*department*
la tienda por departamentos	*department store*
¿Hay una tienda de electrodomésticos también?	*Is there an appliance store, too?*
el electrodoméstico	*household appliance*
los electrodomésticos	*household appliances*
la tienda de electrodomésticos	*appliance store*
también	*too*
Claro que sí. Y una tienda de cómputo.	*Yes, of course. And a computer store.*
claro	*of course*
sí	*yes*
claro que sí	*of course*
la tienda de cómputo	*computer store*

Variantes

Listen, and repeat the same structure from *Diálogo 4*, now with new vocabulary.

Hay once zapaterías en el centro.	*There are **11 shoe stores** downtown.*
doce librerías	*12 bookstores*
trece tiendas de deportes	*13 sporting goods stores*
catorce heladerías	*14 ice cream shops*
quince tiendas de ropa	*15 clothing stores*
dieciséis farmacias	*16 drugstores*
diecisiete teatros	*17 theaters*
dieciocho hoteles	*18 hotels*
diecinueve cibercafés	*19 internet cafés*
veinte restaurantes	*20 restaurants*

¿Hay helado?	*Is there any ice cream?*
No, no hay helado.	*No, there isn't any ice cream.*
No, no hay.	*No, there isn't.*

¿No hay helado?	*Isn't there any ice cream?*
No, no hay.	*No, there isn't.*

¿Hay una tienda de electrodomésticos también?	*Is there an appliance store, too?*
No, no hay.	*No, there isn't.*

¿No hay una joyería también?	*Isn't there a jewelry store, too?*
No, no hay.	*No, there isn't.*

Estructura y Práctica

Compound Nouns

Many Spanish compound nouns are formed with the preposition **de** (*of, from*). The English equivalent of these compound nouns usually consists of two juxtaposed nouns, but in the opposite order of that seen in Spanish.

tienda + zapatos → tienda de zapatos	*store + shoe(s) → shoe store*
tienda + electrodomésticos → tienda de electrodomésticos	*store + appliance(s) → appliance store*
museo + arte → museo de arte	*museum + art → art museum*
base + datos → base de datos	*base + data → database*
libro + texto → libro de texto	*book + text → textbook*
tarjeta + embarque → tarjeta de embarque	*pass + boarding → boarding pass*
tarjeta + crédito → tarjeta de crédito	*card + credit → credit card*
salón + belleza → salón de belleza	*salon + beauty → beauty salon*

Sometimes other prepositions are used instead of **de**.

la tienda **por** departamentos	*department store*

To make a compound noun plural, the noun preceding the preposition is made plural, but the noun following the preposition is not.

las quince nuevas **tiendas de cómputo**   *the 15 new **computer stores***

Compound nouns function like any other noun. They can be the subject or object of a verb, and they can be the object of a preposition.

La tienda por departamentos es muy grande.   *The department store is very big.*

Trabaja en la oficina de turismo.   *He works at the tourist office.*

M *Las tiendas.* Write the name of each store in Spanish; then write its plural form. Include the definite article for both singular and plural. Each one is a compound noun.

1. *the clothing store*   4. *the appliance store*

2. *the computer store*   5. *the sporting goods store*

3. *the shoe store*   6. *the department store*

N Select a noun from the second column that forms a compound noun with a noun from the first column. Join the nouns with the preposition **de**. Write each compound noun; then write the plural of each compound noun. Include the definite article for both singular and plural.

1. libro   a. datos

2. base   b. crédito

3. museo   c. turismo

4. tarjeta   d. texto

5. oficina   e. belleza

6. salón   f. arte

Numbers 1 to 20

Numerals (**los números**) in Spanish present few problems. Here are the numbers from one to twenty.

1	uno	11	once
2	dos	12	doce
3	tres	13	trece
4	cuatro	14	catorce
5	cinco	15	quince
6	seis	16	dieciséis
7	siete	17	diecisiete
8	ocho	18	dieciocho
9	nueve	19	diecinueve
10	diez	20	veinte

The numbers **uno, una** are identical with the indefinite article and agree with the following noun in gender.

un libro	*a book, one book*
una computadora	*a computer, one computer*

The numbers 16 through 19 may be written as three words each, but this is increasingly less common: **diez y seis, diez y siete, diez y ocho, diez y nueve.**

O *Los números 1–20.* Express these noun phrases in Spanish. Write all numbers as words.

1. *1 computer*
2. *2 cities*
3. *3 watches*
4. *4 things*
5. *5 movie theaters*
6. *6 clothing stores*
7. *7 hotels*
8. *8 gifts*
9. *9 cameras*
10. *10 ice cream shops*

11. *11 boxes*
12. *12 internet cafés*
13. *13 backpacks*
14. *14 telephones*
15. *15 days*
16. *16 supermarkets*
17. *17 photos*
18. *18 department stores*
19. *19 packages*
20. *20 sports*

P *¿Cómo?* (What?!) Use *¿Cómo?* (*What?!*) to express surprise or incredulity when your friend tells you how many there are of each item mentioned. Write your response to each statement, using the interrogative words **¿Cuántos?** or **¿Cuántas?** (*How many?*). Note that these interrogative words agree in number and gender with the noun they refer to. Follow the *modelo.*

MODELO   Hay veinte carpetas en la gaveta.
          → ¿Cómo? ¿Cuántas?

1. Hay cuatro cibercafés por aquí.

2. Hay catorce regalos para Antonio.

3. Hay tres farmacias en la esquina.

4. Hay diez libros de texto en la mochila.

5. Hay dieciocho tiendas de cómputo en el centro comercial.

6. Hay seis museos de arte en la ciudad.

7. Hay ocho personas en el carro.

8. Hay dieciséis maletas en el armario.

9. Hay doce cuartos en la casa.

10. Hay tres cámaras en la caja.

Noun Phrases

A noun and the words directly associated with it (articles, numbers, adjectives, demonstratives, possessives) form a noun phrase. In Spanish, almost all of the components of noun phrases change their form to match the gender and number of the noun. This change in form to match the noun is called agreement. In Spanish, an adjective agrees in gender and number with its noun: **un carro cómodo**, **una oficina cómoda**. (See also Chapter 2.)

Q Express each English noun phrase in Spanish. Write all numbers as words.

1. *an art museum*
2. *six months*
3. *the department store*
4. *a credit card*
5. *the shopping center*
6. *eleven computer stores*
7. *twenty packages*
8. *some cities*

Un paso más

Are you ready to take your Spanish a step further? Here are exercises that will enhance your knowledge of the language and encourage you to express yourself freely.

R **Cognates.** An English speaker learning Spanish soon realizes that the two languages share many words. Borrowings from English are common in Spanish, as are borrowings from Spanish in English, and both languages have many words of common origin. **El programa** and **la persona** are two of the many cognates that appear in this chapter. However, some words—like **la librería** (*bookstore*), **la carpeta** (*folder*), and **el idioma** (*language*)—are false cognates. They are similar in form but different in meaning. Write the Spanish words (including the definite article) that are cognates of the following English words.

1. *camera*
2. *document*
3. *system*
4. *telephone*
5. *computer*
6. *analysis*
7. *tourism*
8. *art*
9. *theater*
10. *credit*
11. *pharmacy*
12. *museum*
13. *text*
14. *supermarket*
15. *problem*
16. *department*
17. *map*
18. *bank*

S *Preguntas personales.* Answer each question with a complete Spanish sentence. Replace **su** (*your*) with **mi** (*my*) in your answers.

1. ¿Qué hay en su cartapacio? ¿En su maletín? ¿En su maleta?

2. ¿Hay un (teléfono) celular en su mochila? ¿Qué cosas hay en su mochila?

3. ¿Cuánto dinero hay en su billetero? (**el dólar / los dólares** = *dollar/dollars*)

4. ¿Hay una farmacia por aquí? ¿Un café? ¿Un restaurante? ¿Dónde?

5. ¿Hay un centro comercial por aquí? ¿Qué tiendas hay? ¿Cuántas hay?

6. ¿Hay un regalo en la caja? ¿Qué es? ¿Para quién es?

7. ¿Es cómoda su oficina?

8. ¿Qué libros hay en los estantes?

9. ¿Qué hay en las gavetas?

10. ¿Cuántos cuartos hay en su casa (*house*)?

11. ¿Cuántas personas hay en su familia?

Describing Places and Things

Communication Goals

- Describing places and things
- Asking about hotel accommodations
- Indicating possession
- Vocabulary: qualities and attributes of things, colors, academic subjects

Grammar Topics

- Agreement of Adjectives
- Position of Adjectives
- Short Forms of Adjectives
- **Ser** *to be* (third person plural)
- Contraction **del**
- Possessive Adjectives
- More on Question Formation
- Intensifiers
- Noun Phrase Functions

DIÁLOGO 1 · ¿Cómo es el hotel?

Study the dialogue, then listen to the recording and repeat each line.

DANIEL	¿Es cómodo el hotel?
CAMILA	Sí, muy cómodo y muy moderno.
DANIEL	¿Tu habitación es grande?
CAMILA	Sí, es una habitación grande y muy bonita.

Análisis

Check that you understand the linguistic breakdown of each speech from *Diálogo 1*.

¿Es cómodo el hotel?	*Is the hotel comfortable?*
es	*it is, he is, she is, you* (formal singular) *are* (**ser**)
cómodo	*comfortable*
el hotel	*hotel*

Sí, muy cómodo y muy moderno.	*Yes, very comfortable and very modern.*
muy	*very*
muy cómodo	*very comfortable*
moderno	*modern*
muy moderno	*very modern*

¿Tu habitación es grande?	*Is your room big?*
tu	*your* (informal, before a singular noun)
la habitación	*room* (*especially in a hotel or dorm*)
tu habitación	*your room*
grande	*big*

Sí, es una habitación grande y muy bonita.	*Yes, it's a big room, and very pretty.*
y	*and*
bonito	*pretty*
muy bonita	*very pretty* (feminine)

⏵ Variantes

Listen, and repeat the same structures from *Diálogo 1*, now with new vocabulary.

Mi habitación es grande .	*My room is **big**.*
pequeña	*small*
chiquita	*small*
oscura	*dark*
clara	*bright, light*
hermosa	*beautiful*
fea	*ugly*

Mi habitación es grande.	*My **room** is big.*
casa	*house*
oficina	*office*
patio	*yard, patio*
jardín	*garden, yard*
garaje	*garage*
apartamento	*apartment*
condominio	*condominium*
cuarto	*room*

Mi casa es cómoda.	*My* house is comfortable.
Tu	*Your* (informal)
Su	*His, her, your* (formal), *their*
Nuestra	*Our*

Mis regalos son hermosos.	*My* gifts are beautiful.
Tus	*Your* (informal)
Sus	*His, her, your* (formal), *their*
Nuestros	*Our*

¿Es muy grande su jardín?	*Is their garden very big?*
No, no es muy grande.	*No, it's not very big.*

¿Es oscura nuestra oficina?	*Is our office dark?*
No, no es oscura.	*No, it's not dark.*

Estructura y Práctica

Agreement of Adjectives

Spanish adjectives are part of the noun phrase. They modify or describe the noun that is the head of the noun phrase. Like all modifiers of nouns, Spanish adjectives agree with the noun. Most adjectives agree in gender and number, while some agree only in number.

Spanish adjectives are divided into two broad categories: adjectives that have a masculine singular form ending in -**o** and adjectives that have a masculine singular form ending in a consonant or in a vowel other than -**o**.

Adjectives that have a masculine singular form ending in -**o** have four forms. They agree in both gender and number with the noun they modify or describe. An -**s** is added to the singular forms to form the plural. This **s** is pronounced /s/ like the double *s* in English *class*, not /z/ like the single *s* in *present*.

	MASCULINE	FEMININE
SINGULAR	un reloj **hermoso**	una pulsera **hermosa**
PLURAL	unos relojes **hermosos**	unas pulseras **hermosas**

Adjectives that have a masculine singular form ending in a consonant or in a vowel other than -**o** have two forms. They agree in number with the noun they modify or describe, but they have the same form for both masculine and feminine.

Adjectives ending in a consonant add -**es** to form the plural.

	MASCULINE	FEMININE
SINGULAR	un libro **difícil**	una situación **difícil**
PLURAL	unos libros **difíciles**	unas situaciones **difíciles**

Adjectives ending in **-e** add **-s** to form the plural.

	MASCULINE	FEMININE
SINGULAR	un documento **interesante**	una revista (*magazine*) **interesante**
PLURAL	unos documentos **interesantes**	unas revistas **interesantes**

More Adjectives

bueno *good*   barato *inexpensive, cheap*
malo *bad*   lindo *nice, lovely, pretty* (Spanish America)
nuevo *new*   inteligente *intelligent*
viejo *old*   maravilloso *wonderful*
caro *expensive*   estupendo *great, amazing*

A   *También.* Write sentences stating that the noun asked about has the same quality as the noun in the original sentence. Make necessary changes in the form of the adjective. Follow the *modelo.*

> MODELO   El apartamento es cómodo. ¿Y la oficina?
> → La oficina es cómoda también.

1. La casa es nueva. ¿Y el condominio?

2. El barrio es comercial. ¿Y la zona?

3. El museo de arte es maravilloso. ¿Y la catedral?

4. La heladería es animada (*bustling*). ¿Y el café?

5. El supermercado es grande. ¿Y la tienda por departamentos?

6. La mochila es pequeña. ¿Y el cartapacio?

7. La agenda electrónica es útil. ¿Y el celular?

8. El cuarto es oscuro. ¿Y la habitación?

9. El teléfono es viejo. ¿Y la cámara?

10. El patio es bonito. ¿Y la calle?

B   *Son así* (like this). Write sentences stating that the plural noun asked about has the same quality as the singular noun in the original sentence. Make necessary changes in the form of the adjective. Follow the *modelo.*

> MODELO   El patio es bonito. ¿Y los jardines?
> → Los jardines son bonitos también.

1. El problema es difícil. ¿Y los exámenes?

2. El paquete es chiquito. ¿Y las cajas?

3. La pulsera es hermosa. ¿Y los relojes?

4. El salón de belleza es moderno. ¿Y las tiendas de deportes?

5. El libro es interesante. ¿Y las películas (*films*)?

6. La ropa es cara. ¿Y las joyas?

7. El hospital es grande. ¿Y las farmacias?

8. La maleta es buena. ¿Y los cartapacios?

9. El teléfono celular es útil. ¿Y las computadoras?

10. El cibercafé es malo. ¿Y los restaurantes?

▶ DIÁLOGO 2 · Las calles del centro

Study the dialogue, then listen to the recording and repeat each line.

CAMILA	¿Cómo son las calles del centro?
DANIEL	Son bonitas, pero muy transitadas.
CAMILA	¿Hay mucho ruido?
DANIEL	Sí, las calles del centro son muy ruidosas.

Análisis

Check that you understand the linguistic breakdown of each speech from *Diálogo 2*.

¿Cómo son las calles del centro?	*What are the downtown streets like?*
¿Cómo?	*How?* (here, *What?*)
son	*they are* (**ser**)
¿Cómo son?	*What are they like?*
la calle	*street*
del	*of the* (contraction of **de** + **el**)
las calles del centro	*the downtown streets*
Son bonitas, pero muy transitadas.	*They're pretty, but very heavily trafficked.*
bonito	*pretty*
bonitas	*pretty* (feminine plural)
pero	*but*
transitado	*heavily trafficked, with a lot of traffic*
muy transitadas	*very heavily trafficked* (feminine plural)
¿Hay mucho ruido?	*Is there a lot of noise?*
mucho	*much, a lot (of)*
el ruido	*noise*
Sí, las calles del centro son muy ruidosas.	*Yes, the downtown streets are very noisy.*
ruidoso	*noisy*
muy ruidosas	*very noisy* (feminine plural)

▶ Variantes

Listen, and repeat the same structures from *Diálogo 2*, now with new vocabulary.

Es una calle ruidosa .	*It's a **noisy** street.*
tranquila	*quiet, calm, peaceful*
animada	*bustling, busy*
comercial	*commercial*
peatonal	*pedestrian (allowing no vehicular traffic)*

Es una calle comercial.   *It's a commercial street.*
  un barrio   *neighborhood*
  una zona   *area*
  una avenida   *avenue*
  un paseo   *boulevard*

Estructura y Práctica

Position of Adjectives

In Spanish, adjectives normally follow the noun, rather than precede it as in English.

un hotel **moderno**   *a **modern** hotel*
una casa **cómoda**   *a **comfortable** house*
unos informes **importantes**   *some **important** reports*
unas programadoras **inteligentes**   *some **intelligent** programmers*

However, certain types of adjectives precede the noun they modify.

- Adjectives that express quantity

    mucho, mucha *much, a lot of*
    muchos, muchas *many, a lot of*
    poco, poca *little, not much*
    pocos, pocas *few, not many*
    bastante, bastantes *quite a lot of* (Spanish America); *enough* (Spain)
    suficiente, suficientes *enough*
    ¿cuánto? ¿cuánta? *how much?*
    ¿cuántos? ¿cuántas? *how many?*
    alguno, alguna, algunos, algunas *some*
    ninguno, ninguna *no, none*
    ambos, ambas *both*
    varios, varias *several*

    muchos hoteles viejos   *many old hotels*
    pocos restaurantes baratos   *few inexpensive restaurants*
    ambas zonas comerciales   *both commercial areas*
    suficiente dinero   *enough money*

  The adjective **todo** also belongs in this category. (See also Chapter 3.)

    todo el dinero   *all the money*
    toda la ropa   *all the clothing*
    todos los condominios nuevos   *all the new condominiums*
    todas las maletas grises   *all the gray suitcases*

- Ordinal numbers

    primero *first*   sexto *sixth*
    segundo *second*   séptimo *seventh*
    tercero *third*   octavo *eighth*
    cuarto *fourth*   noveno *ninth*
    quinto *fifth*   décimo *tenth*

el **primer** día	the **first** day
la **primera** semana	the **first** week
el **tercer** día	the **third** day
la **tercera** semana	the **third** week

- Adjectives used in exclamations after **¡Qué!** (See also Chapter 3.)

¡Qué **lindo** barrio!	What a **lovely** neighborhood!
¡Qué **hermosa** ciudad!	What a **beautiful** city!
¡Qué **feo** día!	What a **nasty** day!
¡Qué **maravillosa** tienda!	What a **wonderful** store!

- Adjectives that express a subjective judgment made by the speaker, rather than an objective description. The adjectives **bueno** (*good*), **malo** (*bad*), **mejor** (*better/best*), and **peor** (*worse/worst*) fall into this category.

una **buena** persona	a **good** person
un **mal** día	a **bad** day
los **peores** problemas posibles	the **worst** problems possible
la **mejor** idea	the **best** idea
un **horrible** accidente	a **horrible** accident
una **magnífica** oportunidad	a **magnificent** opportunity
un **bonito** regalo	a **pretty** gift

- Adjectives that express a quality known to all, rather than new information about the noun.

la **verde** hierba	the **green** grass
la **blanca** nieve	the **white** snow

Some adjectives can appear either before or after the noun. In these cases, the meaning changes depending on the position of the adjective.

nuestro **antiguo** profesor	our **former** teacher
un cementerio **antiguo**	an **ancient** cemetery
cierto análisis	a **certain** analysis
una cosa **cierta**	a **sure** thing
un **nuevo** proyecto	**another** project
un proyecto **nuevo**	a **new** project
este **pobre** país	this **poor** country (*unfortunate*)
un país **pobre**	a **poor** country (*economically depressed*)
un **gran** hombre	a **great** man
un hombre **grande**	a **big** man
diferentes posibilidades	**various** possibilities
posibilidades **diferentes**	**different** possibilities
Luis es **medio** español.	Luis is **half** Spanish.
el español **medio**	the **average** Spaniard
Es el **mismo** programa.	It's the **same** program.
El problema es el programa **mismo**.	The problem is the program **itself**.

Las bebidas allí son **pura** agua.	*The drinks there are **nothing but** water.*
Hay que beber agua **pura**.	*You should drink **pure** water.*
un **simple** empleado	*a **mere** employee*
una muchacha **simple**	*a **simple** girl*
cualquier persona	*any person*
una persona **cualquiera**	*a **vulgar** person*
la **única** persona	*the **only** person*
una persona **única**	*a **unique** person*

Short Forms of Adjectives

The adjectives **bueno** (*good*) and **malo** (*bad*), the ordinal numbers **primero** (*first*) and **tercero** (*third*), the indefinite article **uno**, and **alguno** (*some*) and **ninguno** (*no*) lose their final **-o** before a masculine singular noun or before an adjective preceding a masculine singular noun.

un **buen** libro	*a **good** book*
BUT	
una **buena** revista	*a **good** magazine*
un **mal** día	*a **bad** day*
BUT	
una **mala** semana	*a **bad** week*
el **primer** día	*the **first** day*
el **tercer** mes	*the **third** month*

However, if these adjectives follow a masculine singular noun, the full form is used.

Felipe **Segundo**	*Philip **the Second***
el siglo **primero**	*the **first** century*

Alguno (*some*) and **ninguno** (*no*) add an accent mark over the **-u-** when the final **-o** is dropped. Notice that **alguno** and **ninguno** can stand before other adjectives.

algún buen vino chileno	***some** good Chilean wine*
No hay **ningún** restaurante caro.	*There is **no** expensive restaurant.*

The adjective **grande** shortens to **gran** before any singular noun, whether masculine or feminine. **Gran** means *great* when it precedes the noun.

una **gran** bailarina rusa	*a **great** Russian ballet dancer*

Grande does not shorten before plural nouns.

grandes artistas italianos	***great** Italian artists*

The adjective **cualquiera** (*any*) shortens to **cualquier** before any singular noun, whether masculine or feminine.

cualquier celular	*any cell phone*
cualquier computadora	*any computer*

C   Write the form of the adjective in parentheses that correctly completes each sentence.

1. Es un _____ chico. (bueno)

2. Lucía es su _____ hija (*daughter*). (tercero)

3. Hay _____ mapas en el maletín. (alguno)

4. Es el _____ mes del año. (primero)

5. Son muy _____ ideas. (malo)

6. Es una _____ escritora. (grande)

7. No hay _____ cibercafé por aquí. (ninguno)

8. ¿Hay _____ paseo tranquilo? (alguno)

D   Form noun phrases using the elements given. Some of the adjectives precede the noun and others follow it. Change the form of the adjectives and other elements to agree with the noun they refer to. Follow the *modelo*.

> MODELO   flores / mucho / hermoso
> → muchas flores hermosas

1. semana / primero / el

2. avenidas / animado / alguno

3. transitado / cierto / calles

4. peatonal / zona / bastante

5. periódico / cualquiera / importante

6. varios / pesado / revistas

7. computadora / ninguno / viejo

8. mucho / problemas / difícil

9. coche / ninguno / ruidoso

10. barato / poco / ropa

E   Complete each sentence with the Spanish equivalent of the word in parentheses. Rewrite each sentence, placing the word either before or after the noun, depending on the meaning of the word.

1. Son unas _____ niñas _____. (*big*)

2. Es el _____ perro _____. (*same*)

3. Hay algunas _____ personas _____. (*poor, penniless*)

4. Es su _____ oportunidad _____. (*only*)

5. Es una _____ civilización _____. (*ancient*)

6. Es _____ americano _____. (*half*)

7. Es un _____ científico _____. (*great*)

8. Hay _____ cosas _____. (*certain*)

Ser *to be* (third person plural)

The verb form **son** means *you* (plural)/*they are*. It is a form of the irregular verb **ser** (*to be*). (See also Chapters 3 and 4).

¿Cómo **son** las oficinas?	*What **are** the offices like?*
Son grandes y claras.	*They're big and bright.*
¿El patio **es** lindo?	*Is the patio pretty?*
Sí, y el jardín también. **Son** lindos.	*Yes, and the garden, too. **They're** pretty.*

F *¿Cómo es tu barrio?* Describe places and things in your neighborhood by writing sentences with **es** or **son** and the elements given. Change the form of the adjectives to agree with the nouns they refer to. Follow the *modelo*.

MODELO   el hotel / cómodo / muy moderno
   → El hotel es cómodo y muy moderno.

1. la avenida / animado / muy transitado

2. las casas / hermoso / muy caro

3. las calles / comercial / muy ruidoso

4. la biblioteca (*library*) / viejo / muy importante

5. la tienda por departamentos / nuevo / muy grande

6. los condominios / pequeño / muy barato

7. la zona / tranquilo / muy bonito

8. los garajes / oscuro / muy feo

9. el salón de belleza / lindo / muy bueno

10. los jardines / peatonal / muy interesante

G Express the following dialogues in Spanish.

1. *Is there a lot of noise in the neighborhood?*
   No, the area is not very noisy.

2. *What is the house like?*
   It's modern and beautiful.
   And the rooms, what are they like?
   They're light and small.

3. *The gifts are for Raquel.*
   What's in this (esta) *pretty box?*
   It's a bracelet.

4. *Is there a shopping center around here?*
   Yes, there are twenty stores.
   It's not very big.
   No, but (pero) *the stores are very good.*

5. *The garden is lovely and there are many flowers.*
   Aren't they beautiful?
   The garden is very peaceful.
   Yes, it's a wonderful place (el lugar).

Contraction **del**

The preposition **de** contracts with the masculine singular definite article **el** to form **del**: **de** + **el** → **del**.

Es la farmacia **del** barrio.	*It's the neighborhood drugstore.*
Son los papeles **del** director.	*They're the director's papers.*
Salen **del** hotel. (**salir (de)** (*to go out, leave*))	*They're leaving the hotel.*
Es el problema **del banco**.	*It's the bank's problem.*

The preposition **de** does not contract with the other forms of the definite article.

Es el café **de la** esquina.	*It's the corner café.*
Son los papeles **de la** directora.	*They're the director's* (fem.) *papers.*
Salen **de los** jardines.	*They're leaving the gardens.*
Son los problemas **de los bancos**.	*They're the banks' problems.*
Es el cuarto **de las niñas**.	*It's the little girls' room.*

The preposition **de** does not contract with the pronoun **él** (*he, it*).

El condominio no es **de él**.	*It's not **his** condominium.*

H Join each pair of nouns with **de**. Write the corresponding form of the definite article for each noun and use the contraction **del** where needed. Follow the *modelo*.

MODELO   habitación / hotel
→ la habitación del hotel

1. estantes / librería
2. maletín / director
3. cibercafé / esquina
4. temas / documento
5. supermercado / barrio
6. condominio / señorita
7. teatros / centro
8. computadoras / oficina
9. mapa / ciudad
10. luz / día
11. coches / garajes
12. electrodomésticos / casas
13. datos / libro
14. ruido / carro
15. problemas / museos
16. cámaras / banco

I Express the following phrases in Spanish, using **de**.

1. *the corner drugstore*
2. *the director's [masc.] office*
3. *the apartment keys*
4. *the toy store's toys*
5. *the garden's flowers*
6. *the (hotel) room's closets*
7. *the jewelry store's wristwatches*
8. *the neighborhood movie theater*
9. *the commercial area's stores*
10. *the electronic appointment book data*

▶ DIÁLOGO 3 · ¿De qué color es tu carro?

Study the dialogue, then listen to the recording and repeat each line.

DANIEL   ¿De qué color es tu carro?
CAMILA   Es azul.
DANIEL   ¿Y el interior?
CAMILA   Es blanco.

Análisis

Check that you understand the linguistic breakdown of each speech from *Diálogo 3*.

¿De qué color es tu carro?	*What color is your car?*
el color	*color*
¿De qué color?	*What color?*
es	*is* (**ser**)
el carro	*car*
tu carro	*your car*
Es azul.	*It's blue.*
azul	*blue*
¿Y el interior?	*And what about the interior?*
y	*and (what about?)*
el interior	*the interior, the inside*
Es blanco.	*It's white.*
blanco	*white*

▶ Variantes

Listen, and repeat the same structures from *Diálogo 3*, now with new vocabulary.

Mi carro es azul .	*My car is **blue**.*
rojo	*red*
amarillo	*yellow*
gris	*gray*
verde	*green*
negro	*black*
anaranjado	*orange*
marrón	*brown*
beige	*beige*
morado	*purple*
violeta	*purple*
¿De qué color es tu coche?	*What color is your car?*
Mi coche es azul claro.	*My car is light blue.*
Mi coche es azul oscuro.	*My car is dark blue.*
¿De qué color son los zapatos?	*What color are the shoes?*
Son negros.	*They're black.*

¿De qué colores son las maletas?	*What colors are the suitcases?*
Son grises y rojas.	*They're gray and red.*

Estructura y Práctica

> ## FORMS OF ADJECTIVES: COLORS
>
> Some colors are four-form adjectives: **rojo/roja/rojos/rojas**. Other colors are two-form adjectives: **verde/verdes, azul/azules**. The colors **beige** and **violeta** are invariable, that is, they do not change for gender or number. The color *pink* is translated **rosado**, a four-form adjective, and also **rosa**, which is invariable. **Azul claro / azul oscuro** is invariable: **los pantalones** (*pants*) **azul claro, la camisa** (*shirt*) **azul oscuro**.

Possessive Adjectives

Here are the possessive adjectives in Spanish.

	SINGULAR	PLURAL
FIRST PERSON	mi(s)	nuestro/a/os/as
SECOND PERSON	tu(s)	vuestro/a/os/as
THIRD PERSON	su(s)	su(s)

The possessive adjectives **mi, tu, su** are used before singular nouns. They add an -s before plural nouns: **mis, tus, sus**.

mi carpeta	*my folder*	**mis** carpetas	*my folders*
tu mensaje	*your message*	**tus** mensajes	*your messages*
su perro	*his/her/your/its/ your* (pl.)/*their dog*	**sus** perros	*his/her/your/its/ your* (pl.)/*their dogs*

The possessive adjectives **nuestro** (*our*) and **vuestro** (*your*) are four-form adjectives. They agree in gender and number with the noun that follows.

nuestro/vuestro mensaje	nuestros/vuestros mensajes
nuestra/vuestra carpeta	nuestras/vuestras carpetas

Vosotros, the plural of **tú**, is used only in Spain, not in Spanish America. **Vosotros** verb forms and the possessive adjective **vuestro** will not be used actively in this book.

The possessive adjective **su/sus** refers to all third persons, both singular and plural. It can therefore mean *his, her, your, its, your* (plural), *their*. Be careful not to make the mistake of assuming that **su** means *his, her* and that **sus** means *their*. **Su** and **sus** agree with the noun that follows, not with the possessor.

su amigo	*his/her/your/its/your* (pl.)/*their friend*
sus amigos	*his/her/your/its/your* (pl.)/*their friends*

To focus on the referent of **su/sus**, a phrase beginning with **de** + subject pronoun is used. (For subject pronouns, see Chapter 3.)

el amigo de él/de ella/de Ud./de ellos/   *his/her/your/their/their* (fem.)/*your* (pl.)
   de ellas/de Uds.   *friend*
los amigos de él/de ella/de Ud./de ellos/   *his/her/your/their/their* (fem.)/*your* (pl.)
   de ellas/de Uds.   *friends*

J Express the following phrases with possessive adjectives in Spanish. Follow the *modelo*.

     MODELO   *his house*
               → su casa

1. *their class*

2. *my books*

3. *our neighborhood*

4. *her money*

5. *your dogs* (Uds.)

6. *their suitcases*

7. *your wallet* (tú)

8. *my cell phone*

9. *his problems*

10. *her credit cards*

11. *our folders*

12. *your street* (Uds.)

13. *your shoes* (tú)

14. *our city*

15. *its hotel*

16. *our toys*

17. *its computer stores*

18. *their boarding passes*

K *Diálogos.* Write the possessive adjectives that correctly complete each dialogue, using the cues in parentheses.

1. —¿De qué color es _____ carro? (de ellas)

   —_____ carro es negro.

2. —¿Es animado _____ barrio? (de él)

   —Sí, _____ barrio es animado.

3. —¿Es nueva _____ casa? (de Uds.)

   —No, _____ casa es vieja.

4. —¿Son difíciles _____ exámenes? (de ellos)

   —No, _____ exámenes no son difíciles.

5. —¿De qué color son _____ zapatos? (de ella)

   —_____ zapatos son marrones.

6. —¿Es pesado _____ artículo? (de Ud.)

   —No, _____ artículo es muy interesante.

7. —¿Cómo son _____ perros? (de Ud.)

   —_____ perros son tranquilos.

8. —¿Son largos _____ informes? (Uds.)

   —No, _____ informes son cortos.

L *¿De qué color es?* Rewrite each phrase, including the Spanish equivalent of the word(s) in parentheses.

1. la ropa _____ (*black and white*)
2. unos carros _____ (*blue*)
3. mi cuarto _____ (*green*)
4. muchas flores _____ (*red and yellow*)
5. sus maletas _____ (*gray*)

6. tu mochila _____ (*purple*)
7. unas carteras _____ (*brown*)
8. su camiseta (*T-shirt*) _____ (*light blue*)
9. los abrigos (*overcoats*) _____ (*dark blue*)
10. unos bolsos _____ (*beige*)

DIÁLOGO 4 · ¿Qué hay en el maletín?

Study the dialogue, then listen to the recording and repeat each line.

CAMILA   ¿Qué hay en tu maletín?
DANIEL   Hay documentos importantes.
CAMILA   ¿Son largos los documentos?
DANIEL   Sí, son largos y muy pesados.

Análisis

Check that you understand the linguistic breakdown of each speech from *Diálogo 4*.

¿Qué hay en tu maletín?
  tu

What's in your attaché case?
  your (informal, before a singular noun)

Hay documentos importantes.
  importante
  documentos importantes

There are important documents.
  important
  important documents

¿Son largos los documentos?
  largo

Are the documents long?
  long

Sí, son largos y muy pesados.
  son
  muy
  pesado

Yes, they're long and very boring.
  they are (**ser**)
  very
  heavy, boring

Variantes

Listen, and repeat the same structures from *Diálogo 4*, now with new vocabulary.

Hay documentos en el maletín.
  informes
  contratos
  revistas
  periódicos
  artículos
  folletos

*There are **documents** in the attaché case.*
  reports
  contracts
  magazines
  newspapers
  articles
  brochures

El informe es largo .   *The report is long.*
  corto   *short*
  fácil   *easy*
  aburrido   *boring*

Estructura y Práctica

More on Question Formation: Information Questions, Question Words (Interrogatives), Yes/No Questions

Information Questions

You learned in Chapter 1 that information questions expect a piece of information as an answer. Question words introduce information questions. They are always written with an accent mark in Spanish, and they carry stress in questions. Information questions in Spanish usually have the following word order: interrogative word + verb (+ subject) + other elements. The subject position may or may not be occupied, since verb endings indicate the subject.

  ¿Qué hay en la mochila?   ***What** is (there) in the backpack?*
  ¿Cómo son las tiendas?   ***What** are the stores **like**?*
  ¿Cuántos museos hay en la ciudad?   ***How many** museums are (there) in the city?*

Question Words (Interrogatives)

The most important question words in Spanish are the following.

  ¿Cuál? ¿Cuáles?   *Which?*
  ¿Cuándo?   *When?*
  ¿Cuánto? ¿Cuánta?   *How much?*
  ¿Cuántos? ¿Cuántas?   *How many?*
  ¿Cómo?   *How?*
  ¿Dónde?   *Where?*
    ¿Adónde?   *(To) where? (with verbs of motion)*
    ¿De dónde?   *(From) where?*
  ¿Qué?   *What?*
    ¿Para qué?   *For what purpose?*
    ¿Por qué?   *Why?*
  ¿Quién? ¿Quiénes?   *Who?*
    ¿A quién? ¿A quiénes?   *Whom?*
    ¿De quién? ¿De quiénes?   *Whose?*

¿Qué? may be used before a verb or a noun.

  ¿Qué hay en la gaveta?   ***What's (there)** in the drawer?*
  ¿Qué tiendas hay en esta calle?   ***What stores** are there on this street?*

¿Cómo? asks for repetition when you don't hear something clearly.

  Él llega mañana.   *He's arriving tomorrow.*
  ¿Cómo? ¿Cuándo llega?   ***What?** When is he arriving?*

¿**Cómo?** is also used to express astonishment.

Carlos habla siete idiomas.	*Carlos speaks seven languages.*
¿**Cómo?** No lo puedo creer.	***What?!*** *I can't believe it.*

Prepositions associated with an interrogative word must precede it in Spanish. In English, they usually are separated from the question word and appear at the end of the sentence.

¿**De dónde** es Ud.?	***Where*** *are you* ***from?***
¿**De quién** es el carro?	***Whose*** *car is it?*

M *Preguntas informativas.* Write the information question that would elicit the information given in each statement. There may be more than one response possible for some statements.

1. Nuestra casa es grande.

2. Hay tres tarjetas de crédito en su billetero.

3. Mi carro es azul oscuro.

4. Hay un CD en la caja.

5. El restaurante mexicano queda (*is*) en la esquina.

6. Las revistas son aburridas.

7. Los regalos son para Sofía.

8. El museo de arte queda (*is*) por aquí.

9. Hay dieciséis estudiantes (*students*) en la clase.

10. Es una agenda electrónica.

11. Son folletos y contratos.

12. El interior de su casa es blanco.

13. Hay tiendas de cómputo en esta (*this*) avenida.

14. Su (de ellos) jardín es lindo y tranquilo.

QUEDAR

Quedar means *to be located*, referring to things that do not change location.

El café **queda** por aquí.	*The café* ***is*** *around here.*
Mi hotel **queda** cerca.	*My hotel* ***is*** *nearby.*
Nuestra casa **queda** en la esquina.	*Our house* ***is*** *at the corner.*
Las tiendas de cómputo **quedan** en el centro.	*The computer stores* ***are*** *downtown.*

Yes/No Questions

You learned in Chapter 1 that questions not beginning with a question word are called yes/no questions; they ask for either *yes* or *no* as an answer.

When a sentence consists of a form of the verb **ser** and an adjective, the subject may be placed at the end of the sentence to form a question. The pattern of the question is thus verb + adjective + subject.

El artículo es corto.	*The article is short.*
¿Es corto el artículo?	*Is the article short?*
Los documentos son importantes.	*The documents are important.*
¿Son importantes los documentos?	*Are the documents important?*

N *Preguntas de sí o no.* Change each of the following statements into a yes/no question, using the pattern **ser** + adjective + subject. Follow the *modelo.*

> MODELO   El condominio es nuevo.
> → ¿Es nuevo el condominio?

1. Los teléfonos celulares son útiles.
2. Su reloj es caro.
3. Los paseos son muy transitados.
4. La catedral es vieja.
5. Las preguntas son difíciles.
6. Ana y Fernando son inteligentes.
7. El hotel es bueno.
8. Esta (*this*) calle es muy ruidosa.
9. Las flores son hermosas.
10. El profesor es aburrido.

▶ DIÁLOGO 5 · Mis libros

Study the dialogue, then listen to the recording and repeat each line.

DANIEL   Hay libros en la mesa, ¿no sabes?
CAMILA   Ah, sí. Son mis libros de administración de empresas.
DANIEL   ¿Son libros difíciles?
CAMILA   Sí, son bastante difíciles, pero muy útiles.

Análisis

Check that you understand the linguistic breakdown of each speech from *Diálogo 5.*

Hay libros en la mesa, ¿no sabes?	*There are books on the table, you know?*
el libro	*book*
la mesa	*table*
en la mesa	*on the table*
¿no sabes?	*you know?* (literally, *don't you know?*)
Ah, sí. Son mis libros de administración de empresas.	*Oh, yes. They're my business books.*
mis	*my* (before a plural noun)
la administración	*administration*

la empresa	*firm, company, business*
la administración de empresas	*business (administration)*

¿Son libros difíciles?	*Are they difficult books?*
difícil	* difficult*

Sí, son bastante difíciles, pero muy útiles.	*Yes, they're quite difficult, but very useful.*
bastante	* quite, quite a lot*
bastante difícil	* quite difficult*
útil	* useful*

▶ Variantes

Listen, and repeat the same structures from *Diálogo 5*, now with new vocabulary.

Son mis libros de administración de empresas .	*They're my **business** books.*
historia	* history*
economía	* economics*
derecho	* law*
ciencias políticas	* political science*
español	* Spanish*
inglés	* English*
computación	* computer science*
música	* music*
arte	* art*
medicina	* medical* (literally, *medicine*)
contabilidad	* accounting*
enfermería	* nursing*
matemáticas	* math*
química	* chemistry*
biología	* biology*
física	* physics*

¿Son libros difíciles ?	*Are they **difficult** books?*
importantes	* important*
interesantes	* interesting*
nuevos	* new*
viejos	* old*

Estructura y Práctica

Intensifiers

An intensifier is a word, especially an adverb, that is used to emphasize, enhance, or add impact to another adjective, adverb, noun, or verb.

Su casa es **muy** fea.	*Their house is **very** ugly.*
Los exámenes son **bastante** fáciles.	*The exams are **quite** easy.*
Los gemelos son **completamente** diferentes.	*The twins are **completely** different.*

Many intensifiers are adverbs that end in **-mente**. They are formed by adding the suffix **-mente** to the feminine singular form of the adjective. (See also Chapter 8.)

MASCULINE SINGULAR	FEMININE SINGULAR	ADVERB	MEANING
completo	completa	completamente	*completely*

If the adjective has only one form for the masculine and feminine singular, then the suffix **-mente** is added to that form.

SINGULAR	ADVERB	MEANING
fácil	fácilmente	*easily*
suficiente	suficientemente	*sufficiently, adequately*

More adverbs ending in **-mente**

realmente *really*
relativamente *relatively*
sumamente *extremely*
verdaderamente *really*

O *Intensificadores.* Rewrite each of the following sentences, including the intensifier in parentheses to add emphasis to the adjective.

1. Mi clase de historia es interesante. (muy)
2. Las casas son hermosas. (tan (*so*))
3. El libro de arte es maravilloso. (realmente)
4. Es una ciudad grande. (bastante)
5. ¿Son largos los informes? (demasiado (*too*))
6. Nuestra empresa es nueva. (relativamente)
7. Unas calles son transitadas. (poco (*little, not much*))
8. Sus hijos son inteligentes. (sumamente)
9. ¿Es tranquilo tu barrio? (verdaderamente)
10. ¿No son modernas las oficinas? (suficientemente)

Noun Phrase Functions

Nouns and noun phrases function as the subject or object of the verb, as the object of a preposition, or as a short answer to a question. In Chapter 1, you saw examples of these functions. Noun phrases can also follow forms of the verb **ser** (*to be*) in the predicate of a sentence. In traditional grammar, this function is called the predicate nominative.

Es **una fiesta** para Juan.   *It's **a party** for Juan.*
Son **los amigos** de mi hijo.   *They're **friends** of my son.*

THE PREDICATE

The predicate consists of everything in a sentence except the subject. Thus, in the sentence *Philip studies business administration*, the words *studies business administration* form the predicate of the sentence. The predicate contains the verb and its objects, adverbs, prepositional phrases adding to the meaning of the verb, etc.

P **Noun phrases.** Create noun phrases from the elements given. Follow the *modelo*.

> MODELO   camisetas / sus / blancas
> → sus camisetas blancas

1. folletos / largos / quince
2. animadas / avenidas / unas
3. el / en / maletín
4. examen / de / química / mi
5. amarillas / flores / muchas

6. habitaciones / veinte / modernas
7. nuestros / para / amigos
8. rojo / el / carro
9. sus / matemáticas / de / clases
10. paseos / en / transitados / los

Q **Translation.** Express the following dialogues in Spanish.

1. *Is your (tú) neighborhood lively?*
   No, my neighborhood is quite quiet.

2. *Are your (you [pl.]) biology books interesting?*
   No, our biology books are boring.

3. *Is their company new?*
   Yes, their company is new and very important.

4. *Are her suitcases black?*
   No, her suitcases are brown.

5. *Are his articles difficult?*
   No, his articles are easy.

Un paso más

Are you ready to take your Spanish a step further? Here are exercises that will enhance your knowledge of the language and encourage you to express yourself freely.

R **Word families.** You have learned several adjectives that are derived from nouns, as well as some nouns that are derived from adjectives. Many of these words are cognates of English words. Nouns that end in **-dad, -tad, -cia, -eza, -ez** are usually feminine: **la novedad, la dificultad, la importancia, la grandeza, la vejez.** Increasing your recognition of word families and gender endings will make your study of the Spanish language more productive. In the exercise that follows, write the Spanish adjective that is related to the noun provided.

1. la importancia
2. la dificultad
3. el ruido
4. la tranquilidad

5. el comercio
6. la novedad
7. la claridad
8. el interés

9. la hermosura

10. la facilidad

11. la naranja (*orange*)

12. la grandeza

13. el tránsito

14. la oscuridad

15. la bondad

16. la utilidad

17. la comodidad

18. la modernidad

19. el peatón (*pedestrian*)

20. el ánimo (*spirit, energy*)

21. la vejez

22. la maldad

23. la verdad

S *Preguntas personales.* Answer each question with a complete Spanish sentence.

1. ¿Cómo es tu casa?

2. ¿De qué color es?

3. ¿Cuántos cuartos hay?

4. ¿Hay jardín, patio y garaje? ¿Cómo son?

5. ¿Dónde queda tu casa?

6. ¿Cómo es tu barrio?

7. ¿Cómo son las calles, avenidas y tiendas?

8. ¿Cómo es tu carro?

9. ¿De qué color es?

10. ¿Cuál es tu color favorito?

Nationalities, Professions, Food, and Films

Communication Goals

- Asking and telling about nationalities and origins
- Learning about the Spanish-speaking world
- Talking about restaurants and films
- Vocabulary: countries, foreign languages, food, professions

Grammar Topics

- Subject Pronouns
- **Ser** *to be*
- Adjectives of Nationality
- **¡Qué!** in Exclamations
- Information Questions
- Yes/No Questions
- Negative Sentences
- Position of Adjectives
- Prepositions
- Demonstrative Adjectives
- Gender of Nouns That Refer to People

DIÁLOGO 1 · ¿De dónde son?

Study the dialogue, then listen to the recording and repeat each line.

FERNANDA ¿Es Ud. mexicano?
ESTEBAN No, no soy mexicano. Soy costarricense, de San José. ¿Y Ud.?
FERNANDA ¿Yo? Yo soy colombiana. Soy de Bogotá.

Análisis

Check that you understand the linguistic breakdown of each speech from *Diálogo 1*.

¿Es Ud. mexicano?	*Are you Mexican?*
es	*are* (third person singular) (**ser**)
Ud.	*you* (formal singular)
mexicano	*Mexican*

No, no soy mexicano. Soy costarricense, de San José. ¿Y Ud.?	*No, I'm not Mexican. I'm Costa Rican, from San José. And you?*
no	*no* (negative particle)
soy	*am* (first person singular) (**ser**)
costarricense	*Costa Rican*
de	*from*
San José	*San José* (*capital of Costa Rica*)

¿Yo? Yo soy colombiana. Soy de Bogotá.	*Me? I'm Colombian. I'm from Bogotá.*
yo	*I, me* (colloquial)
colombiana	*Colombian* (feminine)
Bogotá	*Bogotá* (*capital of Colombia*)

▶ Variantes

Listen, and repeat the same structures from *Diálogo 1*, now with new vocabulary.

Soy mexicano .	Soy mexicana .	*I'm **Mexican**.*
costarricense	costarricense	*Costa Rican*
cubano	cubana	*Cuban*
colombiano	colombiana	*Colombian*
puertorriqueño	puertorriqueña	*Puerto Rican*
norteamericano	norteamericana	*American*
estadounidense	estadounidense	*American*
panameño	panameña	*Panamanian*
guatemalteco	guatemalteca	*Guatemalan*
salvadoreño	salvadoreña	*Salvadoran*
hondureño	hondureña	*Honduran*
nicaragüense	nicaragüense	*Nicaraguan*
dominicano	dominicana	*Dominican*
chileno	chilena	*Chilean*
argentino	argentina	*Argentinian, Argentine*
peruano	peruana	*Peruvian*
brasileño	brasileña	*Brazilian*
venezolano	venezolana	*Venezuelan*
uruguayo	uruguaya	*Uruguayan*
paraguayo	paraguaya	*Paraguayan*
ecuatoriano	ecuatoriana	*Ecuadoran*
boliviano	boliviana	*Bolivian*
canadiense	canadiense	*Canadian*
inglés	inglesa	*English*
español	española	*Spanish*

italiano	italiana	*Italian*
francés	francesa	*French*
portugués	portuguesa	*Portuguese*
alemán	alemana	*German*
polaco	polaca	*Polish*
irlandés	irlandesa	*Irish*
escocés	escocesa	*Scottish*
griego	griega	*Greek*
ruso	rusa	*Russian*
hindú	hindú	*Indian*
indio	india	*Indian*
vietnamita	vietnamita	*Vietnamese*
coreano	coreana	*Korean*
surcoreano	surcoreana	*South Korean*
norcoreano	norcoreana	*North Korean*
japonés	japonesa	*Japanese*
chino	china	*Chinese*
israelí	israelí	*Israeli*
iraquí	iraquí	*Iraqi*
iraní	iraní	*Iranian*
saudí, saudita	saudí, saudita	*Saudi*

Otras Nacionalidades

austríaco	austríaca	*Austrian*
holandés	holandesa	*Dutch*
belga	belga	*Belgian*
suizo	suiza	*Swiss*
luxemburgués	luxemburguesa	*Luxembourgian*
sueco	sueca	*Swedish*
noruego	noruega	*Norwegian*
danés	danesa	*Danish*
finlandés	finlandesa	*Finnish*
ucranio, ucraniano	ucrania, ucraniana	*Ukrainian*
paquistaní, pakistaní	paquistaní, pakistaní	*Pakistani*
filipino	filipina	*Philippine*
tailandés	tailandesa	*Thai*
taiwanés	taiwanesa	*Taiwanese*
sudafricano	sudafricana	*South African*
egipcio	egipcia	*Egyptian*
jordano	jordana	*Jordanian*
sirio	siria	*Syrian*
turco	turca	*Turkish*
libanés	libanesa	*Lebanese*
marroquí	marroquí	*Moroccan*
libio	libia	*Libyan*
afgano	afgana	*Afghan, Afghani*
australiano	australiana	*Australian*
neozelandés	neozelandesa	*New Zealander*

Estructura y Práctica

Subject Pronouns

Spanish and English have different sets of personal pronouns. Here are the English subject pronouns.

	SINGULAR	PLURAL
FIRST PERSON	*I*	*we*
SECOND PERSON	*you*	*you*
THIRD PERSON	*he, she, it*	*they*

Here are the Spanish subject pronouns.

	SINGULAR	PLURAL
FIRST PERSON	yo	nosotros, nosotras
SECOND PERSON	tú	vosotros, vosotras
THIRD PERSON	él, ella, usted	ellos, ellas, ustedes

NOTE   Verb forms for **vosotros** will be presented but will not be practiced actively throughout the book.

There are several important differences between personal pronouns in English and in Spanish.

1 · The pronoun **yo** is not capitalized unless it is the first word of a sentence.

2 · The Spanish equivalents of *we* make a gender distinction that English does not require. **Nosotros** is used for groups of two or more males or for groups of two or more males and females. **Nosotras** is used for groups of two or more females.

3 · Spanish has four equivalents for English *you*. The pronouns **tú** and **vosotros/vosotras** are informal. **Tú** is used to address one person with whom you have a relationship that Hispanic culture defines as informal: family members, children, fellow students, etc. **Vosotros/vosotras** is used to address two or more people with whom you have an informal relationship. Note that **vosotros/vosotras** makes the same gender distinction as **nosotros/nosotras**, above. **Usted** and **ustedes** are used in formal situations. **Usted** is used to address one person with whom you have a relationship that Hispanic culture defines as formal: strangers, superiors at work, people not part of your usual network, etc. **Ustedes** is used to address two or more people with whom you have a formal relationship.

4 · In the third person plural, groups of two or more males or groups of two or more males and females are referred to as **ellos**. Groups of two or more consisting entirely of females are referred to as **ellas**.

5 · The equivalents of *you* (**vosotros/vosotras**) described in No. 3 above reflect the usage in Spain only. In Spanish America, **vosotros/vosotras** is not used. Instead, **ustedes** is used as the plural of both **tú** and **usted**.

6 · **Usted** is used with a third person singular verb. **Ustedes** is used with a third person plural verb. In writing, **usted** is usually written **Ud.**, and **ustedes** is usually written **Uds.** These abbreviations are pronounced **usted** and **ustedes**, respectively.

7 · The standards of formality that condition the choice of **tú** or **usted** vary within the Spanish-speaking world. Informal address is more frequent in Spain than in countries such as Mexico or Ecuador. Rural aristocratic milieus use **usted** much more than modern urban milieus.

8 · When in doubt, learners of Spanish should use formal address until asked to switch to **tú** by the native speaker they are talking to. American culture places a high value on informality, but in Spanish-speaking cultures, the inappropriate use of **tú** is considered rude, not friendly.

9 · Spanish has no equivalent for English *it* as a subject pronoun. All masculine nouns, whether referring to people or things, are replaced by **él**. All feminine nouns are replaced by **ella**.

10 · In many parts of Spanish America, **tú** is replaced by the pronoun **vos**, which has its own set of verb endings. This phenomenon, called *el voseo,* is characteristic of the speech of Argentina, Uruguay, Paraguay, Bolivia, Chile, Central America except for Panamá, and parts of Venezuela and Colombia. In Argentina, Uruguay, and Nicaragua, **vos** is acceptable in both speech and writing and has become a standard second person singular form.

11 · In Spanish, personal pronouns are not used as much as in English, because the ending of the verb shows who the subject is. The pronouns are used for focus or contrast, as in sentences such as the following.

Él es asesor, pero **ella** es abogada.	*He's a consultant, but **she's** a lawyer.*
Uds. son italianos, pero **nosotros** somos ingleses.	*You are Italian, but **we** are English.*

In the English equivalents of the sentences above, the subject pronouns are stressed.

12 · The pronoun **usted** (**Ud.**) is often used to add a note of politeness or formality to sentences.

A *¿Quiénes son?* Identify the subject or subjects of each of the following sentences. Write the correct subject pronoun or pronouns.

1. Es argentino.

2. Somos rusos.

3. Son panameñas.

4. Soy norteamericano.

5. Es india.

6. Son canadienses.

7. Eres israelí.

8. Somos venezolanas.

Ser *to be*

The verb **ser** is one of the two Spanish verbs meaning *to be*. An irregular verb, its conjugation in present tense is as follows:

ser *to be*

SINGULAR	PLURAL
soy	somos
eres	sois
es	son

Uses of ser

1 · **Ser** links nouns and pronouns.

Yo **soy** ingeniero.	*I'm an engineer.*
¿**Eres** dentista?	*Are you a dentist?*
Alicia y José **son** amigos.	*Alicia and José **are** friends.*

Notice that, unlike English, Spanish omits the indefinite article **un/una** with a profession.

2 · **Ser** is used before (or, in information questions, after) a phrase beginning with **de** that expresses possession, origin, or the material of which something is made.

La oficina **es de** Jorge.	*The office **is** Jorge's.*
¿Uds. **son de** Chile?	*Are you **from** Chile?*
¿**De quién es** este billetero?	*Whose wallet **is** this?*
El reloj **es de** oro.	*The watch **is made of** gold.*

3 · **Ser** is used with color, nationality, aesthetic attributes, and age.

Mi carro **es** negro.	*My car **is** black.*
Somos norteamericanos.	*We **are** American.*
Alonso y Nicolás **son** guapos.	*Alonso and Nicolás **are** handsome.*
El profesor **es** viejo.	*The professor **is** old.*

4 · **Ser** is used to tell time and to give the date. (See also Chapter 4.)

¿Qué hora **es**?	*What time **is it**?*
Es la una.	*It's one o'clock.*
Son las dos y media.	*It's two thirty.*
Hoy **es** el once de marzo.	*Today **is** March 11.*

B   *Es de México.* Write complete sentences, conjugating the verb **ser** to agree with each subject provided. Follow the *modelo*.

MODELO   él → Es de México.

1. tú

2. ellos

3. yo

4. Uds.

5. ella

6. nosotros

7. Ud.

8. ellas

C ***De los Estados Unidos.*** Your new friend thinks that you, your family, and your friends are from other countries, but you're all from the United States. Write responses telling him so. Follow the *modelo.*

MODELO   Claudio es francés, ¿no?
          → De Francia, no. Es de los Estados Unidos.

1. Tus papás son españoles, ¿no?

2. Tu primo es chino, ¿no?

3. Eres australiano, ¿no?

4. María Elena es colombiana, ¿no?

5. Uds. son alemanes, ¿no?

6. Tus amigos son irlandeses, ¿no?

7. Ud. es surcoreano, ¿no?

8. Diego y Fernanda son peruanos, ¿no?

The phrase **¿no?** added to a statement turns it into a question. This is called a tag question. In the *modelo* for Exercise C, it is translated as *isn't he?* The English translation will change based on the subject of the sentence. (See also Chapter 4.)

D ***Nacionalidades.*** Write a complete sentence to respond to each of the following questions, confirming the nationality of the people asked about. Follow the *modelo.*

MODELO   ¿Lorenzo es de Bolivia?
          → Sí, es boliviano.

1. ¿Mateo es de Escocia?

2. ¿Tomás y Lucas son de Tailandia?

3. ¿Clara es de Vietnam?

4. ¿Uds. son de Costa Rica?

5. ¿Benjamín y Raquel son de Israel?

6. ¿Isabel es de Suecia?

7. ¿Joaquín es de Bélgica?

8. ¿Olivia y Amelia son de Taiwán?

9. ¿Josefa es de Irán?

10. ¿Esos estudiantes son de Egipto?

▶ DIÁLOGO 2 · ¿De qué origen son?

Study the dialogue, then listen to the recording and repeat each line.

ESTEBAN	¿De dónde eres?
FERNANDA	Soy de Puerto Rico. ¿Y tú?
ESTEBAN	Yo soy de la Florida, pero de origen cubano.
FERNANDA	¡Qué casualidad! Yo también soy de origen cubano.

Análisis

Check that you understand the linguistic breakdown of each speech from *Diálogo 2.*

¿De dónde eres?	*Where are you from?*
de	*from*
¿dónde?	*where?*
eres	*you are* (second person singular) (**ser**)

Soy de Puerto Rico. ¿Y tú?	*I'm from Puerto Rico. What about you?*
soy	*I am* (first person singular) (**ser**)
Puerto Rico	*Puerto Rico* (*commonwealth of the U.S.;* Estado Libre Asociado de Puerto Rico)
tú	*you* (*informal singular*)
Yo soy de la Florida, pero de origen cubano.	*I'm from Florida, but of Cuban descent.*
yo	*I*
de	*from, of*
la Florida	*Florida*
pero	*but*
el origen	*origin, descent, background*
cubano	*Cuban*
de origen cubano	*of Cuban descent*
¡Qué casualidad! Yo también soy de origen cubano.	*What a coincidence! I am also of Cuban descent.*
¡Qué + *noun*!	*What a + noun!*
la casualidad	*chance, coincidence*
¡Qué casualidad!	*What a coincidence!*
también	*also, too*

▶ Variantes

Listen, and repeat the same structures from *Diálogo 2*, now with new vocabulary.

Yo soy de Puerto Rico .	*I'm from* **Puerto Rico**.
los Estados Unidos	*the United States*
(el) Canadá	*Canada*
México	*Mexico*
Costa Rica	*Costa Rica*
Panamá	*Panama*
Guatemala	*Guatemala*
El Salvador	*El Salvador*
Honduras	*Honduras*
Nicaragua	*Nicaragua*
Colombia	*Colombia*
Chile	*Chile*
(la) Argentina	*Argentina*
(el) Perú	*Peru*
Venezuela	*Venezuela*
Paraguay	*Paraguay*
(el) Uruguay	*Uruguay*
(el) Ecuador	*Ecuador*
Bolivia	*Bolivia*
Cuba	*Cuba*

(el) Brasil	*Brazil*
Inglaterra	*England*
España	*Spain*
Italia	*Italy*
Francia	*France*
Portugal	*Portugal*
Alemania	*Germany*
Austria	*Austria*
Irlanda	*Ireland*
Escocia	*Scotland*
Grecia	*Greece*
Polonia	*Poland*
Rusia	*Russia*
(la) India	*India*
Vietnam	*Vietnam*
Corea	*Korea*
Corea del Sur	*South Korea*
Corea del Norte	*North Korea*
Japón	*Japan*
China	*China*
Israel	*Israel*
Irak	*Iraq*
Irán	*Iran*
Arabia Saudita	*Saudi Arabia*

Mi familia es de origen cubano .	*My family is of **Cuban** descent.*
inglés	*English*
español	*Spanish*
italiano	*Italian*
irlandés	*Irish*
escocés	*Scottish*
francés	*French*
alemán	*German*
griego	*Greek*
portugués	*Portuguese*
ruso	*Russian*
polaco	*Polish*
chino	*Chinese*
japonés	*Japanese*
coreano	*Korean*
indio	*Indian*
hindú	*Indian*
vietnamita	*Vietnamese*
iraquí	*Iraqi*
iraní	*Iranian*

Otros Países

(la) República Dominicana	*(the) Dominican Republic*
Holanda (Países Bajos)	*Holland (Netherlands)*
Bélgica	*Belgium*
Luxemburgo	*Luxembourg*
(la) Suiza	*Switzerland*
Suecia	*Sweden*
Noruega	*Norway*
Dinamarca	*Denmark*
Finlandia	*Finland*
Egipto	*Egypt*
Ucrania	*Ukraine*
Filipinas	*Philippines*
Paquistán, Pakistán	*Pakistan*
Taiwán	*Taiwan*
Sudáfrica	*South Africa*
Jordania	*Jordan*
Siria	*Syria*
Turquía	*Turkey*
el Líbano	*Lebanon*
Marruecos	*Morocco*
Libia	*Libya*
Afganistán	*Afghanistan*
Australia	*Australia*
Nueva Zelanda	*New Zealand*

Estructura y Práctica

Adjectives of Nationality

Some adjectives of nationality do not follow the pattern of other adjectives.

Adjectives of nationality ending in **-o** or **-e** have the expected number of forms. Adjectives of nationality ending in **-o** have four forms; those ending in **-e** have two forms. Note that adjectives of nationality are not capitalized in Spanish.

	MASCULINE	FEMININE
SINGULAR	un restaurante mexicano	una comida mexicana
PLURAL	unos restaurantes mexicanos	unas comidas mexicanas
SINGULAR	un periódico árabe	una revista árabe
PLURAL	unos periódicos árabes	unas revistas árabes

Most adjectives of nationality ending in **-e** end in the suffix **-ense**.

	MASCULINE	FEMININE
SINGULAR	un periódico canadiense	una revista canadiense
PLURAL	unos periódicos canadienses	unas revistas canadienses

Here are some two-form adjectives of nationality ending in vowels other than **-e**.

SINGULAR	PLURAL	MEANING
belga	belgas	*Belgian*
saudita	sauditas	*Saudi*
iraní	iraníes	*Iranian*
iraquí	iraquíes	*Iraqi*
israelí	israelíes	*Israeli*
marroquí	marroquíes	*Moroccan*
hindú	hindúes	*Hindu, Indian*

Adjectives of nationality ending in a consonant have four forms, not two like other adjectives ending in a consonant.

	MASCULINE	FEMININE
SINGULAR	español	española
PLURAL	españoles	españolas

Adjectives of nationality having an accent mark on the final syllable in the masculine singular lose that written accent in the other three forms.

	MASCULINE	FEMININE
SINGULAR	francés	francesa
PLURAL	franceses	francesas
SINGULAR	alemán	alemana
PLURAL	alemanes	alemanas

Other common adjectives of nationality ending in a consonant are the following:

danés *Danish*
escocés *Scottish*
finlandés *Finnish*
galés *Welsh*
holandés *Dutch*
inglés *English*
irlandés *Irish*
japonés *Japanese*

letón *Latvian*
libanés *Lebanese*
luxemburgués *Luxembourgian*
portugués *Portuguese*
tailandés *Thai*
taiwanés *Taiwanese*
ugandés *Ugandan*

"AMERICAN": ADJECTIVES OF NATIONALITY

A citizen of the United States is called **americano** or **norteamericano** (*North American*) in Spanish. In Spanish America, **americano** can also simply mean someone from the Americas. The term **norteamericano** is therefore clearer when referring to a United States citizen. The adjective **estadounidense** may be used in formal language to refer to someone or something from the United States (**los Estados Unidos**).

Adjectives of Nationality Used as Nouns

When accompanied by an article or other determiner, adjectives of nationality are used as nouns.

el **inglés**	*the Englishman*
la **griega**	*the Greek woman*
los **franceses**	*the French*

The masculine singular form of adjectives of nationality, when used with the definite article, also functions as a noun that refers to the language.

el inglés	*English*
el español	*Spanish*
el alemán	*German*
el ruso	*Russian*
el chino	*Chinese*

E *Nacionalidad y origen.* Write a complete sentence that tells the nationality and origin of the people indicated. The first country named is for nationality, the second for origin or descent. Follow the *modelo.*

MODELO   Gonzalo: Puerto Rico / España
  → Gonzalo es puertorriqueño, pero de origen español.

1. Raquel: Ecuador / Alemania

2. Los señores (*Mr. and Mrs.*) Fuentes: Brasil / Dinamarca

3. Yo [*masc.*]: Escocia / Austria

4. María y Catalina: El Salvador / Líbano

5. Tú [*fem.*]: Bélgica / Irán

6. Regina y Mauricio: Uruguay / Ucrania

7. Uds. [*fem.*]: Francia / Paquistán

8. La señorita Rivas: Israel / Polonia

9. Victoria y yo [*masc.*]: Inglaterra / Marruecos

10. Ignacio y Alberto: Nicaragua / Vietnam

F *Idiomas* (**Languages**). Write the name of an official language spoken in each of the following countries. Write your answers in Spanish, and include the definite article.

1. Suecia	9. Vietnam
2. Portugal	10. Holanda
3. Rusia	11. China
4. Finlandia	12. Egipto
5. Francia	13. Austria
6. Alemania	14. Honduras
7. Japón	15. Corea del Sur
8. Italia	16. Tailandia

¡Qué! in Exclamations

¡Qué! is used in exclamations before both nouns and adjectives. The English equivalent is *What a!* when used before a singular noun, *What!* before a plural noun, and *How!* before an adjective.

¡**Qué** casualidad!	**What a** coincidence!
¡**Qué** problemas!	**What** problems!
¡**Qué** divertido!	**How** amusing!
¡**Qué** estupendo!	**How** great! / **How** fantastic!
¡**Qué** padre!	**How** great! / **How** fantastic! (Mexico)
¡**Qué** chévere!	**How** great! / **How** fantastic! (Puerto Rico)

To emphasize a characteristic of a noun, the pattern **¡Qué!** + adjective + noun may be used.

¡**Qué** buen amigo!	**What a** good friend!
¡**Qué** mala suerte!	**What** bad luck!
¡**Qué** lindos juguetes!	**What** nice toys!
¡**Qué** ridículas ideas!	**What** ridiculous ideas!

Perhaps more common in the above function is the pattern **¡Qué!** + noun + **más/tan** + adjective.

¡**Qué** país más interesante!	**What an** interesting country!
¡**Qué** comida tan rica!	**What a** delicious meal!
¡**Qué** películas más divertidas!	**What** entertaining films!
¡**Qué** niños tan traviesos!	**What** mischievous children!

G Rewrite each statement as an exclamation. Use **más** or **tan** in the exclamation, depending on which appears in parentheses. Follow the *modelo*.

MODELO   El museo es muy grande. (más)
  → ¡Qué museo más grande!

1. Los hoteles son muy modernos. (más)
2. La comida es muy sabrosa. (tan)
3. El libro es muy interesante. (más)
4. Las señoras son muy simpáticas. (tan)
5. La ciudad es muy animada. (más)
6. Los temas son muy importantes. (tan)
7. El informe es muy aburrido. (más)
8. Las calles son muy ruidosas. (tan)
9. El jardín es muy tranquilo. (más)
10. Los estudiantes son muy inteligentes. (tan)

H Express the following exclamations with **¡Qué!** in Spanish.

1. *What a day!*
2. *How wonderful!*
3. *What a dessert!*
4. *How ugly!*
5. *How easy!*
6. *What a musician* [masc.]*!*
7. *How authentic!*
8. *What a painter* [fem.]*!*

▶ DIÁLOGO 3 · Somos de Madrid.

Study the dialogue, then listen to the recording and repeat each line.

ESTEBAN	¿De dónde son Uds.?
FERNANDA	Somos españoles, de Madrid.
ESTEBAN	Pues mi esposa y yo también somos madrileños.
FERNANDA	¿De veras? ¿De qué parte de la ciudad?

Análisis

Check that you understand the linguistic breakdown of each speech from *Diálogo 3*.

¿De dónde son Uds.?	*Where are you from?*
Uds.	*you* (plural)
Somos españoles, de Madrid.	*We're Spaniards, from Madrid.*
somos	*we are* (first person plural) (**ser**)
español	*Spanish, Spaniard*
españoles	*Spanish, Spaniards*
Madrid	*Madrid* (*capital of Spain*)
Pues mi esposa y yo también somos madrileños.	*Well, my wife and I are also from Madrid.*
pues	*well* (interjection)
la esposa	*wife*
mi esposa	*my wife*
madrileño	*from Madrid*
¿De veras? ¿De qué parte de la ciudad?	*Really? Where in the city?*
de veras	*really*
la parte	*part*
¿de qué parte?	*where?, from which part?*
de la ciudad	*in the city, of the city*

▶ Variantes

Listen, and repeat the same structures from *Diálogo 3*, now with new vocabulary.

Mi esposa y yo somos madrileños.	*My **wife** and I are from Madrid.*
esposo	*husband*
mujer	*wife*
marido	*husband*
novia	*girlfriend*
novio	*boyfriend*
amigo	*friend* (*male*)
amiga	*friend* (*female*)

Estructura y Práctica

MADRILEÑOS AND OTHER CITY DWELLERS

The residents of Madrid are known as **madrileños**. **Madrileño** is a gentilic (or demonym), a word that identifies the residents or natives of a particular place. You have learned the gentilics or adjectives of nationality of several countries, for example, **España** → **español(a)**. Here are some cities and their gentilics.

Ciudad de México	capitalino/a
Bogotá	bogotano/a
Buenos Aires	bonaerense, porteño/a
Caracas	caraqueño/a
La Habana	habanero/a
Lima	limeño/a
San Juan	sanjuanero/a
Santiago	santiaguino/a
Barcelona	barcelonés/barcelonesa
Sevilla	sevillano/a
Valencia	valenciano/a
Río de Janeiro	carioca
Nueva York	neoyorquino/a
Londres	londinense
París	parisiense, parisino/a
Roma	romano/a
Moscú	moscovita
Beijing (Pequín)	pequinés/pequinesa

Information Questions: Question Words (Interrogatives) with Prepositions

You learned about question formation in Spanish in Chapters 1 and 2. Remember that information questions are introduced by question words (interrogatives). A preposition associated with an interrogative word must precede it in Spanish. In English, a preposition is usually separated from the question word and appears at the end of the sentence.

¿**De dónde** son Uds.?	**Where** are you **from?**
¿**De qué** parte del país?	**Where** in the country?
¿**De quién** es el pasaporte?	**Whose** passport is it?
¿**Para quién** son los paquetes?	**Who** are the packages **for?** (literally, **For whom** are the packages?)
¿**De qué** origen eres?	**What** is your (country of) origin?
¿**De qué** color es su carro?	**What** color is their car?

I Express the following dialogues in Spanish.

1. *Where are you (Ud.) from?*
   I'm [masc.] American, from Los Angeles.
   What a coincidence! I'm also from California, from San Francisco.

2. *My husband and I are English, from London.*
   Really? My wife and I are also from London. Where in the city?

3. *What is your (tú) (country of) origin?*
   I'm of Irish descent. What about you (tú)?
   My family is of Scottish descent.

4. *Whose boarding pass is it?*
   It's Mr. Aguilar's.

5. *Who is the gift for?*
   It's for my girlfriend.

▶ DIÁLOGO 4 · Los estudiantes chilenos

Study the dialogue, then listen to the recording and repeat each line.

FERNANDA   ¿Los estudiantes son de Argentina?
ESTEBAN   No, no son argentinos. Son de Chile.
FERNANDA   ¿De la capital?
ESTEBAN   No, de Santiago no. Son de Valparaíso.

Análisis

Check that you understand the linguistic breakdown of each speech from *Diálogo 4.*

¿Los estudiantes son de Argentina?	*Are the students from Argentina?*
el estudiante	*student*
los estudiantes	*students*
son	*(they) are (third person plural)* (**ser**)
Argentina	*Argentina*
son de Argentina	*(they) are from Argentina*
No, no son argentinos. Son de Chile.	*No, they're not Argentinian. They're from Chile.*
no	*no*
argentino	*Argentinian, Argentine*
son argentinos	*they're Argentinian(s), they're Argentine(s)*
no + *verb*	*(negative particle: not) +* verb
no son argentinos	*they're not Argentinian(s), they're not Argentine(s)*
Chile	*Chile*
Son de Chile.	*They're from Chile.*
¿De la capital?	*From the capital?*
la capital	*capital city*
No, de Santiago no. Son de Valparaíso.	*No, not from Santiago. They're from Valparaíso.*
Santiago	*Santiago (capital of Chile)*
de Santiago	*from Santiago*
de Santiago no	*not from Santiago*
Valparaíso	*Valparaíso (major port on the Pacific Ocean)*
Son de Valparaíso.	*They're from Valparaíso.*

Variantes

Listen, and repeat the same structures from *Diálogo 4*, now with new vocabulary.

¿De dónde son ellos?   *Where are they from?*
Son de Puerto Rico.   *They're from Puerto Rico.*
¿De San Juan?   *From San Juan?*
No, son de Ponce.   *No, they're from Ponce (second largest city).*

Estructura y Práctica

Yes/No Questions

As you learned in Chapters 1 and 2, yes/no questions (those that elicit *yes* or *no* as a response) are formed by changing the intonation from statement intonation to rising question intonation.

Los estudiantes son de Costa Rica.   *Los students are from Costa Rica.*
¿Los estudiantes son de Costa Rica?   *Are the students from Costa Rica?*

When a sentence consists of a form of the verb **ser** and an adjective, the subject may be placed at the end of the sentence to form a question. The pattern is thus verb + adjective + subject.

Los estudiantes son puertorriqueños.   *The students are Puerto Rican.*
¿Son puertorriqueños los estudiantes?   *Are the students Puerto Rican?*

J   *Latinoamérica.* Transform the following statements about the nationalities of people from Latin America into yes/no questions. Follow the *modelo.*

MODELO   Su amiga es colombiana.
           → ¿Es colombiana su amiga?

1. El marido de Anita es peruano.

2. Pilar es hondureña.

3. Los esposos (*husband and wife*) son guatemaltecos.

4. Mi mujer es chilena.

5. Rafael es ecuatoriano.

6. Los novios son costarricenses.

7. Mi marido y yo somos brasileños.

8. Blanca y Consuelo son panameñas.

Negative Sentences

As you learned in Chapter 1, a Spanish sentence is made negative by placing **no** before the verb. The word **no** often appears twice in a Spanish sentence that answers a question: The first **no** is the Spanish word for *no*; the second **no** is a marker of negation, referred to as a negative particle in English.

Ramón **no** es de Ecuador.   *Ramón isn't from Ecuador.*

¿Ramón es de Ecuador?   *Is Ramón from Ecuador?*
No, Ramón **no** es de Ecuador.   *No, Ramón isn't from Ecuador.*

K **No.** Answer the following questions about these people in the negative. Follow the *modelo*.

MODELO   ¿Perla es cubana?
→ No, Perla no es cubana.

1. ¿Jaime es de Venezuela?
2. ¿Tú eres de origen europeo (*European*)?
3. ¿Manuel es el esposo de Carolina?
4. ¿Sus (de él) estudiantes son hindúes?
5. ¿La profesora Arriaga es griega?
6. ¿Santiago y Emilia son novios?
7. ¿Uds. son de la capital?
8. ¿Su familia (de Uds.) es de Marruecos?

DIÁLOGO 5 · Unos restaurantes mexicanos

Study the dialogue, then listen to the recording and repeat each line.

FERNANDA   ¿Hay un restaurante mexicano por aquí?
ESTEBAN   Oh, sí, hay varios restaurantes mexicanos aquí en el centro.
FERNANDA   ¿Son buenos?
ESTEBAN   Sí, son buenos y no muy caros.

Análisis

Check that you understand the linguistic breakdown of each speech from *Diálogo 5*.

¿Hay un restaurante mexicano por aquí? *Is there a Mexican restaurant around here?*
    mexicano *Mexican*
    un restaurante mexicano *a Mexican restaurant*

Oh, sí, hay varios restaurantes mexicanos aquí en el centro. *Oh, yes, there are several Mexican restaurants downtown.*
    varios *several*
    varios restaurantes mexicanos *several Mexican restaurants*

¿Son buenos? *Are they good?*
    son *they are (ser)*
    bueno *good*
    buenos *good (masculine plural)*

Sí, son buenos y no muy caros. *Yes, they're good and not very expensive.*
    no *not*
    muy *very*
    caro *expensive*
    caros *expensive (masculine plural)*
    no muy caros *not very expensive*

▶ Variantes

Listen, and repeat the same structures from *Diálogo 5*, now with new vocabulary.

El pollo es muy bueno aquí.	The **chicken** is very good here.
pavo	*turkey*
pescado	*fish*
cordero	*lamb*
pan	*bread*
arroz	*rice*
postre	*dessert*
pastel	*pastry, cake, pie*
helado	*ice cream*

La comida es muy buena aquí.	The **food** is very good here.
sopa	*soup*
ensalada	*salad*
fruta	*fruit*
torta	*cake*
pasta	*pasta*
pizza	*pizza*
salsa	*salsa, sauce*
salchicha	*sausage*

Los tacos son muy buenos aquí.	The **tacos** are very good here.
frijoles	*beans*
entremeses	*hors d'oeuvres*
sándwiches	*sandwiches*
perros calientes	*hot dogs*
huevos	*eggs*
mariscos	*shellfish*
quesos	*cheeses*

Las quesadillas son muy buenas aquí.	The **quesadillas** are very good here.
enchiladas	*enchiladas*
tapas	*tapas*
tortillas	*tortillas* (Mexico), *omelets* (Spain)
hamburguesas	*hamburgers*
papas fritas	*French fries*
legumbres	*vegetables*

¿Hay vino en la carta?	Is there **wine** on the menu?
cerveza	*beer*
café	*coffee*
té	*tea*
jugo	*juice*
chocolate caliente	*hot chocolate*
agua mineral	*mineral water*
leche	*milk*
limonada	*lemonade*

¿Hay refrescos en la carta?	*Are there* **soft drinks** *on the menu?*
bebidas sin alcohol	*nonalcoholic beverages*
batidos de fruta	*fruit shakes*
La comida es barata aquí.	*The food is* **inexpensive** *here.*
rica	*delicious*
deliciosa	*delicious*
sabrosa	*tasty*
picante	*spicy*

Otros Alimentos

el aceite de oliva	*olive oil*
la aceituna	*olive*
el aguacate	*avocado*
la albóndiga	*meatball*
los alimentos frescos	*fresh food*
el arroz con pollo	*chicken with rice*
el atún	*tuna*
las aves	*poultry (el ave (bird, chicken))*
el azúcar	*sugar*
la batata	*sweet potato*
el bistec/biftec	*steak*
la carne	*meat*
la carne de res/vaca	*beef*
la carne roja	*red meat*
la cebolla	*onion*
el cerdo	*pork*
la cereza	*cherry*
el chocolate	*chocolate*
la comida chatarra	*junk food*
la comida orgánica	*organic food*
la comida rápida	*fast food*
la comida vegetariana	*vegetarian food*
los dulces	*candy*
dulce	*sweet*
el durazno	*peach*
la galleta con chispas/pepitas de chocolate	*chocolate chip cookie*
las golosinas	*candy, sweets, treats*
goloso	*sweet-toothed*
ser goloso	*to have a sweet tooth*
los guisantes	*peas*
el jamón	*ham*
los lácteos	*dairy*
la lechuga	*lettuce*
la mantequilla	*butter*
la mantequilla de cacahuete	*peanut butter*
la manzana	*apple*

la naranja	*orange*
la nuez	*nut*
el pan integral	*whole grain bread*
la papa	*potato*
las pasas	*raisins*
la patata	*potato* (Spain)
la pera	*pear*
la pimienta	*pepper*
la piña	*pineapple*
el plátano	*banana*
el plato acompañante/adicional	*side dish*
la sal	*salt*
la soya/soja	*soy*
la ternera	*veal*
el tocino	*bacon*
el tomate	*tomato*
las uvas	*grapes*
las (uvas) pasas	*raisins*
las verduras	*greens, green vegetables*
el yogurt	*yogurt*
la zanahoria	*carrot*

Estructura y Práctica

NOUNS

Nouns that begin with stressed /a/ (written **a** or **ha**) are feminine and therefore take feminine adjectives. However, they take the masculine article in the singular and **las** in the plural. (See also Chapter 7.)

el agua **fría**	*cold water*
las aguas **frescas**	*cool waters*
el ave **blanca**	*white bird*
las aves **asadas**	*roasted poultry/chicken*
el haba **negra**	*black fava bean*
las habas **secas**	*dried fava beans*

Position of Adjectives

You have learned that, in Spanish, adjectives normally follow the noun, rather than precede it as in English. You also saw certain types of adjectives that precede the noun in Spanish. Preposed adjectives occur with postposed adjectives of nationality in noun phrases.

muchas compañías norteamericanas	*many American companies*
algunos cantantes italianos	*some Italian singers*
varios vinos españoles	*several Spanish wines*

L Write each noun phrase, completing it with the cues in parentheses in their correct positions. Make all necessary agreements when you write the complete phrase. Follow the *modelo.*

MODELO   _____ carne _____ (mucho) (argentino)
            → mucha carne argentina

1. _____ queso _____ (suizo) (ninguno)

2. _____ jamones _____ (varios) (inglés)

3. _____ torta _____ (italiano) (bastante)

4. _____ uvas _____ (poco) (chileno)

5. _____ nueces _____ (alguno) (español)

6. _____ aceite de oliva _____ (griego) (suficiente)

7. _____ pescado _____ (alguno) (japonés)

8. _____ manzanas _____ (estadounidenses) (varios)

M *¡Buen provecho!* **(Enjoy your meal!)** Assign a category for each food on the list. Refer to the vocabulary in *Diálogo 5: Variantes* and *Otros Alimentos* as needed. Write the name of the correct category for each of the foods listed: **frutas**, **legumbres**, **lácteos**, **carnes y aves**, or **postres**.

1. el pollo

2. el queso

3. la manzana

4. la torta

5. la papa

6. la carne de res

7. la cebolla

8. el helado

9. la mantequilla

10. las uvas

11. el yogurt

12. el jamón

13. la piña

14. las galletas con chispas

15. los guisantes

16. las cerezas

17. las zanahorias

18. los dulces

19. la salchicha

20. la leche

▶ DIÁLOGO 6 · Una película mexicana

Study the dialogue, then listen to the recording and repeat each line.

ESTEBAN   ¿Hay cines aquí con películas en español?
FERNANDA   Sí, en el cine Real hay una película mexicana.
ESTEBAN   ¿Es buena la película?
FERNANDA   Sí, es interesante y muy divertida.

Análisis

Check that you understand the linguistic breakdown of each speech from *Diálogo 6*.

¿Hay cines aquí con películas en español?	*Are there movie theaters here with films in Spanish?*
el cine	*movie theater*
la película	*film*
con	*with*
el español	*Spanish*
en español	*in Spanish*

Sí, en el cine Real hay una película mexicana.	*Yes, there's a Mexican film at the Real movie theater.*
mexicana	*Mexican* (feminine singular)
una película mexicana	*a Mexican film*

¿Es buena la película?	*Is the film good?*

Sí, es interesante y muy divertida.	*Yes, it's interesting and very entertaining.*
interesante	*interesting* (masculine and feminine)
divertido	*amusing, entertaining*
divertida	*amusing, entertaining* (feminine)

▶ Variantes

Listen, and repeat the same structures from *Diálogo 6*, now with new vocabulary.

¿Hay películas en español ?	*Are there films in **Spanish**?*
inglés	*English*
francés	*French*
italiano	*Italian*
alemán	*German*
portugués	*Portuguese*
ruso	*Russian*
chino	*Chinese*
japonés	*Japanese*
coreano	*Korean*
hindi	*Hindi*
hebreo	*Hebrew*
árabe	*Arabic*

Estructura y Práctica

Prepositions

Prepositions are words (such as *to, for, in, at, from* in English) that link nouns or pronouns to other elements of the sentence. The group of words consisting of a preposition + noun or pronoun is called a prepositional phrase. The prepositions of one language rarely correspond exactly to the prepositions of another. (See also Chapters 4, 5, and 6.)

In these chapters you have seen the prepositions **con** (*with*), **de** (*of, from, in, about*), **en** (*in, at, on*), and **para** (*for*). **Por** also means *for,* which you have learned as part of **por aquí** (*around here*) and **la tienda por departamentos** (*department store*).

Con *with*

Hay un cine **con** películas en español.	*There's a movie theater **with** films in Spanish.*
Hay arroz **con** pollo en la carta.	*There's chicken **with** rice on the menu.*

De *of, from, in, about*

De expresses possession, origin, and the material of which something is made.

Estos libros son **de** Consuelo.	*These are Consuelo's books.*
Los programadores son **de** Chile.	*The programmers are **from** Chile.*
Marta es **de** origen polaco.	*Marta is **of** Polish descent.*
¿**De** qué parte eres?	*Where (**from** which part) are you **from**?*
¿**De** qué color es su casa?	*(**Of**) What color is their house?*
El reloj es **de** oro.	*The watch is (**made of**) gold.*
La comida **de** este restaurante es rica.	*The food **in** this restaurant is delicious.*
Es un libro **de** animales para niños.	*It's a book **about** animals for children.*

The preposition **de** is used to form compound nouns.

la administración **de** empresas	*business administration*
la tienda **de** cómputo	*computer store*
el museo **de** arte	*art museum*
la tarjeta **de** crédito	*credit card*
el libro **de** texto	*textbook*
la base **de** datos	*database*

The preposition **de** contracts with the masculine singular definite article **el** to form **del**.

Ana es la esposa **del** señor Vega.	*Ana is Mr. Vega's wife.*
Es la ciudad más grande **del** país.	*It's the biggest city **in the** country.*

The preposition **de** occurs in many idiomatic expressions.

de veras	*really*
de nada	*you're welcome*

En *in, at, on*

Hay películas **en** francés.	*There are films **in** French.*
Hay informes **en** el maletín.	*There are reports **in** the attaché case.*
Hay muchos hoteles **en** el centro.	*There are many hotels downtown (**in** the downtown area).*
Hay un cibercafé **en** la esquina.	*There's an internet café **on/at** the corner.*
¿Qué hay **en** la carta?	*What's **on** the menu?*

To specify position, **en** can be replaced by **dentro de** (*inside of*) or **encima de** (*on, on top of*).

En specifies the period of time within which something happens.

Regresamos **en** diez minutos. (**regresar**)   *We're coming back **in** ten minutes.*

Para *for*

Es un regalo **para** Miguel.   *It's a gift **for** Miguel.*

N Complete each phrase with the missing preposition: **con**, **de**, **en**, **para**, or **por**. Write the correct prepositions, and remember to use the contraction **del** when necessary.

1. No hay pescado _____ la carta.

2. —¿_____ quiénes son estos platos? —El sándwich _____ queso es _____ Daniel y la pasta _____ salsa es _____ Elena.

3. Son mis libros _____ administración _____ empresas.

4. El restaurante vegetariano queda (*is located*) _____ la esquina.

5. Sus amigos son _____ Madrid.

6. Hay un pastel _____ manzana _____ la mesa.

7. Perdón, ¿hay un cine _____ películas _____ inglés _____ aquí?

8. ¿_____ qué origen eres?

9. ¿Hay tomate y lechuga _____ la hamburguesa?

10. La pulsera _____ oro es un regalo _____ Beatriz.

11. _____ favor, ¿hay una tienda _____ departamentos _____ este barrio?

12. Son los contratos _____ señor Maldonado.

13. _____ veras, ¿no hay una tienda _____ cómputo _____ el centro?

14. —Muchas gracias, señorita. —_____ nada, señor.

15. El arroz _____ pollo es muy rico _____ este restaurante.

16. El helado _____ chocolate y el café _____ leche son muy buenos _____ este cibercafé.

▶ DIÁLOGO 7 · Un restaurante auténtico

Study the dialogue, then listen to the recording and repeat each line.

FERNANDA   ¿Cómo es la comida de este restaurante?
ESTEBAN   Es muy buena y muy auténtica.
FERNANDA   ¿Hay muchos platos diferentes?
ESTEBAN   Sí, hay platos de todas las regiones del país.

Análisis

Check that you understand the linguistic breakdown of each speech from *Diálogo 7*.

¿Cómo es la comida de este restaurante?	*How's the food in this restaurant?*
¿Cómo?	*How?*
la comida	*food, meal*
¿Cómo es la comida?	*How's the food?*
de	*of, in*
este	*this* (masculine singular)
este restaurante	*this restaurant*
de este restaurante	*in this restaurant*
Es muy buena y muy auténtica.	*It's very good and very authentic.*
auténtico	*authentic*
auténtica	*authentic* (feminine)
¿Hay muchos platos diferentes?	*Are there many different dishes?*
mucho, mucha	*much*
muchos, muchas	*many*
el plato	*plate, dish*
muchos platos	*many dishes*
diferente	*different*
muchos platos diferentes	*many different dishes*
Sí, hay platos de todas las regiones del país.	*Yes, there are dishes from every region of the country.*
todo el, toda la, todos los, todas las	*all, every*
la región	*region*
las regiones	*regions*
todas las regiones	*all the regions, every region*
el país	*country*
del	*of the* (contraction of **de** + **el**)
del país	*of the country*
todas las regiones del país	*every region of the country*

▶ **Variantes**

Listen, and repeat the same structures from *Diálogo 7*, now with new vocabulary.

Este café es bueno.	**This** *café is good.*
Ese	*That*
Aquel	*That*
Estos platos son auténticos.	**These** *dishes are authentic.*
Esos	*Those*
Aquellos	*Those*
Esta calle es bonita.	**This** *street is pretty.*
Esa	*That*
Aquella	*That*

Estas maletas son grandes.	***These*** *suitcases are big.*
Esas	*Those*
Aquellas	*Those*

Estructura y Práctica

Demonstrative Adjectives

Spanish has a set of three demonstrative adjectives, whereas English has only two.

este	*this* (near the speaker)
ese	*that* (near the person spoken to)
aquel	*that* (removed from both the speaker and the person spoken to)

These demonstratives correspond to the Spanish division of place.

aquí	*here* (near the speaker)
ahí	*there* (near the person spoken to)
allí	*there* (removed from both the speaker and the person spoken to)

The demonstratives, like the definite and indefinite articles, agree with the noun they refer to in both gender and number. The masculine singular form is slightly irregular, as it does not end in **-o**. The other three forms look like any other adjective.

MASCULINE SINGULAR	MASCULINE PLURAL	FEMININE SINGULAR	FEMININE PLURAL
este	estos	esta	estas
ese	esos	esa	esas
aquel	aquellos	aquella	aquellas

Este café es bueno.	***This*** *café is good.*
Sí, pero **aquel** café es mejor.	*Yes, but **that** café (over there) is better.*
Esa mochila es linda.	***That*** *backpack is nice.*
Pero **esta** mochila es más útil.	*But **this** backpack is more useful.*

For many Spanish American speakers, **aquel** is replaced by **ese**.

O ***Estas cosas o esas cosas.*** Write the correct form of all three demonstrative adjectives for each of the following nouns. Follow the *modelo*.

MODELO libro
        → este ese aquel libro

1. comida
2. cine
3. países
4. calles
5. pizza

6. billete
7. flores
8. amigos
9. pan
10. región

P   *¿De dónde son?¿Cómo son?* Rewrite each of the following sentences, changing the forms of the definite article to the corresponding forms of **este**. Follow the *modelo*.

> MODELO   La directora es canadiense.
>   → Esta directora es canadiense.

1. Las programadoras son buenas.
2. El asesor es muy inteligente.
3. Los dentistas son viejos.
4. La cocinera es italiana.
5. El escritor es famoso.
6. Los músicos son de Cuba.
7. El cantante es brasileño.
8. La abogada es trabajadora (*hardworking*).
9. Las bailarinas son maravillosas.
10. Los médicos son hindúes.

When **todo** is used as an adjective, it is usually followed by the definite article. Notice the different translations in English.

todo el país	the **whole** country, **all** the country
toda la zona	the **whole** area, the **entire** area
todos los países	**every** country, **all** the countries
todas las zonas	**every** area, **all** the areas
todo el día	**all** day **long**, the **whole** day
todos los días	**every** day
toda la novela	the **entire** novel
todas las novelas	**all** the novels, **every** novel

The forms **todo** and **toda** may precede a singular noun with the meaning *every*, especially in more formal style.

todo informe = todos los informes	**every** report
toda tienda = todas las tiendas	**every** store

Todo as a pronoun in Spanish means *everything*.

Todo es maravilloso aquí.	**Everything** is wonderful here.
Todo es moderno en su casa.	**Everything** is modern in their house.

When the pronoun **todo** is the object of a verb, the pronoun **lo** precedes the verb. Notice that **todo** as direct object may sometimes precede the verb.

Ahora **lo** comprendo **todo**. (**comprender**)	*Now I understand **everything**.*
Todo lo tiene. (**tener**)	*He has **everything**.*

Q   Express the following phrases with **todo** in Spanish. Use **todo** as an adjective followed by the definite article.

1. *the whole city*
2. *every film*
3. *all the wines*
4. *all the downtown area*
5. *the entire country*
6. *all month long*
7. *the whole week*
8. *every meal*
9. *the entire neighborhood*
10. *all the actresses*

🔊 DIÁLOGO 8 · ¿De dónde son los profesores?

Study the dialogue, then listen to the recording and repeat each line.

ESTEBAN	¿De dónde es ese profesor? ¿De Santo Domingo?
FERNANDA	Sí, es dominicano.
ESTEBAN	¿Y aquella profesora?
FERNANDA	Ella es dominicana también.

Análisis

Check that you understand the linguistic breakdown of each speech from *Diálogo 8*.

¿De dónde es ese profesor? ¿De Santo Domingo?	*Where is that professor from? ¿Santo Domingo?*
¿dónde?	*where?*
¿de dónde?	*from where?*
el profesor	*university professor, secondary school teacher* (masculine)
ese profesor	*that teacher*
Santo Domingo	*Santo Domingo* (*capital of the Dominican Republic*)
Sí, es dominicano.	*Yes, he's Dominican.*
sí	*yes*
dominicano	*Dominican*
¿Y aquella profesora?	*What about that (female) professor?*
y	*and, and what about?*
la profesora	*university professor, secondary school teacher* (feminine)
aquella profesora	*that teacher*
Ella es dominicana también.	*She's Dominican, too.*
ella	*she*
dominicana	*Dominican* (feminine)

🔊 Variantes

Listen, and repeat the same structures from *Diálogo 8*, now with new vocabulary.

¿De dónde es ese profesor ?	*Where's that **professor** from?*
abogado	*lawyer*
dentista	*dentist*
médico	*doctor*
asesor	*consultant*
asesor financiero	*financial advisor*
ingeniero	*engineer*
escritor	*writer*
contador	*accountant*
enfermero	*nurse*
analista	*analyst*

¿De dónde es ese profesor ?	Where's that **professor** from?
programador	programmer
músico	musician
cantante	singer
bailarín	dancer
pintor	painter
cocinero	cook, chef
actor	actor

Aquella profesora es dominicana también.	That **professor** is Dominican, too.
abogada	lawyer
dentista	dentist
doctora	doctor
asesora	consultant
asesora financiera	financial advisor
ingeniera	engineer
escritora	writer
contadora	accountant
enfermera	nurse
analista	analyst
programadora	programmer
música	musician
cantante	singer
bailarina	dancer
pintora	painter
cocinera	cook, chef
actriz	actress

Otras Profesiones

el hombre de negocios *businessman*	la mujer de negocios *businesswoman*
el científico *scientist*	la científica *scientist*
el político *politician*	la política *politician*

Estructura y Práctica

Gender of Nouns That Refer to People

When a noun that refers to people ends in **-or**, **-és**, **-ón**, or **-ín**, the noun is usually masculine and adds **-a** to make the feminine form. The written accent is dropped when the suffix **-a** is added.

MASCULINE	FEMININE
el locutor *newscaster*	la locutora *newscaster*
el inglés	la inglesa
el anfitrión *host*	la anfitriona *hostess*
el bailarín	la bailarina

Some nouns that refer to people keep the same form for the feminine as for the masculine, changing only their article. Many of these nouns end in **-e**, **-a**, **-ista**, **-nte**, or a consonant.

el/la intérprete *performer* el/la dependiente *salesperson*
el/la atleta *athlete* el/la agente *agent*
el/la artista *artist, performing artist* el/la albañil *mason, construction worker*

For some nouns ending in **-nte**, a feminine form ending in **-nta** is common: **el estudiante**, **la estudianta**; **el gerente**, **la gerenta**.

R **Profesiones.** Write the feminine form for each of the following nouns of profession.

1. el desarrollador de programas (*software developer*)

2. el desarrollador de web (*web developer*)

3. el administrador de bases de datos (*database administrator*)

4. el arquitecto de red (*computer network architect*)

5. el analista de seguridad de (la) información (*information security analyst*)

6. el enfermero practicante (*nurse practitioner*)

7. el médico asistente (*physician assistant*)

8. el gerente de marketing (mercadeo) (*marketing manager*)

9. el gerente de ventas (*sales manager*)

10. el diseñador de videojuegos (*video game designer*)

Un paso más

Are you ready to take your Spanish a step further? Here are exercises that will enhance your knowledge of the language and encourage you to express yourself freely.

S **Oficios (Occupations).** Write the English translation of each of the following nouns. Then write the feminine form of each of the nouns in Spanish. You have learned vocabulary words that will help you figure out the meanings of most of these words; other words will be familiar to you as cognates of English.

1. el hotelero

2. el electricista

3. el policía

4. el taxista

5. el uberista

6. el mesero

7. el florista

8. el jardinero

9. el panadero

10. el mecánico

11. el carpintero

12. el plomero

13. el periodista

14. el librero

15. el secretario

16. el recepcionista

17. el banquero   20. el carnicero

18. el estilista   21. el farmacéutico

19. el oficinista   22. el joyero

T *Preguntas personales.* Answer each question with a complete Spanish sentence.

1. ¿De dónde es Ud.?

2. ¿De qué origen es?

3. ¿De dónde son sus padres (*parents*)? ¿Y sus abuelos (*grandparents*)?

4. ¿Cuál es su profesión?

5. ¿Hay un restaurante mexicano en su barrio? ¿Qué platos hay en la carta? ¿Cómo es la comida?

6. ¿Hay un restaurante italiano (chino, japonés, francés, tailandés, vegetariano) en su ciudad? ¿Qué platos hay en la carta? ¿Cómo es la comida?

7. ¿Es Ud. vegetariano/vegetariana? ¿Qué alimentos come?

8. ¿Cuáles son sus alimentos favoritos?

9. ¿Cuáles son sus platos favoritos?

10. ¿Es goloso/golosa? ¿Qué dulces come?

Describing People, Emotions, and Health

Communication Goals

- Talking about one's physical state and frame of mind
- Locating people and places
- Telling time and days of the week
- Describing people
- Vocabulary: health, emotions, events, articles of clothing, the family

Grammar Topics

- **Estar** *to be*: Uses
- **Estar** vs. **ser**
- Adverbs of Place with Prepositions
- **Ser** *to be*: Uses
- **Ser** vs. **estar**: Describing Food
- Tag Questions
- **Estar** + Past Participle
- **Ser** and **estar** in Yes/No Questions

DIÁLOGO 1 · ¿Cómo estás?

Study the dialogue, then listen to the recording and repeat each line.

PACO   Hola, Carmen. ¿Cómo estás?
CARMEN   Estoy bien. Y tú, Paco, ¿qué tal?
PACO   Estoy acatarrado.
CARMEN   ¡Pobre!

Análisis

Check that you understand the linguistic breakdown of each speech from *Diálogo 1*.

Hola, Carmen. ¿Cómo estás?	*Hi, Carmen. How are you?*
¿cómo?	*how?*
estás	*you are* (second person singular) (**estar**)
Estoy bien. Y tú, Paco, ¿qué tal?	*I'm fine. And how about you, Paco?*
estoy	*I am* (first person singular) (**estar**)
bien	*well, fine*
Estoy acatarrado.	*I have a cold.*
acatarrado	*sick with a cold*
¡Pobre!	*Poor guy! / You poor thing!*

▶ Variantes

Listen, and repeat the same structures from *Diálogo 1*, now with new vocabulary.

Estoy bien .	*I'm (feeling)* ***fine***.
mal	*ill*
perfectamente	*very well, great*
regular	*so-so*
enfermo	*sick*
Diana está acatarrada .	*Diana has a* ***cold***.
un poco acatarrada	*slight cold*
¿Está enfermo tu hermano?	*Is your brother sick?*
Sí, está resfriado.	*Yes, he has a cold (is sick with a cold).*

Estructura y Práctica

Estar *to be*: Uses

The verbs **ser** and **estar** both mean *to be*, but they are not interchangeable. They are used in different contexts, as you will see in this chapter.

Estar (*to be*) is an irregular **-ar** verb. Its conjugation in the present tense is as follows.

estar *to be*

SINGULAR	PLURAL
estoy	estamos
estás	estáis
está	están

1 · **Estar** is used before adjectives that express a temporary physical state, such as health, or frame of mind, such as happiness.

Sara **está** bien.	*Sara **is** (**feeling**) fine.*
Estamos contentos.	*We're happy.*
Mario, ¿por qué **estás** nervioso?	*Mario, why **are you** nervous?*

Only **estar** (not **ser**) can be used with **contento**.

2 · **Estar** is used to express location, whether temporary or permanent.

¿Dónde **están** los asesores?	*Where **are** the consultants?*
Están en su oficina.	*They're in their office.*
Estoy en México.	*I'm in Mexico.*
La heladería **está** cerca.	*The ice cream store **is** nearby.*

Remember that **queda**, from **quedar** (*to be located*), expresses location that is permanent only.

La biblioteca **queda** en la esquina.	*The library **is** on the corner.*
Las tiendas por departamentos **quedan** en el centro.	*The department stores **are** downtown.*

A Write the form of **estar** that correctly completes each of the following sentences.

1. Juan _____ enfermo.

2. María y Consuelo _____ bien.

3. Yo _____ perfectamente.

4. ¿Por qué (tú) _____ tan estresado?

5. Perla _____ regular.

6. Daniel y yo _____ cansados.

7. ¿Cómo _____ Uds.?

8. Manolo y Luis _____ mal.

DIÁLOGO 2 · Estoy inquieto.

Study the dialogue, then listen to the recording and repeat each line.

CARMEN	¿Cómo está Ud.?
PACO	Yo estoy bien, pero muy inquieto.
CARMEN	¿Inquieto? ¿Por qué?
PACO	¿No sabe? Fernando está en el hospital.

Análisis

Check that you understand the linguistic breakdown of each speech from *Diálogo 2.*

¿Cómo está Ud.?	*How are you?*
está	*you are, he is, she is* (third person singular) (**estar**)
Yo estoy bien, pero muy inquieto.	*I'm well, but very worried.*
inquieto	*worried*
¿Inquieto? ¿Por qué?	*Worried? Why?*
¿No sabe? Fernando está en el hospital.	*Then you don't know? Fernando is in the hospital.*

▶ Variantes

Listen, and repeat the same structures from *Diálogo 2*, now with new vocabulary.

Juan está inquieto .	*Juan is **worried**.*
estresado	*stressed*
emocionado	*excited*
cansado	*tired*
contento	*happy*
deprimido	*depressed*
molesto	*annoyed*

Elena está preocupada .	*Elena is **worried**.*
triste	*sad*
asustada	*scared*
entusiasmada	*enthusiastic*
nerviosa	*nervous*
alegre	*cheerful*
angustiada	*distressed*
aburrida	*bored*

▶ DIÁLOGO 3 · Estamos preocupados.

Study the dialogue, then listen to the recording and repeat each line.

CARMEN	Estamos preocupados. El perro no está en la casa.
PACO	¿No está en el jardín?
CARMEN	Tampoco.
PACO	Ahora yo estoy preocupado también.

Análisis

Check that you understand the linguistic breakdown of each speech from *Diálogo 3*.

Estamos preocupados. El perro no está en la casa.	*We're worried. The dog isn't in the house.*
estamos	*we are* (first person plural) (**estar**)
el perro	*dog*
¿No está en el jardín?	*Isn't he in the garden?*
el jardín	*garden*
Tampoco.	*No, he's not there either.*
tampoco	*neither*
Ahora yo estoy preocupado también.	*Now I'm worried, too.*
ahora	*now*

▶ Variantes

Listen, and repeat the same structures from *Diálogo 3*, now with new vocabulary.

El perro está en el jardín.	*The **dog** is in the garden.*
gato	*cat*

Estructura y Práctica

B *¿Cómo están?* Write a sentence to describe the emotional state or frame of mind of each indicated member of your family. Use the correct form of **estar** plus the adjective provided. Make all necessary agreements. (For Spanish terms for family members, see the *Variantes* section of *Diálogo 19* in this chapter.) Follow the *modelo*.

MODELO   mi primo / aburrido
→ Mi primo está aburrido.

1. mi mamá / entusiasmado
2. mis hijos / emocionado
3. yo [*fem.*] / contento
4. los tíos / triste
5. la cuñada / estresado
6. tú [*fem.*] / preocupado

7. la tía / deprimido
8. mis hermanos y yo / molesto
9. los abuelos / inquieto
10. mi papá / nervioso
11. mis nietas / alegre
12. las sobrinas / angustiado

DIÁLOGO 4 · Estamos muy atrasados.

Study the dialogue, then listen to the recording and repeat each line.

CARMEN   El taxi ya está. ¿Ya están listos?
PACO   No, no estamos listos todavía.
CARMEN   ¡Caramba! Estamos muy atrasados ya.

Análisis

Check that you understand the linguistic breakdown of each speech from *Diálogo 4*.

El taxi ya está. ¿Ya están listos? — *The cab is here already. Are you ready?*
el taxi — *taxi, cab*
ya — *already*
están — *you* (plural) *are, they are* (third person plural) (**estar**)
listo — *ready* (when used with **estar**)

No, no estamos listos todavía. — *No, we're not ready yet.*
todavía — *still, yet*

¡Caramba! Estamos muy atrasados ya. — *My goodness! We're already very late.*
¡Caramba! — *My goodness!*
atrasado — *late, behind schedule*
estar atrasado — *to be behind schedule*

Variantes

Listen, and repeat the same structures from *Diálogo 4*, now with new vocabulary.

Están atrasados en la alta tecnología. — *They are **lagging** in high tech.*
adelantados — *advanced*

Estructura y Práctica

ADJECTIVES

Many of the adjectives you have seen in these *diálogos* end in **-ado** or **-ido**. For example, **emocionado, preocupado, acatarrado, atrasado, adelantado, aburrido, deprimido**.

These adjectives derive from the past participle (the **-do** form) of the present perfect tense. For **-ar** verbs, the ending is **-ado**; for **-er** and **-ir** verbs, the ending is **-ido**. (For the present perfect tense, see Chapter 13.)

▶ DIÁLOGO 5 · ¿Dónde está el museo de arte?

Study the dialogue, then listen to the recording and repeat each line.

PACO   ¿Dónde está el museo de arte?
CARMEN   Queda en la calle Robles al lado del parque.
PACO   ¿Está lejos de la plaza?
CARMEN   En absoluto. Está a una cuadra de la plaza.

Análisis

Check that you understand the linguistic breakdown of each speech from *Diálogo 5*.

¿Dónde está el museo de arte?	*Where is the art museum?*
¿Dónde?	*Where?*
Queda en la calle Robles al lado del parque.	*It's on Robles Street, next to the park.*
queda	*it is* (to express the permanent location of places) (**quedar**)
al lado de	*next to*
el parque	*park*
al lado del parque	*next to the park*
¿Está lejos de la plaza?	*Is it far from the square?*
lejos de	*far from*
la plaza	*square*
lejos de la plaza	*far from the square*
En absoluto. Está a una cuadra de la plaza.	*Not at all. It's a block away from the square.*
En absoluto.	*Not at all.*
a	*at a distance of*
la cuadra	*(city) block*
a una cuadra	*a block away*
a una cuadra de la plaza	*a block away from the square*

Variantes

Listen, and repeat the same structures from *Diálogo 5*, now with new vocabulary.

¿Dónde está el museo de arte ?	*Where is the art museum?*
el museo de ciencias	*science museum*
la biblioteca	*library*
la universidad	*university*
el colegio	*high school*
la escuela	*school*
el zoológico	*zoo*
el monumento	*monument*
la iglesia	*church*
la sinagoga	*synagogue*
la catedral	*cathedral*
el banco	*bank*
el club de jazz	*jazz club*

El hotel está a una cuadra de la plaza.	*The hotel is a block from the square.*
cinco cuadras	*five blocks*
una milla	*a mile*
diez kilómetros	*ten kilometers*

El edificio queda lejos de la plaza.	*The building is far from the square.*
cerca de	*near*
al lado de	*next to*
detrás de	*behind*
delante de	*in front of*
en frente de	*opposite*
a la derecha de	*to the right of*
a la izquierda de	*to the left of*

El perro está debajo de la mesa.	*The dog is under the table.*
encima de	*on top of*

DIÁLOGO 6 · Los gerentes están reunidos.

Study the dialogue, then listen to the recording and repeat each line.

CARMEN	Los gerentes no están en su oficina.
PACO	Es que están reunidos ahora.
CARMEN	¿Dónde es la reunión?
PACO	Es en la sala de conferencias.

Análisis

Check that you understand the linguistic breakdown of each speech from *Diálogo 6*.

Los gerentes no están en su oficina.	*The managers aren't in their offices.*
el gerente	*manager*
su	*their*

Es que están reunidos ahora.	*It's because they're having a meeting now.*
es que	*it's because, it's that, the fact is*
reunido	*at a meeting*
estar reunidos	*to be at a meeting, to be having a meeting*
¿Dónde es la reunión?	*Where is the meeting?*
¿Dónde es?	*Where is? (of events)*
la reunión	*meeting*
Es en la sala de conferencias.	*It's in the conference room.*
la sala de conferencias	*the conference room*

⏵ Variantes

Listen, and repeat the same structures from *Diálogo 6*, now with new vocabulary.

¿Dónde es la reunión ?	*Where is the **meeting**?*
la fiesta	*party*
el partido	*game*
la comida	*dinner*
el concierto	*concert*
el baile	*dance*
el espectáculo	*show*
el examen	*exam*
la conferencia	*lecture*
la boda	*wedding*

Estructura y Práctica

Estar vs. ser

As you have learned, **estar** is used to express location, whether temporary or permanent.

Estamos en Madrid.	***We're** in Madrid.*
¿Dónde **está** el banco?	*Where **is** the bank?*
El banco **está** enfrente del hotel.	*The bank **is** opposite the hotel.*

Ser is used to indicate where an event takes place. **Estar** cannot be used for this purpose.

¿Dónde **es** la conferencia?	*Where **is** the lecture?*
Es en la universidad.	***It's** at the university.*
¿Dónde **es** el concierto?	*Where **is** the concert?*
Es en el Teatro Real.	***It's** in the Teatro Real.*

C **Where is it?** Choose **ser** or **estar** to complete each of the following questions about where things or events are located. Follow the *modelos*.

MODELOS ¿Dónde _está_ el billetero?

¿Dónde _es_ la fiesta?

1. ¿Dónde _____ el zoológico?
2. ¿Dónde _____ el partido?
3. ¿Dónde _____ el taxi?
4. ¿Dónde _____ la boda?
5. ¿Dónde _____ el bailarín?
6. ¿Dónde _____ el jardín?
7. ¿Dónde _____ la sala?
8. ¿Dónde _____ el espectáculo?
9. ¿Dónde _____ el informe?
10. ¿Dónde _____ el paseo?
11. ¿Dónde _____ la reunión?
12. ¿Dónde _____ la joyería?

Adverbs of Place with Prepositions

Prepositions are words that link nouns or pronouns to other elements of the sentence. The group of words consisting of a preposition + a noun or pronoun is called a prepositional phrase.

Adverbs of place can combine with prepositions to form compound prepositions. In Chapter 1, you learned **enfrente** (*across the street*). The preposition **de** can be added to **enfrente**: **enfrente de** (*opposite, across the street from*).

El café está **enfrente**.	*The café is **across the street**.*
El café está **enfrente del** hotel.	*The café is **opposite / across the street from** the hotel.*

Here are some common adverbs of place with the preposition **de** (*of, from*).

a la derecha (de)	*on/to the right (of)*
a la izquierda (de)	*on/to the left (of)*
al lado (de)	*next to*
cerca (de)	*close (to)*
lejos (de)	*far (from)*
debajo (de)	*under*
delante (de)	*in front (of)*
detrás (de)	*behind*
encima (de)	*on top (of)*
al fondo (de)	*at/in the back (of)*

El colegio está **al lado del** museo.	*The high school is **next to** the museum.*
La sinagoga está **cerca de** la catedral.	*The synagogue is **near** the cathedral.*
El perro está **detrás de** su casa.	*The dog is **behind** their house.*

The preposition **a** (*to*) is used to express English *away from, at a distance of*.

La estación está **a tres cuadras** del hotel.	*The train station is **three blocks** from the hotel.*
El centro está **a diez minutos** de aquí.	*The downtown area is **ten minutes** from here.*

D *¿Dónde está?* Answer each of the following questions with a complete Spanish sentence. Use the cue provided and add the correct prepositions as necessary: **a**, **de**, **en**, **por**. Follow the *modelo*.

> MODELO   ¿Dónde está la heladería? (*on a pedestrian street*)
> → Está en una calle peatonal.

1. ¿Dónde está la universidad? (*nine miles from downtown*)
2. ¿Dónde queda el parque? (*behind the church*)
3. ¿Dónde está el perro? (*under the table*)
4. ¿Dónde están los edificios nuevos? (*near the business area*)
5. ¿Dónde está la tienda de deportes? (*at the corner*)
6. ¿Dónde están los documentos? (*on / on top of the shelf*)
7. ¿Dónde queda ese club de jazz? (*a block from the internet café*)
8. ¿Dónde queda el aeropuerto (*airport*)? (*far from the city*)
9. ¿Dónde están la escuela y el colegio? (*around here*)
10. ¿Dónde está la sala de conferencias? (*to the right of our office*)
11. ¿Dónde queda esa tienda de cómputo? (*next to an Italian restaurant*)
12. ¿Dónde está tu carro? (*in front of my house*)
13. ¿Dónde queda la farmacia? (*opposite the hospital*)
14. ¿Dónde están los gatos? (*behind the sofa* (el sofá))
15. ¿Dónde están nuestras maletas? (*in the back of the closet*)
16. ¿Dónde queda la catedral? (*to the left of the square*)

▶ DIÁLOGO 7 · ¿A qué hora es la reunión?

Study the dialogue, then listen to the recording and repeat each line.

PACO	¿A qué hora es la reunión?
CARMEN	A las dos y media.
PACO	¿Dos o doce?
CARMEN	Dos. Es a las dos y media.

Análisis

Check that you understand the linguistic breakdown of each speech from *Diálogo 7*.

¿A qué hora es la reunión?	*At what time is the meeting?*
la hora	*hour, time*
¿A qué hora?	*At what time?*
A las dos y media.	*At two thirty.*
las dos	*two o'clock*
medio	*half*
y media	*and a half (hour)*
las dos y media	*two thirty, 2:30*

¿Dos o doce?   *(Did you say) Two or twelve?*

Dos. Es a las dos y media.   *(I said) Two. It's at 2:30.*

▶ Variantes

Listen, and repeat the same structures from *Diálogo 7*, now with new vocabulary.

La reunión es a las dos .	*The meeting is at **two o'clock**.*
tres y cuarto	*a quarter after three*
cuatro y quince	*4:15*
cinco y media	*5:30*
seis menos cuarto	*a quarter to six*
siete menos quince	*a quarter to seven*
ocho cincuenta	*8:50*

Es la una .	*It's **one o'clock**.*
mediodía	*noon*
medianoche	*midnight*

Son las nueve de la mañana .	*It's **9:00** A.M.*
diez de la noche	*10:00 P.M.*
once en punto	*11:00 on the dot*
doce	*12 o'clock*

▶ DIÁLOGO 8 · El museo no está abierto.

Study the dialogue, then listen to the recording and repeat each line.

CARMEN   El museo no está abierto todavía.
PACO   ¡Qué raro! Ya son las once.
CARMEN   Ay, ¡qué tontos somos! Hoy es lunes.
PACO   Claro. Los lunes todos los museos están cerrados.

Análisis

Check that you understand the linguistic breakdown of each speech from *Diálogo 8*.

El museo no está abierto todavía.	*The museum isn't open yet.*
el museo	*museum*
abierto	*open*
estar abierto	*to be open*
todavía	*still, yet*

¡Qué raro! Ya son las once.	*How strange! It's 11 o'clock already.*
raro	*strange*
¡Qué raro!	*How strange!*
ya	*already*
las once	*eleven o'clock*
son las once	*it's eleven o'clock*

Ay, ¡qué tontos somos! Hoy es lunes.	*Oh, we're so stupid! Today is Monday.*
tonto	*stupid, silly, foolish*
¡qué tontos!	*how stupid!*
somos	*we are* (first person plural) (**ser**)
hoy	*today*
lunes	*Monday*

Claro. Los lunes todos los museos están cerrados.	*Of course. All the museums are closed on Mondays.*
claro	*of course*
los lunes	*on Mondays*
cerrado	*closed*
estar cerrado	*to be closed*

Variantes

Listen, and repeat the same structures from *Diálogo 8*, now with new vocabulary.

¿Qué día es hoy?	*What day is today?*

Hoy es lunes .	*Today is **Monday**.*
martes	*Tuesday*
miércoles	*Wednesday*
jueves	*Thursday*
viernes	*Friday*
sábado	*Saturday*
domingo	*Sunday*

¡Qué raro !	*How **strange**!*
interesante	*interesting*
ridículo	*ridiculous*
impresionante	*impressive, awesome*
tonto	*foolish, stupid, silly*
asombroso	*amazing*

Estructura y Práctica

Ser *to be*: Uses

1 · **Ser** (*to be*) is used to link nouns and pronouns.

Yo **soy** ingeniera.	*I'm an engineer.*
Es arquitecto.	*He's an architect.*
Somos norteamericanos.	*We're American.*
Alicia y José **son** nuestros primos.	*Alicia and José **are** our cousins.*
El señor Pérez **es** el profesor.	*Mr. Pérez **is** the teacher.*

Because the verb ending tells who the subject is, subject pronouns do not appear in these sentences: **Es arquitecto. Somos norteamericanos.**

Unlike English, Spanish omits the indefinite article **un/una** with a profession: **Es arquitecto.** However, when the noun is modified, the indefinite article must be used: **Es un arquitecto exitoso** (*successful*).

2 · **Ser** is used before (or in questions, after) a phrase beginning with **de** that expresses possession, origin, or the material something is made of.

Esta oficina **es del** jefe.	*This office **is the** boss's.*
Somos de los Estados Unidos.	*We're from the United States.*
Las chaquetas **son de** lana.	*The jackets **are made of** wool.*
¿De quién es este celular?	*Whose cell phone **is** this?*

3 · **Ser** is used before adjectives that express inherent qualities and characteristics, such as physical and moral attributes, personality, nationality, age, religion, and color.

Felipe **es** inteligente.	*Felipe **is** intelligent.*
Sus hermanos **son** altos.	*His brother and sister **are** tall.*
Isabel y yo **somos** inglesas.	*Isabel and I **are** English.*
Juan **es** protestante, Samuel **es** judío, José **es** católico, and Alano **es** musulmán.	*Juan **is** Protestant, Samuel **is** Jewish, José **is** Catholic, and Alano **is** Muslim.*
Nuestro coche **es** gris.	*Our car **is** gray.*

4 · **Ser** is used to tell time, dates, and days of the week.

¿Qué hora **es**?	*What time **is it**?*
Es la una.	*It's one o'clock.*
Son las dos y media.	*It's two thirty.*
¿A qué hora **es** la comida?	*At what time **is** the dinner?*
Es a las siete.	*It's at seven o'clock.*
Hoy **es** el siete de diciembre.	*Today **is** December seventh.*
Hoy **es** viernes.	*Today **is** Friday.*

E Write the form of **ser** that correctly completes each of the following sentences.

1. Roberto y Matilde _____ simpáticos.

2. Yo _____ científico.

3. ¿De dónde _____ tú?

4. El abrigo _____ de lana.

5. Nosotros _____ de Costa Rica.

6. Julio _____ muy gracioso.

7. Uds. _____ católicos, ¿no?

8. Elenita _____ mi hermana.

9. Sus zapatos _____ marrones.

10. Mi tía _____ canadiense.

Telling Time

To ask what time it is in Spanish, one says **¿Qué hora es? ¿Qué horas son?** is also used, especially in Spanish America. Phrases telling time begin with **Son las** + the hour. The one exception is **Es la una.** (*It's one o'clock.*). (For cardinal numbers, see Chapter 6.)

Here is the way Spanish tells time on the traditional analog clock.

Son las cinco.	*It's five o'clock.*
Son las cinco y cinco.	*It's five past five. / It's five after five.*
Son las cinco y diez.	*It's ten past five. / It's ten after five.*
Son las cinco y cuarto.	*It's a quarter past five. / It's a quarter after five.*
Son las cinco y veinte.	*It's twenty past five. / It's twenty after five.*
Son las cinco y veinticinco.	*It's twenty-five past five. / It's twenty-five after five.*
Son las cinco y media.	*It's half past five. / It's five thirty.*
Son las seis menos veinticinco.	*It's twenty-five to six.*
Son las seis menos veinte.	*It's twenty to six.*
Son las seis menos cuarto.	*It's a quarter to six.*
Son las seis menos diez.	*It's ten to six.*
Son las seis menos cinco.	*It's five to six.*
Son las seis.	*It's six o'clock.*

The preceding system is typical of Spain and Argentina. In the rest of Spanish America, the times from the half hour to the following hour are usually expressed as follows.

Faltan veinticinco para las seis.	*It's twenty-five to six.*
Faltan veinte para las seis.	*It's twenty to six.*
Faltan quince para las seis.	*It's a quarter to six.*
Faltan diez para las seis.	*It's ten to six.*
Faltan cinco para las seis.	*It's five to six.*

As in the United States, the use of digital clocks and watches in Spanish-speaking countries has changed the way people tell time. Phrases such as the following are replacing the traditional analog times.

Son las cinco y quince.	*It's five fifteen.*
Son las cinco y treinta.	*It's five thirty.*
Son las cinco (y) cuarenta y cinco.	*It's five forty-five.*

The conjunction **y** between the hour and minutes may be left out when stating times from thirty-one to fifty-nine minutes past the hour.

To specify the time at which something happens, the preposition **a** is used.

¿**A** qué hora llega el avión?	*At what time is the plane arriving?*
A las ocho cincuenta.	*At eight fifty.*

Spanish has two ways of expressing A.M. and P.M. In everyday speech, the phrases **de la mañana**, **de la tarde**, and **de la noche** are added to the expression of time.

La reunión es a las ocho **de la mañana**.	*The meeting is at 8 A.M.*

For official time—train and airplane schedules, movie and show times, and class times—a twenty-four hour clock is used.

Hay un tren a las dieciocho (y) veinte.	*There's a train at 6:20 P.M.*
El avión llega a las veintidós (y) cuarenta.	*The plane is arriving at 10:40 P.M.*

Days of the Week

The days of the week are written with a lowercase letter in Spanish, rather than with a capital letter as in English.

lunes	*Monday*
martes	*Tuesday*
miércoles	*Wednesday*
jueves	*Thursday*
viernes	*Friday*
sábado	*Saturday*
domingo	*Sunday*

El domingo es el primer día de la semana.　　　　**Sunday** *is the first day of the week.*

El miércoles es un día ocupado.　　　　**Wednesday** *is a busy day.*

The singular definite article **el** means *on* before the days of the week.

Hay un concierto **el viernes**.　　　　*There's a concert* **on Friday**.

The plural definite article **los** indicates repeated action or regular occurrence.

Este museo está cerrado **los martes**.　　　　*This museum is closed* **on Tuesdays**.

No hay reunión **los jueves**.　　　　*There's no meeting* **on Thursdays**.

DAYS AND TIME: EXPRESSIONS

el anochecer, el atardecer	*dusk, nightfall*
al anochecer, al atardecer	*at dusk, at nightfall*
ayer	*yesterday*
anteayer	*the day before yesterday*
el fin de semana	*weekend*
la madrugada	*early morning, dawn*
madrugador/madrugadora	*early riser*
mañana	*tomorrow*
pasado mañana	*the day after tomorrow*
la medianoche	*midnight*
el mediodía	*noon*
Es tarde.	*It's late.*
Es temprano.	*It's early.*
Mi reloj está adelantado.	*My watch is fast.*
Mi reloj está atrasado/retrasado.	*My watch is slow.*

F *¿Qué hora es?* Rewrite the following sentences in Spanish. Express the time in more than one way whenever possible. Follow the *modelo.*

> MODELO   It's 4:00.
> → Son las cuatro.

1. It's 7:00.   7. It's 3:50.

2. It's 1:00.   8. It's 6:00 A.M.

3. It's 9:30.   9. It's 5:25 P.M.

4. It's 2:15.   10. It's 11:10 P.M.

5. It's 4:45.   11. It's 8:05 A.M.

6. It's 10:20.   12. It's 12:00 A.M. It's 12:00 P.M.

G *Diálogos.* Write mini-dialogues in Spanish. First, ask where and at what time an event is taking place, then respond with the information requested. Write all numbers as words. Follow the *modelo.*

> MODELO   el espectáculo: el teatro / 8:00 P.M.
> → —¿Dónde es el espectáculo?
> —Es en el teatro.
> —¿A qué hora?
> —Es a las ocho.

1. la reunión: la sala de conferencias / 11:30 A.M.

2. la fiesta de cumpleaños (*birthday*): la casa de Bernardo y Josefa / 7:00 P.M.

3. el partido de fútbol (*soccer*): el campo de fútbol (*soccer field*) / 1:30 P.M.

4. la boda: la iglesia / 4:00 P.M.

5. la comida: el hotel / 10:00 P.M.

6. el examen de historia: el salón de clase / 9:15 A.M.

H *Los días de la semana.* Express the following sentences in Spanish.

1. *There's a soccer game on Saturday.*

2. *What day is today?*

3. *The museums are closed on Mondays.*

4. *Their wedding is on Sunday.*

5. *This department store is open every day.*

6. *Mr. Paz is in the office from Monday to Thursday.*

7. *There are lectures at the university on Wednesdays.*

8. *We are having a meeting all day.*

⏵ DIÁLOGO 9 · Nuestro carro está descompuesto.

Study the dialogue, then listen to the recording and repeat each line.

PACO	¿Por qué está tu marido tan enojado?
CARMEN	Es que nuestro carro está descompuesto.
PACO	¿Dónde está el carro ahora?
CARMEN	Está en el taller mecánico.

Análisis

Check that you understand the linguistic breakdown of each speech from *Diálogo 9*.

¿Por qué está tu marido tan enojado?	*Why is your husband so angry?*
¿Por qué?	*Why?*
el marido	*husband*
tu	*your (informal, before a singular noun)*
tu marido	*your husband*
enojado	*angry*
tan	*so*
tan enojado	*so angry*
estar enojado	*to be angry*
Es que nuestro carro está descompuesto.	*It's that our car is broken.*
nuestro	*our*
nuestro carro	*our car*
descompuesto	*out of order, broken*
estar descompuesto	*to be out of order, to be broken*
¿Dónde está el carro ahora?	*Where is the car now?*
ahora	*now*
Está en el taller mecánico.	*It's in the mechanic's shop.*
el taller	*shop, workshop*
el taller mecánico	*mechanic's shop, garage (for repairs)*

⏵ Variantes

Listen, and repeat the same structures from *Diálogo 9*, now with new vocabulary.

¿Por qué está enojado ?	*Why is he **angry**?*
enfadado	*angry*
molesto	*annoyed*
furioso	*furious*
El carro está en el taller mecánico .	*The car is in the **mechanic's shop**.*
el parqueo	*parking lot*
el estacionamiento	*parking lot*
el garaje	*garage (for parking, not repair)*
la gasolinera	*gas station*
La carretera está cerca de aquí.	*The **highway** is near here.*
La autopista	*The turnpike*

▶ DIÁLOGO 10 · La comida está rica.

Study the dialogue, then listen to the recording and repeat each line.

GABRIELA   Esta carne está hecha a la perfección.
HERNANDO   Yo estoy de acuerdo. Está muy rica.
GABRIELA   En realidad toda la comida está deliciosa.
HERNANDO   Por eso este restaurante es tan famoso.

Análisis

Check that you understand the linguistic breakdown of each speech from *Diálogo 10*.

Esta carne está hecha a la perfección.	*This meat is perfectly done.*
la carne	*meat*
hecho	*done*
estar hecho	*to be done*
la perfección	*perfection*
a la perfección	*perfectly, to perfection*
Yo estoy de acuerdo. Está muy rica.	*I agree. It's delicious.*
el acuerdo	*agreement*
de acuerdo	*in agreement*
estar de acuerdo	*to agree*
rico	*delicious*
estar rico	*to be delicious*
En realidad toda la comida está deliciosa.	*Actually, all the food is delicious.*
la realidad	*reality*
en realidad	*actually, really*
la comida	*food*
toda la comida	*all the food*
delicioso	*delicious*
estar delicioso	*to be delicious*
Por eso este restaurante es tan famoso.	*That's why this restaurant is so famous.*
por eso	*that's why*
famoso	*famous*
tan famoso	*so famous*

▶ Variantes

Listen, and repeat the same structures from *Diálogo 10*, now with new vocabulary.

La carne está muy hecha .	*The meat is **too well done**.*
poco hecha	*underdone*

Estructura y Práctica

Ser vs. estar: Describing Food

Ser and **estar** also contrast when describing food. **Ser** is used when referring to food in general. **Estar** is used when describing how a particular food tastes.

El pescado **es** rico.	*Fish **is** delicious.* (general statement)
El pescado **está** rico.	*The fish **is** delicious.* (*This particular fish tastes good.*)
Las legumbres **son** buenas para la salud.	*Vegetables **are** good for your health.* (general statement)
Estas legumbres **están** buenas.	*These vegetables **are** good.* (*These particular vegetables taste good.*)

▶ DIÁLOGO 11 · ¡Yo estoy frito!

Study the dialogue, then listen to the recording and repeat each line.

GABRIELA ¿Por qué estás de mal humor?
HERNANDO Es que la impresora está descompuesta otra vez.
GABRIELA El técnico está en la oficina, ¿no?
HERNANDO No, el jueves es su día libre. ¡Yo estoy frito!

Análisis

Check that you understand the linguistic breakdown of each speech from *Diálogo 11*.

¿Por qué estás de mal humor?	*Why are you in a bad mood?*
de mal humor	*in a bad mood*
estar de mal humor	*to be in a bad mood*
Es que la impresora está descompuesta otra vez.	*Because the printer is broken again.*
la impresora	*printer*
otra vez	*again*
El técnico está en la oficina, ¿no?	*The technician is in the office, isn't he?*
el técnico	*technician*
¿no?	*isn't he?*
No, el jueves es su día libre. ¡Yo estoy frito!	*No, Thursday is his day off. I'm done for!*
el jueves	*Thursday*
el día	*day*
libre	*free*
el día libre	*day off*
frito	*done for, finished, doomed* (literally, *fried*)

▶ Variantes

Listen, and repeat the same structures from *Diálogo 11*, now with new vocabulary.

Estás de mal humor.	*You're in a **bad** mood.*
buen	*good*
El técnico está en la oficina, ¿no?	*The technician is in the office, **isn't he?***
¿verdad?	*isn't he?*

Estructura y Práctica

I *¿Ser o estar?* Choose **ser** or **estar** to complete each of the following sentences, then write the correct form of the verb or verbs needed.

1. El arroz integral (*brown rice*) _____ bueno para la salud.

2. Mi marido _____ diseñador gráfico.

3. Estos platos _____ muy sabrosos.

4. _____ que yo no _____ de acuerdo con Uds.

5. Aquel estacionamiento _____ bastante caro.

6. La gasolinera _____ al lado del parqueo.

7. El carro _____ nuevo pero _____ descompuesto otra vez.

8. Uds. _____ muy atrasados ya.

9. El viernes _____ su día libre.

10. ¿Por qué _____ Eduardo de mal humor?

11. ¡Qué ridículos _____ esos chicos!

12. La hamburguesa _____ muy hecha.

13. Ese cantante _____ muy famoso.

14. La tienda de cómputo _____ abierta hasta (*until*) las nueve.

Tag Questions

Spanish adds phrases such as **¿no?**, **¿verdad?**, **¿no es verdad?**, and **¿no es cierto?** to statements to turn them into questions. These phrases are called tags. Tag questions signal that the speaker expects the answer *yes*. If the statement to be agreed with is negative, only **¿verdad?** can be used as a tag. English uses tags such as *isn't it?* and *aren't you?* to turn statements into questions.

Ya son las siete, **¿no?**	It's already seven o'clock, **isn't it?**
Eres de origen francés, **¿no es cierto?**	You're of French descent, **aren't you?**
El pollo está riquísimo, **¿verdad?**	The chicken is delicious, **isn't it?**
No hay vuelo directo, **¿verdad?**	There's no direct flight, **is there?**

J **Tag Questions.** Write a sentence from each string of elements given, adding the tag in parentheses to turn it into a tag question. Follow the *modelo*.

> MODELO   la / ya / una / es (¿no?)
> → Ya es la una, ¿no?

1. descompuesta / tu / impresora / está (¿no?)

2. esta / picante / está / salsa / muy (¿verdad?)

3. negocios / son / esos / de / costarricenses / hombres (¿no es cierto?)

4. queda / de / carretera / aquí / lejos / la / no (¿verdad?)

5. las / es / economía / a / clase / de / tres / la (¿no es verdad?)

6. el / es / béisbol / de / sábado / partido / el (¿no?)

7. humor / de / estás / no / mal (¿verdad?)

8. día / tu / es / libre / domingo / el (¿no es cierto?)

⏵ DIÁLOGO 12 · Pablo y su computadora

Study the dialogue, then listen to the recording and repeat each line.

HERNANDO ¿Dónde está Pablo?
GABRIELA Está ocupado con su correo electrónico.
HERNANDO Está sentado frente a su computadora como de costumbre. ¡Qué chico!

Análisis

Check that you understand the linguistic breakdown of each speech from *Diálogo 12*.

¿Dónde está Pablo?	*Where's Pablo?*
Está ocupado con su correo electrónico.	*He's busy with his email.*
ocupado	*busy*
estar ocupado	*to be busy*
con	*with*
su	*his*
el correo	*mail*
el correo electrónico	*email*

Está sentado frente a su computadora como de costumbre. ¡Qué chico!	*He's sitting in front of his computer as usual. What a kid!*
estar sentado	*to be sitting*
frente a	*in front of*
la computadora	*computer*
como	*like, as*
la costumbre	*custom, habit*
como de costumbre	*as usual*
el chico	*kid, boy, guy*
¡Qué chico!	*What a kid!*

⏵ Variantes

Listen, and repeat the same structures from *Diálogo 12*, now with new vocabulary.

Está ocupado con su correo electrónico .	*He's busy with his **email**.*
sitio web	*website*

Está sentada frente a la computadora .	*She's sitting in front of **the computer**.*
al televisor	*the television (set)*
a la televisión	*the television*
a la pantalla	*the screen*

Están sentados .	*They're **sitting**.*
parados	*standing*
de pie	*standing*
acostados	*lying down*
dormidos	*sleeping*

¡Qué muchacho !	*What a **boy**!*
muchacha	*girl*

▶ DIÁLOGO 13 · Los señores Ortega están de vacaciones.

Study the dialogue, then listen to the recording and repeat each line.

HERNANDO   ¿Dónde están los señores Ortega?
GABRIELA   Están de vacaciones. Están en Cancún.
HERNANDO   ¡Pobres! Estoy seguro que están tumbados en la playa todo el día.

Análisis

Check that you understand the linguistic breakdown of each speech from *Diálogo 13*.

¿Dónde están los señores Ortega?	*Where are Mr. and Mrs. Ortega?*
los señores Ortega	*Mr. and Mrs. Ortega*

Están de vacaciones. Están en Cancún.	*They're on vacation. They're in Cancún.*
las vacaciones	*vacation*
de vacaciones	*on vacation*
estar de vacaciones	*to be on vacation*
Cancún	*Cancún (world-famous tourist resort on Mexico's Yucatán Peninsula)*

¡Pobres! Estoy seguro que están tumbados en la playa todo el día.	*Poor people! I'm sure they're lying on the beach all day.*
pobre	*poor*
pobres	*poor people*
seguro	*sure*
estar seguro	*to be sure*
estar tumbado	*to be lying down*
la playa	*beach*
el día	*day*
todo el día	*all day*

▶ Variantes

Listen, and repeat the same structures from *Diálogo 13*, now with new vocabulary.

Están de vacaciones .	*They're on **vacation**.*
viaje	*a trip*

Está en casa todo el día .	*She's at home **all day**.*
toda la tarde	*all afternoon*
toda la noche	*all night*

Estructura y Práctica

Estar + Past Participle: Expressing Positions of the Body

Estar is used with the past participle to express positions of the body. The past participle functions as an adjective, thereby agreeing in gender and number with the noun it refers to. English uses the *-ing* form for this purpose. (For the past participle, see Chapter 13.)

Los invitados **están sentados** a la mesa.	*The guests **are sitting** at the table.*
Maite **está recostada**.	*Maite **is lying down**.*

K Rewrite each of the following sentences. Include the correct form of **estar** plus the past participle (cue in parentheses) to describe positions of the body. Make all necessary changes. Follow the *modelo*.

> MODELO   La niña ya _____. (acostado)
> → La niña ya está acostada.

1. Julio y Laura _____ en la sala de conferencias. (sentado)

2. Las hermanas _____ en la cama. (tumbado)

3. El bebé _____. (dormido)

4. Los jardineros (*gardeners*) _____. (arrodillado (*kneeling*)) (la rodilla (*knee*))

5. Algunos pasajeros (*passengers*) _____ en el autobús. (parado)

6. Virginia _____ en el sofá. (echado (*lying down*))

7. El receptor (*catcher*) _____. (agachado (*crouching*))

L *Estoy seguro que...* Express each of the following sentences in Spanish, stating your certainty that some people are doing certain things.

1. *I'm sure that Marta is busy with her website.*

2. *I'm sure that Mr. and Mrs. Martínez are on vacation.*

3. *I'm sure that Paco is lying on the beach as usual.*

4. *I'm sure that my friends [fem.] are sitting in front of the television.*

5. *I'm sure that the boys are on a trip.*

6. *I'm sure that Lorenzo is lying down.*

7. *I'm sure that your (tú) computer is broken.*

8. *I'm sure that you're (Uds.) in the office all day.*

▶ DIÁLOGO 14 · ¿Cómo es el novio de Laura?

Study the dialogue, then listen to the recording and repeat each line.

GABRIELA	¿Cómo es el novio de Laura?
HERNANDO	Miguel es alto, delgado y moreno. Es muy guapo.
GABRIELA	Es simpático, ¿verdad?
HERNANDO	Ah sí. Es un tipo encantador y gracioso.

Análisis

Check that you understand the linguistic breakdown of each speech from *Diálogo 14*.

¿Cómo es el novio de Laura?	*What does Laura's boyfriend look like?*
¿cómo?	*how?*
¿Cómo es?	*What is he like? / What does he look like?*
el novio	*boyfriend, fiancé*
Miguel es alto, delgado y moreno.	*Miguel is tall, thin, and dark.*
Es muy guapo.	*He's very handsome.*
alto	*tall*
delgado	*thin*
moreno	*dark-haired, dark-skinned*
guapo	*handsome, good-looking*
Es simpático, ¿verdad?	*He's nice, isn't he?*
simpático	*nice*
la verdad	*truth*
¿verdad?	*isn't he?* (tag question)
Ah sí. Es un tipo encantador y gracioso.	*Oh, yes. He's a charming and funny guy.*
el tipo	*guy*
encantador	*charming*
gracioso	*funny, witty*

▶ Variantes

Listen, and repeat the same structures from *Diálogo 14*, now with new vocabulary.

Roberto es bajo .	*Roberto is **short**.*
gordo	*fat*
amable	*kind*
antipático	*unpleasant*
honrado	*honest*
divertido	*amusing*
Marta es encantadora .	*Marta is **charming**.*
flaca	*thin*
rubia	*blond*
arrogante	*arrogant*
alegre	*cheerful (by nature)*
atenta	*considerate*

🔘 DIÁLOGO 15 · ¿Cómo es Isabel?

Study the dialogue, then listen to the recording and repeat each line.

HERNANDO   Isabel es trabajadora y emprendedora.
GABRIELA   Es muy inteligente también.
HERNANDO   Por eso es directora de la compañía.

Análisis

Check that you understand the linguistic breakdown of each speech from *Diálogo 15*.

Isabel es trabajadora y emprendedora.
  trabajador
  emprendedor

Isabel is hardworking and enterprising.
  hardworking
  enterprising

Es muy inteligente también.
  inteligente

She's also very intelligent.
  intelligent

Por eso es directora de la compañía.
  la directora
  la compañía
  la directora de la compañía

That's why she's president of the company.
  director, president (feminine)
  company
  president of the company

🔘 Variantes

Listen, and repeat the same structures from *Diálogo 15*, now with new vocabulary.

¿Es trabajadora Isabel?
Sí, es muy trabajadora.

Is Isabel hardworking?
Yes, she's very hardworking.

¿Es rico el director?
Sí, es rico.

Is the director rich?
Yes, he's rich.

Estructura y Práctica

M **¿Cómo son?** Write complete sentences to describe some of Santiago's family members. Make all necessary changes. Follow the *modelo*.

MODELO   mi prima: joven / bonito
          → Mi prima es joven y bonita.

1. mis sobrinos: rubio / bajo

2. mis papás: inteligente / simpático

3. mi hermano: alto / moreno

4. mis hijos: guapo / encantador

5. mis cuñadas: antipático / arrogante

6. mi hermana: emprendedor / rico

7. mis nietos: moreno / delgado

8. mi tía: flaco / lindo

9. mi esposa: honrado / amable

10. mis primas: alegre / atento

11. mis abuelos: trabajador / divertido

12. mi cuñado: gordo / feo

▶ DIÁLOGO 16 · ¿De quién es?

Study the dialogue, then listen to the recording and repeat each line.

HERNANDO   ¿De quién es esta bufanda?
GABRIELA   Es del niño.
HERNANDO   Y esos guantes, ¿de quién son?
GABRIELA   Son de la niña.

Análisis

Check that you understand the linguistic breakdown of each speech from *Diálogo 16*.

¿De quién es esta bufanda?	*Whose scarf is this?*
¿De quién?	*Whose?*
la bufanda	*scarf*
Es del niño.	*It's the boy's.*
el niño	*male child, boy*
del niño	*of the boy, belonging to the boy*
Y esos guantes, ¿de quién son?	*And what about those gloves? Whose are they?*
el guante	*glove*
Son de la niña.	*They're the girl's.*
la niña	*female child, girl*
de la niña	*of the girl, belonging to the girl*

▶ Variantes

Listen, and repeat the same structures from *Diálogo 16*, now with new vocabulary.

¿De quiénes es esta cámara?	*Whose camera is this?*
Es de ellos.	*It's theirs.*
¿De quiénes son esos discos compactos?	*Whose compact discs are those?*
Son de ellas.	*They're theirs. (feminine)*

Estructura y Práctica

N *¿De quién es?* Express the following dialogues in Spanish.

1. *Whose book is this?*
   It's the teacher's [masc.].

2. *These shoes. Whose are they?*
   They're hers.

3. *Whose wallet is that?*
   It's Doctor Lara's.

4. *These socks* (las medias). *Whose are they?*
   They're hers.

5. *Whose* [pl.] *car is it?*
   It's theirs.

▶ DIÁLOGO 17 · ¿De qué son los suéteres?

Study the dialogue, then listen to the recording and repeat each line.

HERNANDO	Señorita, por favor, ¿de qué son estos suéteres?
GABRIELA	Son de algodón.
HERNANDO	¿Hay suéteres de lana?
GABRIELA	Cómo no. Están al fondo, a la derecha.

Análisis

Check that you understand the linguistic breakdown of each speech from *Diálogo 17*.

Señorita, por favor, ¿de qué son estos suéteres?	*Miss, please, what are these sweaters made of?*
señorita	*miss*
por favor	*please*
¿De qué son?	*What are they made of?*
el suéter	*sweater*
Son de algodón.	*They're cotton.*
el algodón	*cotton*
¿Hay suéteres de lana?	*Are there wool sweaters?*
la lana	*wool*
Cómo no. Están al fondo, a la derecha.	*Of course. They're in the back, on the right.*
Cómo no.	*Of course.*
estar al fondo	*to be in the back*
a la derecha	*on the right, to the right*

▶ Variantes

Listen, and repeat the same structures from *Diálogo 17*, now with new vocabulary.

¿De qué es el suéter ?	*What's the **sweater** made of?*
la blusa	*blouse*
la camisa	*shirt*
el traje	*suit*
el abrigo	*coat*
la chaqueta	*jacket*
la falda	*skirt*
el vestido	*dress*
el pantalón	*pants*
el bluejean	*jeans*
la camiseta	*T-shirt*
la corbata	*necktie*
el sombrero	*hat*
el gorro	*cap*
¿De qué son estos zapatos ?	*What are **these shoes** made of?*
estos guantes	*these gloves*
estos pantalones	*these pants*
estas botas	*these boots*

Estructura y Práctica

O *¿De qué es?* Express each of the following sentences in Spanish, using the cue in parentheses to describe what the item of clothing is made of. Follow the *modelo*.

> MODELO ¿De qué es el gorro (*cap*)? (lana)
> → Es de lana.

1. ¿De qué es esta corbata? (seda (*silk*))
2. ¿De qué son las botas? (cuero (*leather*))
3. ¿De qué son esas camisetas? (poliéster)
4. ¿De qué es el vestido? (lino (*linen*))
5. ¿De qué son los pantalones? (pana (*corduroy*))
6. ¿De qué es esta falda? (algodón)

DIÁLOGO 18 · Mi trabajo es aburrido.

Study the dialogue, then listen to the recording and repeat each line.

> GABRIELA ¿Cuál es su profesión?
> HERNANDO Soy programador.
> GABRIELA ¿Es interesante su trabajo?
> HERNANDO No. En realidad es muy aburrido.

Análisis

Check that you understand the linguistic breakdown of each speech from *Diálogo 18*.

¿Cuál es su profesión?	*What is your profession?*
la profesión	*profession*
Soy programador.	*I'm a computer programmer.*
el programador	*computer programmer*
¿Es interesante su trabajo?	*Is your work interesting?*
interesante	*interesting*
el trabajo	*work, job*
No. En realidad es muy aburrido.	*No. Actually, it's very boring.*
en realidad	*actually, really*
ser aburrido	*to be boring*

Variantes

Listen, and repeat the same structures from *Diálogo 18*, now with new vocabulary.

¿Cuál es su profesión ?	*What is your **profession**?*
dirección	*address*
número de teléfono	*telephone number*
nacionalidad	*nationality*
religión	*religion*
fecha de nacimiento	*date of birth*
estado civil	*marital status*
Soy casado .	*I'm **married**.*
divorciado	*divorced*

Estoy casado .	*I'm **married**.*
divorciado	*divorced*
Soy programador .	*I'm **a computer programmer**.*
hombre de negocios	*a businessman*
arquitecto	*an architect*

Estructura y Práctica

¿CUÁL? AND ¿QUÉ?

¿Cuál? before **ser** is used for English *what?* when an identification is asked for.

¿Cuál es la fecha de hoy?	*What's today's date?*
¿Cuál es la capital de España?	*What is the capital of Spain?*
¿Cuál es su apellido?	*What is your last name?*

¿Qué? before **ser** asks for a definition.

¿Qué es el ciberespacio?	*What is cyberspace?*

P Express the following dialogues in Spanish.

1. *Whose suitcase is this?*
   It's his.

2. *What are those suits made of?*
   They're wool.

3. *Please, miss, where are the silk (seda) ties?*
   They're next to the shirts.

4. *Whose [pl.] coats are those?*
   They're theirs.

5. *What is your (Uds.) nationality?*
   We're Peruvian.

6. *What is your (Ud.) profession?*
   I'm a lawyer [fem.].
   What is your nationality?
   I'm Panamanian.
   And your (country of) origin?
   I'm of English descent.

▶ DIÁLOGO 19 · Regalos para mi familia

Study the dialogue, then listen to the recording and repeat each line.

HERNANDO	¿Para quién son estos regalos?
GABRIELA	Bueno, este regalo es para mis padres.
HERNANDO	¿Y los otros?
GABRIELA	Son para mis hermanos.

Análisis

Check that you understand the linguistic breakdown of each speech from *Diálogo 19*.

¿Para quién son estos regalos?	*Whom are these gifts for?*
¿Para quién?	*For whom?*
Bueno, este regalo es para mis padres.	*Well, this gift is for my parents.*
los padres	*parents*

¿Y los otros?   *And what about the other ones?*

Son para mis hermanos.   *They're for my brother and sister.*
  los hermanos   *brother(s) and sister(s), brothers*

▶ Variantes

Listen, and repeat the same structures from *Diálogo 19*, now with new vocabulary.

El iPod es para mi madre .   *The iPod is for my **mother**.*
  padre   *father*
  mamá   *mom*
  papá   *dad*
  hijo   *son*
  hija   *daughter*
  hermano   *brother*
  hermana   *sister*
  abuela   *grandmother*
  abuelo   *grandfather*
  tía   *aunt*
  tío   *uncle*
  cuñado   *brother-in-law*
  cuñada   *sister-in-law*
  madrastra   *stepmother*
  padrastro   *stepfather*

Estos regalos son para nuestros padres .   *These gifts are for our **parents**.*
  papás   *parents*
  hijos   *children*
  abuelos   *grandparents*
  nietos   *grandchildren*
  tíos   *aunt(s) and uncle(s), uncles*
  primos   *cousins*
  sobrinos   *niece(s) and nephew(s), nephews*

Estructura y Práctica

Ser and estar in Yes/No Questions

In Chapter 1, you learned that when a yes/no question includes a form of the verb **ser** + an adjective, the subject is placed at the end of the sentence. The pattern of the question is thus verb + adjective + subject.

Estos programadores son trabajadores.   *These computer programmers are hardworking.*

¿Son trabajadores estos programadores? *Are these computer programmers hardworking?*

Eugenia es simpática.   *Eugenia is pleasant.*
¿Es simpática Eugenia?   *Is Eugenia pleasant?*

Similarly, in questions containing a form of the verb **estar** + an adjective, the subject is placed at the end of the sentence.

Los chicos están contentos.	*The kids are happy.*
¿Están contentos los chicos?	*Are the kids happy?*
La tienda de cómputo está abierta.	*The computer store is open.*
¿Está abierta la tienda de cómputo?	*Is the computer store open?*

For information questions in Spanish, a preposition associated with an interrogative word must precede it. In English, prepositions are usually separated from the question word and appear at the end of the sentence.

¿De quién es aquella casa?	***Whose*** *house is that?*
¿De dónde son tus abuelos?	***Where*** *are your grandparents **from**?*
¿De qué es el traje?	***What*** *is the suit **made of**?*
¿Para quién es el reloj?	***Whom*** *is the watch **for**?*

Q *¿Cuál es la pregunta?* Write the information question that would elicit each of the following responses. Follow the *modelo*.

MODELO   Estas maletas son de Daniel.
        → ¿De quién son estas maletas?

1. Los señores Arriaga están de vacaciones en Europa.
2. Es ingeniero mecánico.
3. Las chicas están perfectamente.
4. Es la una y media.
5. Las camisetas son de algodón.
6. Santiago es la capital de Chile.
7. La novia de Arturo es encantadora.
8. Hoy es viernes.
9. La reunión es en la oficina del director.
10. La fiesta es a las nueve.
11. Los zapatos son del niño.
12. La pulsera es para Emilia.
13. Estos platos están muy sabrosos.
14. Estoy casado.
15. Calle Flores, número dieciocho.
16. Son protestantes.

R Transform the following sentences with **ser** and **estar** into yes/no questions. Follow the *modelo*.

MODELO   Sus primos son argentinos.
        → ¿Son argentinos sus primos?

1. Las tiendas por departamentos están abiertas.
2. Su trabajo es aburrido.
3. Sus hijos están emocionados.
4. La novia de Juan Antonio es atenta.
5. Los niños están asustados.
6. Este contador está muy ocupado.
7. Sus papás son simpáticos.
8. Tu coche está descompuesto.
9. Esos museos son impresionantes.
10. Lola y Diego son casados.
11. Su hermano es emprendedor.
12. Estos países están muy adelantados.

Un paso más

Are you ready to take your Spanish a step further? Here are exercises that will enhance your knowledge of the language and encourage you to express yourself freely.

S Here is a list of nouns related to adjectives that appear in Chapter 4. Write the adjective related to each of the nouns. Learning the adjective related to the noun will help you increase your vocabulary.

1. el aburrimiento
2. el catarro
3. el adelanto
4. la alegría
5. la angustia
6. el susto
7. la reunión
8. el cansancio
9. la emoción
10. la enfermedad
11. el entusiasmo
12. el estrés
13. la inquietud
14. la molestia
15. el nervio
16. la preocupación
17. el atraso
18. la tristeza
19. el divorcio
20. la gracia

T *Preguntas personales.* Answer each question with a complete Spanish sentence.

1. ¿Qué día es hoy?
2. ¿Qué hora es?
3. ¿Hay una reunión (un concierto, una fiesta, un partido) hoy?
4. ¿Dónde es? ¿A qué hora es?
5. ¿Dónde queda tu casa?
6. ¿Dónde queda tu lugar de trabajo (*workplace*)?
7. ¿Cómo es tu carro? ¿Está descompuesto?
8. ¿Hay un taller mecánico cerca de tu casa? ¿Dónde está?

U Write a paragraph in Spanish telling about yourself and some family members. Use these questions as a guide.

1. ¿Cómo eres?
2. ¿Cuál es tu profesión?
3. ¿Cuál es tu estado civil?
4. ¿Cuál es tu nacionalidad?
5. ¿De qué origen eres?
6. ¿Cuál es tu religión?
7. ¿Cuál es tu fecha de nacimiento?
8. ¿Cómo estás actualmente (*these days*)? (la salud (*health*); el ánimo (*spirits*))
9. ¿Cómo son tus papás (hijos, hermanos, abuelos, nietos, tíos, primos, cuñados)?
10. ¿Cómo están actualmente?

Work and Leisure

Communication Goals

- Talking about work, vacation and travel, and leisure activities
- Telling how you celebrate your birthday
- Telling when things happen
- Vocabulary: sports, music, the computer, the seasons, months, meals

Grammar Topics

- The Present Tense of Regular **-ar** Verbs
- Uses of the Present Tense
- **Hacer** *to do, make*
- **Ir** *to go*
- **Ir** + **a** + Infinitive
- Contraction **al**
- Direct Objects and the Personal **a**
- Relative Pronoun **que**
- Negative Words
- Compound Nouns
- Nouns
- Adverbs of Time

DIÁLOGO 1 · Hacen ejercicio.

Study the dialogue, then listen to the recording and repeat each line.

JUAN   ¿Haces mucho ejercicio?
ISABEL   Sí, troto cinco veces por semana y levanto pesas.
JUAN   Yo troto también, pero no levanto pesas.
ISABEL   Pues vamos a trotar juntos mañana.

Análisis

Check that you understand the linguistic breakdown of each speech from *Diálogo 1*.

¿Haces mucho ejercicio?	*Do you exercise a lot?*
hacer	*to do, make*
haces	*you do*
el ejercicio	*exercise, workout*
mucho ejercicio	*a lot of exercise*

Sí, troto cinco veces por semana y levanto pesas.	*Yes, I jog five times a week and I lift weights.*
trotar	*to jog*
troto	*I jog*
la vez	*time (occasion, occurrence)*
las veces	*times (occasions, occurrences)*
cinco veces	*five times*
la semana	*week*
por semana	*weekly*
levanto	*I lift*
la pesa	*weight*
las pesas	*weights, dumbbells*

Yo troto también, pero no levanto pesas.	*I jog, too, but I don't lift weights.*

Pues vamos a trotar juntos mañana.	*Well, let's jog together tomorrow.*
pues	*well* (interjection)
vamos	*we go, we're going*
vamos a + *infinitive*	*let's (do something)*
vamos a trotar	*let's jog*
juntos	*together*
mañana	*tomorrow*

▶ Variantes

Listen, and repeat the same structures from *Diálogo 1*, now with new vocabulary.

Vamos a trotar juntos mañana.	*Let's **jog** together tomorrow.*
nadar	*swim*
patinar	*skate*
caminar	*walk*
montar en bicicleta	*take a bicycle ride*
montar a caballo	*go horseback riding*

Vamos al gimnasio .	*We're going **to the gym**.*
al estadio	*to the stadium*
a la piscina	*to the pool*
a la pista	*to the track*
a la cancha de tenis	*to the tennis court*
a la cancha de baloncesto	*to the basketball court*
al campo de fútbol americano	*to the football field*
a la playa	*to the beach*

al bosque nacional	*to the national park*
al campo	*to the countryside*
al mar	*to the seashore*
¿Haces ejercicio ?	*Do you **exercise**?*
deportes	*play sports, do sports*
yoga	*do yoga*
camping	*go camping*
jogging	*jog, go jogging*

Estructura y Práctica

The Present Tense of Regular -ar Verbs

The Spanish verb system is characterized by a large number of forms, each one of which shows person and tense. This is very different from English, where person and tense are signaled by separate words that are often contracted.

SPANISH	ENGLISH
llego	*I arrive, I am arriving, I'm arriving*
estudiamos	*we study, we are studying, we're studying*

Spanish verbs are divided into three classes, called conjugations, distinguished by the vowel of the infinitive. The infinitive is the form of the verb that does not show person or tense and is the form used for listing verbs in dictionaries and vocabularies. Spanish infinitives may end in **-ar**, **-er**, or **-ir**. When the infinitive ending is removed, the stem of the verb is left. Endings are added to the stem.

The present indicative tense in Spanish is formed by adding the present tense endings to the stem of the verb. You will learn the **-ar** conjugation in this chapter. In Chapter 6, you will learn the **-er** and **-ir** conjugations.

comprar *to buy*			
yo	compr**o**	nosotros	compr**amos**
tú	compr**as**	vosotros	compr**áis**
él/ella/Ud.	compr**a**	ellos/ellas/Uds.	compr**an**

Note that **-ar** verbs have the vowel **a** in all the endings except the **yo** form.

Stress is a very important feature of the Spanish verb system. The forms of **-ar**, **-er**, and **-ir** verbs are stressed on the stem in the singular (**yo/tú/él/ella/Ud.**) and the third person plural (**ellos/ellas/Uds.**) forms, and on the ending in the **nosotros** and **vosotros** forms.

hablo, hablas, habla, hablan, hablamos, habláis

Uses of the Present Tense

1 · The present tense forms of Spanish verbs express both the English simple present (*I speak*) and the English present progressive (*I'm speaking*).

Tocas el piano.	{ *You play* the piano. { *You're playing* the piano.
¿**Trabajan** Uds. en casa?	{ *Do you work* at home? { *Are you working* at home?

2 · The **yo** form and the **nosotros** form of the present tense are often used to ask for instructions.

¿**Entrego** los documentos hoy?	*Shall I submit* the documents today?
¿**Tomamos** un vino tinto?	*Shall we have* a red wine?

3 · After ¿**Por qué no...?**, the present tense is used to make a suggestion.

¿**Por qué no** cenas con nosotros?	*Why don't* you have dinner with us?
¿**Por qué no** vamos de vacaciones en mayo?	*Why don't* we go on vacation in May?

4 · The present tense may be used to express the future when another element of the sentence (such as an adverb of time) makes the future reference clear.

Mañana **montan** a caballo.	*Tomorrow they'll go* horseback *riding*.

Hacer *to do, make*

You will see in Chapter 6 that **-er** verbs are conjugated like **-ar** verbs, except that they have **-e-** in the ending where **-ar** verbs have **-a-**. **Hacer**, like a number of common **-er** verbs, has an irregular **yo** form: a **-g-** inserted before the **-o** ending. Verbs with this irregularity are called **-g-** verbs. Thus, the **yo** form of **hacer** (**hago**) is irregular, but the rest of its present tense forms are regular.

hacer *to do, make*

yo	ha**go**	nosotros	hacemos
tú	haces	vosotros	hacéis
él/ella/Ud.	hace	ellos/ellas/Uds.	hacen

¿Haces mucho ejercicio?	*Do you exercise a lot?*
Hago deportes pero no mucho.	*I play sports, but not a lot.*

 Los deportes. Write sentences using the string of elements given to tell what sports and exercises you and your friends do. Follow the *modelo*.

> MODELO   Pablo / trotar
> → Pablo trota.

1. tú / montar en bicicleta

2. Uds. / nadar

3. yo / patinar sobre hielo (*ice-skate*)

4. mis amigos y yo / montar a caballo

5. Ud. / caminar ocho millas diarias (*daily*)

6. Marta y Simón / trotar

7. Nicolás / levantar pesas

8. Diana / patinar sobre ruedas (*roller-skate*)

B *¡No hacen nada!* Write the form of **hacer** that correctly completes each of the following sentences about the sports and workouts these people refuse to do!

1. Uds. no _____ camping.

2. Yo no _____ deportes.

3. Él no _____ jogging.

4. Ellos no _____ una caminata (*walk around*).

5. Ud. no _____ ejercicio.

6. Tú no _____ yoga.

7. Nosotros no _____ rafting.

8. Ella no _____ Pilates.

C Express the following sentences in Spanish.

1. *I swim twice a week.*

2. *Shall we take a bicycle ride today?*

3. *I'll exercise tomorrow.*

4. *Why don't we go to the gym together?*

5. *My friends don't play sports.*

6. *Let's walk to the basketball court.*

DIÁLOGO 2 · Vamos al club.

Study the dialogue, then listen to the recording and repeat each line.

ISABEL	¿Por qué no vamos al club Maracas?
JUAN	Ah, tú hablas del club donde tocan música latina, ¿no?
ISABEL	Precisamente. Vamos a tomar una copa y escuchar música.
JUAN	¡Y bailar salsa! ¿Qué esperamos? Vamos ahora mismo.

Análisis

Check that you understand the linguistic breakdown of each speech from *Diálogo 2*.

¿Por qué no vamos al club Maracas?	*Why don't we go to Club Maracas?*
vamos	*we go*
no vamos	*we don't go*
¿Por qué no vamos?	*Why don't we go?*
el club	*club*
al	*to the* (contraction of **a** + **el**)
al club	*to the club*

Ah, tú hablas del club donde tocan música latina, ¿no?	*Ah, you mean the club where they play Latin music, right?*
hablar	*to speak, talk*
de	*about*
del	*of the, about the* (contraction of **de** + **el**)
tocar	*to play (a musical instrument)*
la música	*music*
latino	*Latin*

Precisamente. Vamos a tomar una copa y escuchar música.	*Exactly. We'll have a drink and listen to music.*
precisamente	*exactly*
tomar	*to take; to drink*

una copa	*an alcoholic drink* (literally, *wine glass, stem glass*)
tomar una copa	*to have a drink*
escuchar	*to listen to*
¡Y bailar salsa! ¿Qué esperamos?	*And dance salsa! What are we waiting for?*
Vamos ahora mismo.	*Let's go right now.*
bailar	*to dance*
la salsa	*salsa dance music* (literally, *sauce*)
esperar	*to wait for*
¿Qué esperamos?	*What are we waiting for?*
Vamos.	*Let's go.*
ahora	*now*
ahora mismo	*right now*

▶ Variantes

Listen, and repeat the same structures from *Diálogo 2*, now with new vocabulary.

Vamos al club .	*Let's go **to the club**.*
a la discoteca	*to the discotheque*
al bar	*to the bar*
al concierto	*to the concert*
a la exposición de arte	*to the art exhibit*
¿De qué hablas?	*What are you talking about?*
Hablo del club .	*I'm talking **about the club**.*
de la discoteca	*about the discotheque*
del cine	*about the movie theater*
de la galería de arte	*about the art gallery*
del espectáculo	*about the show*
de la obra de teatro	*about the play*
Tocan música latina en el iPod.	***They play** Latin music on the iPod.*
Escuchan	*They listen to*
Disfrutan de	*They enjoy*
Graban	*They record*
Cargan	*They upload*
Descargan	*They download*
Toco el piano .	*I play **the piano**.*
el clarinete	*the clarinet*
la flauta	*the flute*
la guitarra	*the guitar*
el violín	*the violin*
el saxofón	*the saxophone*
Vamos a tomar una copa .	*Let's have **a drink**.*
algo	*something*
el desayuno	*breakfast*
el almuerzo	*lunch*
la merienda	*a snack*

Estructura y Práctica

Ir *to go*

Ir (*to go*) is an irregular verb and one of the small number of verbs ending in **-oy** in the first person singular: **voy**.

ir *to go*			
yo	**voy**	nosotros	vamos
tú	vas	vosotros	vais
él/ella/Ud.	va	ellos/ellas/Uds.	van

¿Adónde van Uds.?	*Where are you going?*
Yo voy a la cancha de tenis y Diego va a la piscina.	*I'm going to the tennis court and Diego is going to the pool.*

D ***¿Adónde van?*** Write sentences using the verb **ir** with the elements given to tell where these people are going. Follow the *modelo*.

MODELO   los chicos / la discoteca
            → Los chicos van a la discoteca.

1. Felipe y yo / el campo
2. Uds. / la cancha de tenis
3. Mercedes / la piscina
4. los señores Vargas / la playa
5. yo / el concierto
6. tú / el bar
7. Mauricio / el bosque nacional
8. Ud. / la galería de arte

Ir + a + Infinitive

In both English and Spanish, the infinitive can follow a conjugated verb. In the **ir** + **a** + infinitive construction, the verb **ir** is conjugated and connected to the infinitive by the preposition **a**.

Van a tomar el almuerzo.	*They're going to have lunch.*

Ir + **a** + infinitive is a frequent substitute for the future tense.

¿Cuándo vamos a cenar?	*When are we going to have dinner?*
Voy a servir (*to serve*) la cena a las ocho.	*I'm going to serve dinner at eight o'clock.*

Vamos a + infinitive often means *let's (do something)*. However, when used in the negative, it can only mean *we are not going to do something*.

Vamos a hacer un viaje en mayo.	*Let's take a trip in May.*
No vamos a hacer un viaje en mayo.	*We're not going to take a trip in May.*

E *¿Qué van a hacer?* Expand each of the following sentences using the **ir** + **a** + infinitive construction to state what people are going to do at the party. Follow the *modelo*.

MODELO   Ellos hacen una pizza.
→ Ellos van a hacer una pizza.

1. Uds. toman una copa.
2. Mario descarga música brasileña.
3. Yo hago las tapas.
4. Manuel y Leticia bailan el tango.
5. Tú hablas con los invitados (*guests*).
6. Alicia y yo tocamos el piano.
7. Clara graba un video.
8. ¡Nosotros disfrutamos de una fiesta muy divertida!

Contraction al

You learned in Chapter 2 that the preposition **de** contracts with the masculine singular definite article **el** to form **del**: **de** + **el** → **del**.

Es la oficina **del** gerente.   *It's the manager's office.*

Similarly, the preposition **a** contracts with the masculine singular definite article **el** to form **al**: **a** + **el** → **al**.

Voy **al** museo.   *I'm going **to the** museum.*

The preposition **a**, like **de**, does not contract with other forms of the definite article or with the pronoun **él** (*he, it*).

¿Vas **a los** conciertos pop?   *Do you go **to** pop concerts?*
Van **a la** playa.   *They're going **to the** beach.*
¿Por qué se lo entregaste **a él**?   *Why did you hand it **to him**?*

F *A o al.* Rewrite each of the following sentences, completing each one by writing the preposition **a** or the contraction **al** as necessary. Make any necessary changes.

1. —¿Uds. van _____ ir _____ el mar mañana?

   —Sí, vamos _____ ir _____ la playa mañana en la tarde.

2. —¿Vas _____ el gimnasio?

   —No, voy _____ el club.

3. —¿Ud. camina _____ la tienda de cómputo?

   —Sí, pero primero voy _____ la heladería.

4. —¿Tus amigos van _____ la universidad?

   —No, van _____ el campo de fútbol.

5. —La reunión es _____ las dos, ¿verdad?

   —No, es _____ la una.

6. —El teatro está _____ una cuadra de aquí, ¿no?

   —Ah sí. Queda _____ el lado de una galería de arte.

G Express the following sentences in Spanish.

1. *I'm going to have lunch.*
2. *Let's go to the museum.*
3. *What are you (Uds.) talking about?*
4. *We're talking about the show.*
5. *What are you (tú) listening to?*
6. *I'm downloading Spanish music.*
7. *Why don't we ice-skate* (patinar sobre hielo)?

DIÁLOGO 3 · ¿Esperas a alguien?

Study the dialogue, then listen to the recording and repeat each line.

JUAN	¿Qué haces? ¿Esperas a alguien?
ISABEL	Sí, espero a mi amigo Gabriel.
JUAN	Ah claro, Gabriel, tu amigo que hace programación.
ISABEL	Sí, él y yo trabajamos juntos. Mira, ya llega.

Análisis

Check that you understand the linguistic breakdown of each speech from *Diálogo 3*.

¿Qué haces? ¿Esperas a alguien?	*What are you doing? Are you waiting for someone?*
esperar	*to wait for*
esperas	*you wait for*
a	(personal **a** required before an animate direct object)
alguien	*someone*
esperar a alguien	*to wait for someone*
Sí, espero a mi amigo Gabriel.	*Yes, I'm waiting for my friend Gabriel.*
Ah claro, Gabriel, tu amigo que hace programación.	*Oh, of course, Gabriel, your friend who does computer programming.*
claro	*of course*
que	*who, which, that*
hacer	*to do, make*
hace	*he does*
la programación	*(computer) programming*
Sí, él y yo trabajamos juntos. Mira, ya llega.	*Yes, he and I work together. Look, here he comes.*
trabajar	*to work*
trabajamos	*we work*
juntos	*together*
mirar	*to look at*
Mira	*look* (**tú** command form of **mirar**)
ya	*already, now*
llegar	*to arrive*
llega	*he arrives*
ya llega	*here he comes*

▶ Variantes

Listen, and repeat the same structures from *Diálogo 3*, now with new vocabulary.

¿ Esperas a alguien?	***Are you waiting for*** *someone?*
Llevas	*Are you taking*
Ayudas	*Are you helping*
Visitas	*Are you visiting*
Buscas	*Are you looking for*
Llamas	*Are you calling*

¿A quién esperas ?	*Whom are you **waiting for**?*
llevas	*taking*
ayudas	*helping*
visitas	*visiting*
buscas	*looking for*
llamas	*calling*
miras	*looking at*

Busco al programador .	*I'm looking for **the computer programmer**.*
a la cocinera	*the chef*
a los asesores	*the consultants*
a las profesoras	*the teachers*
a Juan Carlos	*Juan Carlos*
a sus primos	*their cousins*
al señor Machado	*Mr. Machado*
a la señorita Salinas	*Ms. Salinas*
a mi perro	*my dog*

Busco el correo electrónico .	*I'm looking for **the email**.*
la estación de tren	*the train station*
una tienda de cómputo	*a computer store*
mis llaves	*my keys*
nuestros discos compactos	*our compact discs*

Es mi amigo que hace programación .	*It's my friend who **does programming**.*
diseña sitios web	*designs websites*
desarrolla software	*develops software*
navega en la red	*surfs the internet*
toma fotos	*takes pictures*

¿Llamas a alguien?	*Are you calling someone?*
No, no llamo a nadie.	*No, I'm not calling anyone.*

¿Miras algo?	*Are you looking at something?*
No, no miro nada.	*No, I'm not looking at anything.*

Estructura y Práctica

Direct Objects and the Personal **a**

The direct object is a noun or pronoun that completes the idea of a verb by labeling the goal of the action. Spanish distinguishes between two kinds of direct objects.

1 · Inanimate direct objects are connected to the verb without a preposition.

Llevo **los paquetes** a casa.	*I'm taking **the packages** home.*
El cocinero hace **un plato** rico.	*The chef is making **a** delicious **dish**.*
Toca **la flauta**.	*She plays **the flute**.*

2 · Animate direct objects are connected to the verb by means of the preposition **a**. This use of **a** is called personal **a**. The animate object must be specific and identifiable to require the use of personal **a**.

Llevo **a mis hijos** a casa.	*I'm taking **my children** home.*
Llamo **a Carmen** más tarde.	*I'll call **Carmen** later.*

Some English verbs that require a preposition (for example, *for*, *to*, *at*) before the direct object have Spanish verb equivalents that are followed immediately by a direct object.

buscar otro empleo	*to **look for** another job*
escuchar música	*to **listen to** music*
esperar el autobús	*to **wait for** the bus*
mirar estos contratos	*to **look at** these contracts*

If, however, the direct object is a definite animate being, it is preceded by the personal **a**.

Busca **al** programador.	*He's looking for the computer programmer.*
Escuchamos **a** la cantante.	*We're listening to the singer.*
Esperan **a** sus amigos.	*They're waiting for their friends.*
¿Por qué miras **a** ese tipo?	*Why are you looking at that guy?*

The words **alguien** (*somebody, someone*) and **nadie** (*nobody, no one*) are also preceded by personal **a** when they are the direct object of the verb.

¿Buscas **a alguien**?	*Are you looking for someone?*
No, no busco **a nadie**.	*No, I'm not looking for anyone.*

H ¿*La a personal o no*? Determine whether or not the personal **a** is needed in each of the following sentences. Rewrite the sentences that require the personal **a**, making any necessary changes. Write an X if the sentence does not need the personal **a**.

1. Busco _____ mi celular.

2. ¿Vas a visitar _____ tus primos?

3. Esperan _____ el tren.

4. Voy a llamar _____ mis suegros (*in-laws*).

5. Llevan _____ muchas cajas.

6. ¿_____ quién miras?

7. Vamos a ayudar _____ el asesor.

8. No miramos _____ nada.

9. Buscan _____ su perro.

10. Armando lleva _____ su esposa al centro.

11. Escucho _____ música clásica.

12. ¿Esperas _____ alguien?

Relative Pronoun **que**

Relative pronouns introduce relative clauses. A relative clause is a sentence that is incorporated into a larger sentence and that functions as an adjective within the larger sentence. In other words, it describes a noun. Relative clauses are also called adjective clauses. See the following English examples.

*They live in a **new** house.*
*They live in a house **that they bought last year**.*

Both *new* and *that they bought last year* modify the noun *house*. *New* is an adjective and *that they bought last year* is a relative clause that functions as an adjective.

The Spanish relative pronoun **que** can refer to people or things and can be either the subject or object of its clause.

1 · **Que** as the subject of the verb

mi amigo **que** trabaja en Inglaterra	*my friend **who** works in England*
un programa **que** es innovador	*a program **that** is innovative*

2 · **Que** as the direct object of the verb

la señora **que** voy a llamar	*the woman (**that**) I'm going to call*
los sitios web **que** diseñan	*the websites (**that**) they design*

In English, when the relative pronoun is the object of the verb in the relative clause, the pronoun is often omitted. It is never omitted in Spanish.

la casa **que** van a comprar	*the house (**that**) they're going to buy*
los asesores **que** contratamos	*the consultants (**that**) we hired*

When **que** is the object of the verb in the relative clause and it refers to people, it may be replaced by **a quien** or **a quienes**, depending on whether it refers to a singular or plural noun. **A quien** and **a quienes** are more formal in style than **que**.

el asesor **a quien** contratamos	*the consultant (**whom**) we hired*
los asesores **a quienes** contratamos	*the consultants (**whom**) we hired*

I   *Mis amigos.* Write sentences using a relative clause introduced by the relative pronoun **que** to tell about your friends. Use the cues in parentheses. Follow the *modelo*.

MODELO   Ana es mi amiga. (Mi amiga habla italiano.)
       → Ana es mi amiga que habla italiano.

1. Pedro es mi amigo. (Mi amigo toca el saxofón.)

2. Rebeca y Nora son mis amigas. (Mis amigas estudian física.)

3. Lorenzo es mi amigo. (Mi amigo diseña sitios web.)

4. Elena es mi amiga. (Mi amiga cocina muy bien.)

5. Antonio y Matilde son mis amigos. (Mis amigos trabajan en mi oficina.)

6. Ricardo es mi amigo. (Mi amigo hace programación.)

J *¿Qué es precisamente?* Use a relative clause to tell which person or object is being referred to in each question. Use the cues in parentheses. Follow the *modelo*.

> MODELO   ¿Qué libro? (El libro está en el estante.)
> → El libro que está en el estante.

1. ¿Qué museo? (El museo está abierto los lunes.)

2. ¿Qué mujeres de negocios? (Las mujeres de negocios ganan mucho dinero.)

3. ¿Qué asesor? (El asesor habla tres idiomas.)

4. ¿Qué coche? (El coche negro está descompuesto.)

5. ¿Qué estudiantes? (Los estudiantes hacen deportes.)

6. ¿Qué cancha de tenis? (La cancha de tenis queda enfrente de la piscina.)

7. ¿Qué profesores? (Los profesores enseñan (*teach*) administración de empresas.)

8. ¿Qué trajes? (Los trajes son de lana.)

Negative Words

Nada (*nothing*) and **nadie** (*no one*) are negative words. They have negative meaning when used in isolation.

¿Qué buscas?	*What are you looking for?*
Nada.	***Nothing.***
¿Quién hace la cena?	*Who's making dinner?*
Nadie.	***No one.***

Nada and **nadie** can function as the subject of a verb.

Nada es imposible.	***Nothing*** *is impossible.*
Nadie habla inglés aquí.	***No one*** *speaks English here.*

Nada and **nadie** can also function as the object of a verb. When a negative word follows the verb in Spanish, **no** must be used before the verb. When **nadie** is the direct object of a verb, it is preceded by the personal **a**.

No hago **nada** hoy.	*I'm not doing anything today.*
Ellos **no** ayudan **a nadie**.	*They don't help anyone.*

Here is a list of the most common negative words in Spanish, together with their affirmative counterparts.

NEGATIVE WORDS	AFFIRMATIVE COUNTERPARTS
nada *nothing*	algo *something*
nadie *no one, nobody*	alguien *someone, somebody*
ninguno (ningún), ninguna *no, none*	alguno (algún), alguna *some*
	algunos, algunas *some*
nunca, jamás *never*	algunas veces, a veces,
	alguna vez *sometimes*
	siempre *always*
	muchas veces, a menudo *often*

NEGATIVE WORDS	AFFIRMATIVE COUNTERPARTS
tampoco *neither*	o *or*
ni... ni *neither . . . nor*	o... o *either . . . or*
ya no *no longer*	todavía *still*

Ninguno and **alguno** are used before nouns, functioning as adjectives or pronouns. (For the forms **ningún** and **algún** before a masculine singular noun, see Chapter 2.)

ninguna calle	**no** *street,* **no** *streets*
ningún medico	**no** *doctor,* **no** *doctors*

Ninguno is only used in the plural when the following noun is inherently plural and has no singular. For all other nouns, the singular is used.

ningunos anteojos	**no** *eyeglasses* (los anteojos)
ningunas tijeras	**no** *scissors* (las tijeras)

Spanish, unlike English, allows two or more negative words in a sentence.

Nadie hace **nada nunca**.	*Nobody ever does anything.*

EXPRESSIONS WITH NEGATIVE WORDS

EXPRESSIONS WITH NEGATIVE WORDS	AFFIRMATIVE COUNTERPARTS
en/por ninguna parte *nowhere*	en/por alguna parte *somewhere*
en/por ningún lado *nowhere*	en/por algún lado *somewhere*
de ninguna manera *in no way, not at all*	de alguna manera *somehow, in some way*
de ningún modo *in no way*	de algún modo *somehow, in some way*

casi nunca *hardly ever*
nunca jamás *never ever*
nunca más *never again, no more*
¡Hasta nunca! *Goodbye forever!*
ni hablar *nothing doing*
ni modo *nothing doing*
nada de eso *nothing of the sort*
nada de extraordinario *nothing unusual*
nada más *that's all*
por nada del mundo *for nothing in the world*
nadie más *nobody else*
Es un don nadie. *He's a nobody.*

K *¡Siempre negativo!* Write negative responses to each of the following questions, using **no** plus the negative words that correspond to their affirmative counterparts. Follow the *modelo*.

MODELO   ¿Vas a tomar algo?
         → No, no voy a tomar nada.

1. ¿Uds. esperan a alguien?

2. ¿Roberto va a bailar salsa alguna vez?

3. ¿Los cocineros preparan algunos platos de pollo?

4. ¿Leonor habla ruso también?

5. ¿Siempre estudias en la biblioteca?

6. ¿Todavía patinas sobre hielo?

7. ¿Julio busca o a su perro o a su gato?

8. ¿Algunas abogadas trabajan los sábados?

DIÁLOGO 4 · Una fiesta de cumpleaños

Study the dialogue, then listen to the recording and repeat each line.

ISABEL ¿Vas a celebrar tu cumpleaños con una fiesta?
JUAN Sí, y voy a invitar a todos mis amigos.
ISABEL ¿Vas a invitar a Jaime Sandoval también?
JUAN ¡Qué va! Él es muy antipático y siempre toma demasiado.

Análisis

Check that you understand the linguistic breakdown of each speech from *Diálogo 4*.

¿Vas a celebrar tu cumpleaños con una fiesta?	*Are you going to celebrate your birthday with a party?*
ir a + *infinitive*	*to be going to (do something)*
celebrar	*to celebrate*
vas a celebrar	*you're going to celebrate*
el cumpleaños	*birthday*
la fiesta	*party*
Sí, y voy a invitar a todos mis amigos.	*Yes, and I'm going to invite all my friends.*
voy a invitar	*I'm going to invite*
a	*(personal **a** required before an animate direct object)*
todos mis amigos	*all my friends*
¿Vas a invitar a Jaime Sandoval también?	*Are you going to invite Jaime Sandoval, too?*
¡Qué va! Él es muy antipático y siempre toma demasiado.	*Are you kidding? He is very unpleasant and always drinks too much.*
¡Qué va!	*Are you kidding?*
antipático	*unpleasant*
siempre	*always*
tomar	*to take; to drink*
demasiado	*too much*
toma demasiado	*he drinks too much*

▶ Variantes

Listen, and repeat the same structures from *Diálogo 4*, now with new vocabulary.

Jaime toma demasiado.	*Jaime **drinks** too much.*
habla	*talks*
trabaja	*works*
viaja	*travels*

¿A quiénes vas a invitar?	*Whom are you going to invite?*
Voy a invitar a todos mis amigos.	*I'm going to invite all my friends.*

¿No vas a invitar a Susana?	*Aren't you going to invite Susana?*
No, y no voy a invitar a Laura tampoco.	*No, and I'm not going to invite Laura either.*

Estructura y Práctica

Compound Nouns

The compound nouns you learned in Chapter 1 consisted of two nouns with the preposition **de**: **el museo de arte**, **la tienda de zapatos**. The compound nouns in this chapter are composed of a verb in third person singular of the present tense + a plural noun. The verb precedes the noun in Spanish, unlike its English counterpart. These compound nouns function as a masculine singular noun and take the definite article **el**. The plural of these compound nouns uses the plural form of the article, but the noun remains the same.

el cumpleaños *birthday* (cumplir (*to turn, reach*)) + años (*years*)
los cumpleaños *birthdays*

el aguafiestas *wet blanket, party pooper, spoilsport* (aguar (*to spoil*)) + fiestas (*parties*)
los aguafiestas *wet blankets, party poopers, spoilsports*

L **Compound nouns.** For each of the following items, form a compound noun by combining the third person singular form of the given verb with the plural of the given noun. Write each compound noun with its definite article, then write the English translation of each noun. Note that the third person singular form of **-ir** verbs in present tense ends in **-e**. Follow the *modelo*.

MODELO   quitar (*to remove*) + mancha (*stain*)
            → el quitamanchas (*stain remover*)

1. lavar (*to wash*) + el plato (*dish*)

2. rascar (*to scrape*) + el cielo (*sky*)

3. cortar (*to cut*) + la uña (*fingernail*)

4. cubrir (*to cover*) + la cama (*bed*)
   [*cama* remains singular]

5. parar (*to stop*) + la caída (*fall*)

6. abrir (*to open*) + la lata (*can*)

7. cortar (*to cut*) + el césped (*grass, lawn*)
   [*césped* remains singular]

8. sacar (*to take out, get out*) + el corcho (*cork*)

DIÁLOGO 5 · Vamos a ir de vacaciones.

Study the dialogue, then listen to the recording and repeat each line.

JUAN   Ud. va a ir de vacaciones en el verano, ¿verdad?

ISABEL   Sí, hago un viaje con mis amigos a España en julio. ¡Ya hacemos las maletas!

JUAN   ¡Qué estupendo! ¿Uds. van a hacer turismo entonces?

ISABEL   Ah sí, vamos a viajar por todo el país. Y vamos a tomar muchas fotos.

Análisis

Check that you understand the linguistic breakdown of each speech from *Diálogo 5*.

Ud. va a ir de vacaciones en el verano, ¿verdad?	*You're going to go on vacation in the summer, aren't you?*
las vacaciones	*vacation*
de vacaciones	*on vacation*
ir de vacaciones	*to go on vacation*
el verano	*summer*
¿verdad?	*aren't you?*
Sí, hago un viaje con mis amigos a España en julio. ¡Ya hacemos las maletas!	*Yes, I'm taking a trip with my friends to Spain in July. We're already packing!*
el viaje	*trip*
hacer un viaje	*to take a trip*
hago un viaje	*I'm taking a trip*
España	*Spain*
julio	*July*
la maleta	*suitcase*
hacer las maletas	*to pack*
hacemos las maletas	*we're packing*
¡Qué estupendo! ¿Uds. van a hacer turismo entonces?	*How wonderful! So you are going to go sightseeing?*
estupendo	*terrific, wonderful, great*
¡Qué + *adjective*!	*How + adjective!*
hacer turismo	*to go sightseeing*
entonces	*then, so, in that case*
Ah sí, vamos a viajar por todo el país. Y vamos a tomar muchas fotos.	*Oh, yes, we are going to travel around the whole country. And we are going to take a lot of pictures.*
viajar	*to travel*
vamos a viajar	*we are going to travel*
por	*through, around*
todo el país	*the whole country, the entire country*
la foto	*photograph, picture*
tomar fotos	*to take pictures*

▶ Variantes

Listen, and repeat the same structures from *Diálogo 5*, now with new vocabulary.

¿Ud. va a ir de vacaciones en el verano ?   *Are you going to go on vacation in **the***
                                                 summer?
    el otoño   *the fall*
    el invierno   *the winter*
    la primavera   *the spring*

Hago un viaje en julio .   *I'll be taking a trip in **July**.*
    agosto   *August*
    septiembre   *September*
    octubre   *October*
    noviembre   *November*
    diciembre   *December*
    enero   *January*
    febrero   *February*
    marzo   *March*
    abril   *April*
    mayo   *May*
    junio   *June*

Toman un avión .   *They're taking **a plane**.*
    un tren   *a train*
    un taxi   *a taxi*
    un autobús   *a bus*
    el metro   *the subway*
    un barco   *a boat*

Estructura y Práctica

Nouns

Some nouns in Spanish have unpredictable genders. (See Chapter 1.)

la foto (la fotografía) *photograph*   el día *day*
la moto (la motocicleta) *motorcycle*   el mapa *map*
la mano *hand*

Some nouns in Spanish are always plural.

los anteojos *eyeglasses*   las tijeras *scissors*
las gafas *eyeglasses*   los auriculares *earphones*
los gemelos *twins, binoculars, cufflinks*

Some nouns in Spanish are usually plural.

las vacaciones *vacation*   las afueras *outskirts*
las elecciones *election*   los celos *jealousy*
los bienes *goods*

M *¡De vacaciones!* Choose the item from the second column that correctly completes the phrase in the first column to learn about the López's family trip. Write the complete phrase.

1. preparan	a. varios museos
2. viajan	b. en la piscina
3. visitan	c. turismo
4. llegan	d. las maletas
5. sacan	e. al aeropuerto
6. hacen	f. salsa
7. bailan	g. en avión
8. nadan	h. las tarjetas de embarque

 # DIÁLOGO 6 · Encargamos una pizza.

Study the dialogue, then listen to the recording and repeat each line.

ISABEL ¿Qué vamos a cenar esta noche? ¿Cenamos fuera o preparamos algo en casa?

JUAN Vamos a cenar en casa, pero sin cocinar. ¿Por qué no encargamos una pizza?

ISABEL ¡Estupendo! Ahora mismo yo llamo al restaurante Roma para encargar la pizza.

JUAN Y yo voy a comprar una botella de vino y alquilar una película.

Análisis

Check that you understand the linguistic breakdown of each speech from *Diálogo 6*.

¿Qué vamos a cenar esta noche?	*What are we going to have for dinner?*
¿Cenamos fuera o preparamos algo en casa?	*Shall we eat out or shall we prepare something at home?*
cenar	*to have dinner*
cenar algo	*to have something for dinner*
la noche	*night*
esta noche	*tonight*
fuera	*out, outside*
cenar fuera	*to have dinner out*
¿Cenamos fuera?	*Shall we have dinner out?*
preparar	*to prepare*
¿Preparamos algo?	*Shall we prepare something?*
la casa	*house*
en casa	*at home*

Vamos a cenar en casa, pero sin cocinar.	*Let's eat at home, but without cooking.*
¿Por qué no encargamos una pizza?	*Why don't we order a pizza?*
vamos a + *infinitive*	*let's (do something)*
vamos a cenar	*let's have dinner*
sin	*without*
cocinar	*to cook*
sin cocinar	*without cooking*
encargar	*to order*
¿Por qué no encargamos?	*Why don't we order?*
la pizza	*pizza*
¡Estupendo! Ahora mismo yo llamo al restaurante Roma para encargar la pizza.	*Great! I'll call the Roma restaurant right now to order the pizza.*
estupendo	*terrific, wonderful, great*
ahora mismo	*right now*
llamar	*to call*
yo llamo	*I call, I'll call*
llamar a un lugar	*to call a place*
para + *infinitive*	*in order (to do something)*
para encargar la pizza	*(in order) to order the pizza*
Y yo voy a comprar una botella de vino y alquilar una película.	*And I'm going to buy a bottle of wine and rent a movie.*
comprar	*to buy*
la botella	*bottle*
el vino	*wine*
una botella de vino	*a bottle of wine*
alquilar	*to rent*
la película	*movie, film*

▶ Variantes

Listen, and repeat the same structures from *Diálogo 6*, now with new vocabulary.

¿ Preparamos un plato vegetariano?	***Should we prepare*** *a vegetarian dish?*
Hacemos	*Should we make*
Cocinamos	*Should we cook*
Compramos	*Should we buy*
Encargamos	*Should we order*
Yo llamo al restaurante ahora mismo.	*I'll call* ***the restaurant*** *right now.*
a la empresa	*the firm*
al número (de teléfono)	*the number*
a la oficina	*the office*
al bufete	*the lawyer's office*

Vamos a ir de compras ahora .	*Let's go shopping **now**.*
tarde	*late*
temprano	*early*
más tarde	*later*
más temprano	*earlier*
pronto	*soon*
después	*afterwards*
hoy	*today*
mañana	*tomorrow*
pasado mañana	*the day after tomorrow*

Estructura y Práctica

Adverbs of Time

Adverbs of time only modify verbs. They are usually not derived from adjectives in Spanish or English.

¿Tomas el desayuno **temprano**?	*Do you have breakfast **early**?*
Vamos al concierto **mañana**.	*We're going to the concert **tomorrow**.*
¿Uds. **ya** ganan mucho dinero?	*Are you **already** earning a lot of money?*

N *¿Cuándo?* Express each sentence in Spanish to find out when things are happening.

1. *Let's go sightseeing tomorrow.*

2. *I'm packing right now.*

3. *I always help my parents.*

4. *Shall we take a trip in the summer?*

5. *Why don't we have dinner out on Friday?*

6. *Are you (Uds.) going to the national park early?*

7. *Yes, we're going to go at seven in the morning.*

8. *Emilia is visiting her brother the day after tomorrow.*

9. *The web designers are going to work together very soon.*

10. *We'll take the children to the shoe store later.*

▶ DIÁLOGO 7 · En tus horas libres

Study the dialogue, then listen to the recording and repeat each line.

JUAN ¿Qué haces en tus horas libres?

ISABEL Dibujo, canto en una banda y hago deportes. ¿Tú?

JUAN Yo cuando estoy libre hago programas y páginas web para pequeñas empresas.

ISABEL ¡Qué emprendedor eres! Así ganas dinero en tus ratos libres.

Análisis

Check that you understand the linguistic breakdown of each speech from *Diálogo 7*.

¿Qué haces en tus horas libres?	*What do you do in your free time?*
la hora	*hour, time*
libre	*free*
las horas libres	*free time* (literally, *free hours*)
en tus horas libres	*in your free time, when you are free*

Dibujo, canto en una banda y hago deportes. ¿Tú?	*I draw, I sing in a band, and I play sports. How about you?*
dibujar	*to draw*
dibujo	*I draw*
cantar	*to sing*
canto	*I sing*
la banda	*band*
el deporte	*sport*
hacer deportes	*to play sports*
hago deportes	*I play sports*

Yo cuando estoy libre hago programas y páginas web para pequeñas empresas.	*When I'm free, I do programs and web pages for small businesses.*
estar libre	*to be free, be at leisure*
estoy libre	*I'm free*
el programa	*program*
la página	*page*
la página web	*web page*
pequeño	*small*
la empresa	*business, firm*
la pequeña empresa	*small business*

¡Qué emprendedor eres! Así ganas dinero en tus ratos libres.	*How enterprising you are! That way you earn money in your free time.*
emprendedor	*enterprising*
así	*that way, in that way, thus*
ganar	*to earn*
el dinero	*money*
ganar dinero	*to earn money*
ganas dinero	*you earn money*

▶ Variantes

Listen, and repeat the same structures from *Diálogo 7*, now with new vocabulary.

Ganas mucho dinero.	***You earn** a lot of money.*
Gastas	*You spend*
Ahorras	*You save*
Pagas	*You pay*

Llevas	*You carry*
Deseas	*You want*
Haces	*You make*

En mis horas libres, canto en una banda .	*In my free time, **I sing in a band**.*
saco fotos	*I take pictures*
practico mi español	*I practice my Spanish*
saco a pasear a mi perro	*I take my dog out for a walk*
pinto cuadros	*I paint pictures*

Estructura y Práctica

O *Las actividades de ocio* **(Leisure activities).** Write the present tense form of the verb that correctly completes each of the following sentences to tell what you and your friends do as leisure activities. Follow the *modelo*.

MODELO   Alonso __*pasea*__ por las calles del centro. (pasear (*to go for a walk*))

1. Maite _____ en la red. (navegar)

2. Yo _____ música. (escuchar)

3. Tú _____ una clase en línea. (tomar)

4. Ignacio y Héctor _____ bricolaje (*do-it-yourself projects*). (hacer)

5. Ud. _____ a la gente en los cafés. (observar (*to watch*))

6. Uds. _____ en bicicleta. (montar)

7. Juanita _____ sitios web. (diseñar)

8. ¡Todos nosotros _____ de la vida! (disfrutar (*to enjoy*))

Un paso más

Are you ready to take your Spanish a step further? Here are exercises that will enhance your knowledge of the language and encourage you to express yourself freely.

P **Forming nouns from verbs.** Nouns are formed from verbs in multiple ways. (1) Some nouns related to verbs consist of the verb stem + **-o** or **-a**. (2) Many nouns are formed from **-ar** verbs with the suffix **-ción**. Most of these have English cognates ending in *-tion*. (3) Many nouns are formed from the past participle of verbs. They consist of the verb stem + the suffix **-ada** (for **-ar** verbs) or **-ida** (for **-er** and **-ir** verbs). Write the English translation for each of the following nouns; then write the Spanish verb from which it derives.

1. el trabajo

2. la canción

3. la espera

4. la invitación

5. la mirada

6. la ayuda

7. la visita

8. el desarrollo

9. la práctica	16. el ahorro
10. la celebración	17. el gasto
11. el dibujo	18. la navegación
12. la llegada	19. el pago
13. la preparación	20. la grabación
14. la compra	21. la llamada
15. la cocina	22. el diseño

Q *Preguntas personales.* Answer each question with a complete Spanish sentence.

1. ¿Qué deportes hace Ud.?

2. ¿Qué ejercicio hace?

3. ¿Escucha música latina? ¿Qué otra música escucha?

4. ¿Toca un instrumento musical? ¿Cuál? ¿Cuánto practica todos los días?

5. ¿Cuándo es su cumpleaños? ¿Cómo celebra su cumpleaños?

6. ¿Cuándo va Ud. de vacaciones? ¿Adónde va? ¿Con quién(es) va?

7. ¿Qué meses son buenos para viajar? ¿Cuál es su estación (*season*) favorita?

8. ¿Cocina platos de alta cocina (*haute cuisine, gourmet*)? ¿Cuáles son?

9. ¿A qué restaurantes va?

10. ¿Encarga comida a domicilio (encargar comida a domicilio (*to order take out*))? ¿Qué comida encarga?

11. ¿Qué hace en sus horas libres?

12. ¿Cómo gana dinero? ¿Cuánto dinero gasta al mes? ¿Cuánto dinero ahorra al mes?

13. ¿A qué tiendas va para comprar comida (ropa, libros, zapatos, medicamentos y productos de belleza y cuidado personal (*medicine and beauty and personal care products*), dispositivos electrónicos (*electronic devices*))?

14. ¿Usa el e-comercio? ¿Qué compra por internet?

The Weather, Foreign Languages, and Sports

Communication Goals

- Talking about learning a foreign language, making plans, cooking and eating
- Telling what you want, need, prefer, are able, intend, and know how to do
- Telling how long you have been doing something
- Vocabulary: foreign languages, weather expressions, business, numbers, sports

Grammar Topics

- The Present Tense of Regular **-er** and **-ir** Verbs
- Review: Uses of the Present Tense
- **Hace** + Expression of Time + Verb in Present Tense
- Stem-changing Verbs
- **Tener** *to have*
- Verb + Infinitive Construction, Verb + Connector + Infinitive Construction
- **Para** vs. **por**
- **Saber** and **conocer**
- Direct Object Pronouns
- Stem-changing Verbs: **servir** and **pedir**
- Prepositional Pronouns
- Numbers
- **Seguir**
- **Jugar**

▶ DIÁLOGO 1 · Estudiamos español.

Study the dialogue, then listen to the recording and repeat each line.

LAURA   Yo comienzo a tomar una clase de español a distancia.
MATEO   ¿Necesitas usar el español en tu trabajo?
LAURA   Sí, y hace cinco años que yo estudio español, pero no hablo muy bien
         el idioma.
MATEO   Pues hay que practicar mucho para dominar un idioma.

Análisis

Check that you understand the linguistic breakdown of each speech from *Diálogo 1*.

Yo comienzo a tomar una clase de español a distancia.	*I'm starting to take an online Spanish course.*
comenzar (**e** > **ie**)	*to begin*
comenzar a + *infinitive*	*to start to (do something), begin (doing something)*
tomar una clase	*to take a class*
comienzo a tomar	*I'm starting to take*
la distancia	*distance*
a distancia	*at a distance*
una clase a distancia	*an online course, a distance learning course*

¿Necesitas usar el español en tu trabajo?	*Do you need to use Spanish in your work?*
necesitar	*to need*
necesitar + *infinitive*	*to need to (do something)*
usar	*to use*
en	*in*
el trabajo	*work, job*

Sí, y hace cinco años que yo estudio español, pero no hablo muy bien el idioma.	*Yes, and I've been studying Spanish for five years, but I don't speak the language very well.*
hace + *expression of time*	*for* + expression of time
hace cinco años	*for five years*
estudio	*I study* (here, *I have been studying*)
bien	*well*
muy bien	*very well*
el idioma	*language*

Pues hay que practicar mucho para dominar un idioma.	*Well, you have to practice a lot to master a language.*
pues	*well* (interjection)
hay que + *infinitive*	*one must (do something), it is necessary to (do something), you have to (do something)*

mucho	*a lot*
para	*for, in order to*
dominar	*to master*

▶ Variantes

Listen, and repeat the same structures from *Diálogo 1*, now with new vocabulary.

Comienzo a hablar español.	**I'm beginning to** speak Spanish.
Empiezo a	*I'm beginning to*
Aprendo a	*I'm learning to*
Voy a	*I'm going to*

¿ Necesitas usar el español?	**Do you need to** use Spanish?
Debes	*Should you*
Puedes	*Can you*
Prefieres	*Do you prefer to*
Quieres	*Do you want to*
Piensas	*Do you intend to*
Deseas	*Do you want to*
Esperas	*Do you hope to, Do you expect to*
Sabes	*Do you know how to*

Hay que practicar el español todos los días .	*You have to* **practice Spanish every day**.
comprender su punto de vista	*understand her point of view*
compartir las ideas	*share the ideas*
pensar en el problema	*think about the problem*
meter la tarjeta en el parquímetro	*put the card into the parking meter*

¿Cuánto (tiempo) hace que estudias español ?	*How long have you been* **studying Spanish**?
vives en el centro	*living downtown*
asistes a estos conciertos	*attending these concerts*
escribes novelas	*writing novels*
recibes sus correos electrónicos	*receiving their emails*

Hace cinco años que estudio español .	**I've been studying Spanish** *for five years.*
vivo en el centro	*I've been living downtown*
asisto a estos conciertos	*I've been attending these concerts*
escribo novelas	*I've been writing novels*
recibo sus correos electrónicos	*I've been receiving their emails*

Hace cinco años que estudio español.	*I've been studying Spanish* **for five years**.
Hace un año	*for a year*
Hace ocho meses	*for eight months*
Hace mucho tiempo	*for a long time*
Hace poco tiempo	*for a short time*
Hace un semestre	*for a semester*

Estructura y Práctica

The Present Tense of Regular -er and -ir Verbs

As you learned in Chapter 5, Spanish verbs are divided into three classes, called conjugations, distinguished by the vowel of the infinitive. Spanish infinitives may end in -ar, -er, or -ir.

The present indicative tense in Spanish is formed by adding the present tense endings to the stem of the verb. You learned the -ar conjugation in Chapter 5. Here are the -er and -ir conjugations.

comprender *to understand*		escribir *to write*	
comprendo	comprendemos	escribo	escribimos
comprendes	comprendéis	escribes	escribís
comprende	comprenden	escribe	escriben

Note that the endings of the -er and -ir verbs are identical except in the first and second person plural (**nosotros** and **vosotros** forms). The endings of the three conjugations are similar. The characteristic difference is the vowel of the ending: -ar verbs have an -a- in five of the six endings, while -er verbs have an -e-. -Ir verb endings are identical to -er verb endings in all but two persons, as shown.

A **Regular -er and -ir verbs.** Write the present tense form of the regular -er or -ir verb that correctly completes each of the following sentences. Use the verbs in parentheses.

1. Ellos _____ (correr) diez millas todos los días.

2. Nosotros _____ (vivir) en el centro.

3. Ella _____ (romper) con su novio.

4. Yo _____ (creer) que va a llover más tarde.

5. ¿Ya (tú) _____ (subir) al tren?

6. Él no _____ (compartir) sus ideas con nadie.

7. ¿Cuándo _____ (vender) Uds. su casa?

8. Ud. no _____ (resistir) a la tentación, ¿verdad?

B *¿Qué hacen en la universidad?* Write sentences from the strings of elements given to tell what you and other people are doing in the university today. Follow the *modelo*.

MODELO   los problemas / discutir / los estudiantes
         → Los estudiantes discuten los problemas.

1. un informe / escribir / Mario

2. en la biblioteca / leer / nosotros

3. yo / una conferencia / asistir a

4. abrir / Uds. / los libros de texto

5. las teorías de la física / comprender / tú

6. imprimir / un artículo / María Elena

7. subir (*to upload*) / Rodrigo y Mateo / unos archivos

8. Ud. / para el laboratorio / salir

Review: Uses of the Present Tense

You learned the uses of the present tense in Chapter 5. Here is a brief review.

1 · The present tense forms of Spanish verbs express both the English simple present (*I speak*) and the English present progressive (*I'm speaking*).

Lee libros de cocina.	{ ***She reads*** *cookbooks.* { ***She's reading*** *cookbooks.*
Escribo libros de texto.	{ ***I write*** *textbooks.* { ***I'm writing*** *textbooks.*

2 · The **yo** form and the **nosotros** form of the present tense are often used to ask for instructions.

¿**Asisto** al concierto?	***Shall I attend*** *the concert?*
¿**Vivimos** en este barrio?	***Shall we live*** *in this neighborhood?*

3 · After ¿**Por qué no…?**, the present tense is used to make a suggestion.

¿**Por qué no compartes** tu idea?	***Why don't you share*** *your idea?*
¿**Por qué no corren** el maratón?	***Why don't you run*** *the marathon?*

4 · The present tense may be used to express the future when another element of the sentence (such as an adverb of time) makes the future reference clear.

Vuelven de su viaje el jueves.	***They'll return*** *from their trip on Thursday.*
Servimos la cena a las ocho.	***We'll serve*** *dinner at 8 o'clock.*

Hace + Expression of Time + Verb in Present Tense

The present tense is used in Spanish to express actions beginning in the past but continuing into the present (English *have/has been doing something*). The period of time during which the action has been going on is expressed in a phrase beginning with **hace**.

Hace seis meses que trabajo aquí.	*I have been working here **for six months**.*
Él estudia español **hace tres años**.	*He's been studying Spanish **for three years**.*

Note that the time phrase with **hace** can be placed either at the beginning of the sentence or at the end. When it is placed at the beginning, the conjunction **que** is used to connect it to what follows.

To ask a question using this construction, the form ¿**Cuánto (tiempo) hace que** + verb in present tense? is used. (The word **tiempo** is optional.)

¿**Cuánto (tiempo) hace que** Ud. vive en la ciudad?	***How long** have you been living in the city?*

¿*Cuánto tiempo hace...*? Form questions using **¿Cuánto tiempo hace que...?** and the elements given. Then answer each question in two ways, using the time phrase in parentheses. Follow the *modelo*.

> MODELO   Ana / estudiar español (siete años)
> → —¿Cuánto tiempo hace que Ana estudia español?
> —Hace siete años que estudia español.
> —Estudia español hace siete años.

1. tú / esperar / a tus amigos (quince minutos)

2. los niños / buscar a su perro (dos días)

3. Uds. / vivir en este barrio (dieciséis años)

4. Pedro / tomar clases a distancia (un año)

5. Uds. / hacer deportes (cuatro meses)

6. Susana y Fernando / buscar casa (varios meses)

7. nosotros / asistir a estos conciertos (mucho tiempo)

8. Ud. / mandar emails (una hora)

Stem-changing Verbs

Many Spanish verbs show a change in the vowel of the stem in the present tense. This occurs in those forms where the vowel of the stem is stressed—all three singular forms and the third person plural; only the **nosotros** and **vosotros** forms are not affected. These are called stem-changing verbs. For -**ar** and -**er** verbs, the stem changes are **e > ie** and **o > ue**. Stem changes in -**ir** verbs are **e > i**, **e > ie**, and **o > ue**.

You cannot predict from the infinitive which verbs will have a stem change and which will not, so you must memorize the verbs that have a stem change. These changes are indicated in infinitive listings in this book as follows.

> pensar (**e > ie**)
> volver (**o > ue**)
> servir (**e > i**)

1 · Here are present tense forms of the -**ar** and -**er** stem-changing verbs **pensar** (*to think*), **querer** (*to want*), **contar** (*to count, tell*), and **volver** (*to return*).

pensar (e > ie) *to think*		**querer (e > ie)** *to want*	
pienso	pensamos	quiero	queremos
piensas	pensáis	quieres	queréis
piensa	piensan	quiere	quieren

contar (o > ue) *to count, tell*		**volver (o > ue)** *to return*	
cuento	contamos	vuelvo	volvemos
cuentas	contáis	vuelves	volvéis
cuenta	cuentan	vuelve	vuelven

Additional verbs that pattern like **pensar** and **querer** (**e > ie**) are **cerrar** (*to close*), **comenzar** (*to begin*), **empezar** (*to begin*), **entender** (*to understand*), **helar** (*to freeze*), **merendar** (*to have an afternoon snack*), **nevar** (*to snow*), and **reventar** (*to burst*). Impersonal verbs like **helar** and **nevar** are conjugated only in the third person singular.

Additional verbs that pattern like **contar** and **volver** (**o > ue**) are **almorzar** (*to have lunch*), **costar** (*to cost*), **devolver** (*to return (something), to give back (something)*), **encontrar** (*to find*), **jugar** (*to play (a sport or game)*), **llover** (*to rain*), **poder** (*to be able, can*), **probar** (*to try, taste*), and **tronar** (*to thunder*). **Jugar** is conjugated as if it had -o- as its stem vowel. Impersonal verbs like **llover** and **tronar** are conjugated only in the third person singular.

2 · Here are present tense forms of the -**ir** stem-changing verbs **servir** (*to serve*), **preferir** (*to prefer*), and **dormir** (*to sleep*).

servir (e > i) *to serve*	
sirvo	servimos
sirves	servís
sirve	sirven

preferir (e > ie) *to prefer*	
prefiero	preferimos
prefieres	preferís
prefiere	prefieren

dormir (o > ue) *to sleep*	
duermo	dormimos
duermes	dormís
duerme	duermen

Additional verbs that pattern like **servir** (**e > i**) are **pedir** (*to ask for, request*) and **seguir** (*to follow, continue*). The verb **morir** (*to die*) is conjugated like **dormir**. The verb **sentir** (*to feel*) is conjugated like **preferir**. (For more on **seguir**, see *Diálogo 10* in this chapter.)

D **Stem-changing verbs.** Write the present tense form of the stem-changing verb that correctly completes each of the following sentences. Use the verbs in parentheses.

1. El concierto _____ (comenzar) a las siete y media.

2. Ellos _____ (volver) de su viaje el domingo.

3. Yo _____ (querer) más carne, por favor.

4. ¿No (tú) _____ (encontrar) tus llaves?

5. ¿Uds. _____ (pedir) algo de postre?

6. Él _____ (pensar) en su futuro.

7. ¿Cuánto _____ (costar) esos trajes?

8. Ella _____ (preferir) la falda azul de lana.

9. ¿Por qué no _____ (probar) Ud. este plato?

10. El bebé _____ (dormir) muy poco.

11. ¿A qué hora _____ (empezar) los partidos?

12. Es que nosotros no _____ (entender) el problema.

13. Yo _____ (almorzar) con Uds. pasado mañana.

14. Ellas no _____ (servir) la cena hasta las seis.

15. ¿Tú _____ (jugar) al golf o al tenis?

16. Nosotros _____ (merendar) hoy a las cuatro y media.

▶ DIÁLOGO 2 · ¿Tú sabes francés?

Study the dialogue, then listen to the recording and repeat each line.

LAURA	Tú sabes francés, ¿verdad?
MATEO	Yo leo y escribo francés, pero no entiendo muy bien el francés hablado.
LAURA	Dominar el idioma hablado es difícil.
MATEO	Por eso espero pasar unos meses en Francia el año que viene.

Análisis

Check that you understand the linguistic breakdown of each speech from *Diálogo 2*.

Tú sabes francés, ¿verdad?	*You know French, don't you?*
saber	*to know*
sabes	*you know*
el francés	*French*
¿verdad?	*don't you?*
Yo leo y escribo francés, pero no entiendo muy bien el francés hablado.	*I read and write French, but I don't understand spoken French very well.*
leer	*to read*
escribir	*to write*
entender (**e** > **ie**)	*to understand*
hablado	*spoken* (past participle of **hablar**)
el francés hablado	*spoken French*
Dominar el idioma hablado es difícil.	*It's difficult to master the spoken language.*
dominar	*to master*
el idioma hablado	*the spoken language*
difícil	*difficult*
Por eso espero pasar unos meses en Francia el año que viene.	*That's why I hope to spend a few months in France next year.*
por eso	*that's why, therefore*
esperar + *infinitive*	*to hope to (do something)*
el mes	*month*
unos meses	*a few months*
Francia	*France*
el año	*year*
que viene	*next* (literally, *that's coming*)
el año que viene	*next year*

▶ Variantes

Listen, and repeat the same structures from *Diálogo 2*, now with new vocabulary.

¿Sabes francés ?	*Do you know **French**?*
inglés	*English*
español	*Spanish*
italiano	*Italian*
alemán	*German*
ruso	*Russian*
chino	*Chinese*

▶ DIÁLOGO 3 · Hace mal tiempo.

Study the dialogue, then listen to the recording and repeat each line.

MATEO	Llueve fuerte. Yo no tengo ganas de salir.
LAURA	Yo tampoco. Además, hace frío y viento.
MATEO	Y ahora yo creo que empieza a nevar. ¡Qué día más feo!
LAURA	Menos mal que no tenemos que ir a ninguna parte hoy.

Análisis

Check that you understand the linguistic breakdown of each speech from *Diálogo 3*.

Llueve fuerte. Yo no tengo ganas de salir.	*It's raining hard. I don't feel like going out.*
llover (**o** > **ue**)	*to rain*
fuerte	*strong, hard, loud*
tengo	*I have*
no tengo ganas de + *infinitive*	*I don't feel like (doing something)*
Yo tampoco. Además, hace frío y viento.	*Neither do I. Besides, it's cold and windy.*
tampoco	*neither*
yo tampoco	*neither do I*
además	*besides*
hacer	*to do, make*
el frío	*cold*
hace frío	*it's cold*
el viento	*wind*
hace viento	*it's windy*
Y ahora yo creo que empieza a nevar. ¡Qué día más feo!	*And now I think it's beginning to snow. What an awful day!*
creer	*to believe*
creo	*I believe*
empezar (**e** > **ie**)	*to begin*
empezar a hacer algo	*to begin to do something, start to do something*
nevar (**e** > **ie**)	*to snow*
feo	*ugly*
¡Qué día más feo!	*What an awful day!*

Menos mal que no tenemos que ir a ninguna parte hoy.	It's lucky that we don't have to go anywhere today.
menos mal	fortunately, at least
menos mal que	it's lucky that
tener que + infinitive	to have to (do something)
ir	to go
tenemos que ir	we have to go
a ninguna parte	anywhere, nowhere (with verb of motion)

▶ Variantes

Listen, and repeat the same structures from *Diálogo 3*, now with new vocabulary.

Yo no tengo ganas de salir .	I don't feel like **going out**.
entrar	going in
regresar	going back
discutir	arguing, discussing
subir	going up
dormir	sleeping

Hace frío .	It's **cold**.
calor	hot
fresco	cool
viento	windy
sol	sunny

Empieza a nevar .	It's beginning to **snow**.
llover	rain
tronar	thunder
despejar	clear up

No tenemos que ir .	We don't have to **go**.
seguir	continue
volver	go back
comenzar	begin
correr	run

¿Qué tiempo hace?	What's the weather like?
Hace buen/mal tiempo.	The weather's good/bad.

¿Qué temperatura hace?	What's the temperature?
Hace setenta grados.	It's seventy degrees.

Estructura y Práctica

E *¿Qué tiempo hace?* Express the following sentences in English to describe the weather in some American cities. Write numbers as words.

1. *It's hot in Miami.*

2. *It's raining in Seattle.*

3. *It's cool in Philadelphia.*

4. *The weather's good in San Diego.*

5. *It's very windy in Chicago.*

6. *It's snowing in Boston.*

7. *It's very cold in Anchorage.*

8. *It's 75 degrees in Washington, D.C.*

9. *It's thundering in New York.*

10. *It's sunny in Dallas.*

11. *The weather's bad in Baton Rouge.*

Tener *to have*

Tener is an irregular verb—one that does not follow the standard pattern of formation. The most common pattern of irregular verbs in the present tense is an irregular **yo** form, most often a **-g-** inserted before the **-o** ending. Verbs with this irregularity, called **-g-** verbs, may also have irregularities in the other forms. **Tener** is one such verb.

tener *to have*	
tengo	tenemos
tienes	tenéis
tiene	tienen

Tener is used in the verb + connector + infinitive construction **tener que** (*to have to (do something)*).

Verb + Infinitive Construction, Verb + Connector + Infinitive Construction

In both Spanish and English, the infinitive can follow a conjugated verb. In this function, the infinitive serves as a complement, much like an object. Depending on the first verb (the conjugated verb) in this construction, the infinitive may follow the verb directly or be linked to it by a connector, most commonly the preposition **a** or **de**. All the examples that follow appear in Chapter 6.

1 · Here are some of the most common verbs that are followed directly by the infinitive.

deber *should, ought to, must*
Debemos ayudarlo.

We should / ought to / must help him.

desear *to want to*
Desea vivir en este barrio.

She wants to live in this neighborhood.

esperar *to hope to*
Esperamos graduarnos en mayo.

We hope to graduate in May.

lograr *to succeed in, manage to*
A ver si logro salir un poco antes.

Let's see if I can manage to get out a little early.

necesitar *to need to*
Necesitas estudiar un poco más.

You have to study a little more.

pensar *to intend to*
Pienso ir de vacaciones en junio.

I intend to go on vacation in June.

poder *to be able to, can*
¿Ud. no puede terminar el informe   *Can't you finish the report today?*
  hoy?

preferir *to prefer to*
Prefiere ir por tren.   *He prefers to go by train.*

querer *to want to*
Quiero buscar otro empleo.   *I want to look for another job.*

saber *to know how to*
Esos niños ya saben nadar.   *Those children already know how to swim.*

2 · Here are some of the most common verbs that are followed by **a** + infinitive.

aprender a *to learn to*
¿Dónde aprendió Ud. a hablar   *Where did you learn to speak Spanish?*
  español?

ayudar (a uno) a *to help (someone) to*
Ayúdeme a elaborar el presupuesto.   *Help me draw up the budget.*

comenzar a *to begin to, start to*
¿Cuándo comienza Ud. a trabajar?   *When do you start to work?*

empezar a *to begin to, start to*
Empiezo a comprender el problema.   *I'm beginning to understand the problem.*

ir a *to be going to*
Voy a servir la cena a las ocho.   *I'm going to serve dinner at eight o'clock.*

3 · Here are some of the most common verbs that are followed by **de** + infinitive.

acabar de *to have just*
Acabo de entregarle los datos.   *I have just submitted the data to him.*

tener ganas de *to feel like*
No tenemos ganas de salir esta noche. *We don't feel like going out tonight.*

tratar de *to try to*
Trate Ud. de comprenderme.   *Try to understand me.*

4 · There are two verbs that use **que** as the connector to the following infinitive.

tener que *to have to*
¿Qué tienes que hacer hoy?   *What do you have to do today?*

hay que *one has to, one must*
Hay que estudiar idiomas.   *One has to study languages.*

F **Connectors.** Write the connector (**a**, **de**, or **que**) that correctly completes each of the following sentences. Write an X if no connector is required.

1. Piensa _____ tomar una clase a distancia.

2. ¿Vas _____ asistir a la reunión?

3. Debemos _____ ahorrar más dinero.

4. Comienzo _____ escribir el informe.

5. No quieren _____ salir todavía.

6. Tienes _____ conocer bien el mercado.

7. Acaba _____ regresar de la playa.

8. Esperan _____ tener éxito en los negocios.

9. Trata _____ dominar el idioma.

10. Empiezas _____ comprender el problema, ¿no?

11. ¡No pueden _____ discutir más!

12. Aprendes _____ jugar al béisbol, ¿verdad?

13. Hay _____ aprovechar las ofertas.

14. Necesita _____ practicar el español todos los días.

15. Prefieren _____ ir de vacaciones en abril.

16. ¿No tienes ganas _____ hacer nada?

17. Sabemos _____ bailar salsa muy bien.

18. No logra _____ devolver la pelota.

G *Expansión.* Rewrite each sentence, using the verb in parentheses to expand it. Add the correct connector as necessary. Follow the *modelo.*

MODELO   Compro un libro de recetas de cocina. (necesitar)
          → Necesito comprar un libro de recetas de cocina.

1. Es experto en su campo. (querer)

2. ¿No encuentras tus gafas? (poder)

3. ¿Escribes el informe en español? (tener)

4. Conozco a los asesores chilenos. (acabar)

5. Entiende el inglés muy bien. (empezar)

6. Hago programación. (saber)

7. El niño cuenta hasta cien. (aprender)

8. Tienen mucho éxito con su empresa. (esperar)

9. Vuelven de México la semana entrante. (pensar)

10. Prueba las tapas, ¿no? (ir)

11. Juegan al fútbol. (preferir)

12. Resisten a la tentación. (tratar)

▶ DIÁLOGO 4 · Quiero aprender a cocinar.

Study the dialogue, then listen to the recording and repeat each line.

LAURA   Quiero aprender a cocinar pero no sé por dónde empezar.
MATEO   ¿Conoces un buen libro de recetas de cocina?
LAURA   Acabo de comprar este libro. Tiene cien recetas.
MATEO   Pues vamos a probar esta receta sencilla para hacer huevos revueltos.

Análisis

Check that you understand the linguistic breakdown of each speech from *Diálogo 4*.

Quiero aprender a cocinar pero no sé por dónde empezar.	*I want to learn how to cook, but I don't know where to begin.*
querer (**e** > **ie**)	*to want*
querer + *infinitive*	*to want to (do something)*
aprender	*to learn*
aprender a + *infinitive*	*to learn how to (do something)*
cocinar	*to cook*
aprender a cocinar	*to learn how to cook*
sé	*I know*
por	*for, through, around*
por dónde	*where, in what place*
¿Conoces un buen libro de recetas de cocina?	*Do you know a good cookbook?*
conocer	*to know, be familiar with*
buen	*good*
la receta	*recipe*
la cocina	*kitchen, cooking*
un libro de recetas de cocina	*a cookbook*
Acabo de comprar este libro. Tiene cien recetas.	*I've just bought this book. It has one hundred recipes.*
acabar de + *infinitive*	*to have just (done something)*
cien	*one hundred*
Pues vamos a probar esta receta sencilla para hacer huevos revueltos.	*Well, let's try this simple recipe to make scrambled eggs.*
pues	*well, in that case* (interjection)
vamos a + *infinitive*	*let's (do something)*
probar (**o** > **ue**)	*to try; to taste*
vamos a probar	*let's try*
sencillo	*simple*
para + *infinitive*	*in order to (do something)*
hacer	*to do, make*
el huevo	*egg*
revuelto	*scrambled*
huevos revueltos	*scrambled eggs*

Variantes

Listen, and repeat the same structures from *Diálogo 4*, now with new vocabulary.

Quiero aprender a cocinar .	*I want to learn to **cook**.*
coser	*sew*
manejar	*drive*
programar	*program*

Acabo de comprar el libro.	***I've just bought** the book.*
Acabo de leer	*I've just read*
Acabo de vender	*I've just sold*
Acabo de escribir	*I've just written*
Acabo de abrir	*I've just opened*
Acabo de romper	*I've just torn*

Prueban la comida.	*They're trying the food. / They're tasting the food.*

Ahora comen .	*They're **eating** now.*
almuerzan	*having lunch*
meriendan	*having a snack* (usually in the afternoon)

Estructura y Práctica

Para vs. por

The prepositions **para** and **por** are often confusing to English-speaking students of Spanish, because both of them can be translated as *for*.

1 · **Para** labels the goal of an action. This goal may be the destination of motion, the time by which something is done, or the beneficiary of the action.

Daniel salió **para** la oficina.	*Daniel left **for** the office.*
Tiene que terminar el informe **para** el jueves.	*He has to finish the report **by** Thursday.*
El anillo es **para** Fernanda.	*The ring is **for** Fernanda.*
Lo hago **para** ti.	*I'm doing it **for** you. (for your benefit)*

Para is used before an infinitive to label the purpose of an action.

Ahorro dinero **para** comprar una casa.	*I'm saving money (**in order**) to buy a house.*
Estudia mucho **para** sacar buenas notas.	*She studies a lot **in order** to get good grades.*

Para appears in several idiomatic expressions.

para siempre	*forever*
para variar	*for a change*
estar **para**	*to be about to*

2 · **Por** expresses motion through a place or imprecise location.

Deben seguir **por** esta calle.	*You should continue **along** this street.*
¿Vas a caminar **por** el parque?	*Are you going to walk **through** the park?*
Creo que viven **por** aquí.	*I think they live **around** here.*

Por expresses duration in time.

Trabajó con nosotros **por** muchos meses.	*He worked with us **for** many months.*

Por expresses the cause or reason for an action.

Se enoja **por** cualquier cosa.	*He gets angry **for** any little thing.*
No quieren vivir aquí **por** el frío.	*They don't want to live here **because of** the cold.*
Lo hacemos **por** ti.	*We're doing it **because of** you.*

Por appears in many idiomatic expressions.

por ahora	*for now*
por aquí	*around here*
por casualidad	*by chance*
por ciento	*percent*
por desgracia	*unfortunately*
por eso	*therefore, that's why*
por favor	*please*
por todas partes	*everywhere*
por todos lados	*everywhere*

3 · **Para** and **por** contrast with each other in the following contexts.

¿**Para** quién trabaja Ud.?	*For whom are you working?*
Trabajo **para** el señor López.	*I'm working **for** Mr. López. (He's my boss.)*
¿**Por** quién trabaja Ud.?	*For whom are you working?*
Trabajo **por** el señor López.	*I'm working **for** Mr. López. (I'm working in his place.)*

H *Para y por.* Choose either **para** or **por** to correctly complete each of the following sentences.

1. Estos regalos son _____ mis sobrinos.

2. Tienes que seguir _____ aquella avenida.

3. Necesito ganar dinero _____ pagar la matrícula (*tuition*).

4. Ni sabemos _____ dónde comenzar el proyecto.

5. ¿Piensas regresar a la ciudad _____ la semana entrante?

6. ¿A qué hora debemos salir _____ el teatro?

7. Mi hija va a estudiar español en Madrid _____ un año.

8. Los Ortega no quieren vivir aquí _____ el calor.

9. Uds. están _____ merendar, ¿no?

10. Ya salgo _____ la oficina. Necesito estar _____ las nueve.

11. ¿Sabes _____ casualidad dónde está el perro? Lo acabo de buscar _____ todos lados.

▶ DIÁLOGO 5 · No conozco al nuevo gerente.

Study the dialogue, then listen to the recording and repeat each line.

MATEO	¿Tú conoces al hombre que acaba de entrar?
LAURA	No, no lo conozco pero creo que es el nuevo gerente.
MATEO	¿Sabes si tiene mucha experiencia?
LAURA	Yo sé que conoce bien el mercado. Es reconocido como experto en su campo.

Análisis

Check that you understand the linguistic breakdown of each speech from *Diálogo 5*.

¿Tú conoces al hombre que acaba de entrar?	*Do you know the man who has just come in?*
conocer	*to know a person*
conoces al hombre	*you know the man*
que	*who*
acabar de + *infinitive*	*to have just (done something)*
acaba de entrar	*he has just come in*

No, no lo conozco pero creo que es el nuevo gerente.	*No, I don't know him, but I think he's the new manager.*
lo	*him* (masculine direct object pronoun)
conozco	*I know*
creer	*to believe, think*
que	*that* (conjunction)
el gerente	*manager*

¿Sabes si tiene mucha experiencia?	*Do you know whether he has a lot of experience?*
sabes	*you know*
si	*if, whether*
la experiencia	*experience*

Yo sé que conoce bien el mercado. Es reconocido como experto en su campo.	*I know that he knows the market well. He is recognized as an expert in his field.*
sé	*I know*
conoce	*he knows*
el mercado	*market*

reconocido	recognized
ser reconocido	to be recognized
como	as
el experto	expert
el campo	field

▶ Variantes

Listen, and repeat the same structures from *Diálogo 5*, now with new vocabulary.

¿Conoces al hombre que acaba de entrar?	Do you know **the man** who has just come in?
a la mujer	the woman
a la persona	the person
a ese señor	that man
a esa señorita	that young woman
al tipo	the guy
a aquel joven	that young man
al empleado	the employee

No lo conozco.	I don't **know** him.
comprendo	understand
visito	visit

No lo llevo.	I'm not **taking** him.
llamo	calling
busco	looking for
espero	waiting for
miro	looking at
ayudo	helping

Creo que es el nuevo gerente.	I think **he's the new manager**.
conoce bien el mercado	he knows the market well
está en su oficina	he's in his office
hace programación	he does programming
diseña sitios web	he designs websites
desarrolla software	he develops software

Sé que conoce bien el mercado.	I know **he knows the market well**.
tiene buenas ideas	he has good ideas
sabe resolver problemas	he knows how to solve problems
vuelve de un viaje de negocios hoy	he's returning from a business trip today
habla tres idiomas	he speaks three languages
va a tener mucho éxito	he's going to be very successful

¿Sabes si tiene mucha experiencia?	Do you know if **he has a lot of experience**?
habla español	he speaks Spanish
gana mucho dinero	he earns a lot of money
conoce a los asesores	he knows the consultants
puede trabajar los fines de semana	he can work on weekends
piensa cerrar unas tiendas	he intends to close some stores

Estructura y Práctica

Saber and conocer

Spanish has two verbs that mean *to know*: **saber** and **conocer**. Both are irregular verbs.

1 · **Saber** has an irregularity in the first person singular (**yo** form) but is regular in the rest of the conjugation.

saber *to know*	
sé	sabemos
sabes	sabéis
sabe	saben

Saber means to know something that you have learned or can repeat or state.

Sé la fecha.	*I know the date.*
Sabemos la respuesta.	*We know the answer.*

Saber is used before a following clause beginning with **si** or **que**.

¿Sabes si van a venir?	*Do you know if they are going to come?*
Sé que ella enseña en esta escuela.	*I know that she teaches at this school.*

Saber is used before an infinitive with the meaning *to know how to (do something)*.

Esta niña ya **sabe** leer.	*This child already **knows how to** read.*

2 · **Conocer** has **-zc-** before the **-o** ending of the **yo** form. All other forms are regular.

conocer *to know*	
conozco	conocemos
conoces	conocéis
conoce	conocen

Conocer means *to know* in the sense of being familiar with or having an acquaintance with. It is used with people and places.

¿Conocen Uds. a mi primo Javier?	*Do you know my cousin Javier?*
Él **conoce** muy bien Madrid.	*He **knows** Madrid very well.*
No **conozco** la República Dominicana.	*I **haven't been to** the Dominican Republic.*

The phrases **conocer la dirección** (*to know the address*) and **conocer el número de teléfono** (*to know the phone number*) are also very common.

I   *Saber y conocer.* Write the present tense form of **saber** or **conocer** that correctly completes each of the following sentences.

1. Pienso que él no _____ nada.

2. Tú _____ que Olivia es una compradora compulsiva.

3. Yo no _____ a nadie en esta ciudad.

4. Ellos no _____ por dónde empezar.

5. Ud. _____ aquella tienda de cómputo, ¿no?

6. Yo _____ que tú me _____ muy bien.

7. ¿Quién _____ la dirección de Carlos?

8. Nosotros no _____ al nuevo ingeniero pero _____ quién es.

9. ¿Ud. _____ qué tiempo va a hacer mañana?

10. Uds. no _____ Costa Rica, ¿verdad?

11. ¿Tú _____ si debemos seguir por esta carretera?

12. ¿Los señores Álvarez? Claro que yo los _____.

Direct Object Pronouns

Direct object nouns may be replaced by direct object pronouns once it is clear to whom or what they refer. In this chapter, we present **lo**, the third person singular direct object pronoun that refers to people and things that are grammatically masculine. **Lo** means *him* and *it*; **lo** also means *you* when referring to **Ud.** (For more on direct object pronouns, see Chapter 7.)

J　*Lo.* Write sentences to answer each of the following questions, changing the direct object noun in the question to a direct object pronoun in your answer. Answer *yes* or *no*, based on the cue in parentheses. Follow the *modelos*.

> MODELOS　¿Ella prepara el pollo? (sí)
> 　　　　　→ Sí, lo prepara.
>
> 　　　　　¿Ella prepara el pollo? (no)
> 　　　　　→ No, no lo prepara.

1. ¿Ellos leen el chino?　(sí)

2. ¿Ud. conoce al profesor de historia?　(no)

3. ¿Llamas al diseñador de sitios web?　(sí)

4. ¿Uds. sirven el pastel?　(no)

5. ¿Ella visita al abuelo?　(sí)

6. ¿Él busca a su perro?　(no)

7. ¿Ayudas a tu hermano?　(sí)

8. ¿Uds. empiezan el proyecto?　(sí)

9. ¿Él cuenta el dinero?　(no)

10. ¿Uds. encuentran su maletín?　(no)

▶ DIÁLOGO 6 · ¡Yo no puedo comer nada más!

Study the dialogue, then listen to the recording and repeat each line.

LAURA	¡Qué comida más rica! Siempre comemos muy bien aquí.
MATEO	Y sirven los mejores postres del mundo. ¿Qué pides de postre?
LAURA	¿De postre? Yo no puedo comer nada más. ¡Estoy para reventar!

Análisis

Check that you understand the linguistic breakdown of each speech from *Diálogo 6*.

¡Qué comida más rica! Siempre comemos muy bien aquí.	*What delicious food! We always eat very well here.*
comer	*to eat*
comemos	*we eat*
siempre	*always*
Y sirven los mejores postres del mundo. ¿Qué pides de postre?	*And they serve the best desserts in the world. What are you having for dessert?*
servir (**e** > **i**)	*to serve*
sirven	*they serve*
mejor	*better, best*
el postre	*dessert*
los mejores postres	*the best desserts*
de	*in (after a superlative)*
del mundo	*of the world, in the world*
pedir (**e** > **i**)	*to ask for, order*
pides	*you ask for, you order*
de postre	*for dessert*
¿De postre? Yo no puedo comer nada más. ¡Estoy para reventar!	*For dessert? I can't eat anything else. I'm about to burst!*
poder (**o** > **ue**)	*to be able, can*
poder + *infinitive*	*to be able to (do something)*
nada	*nothing*
más	*more, else*
nada más	*nothing else*
estar para + *infinitive*	*to be about to (do something)*
reventar (**e** > **ie**)	*to burst*
¡Estoy para reventar!	*I'm about to burst!*

▶ Variantes

Listen, and repeat the same structures from *Diálogo 6*, now with new vocabulary.

Yo no puedo comer nada más.	*I can't **eat** another thing.*
beber	*drink*
tomar	*drink*
probar	*try, taste*
¿Qué pides de postre?	*What are you **ordering** for dessert?*
sirves	*serving*

Estructura y Práctica

Stem-changing Verbs: **servir** and **pedir**

Here are the present tense forms of the -**ir** stem-changing verbs **servir** (*to serve*) and **pedir** (*to ask for, request*).

servir (e > i) *to serve*		**pedir (e > i)** *to ask for, request*	
sirvo	servimos	pido	pedimos
sirves	servís	pides	pedís
sirve	sirven	pide	piden

K Write the form of the verb **servir** or **pedir** that correctly completes each of the following sentences.

1. Este jugador _____ bien la pelota.

2. Nosotros _____ unos libros por internet.

3. Las meseras _____ la cena.

4. ¿Por qué no (tú) _____ la cuenta (*bill*)?

5. Yo no _____ postre porque no puedo comer nada más.

6. Nosotros _____ a la patria (*native country*).

7. Tú _____ de ejemplo (*set an example*) para los niños.

8. El culpable (*culprit*) ni _____ perdón (*to apologize*).

9. Hago un pastel y lo _____ con helado.

10. ¿Uds. _____ pizza a domicilio? (*takeout*)

⏵ DIÁLOGO 7 · No puedo imprimir el informe.

Study the dialogue, then listen to the recording and repeat each line.

MATEO	Oye, trabajas muy tarde hoy. ¿Lees tu correo electrónico?
LAURA	Ya no. Ahora tengo que terminar mi informe.
MATEO	Y luego vas a imprimir el informe, ¿verdad?
LAURA	Por desgracia no puedo. La impresora está descompuesta.

Análisis

Check that you understand the linguistic breakdown of each speech from *Diálogo 7*.

Oye, trabajas muy tarde hoy. ¿Lees tu correo electrónico?	*Hey, you're working very late today. Are you reading your email?*
oye	*say, hey* (literally, *hear*)
leer	*to read*
lees	*you read, you are reading*

el correo	mail
electrónico	electronic
el correo electrónico	email

Ya no. Ahora tengo que terminar mi informe.	*Not anymore. Now I have to finish my report.*
ya no	*no longer, not anymore*
tener que + *infinitive*	*to have to (do something)*
terminar	*to finish*
tengo que terminar	*I have to finish*
el informe	*report*

Y luego vas a imprimir el informe, ¿verdad?	*And then you are going to print the report, aren't you?*
luego	*then, later, afterward*
ir a + *infinitive*	*to be going to (do something)*
imprimir	*to print*
vas a imprimir	*you are going to print*
¿verdad?	*aren't you?*

Por desgracia no puedo. La impresora está descompuesta.	*Unfortunately, I can't. The printer is broken.*
por desgracia	*unfortunately*
poder (**o** > **ue**)	*to be able, can*
puedo	*I can, I am able*
la impresora	*printer*
descompuesto	*out of order, broken*
estar descompuesto	*to be out of order, be broken*

▶ Variantes

Listen, and repeat the same structures from *Diálogo 7*, now with new vocabulary.

Tengo que terminar el informe.	*I have to **finish** the report.*
escribir	*write*
leer	*read*
imprimir	*print*
comenzar	*begin*
guardar	*save (computer file)*
descargar	*download*

¿ Vas a imprimir el informe?	***Are you going to** print the report?*
Tienes que	*Do you have to*
Debes	*Must you*
Prefieres	*Do you prefer to*
Puedes	*Are you able to*
Empiezas a	*Are you beginning to*
Tratas de	*Are you trying to*

▶ DIÁLOGO 8 · Tenemos planes para el fin de semana.

Study the dialogue, then listen to the recording and repeat each line.

LAURA	¿Ya tienes planes para el fin de semana?
MATEO	Sí. Felipe y yo pensamos visitar a Elena y Tomás.
LAURA	¿Tus amigos que viven en la costa? Entonces vas al mar.
MATEO	No, ellos vuelven a su apartamento en la ciudad el sábado.

Análisis

Check that you understand the linguistic breakdown of each speech from *Diálogo 8*.

¿Ya tienes planes para el fin de semana?	*Do you have plans for the weekend already?*
ya	*already*
tienes	*you have*
el plan	*plan*
para	*for*
fin	*end*
el fin de semana	*weekend*

Sí. Felipe y yo pensamos visitar a Elena y Tomás.	*Yes, Felipe and I intend to visit Elena and Tomás.*
pensar (**e** > **ie**)	*to think*
pensar + *infinitive*	*to intend to (do something)*
pensamos visitar	*we intend to visit*

¿Tus amigos que viven en la costa? Entonces vas al mar.	*Your friends who live at the shore? So you're going to the ocean.*
que	*who*
vivir	*to live*
la costa	*coast, shore*
el mar	*sea, ocean*

No, ellos vuelven a su apartamento en la ciudad el sábado.	*No, they're coming back to their apartment in the city on Saturday.*
volver (**o** > **ue**)	*to return, come back*
el apartamento	*apartment*
la ciudad	*city*
el sábado	*Saturday, on Saturday*

▶ Variantes

Listen, and repeat the same structures from *Diálogo 8*, now with new vocabulary.

¿Tienes planes para el fin de semana ?	*Do you have plans for **the weekend**?*
el sábado	*Saturday*
el domingo	*Sunday*
mañana	*tomorrow*

esta noche	*tonight*
la semana entrante	*next week*
el mes próximo	*next month*
el verano	*the summer*

Pensamos visitar a Elena.	**We intend to** *visit Elena.*
Queremos	*We want to*
Preferimos	*We prefer to*
Debemos	*We should*
Necesitamos	*We need to*
Podemos	*We're able to*
Esperamos	*We hope to*
Tenemos que	*We have to*

DIÁLOGO 9 · Las gangas—¡no puedo resistir a la tentación!

Study the dialogue, then listen to the recording and repeat each line.

MATEO   Pienso ir al centro comercial hoy. ¿Quieres ir conmigo? Podemos aprovechar las ofertas de enero.

LAURA   No necesito ropa ni nada para la casa. Debo ahorrar mi dinero para comprar un coche.

MATEO   Mujer, tú sabes que eres una compradora compulsiva. Anda, vamos.

LAURA   Qué bien me conoces. Cuando hay gangas, ¡no puedo resistir a la tentación!

Análisis

Check that you understand the linguistic breakdown of each speech from *Diálogo 9*.

Pienso ir al centro comercial hoy.	*I intend to go to the shopping center today.*
¿Quieres ir conmigo? Podemos	*Do you want to go with me? We can take*
aprovechar las ofertas de enero.	*advantage of the January sales.*
pensar (**e** > **ie**)	*to think*
pensar + *infinitive*	*to intend to (do something)*
pienso ir	*I intend to go*
el centro comercial	*shopping center, mall*
al	*to the* (contraction of **a** + **el**)
querer (**e** > **ie**)	*to want*
querer + *infinitive*	*to want to (do something)*
conmigo	*with me*
¿Quieres ir conmigo?	*Do you want to go with me?*
poder (**o** > **ue**)	*to be able, can*
poder + *infinitive*	*to be able to (do something)*
aprovechar	*to take advantage of*
la oferta	*sale*

podemos aprovechar las ofertas	*we can take advantage of the sales*
enero	*January*
las ofertas de enero	*the January sales*

No necesito ropa ni nada para la casa. Debo ahorrar mi dinero para comprar un coche.

I don't need clothing or anything for the house. I should save my money to buy a car.

la ropa	*clothing*
ni	*nor*
nada	*nothing*
deber	*ought to, should, must*
deber + *infinitive*	*ought to / should / must (do something)*
ahorrar	*to save*
el dinero	*money*
debo ahorrar mi dinero	*I should save my money*
para	*in order to*
el coche	*car* (Spain, Argentina)

Mujer, tú sabes que eres una compradora compulsiva. Anda, vamos.

Oh, you know that you are a compulsive shopper. Come on, let's go.

mujer	*oh; oh, come on now; well; hey* (interjection) (literally, *woman*; addressed to a woman)
sabes	*you know*
que	*that*
la compradora	*shopper* (feminine)
compulsivo	*compulsive*
anda	*come on* (**tú** command form of **andar**)
vamos	*let's go* (**nosotros** command form of **ir**)

Qué bien me conoces. Cuando hay gangas, ¡no puedo resistir a la tentación!

How well you know me. When there are bargains, I can't resist the temptation!

qué bien	*how well*
me	*me* (direct object pronoun)
me conoces	*you know me*
la ganga	*bargain*
puedo	*I can*
resistir	*to resist*
resistir a algo	*to resist something*
la tentación	*temptation*
resistir a la tentación	*to resist temptation*

Variantes

Listen, and repeat the same structures from *Diálogo 9*, now with new vocabulary.

Pienso ir al centro comercial hoy.	*I intend to go to the mall today.*
Prefiero	*I prefer to*
Puedo	*I can*
Espero	*I hope to*
Necesito	*I need to*
Deseo	*I want to*
Debo	*I ought to*
¿Quieres ir ?	*Do you want to go?*
subir	*go up*
bajar	*go down*
regresar	*go back*
volver	*go back*
¿Quieres ir conmigo ?	*Do you want to go with me?*
con él	*with him*
con ella	*with her*
con nosotros	*with us*
con ellos	*with them*
Quiero ir contigo .	*I want to go with you.*
con Ud.	*with you*
con Uds.	*with you*
con ellas	*with them*
Cuentan conmigo .	*They count on me.*
contigo	*on you*
con nosotros	*on us*
con Uds.	*on you*
con él	*on him*
¿Cuánto cuesta esta camisa?	*How much does this shirt cost?*
Cuesta sesenta y cinco dólares.	*It costs sixty-five dollars.*
noventa y un	*ninety-one*
¿Cuánto cuestan los zapatos?	*How much do the shoes cost?*
Cuestan cien dólares.	*They cost one hundred dollars.*
ciento cuarenta	*one hundred forty*
El carro cuesta treinta y cinco mil dólares.	*The car costs thirty-five thousand dollars.*
cincuenta y un mil	*fifty-one thousand*
La casa cuesta trescientos mil dólares.	*The house costs three hundred thousand dollars.*
setecientos cincuenta mil	*seven hundred fifty thousand*
un millón de	*a million*
dos millones de	*two million*

Hay veintiún paquetes y veintiuna cajas.   *There are twenty-one packages and twenty-one boxes.*

Hay quinientos paquetes y setecientas cajas.   *There are five hundred packages and seven hundred boxes.*

Estructura y Práctica

Prepositional Pronouns

In Spanish, there is a special set of pronouns that is used after prepositions. These pronouns are identical with the subject pronouns except in the first and second persons singular.

Here is the set of prepositional pronouns after **para**.

para **mí**	para **nosotros/nosotras**
para **ti**	para **vosotros/vosotras**
para **él/ella/Ud.**	para **ellos/ellas/Uds.**

Note that the prepositional pronoun **mí** has a written accent, though the prepositional pronoun **ti** does not.

After **con** there are three irregular forms.

con + mí → **conmigo**	*with me*
con + ti → **contigo**	*with you* (informal singular)
consigo	*with himself, with herself, with yourself* (formal singular), *with yourselves* (formal plural), *with themselves*

L   **Prepositional pronouns.** Write each preposition with the correct prepositional pronoun indicated by the subject pronoun in parentheses. Follow the *modelo*.

MODELO   de (yo)
→ de mí

1. para (ella)
2. con (tú)
3. de (él)
4. para (yo)
5. con (nosotros)
6. de (Uds.)
7. por (yo)
8. con (yo)

9. a (tú)
10. para (tú)
11. por (Ud.)
12. a (yo)
13. por (tú)
14. en (él)
15. de (tú)
16. en (ellos)

Numbers

Here's a review of the numbers from one to twenty as presented in Chapter 1.

1	uno	11	once
2	dos	12	doce
3	tres	13	trece
4	cuatro	14	catorce
5	cinco	15	quince
6	seis	16	dieciséis
7	siete	17	diecisiete
8	ocho	18	dieciocho
9	nueve	19	diecinueve
10	diez	20	veinte

Here are the numbers from twenty-one through thirty-nine.

21	veintiuno (-una)	31	treinta y uno (una)
22	veintidós	32	treinta y dos
23	veintitrés	33	treinta y tres
24	veinticuatro	34	treinta y cuatro
25	veinticinco	35	treinta y cinco
26	veintiséis	36	treinta y seis
27	veintisiete	37	treinta y siete
28	veintiocho	38	treinta y ocho
29	veintinueve	39	treinta y nueve
30	treinta		

All numbers ending in *one* have a masculine and a feminine form: **veintiuno**, **veintiuna**; **treinta y uno**, **treinta y una**. They agree with the following noun in gender. Before a masculine noun, **veintiuno** shortens to **veintiún** and **uno** shortens to **un**.

veintiún libros	*twenty-one books*
treinta y un libros	*thirty-one books*
veintiuna páginas	*twenty-one pages*
treinta y una páginas	*thirty-one pages*

However, the masculine form is sometimes used colloquially before feminine nouns as well.

veintiún páginas	*twenty-one pages*
treinta y un páginas	*thirty-one pages*

The numbers 21 through 29 may be written as three words each, but this is increasingly less common: **veinte y uno/una**, **veinte y dos**, **veinte y tres**, etc.

The numbers 31 through 39 are occasionally written as one word each in some countries: **treintiuno/treintiuna**, **treintidós**, **treintitrés**, etc.

Note that the forms **veintiún**, **veintidós**, **veintitrés**, and **veintiséis** have written accents, according to the rules for the placement of accent marks in Spanish.

Here are the numbers from 40 to 99.

40	cuarenta	70	setenta
41	cuarenta y uno (una)	71	setenta y uno (una)
42	cuarenta y dos	80	ochenta
43	cuarenta y tres	81	ochenta y uno (una)
50	cincuenta	90	noventa
51	cincuenta y uno (una)	91	noventa y uno (una)
52	cincuenta y dos	99	noventa y nueve
60	sesenta		
61	sesenta y uno (una)		

Here are the hundreds in Spanish.

100	cien	600	seiscientos/seiscientas
200	doscientos/doscientas	700	setecientos/setecientas
300	trescientos/trescientas	800	ochocientos/ochocientas
400	cuatrocientos/cuatrocientas	900	novecientos/novecientas
500	quinientos/quinientas		

The forms **quinientos/quinientas**, **setecientos/setecientas**, and **novecientos/novecientas** are irregular in their formation.

The numeral **cien** becomes **ciento** before another number. **Ciento** has no feminine form. **Ciento** + number is used before both masculine and feminine nouns.

101	ciento uno (una)
102	ciento dos
110	ciento diez
155	ciento cincuenta y cinco

The word **y** is not used between **ciento** and a following number.

Multiples of **cien** agree in gender and number with the noun they refer to. They agree even when another number intervenes.

doscient**os** cafés	*two hundred cafés*
doscient**os** cincuenta y ocho cafés	*two hundred fifty-eight cafés*
doscient**as** tiendas	*two hundred stores*
doscient**as** cincuenta y ocho tiendas	*two hundred fifty-eight stores*
quinient**os** pesos	*five hundred pesos*
quinient**os** dieciocho pesos	*five hundred eighteen pesos*
quinient**as** computadoras	*five hundred computers*
quinient**as** dieciocho computadoras	*five hundred eighteen computers*
novecient**os** archivos	*nine hundred files*
novecient**os** treinta y un archivos	*nine hundred thirty-one files*
novecient**as** calles	*nine hundred streets*
novecient**as** treinta y un**a** calles	*nine hundred thirty-one streets*

The word for 1,000 is **mil**.

1,000	mil
1,050	mil cincuenta

1,200	mil doscientos/doscientas
1,278	mil doscientos/doscientas setenta y ocho
2,000	dos mil
2,100	dos mil cien
2,912	dos mil novecientos/novecientas doce
3,000	tres mil
4,000	cuatro mil
5,000	cinco mil
6,000	seis mil
7,000	siete mil
8,000	ocho mil
9,000	nueve mil
10,000	diez mil
20,000	veinte mil
100,000	cien mil
200,000	doscientos/doscientas mil
500,000	quinientos/quinientas mil
1,000,000	un millón

NOTES

1 · The word **un** is not used before **cien** or **mil** to mean 100 or 1,000. Contrast this with English *one hundred, one thousand.*

2 · Agreements of multiples of 100,000 take place across intervening numbers.

trescien**tos** mil mensajes	*three hundred thousand messages*
trescien**tos** cincuenta mil mensajes	*three hundred fifty thousand messages*
trescien**tas** mil viviendas	*three hundred thousand dwellings*
trescien**tas** cincuenta mil viviendas	*three hundred fifty thousand dwellings*

3 · **Un, una** do not agree with the noun when they precede **mil** directly. Only **un** is used even if the noun is feminine.

trescientas cincuenta y **un mil** viviendas	*three hundred fifty-one thousand dwellings*

However, agreement with a feminine noun is not uncommon in colloquial usage.

treinta y **una mil** cuentas de banco	*thirty-one thousand bank accounts*

4 · In some countries of the Spanish-speaking world, a period is used to separate thousands when writing numbers, and the comma serves as a decimal point.

1.500.000	un millón quinientos mil
$10,25	diez dólares veinticinco centavos

5 · The word **millón** is a masculine noun. It is preceded by **un** and followed by **de** when a noun follows directly. It is made plural (**millones**) after numbers higher than *one.*

un millón de dólares	*a million dollars*
diez millones de dólares	*ten million dollars*

The preposition **de** is not used if another number intervenes.

un millón quinientos mil dólares	*one million five hundred thousand dollars*
diez millones quinientos mil dólares	*ten million five hundred thousand dollars*

6 · In most Spanish-speaking countries, **un billón** means *a trillion. A billion* is **mil millones**.

M ¿*Cuántos hay?* Express each of the following numbers in Spanish words.

1. 41 _____ días
2. 84 _____ idiomas
3. 100 _____ años
4. 731 _____ zonas
5. 976 _____ edificios
6. 1,000 _____ empresas
7. 1,495 _____ ciudades
8. 3,581 _____ ciudadanos (*citizens*)
9. 10,729 _____ mujeres
10. 265,000 _____ hombres
11. 1,000,000 _____ habitantes (*inhabitants*)
12. 92,000,000 _____ dólares

DIÁLOGO 10 · No sé dónde queda su casa.

Study the dialogue, then listen to the recording and repeat each line.

LAURA   Sé que Victoria y Pablo viven en la calle Castaño. ¿Sabes su dirección?
MATEO   Creo que es el número setenta y tres.
LAURA   Pues no encuentro su calle en el plano.
MATEO   No tienes que leer el plano. Yo conozco la calle Castaño. Si sigues por
        la avenida Conde vas a llegar.

Análisis

Check that you understand the linguistic breakdown of each speech from *Diálogo 10*.

Sé que Victoria y Pablo viven en la calle Castaño. ¿Sabes su dirección?	*I know that Victoria and Pablo live on Castaño Street. Do you know their address?*
sé	*I know*
que	*that*
vivir	*to live*
viven	*they live*

en	*in, on*
la calle	*street*
la calle Castaño	*Castaño Street*
sabes	*you know*
su	*their*
la dirección	*address*

Creo que es el número setenta y tres.	*I think it is number seventy-three.*
creer	*to believe, think*
creo	*I believe, I think*
que	*that*
el número	*number*
setenta y tres	*seventy-three*

Pues no encuentro su calle en el plano.	*Well, I can't find their street on the city map.*
encontrar (**o** > **ue**)	*to find*
encuentro	*I find*
no encuentro	*I don't find, I can't find*
el plano	*street map, city map*

No tienes que leer el plano. Yo conozco la calle Castaño. Si sigues por la avenida Conde vas a llegar.	*You don't have to read the map. I know Castaño Street. If you continue along Conde Avenue, you'll get there.*
tener que	*to have to*
leer	*to read*
no tienes que leer el plano	*you don't have to read the map*
conozco	*I know*
seguir (**e** > **i**)	*to follow, continue*
por	*for, through*
seguir por	*to continue along*
la avenida	*avenue*
ir a + *infinitive*	*to be going to (do something)*
llegar	*to arrive, get there*
vas a llegar	*you'll get there*

▶ Variantes

Listen, and repeat the same structures from *Diálogo 10*, now with new vocabulary.

Sé que viven en la calle Castaño .	*I know **they live on Castaño Street**.*
es una calle tranquila	*it's a quiet street*
hay un museo de arte en frente	*there's an art museum opposite*
sus vecinos son simpáticos	*their neighbors are nice*

¿Sabes su dirección ?	*Do you know her **address**?*
número de teléfono	*telephone number*
dirección electrónica	*email address*
fecha de nacimiento	*date of birth*

No tienes que leer el plano.	***You don't have to*** *read the street map.*
No debes	*You shouldn't*
No puedes	*You can't*
No necesitas	*You don't need to*
No logras	*You don't manage to*
No sabes	*You don't know how to*
No quieres	*You don't want to*

Yo conozco la calle Castaño .	*I'm familiar with **Castaño Street**.*
este barrio	*this neighborhood*
Ciudad de México	*Mexico City*
Madrid	*Madrid*
Puerto Rico	*Puerto Rico*

Estructura y Práctica

Seguir

Seguir (**e** > **i**) (*to follow, continue*) is a stem-changing verb that also has a spelling change in the present tense. For verbs that end in -**guir**, **gu** changes to **g** before **o** and **a**. In the present tense, the change occurs only in the first person singular (**yo** form). Here is the conjugation of **seguir** in present tense.

seguir (**e** > **i**) *to follow, continue*	
si**g**o	seguimos
sigues	seguís
sigue	siguen

Verbs ending in -**seguir** are conjugated like **seguir**: **conseguir** (*to get, acquire*), **perseguir** (*to pursue, persecute*), **proseguir** (*to proceed*). Their respective first person singular forms are **consigo**, **persigo**, and **prosigo**.

N Rewrite each of the following sentences, changing the verb + infinitive construction to the correct present tense form of **seguir**. Follow the *modelo*.

MODELO   Ellos deben seguir por esa avenida.
             → Siguen por esa avenida.

1. Uds. van a seguir por la autopista.

2. Puedes seguir la conversación.

3. El perro trata de seguir a los niños.

4. ¿Ud. espera seguir un curso de inglés a distancia?

5. Pienso seguir los consejos (*advice*) de mis padres.

6. Acabamos de seguir por una avenida bajo construcción.

7. Él tiene que seguir las órdenes (*orders*) del médico.

8. Quieren seguir el ejemplo (*example*) de su abuelo.

⏵ DIÁLOGO 11 · Pablo juega al tenis.

Study the dialogue, then listen to the recording and repeat each line.

LAURA   Hola, Pablo, veo que tienes tu raqueta de tenis. ¿Vas a jugar ahora?

PABLO   No, yo vuelvo de la cancha de tenis. Juego al tenis todas las tardes.

LAURA   Yo sé que eres un magnífico jugador. ¿Con quién juegas?

PABLO   Con Rafa. Es mejor que yo. Cuando él sirve yo no puedo devolver la pelota.

Análisis

Check that you understand the linguistic breakdown of each speech from *Diálogo 11*.

Hola, Pablo, veo que tienes tu raqueta de tenis. ¿Vas a jugar ahora?

Hi, Pablo, I see that you have your tennis racket. Are you going to play now?

ver	*to see*
veo	*I see*
que	*that*
tienes	*you have*
la raqueta	*racket*
el tenis	*tennis*
la raqueta de tenis	*tennis racket*
ir a + *infinitive*	*to be going to (do something)*
jugar (**u** > **ue**)	*to play (a sport or game)*
vas a jugar	*you are going to play*
ahora	*now*

No, yo vuelvo de la cancha de tenis. Juego al tenis todas las tardes.

No, I'm coming back from the tennis court. I play tennis every afternoon.

volver (**o** > **ue**)	*to return, come back*
vuelvo	*I return, I come back*
de	*from*
la cancha	*court*
la cancha de tenis	*tennis court*
la tarde	*afternoon*
todas las tardes	*every afternoon*

Yo sé que eres un magnífico jugador. ¿Con quién juegas?

I know that you are a great player. Who do you play with?

sé	*I know*
que	*that*
ser	*to be*
eres	*you are*
magnífico	*magnificent, terrific, great*
el jugador	*player*
un magnífico jugador	*a great player*
con	*with*
quién	*who, whom*

con quién	*with whom*
juegas	*you play*

Con Rafa. Es mejor que yo.	*With Rafa. He's better than I am.*
Cuando él sirve yo no puedo devolver la pelota.	*When he serves, I can't return the ball.*
Rafa	(nickname for *Rafael*)
mejor	*better*
que	*than*
mejor que yo	*better than I*
servir (**e** > **i**)	*to serve*
sirve	*he serves*
puedo	*I can*
devolver (**o** > **ue**)	*to give back (something), return (something)*
devolver la pelota	*to return the ball*

⏵ Variantes

Listen, and repeat the same structures from *Diálogo 11*, now with new vocabulary.

Juego al tenis .	*I play **tennis**.*
béisbol	*baseball*
fútbol	*soccer*
fútbol americano	*football*
baloncesto	*basketball*
golf	*golf*

¿Con quién juegas ?	*Whom **do you play** with?*
vas	*do you go*
compartes	*do you share*
discutes	*do you argue*
vives	*do you live*
comes	*do you eat*
hablas	*do you talk*
trabajas	*do you work*

Estructura y Práctica

Jugar

Jugar (*to play (a sport or game)*), a stem-changing verb, is conjugated as if it had **-o-** as its stem vowel.

jugar (u > ue) *to play (a sport or game)*	
ju**e**go	jugamos
ju**e**gas	jugáis
ju**e**ga	ju**e**gan

Jugar is used with the preposition **a** and the definite article to indicate the game or sport played.

jugar al tenis	*to play tennis*
jugar al béisbol	*to play baseball*
jugar a las cartas	*to play cards*

Some Spanish speakers omit the preposition **a** and the definite article before the name of the game: **jugar tenis**, **jugar béisbol**, **jugar cartas**.

JUGAR AND TOCAR: *TO PLAY*

Remember that Spanish has another word meaning *to play*. **Tocar**, not **jugar**, is used to express *to play a musical instrument*.

Toco el clarinete.	*I play the clarinet.*
Sofía toca el violín.	*Sofía plays the violin.*
¿Tocas un instrumento de viento o de cuerda?	*Do you play a wind or a string instrument?*

O *¡Vamos a jugar!* Rewrite each of the following sentences, changing the verb + infinitive construction to the correct present tense form of **jugar**. Follow the *modelo*.

MODELO   Los chicos desean jugar al baloncesto.
         → Juegan al baloncesto.

1. Joaquín y yo sabemos jugar al ajedrez (*chess*).

2. Estos dos equipos (*teams*) logran jugar en la Serie Mundial (*World Series*).

3. Nunca quiero jugar al tenis de mesa (*Ping-Pong*).

4. Carlitos comienza a jugar a los videojuegos.

5. ¿Tienes ganas de jugar a las cartas?

6. Ud. sabe jugar al vólibol, ¿no?

7. Uds. aprenden a jugar al dominó.

8. Blanca acaba de jugar un juego de sociedad (*board game*).

Un paso más

Are you ready to take your Spanish a step further? Here are exercises that will enhance your knowledge of the language and allow you to express yourself freely.

P **Synonyms and antonyms.** A synonym is a word that means the same or nearly the same as another word. An antonym is a word having the meaning opposite to that of another word. As you study Spanish, you will learn nuance in meaning and be able to select the precise word in any given situation. Learning synonyms and antonyms will increase your vocabulary, thereby expanding your freedom of expression in the language.

Sinónimos. Write a synonym for each of the following verbs, using a verb from Chapter 6.

1. empezar

2. volver

3. bajar

4. tomar

5. subir

6. querer

7. entender

Antónimos. Write the adjective from the second column that is an antonym for each adjective in the first column.

1. feliz	a. pobre
2. adelantado	b. tranquilo
3. abierto	c. barato
4. inquieto	d. claro
5. delgado	e. aburrido
6. caro	f. cerrado
7. interesante	g. triste
8. joven	h. gordo
9. feo	i. antipático
10. rico	j. atrasado
11. oscuro	k. hermoso
12. simpático	l. viejo

Q **Translation.** Express the following sentences in Spanish.

1. *The weather is nasty. It's cold and windy.*

2. *And it's beginning to rain.*

3. *Benjamín has been working in this field for twenty-one years.*

4. *He knows the market very well.*

5. *The students intend to take an online Spanish course.*

6. *They know they have to practice a lot to master the spoken language.*

7. *This restaurant serves the best desserts in the city.*

8. *That's why I'm ordering two. I can't resist the temptation!*

9. *Do you* (tú) *know how to play tennis?*

10. *No, but I want to learn to play.*

11. *I feel like going to the beach. Do you* (tú) *want to go with me?*

12. *I've just come back from the shore. I prefer to go to the country.*

R *Preguntas personales.* Answer each question with a complete Spanish sentence.

1. ¿Cuánto tiempo hace que Ud. estudia español?

2. ¿Qué otros idiomas estudia (habla, lee, escribe)?

3. ¿Necesita usar el español en su trabajo? ¿Cómo lo usa?

4. ¿Qué hace para dominar el idioma?

5. ¿Qué tiempo hace hoy?

6. ¿Ud. prefiere el calor o el frío? ¿Por qué?

7. ¿Qué deportes juega en verano (invierno)? ¿Juega bien?

8. ¿Con quiénes juega?

9. ¿Sabe cocinar? ¿Qué cocina?

10. ¿Qué planes tiene para el fin de semana?

11. ¿Es un comprador compulsivo / una compradora compulsiva?

12. Cuando va de compras (*shopping*), ¿trata de aprovechar las ofertas? ¿Busca gangas?

13. ¿Cuánto dinero gasta en comida, ropa y otras cosas todos los meses?

Entertaining at Home

Communication Goals

- Talking about being hungry, thirsty, warm, cold, sleepy
- Telling how you prepare for a dinner party
- Talking about television and the movies
- Vocabulary: home appliances, entertainment

Grammar Topics

- Irregular Verbs
- Expressions with **tener**
- **El** with Feminine Nouns
- Direct Object Pronouns
- **Haber** *to have*
- Direct Object Pronouns with Verb + Infinitive Constructions
- Word Order

▶ DIÁLOGO 1 · Los invitados vienen a cenar.

Study the dialogue, then listen to the recording and repeat each line.

OLIVIA   Son las siete. Pronto vienen los invitados.
NICOLÁS   Eso espero. Yo tengo mucha hambre.
OLIVIA   Paciencia, chico. El arroz con pollo ya está y voy a hacer la ensalada.
NICOLÁS   Y yo pongo la mesa ahora mismo. Ah, oigo el timbre. Ya están. ¡Por fin!

Análisis

Check that you understand the linguistic breakdown of each speech from *Diálogo 1*.

Son las siete. Pronto vienen los invitados.	*It's seven o'clock. The guests are coming soon.*
las siete	*seven o'clock*
son las siete	*it's seven o'clock*
pronto	*soon*
venir	*to come*
el invitado	*guest*
vienen los invitados	*the guests are coming*
Eso espero. Yo tengo mucha hambre.	*I hope so. I am very hungry.*
eso	*that*
esperar	*to hope*
eso espero	*that's what I hope, I hope so*
tener	*to have*
el hambre	*hunger (feminine)*
tener hambre	*to be hungry (literally, to have (feel) hunger)*
tener mucha hambre	*to be very hungry (literally, to have (feel) a lot of hunger)*
Paciencia, chico. El arroz con pollo ya está y voy a hacer la ensalada.	*Patience. The chicken with rice is already done and I'm going to make the salad.*
la paciencia	*patience*
chico	*boy (interjection; often not translated in this usage)*
el arroz	*rice*
el pollo	*chicken*
el arroz con pollo	*chicken with rice (traditional Hispanic dish)*
ya	*already*
estar	*to be ready, be done*
la ensalada	*salad*
Y yo pongo la mesa ahora mismo. Ah, oigo el timbre. Ya están. ¡Por fin!	*And I'll set the table right now. Oh, I hear the bell. They're here now. At last!*
poner	*to put*
pongo	*I put*
poner la mesa	*to set the table*
ahora mismo	*right now*
oír	*to hear*
oigo	*I hear*
el timbre	*doorbell*
estar	*to be here*
ya están	*they're here now*
por fin	*finally, at last*

▶ Variantes

Listen, and repeat the same structures from *Diálogo 1*, now with new vocabulary.

Los invitados vienen .	The guests **are coming**.
salen	*are leaving*
van	*are going*
vuelven	*are coming back*

Yo tengo hambre .	I'm **hungry**.
sed	*thirsty*
calor	*warm*
frío	*cold*
sueño	*sleepy*
razón	*right*

Él tiene mucha prisa .	He's **in a big hurry**.
mucho miedo	*very afraid*
mucha paciencia	*very patient*
muchos celos	*very jealous*
mucha suerte	*very lucky*

Oigo el timbre .	I hear **the doorbell**.
un ruido	*a noise*
un sonido	*a sound*
una voz	*a voice*
gritos	*shouts, screams*

¿Oyes al profesor?	*Do you hear the professor?*
Sí, lo oigo.	*Yes, I hear him.*

¿Oyes esos anuncios?	*Do you hear those announcements?*
No, no los oigo.	*No, I don't hear them.*

¿Oyes su voz?	*Do you hear her voice?*
Sí, la oigo.	*Yes, I hear it.*

¿Oyes a las actrices?	*Do you hear the actresses?*
No, no las oigo.	*No, I don't hear them.*

Estructura y Práctica

Irregular Verbs

Many Spanish verbs do not follow the standard pattern of formation in the present tense. These are called irregular verbs.

1 · Most irregular verbs in the present tense show an irregular **yo** form, with the rest of the forms being regular. The most common **yo** form irregularity is a **-g-** inserted before the **-o** ending. Verbs with this irregularity are called **-g-** verbs. (For the irregular verbs **ser** and **estar**, see Chapters 1, 3, and 4; for the irregular verbs **hacer** and **ir**, see Chapter 5.)

caer *to fall*	
caigo	caemos
caes	caéis
cae	caen

hacer *to do, make*	
hago	hacemos
haces	hacéis
hace	hacen

poner *to put*	
pongo	ponemos
pones	ponéis
pone	ponen

salir *to go out, leave*	
salgo	salimos
sales	salís
sale	salen

traer *to bring*	
traigo	traemos
traes	traéis
trae	traen

valer *to be worth, cost*	
valgo	valemos
vales	valéis
vale	valen

2 · Some -**g**- verbs show other irregularities or have stem changes in the present.

decir *to say, tell*	
digo	decimos
dices	decís
dice	dicen

oír *to hear*	
oigo	oímos
oyes	oís
oye	oyen

tener *to have*	
tengo	tenemos
tienes	tenéis
tiene	tienen

venir *to come*	
vengo	venimos
vienes	venís
viene	vienen

3 · A variant of -**g**- verbs shows -**zc**- before the -**o** ending of the **yo** form. These verbs have infinitives that end in -**cer** or -**cir** preceded by a vowel.

conocer *to know*	
conozco	conocemos
conoces	conocéis
conoce	conocen

parecer *to seem*	
parezco	parecemos
pareces	parecéis
parece	parecen

traducir *to translate*	
traduzco	traducimos
traduces	traducís
traduce	traducen

4 · A few verbs have other irregularities in the first person singular, but regular forms in the rest of the conjugation.

caber *to fit*	
quepo	cabemos
cabes	cabéis
cabe	caben

saber *to know*	
sé	sabemos
sabes	sabéis
sabe	saben

ver *to see*	
veo	vemos
ves	veis
ve	ven

5 · Verbs ending in -**uir** (not including those ending in -**guir**) add -**y**- between the **u** and the ending in all forms of the singular and in the third person plural, that is, in all forms except the **nosotros** and **vosotros** forms.

construir *to build*	
construyo	construimos
construyes	construís
construye	construyen

Other verbs that pattern like **construir** are **concluir** (*to conclude*), **destruir** (*to destroy*), **huir** (*to flee*), and **incluir** (*to include*).

6 · A small number of verbs end in **-oy** in the first person singular. **Estar** and **ser** show additional irregularities in their conjugations; the form **estoy** is stressed on the second syllable. Notice that in **vosotros** forms of one syllable (**dais**, **vais**, **sois**, and also **veis**, above), the written accent mark is omitted.

dar *to give*		**estar** *to be*	
doy	damos	**estoy**	estamos
das	dais	estás	estáis
da	dan	está	están

ir *to go*		**ser** *to be*	
voy	vamos	**soy**	somos
vas	vais	eres	sois
va	van	es	son

A   **Irregular verbs.** Write the present tense form of the verb that correctly completes each of the following dialogues. Use the irregular verbs in parentheses.

1. —_____ mal tiempo. Va a nevar. (hacer)

   —Mira. La nieve ya _____. (caer)

2. —¿Qué regalo _____ Ud.? (traer)

   —Yo _____ una cámara digital. (traer)

3. —Eva, Mateo _____ tu novio, ¿no? (ser)

   —Ya no. _____ con Jacobo. (salir)

4. —¿Uds. no _____ el timbre? (oír)

   —No, no _____ nada. (oír)

5. —Tú _____ a verme mañana, ¿no? (venir)

   —No, _____ pasado mañana. (venir)

6. —¿Qué película _____ (ellos) en el cine Metro? (poner)

   —Es un nuevo film inglés. Todo el mundo _____ que es fabuloso. (decir)

7. —¿Tú _____ las noticias ahora? (ver)

   —No, _____ una telenovela. (ver)

8. —Yo _____ la comida pronto. (hacer)

   —Y yo _____ a poner la mesa. (ir)

9. —¿Todos nosotros _____ en el taxi? (caber)

   —No todos. Yo no _____. (caber)

10. —¿Cómo se _____ *car* en español? (decir)

    —Bueno, en México nosotros _____ "carro". (decir)

11. —¿De dónde (tú) _____? (ser)

    —_____ español. (ser)

12. —¿Cómo _____ Uds.? (estar)

    —Yo _____ perfectamente, pero Elena _____ acatarrada. (estar)

Expressions with **tener**

Many English phrases consisting of *to be* + adjective and referring to mental or physical states have Spanish equivalents consisting of **tener** + noun. These expressions are used only for people, not for things.

NOUN	IDIOM	MEANING
el hambre *hunger*	tener hambre	*to be hungry*
la sed *thirst*	tener sed	*to be thirsty*
el calor *heat*	tener calor	*to be warm*
el frío *cold*	tener frío	*to be cold*
la prisa *hurry, haste*	tener prisa	*to be in a hurry*
la vergüenza *shame*	tener vergüenza	*to be ashamed*
el éxito *success*	tener éxito	*to be successful*
el cuidado *care, caution*	tener cuidado	*to be careful*
la razón *right, reason*	tener razón	*to be right*
la suerte *luck*	tener suerte	*to be lucky*
el sueño *sleep, sleepiness*	tener sueño	*to be sleepy*
las ganas *desire*	tener ganas de + *infinitive*	*to feel like (doing something)*

Since the word following **tener** in these idioms is a noun, it cannot be modified by **muy**, but must be modified by quantity words such as **mucho**, **poco**, **tanto**, and **demasiado**. These modifiers agree with the noun in gender and number.

¿Tienes **mucha** sed?	*Are you **very** thirsty?*
Hoy tengo **poca** hambre.	*Today I'm **not very** hungry.*
Tenemos **muchas** ganas de conocerla.	*We're **very** eager to meet her.*
¡Tengo **tanto** sueño!	*I am **so** sleepy!*
Tengo **demasiado** frío aquí.	*I am **too** cold here.*
Debes tener **mucho** cuidado.	*You must be **very** careful.*
¿Por qué tiene Ud. **tanta** prisa?	*Why are you in **such a** hurry?*

B **Tener: Expresiones.** Express each sentence in Spanish, using the correct form of the verb **tener** to describe the physical state or frame of mind of these people. Follow the *modelo*.

MODELO *You (Ud.) are very patient.*
        → Tiene mucha paciencia.

1. *They are very hungry.*

2. *Are you (tú) not very thirsty?*

3. *We're right.*

4. *He is very lucky.*

5. *Why are you (Ud.) so ashamed?*

6. *I am not in a hurry.*

7. *Are you (Uds.) too cold?*

8. *She is too careful.*

9. *Why are they so sleepy?*

10. *We're very eager to see him.*

11. *I hope to be successful.*

12. *Are you (tú) not very warm?*

El with Feminine Nouns

When a feminine noun begins with a stressed /a/ sound (written **a** or **ha**), it takes the singular article **el**, not **la**.

> el agua *water*
> el hambre *hunger*

Adjectives that modify these nouns are feminine singular.

> el agua fría *cold water*
> tanta hambre *so much hunger*

In the plural, **las** is used: **las aguas**.

C Write a noun phrase for each of the following nouns beginning with a stressed /a/. Include the correct definite article and the correct form of the adjective in parentheses.

1. _____ agua _____ (potable (*drinking*))

2. _____ aguas _____ (destilado)

3. _____ hambre _____ (extremo)

4. _____ ave _____ (negro)

5. _____ aves _____ (rapaz (*of prey*))

6. _____ alma (*soul*) _____ (divino)

7. _____ almas _____ (humano)

8. _____ área _____ (grande)

9. _____ áreas _____ (protegido)

10. _____ haba (*fava bean*) _____ (blanco)

11. _____ habas _____ (fresco)

12. _____ hacha (*hatchet*) _____ (afilado (*sharp*))

ESO *THAT*

Spanish has several forms ending in **-o** that are called neuters. There are three neuter demonstrative pronouns: **esto**, **eso**, and **aquello**. These pronouns refer to situations or ideas, not to specific nouns.

Paco no dice la verdad.	*Paco doesn't tell the truth.*
Eso es muy malo.	*That's very bad.* (**eso** = *the fact that he doesn't tell the truth*)

(For demonstrative adjectives, see Chapter 3; for demonstrative pronouns, see Chapter 12.)

⏵ DIÁLOGO 2 · Vemos televisión.

Study the dialogue, then listen to the recording and repeat each line.

NICOLÁS	Ya es hora de ver la telenovela. Prendo la tele.
OLIVIA	Ah sí, quiero verla. Pero ponen una película muy buena a la misma hora.
NICOLÁS	Pues, ¿por qué no vemos la película ahora? Y...
OLIVIA	¡Claro! Podemos grabar la telenovela y verla después. Perfecto.

Análisis

Check that you understand the linguistic breakdown of each speech from *Diálogo 2*.

Ya es hora de ver la telenovela. Prendo la tele.	*It's already time to watch the soap opera. I'll turn on the TV.*
la hora	*hour, time*
ser hora de	*to be time to*
ver	*to see, watch*
la telenovela	*serialized TV drama, soap opera*
es hora de ver la telenovela	*it's time to watch the soap opera*
prender	*to turn on, put on*
prendo	*I'll turn on, I'll put on*
prender la tele	*to turn on the TV*
Ah sí, quiero verla. Pero ponen una película muy buena a la misma hora.	*Yes, I want to see it. But they're showing a very good movie at the same time.*
la	*it (feminine singular pronoun)*
verla	*to see it, watch it*
quiero verla	*I want to see it*
la película	*movie, film*
mismo	*same*
a la misma hora	*at the same time*
Pues, ¿por qué no vemos la película ahora? Y...	*Well then, why don't we watch the movie now? And . . .*
pues	*well, well now, well then* (interjection)
vemos	*we see, we watch*
¿por qué no vemos?	*why don't we watch?*
¡Claro! Podemos grabar la telenovela y verla después. Perfecto.	*Of course! We can record the soap opera and watch it afterward. Perfect.*
¡Claro!	*Of course!*
grabar	*to record*
podemos grabar	*we can record*
la	*it (feminine singular pronoun)*
verla	*to see it, watch it*
después	*afterward*

Variantes

Listen, and repeat the same structures from *Diálogo 2*, now with new vocabulary.

Prendo la tele .	*I'll turn the TV on.*
la radio	*the radio*
el microondas	*the microwave*
la lavadora	*the washing machine*
la secadora	*the dryer*
el lavaplatos	*the dishwasher*
el aire acondicionado	*the air conditioning*
la calefacción	*the heat*
¿La tele? Sí, quiero verla.	*TV? Yes, I want to watch it.*
¿El documental? Sí, quiero verlo.	*The documentary? Yes, I want to watch it.*
¿Las noticias? Sí, quiero verlas.	*The news? Yes, I want to watch it.*
¿Los programas? Sí, quiero verlos.	*The programs? Yes, I want to watch them.*

Estructura y Práctica

Ver *to see*

Review the conjugation of **ver** in present tense.

ver *to see*	
veo	vemos
ves	veis
ve	ven

D **¿Qué ven?** Write the form of the verb **ver** that correctly completes each of the following sentences to find out what people are watching on television.

1. Yo _____ un documental.

2. Carlitos _____ dibujos animados (*cartoons*).

3. Uds. _____ una película.

4. Claudia _____ las noticias.

5. Tú _____ un programa de cocina (*cooking show*).

6. Ud. _____ un programa de detectives (*crime show*).

7. Nosotros _____ una telenovela (*serial drama*).

8. Ellos _____ una comedia de situación (*sitcom*).

Poner *to put*

Review the conjugation of **poner** in present tense.

poner *to put*	
pongo	ponemos
pones	ponéis
pone	ponen

Direct Object Pronouns

Direct object nouns may be replaced by direct object pronouns once it is clear to whom or what they refer.

Here are the direct object pronouns in standard Spanish American usage.

	SINGULAR	PLURAL
FIRST PERSON	me	nos
SECOND PERSON	te	(os)
THIRD PERSON	lo, la	los, las

Note that **lo** and **la** refer to both people and things. The direct object pronoun **lo** replaces both people and things that are grammatically masculine singular: **lo** means both *him* and *it*. The direct object pronoun **la** replaces both people and things that are grammatically feminine singular: **la** means both *her* and *it*. In the plural, note that Spanish **los**, **las** refer to both people and things just like English *them*, but Spanish **los**, **las** reflect the gender of the nouns they replace as well. (The pronoun **os** appears in parentheses because the **vosotros** form is not used in Spanish America.)

The direct object pronouns **lo**, **la**, **los**, **las** also mean *you* when referring to **usted** or **ustedes**.

Creo que **lo** conozco, señor.	*I think I know **you**, sir.*
Creo que **la** conozco, señora.	*I think I know **you**, ma'am.*
Creo que **los** conozco, señores.	*I think I know **you**, gentlemen.*
Creo que **las** conozco, señoras.	*I think I know **you**, ladies.*

REGIONAL USAGE

In parts of Spain, **lo** is replaced by **le** when referring to a person, but not when referring to an object. In these varieties of Spanish, the following sentences are distinct.

¿Qué es ese libro? No **lo** conocemos.	*What book is that? We are not familiar with **it**.*
¿Quién es ese señor? No **le** conocemos.	*Who is that man? We don't know **him**.*

In Spanish America, both sentences would read **No lo conocemos.**

The plural **los** may be replaced by **les** when referring to people, but this is less common.

In many parts of Spanish America, **le** and **les** are used as the direct object pronouns corresponding to **Ud.** and **Uds.**, respectively.

Si hay un problema, nosotros **le** contactamos.	*If there is a problem, we will contact **you**.*

E **Direct object nouns to pronouns.** Write sentences to answer each of the following questions, changing the direct object nouns to pronouns in your responses. Use the cues in parentheses, which indicate whether your response should be affirmative or negative. Follow the *modelo.*

MODELO   ¿Lees el ruso? (sí)
→ Sí, lo leo.

¿Lees el ruso? (no)
→ No, no lo leo.

1. ¿Sara pone la mesa? (sí)

2. ¿Ellos venden su casa? (no)

3. ¿Uds. sirven estas galletas? (sí)

4. ¿Martín sube los archivos? (no)

5. ¿Ud. comprende esta idea? (no)

6. ¿Conoces a mis compañeros de trabajo? (sí)

7. ¿Isabel y Ud. prefieren esos vestidos? (sí)

8. ¿Sabes la dirección de los Fernández? (no)

9. ¿Uds. oyen el ruido? (sí)

10. ¿Ud. me [*masc.*] entiende? (sí)

11. ¿Ud. nos [*fem.*] lleva al centro? (no)

12. ¿Alonso comienza la base de datos? (sí)

F *¡Ponemos a Cristóbal por las nubes!* **(We praise Cristóbal to the skies!)** Write the form of **poner** that correctly completes each of the following sentences to tell who is a fan of Cristóbal's music (**la nube** = *cloud*).

1. Ricardo lo _____ por las nubes.

2. Uds. lo _____ por las nubes.

3. Yo lo _____ por las nubes.

4. Ud. lo _____ por las nubes.

5. Margarita lo _____ por las nubes.

6. Tú lo _____ por las nubes.

7. Todos sus aficionados (*fans*) lo _____ por las nubes.

8. Ud. y yo lo _____ por las nubes.

G *Lo, la, los, las* **referring to** *Ud.* **and** *Uds.* Write sentences that correctly answer the questions, using the direct object pronouns that replace **Ud.** and **Uds.** Write the answers in two ways where possible. Follow the *modelo.*

MODELO   ¿Me lleva Ud.?
→ No, señor, no lo llevo.

1. ¿Me conoce Ud.?

No, señora, _____.

2. ¿Nos busca Ud.?

No, señores, _____.

3. ¿Nos llama Ud.?

No, señoras, _____.

4. ¿Me comprende Ud.?

No, señorita, _____.

5. ¿Me ayuda Ud.?

No, señor, _____.

6. ¿Nos conoce Ud.?

No, señoritas, _____.

7. ¿Me quiere Ud. visitar?

No, señor, _____.

8. ¿Nos piensa Ud. invitar?

No, señores, _____.

9. ¿Me va Ud. a llevar?

No, señora, _____.

10. ¿Nos necesita ver?

No, señor, _____.

H **Translation.** Express the following sentences in Spanish, using the correct form of the direct object pronoun. Write the answers in two ways where possible.

1. *I see her.*

2. *He's calling me.*

3. *We're going to take them* [fem.].

4. *Are you* (tú) *looking for him?*

5. *Do you* (Uds.) *want to wait for us?*

6. *She hopes to meet you* (tú).

7. *Do you* (Ud.) *intend to help them* [masc.]?

8. *They* [fem.] *can't understand you* (Ud.) [fem.].

9. *I want to invite you* (Uds.) [masc.].

10. *I'm not going to visit her.*

DIÁLOGO 3 · Dan una película.

Study the dialogue, then listen to the recording and repeat each line.

OLIVIA   Quiero ver la película que dan en el cine Ritz.
NICOLÁS   Yo también la quiero ver. Dicen que es excelente.
OLIVIA   Si quieres verla hoy, más vale salir ahora porque va a haber mucha gente.
NICOLÁS   Es cierto. De todas formas vamos a tener que hacer cola.

Análisis

Check that you understand the linguistic breakdown of each speech from *Diálogo 3*.

Quiero ver la película que dan en el cine Ritz.
    dar una película
    que
    que dan
    el cine

I want to see the movie that they're showing at the Ritz movie theater.
    to show a movie
    that (conjunction)
    that they are showing
    movie theater

Yo también la quiero ver. Dicen que es excelente.
    la
    decir
    que
    excelente

I want to see it, too. They say it's excellent.

    it (replacing feminine singular noun)
    to say, tell
    that (conjunction)
    excellent

Si quieres verla hoy, más vale salir ahora porque va a haber mucha gente.	If you want to see it today, we should leave now, because there will be a lot of people (there).

la	it
verla	to see it, watch it
quieres verla	you want to see it
más vale + *infinitive*	it's better to (do something)
salir	to leave, go out
haber	to be there (infinitive of **hay**)
la gente	people (singular in Spanish)
mucha gente	a lot of people
va a haber mucha gente	there will be a lot of people (there)

Es cierto. De todas formas vamos a tener que hacer cola.	That's right. In any case, we're going to have to stand in line.

cierto	correct, true, right
de todas formas	in any case
ir a + *infinitive*	to be going to (do something)
tener que + *infinitive*	to have to (do something)
la cola	line (of people)
hacer cola	to stand in line, wait in line
vamos a tener que hacer cola	we're going to have to stand in line

Variantes

Listen, and repeat the same structures from *Diálogo 3*, now with new vocabulary.

¿La película? La quiero ver.	The film? I want to see it.
¿El film? Lo quiero ver.	The film? I want to see it.
¿Los videos? Los quiero ver.	The videos? I want to see them.
¿Las diapositivas? Las quiero ver.	The slides? I want to see them.

Dicen que es excelente .	They say **it's excellent**.
que va a llover	it's going to rain
que vienen el sábado	they're coming on Saturday
que sí	yes
que no	no

Va a haber mucha gente .	There will be **many people**.
muchas personas	many people
una gran cantidad de gente	a great many people
mucho público	a big audience

Estructura y Práctica

Dar *to give*

Review the conjugation of **dar** in present tense.

dar *to give*

doy	damos
das	dais
da	dan

I *¿Dan consejos?* Write sentences using the elements given to say that these people never give advice. Make all necessary changes. Follow the *modelo*.

MODELO   Ud. / nunca / dar consejos (*to give advice*)
           → Ud. nunca da consejos.

1. Antonio y yo / nunca / dar consejos

2. Juan / nunca / dar consejos

3. María y Susana / nunca / dar consejos

4. yo / nunca / dar consejos

5. tú / nunca / dar consejos

6. la hermana de Pablo / nunca / dar consejos

7. Uds. / nunca / dar consejos

Decir *to say, tell*

Review the conjugation of **decir** in present tense.

decir *to say, tell*

di**go**	decimos
dices	decís
dice	dicen

J *¡Todos callados!* **(Everyone quiet!)** Write sentences using the elements given to explain that nobody is saying anything. Make all necessary changes. Follow the *modelo*.

MODELO   nosotros / no decir / nada
           → Nosotros no decimos nada.

1. tú / no decir / nada

2. nuestros amigos / no decir / nada

3. Raúl / no decir / nada

4. Ud. / no decir / nada

5. yo / no decir / nada

6. Camila / no decir / nada

7. Uds. / no decir / nada

8. Ana María y yo / no decir / nada

Salir *to go out, leave*

Review the conjugation of **salir** in present tense.

salir *to go out, leave*

sal**go**	salimos
sales	salís
sale	salen

K **¿Cuándo salen?** Write sentences using the elements given to tell when people are leaving the office. Use the correct form of **salir** with the time cue. Follow the *modelo*.

MODELO   ellos / en una hora
          → Ellos salen en una ahora.

1. nosotros / a las seis y media

2. Roberto / dentro de unos minutos

3. yo / en veinte minutos

4. Ud. / muy pronto

5. los empleados / ahora mismo

6. tú / un poco tarde

7. Uds. / a la hora de cenar

8. Timoteo y Rebeca / temprano

Valer *to be worth, cost*

Review the conjugation of **valer** in present tense.

valer *to be worth, cost*	
valgo	valemos
vales	valéis
vale	valen

L Express the following sentences in Spanish. Use the expression **más vale...** to say that it's better to do something.

1. *It's better to leave at noon.*

2. *It's better to discuss the problems.*

3. *It's better not to go.*

4. *It's better to share the information.*

Haber *to have*

Haber (*to have*) is used almost exclusively as an auxiliary verb to form the compound tenses. (See Chapter 13.) In this chapter, we introduce **haber** in its infinitive form as part of the verb + **a** + infinitive construction.

haber *to have*	
he	hemos
has	habéis
ha	han

Va a haber mucha gente.   *There will be many people.*
Va a haber muchos invitados.   *There will be many guests.*

Haber is also the infinitive of **hay** (*there is, there are*), which you learned in Chapter 1. **Hay** is a modified form of the third person singular form **ha**. **Hay** may be followed by either a singular or a plural noun. The noun that follows **hay** is considered to be the direct object of the verb.

Hay un concierto hoy a las ocho.   *There's a concert today at eight o'clock.*
¿**Hay** suficientes médicos?   *Are there enough doctors?*
No, no los **hay**.   *No, there aren't (enough of them).*

Hay is used in the expression **hay que** (*one must / you must / it is necessary to* (*do something*)). In this expression, **hay** is linked to an infinitive by the connector **que**.

Hay que practicar el español.	*You must practice Spanish.*
Hay que hacer cola.	*It's necessary to wait in line.*
Hay que tener cuidado.	*One must be careful.*

M Express the following sentences in Spanish. Use the expression **hay que...** to say that it's necessary to do something.

1. *It's necessary to master a language.*

2. *You must be lucky.*

3. *Sometimes you must resist temptation.*

4. *It's necessary to be patient.*

Direct Object Pronouns with Verb + Infinitive Constructions

Direct object pronouns precede the conjugated verb. In verb + infinitive constructions, direct object pronouns may either precede the conjugated verb or follow the infinitive. When they follow, they are attached to the infinitive in writing.

Lo quiero ver. ⎫ Quiero ver**lo**. ⎭	*I want to see it.*
Las vamos a traer. ⎫ Vamos a traer**las**. ⎭	*We're going to bring them.*

N **Direct object pronouns with the verb + infinitive construction.** Expand each sentence using the verb (or verb + connector) that appears in parentheses to make a verb + infinitive construction. Change the direct object noun to a pronoun. Write each expanded sentence in two ways, according to the *modelo*.

> MODELO   Daniel imprime el informe. (necesitar)
> → Daniel necesita imprimirlo.
> → Daniel lo necesita imprimir.

1. Devuelves la pelota. (deber)

2. ¿Uds. no prueban las quesadillas? (querer)

3. Tienen mucho éxito. (empezar a)

4. No traduzco los documentos. (poder)

5. Vemos a nuestros primos. (esperar)

6. Traigo las flores. (ir a)

7. Ayudamos a los niños. (tener que)

8. Ud. domina el idioma. (lograr)

9. Alicia diseña páginas web. (saber)

10. ¿Ud. la llama? (pensar)

11. Entiendo su punto de vista. (tratar de)

12. Encuentra su cartera. (acabar de)

⏯ DIÁLOGO 4 · ¿Oímos música?

Study the dialogue, then listen to the recording and repeat each line.

NICOLÁS	¿Oímos música? Traigo unos viejos discos de vinilo. Están rayados pero la música es increíble.
OLIVIA	¡Fabuloso! Y yo tengo una app para descargar música en el iPod. También podemos transmitir videos musicales de YouTube a la tele.

Análisis

Check that you understand the linguistic breakdown of each speech from *Diálogo 4*.

¿Oímos música? Traigo unos viejos discos de vinilo. Están rayados pero la música es increíble.	*Shall we listen to music? I have some old vinyl records. They're scratched, but the music is incredible.*

oír	*to hear, listen to*
¿oímos?	*shall we listen to?*
traer	*to bring, have with one*
traigo	*I'm bringing (something), I have (something) with me*
el disco de vinilo	*vinyl record*
rayado	*scratched*
están rayados	*they're scratched*
increíble	*incredible*

¡Fabuloso! Y yo tengo una app para descargar música en el iPod. También podemos transmitir videos musicales de YouTube a la tele.	*Terrific! And I have an app for downloading music to the iPod. We can also send music videos from YouTube to the TV.*

fabuloso	*fabulous, terrific*
una app	*app (application)*
descargar	*to download*
transmitir	*to transmit, send*
el video musical	*music video*

Estructura y Práctica

Oír *to hear*

Review the conjugation of **oír** in present tense.

oír *to hear*	
oigo	oímos
oyes	oís
oye	oyen

O **¿Qué oyen?** Write sentences using the correct form of **oír** and the elements given to find out what people are hearing or listening to. Follow the *modelo*.

MODELO   Miguel / los ruidos de la calle
→ Miguel oye los ruidos de la calle.

1. Marta y yo / el timbre
2. Ud. / música
3. ellos / unos sonidos
4. yo / voces
5. tú / gritos
6. Uds. / el teléfono
7. Leonor / una conversación

DIÁLOGO 5 · ¿Cómo se dice?

Study the dialogue, then listen to the recording and repeat each line.

OLIVIA	Traduzco mi sitio web al inglés. ¿Quieres verlo?
NICOLÁS	Claro. Oye, ¿cómo se dice "sitio web" en inglés?
OLIVIA	Se dice *website*.

Análisis

Check that you understand the linguistic breakdown of each speech from *Diálogo 5*.

Traduzco mi sitio web al inglés.	*I'm translating my website into English.*
¿Quieres verlo?	*Do you want to see it?*
traducir	*to translate*
traduzco	*I translate, I'm translating*
el sitio	*place, site*
el sitio web	*website*
el inglés	*English (language)*
traducir al inglés	*to translate into English*
lo	*it* (replacing masculine singular noun)
verlo	*to see it*
Claro. Oye, ¿cómo se dice "sitio web" en inglés?	*I certainly do. Say, how do you say "website" in English?*
claro	*of course*
oye	*say, hey* (literally, *hear*)
se dice	*you say, one says*
¿cómo se dice?	*how do you say?*
Se dice *website*.	*You say "website."*

⏵ Variantes

Listen, and repeat the same structures from *Diálogo 5*, now with new vocabulary.

¿Cómo se dice *computer* en español?	*How do you say "computer" in Spanish?*
Se dice "computadora". Y en España, "ordenador".	*You say* computadora. *And in Spain,* ordenador.

Estructura y Práctica

Conocer *to know*

Review the conjugation of **conocer** in present tense.

conocer *to know*	
conozco	conocemos
conoces	conocéis
conoce	conocen

Traducir *to translate*

Review the conjugation of **traducir** in present tense.

traducir *to translate*	
traduzco	traducimos
traduces	traducís
traduce	traducen

▶ DIÁLOGO 6 · Cae la nieve.

Study the dialogue, then listen to the recording and repeat each line.

NICOLÁS   Hace muy mal tiempo. Está nublado. Parece que va a llover.
OLIVIA   ¿Llover? ¿No ves? Cae la nieve.

Análisis

Check that you understand the linguistic breakdown of each speech from *Diálogo 6*.

Hace muy mal tiempo. Está nublado.	*The weather is very bad. It's cloudy.*
Parece que va a llover.	*It looks like it's going to rain.*
el tiempo	*weather*
mal tiempo	*bad weather*
hace mal tiempo	*the weather is bad*
nublado	*cloudy*
estar nublado	*to be cloudy*
parecer	*to seem, look like*
que	*that (conjunction)*
llover (**o** > **ue**)	*to rain*
va a llover	*it's going to rain*

¿Llover? ¿No ves? Cae la nieve.	*Rain? Can't you see? Snow is falling.*
ves	*you see*
¿No ves?	*Can't you see? / Don't you see?*
caer	*to fall*
la nieve	*snow*
Cae la nieve.	*Snow is falling.*

▶ Variantes

Listen, and repeat the same structures from *Diálogo 6*, now with new vocabulary.

La nieve cae.	***Snow** is falling.*
La lluvia	*Rain*
La noche cae.	*It's nightfall.*

Estructura y Práctica

Parecer *to seem*

Review the conjugation of **parecer** in present tense.

parecer *to seem*	
parezco	parecemos
pareces	parecéis
parece	parecen

Caer *to fall*

Review the conjugation of **caer** in present tense.

caer *to fall*	
caigo	caemos
caes	caéis
cae	caen

▶ DIÁLOGO 7 · Los libros no caben.

Study the dialogue, then listen to the recording and repeat each line.

| OLIVIA | ¿Y aquellos libros? Los vas a meter en la caja, ¿verdad? |
| NICOLÁS | ¿No ves? No cabe ni un solo libro más. |

Análisis

Check that you understand the linguistic breakdown of each speech from *Diálogo 7*.

¿Y aquellos libros? Los vas a meter en la caja, ¿verdad?	*And what about those books? You're going to put them into the box, aren't you?*
y	*and, and what about?*
aquel	*that*
los	*them*
meter	*to put inside of*
los vas a meter	*you're going to put them in*
¿verdad?	*aren't you?*

¿No ves? No cabe ni un solo libro más.	*Can't you see? Not even one more book can fit.*
ves	*you see*
¿No ves?	*Can't you see?*
caber	*to fit*
no cabe	*it doesn't fit*
ni	*not even*
solo	*single*
un solo	*one single*
ni un solo libro	*not even one single book*
más	*more*
ni un solo libro más	*not even one more book*

Estructura y Práctica

Caber *to fit*

Review the conjugation of **caber** in present tense.

caber *to fit*	
quepo	cabemos
cabes	cabéis
cabe	caben

▶ DIÁLOGO 8 · Una chica pesada

Study the dialogue, then listen to the recording and repeat each line.

NICOLÁS Yo no tengo ganas de ver a Lorenza.
OLIVIA ¿Por qué? ¿No la encuentras simpática?
NICOLÁS De ningún modo. La chica es muy pesada. Siempre da consejos.

Análisis

Check that you understand the linguistic breakdown of each speech from *Diálogo 8*.

Yo no tengo ganas de ver a Lorenza.	*I don't feel like seeing Lorenza.*
tener ganas de + *infinitive*	*to feel like (doing something)*
¿Por qué? ¿No la encuentras simpática?	*Why? Don't you find her to be nice?*
la	*her*
encontrar (**o** > **ue**)	*to find*
la encuentras	*you find her*
simpático	*nice, appealing, pleasant* (of people)

De ningún modo. La chica es muy pesada. Siempre da consejos.	*Not at all. The girl is very annoying. She's always giving advice.*
de ningún modo	*not at all*
la chica	*girl*
pesado	*annoying, boring*
siempre	*always*
el consejo	*piece of advice*
consejos	*advice*
dar consejos	*to give advice*

⏵ Variantes

Listen, and repeat the same structures from *Diálogo 8*, now with new vocabulary.

La encuentro simpática.	*I find her nice.*
Lo encuentro simpático.	*I find him nice.*
Las encuentro simpáticas.	*I find them nice. (females)*
Los encuentro simpáticos.	*I find them nice. (males or males and females)*

⏵ DIÁLOGO 9 · ¿A qué hora vienes?

Study the dialogue, then listen to the recording and repeat each line.

OLIVIA	Tengo que verte. Paso por tu casa mañana.
NICOLÁS	Muy bien. ¿A qué hora vienes a verme?

Análisis

Check that you understand the linguistic breakdown of each speech from *Diálogo 9*.

Tengo que verte. Paso por tu casa mañana.	*I've got to see you. I'll come by your house tomorrow.*
tener que + *infinitive*	*to have to (do something)*
te	*you*
verte	*to see you*
tengo que verte	*I have to see you*
pasar	*to pass, come by*
pasar por tu casa	*to come by your house*
mañana	*tomorrow*
Muy bien. ¿A qué hora vienes a verme?	*That's fine. What time are you coming to see me?*
¿a qué hora?	*at what time?*
vienes	*you're coming*
venir a + *infinitive*	*to be coming to (do something)*
me	*me*
verme	*to see me*

Variantes

Listen, and repeat the same structures from *Diálogo 9*, now with new vocabulary.

Tengo que verte .	*I have to **see you**.*
verlo	*see him, you* (**Ud.**, male)
verla	*see her, you* (**Ud.**, female)
verlos	*see them* (males or males and females), *you* (**Uds.**, males or males and females)
verlas	*see them* (females), *you* (**Uds.**, females)
¿Vienes a verme ?	*Are you coming to **see me**?*
vernos	*see us*
verlo	*see him*
verlas	*see them* (females)

Estructura y Práctica

Venir *to come*

Review the conjugation of **venir** in present tense.

venir *to come*	
vengo	venimos
vienes	venís
viene	vienen

P *¿Cuándo vienen?* Write sentences using the correct form of **venir** and the time cue given to find out when these people are coming. Follow the *modelo*.

MODELO   Alberto / mañana
→ Alberto viene mañana.

1. los chicos / en la tarde
2. Ud. / el jueves
3. yo / a las ocho
4. Uds. / por la mañana
5. Anita y yo / esta noche
6. tú / el miércoles
7. Javier / a la una y media

DIÁLOGO 10 · No los puedo llevar.

Study the dialogue, then listen to the recording and repeat each line.

NICOLÁS   Nos llevas al centro comercial esta tarde, ¿no?
OLIVIA   Lo siento. Hoy no los puedo llevar. Mañana, quizás.

Análisis

Check that you understand the linguistic breakdown of each speech from *Diálogo 10*.

Nos llevas al centro comercial esta tarde, ¿no?	*You'll take us to the mall this afternoon, won't you?*
llevar	*to take (someone somewhere)*
nos	*us*
nos llevas	*you'll take us*
¿no?	*won't you?, right?*

Lo siento. Hoy no los puedo llevar. Mañana, quizás.	*I'm sorry. I can't take you today. Maybe tomorrow.*
sentir (**e** > **ie**)	*to feel, feel sorry about*
Lo siento.	*I'm sorry.*
los	*you (**Uds.**)*
no los puedo llevar	*I can't take you*
quizás	*maybe, perhaps*

Variantes

Listen, and repeat the same structures from *Diálogo 10*, now with new vocabulary.

Los puedo llevar.	*I **can** take you.*
quiero	*want to*
debo	*should*
necesito	*need to*
pienso	*intend to*
prefiero	*prefer to*
espero	*hope to*

DIÁLOGO 11 · Yo lo llamo a Ud.

Study the dialogue, then listen to the recording and repeat each line.

NICOLÁS Ud. me va a llamar mañana, ¿verdad?
OLIVIA Sí, señor, yo lo llamo mañana por la mañana.

Análisis

Check that you understand the linguistic breakdown of each speech from *Diálogo 11*.

Ud. me va a llamar mañana, ¿verdad?	*You're going to call me tomorrow, aren't you?*
me	*me*
llamar	*to call*
me va a llamar	*you're going to call me*
¿verdad?	*aren't you?*

Sí, señor, yo lo llamo mañana por la mañana.	*Yes, sir. I'll call you tomorrow morning.*
lo	*you (**Ud.**)*
yo lo llamo	*I'll call you*
mañana por la mañana	*tomorrow morning*

▶ Variantes

Listen, and repeat the same structures from *Diálogo 11*, now with new vocabulary.

Ud. me va a llamar.	*You're going to call **me**.*
nos	*us*
lo	*him*
la	*her*
los	*them (males or males and females)*
las	*them (females)*

Yo lo llamo mañana.	*I'll call **you** tomorrow.*
la	*you (**Ud.**, female)*
los	*you (**Uds.**, males or males and females)*
las	*you (**Uds.**, females)*

▶ DIÁLOGO 12 · Yo la ayudo.

Study the dialogue, then listen to the recording and repeat each line.

OLIVIA Por favor, ¿puede Ud. ayudarme con la base de datos?
NICOLÁS Claro que sí, señorita. Yo la ayudo en seguida.

Análisis

Check that you understand the linguistic breakdown of each speech from *Diálogo 12*.

Por favor, ¿puede Ud. ayudarme con la base de datos?	*Excuse me, can you help me with the database?*
por favor	*please, excuse me*
me	*me*
ayudar	*to help*
ayudarme	*to help me*
la base de datos	*database*

Claro que sí, señorita. Yo la ayudo en seguida.	*Certainly, miss. I'll help you right away.*
claro que sí	*of course I can, of course I will*
señorita	*miss*
la	*you (**Ud.**)*
yo la ayudo	*I'll help you*
en seguida	*right away*

⏵ Variantes

Listen, and repeat the same structures from *Diálogo 12*, now with new vocabulary.

¿Puede Ud. ayudarme ?	*Can you **help me**?*
ayudarnos	*help us*
ayudarlos	*help them (males or males and females)*
ayudarlas	*help them (females)*

⏵ DIÁLOGO 13 · No lo conozco.

Study the dialogue, then listen to the recording and repeat each line.

OLIVIA ¿Verdad que conoces a mi amigo Eduardo?
NICOLÁS No, no lo conozco. Espero conocerlo algún día.

Análisis

Check that you understand the linguistic breakdown of each speech from *Diálogo 13*.

¿Verdad que conoces a mi amigo Eduardo?	*You know my friend Eduardo, don't you?*
¿Verdad que...?	*Is it true that . . . ?*
conocer	*to know (a person)*
a	*(personal **a**)*
No, no lo conozco. Espero conocerlo algún día.	*No, I don't know him. I hope to meet him someday.*
lo	*him*
no lo conozco	*I don't know him*
esperar	*to hope*
esperar + *infinitive*	*to hope to (do something)*
conocer	*to meet (a person)*
conocerlo	*to meet him*
espero conocerlo	*I hope to meet him*
alguno	*some*
algún día	*someday*

⏵ Variantes

Listen, and repeat the same structures from *Diálogo 13*, now with new vocabulary.

No lo conozco.	*I don't know **him**.*
la	*her*
los	*them (males or males and females)*
las	*them (females)*

▶ DIÁLOGO 14 · Tienes prisa.

Study the dialogue, then listen to the recording and repeat each line.

NICOLÁS	¿Por qué tienes tanta prisa?
OLIVIA	Es que el avión sale a las siete.

Análisis

Check that you understand the linguistic breakdown of each speech from *Diálogo 14*.

¿Por qué tienes tanta prisa?	*Why are you in such a hurry?*
la prisa	*hurry, haste*
tanta prisa	*such a hurry*
tener prisa	*to be in a hurry*
tener tanta prisa	*to be in such a hurry*

Es que el avión sale a las siete.	*Because the plane leaves at seven.*
es que	*the fact is that, because*
el avión	*airplane*
salir	*to go out, leave*
las siete	*seven o'clock*
a las siete	*at seven o'clock*

▶ DIÁLOGO 15 · ¿Quién trae el vino?

Study the dialogue, then listen to the recording and repeat each line.

OLIVIA	Yo traigo tapas a la fiesta. Tú traes el vino, ¿no?
NICOLÁS	No, yo no. Lo trae Diego.

Análisis

Check that you understand the linguistic breakdown of each speech from *Diálogo 15*.

Yo traigo tapas a la fiesta. Tú traes el vino, ¿no?	*I'm bringing hors d'oeuvres to the party. You're bringing the wine, aren't you?*
traer	*to bring*
traigo	*I bring, I'm bringing*
las tapas	*hors d'oeuvres*
la fiesta	*party*
traes	*you're bringing*
el vino	*wine*
¿no?	*aren't you?*

No, yo no. Lo trae Diego.	*No, not me. Diego is bringing it.*
yo no	*not I, not me*
lo	*it (replacing masculine singular noun)*
lo trae Diego	*Diego is bringing it*

Variantes

Listen, and repeat the same structures from *Diálogo 15*, now with new vocabulary.

¿El vino? Lo trae Diego.	*The wine? Diego is bringing it.*
¿Los sándwiches? Los trae Diego.	*The sandwiches? Diego is bringing them.*
¿La torta? La trae Diego.	*The cake? Diego is bringing it.*
¿Las tapas? Las trae Diego.	*The tapas? Diego is bringing them.*

Estructura y Práctica

Word Order

The typical Spanish word order in a sentence is the same as English: subject-verb-object. However, word order in Spanish often appears freer than word order in English. Spanish uses word order the way English uses intonation—to focus on the new information or key information in a sentence. English word order is relatively fixed, so a rise in intonation signals the focus of the sentence.

*I think **Susan** is going out.*
*No, **Philip** is going out.*

In Spanish, new information is placed at the end of the sentence, even if it is the subject.

Creo que sale **Susana**.	*I think **Susana** is going out.*
No, sale **Felipe**.	*No, **Felipe** is going out.*

The words **sale** and **llega** go at the end of the sentences when the verb is what is focused on.

¿Felipe **sale**?	*Is Felipe **going out**?*
No, Felipe **llega**.	*No, Felipe **is arriving**.*

Q **Word order.** Write sentences to tell who is bringing each item to the party by correcting your friend's incorrect information. Note that the subject is placed at the end of the sentence in the response. Change each direct object noun to a pronoun. Follow the *modelo*.

MODELO   Alfredo trae los refrescos, ¿no? (Rafael)
→ No, los trae Rafael.

1. Patricia trae los sándwiches, ¿no? (Lucas y Laura)

2. Paco y Lidia traen el vino, ¿no? (yo)

3. Tú traes las ensaladas, ¿no? (Uds.)

4. Nosotros traemos la pizza, ¿no? (Guillermo)

5. Tú y Franco traen los postres, ¿no? (tú)

6. Santiago trae la cerveza, ¿no? (nosotros)

7. Luz trae las empanadas, ¿no? (Uds.)

Un paso más

Are you ready to take your Spanish a step further? Here are exercises that will enhance your knowledge of the language and allow you to express yourself freely.

Idioms and Expressions with Irregular Verbs

There are many idioms and expressions formed with some of the irregular verbs you learned in this chapter: **tener, dar, poner, valer, oír,** and **ver.** Using these colorful idiomatic expressions will make your Spanish sound more authentic!

tener *to have*
> **tener la culpa de** *to be to blame for* (la culpa = *blame, fault*)
> **tener lugar** *to take place*
> **tener mala cara** *to look bad* (la cara = *face*)
> **no tener ni pies ni cabeza** *to not make sense, have no rhyme or reason*
>   (el pie = *foot*; la cabeza = *head*)

dar *to give*
> **dar guerra** *to cause, make trouble* (la guerra = *war*)
> **dar (la) lata** *to pester, make a nuisance of oneself* (la lata = *can*)
> **dar una vuelta** *to take a walk/ride* (la vuelta = *walk, ride*)

poner *to put*
> **poner las cartas sobre la mesa** *to put one's cards on the table*

valer *to be worth, cost*
> **valer la pena** *to be worthwhile, be worth it* (la pena = *effort, trouble*)

oír *to hear*
> **Las paredes oyen.** *The walls have ears.* (la pared = *wall*)

ver *to see*
> **Ojos que no ven, corazón que no siente.** *Out of sight, out of mind.*
>   (el ojo = *eye*; el corazón = *heart*)

R *Modismos y expresiones* (Idioms and expressions). Express each of the following sentences in Spanish, using the idioms and expressions above. Make all necessary changes.

1. *The meeting is taking place in the director's office.*

2. *It's necessary to put one's cards on the table.*

3. *Clara no longer has a boyfriend. Out of sight, out of mind.*

4. *An excellent job? It's worth waiting for it.*

5. *Juanito always causes trouble. And his sister makes a nuisance of herself.*

6. *Their plan doesn't make sense.*

7. *We shouldn't say anything. The walls have ears.*

8. *Nobody is to blame for that.*

9. *Diego, are you sick? You look bad.*

10. *I'm taking a walk in the park. Are you (tú) coming with me?*

S *Preguntas personales.* Answer each question with a complete Spanish sentence.

1. ¿Tienes hambre? ¿Qué quieres comer?

2. ¿Tienes sed? ¿Qué vas a beber?

3. ¿Qué haces para preparar una comida para tus invitados?

4. ¿Qué comida sirves?

5. ¿Qué programas prefieres ver en la televisión?

6. Si tus amigos te invitan a una fiesta en su casa, ¿qué traes de regalo?

7. ¿Qué tiempo hace hoy? ¿Qué tiempo va a hacer mañana?

8. ¿Tienes paciencia (éxito, suerte, miedo, celos)? Explica (*Explain*).

T **Translation.** Express the following dialogues in Spanish.

1. *It's time for lunch. Are you (tú) hungry?*
   No, I'm not hungry, but I'm very thirsty.

2. *Sir, can you please help me with my computer?*
   Of course, ma'am, I'll help you right away.

3. *Our friends say the film they're showing in that movie theater is terrific. I'm very eager to see it.*
   They're right. I just saw it.

4. *It's twenty-five degrees and very windy. I'm cold.*
   Yes, it's cold and snow is falling, but I'm not very cold.

5. *I want to see the crime show.*
   I want to see it, too.

6. *Do you (Ud.) know the businessmen who are coming this afternoon?*
   No, I don't know them, but I intend to meet them.

7. *There will be a lot of people at the theater.*
   I know. We're going to have to stand in line. And I'm not patient!

8. *How do you say "advice" in Spanish?*
   You say consejos.

The Daily Routine

Communication Goals

- Talking about your daily routine
- Telling how you take care of yourself by eating well and exercising
- Talking about feelings and relationships
- Understanding Hispanic naming customs
- Vocabulary: emotional states such as feeling happy, excited, or angry, falling in love; everyday activities such as getting up, getting dressed

Grammar Topics

- Reflexive Verbs: Formation
- Reflexive Verbs: Uses
- Reflexive Verbs and Their Non-reflexive (Transitive) Counterparts
- Reflexive Verbs Existing Only as Reflexives
- Reflexive Verbs: Reciprocal Meaning
- Reflexive Pronouns
- Reflexive Verbs: Verb + Infinitive Construction
- Adverbs with the Suffix **-mente**
- **Al** + Infinitive
- Prepositions with Reflexive Verbs
- Ordinal Numbers

DIÁLOGO 1 · Carlos el aguafiestas

Study the dialogue, then listen to the recording and repeat each line.

PALOMA ¡Qué fiesta más divertida! Parece que todos los invitados se divierten mucho.

CARLOS No todos. Yo me aburro rotundamente.

PALOMA Carlos, tú me exasperas. Siempre eres el aguafiestas.

Análisis

Check that you understand the linguistic breakdown of each speech from *Diálogo 1*.

¡Qué fiesta más divertida! Parece que todos los invitados se divierten mucho.	*What a fun party! It looks like all the guests are having a very good time.*
la fiesta	*party*
divertido	*amusing, fun*
parecer	*to seem*
parece que	*it seems that*
el invitado	*guest*
todos los invitados	*all the guests*
divertirse (**e** > **ie**)	*to have a good time, have fun*
mucho	*a lot*
No todos. Yo me aburro rotundamente.	*Not all. I am bored stiff.*
todos	*all, everyone*
aburrirse	*to be bored*
rotundo	*definite, emphatic*
rotundamente	*definitely, emphatically*
Carlos, tú me exasperas. Siempre eres el aguafiestas.	*Carlos, you exasperate me. You are always the party pooper.*
exasperar	*to exasperate*
siempre	*always*
el aguafiestas	*party pooper, wet blanket*

▶ Variantes

Listen, and repeat the same structures from *Diálogo 1*, now with new vocabulary.

Todos se divierten .	*Everyone **is having a good time**.*
se alegran	*is happy*
se entusiasman	*is getting excited, is feeling thrilled*
se ríen	*is laughing*
se emocionan	*is getting excited*
se animan	*is cheering up*
Yo me aburro .	*I **am getting bored**.*
me asusto	*am getting frightened*
me enfado	*am getting angry*
me enojo	*am getting angry*
me molesto	*am getting annoyed*
me ofendo	*am getting insulted*
Tú me exasperas .	*You're **making me lose my patience**.*
me aburres	*boring me*
me asustas	*frightening me*
me enfadas	*making me angry*
me enojas	*making me angry*
me molestas	*annoying me*
me ofendes	*insulting me*

Estructura y Práctica

Reflexive Verbs: Formation

Reflexive verbs are a class of verbs in Spanish that always appear with an object pronoun that refers to the subject. This pronoun is called the reflexive pronoun. English also has reflexive verbs. In English, reflexive pronouns end in *-self* or *-selves*: *I hurt myself, they hurt themselves.* English reflexive verbs are a limited class and stress that the subject performs the action upon himself. In Spanish, however, reflexive verbs are a broad category with several different functions that do not correspond at all to English reflexives. Reflexive verbs appear in vocabulary lists with **-se** attached to the infinitive: **levantarse, enojarse, ofenderse, divertirse (e > ie), reírse (e > i), aburrirse.**

Study the conjugation of the reflexive verb **levantarse** (*to get up*) in the present tense. Note that the reflexive pronouns are the same as the direct object pronouns in the first and second persons (**yo, tú, nosotros,** and **vosotros** forms). In the third person, the reflexive pronoun is **se** in both the singular and the plural.

levantarse *to get up*	
me levanto	**nos** levantamos
te levantas	**os** levantáis
se levanta	**se** levantan

Some reflexive verbs are also stem-changing verbs. Study the conjugation of **reírse (e > i)** in the present tense.

reírse (e > i) *to laugh*	
me río	nos reímos
te ríes	os reís
se ríe	se ríen

Reflexive Verbs: Uses

Spanish reflexive verbs correspond most often to intransitive verbs or verb phrases in English. Their English equivalents often contain *get* or *be*. Intransitive verbs in Spanish are those that cannot take a direct object, for example, **ir** (*to go*) and **llegar** (*to arrive*).

aburrirse *to get bored, be bored*
asustarse *to get scared*
divertirse *to have a good time*
enojarse *to get angry*
marearse *to get dizzy*
ofenderse *to get insulted, be offended*
pasearse *to stroll*
sorprenderse *to be surprised*
tranquilizarse *to calm down, stop worrying*

Me aburro en la oficina.	*I get bored at the office.*
Ella se marea en el avión.	*She gets dizzy on the plane.*
Él se ofende por tonterías.	*He gets insulted by silly things.*
Me divierto mucho en Costa Rica.	*I'm having a very good time in Costa Rica.*

A *¿Cómo reaccionan?* Write sentences that describe how people are feeling and reacting. Use the reflexive verbs in parentheses. Follow the *modelo*.

MODELO yo (alegrarse)
→ Yo me alegro.

1. Julio (molestarse)

2. Uds. (aburrirse)

3. Victoria y yo (entusiasmarse)

4. tú (reírse)

5. Alfonso y Edit (asustarse)

6. Ud. (emocionarse)

7. yo (divertirse)

8. Consuelo y Javier (ofenderse)

9. María Elena (enojarse)

10. Juan Carlos y yo (animarse)

B **Reflexive verbs.** Express the following dialogues in Spanish.

1. *I'm getting bored. And you (tú)?*
   Are you kidding? I'm having a great time.

2. *Does he get insulted easily?*
   Yes, and he often gets annoyed.

3. *The children are getting excited.*
   Yes, they're laughing a lot.

4. *Why are you (Uds.) getting angry?*
   We're not getting angry but, yes, we're losing our patience.

Reflexive Verbs and Their Non-reflexive (Transitive) Counterparts

Many reflexive verbs have a non-reflexive counterpart. The non-reflexive verb is transitive and is used with a direct object. Compare the following pairs of expressions.

acostar (**o** > **ue**) al niño *to put the child to bed*	acostarse (**o** > **ue**) *to go to bed*
asustar al gato *to scare the cat*	asustarse *to get scared*
calmar a las víctimas *to calm the victims down*	calmarse *to calm down*
lavar el carro *to wash the car*	lavarse *to wash up*
pasear al perro *to walk the dog*	pasearse *to take a walk*
sentar (**e** > **ie**) a la gente *to seat people*	sentarse (**e** > **ie**) *to sit down*

Acuesto a los niños y después me acuesto.	*I put the children to bed and then I go to bed.*
Juan se despierta y luego despierta a su hermana.	*Juan wakes up and then he wakes his sister up.*

C **Reflexive or transitive verb?** Select one of the verbs in parentheses (reflexive or transitive) to correctly complete each of the following sentences, then write its correct form.

1. Nos _____ (aburrir / aburrirse) esta obra de teatro.

2. Parece que Uds. _____ (enojar / enojarse) por algo.

3. Rafael y yo _____ (emocionar / emocionarse) en los partidos de fútbol.

4. Últimamente Luisa me _____ (exasperar / exasperarse) mucho.

5. Esas películas de terror te _____ (asustar / asustarse), ¿verdad?

6. Yo _____ (divertir / divertirse) mucho en los conciertos.

7. ¿Por qué _____ (preocupar / preocuparse) Ud. por ellos?

8. Ramón los _____ (animar / animarse) con sus chistes (*jokes*) tontos.

9. Su actitud me _____ (sorprender / sorprenderse) mucho.

10. ¿Por qué no (Uds.) _____ (sentar / sentarse) en esta fila (*row*)?

D **Transitive verbs.** Express the following sentences in Spanish.

1. *You (tú) are frightening us.*

2. *We're calming her down.*

3. *She's raising her hand.*

4. *I'm cheering him up.*

5. *You (Uds.) are annoying me.*

6. *They're boring their friends.*

DIÁLOGO 2 · Comprometerse y casarse

Study the dialogue, then listen to the recording and repeat each line.

PALOMA   ¿No sabes? Liliana y Jorge acaban de comprometerse.
CARLOS   Me alegro de saberlo. Yo sé que los prometidos están muy enamorados.
PALOMA   Es verdad. Dicen que van a casarse en julio.

Análisis

Check that you understand the linguistic breakdown of each speech from *Diálogo 2.*

¿No sabes? Liliana y Jorge acaban de comprometerse.	*You know? Liliana and Jorge have just gotten engaged.*
¿No sabes?	*You know?*
acabar de + *infinitive*	*to have just (done something)*
comprometerse	*to get engaged*
Me alegro de saberlo. Yo sé que los prometidos están muy enamorados.	*I'm glad to know that. I know that the engaged couple is very much in love.*
alegrarse de + *infinitive*	*to be happy to (do something), glad to (do something)*
los prometidos	*engaged couple*
estar enamorado	*to be in love*

Es verdad. Dicen que van a casarse en julio.	*It's true. They say that they are going to get married in July.*
la verdad	*truth*
es verdad	*it's true*
casarse	*to get married*

▶ Variantes

Listen, and repeat the same structures from *Diálogo 2*, now with new vocabulary.

Acaban de comprometerse .	*They've just **gotten engaged**.*
casarse	*gotten married*
reunirse	*gotten together*
mudarse	*moved (changed residence)*
instalarse	*moved in*
Van a casarse en julio.	*They're going to **get married** in July.*
comprometerse	*get engaged*
divorciarse	*get divorced*
Liliana se casa con Jorge.	*Liliana **is getting married to** Jorge.*
se compromete con	*is getting engaged to*
Ella se enamora de él.	*She **falls in love with** him.*
se acuerda de	*remembers*
se olvida de	*forgets*
se fía de	*trusts*
se ocupa de	*takes care of*
se despide de	*says goodbye to*

Estructura y Práctica

Reflexive Verbs Existing Only as Reflexives

A small number of Spanish verbs exist only as reflexives.

arrepentirse (**e** > **ie**) de algo *to regret something*
atreverse a hacer algo *to dare to do something*
desmayarse *to faint*
divorciarse *to get divorced*
jactarse de algo *to boast about something, brag about something*
quejarse de algo *to complain about something*
suicidarse *to commit suicide*

E **Reflexive verbs existing only as reflexives.** Write a sentence for each of the following strings of elements. Follow the *modelo*.

MODELO   Gustavo / arrepentirse de / su comportamiento (*behavior*)
          → Gustavo se arrepiente de su comportamiento.

1. yo / jactarse de / mis hijos

2. tú / quejarse de / todo

3. nosotros / no atreverse a / hablar de eso

4. Pedro y Elena / divorciarse / por falta de comunicación

5. Maite y su hermano / desmayarse / por tener la tensión baja (*low blood pressure*)

F   *Oraciones con verbos reflexivos* (**Sentences with reflexive verbs**). Express the
following dialogues in Spanish.

1. *They say that Lucía is getting engaged to Benjamín.*
   And it seems that Margarita is getting married to Leonardo.

2. *Do you (Ud.) remember Armando's address?*
   I'm sorry. I forget everything!

3. *You know? We're moving into our new house today.*
   I'm very glad to know that.

4. *Who is taking care of the details* (los detalles) *of the meeting?*
   I'm taking care of the reports and Diego is tending to the other documents.

5. *Why are you (tú) saying goodbye to all the guests?*
   It's that the party is very boring. I'm leaving!

▶ DIÁLOGO 3 · Los novios se quieren.

Study the dialogue, then listen to the recording and repeat each line.

CARLOS	Benjamín y Jimena se entienden perfectamente.
PALOMA	Los novios se ven y se hablan por celular todos los días.
CARLOS	Y se escriben correos electrónicos todo el día.
PALOMA	Es obvio que se quieren, ¿no?

Análisis

Check that you understand the linguistic breakdown of each speech from *Diálogo 3*.

Benjamín y Jimena se entienden perfectamente.	*Benjamín and Jimena get along perfectly.*
entenderse (**e** > **ie**)	*to get along*
perfecto	*perfect*
perfectamente	*perfectly*
Los novios se ven y se hablan por celular todos los días.	*The boyfriend and girlfriend see each other and talk to each other by cell phone every day.*
los novios	*the boyfriend and girlfriend, the couple*
verse	*to see each other*
se ven	*they see each other*
hablarse	*to talk to each other*
se hablan	*they talk to each other*
por celular	*by cell phone*

Y se escriben correos electrónicos todo el día.	*And they write each other emails all day long.*
escribirse	*to write to each other*
se escriben	*they write to each other*
se escriben correos electrónicos	*they write emails to each other*
Es obvio que se quieren, ¿no?	*It's obvious that they love each other, isn't it?*
obvio	*obvious*
es obvio que	*it's obvious that*
quererse	*to love each other*
se quieren	*they love each other*

▶ Variantes

Listen, and repeat the same structures from *Diálogo 3*, now with new vocabulary.

Se entienden.	*They understand each other.*
Se comprenden.	*They understand each other.*
Se conocen.	*They know each other.*
Se ayudan.	*They help each other.*
Se quieren.	*They love each other.*
Se besan.	*They kiss each other.*
Se abrazan.	*They hug each other.*
Nos entendemos.	*We understand each other.*
Nos comprendemos.	*We understand each other.*
Nos conocemos.	*We know each other.*
Nos ayudamos.	*We help each other.*
Nos queremos.	*We love each other.*
Nos besamos.	*We kiss each other.*
Nos abrazamos.	*We hug each other.*
Nos tuteamos.	*We address each other as* tú (*informally*).

Estructura y Práctica

Reflexive Verbs: Reciprocal Meaning

Reflexive verbs used in the plural may convey a reciprocal meaning equivalent to English "each other."

Pablo y Beatriz **se ven** todos los días.	*Pablo and Beatriz **see each other** every day.*
Ellos **se quieren**.	*They **love each other**.*
¿Por qué no **nos tuteamos**?	*Why don't **we use the** tú **form with each other**?*
Nos enviamos emails.	***We send each other** emails.*

G **Reflexive verbs with reciprocal meaning.** Express the following sentences in Spanish.

1. *You (Ud.) and Jorge understand each other very well.*

2. *Micaela and I see each other every day.*

3. *Why don't we address each other as tú?*

4. *The children are hugging each other.*

5. *Shall we help each other with the project?*

6. *Roberto and Alejandra love each other a lot.*

7. *We know each other quite well.*

8. *Eunice and her cousin write to each other once a year.*

DIÁLOGO 4 · Nos damos prisa.

Study the dialogue, then listen to the recording and repeat each line.

CARLOS   Se hace tarde. Debemos darnos prisa.
PALOMA   Me visto, me peino, me pinto la cara y nos vamos.
CARLOS   Bueno, yo me pongo el abrigo y te espero abajo.

Análisis

Check that you understand the linguistic breakdown of each speech from *Diálogo 4*.

Se hace tarde. Debemos darnos prisa.	*It's getting late. We should hurry.*
hacerse	*to become*
hacerse tarde	*to get late*
darse prisa	*to hurry up, get moving*
Me visto, me peino, me pinto la cara y nos vamos.	*I'll get dressed, comb my hair, put on makeup, and we'll leave.*
vestirse (**e** > **i**)	*to get dressed*
peinarse	*to comb one's hair*
pintar	*to paint*
la cara	*face*
pintarse la cara	*to put on makeup*
irse	*to go away, leave*
nos vamos	*we'll leave*
Bueno, yo me pongo el abrigo y te espero abajo.	*OK, I'll put on my coat and I'll wait for you downstairs.*
ponerse + *article of clothing*	*to put (article of clothing) on*
el abrigo	*coat*
ponerse el abrigo	*to put one's coat on*
abajo	*downstairs*

Variantes

Listen, and repeat the same structures from *Diálogo 4*, now with new vocabulary.

Debemos darnos prisa .	*We should **hurry up**.*
levantarnos	*get up*
sentarnos	*sit down*

pasearnos	*go for a walk*
apresurarnos	*hurry up*

Me visto.	*I'm getting dressed.*
Me pongo la ropa.	*I'm putting my clothes on.*
Me desnudo.	*I'm getting undressed.*
Me quito la ropa.	*I'm taking my clothes off.*
Me arreglo.	*I'm getting ready.*
Me maquillo.	*I'm putting on makeup.*

Nos vamos.	*We're leaving.*
Nos quedamos.	*We're staying.*
Nos acercamos.	*We're approaching.*
Nos alejamos.	*We're moving far away.*

Yo me pongo el abrigo .	*I'm putting on **my coat**.*
la chaqueta	*my jacket*
los pantalones	*my pants*
la camisa	*my shirt*
los guantes	*my gloves*

Ella se quita el suéter .	*She's taking off **her sweater**.*
el vestido	*her dress*
la falda	*her skirt*
la blusa	*her blouse*
el reloj	*her watch*

Yo me pruebo el traje.	*I'm trying the suit on.*
Él se prueba los zapatos.	*He's trying the shoes on.*

Estructura y Práctica

Reflexive Pronouns

Spanish reflexive pronouns are often the equivalent of English possessive adjectives with parts of the body or articles of clothing. Note that, in this case, the reflexive pronoun is an indirect object and the definite article is used before the noun. Spanish uses a singular noun for articles of clothing and parts of the body, even with plural subjects. It is assumed that each person has one item, unless the item comes in pairs. (For more on indirect objects, see Chapter 9.)

lastimarse el pie *to hurt one's foot*
lavarse las manos *to wash one's hands*
limpiarse los dientes *to brush one's teeth, clean one's teeth*
ponerse los zapatos *to put on one's shoes*
quitarse el abrigo *to take off one's coat*
romperse el brazo *to break one's arm*

Nos ponemos el abrigo.	*We're putting on our coats.*
Se lavan la cara.	*They're washing their faces.*

Paco acaba de lastimarse el pie.   *Paco has just hurt his foot.*
¿Por qué no te pruebas el traje azul?   *Why don't you try on the blue suit?*

H Express the following sentences in Spanish.

1. *I'm trying the blouse and skirt on.*
2. *The children are taking their shoes off.*
3. *María Elena is combing her hair.*
4. *Are you (tú) getting dressed right now?*
5. *We get up at 7:00 A.M. every day.*
6. *It's getting late. You (Uds.) have to hurry up!*
7. *Each time Samuel plays soccer, he hurts his foot.*
8. *We're getting ready and we're leaving.*

PONER

The reflexive verb **ponerse** is used in the following ways in Chapter 8.

ponerse *to put on (clothing)*
ponerse a + *infinitive to begin to (do something)*
ponerse en contacto *to get in touch*
ponerse en forma *to get into shape*

Ponerse is also used with an adjective to mean *to become* when referring to a physical or emotional change.

Me pongo feliz al ver a mis hijos.   *I get happy when I see my children.*
Se pone roja cuando siente   *She blushes (gets red) when she feels*
  vergüenza.   *ashamed.*
¿Por qué **se ponen** tan nerviosos?   *Why are you getting so nervous?*

DIÁLOGO 5 · Cómo cuidarte mejor

Study the dialogue, then listen to the recording and repeat each line.

CARLOS   Te acatarras con frecuencia. Debes cuidarte mejor.
PALOMA   Es verdad que no me mantengo en forma y no me alimento bien.
CARLOS   Bueno, debes comenzar a hacer ejercicio lo antes posible.
PALOMA   ¡Y voy a dejar de comer comida basura hoy mismo!

Análisis

Check that you understand the linguistic breakdown of each speech from *Diálogo 5*.

Te acatarras con frecuencia. Debes   *You often catch colds. You should take better*
cuidarte mejor.   *care of yourself.*
  acatarrarse   *to catch a cold*
  la frecuencia   *frequency*
  con frecuencia   *often, frequently*
  cuidarse   *to take care of oneself*
  mejor   *better*

Es verdad que no me mantengo en forma y no me alimento bien.	*It's true that I don't keep in shape and I don't eat right.*
mantener	*to keep* (conjugated like **tener**)
mantenerse	*to keep oneself*
la forma	*shape*
mantenerse en forma	*to keep in shape*
alimentarse	*to feed oneself, eat*
alimentarse bien/mal	*to eat well/badly, eat right/poorly*
bien	*well, right*
mal	*badly, poorly*

Bueno, debes comenzar a hacer ejercicio lo antes posible.	*Well, you should begin exercising as soon as possible.*
bueno	*well, okay*
comenzar (**e** > **ie**) a + *infinitive*	*to begin (doing something)*
hacer ejercicio	*to exercise*
antes	*before*
lo antes posible	*as soon as possible*

¡Y voy a dejar de comer comida basura hoy mismo!	*And I'm going to stop eating junk food this very day!*
dejar de + *infinitive*	*to stop (doing something)*
la comida basura	*junk food*
hoy	*today*
mismo	*very, same*
hoy mismo	*this very day*

▶ Variantes

Listen, and repeat the same structures from *Diálogo 5*, now with new vocabulary.

Te acatarras con frecuencia.	***You catch a cold*** *frequently.*
Te resfrías	*You catch a cold*
Te enfermas	*You get sick*
Te sientes mal	*You feel ill*

Debes cuidarte .	*You should* ***take care of yourself***.
relajarte	*relax*
tranquilizarte	*calm down*
calmarte	*calm down*
ponerte en forma	*get into shape*
pasearte	*go for a walk*

Hago ejercicio con frecuencia .	*I exercise* ***frequently***.
con cuidado	*carefully*
con facilidad	*easily*
con dificultad	*with difficulty*

¿Hacen ejercicio frecuentemente ?	*Do they exercise* ***frequently***?
cuidadosamente	*carefully*
fácilmente	*easily*
difícilmente	*with difficulty*

Estructura y Práctica

Reflexive Verbs: Verb + Infinitive Construction

When a reflexive verb appears in its infinitive form in a verb + infinitive construction, the **se** of the infinitive must change to agree with the subject of the sentence. Like other object pronouns, the reflexive pronoun may be placed either before the first verb or after the infinitive, in which case it is attached to it in writing. There is no difference in meaning.

Me debo calmar.	Debo calmar**me**.
Te debes calmar.	Debes calmar**te**.
Se debe calmar.	Debe calmar**se**.
Nos debemos calmar.	Debemos calmar**nos**.
Os debéis calmar.	Debéis calmar**os**.
Se deben calmar.	Deben calmar**se**.

I **Reflexive Verbs: Expansion.** Expand each sentence using the verb + infinitive or verb + connector + infinitive construction. Use the verb that appears in parentheses. Write all sentences, following the word order in the *modelo*.

> MODELO   Se quedan unos días más. (desear)
> → Desean quedarse unos días más.

1. Se dan prisa. (deber)
2. ¿Te despiertas temprano? (ir a)
3. Manolo se prueba el traje. (acabar de)
4. Ud. se alimenta bien. (comenzar a)
5. Nos cuidamos lo más posible. (tratar de)
6. Se divierten mucho en la playa. (querer)
7. Me mantengo en forma. (tener que)
8. ¿Arturo no se pone en forma? (poder)
9. Las chicas se acatarran. (empezar a)
10. Nos relajamos un poco. (necesitar)
11. ¿Te duchas por la mañana? (preferir)
12. Se instalan en el condominio. (lograr)

J **Reflexive Verbs: Expansion.** Expand each sentence using the verb + infinitive or verb + connector + infinitive construction. Use the verb that appears in parentheses. Write all sentences, following the word order in the *modelo*.

> MODELO   No te enfadas. (deber)
> → No te debes enfadar.

1. Me gradúo en junio. (ir a)
2. Se sientan cerca de nosotros. (querer)
3. El niñito se viste solo. (saber)
4. No se meten en todo. (deber)
5. Me reúno con Uds. la semana próxima. (preferir)
6. Nos apresuramos o perdemos el avión. (tener que)
7. Se ríen. (empezar a)
8. ¿Te casas con Federico? (pensar)
9. Nos vemos pronto. (esperar)
10. ¿Catalina se enamora? (volver a)
11. Se acuerda de la fecha. (acabar de)
12. Pablo se coloca en una empresa importante. (lograr)

Adverbs with the Suffix -mente

Most adverbs of manner in Spanish are formed by adding the suffix -**mente** to the feminine singular form of the adjective.

MASCULINE SINGULAR	FEMININE SINGULAR	ADVERB	MEANING
cómodo	cómoda	cómodamente	*comfortably*
cuidadoso	cuidadosa	cuidadosamente	*carefully*
generoso	generosa	generosamente	*generously*
lento	lenta	lentamente	*slowly*
nervioso	nerviosa	nerviosamente	*nervously*

If the adjective has only one form for the masculine and feminine singular, then the suffix -**mente** is added to that form.

SINGULAR	ADVERB	MEANING
fácil	fácilmente	*easily*
inteligente	inteligentemente	*intelligently*
regular	regularmente	*regularly*

Adverbs ending in -**mente** have two stresses in speech, one on the original stressed syllable of the adjective and one on the first **e** of the suffix -**mente**.

inteligent**e**mente	*intelligently*
gener**o**samente	*generously*

If the adjective itself has a written accent mark, the accent mark is retained when the suffix -**mente** is added.

difícilmente	*with difficulty*
rígidamente	*rigidly*

Spanish often uses a phrase consisting of **con** + a noun instead of an adverb ending in -**mente**.

Lo hacen **con cuidado**.	*They do it **carefully**.*
Ella se viste **con elegancia**.	*She dresses **elegantly**.*
Trabajan **con entusiasmo**.	*They work **enthusiastically**.*

Adverbs modify verbs or adjectives. They add the idea of time, place, quantity, doubt, or manner to the sentence. Adverbs of time, place, quantity, doubt, and manner are usually not derived from adjectives in Spanish or in English.

hoy *today*
  No sé si vienen **hoy**.   *I don't know if they're coming **today**.*

aquí *here*
  Todos se reúnen **aquí**.   *Everyone gets together **here**.*

mucho *a lot*
  Ese hombre trabaja **mucho**.   *That man works **a lot**.*

bien *well*

La niña lee **bien**.   *The little girl reads **well**.*

tal vez *perhaps*

Tal vez se arreglan.   ***Perhaps** they're getting ready.*

The masculine singular form of adjectives is often used as an adverb, especially in informal speech.

¿Es mejor jugar **feo** y ganar o jugar   *Is it better to play **dirty** and win or play*
   bonito y perder?   ***fair** and lose?*
No te entienden porque no hablas **claro**.   *They don't understand you, because you*
                                                  *don't speak **clearly**.*

K   *Adverbios.* Write the adverb with the suffix -**mente** that is derived from each of the following adjectives.

1. hermoso	6. alegre	11. cómodo
2. estupendo	7. nervioso	12. fácil
3. inteligente	8. compulsivo	13. atento
4. honrado	9. comercial	14. arrogante
5. regular	10. triste	15. asustado

L   *Adverbios.* Write the masculine singular form of the adjective (the base form) from which each adverb is derived.

1. perfectamente	6. difícilmente	11. normalmente
2. generalmente	7. frecuentemente	12. graciosamente
3. cuidadosamente	8. rotundamente	13. pobremente
4. recientemente	9. pesadamente	14. amablemente
5. últimamente	10. fríamente	15. tranquilamente

M   Write the adverb ending in -**mente** that is equivalent to each of the following phrases with **con** + a noun.

1. con frecuencia	6. con tranquilidad	11. con arrogancia
2. con claridad	7. con atención	12. con felicidad
3. con inteligencia	8. con comodidad	13. con sinceridad
4. con dificultad	9. con tristeza	14. con oscuridad
5. con alegría	10. con amabilidad	15. con ruido

▶ DIÁLOGO 6 · La rutina diaria

Study the dialogue, then listen to the recording and repeat each line.

PALOMA ¿Qué haces al despertarte por la mañana?

CARLOS Me cepillo los dientes, me ducho, me visto y me peino.

PALOMA Yo también, y me limpio los dientes dos veces—al despertarme
        y después de desayunar.

CARLOS ¿Te lavas el pelo todos los días? Yo sí.

Análisis

Check that you understand the linguistic breakdown of each speech from *Diálogo 6*.

¿Qué haces al despertarte por la mañana?	*What do you do when you wake up in the morning?*
al + *infinitive*	*when (doing something), upon (doing something)*
despertarse (**e** > **ie**)	*to wake up*
al despertarte	*when you wake up*
por la mañana	*in the morning*
Me cepillo los dientes, me ducho, me visto y me peino.	*I brush my teeth, I shower, I get dressed, and I comb my hair.*
cepillar	*to brush*
cepillarse los dientes	*to brush one's teeth*
ducharse	*to shower, take a shower*
vestirse (**e** > **i**)	*to get dressed*
peinarse	*to comb one's hair*
Yo también, y me limpio los dientes dos veces—al despertarme y después de desayunar.	*Me, too, and I brush my teeth twice— when I get up and after having breakfast.*
limpiar	*to clean*
limpiarse los dientes	*to brush one's teeth*
la vez	*time (occurrence)*
dos veces	*twice, two times*
después de + *infinitive*	*after (doing something)*
¿Te lavas el pelo todos los días? Yo sí.	*Do you wash your hair every day? I do.*
lavar	*to wash*
lavarse el pelo	*to wash one's hair*

▶ Variantes

Listen, and repeat the same structures from *Diálogo 6*, now with new vocabulary.

¿Qué haces al despertarte?	*What do you do when you wake up?*
Al despertarme, me limpio los dientes.	*When I wake up, I brush my teeth.*
¿Qué hace Elena al levantarse?	*What does Elena do when she gets up?*
Al levantarse, se lava la cara.	*When she gets up, she washes her face.*

¿Qué hacen Uds. al reunirse?	*What do you do when you get together?*
Al reunirnos, nos ponemos a trabajar.	*When we get together, we begin to work.*
¿Qué vas a hacer al graduarte?	*What are you going to do when you graduate?*
Al graduarme, voy a colocarme en una empresa.	*When I graduate, I'm going to get a position in a company.*
¿Te limpias los dientes antes de desayunar?	*Do you brush your teeth before you have breakfast?*
Claro, y después de desayunar también.	*Of course, and after I have breakfast, too.*
Se duchan.	*They take a shower.*
Se bañan.	*They take a bath.*
Se afeitan.	*They shave.*
Se pintan.	*They put on makeup.*
Se pinta la cara .	*She puts on **makeup** (face).*
los labios	*lipstick (lips)*
las uñas	*nail polish (nails)*
Me cepillo los dientes .	*I brush **my teeth**.*
el pelo	*my hair*
Te lavas el pelo.	***You wash** your hair.*
Te cortas	*You cut*
Te secas	*You dry*
Nos lavamos el pelo .	*We're washing **our hair**.*
la cabeza	*our hair*
la cara	*our faces*
las manos	*our hands*
los pies	*our feet*

Estructura y Práctica

N ***Al levantarse por la mañana.*** Write sentences using reflexive verbs to describe what people do when they get up in the morning. Follow the *modelo*.

MODELO   los niños / bañarse
         → Los niños se bañan.

1. tú / cepillarse los dientes

2. Pilar y yo / lavarse la cabeza

3. Roberto / afeitarse

4. Uds. / secarse el pelo

5. Ignacio / ponerse la ropa

6. yo / pasarse el hilo dental (*to floss*)

7. Marisol y Julieta / pintarse los labios

8. Ud. / ducharse

MORE VOCABULARY

El aseo personal (*personal grooming*): **productos de belleza y cuidado personal** (*beauty and personal care products*)

los aceites de baño *bath oils*
el acondicionador (para el pelo) *hair conditioner*
la afeitadora *razor*
el aftershave *aftershave (lotion)*
el agua de colonia *cologne*
el bronceador *suntan lotion*
el cepillo de dientes *toothbrush*
el cepillo para el pelo *hairbrush*
el champú *shampoo*
el cortaúñas *nail clippers*
la crema de afeitar *shaving cream*
la crema hidratante *moisturizing cream*
el depilatorio *depilatory, hair remover*
el desodorante *deodorant*
el enjuague (bucal) *mouthwash* (bucal < boca (*mouth*))
el esmalte de uñas *nail polish*
el hilo dental *dental floss*
la hoja de afeitar *razor blade*
el jabón *soap*
el lápiz para los labios *lipstick*
la lima de uñas *nail file*
la loción para después del afeitado *aftershave (lotion)*
el maquillaje *makeup*
la máquina (maquinilla) de afeitar *electric razor*
la pasta de dientes *toothpaste*
el peine *comb*
el perfume *perfume*
las pinzas *tweezers*
el protector solar *sunscreen*
la rasuradora *razor*
las sales de baño *bath salts*
el secador de pelo/cabello *hair dryer*
el suavizante (para el pelo) *hair conditioner*
el tinte para el cabello *hair coloring*

Al + Infinitive

The **al** + infinitive phrase can replace a clause beginning with **cuando** when the subjects of the two clauses are the same. Note that the **al** + infinitive phrase can occur either after the main clause or at the beginning of the sentence.

Siempre lo veo **cuando salgo**.
Siempre lo veo **al salir**. }   *I always see him when I go out.*

Cuando me levanto, me cepillo los dientes.
Al levantarme, me cepillo los dientes. } *When I get up, I brush my teeth.*

Note that the English construction consisting of *upon* plus the *-ing* form of the verb is the equivalent of the Spanish **al** + infinitive phrase.

Al oír esto, me enfado.   ***Upon hearing this**, I get angry.*

This English construction, however, is typical of formal or literary language. The Spanish **al** + infinitive phrase is used in informal as well as formal language.

O *Al* + **infinitive.** Rewrite each of the following sentences, replacing the clauses that begin with **cuando** with the **al** + infinitive construction. Write each sentence in two ways. Follow the *modelo*.

> MODELO   Cuando hablo con ese tipo, me molesto mucho.
> → Me molesto mucho al hablar con ese tipo.
> → Al hablar con ese tipo, me molesto mucho.

1. Cuando oigo música, me emociono mucho.

2. Cuando Mario sale de la oficina, va a casa.

3. Cuando te acuestas, ¿te duermes en seguida?

4. Cuando Eva sabe qué pasa, se enoja.

5. Cuando Uds. terminan de ducharse, se visten.

6. Cuando te despiertas, te limpias los dientes.

7. Cuando los niños llegan del parque, se bañan.

8. Cuando Ud. se levanta, ¿se lava el pelo?

9. Cuando me reúno con mis amigos, me divierto mucho.

10. Cuando vemos que todo está bien, nos tranquilizamos.

▶ DIÁLOGO 7 · No se llevan bien.

Study the dialogue, then listen to the recording and repeat each line.

PALOMA   Me fijo en que Javier y Pablo no se llevan bien últimamente.
CARLOS   Tú conoces a Javier. Se enoja fácilmente y se ofende por cualquier cosa.
PALOMA   Y Pablo lo enoja y lo ofende.
CARLOS   En efecto. ¡Qué dos!

Análisis

Check that you understand the linguistic breakdown of each speech from *Diálogo 7*.

Me fijo en que Javier y Pablo no se llevan bien últimamente.	*I notice that Javier and Pablo aren't getting along lately.*
fijarse en	*to notice*
bien	*well, right*
llevarse bien	*to get along*
mal	*badly*
llevarse mal	*not to get along*
últimamente	*lately*

Tú conoces a Javier. Se enoja fácilmente y se ofende por cualquier cosa.	*You know Javier. He gets angry easily and takes offense at every little thing.*

    enojar — *to anger*
    enojarse — *to get angry*
    fácilmente — *easily*
    ofender — *to offend, insult*
    ofenderse — *to get offended, get insulted*
    la cosa — *thing*
    cualquier — *any*
    por cualquier cosa — *for any little thing*

Y Pablo lo enoja y lo ofende. — *And Pablo makes him angry and insults him.*
    lo enoja — *angers him*
    lo ofende — *offends him, insults him*

En efecto. ¡Qué dos! — *That's right. What a pair!*

▶ Variantes

Listen, and repeat the same structures from *Diálogo 7*, now with new vocabulary.

¿En qué te fijas? — *What are you noticing?*
Me fijo en que se llevan mal. — *I'm noticing that they don't get along.*

Lo enoja. — *He makes him angry.*
Lo ofende. — *He insults him.*
Lo molesta. — *He annoys him.*
Lo preocupa. — *He worries him.*

Las tranquilizamos. — *We're calming them down.*
Las preocupamos. — *We're worrying them.*
Las animamos. — *We're encouraging them.*
Las asustamos. — *We're frightening them.*

Uds. se quejan de todo. — *You **complain about** everything.*
    se ocupan de — *take care of*
    se interesan en — *are interested in*
    se meten en — *meddle in*

No se reúnen últimamente. — *They don't get together **lately**.*
    recientemente — *recently*
    generalmente — *generally*
    normalmente — *normally*

Estructura y Práctica

Prepositions with Reflexive Verbs

You have learned many reflexive verbs that appear with certain prepositions. It is important to learn the prepositions that are used with specific reflexive verbs.

Nos acercamos **a** la carretera.　　*We're approaching the highway.*
Se olvida **de** unas fechas importantes.　　*He forgets some important dates.*

P **Prepositions.** Write the preposition that correctly completes each of the following sentences.

1. Ya nos despedimos _____ los invitados.
2. ¿Por qué no te fías _____ él?
3. Me pongo _____ trabajar.
4. Nos interesamos _____ la música clásica.
5. Beatriz se casa _____ Esteban.
6. Nadie se atreve _____ hablar del asunto.
7. ¿_____ qué se fijan?
8. Nunca se acuerda _____ los cumpleaños.
9. Marco se compromete _____ Sofía.
10. Siempre te quejas _____ algo.
11. No te enamoras _____ nadie, ¿verdad?
12. Nos alegramos _____ verlos.
13. El perro se aleja _____ la casa.
14. Daniel se ocupa _____ la oficina.

DIÁLOGO 8 · Matricularse o graduarse

Study the dialogue, then listen to the recording and repeat each line.

PALOMA　Tengo que matricularme para el segundo semestre. Tú también, ¿no?
CARLOS　Nada de matrícula para mí. ¡Yo me gradúo en junio!
PALOMA　Felicidades, chico. Así que vas a despedirte de todos nosotros.
CARLOS　¡Qué va! Claro que nos vamos a mantener en contacto.

Análisis

Check that you understand the linguistic breakdown of each speech from *Diálogo 8*.

Tengo que matricularme para el segundo semestre. Tú también, ¿no?	*I have to register for the second semester. You do, too, don't you?*
matricularse	*to register (for classes)*
tengo que matricularme	*I have to register*
el semestre	*semester*
segundo	*second*

Nada de matrícula para mí. ¡Yo me gradúo en junio!	*No registration for me. I'm graduating in June!*
nada de + *noun*	*no* + noun, *none of* + noun
la matrícula	*registration*
graduarse	*to graduate*
yo me gradúo	*I graduate, I'm graduating*

Felicidades, chico. Así que vas a despedirte de todos nosotros.	*Congratulations, buddy. So you're going to say goodbye to all of us.*
felicidades	*congratulations*
chico	*man, buddy, guy* (interjection)
despedirse de uno	*to say goodbye to someone*
vas a despedirte	*you'll say goodbye*
todos nosotros	*all of us*

¡Qué va! Claro que nos vamos a mantener en contacto.	*Not true! Of course we will stay in touch with each other.*
¡Qué va!	*Are you kidding? / Not true! / Of course not!*
claro que + *verb*	*of course* + verb
el contacto	*contact*
mantenerse en contacto	*to keep in touch, stay in touch*

▶ Variantes

Listen, and repeat the same structures from *Diálogo 8*, now with new vocabulary.

Tengo que matricularme .	*I have to **register**.*
inscribirme	*register*
suscribirme	*subscribe*

Es el primer año.	*It's the **first** year.*
segundo	*second*
tercer	*third*
cuarto	*fourth*
quinto	*fifth*
sexto	*sixth*
séptimo	*seventh*
octavo	*eighth*
noveno	*ninth*
décimo	*tenth*

Es la primera semana.		It's the **first** week.	
segunda		second	
tercera		third	
cuarta		fourth	
quinta		fifth	
sexta		sixth	
séptima		seventh	
octava		eighth	
novena		ninth	
décima		tenth	

¿Te gradúas este año?   *Are you graduating this year?*
No, me gradúo el año próximo.   *No, I'm graduating next year.*

¿Te despides de nosotros?   *Are you saying goodbye to us?*
Sí, ya me voy.   *Yes, I'm going away.*

Nos vamos a mantener en contacto .   *We're going to **stay in touch** (with each other).*

   poner en contacto   *get in touch*

Estructura y Práctica

Ordinal Numbers

You learned about ordinal numbers in Chapter 2, where they were presented as a type of adjective that precedes the noun it modifies. Here is a review of the ordinal numbers in Spanish from first to tenth.

primero	*first*	sexto	*sixth*
segundo	*second*	séptimo	*seventh*
tercero	*third*	octavo	*eighth*
cuarto	*fourth*	noveno	*ninth*
quinto	*fifth*	décimo	*tenth*

NOTES

1 · The ordinals **primero** and **tercero** are shortened to **primer** and **tercer**, respectively, before a masculine singular noun.

    el **primer** mensaje   *the **first** message*
    el **tercer** mes   *the **third** month*

2 · The ordinal numbers, except for **primero**, are not used in giving the date. The cardinal numbers (**dos, tres, cuatro, cinco**, etc.) are used instead.

    el **cuatro** de julio   *the **fourth** of July*
    el **once** de enero   *January **eleventh***
    el **veinticinco** de agosto   *August **twenty-fifth***
    el **seis** de junio   *June **sixth***
    el **veintinueve** de marzo   *March **twenty-ninth***

BUT

> el **primero** de febrero   *February **first***

Some speakers say **el uno de febrero**.

3 · After *tenth*, Spanish usually uses the cardinal number in place of the ordinal.

> Ellos viven en el piso **doce**.   *They live on the **twelfth** floor.*

Q **Ordinal numbers.** Replace the cardinal number with the ordinal number in each sentence. Follow the *modelo.*

MODELO   Es la reunión número dos.
         → Es la segunda reunión.

1. Leemos el libro número cinco.
2. Juego en el partido número ocho.
3. Escribo el correo electrónico número seis.
4. Siguen el plan número tres.
5. Es la semana número siete del viaje.
6. Hacen la práctica número dos.
7. Tomas la clase a distancia número nueve.
8. Se reúnen el miércoles número uno del mes.
9. Es la vez número cuatro que los visitamos.
10. Es la conferencia número uno de la serie.
11. Es el año número diez de la empresa.
12. ¿Conoces a su hija número tres?

▶ DIÁLOGO 9 · ¿Cuál es su nombre?

Study the dialogue, then listen to the recording and repeat each line.

PALOMA   Señor, ¿cómo se llama Ud.?
JOSÉ   Me llamo José Arias Herrera.
PALOMA   Y su esposa, ¿cómo se llama?
JOSÉ   Ella se llama Beatriz Paz Arroyo.

Análisis

Check that you understand the linguistic breakdown of each speech from *Diálogo 9.*

Señor, ¿cómo se llama Ud.?   *Sir, what is your name?*
  llamarse   *to be called, be named*
  se llama   *his/her/your name is*

Me llamo José Arias Herrera.   *My name is José Arias Herrera.*
  me llamo   *my name is*

Y su esposa, ¿cómo se llama?   *And what is your wife's name?*

Ella se llama Beatriz Paz Arroyo.   *Her name is Beatriz Paz Arroyo.*

 Variantes

Listen, and repeat the same structures from *Diálogo 9*, now with new vocabulary.

Y sus hijos, ¿cómo se llaman?   *And what are your children's names?*
Mi hijo se llama Miguel Arias Paz y   *My son's name is Miguel Arias Paz and*
  mi hija se llama Maite Arias Paz.   *my daughter's name is Maite Arias Paz.*

Niño, ¿cómo te llamas?   *Little boy, what's your name?*
Me llamo Juanito Fuentes.   *My name is Juanito Fuentes.*

Estructura y Práctica

HISPANIC NAMES

Hispanic naming customs are different from those in the Anglo-Saxon world. Many Spanish speakers have compound first names: **Juan Carlos**, **Ana María**, **José Luis**. **María**, honoring the Virgin Mary, may appear as the second name in compound names for males as well as for females: **José María**. Women having one of these names are usually called by the latter part of the compound: **Carmen** for **María del Carmen**, **Dolores** for **María de los Dolores**.

Hispanic family names (*apellidos*) also have different patterns. In most Spanish-speaking countries, people use their mother's maiden name after their father's family name. Thus, if you meet someone named **Ricardo Solana Cabreras**, you can assume that **Solana** is his father's family name and **Cabreras** his mother's. For someone named **Susana Durán Ribera**, **Durán** would be her father's family name and **Ribera** her mother's maiden name. In most Spanish-speaking countries, women do not change their names when they marry. Sometimes, for more formal social purposes, **Susana Durán Ribera** would use her husband's name and would be called **Susana Durán de Solana**. The children of **Ricardo Solana Cabreras** and **Susana Durán Ribera** would be **Diego Solana Durán** and **Jimena Solana Durán.**

R *¿Cómo se llama Ud.?* Express the following dialogues in Spanish, using the correct forms of **llamarse**.

1. *Ma'am, what is your (Ud.) name?*
   My name is Isabel Ortega Castellanos.

2. *What is his name?*
   His name is Antonio Herrera Calderón.

3. *Little boy, what is your (tú) name?*
   My name is Juan Manuel Echevarría.

4. *What is her name?*
   Her name is Alicia Marqués Goya.

Un paso más

Are you ready to take your Spanish a step further? Here are exercises that will enhance your knowledge of the language and allow you to express yourself freely.

S **More reflexive verbs.** Select a verb from the list below to complete each of the following sentences. Write the form of the verb that correctly completes each one.

aprovecharse (de) *to take advantage of*
burlarse (de) *to make fun of*
callarse *to become quiet*
equivocarse *to be wrong*
hacerse + *profession to become* + profession
mejorarse *to get better*
morirse (**o** > **ue**) *to die*
portarse bien/mal *to behave well/badly*

1. Los estudiantes _____ cuando entra el profesor.

2. Berta _____ al casarse con ese tipo.

3. Hace una semana que Paco está resfriado pero ya _____.

4. Debemos _____ de esta gran oportunidad.

5. Esteban _____ ingeniero.

6. Están muy tristes porque su perro _____.

7. Estos niños nos exasperan. Los tres _____ mal.

8. Es muy feo _____ de la gente.

T **Translation.** Express the following first person narratives in Spanish.

1. **La rutina diaria**

   My name is Gabriela Torres Ribera. Upon waking up, I brush my teeth, take a shower, and wash my hair. After I get dressed, I put on makeup and comb my hair. My husband Fernando showers, shaves, and gets dressed. After having breakfast, I dress the children and Fernando takes them to school. My husband and I leave for the office.

2. **Hago planes**

   My name is Antonio Lapesa Mondragón. I've just graduated from the university and I'm looking for a job. I'm an accountant. I hope to get a position with a large firm. I've also just gotten engaged. My fiancée Pilar, who is a web designer, wants to get married this year, but I think we shouldn't hurry. We have to work a few years in order to be able to buy a house. We don't worry because we love each other, we understand each other, and we always help each other. We know we'll be successful.

3. **Necesito cuidarme**

   My name is Mario Sánchez Vargas. I catch colds frequently. I've been feeling sick for six weeks. The doctor tells me I'm fine but that I should take better care of myself. That's why I'm going to start exercising. I want to get into shape. I'm going to jog and lift weights. I have to stop eating junk food and start to eat well. I know that I should relax more, go to bed earlier, and live more calmly. I'm going to get bored, but I'll feel great!

U *Preguntas personales.* Answer each question with a complete Spanish sentence.

1. ¿Cómo se llama Ud.?

2. ¿Está casado/casada? ¿Cómo se llama su esposo/esposa? (¿Piensa casarse? ¿Con quién?)

3. ¿Cómo se llaman sus amigos y colegas?

4. ¿Uds. se llevan bien? ¿Cuándo se ven (se hablan por teléfono, se escriben)?

5. ¿Ud. se mantiene en contacto con sus amigos de la universidad? ¿Se mandan textos o emails?

6. ¿Cómo es su rutina diaria?

7. ¿Qué productos de belleza y cuidado personal usa para su aseo personal?

8. ¿Qué hace para cuidarse bien y mantener una buena salud física y mental?

9. ¿En qué cosas o actividades se interesa mucho?

10. ¿Qué lo/la emociona (aburre, entusiasma, molesta, asusta, alegra, enoja)?

11. ¿Es Ud. quejumbroso/quejumbrosa (*a complainer*)? ¿De qué se queja? ¿Tiene aversión (*pet peeve*)? ¿A qué cosas?

12. ¿Ud. se matricula en la universidad? ¿En qué universidad? ¿Cuándo se gradúa?

9

Travel, Likes and Dislikes

Communication Goals

- Talking about past events
- Describing airplane, train, and car trips
- Talking about likes and dislikes
- Vocabulary: travel, the airport, traffic, cardinal points and geographical regions

Grammar Topics

- The Preterit Tense: Formation
- Preterit of **-er** and **-ir** Verbs with Stems Ending in a Vowel
- Preterit of Verbs with Stem Changes
- Irregular Preterits
- Preterit of Verbs with Spelling Changes
- The Indirect Object
- Reverse Construction Verbs
- Verbs with a Different Meaning in the Preterit

▶ DIÁLOGO 1 · Un vuelo directo

Study the dialogue, then listen to the recording and repeat each line.

ROBERTO	¿Encontraste un vuelo a Madrid? ¿Pudiste reservar los billetes en línea?
SOFÍA	Sí, encontré un vuelo directo. Hice todos los trámites en línea.
ROBERTO	Menos mal. La última vez que viajamos tuvimos que hacer escala.
SOFÍA	¡Fue un viaje interminable! No nos gustó para nada.

Análisis

Check that you understand the linguistic breakdown of each speech from *Diálogo 1*.

¿Encontraste un vuelo a Madrid?	*Did you find a flight to Madrid?*
¿Pudiste reservar los billetes en línea?	*Could you make the reservations online?*
encontrar (**o** > **ue**)	*to find*
encontraste	*you found*
el vuelo	*flight*
pudiste	*you could*
reservar	*to reserve*
el billete	*ticket*
la línea	*line*
en línea	*online*

Sí, encontré un vuelo directo. Hice todos los trámites en línea.	*Yes, I found a nonstop flight. I did the whole procedure online.*
encontré	*I found*
el vuelo directo	*nonstop flight*
hice	*I did*
el trámite	*step, procedure*

Menos mal. La última vez que viajamos tuvimos que hacer escala.	*That's fortunate. The last time we traveled, we had to make a stopover.*
menos mal	*that's fortunate, fortunately*
la vez	*time (occasion)*
último	*last*
viajamos	*we traveled*
tuvimos	*we had*
tuvimos que	*we had to*
la escala	*stopover*
hacer escala	*to make a stopover*

¡Fue un viaje interminable! No nos gustó para nada.	*It was an endless trip! We didn't like it at all.*
fue	*it was*
el viaje	*trip*
interminable	*endless*
un viaje interminable	*an endless trip*
gustó	*it was appealing*
nos	*to us, for us*
no nos gustó	*we didn't like it*
para nada	*(not) at all*

▶ Variantes

Listen, and repeat the same structures from *Diálogo 1*, now with new vocabulary.

Encontré un vuelo directo.	***I found*** a direct flight.
Tomé	*I took*
Reservé	*I reserved*
Pedí	*I asked for*
Preferí	*I preferred*
Elegí	*I chose*

¿Pudiste reservar los billetes en línea?	*¿Did you manage **to reserve** the tickets online?*
comprar	*to buy*
pagar	*to pay for*

¿Hiciste los trámites en línea?	*Did you make the arrangements online?*
Sí, lo hice todo a través de internet.	*Yes, I did everything online.*

Viajamos a España.	***We traveled to*** Spain.
Regresamos a	*We went back to*
Volvimos a	*We went back to*
Conocimos	*We got to know*
Recorrimos	*We traveled around*

Tuvimos que hacer escala.	*We had to **make a stopover**.*
hacer vuelo de conexión	*make a connecting flight*
cambiar el vuelo	*change the flight*

Hicimos preparativos para el viaje.	*We **got ready for the trip**.*
un viaje	*took a trip*
las maletas	*packed*
escala en Barcelona	*made a stopover in Barcelona*

Fue un viaje interminable.	*It was **a very long trip**.*
un vuelo agotador	*an exhausting flight*
un avión grande	*a big airplane*

No nos gustó.	*We didn't like it.*
No nos importó.	*We didn't care about it. / We didn't mind it.*
No nos interesó.	*We weren't interested in it.*
No nos convino.	*It wasn't good for us.*

¿Te gustó el viaje?	*Did you like the trip?*
Sí, me gustó.	*Yes, I liked it.*

¿Te gustan los vuelos directos?	*Do you like direct flights?*
Sí, me gustan.	*Yes, I like them.*

¿Te gusta viajar?	*Do you like to travel?*
Sí, me gusta viajar.	*Yes, I like to travel.*

¿Les conviene viajar la semana próxima?	*Is it good for you to travel next week?*
No, no nos conviene.	*No, it's not good for us.*

Estructura y Práctica

The Preterit Tense: Formation

The preterit tense in Spanish is used to express completed actions in the past.

The preterit is signaled by sets of endings added to the verb stem. The characteristic feature of the preterit is that its endings are all stressed.

The preterit of **-er** and **-ir** verbs have the same endings. They differ from the preterit endings of the **-ar** verbs in having an **i** rather than an **a** as the characteristic vowel.

Here are the preterit conjugations of regular verbs.

comprar *to buy*		**vender** *to sell*		**escribir** *to write*	
compré	compramos	vendí	vendimos	escribí	escribimos
compraste	comprasteis	vendiste	vendisteis	escribiste	escribisteis
compró	compraron	vendió	vendieron	escribió	escribieron

Note that in the **nosotros** form of **-ar** and **-ir** verbs, the preterit forms are identical with those of the present tense.

PRESENT AND PRETERIT

compramos	*we buy* OR *we bought*
escribimos	*we write* OR *we wrote*

Context clarifies whether the verb form is in the present or preterit tense.

For **-er** verbs, the present and preterit forms are distinct.

PRESENT	PRETERIT
vendemos *we sell*	vendimos *we sold*

A **Preterit of regular verbs.** Write the preterit form of the verb that corresponds with each present tense form given.

1. trabaja
2. esperas
3. comprendemos
4. miro
5. imprimen
6. llevan
7. compra
8. comen
9. viajo
10. debes
11. corres
12. aprendo
13. bebe
14. abrimos
15. vende
16. manejo
17. escribe
18. regresamos
19. vives
20. toman

Preterit of -**er** and -**ir** Verbs with Stems Ending in a Vowel

-**Er** and -**ir** verbs whose stems end in a vowel change the endings -**ió** to -**yó** and -**ieron** to -**yeron**. These verbs also add a written accent to the -**i**- of the endings of the **tú, nosotros,** and **vosotros** forms of the preterit.

caer *to fall*		leer *to read*	
caí	caímos	leí	leímos
caíste	caísteis	leíste	leísteis
cayó	cayeron	leyó	leyeron

construir *to build*		oír *to hear*	
construí	construímos	oí	oímos
construíste	construísteis	oíste	oísteis
construyó	construyeron	oyó	oyeron

Verbs ending in -**guir** do not follow this pattern.

seguir *to follow*	
seguí	seguimos
seguiste	seguisteis
siguió	siguieron

Preterit of Verbs with Stem Changes

In the preterit, there are no stem changes in -**ar** and -**er** verbs, even if they have a stem change in the present. (For more on stem-changing verbs, see Chapter 6.)

pensar *to think*			
PRESENT		PRETERIT	
pienso	pensamos	pensé	pensamos
piensas	pensáis	pensaste	pensasteis
piensa	piensan	pensó	pensaron

volver *to return*			
PRESENT		PRETERIT	
vuelvo	volvemos	volví	volvimos
vuelves	volvéis	volviste	volvisteis
vuelve	vuelven	volvió	volvieron

-**Ir** verbs that have a change in the vowel of the stem in the present have a vowel change in the third person forms of the preterit. Verbs that change **e > ie** or **e > i** in the present have -**i**- in the third person singular and plural of the preterit. The verbs **morir** and **dormir** have -**u**- in the third person singular and plural of the preterit.

sentirse *to feel*

PRESENT		PRETERIT	
me siento	nos sentimos	me sentí	nos sentimos
te sientes	os sentís	te sentiste	os sentisteis
se siente	se sienten	se sintió	se sintieron

pedir *to ask for*

PRESENT		PRETERIT	
pido	pedimos	pedí	pedimos
pides	pedís	pediste	pedisteis
pide	piden	pidió	pidieron

morir *to die*

PRESENT		PRETERIT	
muero	morimos	morí	morimos
mueres	morís	moriste	moristeis
muere	mueren	murió	murieron

dormir *to sleep*

PRESENT		PRETERIT	
duermo	dormimos	dormí	dormimos
duermes	dormís	dormiste	dormisteis
duerme	duermen	durmió	durmieron

Irregular Preterits

A number of common verbs in Spanish have irregular preterit forms. Almost all of these verbs have the following characteristics.

1 · The preterit is formed from an irregular stem.

2 · The endings are those of -**er** and -**ir** verbs except in the first and third person singular forms: the **yo** and **él/ella/Ud.** forms.

3 · The **yo** and **él/ella/Ud.** forms are stressed on the stem, not on the endings.

4 · The ending for the **yo** form is -**e** and the ending for the **él/ella/Ud.** form is -**o**.

5 · In most cases, the irregular stem has the vowel -**i**- or -**u**-.

venir *to come*

vine	vinimos
viniste	vinisteis
vino	vinieron

tener *to have*

tuve	tuvimos
tuviste	tuvisteis
tuvo	tuvieron

hacer *to do, make*

hice	hicimos
hiciste	hicisteis
hizo	hicieron

poder *to be able, can*		**poner** *to put*		**andar** *to walk*	
pude	pudimos	puse	pusimos	anduve	anduvimos
pudiste	pudisteis	pusiste	pusisteis	anduviste	anduvisteis
pudo	pudieron	puso	pusieron	anduvo	anduvieron

querer *to want, love*		**caber** *to fit*		**saber** *to know*	
quise	quisimos	cupe	cupimos	supe	supimos
quisiste	quisisteis	cupiste	cupisteis	supiste	supisteis
quiso	quisieron	cupo	cupieron	supo	supieron

The verbs **decir**, **traer**, and verbs ending in **-ducir** have preterit stems ending in **-j-**. In the **ellos/ellas/Uds.** form of these verbs, the ending is **-eron**, not **-ieron**.

decir *to say, tell*		**traer** *to bring*		**conducir** *to drive*	
dije	dijimos	traje	trajimos	conduje	condujimos
dijiste	dijisteis	trajiste	trajisteis	condujiste	condujisteis
dijo	dijeron	trajo	trajeron	condujo	condujeron

NOTES

1 · In the third person singular form of **hacer** in the preterit, the stem is spelled **hiz-** (**hizo**). The spelling change **c > z** before **o** retains the pronunciation /s/.

2 · Compound forms of the verbs **hacer** (**rehacer**, etc.), **poner** (**proponer**, etc.), **tener** (**mantener**, etc.), **traer** (**atraer**, etc.), **venir** (**convenir**, etc.) are conjugated in the same way as the main verb.

3 · The preterit of **hay** is **hubo**.

The verb **dar** is conjugated like an **-er/-ir** verb in the preterit. The preterit forms of **dar** and **ver** have no written accent marks.

dar *to give*		**ver** *to see*	
di	dimos	vi	vimos
diste	disteis	viste	visteis
dio	dieron	vio	vieron

The verbs **ser** (*to be*) and **ir** (*to go*) have identical conjugations in the preterit. Context usually clarifies which verb is intended.

ser *to be* / **ir** *to go*	
fui	fuimos
fuiste	fuisteis
fue	fueron

Preterit of Verbs with Spelling Changes

-**Ar** verbs whose stem ends in **c**, **g**, or **z** change those letters to **qu**, **gu**, and **c**, respectively, in the **yo** form of the preterit. These forms are regular in speech; the written changes in the **yo** form are in accordance with the rules of Spanish spelling. The following list includes verbs that you have learned through Chapter 9.

INFINITIVE	**yo** FORM OF THE PRETERIT
buscar	bus**qué**
colocar	colo**qué**
explicar	expli**qué**
sacar	sa**qué**
tocar	to**qué**
apagar	apa**gué**
entregar	entre**gué**
jugar	ju**gué**
llegar	lle**gué**
madrugar	madru**gué**
navegar	nave**gué**
pagar	pa**gué**
actualizar	actuali**cé**
almorzar	almor**cé**
analizar	anali**cé**
comenzar	comen**cé**
empezar	empe**cé**
organizar	organi**cé**
tranquilizar	tranquili**cé**

B   *Viajes.* Rewrite each sentence, changing the verb from the present tense to the preterit. Follow the *modelo*.

MODELO   Regresan a los Estados Unidos.
          → Regresaron a los Estados Unidos.

1. Subes al avión.
2. Prefiere un vuelo directo.
3. Viajamos a Ciudad de Panamá.
4. Voy al aeropuerto en taxi.
5. Hacen escala en Miami.
6. Saco mi tarjeta de embarque.
7. Facturan el equipaje.
8. Vuelve de Panamá el domingo.
9. Pago los billetes en línea.
10. ¿No puedes encontrar tu maleta?
11. Se abrochan el cinturón de seguridad.
12. Pierde el vuelo.
13. Llego a la terminal A.
14. ¡Es un viaje maravilloso!

⏵ DIÁLOGO 2 · En el aeropuerto

Study the dialogue, then listen to the recording and repeat each line.

SOFÍA ¿Te salió bien en el aeropuerto? ¿Nada de líos?

ROBERTO Pan comido. Llegué temprano, facturé mi equipaje y saqué mi tarjeta de embarque.

SOFÍA ¿Luego seguiste a la puerta de embarque?

ROBERTO Primero fui a comer algo y compré unas revistas.

Análisis

Check that you understand the linguistic breakdown of each speech from *Diálogo 2.*

¿Te salió bien en el aeropuerto? ¿Nada de líos?	*Did everything go all right for you at the airport? No problems?*
te	*to you*
le	*to him, to her, to you*
salirle bien/mal a uno	*to turn out well/badly for someone*
el aeropuerto	*airport*
nada de + *noun*	*no* + noun
el lío	*problem, complication, bit of trouble*
Pan comido. Llegué temprano, facturé mi equipaje y saqué mi tarjeta de embarque.	*Piece of cake. I got there early, checked my luggage, and got my boarding pass.*
pan comido	*easy as pie, piece of cake*
llegué	*I arrived*
facturar	*to check (baggage)*
facturé	*I checked*
el equipaje	*luggage*
sacar	*to take out, get*
saqué	*I got*
la tarjeta	*card*
el embarque	*boarding*
la tarjeta de embarque	*boarding pass*
¿Luego seguiste a la puerta de embarque?	*Then you went on to the boarding gate?*
luego	*then, after that*
seguir (**e** > **i**)	*to follow, continue on to*
seguiste	*you continued on to*
la puerta	*gate*
la puerta de embarque	*boarding gate*
Primero fui a comer algo y compré unas revistas.	*First I went to eat something, and I bought some magazines.*
primero	*first*
fui	*I went*
algo	*something*
compré	*I bought*
la revista	*magazine*

▶ Variantes

Listen, and repeat the same structures from *Diálogo 2*, now with new vocabulary.

¿Te salió bien en el aeropuerto?	*Did it go smoothly for you at the airport?*
Sí, me salió muy bien.	*Yes, very smoothly (for me).*
¿Les salió bien en el aeropuerto?	*Did it go smoothly for you at the airport?*
Sí, nos salió muy bien.	*Yes, very smoothly (for us).*
¿Le salió bien en el aeropuerto?	*Did it go smoothly for him at the airport?*
Sí, le salió muy bien.	*Yes, very smoothly (for him).*
¿Le salió bien en el aeropuerto?	*Did it go smoothly for her at the airport?*
Sí, le salió muy bien.	*Yes, very smoothly (for her).*

Llegué temprano.
  Fui
  Salí
  Vine

I arrived early.
  I went
  I left
  I came

Coloqué mi equipaje.
  Busqué
  Saqué
  Toqué

I placed my luggage.
  I looked for
  I took out
  I touched

Fui a comer algo.
  tomar
  beber
  comprar
  buscar

I went to eat something.
  have
  drink
  buy
  look for

Compré unas revistas.
  Leí
  Vi

I bought some magazines.
  I read
  I saw

Llegamos anoche.
  ayer
  anteayer
  la semana pasada
  el mes pasado
  el año pasado
  hace una semana
  hace un mes
  hace un año
  hace varios días

We arrived last night.
  yesterday
  the day before yesterday
  last week
  last month
  last year
  a week ago
  a month ago
  a year ago
  several days ago

Estructura y Práctica

The Indirect Object

The indirect object labels the secondary goal of the action of the verb. The primary goal is the direct object. The direct object is connected directly to the verb without the aid of a preposition. In Spanish, the indirect object is connected to the verb by the preposition **a** (usually *to* or *for* in English). Indirect objects almost always refer to people. (For more on direct object pronouns, see Chapter 7.)

For example, in the sentence *Michael sends an email*, the first goal of the action is *an email*. It is the direct object of the verb. A second goal can be added: *Michael sends an email to Emily.* In this sentence, *Emily* is the indirect object (the secondary goal of the action), joined to the verb *sends* by the preposition *to*. In English, the indirect object can also be placed before the direct object, and when this word order is used, the preposition *to* is omitted: *Michael sends Emily an email.*

Indirect Object Pronouns

Here are the indirect object pronouns in Spanish.

	SINGULAR	PLURAL
FIRST PERSON	me	nos
SECOND PERSON	te	os
THIRD PERSON	le	les

Note that the indirect object pronouns for first and second persons are the same as the corresponding direct object pronouns.

Position of Indirect Object Pronouns

Both direct object pronouns and indirect object pronouns follow the same rules for placement in the sentence.

Indirect object pronouns precede the conjugated verb.

Ella **me** trajo un lindo regalo.	*She brought **me** a lovely gift.*
Le escribí una vez por semana.	*I wrote to **him** once a week.*
No **les** mandamos nada.	*We didn't send **them** anything.*

In verb + infinitive constructions, the indirect object pronoun may precede the first verb or follow the infinitive. When it follows the infinitive, it is attached to it in writing. There is no difference in meaning.

Te quiero **mostrar** mi carro nuevo. ⎫
Quiero **mostrarte** mi carro nuevo. ⎬ *I want to **show you** my new car.*

Les va a **decir** la verdad. ⎫
Va a **decirles** la verdad. ⎬ *He's going to **tell them** the truth.*

Use of Indirect Object Pronouns with Indirect Object Nouns

In Spanish, an indirect object noun is usually accompanied by the corresponding indirect object pronoun.

Jaime **le** envió el texto **a Inés**.	*Jaime sent the text **to Inés**.*

Here are some additional examples.

Le contamos **a Magdalena** lo que pasó.	*We told **Magdalena** what happened.*
Les expliqué el problema **a mis colegas**.	*I explained the problem **to my colleagues**.*
Le voy a pedir un aumento de sueldo **al gerente**.	*I'm going to ask **the manager** for a raise.*

C **Indirect object pronouns.** Rewrite each of the following sentences, changing the indirect object pronoun based on the cue in parentheses. Follow the *modelo*.

> MODELO   Le escribió un texto. (a ellos)
> → Les escribió un texto.

1. Le mandó un email. (a mí)

2. Te expliqué mi idea. (a ella)

3. Me recordaron la fecha. (a nosotros)

4. Le entregó los documentos. (a Uds.)

5. Nos vendiste tu carro. (a él)

6. Les devolvimos el dinero. (a ti)

7. Le contó la historia. (a Ud.)

8. Me enseñaron la casa. (a ellas)

D **Indirect object pronouns.** Write sentences that have a verb in the preterit and an indirect object pronoun, using the elements given. Use the cue in parentheses to determine the indirect object pronoun. Follow the *modelo*.

> MODELO   ella / preguntar / la dirección (a ellos)
> → Ella les preguntó la dirección.

1. ellos / pedir / un favor (a nosotros)

2. tú / leer / un libro (a él)

3. yo / traer / el periódico (a Uds.)

4. nosotros / decir / lo que pasó (a ti)

5. Ud. / explicar / el plan (a ella)

6. él / regalar / unas flores (a mí)

7. ellas / hacer / una comida muy rica (a Ud.)

8. Uds. / dar / un regalo (a ellas)

E **Indirect object pronouns.** Write sentences that have a verb in the preterit, an indirect object (noun), and its corresponding indirect object pronoun, using the elements given. Follow the *modelo*.

> MODELO   él / enviar / un regalo / a sus papás
> → Él les envió un regalo a sus papás.

1. tú / entregar / el informe / al director

2. Manolo / mostrar / su nuevo apartamento / a sus amigos

3. yo / hacer / unas preguntas / al asesor

4. ellos / pedir / la cuenta / a la mesera

5. Daniela / servir / unas tapas / a los invitados

6. Uds. / dar / el software / al programador

7. ella / decir / la verdad / a su abogada

8. tú / escribir / un email / a tus abuelos

9. nosotros / vender / el coche / a nuestra vecina

10. los profesores / explicar / los problemas / a sus estudiantes

Reverse Construction Verbs

Reverse construction verbs usually appear with an indirect object pronoun. They are called reverse construction verbs because the English subject in equivalent sentences corresponds to the Spanish indirect object, and the English direct object corresponds to the subject of the corresponding Spanish sentence.

For instance, the verb **gustar** is the equivalent of English *to like*, but the structure of sentences containing **gustar** is very different from those containing *to like* in English.

In the following English sentence, the subject of the sentence is *I*: *I like this computer.* The noun phrase *this computer* is the direct object of the verb *like*. The Spanish equivalent of this sentence is **Me gusta esta computadora.** In the Spanish sentence, **me** is the indirect object of the verb **gustar**. The subject of the sentence is **la computadora**, and therefore the verb must be in the third person singular to agree with the subject.

Note that the verb changes to the third person plural when the subject is plural.

Me gustan estas computadoras.　　　　　*I like these computers.*

Reverse construction verbs are usually in third person singular or plural; they appear only rarely in first or second person.

When the subject of a reverse construction verb is an infinitive, the verb is in the third person singular.

Me gusta ver las noticias antes de acostarme.　　　*I like to watch the news before going to bed.*

¿Te interesa trabajar en Chile?　　　*Are you interested in working in Chile?*

Note that subject nouns used with **gustar** are usually preceded by the definite article or some other determiner. This can create ambiguity in the meaning of the sentence, as illustrated in the first example below.

Le gusta **el** helado.　　　⎰ *He likes ice cream. (general statement)*
　　　　　　　　　　　　　⎱ *He likes the ice cream. (what he's eating now)*

Nos gustan **los** documentales.　　　*We like documentaries.*

Here are some common reverse construction verbs. The phrase **a uno** represents the indirect object.

caerle bien/mal a uno *to like/dislike (usually a person)*
convenirle a uno *to be suitable for someone*
encantarle a uno *to love something*
entusiasmarle a uno *to be/get excited about something*
faltarle a uno *to be short of something, not have something*
fascinarle a uno *to charm/captivate someone, to love something*
hacerle falta a uno *to need something*
importarle a uno *to matter to someone*
interesarle a uno *to be interested in something*
quedarle a uno *to have something left*
sobrarle a uno *to have more than enough of something*
tocarle a uno *to be someone's turn*

Les cae bien su profesor.	*They like their professor.*
Creo que **te conviene** esta universidad.	*I think this university is good for you.*
Me encanta el café colombiano.	*I love Colombian coffee.*
Nos entusiasmó mucho el partido.	*We got very excited about the game.*
Le falta paciencia.	*He has no patience.*
Nos fascina el teatro.	*We're captivated by the theater.*
Me hace falta tu apoyo.	*I need your support.*
¿No te importa el medio ambiente?	*Don't you care about the environment?*
Me interesan los altibajos de la economía.	*I'm interested in the fluctuations of the economy.*
¿Cuánto dinero **les queda**?	*How much money do you have left?*
Me sobra trabajo.	*I have more than enough work.*
A ti te toca ahora.	*It's your turn now.*

To focus on the person involved in sentences with reverse construction verbs, a phrase consisting of the preposition **a** + prepositional pronoun is used.

A mí me importa el futuro, pero **a él**, nada.	*I care about the future, but he doesn't at all.*

Some reverse construction verbs can be used in other constructions with a difference in meaning.

REVERSE CONSTRUCTION	**A ella le falta** paciencia.	*She lacks patience.*
REGULAR CONSTRUCTION	**Ella falta** mucho a clase.	*She is often absent from class.*
REVERSE CONSTRUCTION	**Me quedó** poco dinero.	*I had little money left.*
REGULAR CONSTRUCTION	**Quedé** en verlo mañana.	*I agreed to see him tomorrow.*
REVERSE CONSTRUCTION	**Les toca** jugar ahora.	*It's their turn to play now.*
REGULAR CONSTRUCTION	**Ellos tocan** la guitarra.	*They play the guitar.*

F **Reverse construction verbs.** Rewrite each sentence, changing the subject from singular to plural. Make all necessary changes. Follow the *modelo*.

MODELO   Le gusta la cámara.
→ Le gustan las cámaras.

1. Me interesa tu idea.
2. Les encanta esta novela.
3. Le falta una reservación.
4. Nos entusiasma el partido de béisbol.
5. Me gusta este concierto.

6. ¿Te cae bien el gerente?
7. Le queda un proyecto.
8. Nos hace falta otra computadora.
9. Les fascina aquella tienda de ropa.
10. ¿No te importa su problema?

G **Reverse construction verbs.** Rewrite each sentence, changing the verb from present to preterit. Follow the *modelo*.

MODELO   Les sobra trabajo.
→ Les sobró trabajo.

1. Nos interesa esa película.
2. Le gustan los programas.
3. ¿Te cae mal este tipo?
4. Les hace falta más dinero.

5. Me encanta la obra de teatro.
6. Nos falta tiempo para terminar el proyecto.
7. Le queda el examen de química.
8. Les entusiasman las conferencias.

H **Translation.** Express each of the following sentences in Spanish, using a reverse construction verb in the preterit.

1. *I liked it.*
2. *She didn't care about them.*
3. *They loved it.*
4. *Did you (tú) need them?*
5. *It was good for them.*
6. *We were very interested in it.*

7. *You (Uds.) had more of them than you needed.*
8. *I was excited to see them.*
9. *They disliked him.*
10. *Was he interested in working in Europe?*
11. *We loved driving through the desert.*
12. *Did you (tú) mind going through security?*

I **Expansion of reverse construction verbs.** Expand each sentence by adding the **ir a** + infinitive construction to the reverse construction verb. Follow the *modelo*.

MODELO   Le gusta la excursión.
→ Le va a gustar la excursión.

1. Nos interesan esos libros.
2. Le hace falta un mapa.
3. Les sobra comida.
4. Te caen bien nuestros amigos.

5. Me encanta viajar en tren.
6. No les importa llegar tarde.
7. Te conviene conocer al director de mercadeo.
8. Le toca jugar pronto.

▶ DIÁLOGO 3 · A bordo del avión

Study the dialogue, then listen to the recording and repeat each line.

ROBERTO   Luego subí al avión y el auxiliar de vuelo me ayudó a colocar mi
            equipaje de mano arriba.

SOFÍA   Entonces te acomodaste en tu asiento. ¿Un asiento de ventana?

ROBERTO   No, un asiento de pasillo. Me abroché el cinturón de seguridad.
            A los quince minutos el avión despegó.

Análisis

Check that you understand the linguistic breakdown of each speech from *Diálogo 3*.

Luego subí al avión y el auxiliar de vuelo me ayudó a colocar mi equipaje de mano arriba.	*Then I got on the plane and the flight attendant helped me put my carry-on overhead.*
subir	*to go up, get on*
subí	*I got on*
subir al avión	*to get on the plane*
el auxiliar de vuelo	*flight attendant*
ayudar	*to help*
ayudó	*he/she helped*
colocar	*to place, put*
la mano	*hand*
el equipaje de mano	*hand luggage, carry-on (bag)*
arriba	*above, upstairs, overhead*
Entonces te acomodaste en tu asiento. ¿Un asiento de ventana?	*Then you settled into your seat. A window seat?*
acomodarse	*to get comfortable in, settle in(to)*
te acomodaste	*you settled into*
el asiento	*seat*
la ventana	*window*
el asiento de ventana	*window seat*
No, un asiento de pasillo. Me abroché el cinturón de seguridad. A los quince minutos el avión despegó.	*No, an aisle seat. I buckled my seatbelt. Fifteen minutes later, the plane took off.*
el pasillo	*aisle*
el asiento de pasillo	*aisle seat*
abrocharse el cinturón	*to buckle one's (seat)belt, fasten one's (seat)belt*
me abroché	*I buckled, I fastened*
me abroché el cinturón de seguridad	*I buckled my seatbelt, I fastened my seatbelt*
a los quince minutos	*fifteen minutes from then, fifteen minutes later*
despegar	*to take off*
despegó	*it took off*

Variantes

Listen, and repeat the same structures from *Diálogo 3*, now with new vocabulary.

¿Dónde colocó su equipaje de mano?	*Where did you put your carry-on bag?*
Lo coloqué arriba.	*I placed it above.*

Se acomodó en el asiento .	*She settled into **the seat**.*
el sofá	* the couch*
el sillón	* the armchair*
su cama	* her bed*
los brazos de su mamá	* her mother's arms*

Se abrochó el cinturón de seguridad.	*He fastened his seatbelt.*
Se desabrochó el cinturón de seguridad.	*He unfastened his seatbelt.*
El avión despegó.	*The plane took off.*
Dos horas después, el avión aterrizó.	*Two hours later, the plane landed.*
Me falta mi equipaje de mano.	*I'm missing my carry-on bag.*
Le faltan sus maletas.	*She's missing her suitcases.*
Me cayó bien el auxiliar de vuelo.	*I liked the flight attendant.*
Y yo le caí bien a él.	*And he liked me.*
A los auxiliares de vuelo les caen bien los pasajeros.	*The flight attendants like the passengers.*

DIÁLOGO 4 · El vuelo

Study the dialogue, then listen to the recording and repeat each line.

SOFÍA   ¿Qué tal el vuelo? ¿Agradable? Yo sé que despegó con un poco de retraso.

ROBERTO   Ah sí, pero una vez en el aire, todo bien.

SOFÍA   ¿Qué hiciste? ¿Te dormiste?

ROBERTO   No, pedí un vino, me puse los auriculares para oír música y leí unas revistas.

Análisis

Check that you understand the linguistic breakdown of each speech from *Diálogo 4*.

¿Qué tal el vuelo? ¿Agradable? Yo sé que despegó con un poco de retraso.	*How was the flight? Pleasant? I know that it took off a little late.*
el vuelo	* flight*
agradable	* pleasant*
un poco de	* a little, some*
el retraso	* delay*
un poco de retraso	* a little delay*

Ah sí, pero una vez en el aire, todo bien.	*Oh, yes, but once we were in the air, everything was fine.*
una vez	* once*
en el aire	* in the air, airborne*
todo bien	* everything is/was fine*

¿Qué hiciste? ¿Te dormiste?	What did you do? Did you fall asleep?
hiciste	you did
dormir (**o** > **ue**)	to sleep
dormirse (**o** > **ue**)	to fall asleep
te dormiste	you fell asleep

No, pedí un vino, me puse los auriculares para oír música y leí unas revistas.	No, I ordered a glass of wine, put on the earphones to listen to music, and read some magazines.
pedir (**e** > **i**)	to order, ask for
pedí	I ordered
puse	I put
me puse	I put on
los auriculares	earphones
leí	I read

▶ Variantes

Listen, and repeat the same structures from *Diálogo 4*, now with new vocabulary.

Una vez en el aire , todo bien.	Once we were **in the air**, everything was fine.
en la tierra	on the ground (*landed*)
a bordo	on board
en la puerta de embarque	at the gate

¿Qué hiciste?	What did you do?
No hice nada.	I didn't do anything.

¿Qué dijiste?	What did you say?
No dije nada.	I didn't say anything.

¿Qué trajiste?	What did you bring?
No traje nada.	I didn't bring anything.

¿Qué viste?	What did you see?
No vi nada.	I didn't see anything.

¿Qué tuviste?	What did you get?
No tuve nada.	I didn't get anything.

¿Uds. se durmieron?	Did you fall asleep?
No, no nos dormimos.	No, we didn't fall asleep.

¿Se dieron prisa?	Did you rush?
No, no nos dimos prisa.	No, we didn't rush.

¿Se pusieron de pie?	Did you stand up?
No, no nos pusimos de pie.	No, we didn't stand up.

¿Se sintieron mareados?	Did you feel dizzy?
No, no nos sentimos mareados.	No, we didn't feel dizzy.

¿Se fueron?	Did you go away?
No, no nos fuimos.	No, we didn't go away.

¿Se perdieron?	*Did you get lost?*
No, no nos perdimos.	*No, we didn't get lost.*

Le pidió un vino.	**He asked her for** *a glass of wine.*
Le sirvió	*He served her*
Le dio	*He gave her*
Le trajo	*He brought her*
Le ofreció	*He offered her*

Me puse los auriculares.	**I put on** *the headphones.*
Me quité	*I took off*

¿Ud. leyó la revista?	*Did you read the magazine?*
Sí, la leí.	*Yes, I read it.*

¿Ud. oyó la música?	*Did you listen to the music?*
Sí, la oí.	*Yes, I listened to it.*

¿Ud. siguió el camino?	*Did you follow the path?*
No, no lo seguí.	*No, I didn't follow it.*

Estructura y Práctica

J *El pretérito.* Review the preterit of **-er** and **-ir** verbs with stems ending in a vowel, verbs with stem changes, and irregular preterits. Write the preterit form of the verb that corresponds with each present tense form given.

1. cree
2. construyo
3. leen
4. distribuimos
5. cuenta
6. vuelven
7. quiero
8. entendemos
9. comenzamos
10. llueve
11. piensas
12. digo
13. pueden
14. sé
15. traemos
16. viene
17. sigues
18. duermen
19. estoy
20. da
21. pongo
22. vamos
23. haces
24. son
25. pide
26. hay
27. conduzco
28. tienen
29. ves
30. prefiere

K *Ya pasó.* Write answers to each of the following questions, using a verb in the preterit to explain that the things being asked about already happened. For questions that include a direct object noun, change the noun to a pronoun in your answer. Follow the *modelo.*

MODELO   ¿Miguel va a comer las enchiladas?
→ Ya las comió.

1. ¿Julia va a ver a sus primos?

2. ¿Ud. y sus colegas van a reunirse el miércoles?

3. ¿Ellos van a pedir el vino?

4. ¿Vas a matricularte para el segundo semestre?

5. ¿Ana va a casarse con su prometido?

6. ¿Uds. van a traer los documentos?

7. ¿Ud. va a comenzar el proyecto este mes?

8. ¿Ellos van a construir la casa?

9. ¿Vas a hacer los trámites para el viaje?

10. ¿Esteban va a ponerse en contacto contigo?

11. ¿Los empleados van a seguir las instrucciones?

12. ¿Ud. va a almorzar ahora?

13. ¿Uds. van a ir al museo de arte?

14. ¿Vas a buscar al gato?

15. ¿Marcos va a recoger el equipaje?

L *Una narrativa.* Write the correct preterit form of each of the following verbs in parentheses to learn about Daniel Arriaga's day.

La alarma de Daniel no (1) _____ (sonar) esta mañana. Él (2) _____

(asustarse) al ver la hora. Él (3) _____ (levantarse), (4) _____ (afeitarse),

(5) _____ (ducharse) y (6) _____ (vestirse). (7) _____

(Darse) prisa por llegar a la estación de tren. (8) _____ (Llegar) a la oficina justo

a tiempo (*just in time*). (9) _____ (Correr) a la sala de conferencias donde

(10) _____ (tener) una reunión con su equipo de asesores.

▶ DIÁLOGO 5 · Recuerdos: Viaje de vuelta a Estados Unidos

Study the dialogue, then listen to the recording and repeat each line.

ROBERTO ¿Te acuerdas del aterrizaje? Tomamos tierra en el aeropuerto de Filadelfia pero no nos dejaron bajar del avión por una hora.

SOFÍA Ah sí, fue horrendo. Por fin pudimos bajar y fuimos a recoger nuestro equipaje.

ROBERTO Luego pasamos por la aduana donde mostramos el pasaporte. Cogimos un taxi para irnos a casa.

SOFÍA ¡Qué jetlag tuvimos al día siguiente! ¡Y qué lindos recuerdos de nuestro viaje!

Análisis

Check that you understand the linguistic breakdown of each speech from *Diálogo 5*.

¿Te acuerdas del aterrizaje? Tomamos tierra en el aeropuerto de Filadelfia pero no nos dejaron bajar del avión por una hora.	*Do you remember the landing? We landed at the Philadelphia airport, but they didn't let us get off the plane for an hour.*
acordarse de (**o** > **ue**)	*to remember*
el aterrizaje	*landing*
tomar tierra	*to land, touch down*
el aeropuerto	*airport*
dejar	*to leave, let*
dejar a uno hacer algo	*to let someone do something*
dejaron	*they let*
no nos dejaron bajar	*they didn't let us get off*
bajar de	*to get off (a conveyance)*
bajar del avión	*to get off the plane*
por + *time expression*	*for/during* + a period of time
por una hora	*for an hour*
Ah sí, fue horrendo. Por fin pudimos bajar y fuimos a recoger nuestro equipaje.	*Oh, yes, it was horrible. We finally were able to get off and get our luggage.*
fue	*it was*
horrendo	*horrible, awful*
por fin	*finally*
pudimos	*we were able to*
fuimos	*we went*
recoger	*to pick up, get* (not used in all countries)
el equipaje	*luggage*
fuimos a recoger nuestro equipaje	*we went to get our luggage*

Luego pasamos por la aduana donde mostramos el pasaporte. Cogimos un taxi para irnos a casa.	*Then we went through customs, where we showed our passports. We took a cab to go home.*
luego	*then*
pasar por	*to go through*
pasamos	*we went through*
la aduana	*customs*
mostrar (**o** > **ue**)	*to show*
mostramos	*we showed*
el pasaporte	*passport*
coger	*to take, grab* (not used in all countries)
cogimos	*we took*
el taxi	*taxi*
para	*in order to*
irse	*to leave*
irse a	*to leave for, go to*
irse a casa	*to go home, leave for home, depart for home*

¡Qué jetlag tuvimos al día siguiente! ¡Y qué lindos recuerdos de nuestro viaje!	*What jet lag we had the next day! And what lovely memories of our trip!*
el jetlag	*jet lag*
tuvimos	*we had*
siguiente	*following*
al día siguiente	*the next day*
lindo	*pretty, lovely*
el recuerdo	*memory, remembrance*

▶ Variantes

Listen, and repeat the same structures from *Diálogo 5*, now with new vocabulary.

| ¿Te acuerdas del aterrizaje ? | *Do you remember **the landing**?* |
| del despegue | *the takeoff* |

| No nos dejaron bajar del avión . | *We weren't allowed **to get off the plane**.* |
| subir al avión | *to get on the plane* |

Por fin pudimos bajar .	*Finally we could **get off**.*
subir	*get on*
sentarnos	*sit down*
ponernos de pie	*stand up*
prender el celular	*turn our cell phones on*
apagar el celular	*shut off our cell phones*

Pasamos por la aduana .	*We went/passed through **customs**.*
el control de seguridad	*security*
la terminal	*the terminal*

| Le mostramos los pasaportes al aduanero. | *We showed our passports to the customs inspector.* |

Les mostramos los pasaportes a los aduaneros.	*We showed our passports to the customs inspectors.*
Le entregué mi billete.	*I handed him my ticket.*
Él me entregó la tarjeta de embarque.	*He handed me my boarding pass.*

Estructura y Práctica

M *Una narrativa.* Write the correct preterit form of each of the following verbs in parentheses to learn about Isabel Rubio's trip.

El año pasado yo (1) _____ (hacer) un viaje a Europa con mi esposo y mis dos

hijos. Primero nosotros (2) _____ (viajar) a Inglaterra donde (3) _____

(pasar) una semana en Londres. Después (4) _____ (tomar) el tren del Eurotúnel

(del Canal de la Mancha) a Francia y (5) _____ (quedarse) cinco días en París.

Por fin nosotros (6) _____ (llegar) a España donde (7) _____ (tener)

que quedarnos tres semanas porque tenemos mucha familia en Madrid. Claro que no

(8) _____ (poder) irnos sin verlos a todos. (9) ¡_____ (Ser) un viaje

maravilloso!

⊳ DIÁLOGO 6 · Nuestro viaje al sudoeste

Study the dialogue, then listen to the recording and repeat each line.

SOFÍA	Hace dos años Juan, Pedro y yo alquilamos una furgoneta para recorrer el suroeste de Estados Unidos.
ROBERTO	Pedro me dijo que hicieron un viaje maravilloso. Se divirtieron mucho, ¿no?
SOFÍA	Como nunca. Vimos desiertos, montañas y cactos. ¡Qué paisajes más impresionantes!
ROBERTO	Creo que el suroeste te interesó mucho.

Análisis

Check that you understand the linguistic breakdown of each speech from *Diálogo 6*.

Hace dos años Juan, Pedro y yo alquilamos una furgoneta para recorrer el suroeste de Estados Unidos.	*Two years ago, Juan, Pedro, and I rented a station wagon to travel through the southwest United States.*
hace + *time expression* + *verb in preterit*	*ago*
hace dos años	*two years ago*
alquilar	*to rent*
alquilamos	*we rented*
la furgoneta	*station wagon*
recorrer	*to travel through*
el suroeste	*the southwest*

Pedro me dijo que hicieron un viaje maravilloso. Se divirtieron mucho, ¿no?	*Pedro told me that you had a wonderful trip. You had a very good time, didn't you?*
me	*to me, for me*
dijo	*he said, he told*
me dijo	*he told me*
que	*that* (subordinating conjunction)
me dijo que...	*he told me that . . .*
hicieron	*you made, you did*
hacer un viaje	*to take a trip*
hicieron un viaje	*you took a trip, you had a trip*
maravilloso	*wonderful*
se divirtieron	*you had a good time*

Como nunca. Vimos desiertos, montañas y cactos. ¡Qué paisajes más impresionantes!	*You can't imagine. We saw deserts, mountains, and cacti. What impressive scenery!*
como nunca	*you can't imagine* (literally, *as never before*)
vimos	*we saw*
el desierto	*desert*
la montaña	*mountain*
el cacto	*cactus*
el paisaje	*scenery, landscape*
impresionante	*impressive*

Creo que el suroeste te interesó mucho.	*I think you found the Southwest very interesting.*
el suroeste	*the Southwest*
te	*to you, for you*
interesó	*it interested*
te interesó	*it interested you*
te interesó mucho	*you found it very interesting*

▶ Variantes

Listen, and repeat the same structures from *Diálogo 6*, now with new vocabulary.

Alquilamos una furgoneta.	**We rented** *a van.*
Compramos	*We bought*
Manejamos	*We drove*
Condujimos	*We drove*

Recorrimos el suroeste.	*We toured **the Southwest**.*
el sur	*the South*
el oeste	*the West*
el norte	*the North*
el este	*the East*
el sudeste	*the Southeast*
el nordeste	*the Northeast*
el noroeste	*the Northwest*

El suroeste te interesó mucho, ¿no?	*You were very interested in the Southwest, weren't you?*
Sí, me encantó.	*Yes, I loved it.*
Me encantaron los paisajes. ¿Y a ti? A mí me encantaron también.	*I loved the landscapes. How about you? I loved them, too.*

Estructura y Práctica

N *Una narrativa.* Write the correct preterit form of each of the following verbs in parentheses to learn about a birthday party.

Mi amiga Sofía (1) _____ (cumplir) veintisiete años ayer. Anoche yo

(2) _____ (asistir) a su fiesta de cumpleaños. Todos nosotros los invitados

(3) _____ (comer) platos riquísimos y (4) _____ (beber) mucho vino.

Sofía (5) _____ (alegrarse) al abrir sus regalos. Yo le (6) _____ (traer)

flores y una linda cartera. A la una de la mañana, Javier (7) _____ (tener) la idea

de ir a un club de salsa. Todo el mundo (8) _____ (entusiasmarse) mucho.

Nosotros (9) _____ (ir) a un club donde (10) _____ (oír) música y

(11) _____ (bailar) hasta las cuatro de la mañana. ¡Nosotros (12) _____

(divertirse) mucho!

▶ DIÁLOGO 7 · Los viajes de negocios

Study the dialogue, then listen to the recording and repeat each line.

SOFÍA	¿Cuándo volvió de su viaje de negocios?
ROBERTO	Del viaje a la ciudad de México, el miércoles. Pero al día siguiente me fui de viaje otra vez. Esta vez viajé a Santiago de Chile.
SOFÍA	Conoció a los directores de la compañía, ¿verdad?
ROBERTO	Sí, y les expliqué nuestro plan de mercadeo. Todos los días madrugué y me acosté muy tarde. ¡Estoy agotado!

Análisis

Check that you understand the linguistic breakdown of each speech from *Diálogo* 7.

¿Cuándo volvió de su viaje de negocios?	*When did you get back from your business trip?*
volver de	*to come back from*
volvió	*you got back*
el viaje de negocios	*business trip*
Del viaje a la ciudad de México, el miércoles. Pero al día siguiente me fui de viaje otra vez. Esta vez viajé a Santiago de Chile.	*From my trip to Mexico City, on Wednesday. But the next day I left on another trip. This time I traveled to Santiago, Chile.*

la ciudad de México	*Mexico City*
al día siguiente	*next day*
irse de viaje	*to leave on a trip*
me fui	*I left*
viajar	*to travel*

Conoció a los directores de la compañía, ¿verdad?	*You met the directors of the company, didn't you?*
conoció	*you met*
el director	*director*
la compañía	*company*

Sí, y les expliqué nuestro plan de mercadeo. Todos los días madrugué y me acosté muy tarde. ¡Estoy agotado!	*Yes, and I explained our marketing plan to them. Every day I got up very early and went to bed very late. I'm exhausted!*
les	*to them*
explicar	*to explain*
expliqué	*I explained*
el plan	*plan*
el mercadeo	*marketing*
el plan de mercadeo	*marketing plan*
madrugar	*to get up very early*
madrugué	*I got up very early*
agotado	*exhausted*
estar agotado	*to be exhausted*

⏵ Variantes

Listen, and repeat the same structures from *Diálogo 7*, now with new vocabulary.

Viajaron a la ciudad de México.	*They traveled to Mexico City.*
Volvieron	*They returned*
Fueron	*They went*
Vinieron	*They came*
Hicieron un viaje	*They took a trip*

Les expliqué nuestro plan de mercadeo.	*I explained our marketing plan to them.*
mostré	*I showed*
traje	*I brought*
di	*I gave*

Les actualicé el plan de mercadeo.	*I updated the marketing plan for them.*
organicé	*I organized*
escribí	*I wrote*
conseguí	*I got*

Me acosté.	*I went to bed.*
desperté	*woke up*
levanté	*got up*
coloqué	*got a job*
vestí	*got dressed*
tranquilicé	*stopped worrying*

Estructura y Práctica

O *Una narrativa.* Write the correct preterit form of each of the following verbs in parentheses to learn about Felipe and Blanca's life.

Felipe y Blanca (1) _____ (estudiar) administración de empresas en la universidad.

Ellos (2) _____ (graduarse) hace siete años. Blanca (3) _____ (colocarse)

en una empresa de mercadeo y Felipe (4) _____ (empezar) a trabajar en una

compañía de software. Felipe y Blanca (5) _____ (comprometerse) y al año

siguiente (6) _____ (casarse). Ellos (7) _____ (comprar) una casa

y (8) _____ (tener) un hijo. ¡Son muy felices!

▶ DIÁLOGO 8 · ¡Qué tráfico!

Study the dialogue, then listen to the recording and repeat each line.

SOFÍA   ¡Qué embotellamiento! Nunca vamos a llegar a la estación. Creo que
         ya perdimos el tren.

ROBERTO No te preocupes. Yo descubrí un atajo el otro día. Y ya tenemos
         reservaciones.

SOFÍA   Bueno, podemos sacar los boletos en la máquina. En la taquilla lleva
         más tiempo.

Análisis

Check that you understand the linguistic breakdown of each speech from *Diálogo 8*.

¡Qué embotellamiento! Nunca vamos a llegar a la estación. Creo que ya perdimos el tren.	*What a traffic jam! We'll never get to the station. I think we missed the train already.*
el embotellamiento	* traffic jam*
la estación	* station*
perder el tren	* to miss the train*
perdimos	* we missed*
No te preocupes. Yo descubrí un atajo el otro día. Y ya tenemos reservaciones.	*Don't worry. I discovered a shortcut the other day. And we already have reservations.*
preocuparse	* to worry*
no te preocupes	* don't worry*
descubrir	* to discover*
descubrí	* I discovered*
la reservación	* reservation*
Bueno, podemos sacar los boletos en la máquina. En la taquilla lleva más tiempo.	*Well, we can buy the tickets from the machine. It's faster than at the ticket window.*
sacar	* to take out*
sacar los boletos	* to buy the tickets, get the tickets*
la máquina	* machine*

la taquilla	box office, ticket window
llevar más tiempo	to take more time
En la taquilla lleva más tiempo.	(literally) At the ticket window, it takes more time.

▶ Variantes

Listen, and repeat the same structures from *Diálogo 8*, now with new vocabulary.

Tomé un atajo en las horas punta.	I took a shortcut at rush hour.
Nos faltó tiempo.	We didn't have enough time.
Nos sobró tiempo.	We had more than enough time.

| ¿Cuánto dinero le falta? | How much money is he short? |
| Le faltan mil dólares. | He's a thousand dollars short. |

| Nos queda mucho dinero. ¿Y a ti? | We have a lot of money left. How about you? |
| A mí también. | I do, too. |

| ¿Les hacen falta los boletos? | Do you need the tickets? |
| Sí, nos hace falta comprarlos. | Yes, we need to buy them. |

▶ DIÁLOGO 9 · Una excursión a Toledo

Study the dialogue, then listen to the recording and repeat each line.

ROBERTO   Hicimos una excursión de Madrid a Toledo. Tomamos el tren de alta
           velocidad y llegamos en media hora.

SOFÍA   Vieron la casa y la pintura de El Greco, ¿verdad?

ROBERTO   Claro. Para eso fuimos. Además, conocimos las iglesias, las sinagogas
           y El Alcázar. Y caminamos por las espléndidas calles medievales.

Análisis

Check that you understand the linguistic breakdown of each speech from *Diálogo 9*.

Hicimos una excursión de Madrid a Toledo. Tomamos el tren de alta velocidad y llegamos en media hora.	We took a trip from Madrid to Toledo. We took the high-speed train and got there in half an hour.
hicimos	we did, we made
la excursión	tour, trip
la velocidad	speed
alta velocidad	high speed
media hora	half hour

Vieron la casa y la pintura de El Greco, ¿verdad?	You saw El Greco's house and paintings, didn't you?
vieron	you saw
la pintura	painting, paintings

Claro. Para eso fuimos. Además, conocimos las iglesias, las sinagogas y El Alcázar. Y caminamos por las espléndidas calles medievales.	*Of course. That's why we went. In addition, we visited the churches, the synagogues, and the Alcázar. And we walked along the splendid medieval streets.*
para eso	* for that purpose*
fuimos	* we went*
Para eso fuimos.	* That's why we went.*
además	* besides, in addition*
conocimos	* we visited* (of places)
la iglesia	* church*
la sinagoga	* synagogue*
El Alcázar	* El Alcázar* (*fortress overlooking Toledo*)
caminamos	* we walked*
por	* through, along*
medieval	* medieval*

⏵ Variantes

Listen, and repeat the same structures from *Diálogo 9*, now with new vocabulary.

Para eso fuimos .	*That's why **we went**.*
volvimos	* we returned*
vinimos	* we came*
salimos	* we left*
No conoció nada.	*She didn't become familiar with anything.*
No supo nada.	*She didn't find out anything.*
¿A quién le van a gustar estas calles medievales?	*Who is going to like these medieval streets?*
A mí.	*I am.*
¿A quiénes les va a interesar esta pintura?	*Who is going to be interested in this painting?*
A ellos.	*They are.*

Estructura y Práctica

P **Translation: Reverse construction verbs.** Express the following sentences in Spanish, using reverse construction verbs. Note that the verbs have a noun or an infinitive as the subject.

1. *They're short one aisle seat.*

2. *They have three window seats left.*

3. *It's your (Ud.) turn to pass through customs.*

4. *It's not good for us to make a stopover.*

5. *I like these flight attendants.*

6. *Does he need to get his boarding pass?*

7. *You (tú) like to travel by plane, but I love to take the high-speed train!*

Verbs with a Different Meaning in the Preterit

Some verbs take on a different meaning when they are used in the preterit. The distinction in meaning will be especially important when you study the difference between the preterit tense and the imperfect tense, which are two ways of looking at past time. (See Chapters 10 and 11.) In the case of the following verbs, when used in the preterit they focus on the beginning or completion of an action. For example, **supe** means *I began to know,* that is, *I found out.*

VERB	SPANISH	ENGLISH
saber *to know*	Supe su nombre hoy.	*I found out his name today.*
conocer *to know*	Los conocimos ayer.	*We met them yesterday.*
tener *to have*	Tuvo una idea.	*He got an idea.*
poder *to be able to*	¿No pudiste verla?	*Didn't you manage to see her?*
querer *to want*	No quiso ir.	*He refused to go.*

Q **Verbs with a different meaning in the preterit.** Express each of the following sentences in Spanish, using a verb from the list above.

1. *We managed to tour six countries.*
2. *I finally found out their address.*
3. *He got a great idea.*
4. *The passenger [fem.] refused to shut off her cell phone.*
5. *Did you (tú) manage to check your luggage?*
6. *When did you (tú) meet Mr. and Mrs. Díaz?*

Un paso más

Are you ready to take your Spanish a step further? Here are exercises that will enhance your knowledge of the language and allow you to express yourself freely.

R **Compound nouns.** Select a noun in the second column that forms a compound noun with a noun in the first column. Join the nouns with the preposition **de** and then write each compound noun with its definite article.

1. viaje	a. embarque
2. asiento	b. seguridad
3. auxiliar	c. negocios
4. puerta	d. conexión
5. equipaje	e. mano
6. control	f. vuelo
7. vuelo	g. mercadeo
8. tren	h. ventana
9. plan	i. alta velocidad

S *Diálogos.* Express the following dialogues about travel in Spanish.

1. *We took a trip to Chile five years ago.*
   It was an exhausting flight, wasn't it?

2. *The plane took off, and twenty minutes later, I unbuckled my seatbelt.*
   And I settled into my seat and fell asleep immediately.

3. *Did you (tú) like the scenery in the Southwest?*
   Yes, I loved it. We drove through the desert and saw impressive cactuses.

4. *Did you (Uds.) have to make a stopover?*
   No, it was a direct flight.

5. *What did you (Ud.) do when you got off the plane?*
   I picked up my luggage and went through customs.

6. *Did you (tú) show your passport at the gate?*
   No, but I handed the boarding pass to the young woman.

7. *Did you (Ud.) check your suitcase?*
   No, the flight attendant put it in the overhead compartment (el compartimiento de arriba).

8. *What a traffic jam! We're going to miss our flight.*
   Nonsense! I know a shortcut.

T *Preguntas personales.* Answer each question with a complete Spanish sentence.

1. ¿Qué cosas o actividades te gustan?

2. ¿Qué te importa más que nada en la vida? ¿Por qué?

3. ¿Te gusta viajar? ¿Por qué?

U *Una narrativa personal.* Write a personal narrative in Spanish about a plane, train, or car trip you took, using words and expressions from Chapter 9. Use the following questions as a guide.

1. ¿Fue un viaje de vacaciones o de negocios?

2. ¿Qué preparativos y trámites hiciste?

3. ¿Adónde fuiste?

4. ¿Cuándo fuiste?

5. ¿Cómo viajaste?

6. ¿Con quiénes viajaste?

7. ¿Hiciste turismo? ¿Qué viste?

8. ¿Qué comiste? ¿Te gustó la comida?

9. ¿El viaje te salió bien/mal? Explica (*Explain*).

Childhood, Family History, University

Communication Goals

- Talking about time, weather, and repeated actions in the past
- Talking about what you did as a child and your family history
- Telling about pre-Columbian peoples and the pyramids in Mexico
- Vocabulary: childhood memories, university, working in a restaurant, immigrants

Grammar Topics

- The Imperfect Tense
- Long-form Possessive Adjectives
- The Passive Voice
- **Se** Construction
- Double Object Pronouns
- The Reflexive Pronoun as Indirect Object
- Imperfect vs. Preterit: Two Aspects of Past Time
- Double Object Pronouns in Verb + Infinitive Constructions
- Verbs with Different Meanings in Imperfect and Preterit
- Expressions with **dar**
- **Hacía** + Expression of Time + **que** + Verb in Imperfect Tense
- Preterit and Imperfect in Indirect Discourse (Reported Speech)

▶ DIÁLOGO 1 · Cuando yo era niño...

Study the dialogue, then listen to the recording and repeat each line.

JOSÉ   Cuando yo era niño, mi familia y yo íbamos al mar todos los veranos.
        ¿Cómo pasabas tú los veranos?
ELENA   Cuando yo era niña, mis papás me llevaban de viaje. Yo conocía las
        grandes capitales del mundo.
JOSÉ   Disfrutabas de unas vacaciones muy interesantes.
ELENA   Y las vacaciones tuyas eran muy tranquilas y relajadas.

Análisis

Check that you understand the linguistic breakdown of each speech from *Diálogo 1*.

Cuando yo era niño, mi familia y yo
íbamos al mar todos los veranos.
¿Cómo pasabas tú los veranos?

*When I was a child, my family and I used
to go to the seashore every summer.
How did you spend the summers?*

era	*I was*
el niño	*child*
la familia	*family*
mi familia	*my family*
íbamos	*we used to go*
el mar	*sea*
el verano	*summer*
todos los veranos	*every summer*
pasar	*to spend* (*time*)
pasabas	*you spent, you used to spend*

Cuando yo era niña, mis papás me
llevaban de viaje. Yo conocía las
grandes capitales del mundo.

*When I was a child, my parents took me
traveling. I visited the great capitals
of the world.*

la niña	*child*
mis papás	*my parents* (especially in Spanish America)
llevar	*to take* (*someone somewhere*)
llevar a uno de viaje	*to take someone on a trip*
llevaban	*they used to take*
me llevaban de viaje	*used to take me traveling*
conocer + *place*	*to visit* + place
yo conocía	*I visited*
la capital	*capital city*
el mundo	*world*

Disfrutabas de unas vacaciones muy   *You had very interesting vacations.*
interesantes.
   disfrutar de algo   *to enjoy something*
   disfrutabas   *you enjoyed, you had*
   las vacaciones   *vacation* (always plural in Spanish)
   interesante   *interesting*

Y las vacaciones tuyas eran muy   *And your vacations were very calm and*
tranquilas y relajadas.   *relaxed.*
   las vacaciones tuyas   *your vacation*
   tranquilo   *quiet, calm*
   relajado   *relaxed*

▶ Variantes

Listen, and repeat the same structures from *Diálogo 1*, now with new vocabulary.

Íbamos al mar todos los veranos.   ***We went** to the seashore every summer.*
   Viajábamos   *We traveled*
   Manejábamos   *We drove*
   Conducíamos   *We drove*

Las vacaciones tuyas eran tranquilas.   ***Your** vacation was restful.*
   mías   *My*
   suyas   *His, Her, Your, Their*
   nuestras   *Our*

Estructura y Práctica

The Imperfect Tense

The forms of the imperfect tense are almost entirely regular. Two sets of endings are used, one for **-ar** verbs and another for **-er** and **-ir** verbs. **-Ar** verbs have **-aba-** in all forms; **-er** and **-ir** verbs have **-ía-** in all forms.

tomar *to take; to drink*		**comer** *to eat*		**vivir** *to live*	
tomaba	**tomábamos**	comía	comíamos	vivía	vivíamos
tomabas	tomabais	comías	comíais	vivías	vivíais
tomaba	tomaban	comía	comían	vivía	vivían

NOTES

1 · The first and third person singular forms are identical for all verbs in the imperfect: **yo/él/ella/Ud. hablaba/aprendía/escribía.**

2 · For -ar verbs, the **nosotros** form is the only one with a written accent: **hablábamos.**

3 · For -er and -ir verbs, all forms have a written accent over the -í- of the imperfect ending.

4 · The imperfect of **hay** is **había** (*there was, there were*).

Only the verbs **ser**, **ir**, and **ver** are irregular in the imperfect.

ser *to be*		**ir** *to go*		**ver** *to see*	
era	éramos	iba	íbamos	veía	veíamos
eras	erais	ibas	ibais	veías	veíais
era	eran	iba	iban	veía	veían

Uses of the Imperfect

The imperfect tense is used to express an event or action going on in the past without any reference to its beginning or end. Therefore, it is the tense used to express repeated actions in past time. Adverbs and adverbial phrases such as **todos los días**, **siempre**, and **muchas veces** are often clues for the selection of the imperfect rather than the preterit.

The imperfect is therefore also the tense used for description and expressing background in the past. Common English equivalents for the Spanish imperfect are *used to do, was doing*.

¿**Jugabas** al tenis todos los días?	*Did you play tennis every day?*
No, **jugaba** solamente los sábados.	*No, I only played on Saturdays.*

¿Qué tiempo **hacía**?	*What was the weather like?*
Hacía calor y **estaba** nublado.	*It was warm and (it was) cloudy.*

The imperfect tense is used to tell what time it was in the past. The preterit is never used in this function. (See *Diálogo 14* in this chapter.)

¿Qué hora **era**?	*What time was it?*
Eran las tres de la tarde.	*It was 3:00 P.M.*

The imperfect tense is used in indirect discourse, or reported speech (reporting what someone said), after the preterit form of verbs such as **decir** and **escribir**. (See *Diálogo 17* in this chapter.)

¿Qué te **dijo** Mario?	*What did Mario tell you?*
Me **dijo** que **volvía** tarde.	*He told me he was coming back late.*

¿Le **escribiste** a Carmen?	*Did you write to Carmen?*
Sí, le **escribí** que **me mudaba**.	*Yes, I wrote her that I was moving.*

(For the presentation of the preterit tense, see Chapter 9. For an explanation of the imperfect vs. the preterit, see *Diálogo 5* of this chapter.)

A Write the imperfect form of the verb that corresponds with each present tense form given.

1. hablo

2. comen

3. escribimos

4. son

5. crees

6. tengo

7. vuelven

8. sé

9. dices

10. ve

11. vienen

12. hay

13. tomamos

14. hago

15. vives

16. puede

17. quieren

18. pide

19. voy

20. juegas

21. suben

22. entiendo

23. leemos

24. damos

25. estoy

26. pongo

27. piensan

28. almuerzas

29. sigo

30. construye

B *¿Qué hacían?* Write the imperfect form of the verb in parentheses that correctly completes each of the following sentences. Follow the *modelo.*

MODELO   Ella __*abría*__ las cajas. (abrir)

1. Ellos _____ en una tienda de deportes. (trabajar)

2. ¿Tú _____ las grandes capitales? (recorrer)

3. Él _____ a ir de vacaciones en agosto. (ir)

4. Nosotros _____ en mi oficina. (reunirse)

5. _____ muy buen tiempo. (Hacer)

6. Yo _____ unos pájaros hermosos. (ver)

7. Esos inmigrantes _____ de origen griego. (ser)

8. Uds. _____ comida sana. (servir)

9. Ella nos _____ una foto de su familia. (enseñar)

10. No _____ tren hasta las cuatro de la tarde. (haber)

11. Les _____ el mar. (encantar)

12. Ella y yo _____ un paseo todas las tardes. (dar)

13. Los niños _____ ir al jardín zoológico, ¿verdad? (querer)

14. Yo _____ una clase a distancia. (tomar)

15. Tú _____ aprovechar las ofertas de enero, ¿verdad? (pensar)

16. ¿Ud. _____ jugar al fútbol? (saber)

17. Nos _____ merendar al aire libre. (gustar)

18. La abuela _____ a sus nietecitas. (vestir)

19. Los Sánchez _____ en pleno centro. (vivir)

20. Nosotros no _____ de acuerdo con ellos. (estar)

C ***Todos los días.*** Rewrite each sentence in the imperfect, adding the adverb or adverbial phrase of frequency in parentheses. Follow the *modelo*.

MODELO   Jorge se despierta a las siete. (todos los días)
          → Jorge se despertaba a las siete todos los días.

1. Yo me reúno con mis amigos. (todos los domingos)

2. ¿Uds. van a la sierra? (todos los inviernos)

3. María Elena almuerza con nosotros. (cada semana)

4. Rodrigo y yo asistimos a un concierto. (todas las semanas)

5. ¿No puedes hacer un viaje? (cada año)

6. Les doy muchos regalos. (todos los años)

7. Se divierten mucho en las fiestas. (siempre)

8. Los chicos ven ese programa. (a menudo)

Long-form Possessive Adjectives

Most Spanish speakers don't stress possessive adjectives to contrast them the way we do in English.

> He likes **his** computer, not **my** computer.
> **Your** house is bigger than **their** house.

In order to stress possessive adjectives, Spanish uses long-form possessives. These consist of the definite article + noun + long-form possessive. All the long-form possessive adjectives agree with the noun in gender and number.

el boleto **mío**	la oficina **mía**	el boleto **nuestro**	la oficina **nuestra**
los boletos **míos**	las oficinas **mías**	los boletos **nuestros**	las oficinas **nuestras**
el boleto **tuyo**	la oficina **tuya**	el boleto **vuestro**	la oficina **vuestra**
los boletos **tuyos**	las oficinas **tuyas**	los boletos **vuestros**	las oficinas **vuestras**
el boleto **suyo**	la oficina **suya**	el boleto **suyo**	la oficina **suya**
los boletos **suyos**	las oficinas **suyas**	los boletos **suyos**	las oficinas **suyas**

A prepositional phrase beginning with **de** can replace forms of **suyo** to provide a focus on the person referred to.

> el boleto de él / de ella / de Ud. / de ellos / de ellas / de Uds.
> los boletos de él / de ella / de Ud. / de ellos / de ellas / de Uds.

In noun phrases with long-form possessive adjectives, the indefinite article, a demonstrative adjective, or a numeral can replace the definite article.

una oficina nuestra	*an office of ours*
estos boletos suyos	*these tickets of yours*
dos amigos míos	*two friends of mine*

(For possessive adjectives, see Chapter 2.)

D *¿De quién es?* Write phrases using long-form possessive adjectives to tell whose items these are. Follow the *modelo*.

MODELO   el billetero (él)
          → el billetero suyo

1. los maletines _____ (nosotros)

2. el cartapacio _____ (yo)

3. las cámaras _____ (ellos)

4. el gorro _____ (Ud.)

5. el celular _____ (tú)

6. el abrigo _____ (ella)

7. las tarjetas de crédito _____ (Uds.)

8. el coche _____ (él)

9. la cartera _____ (yo)

10. la pintura _____ (nosotras)

11. los aretes (*earrings*) _____ (tú)

12. la casa de campo _____ (Uds.)

E Express the following phrases in Spanish, using long-form possessive adjectives. Follow the *modelo*.

MODELO   *that farm of his*
          → esa finca suya

1. *these reports of yours* (tú)

2. *three friends* [fem.] *of hers*

3. *an apartment of theirs*

4. *an idea of mine*

5. *these problems of yours* (Uds.)

6. *that car of his*

7. *a company of ours*

8. *some plans of yours* (Ud.)

9. *this watch of mine*

10. *that sister-in-law of hers*

▶ DIÁLOGO 2 · En la finca

Study the dialogue, then listen to the recording and repeat each line.

JOSÉ   Todos los años mi esposa y yo llevábamos a nuestros hijos a una finca.

ELENA   Me imagino que a los niños les gustaba ver los animales.

JOSÉ   Sí, muchísimo. Había vacas, caballos, gallinas, cabras y ovejas.

ELENA   Supongo que toda la comida fue cultivada en la finca misma. ¡Qué vida más sana!

Análisis

Check that you understand the linguistic breakdown of each speech from *Diálogo 2*.

Todos los años mi esposa y yo
llevábamos a nuestros hijos a una finca.
   todos los años
   llevábamos
   los hijos
   a nuestros hijos
   la finca

Every year, my wife and I used to take our
children to a farm.
   every year
   we used to take
   children
   our children
   farm

Me imagino que a los niños les gustaba
ver los animales.
   imaginarse
   me imagino
   a los niños
   les gustaba
   les gustaba ver
   el animal

I imagine that the children liked to see the
animals.
   to imagine
   I imagine
   the children
   they liked
   they liked to see
   animal

Sí, muchísimo. Había vacas, caballos,
gallinas, cabras y ovejas.
   muchísimo
   había
   la vaca
   el caballo
   la gallina
   la cabra
   la oveja

Yes, very much. There were cows, horses,
chickens, goats, and sheep.
   very much
   there was, there were
   cow
   horse
   hen, chicken
   goat
   sheep

Supongo que toda la comida fue
cultivada en la finca misma. ¡Qué vida
más sana!
   suponer
   supongo
   la comida
   toda la comida
   cultivar
   fue cultivada
   mismo
   en la finca misma

   la vida
   sano
   ¡Qué vida más sana!

I suppose that all the food was grown right
there on the farm. What a healthy life!

   to suppose (conjugated like **poner**)
   I suppose
   food
   all the food
   to grow (transitive)
   was grown
   the very (when it follows the noun)
   on the very farm, on the farm itself,
     right there on the farm

   life
   healthy
   What a healthy life!

▶ Variantes

Listen, and repeat the same structures from *Diálogo 2*, now with new vocabulary.

Comían comida sana.	**They ate** healthy food.
Pedían	They ordered
Servían	They served
Hacían	They made
Cocinaban	They cooked
Preparaban	They prepared

La comida fue cultivada por el agricultor.	**The food was grown** by the farmer.
Las papas fueron cultivadas	The potatoes were grown
El maíz fue cultivado	The corn was grown
Los frijoles fueron cultivados	The beans were grown

Estructura y Práctica

F *Una narrativa.* Write the correct imperfect form of each of the following verbs in parentheses to create a narrative.

Habla Ricardo. Cuando yo (1) _____ (ser) niño, mis hermanos y yo

(2) _____ (ir) a una finca que (3) _____ (quedar) en la sierra.

A veces a mis papás les (4) _____ (gustar) tomar las vacaciones en verano,

a veces (5) _____ (preferir) tomarlas en invierno. Es que nos (6) _____

(encantar) los deportes de verano y también los de invierno. Cuando (7) _____

(hacer) calor, nosotros (8) _____ (nadar) en el río y cuando (9) _____

(nevar), nosotros (10) _____ (esquiar). En verano, yo (11) _____

(montar) a caballo todos los días. Mi caballo favorito (12) _____ (llamarse)

Campeón. A mis hermanos menores les (13) _____ (fascinar) darles de comer

a los animales.

POSITION OF ADJECTIVES

In Chapter 2, you learned that some adjectives can appear either before or after the noun and that the meaning changes depending on the position of the adjective.

In *Diálogo 2*, **en la finca misma** is translated as *right there on the farm, on the farm itself.* If the adjective **mismo** precedes the noun—**en la misma finca**—the meaning changes to *on the same farm.* Here are some other examples.

cierta tradición *a certain tradition*	una cosa **cierta** *a sure thing*
un **gran** hombre *a great man*	un hombre **grande** *a large man*
esa **pobre** gente *those poor people (unfortunate)*	esa gente **pobre** *those poor people (lacking money)*
la **única** persona *the only person*	una persona **única** *a unique person*

The Passive Voice

The passive voice in Spanish consists of a form of **ser** + the past participle. In Spanish, the past participle agrees in gender and number with the subject of the sentence. Similarly, English forms the passive voice with a form of the auxiliary verb *to be* + the past participle.

You will learn about the past participle in Chapter 13. For now, it is enough to know that for regular verbs, the past participle in Spanish ends in **-do**. (Some irregular verbs have past participles ending in **-to** or **-cho**.)

The past participle consists of the following elements:

verb stem + the vowel **a** for **-ar** verbs / the vowel **i** for **-er** and **-ir** verbs + **-do**

tomar	tom + a + do → **tomado**	*taken*
comer	com + i + do → **comido**	*eaten*
vivir	viv + i + do → **vivido**	*lived*

La computadora **fue reparada** ayer.	*The computer **was fixed** yesterday.*
Los archivos **fueron descargados** ya.	*The files **were downloaded** already.*
El informe no **fue recibido**.	*The report **was not received**.*
¿**Fueron pagadas** las cuentas?	***Were** the bills **paid**?*

The passive voice sometimes uses an agent phrase beginning with **por**.

Los cheques **fueron cobrados**.	*The checks **were cashed**.*
Los cheques **fueron cobrados por el contador**.	*The checks **were cashed by the accountant**.*

The passive is used to move the focus of the sentence to the direct object of the verb by making it the subject. The passive voice thus deemphasizes the performer of the action.

El jefe despidió **a los empleados**. →	**Los empleados** fueron despedidos por el jefe.
La profesora explicó **el problema**. →	**El problema** fue explicado por la profesora.

The passive voice is much more common in English than in Spanish. Spanish prefers the **se** construction to remove the focus from the performer of the action. (See *Diálogo 3* in this chapter.)

G **Passive voice.** Write the preterit form of **ser** + the past participle (verb in parentheses) that correctly completes each of the following sentences in the passive voice. Note the agent phrase in each sentence. Follow the *modelo*.

MODELO   La cena _fue preparada_ por el cocinero. (preparar)

1. Los cuartos _____ por el pintor. (pintar)

2. La computadora _____ por el programador. (prender)

3. Las cartas _____ por el secretario. (entregar)

4. El condominio _____ por los señores Ayala. (vender)

5. Los niños _____ por sus papás. (acostar)

6. El pescado _____ por el mesero. (servir)

7. Las manzanas _____ por el agricultor. (cultivar)

8. La empresa _____ por mis abuelos. (fundar)

9. Los problemas _____ por los abogados del bufete. (discutir)

10. El maletín _____ por el auxiliar de vuelo. (subir)

11. Los empleados _____ por el gerente. (despedir)

12. La canción _____ por la soprano. (cantar)

H **La voz pasiva.** Rewrite each of the following sentences, changing the active construction to a passive construction. Follow the *modelo*.

MODELO   Raúl grabó las canciones.
→ Las canciones fueron grabadas por Raúl.

1. El director firmó los papeles.

2. La doctora Vega explicó la teoría.

3. Los asesores terminaron el informe.

4. Los turistas italianos tomaron las fotos.

5. Un amigo mío diseñó mi sitio web.

6. Consuelo cosió el botón.

7. Los estudiantes aprendieron todas las fechas.

8. El desarrollador de programas entró los datos.

9. El equipo peruano ganó el partido.

10. Guillermo prendió la tele.

DIÁLOGO 3 · De vacaciones en Costa Rica

Study the dialogue, then listen to the recording and repeat each line.

ELENA   Uds. hacían ecoturismo en Costa Rica durante el verano, ¿verdad?
JOSÉ   Sí. Recorríamos varias selvas tropicales donde había una gran cantidad de mariposas hermosas.
ELENA   ¿Visitaban los cafetales?
JOSÉ   Desde luego. Veíamos cómo se producía el café. Nos interesaba mucho.

Análisis

Check that you understand the linguistic breakdown of each speech from *Diálogo 3*.

Uds. hacían ecoturismo en Costa Rica durante el verano, ¿verdad?	*You used to do ecotourism in Costa Rica during the summer, didn't you?*
hacer turismo	*to go sightseeing*
hacer ecoturismo	*to do ecotourism*
hacían	*used to do*
durante	*during*
el verano	*summer*
¿verdad?	*didn't you?*

Sí. Recorríamos varias selvas tropicales donde había una gran cantidad de mariposas hermosas.

Yes, we traveled around several tropical jungles where there was a large number of beautiful butterflies.

recorrer	*to travel around, travel through*
recorríamos	*we traveled around*
varios	*several*
la selva	*jungle*
tropical	*tropical*
la cantidad	*quantity*
una gran cantidad de	*a large amount of, a large number of*
la mariposa	*butterfly*
hermoso	*beautiful*

¿Visitaban los cafetales?

Did you (use to) visit the coffee plantations?

visitaban	*you used to visit*
el cafetal	*coffee plantation*

Desde luego. Veíamos cómo se producía el café. Nos interesaba mucho.

Of course. We would see how coffee was produced. We were very interested in that.

desde luego	*of course*
veíamos	*we would see, we used to see*
cómo	*how*
producir	*to produce*
se produce el café	*coffee is produced*
se producía el café	*coffee was produced*
interesarle a uno	*to be interested in something*
nos interesaba	*we were interested in it*

▶ Variantes

Listen, and repeat the same structures from *Diálogo 3*, now with new vocabulary.

Recorríamos una selva tropical.	***We traveled around** a tropical forest.*
Visitábamos	*We visited*
Veíamos	*We saw*

¿ Visitaban los cafetales?	***Did you visit** the coffee plantations?*
Veían	*Did you see*
Recorrían	*Did you travel around*

Se producía petróleo.	*They produced oil.*
Se producía vino.	*They produced wine.*
Se producían automóviles.	*They produced cars.*
Se producían productos petroquímicos.	*They produced petrochemical products.*

Se habla español en Costa Rica.	*Spanish is spoken in Costa Rica.*

¿Cómo se dice *coffee plantation* en español?	*How do you say "coffee plantation" in Spanish?*
Se dice "cafetal".	*You say cafetal.*
¿Cómo se deletrea la palabra "verano"?	*How do you spell the word* verano?
Se escribe ve chica, e, ere, a, ene, o.	*It's written v, e, r, a, n, o.*
Se come bien en esta ciudad.	*You eat well in this city.*
Se comen granos integrales.	*You eat whole grains.*
Se debe comer granos integrales.	*You should eat whole grains.*
Uno se divierte mucho en Madrid.	*People have a great time in Madrid.*
Nos interesaba.	***We were interested in*** *it.*
Nos gustaba.	*We liked*
Nos encantaba.	*We loved*
Nos fascinaba.	*We were fascinated by*
Nos entusiasmaba.	*We were enthusiastic about*

Estructura y Práctica

Se Construction

To understand the **se** construction, it is important to understand the difference between the subject of the sentence and the performer of the action. Subject is a grammatical category. The subject of a sentence determines the ending of the verb.

Usually, the subject is also the performer of the action, but not always. In the examples below, the subjects of the sentences are the nouns *water* and *meat*.

The water boiled.
The meat was cooking.

The performers of the actions, however, are left unspecified.

Spanish removes the focus from the performer of the action by using the **se** construction. The **se** construction consists of the pronoun **se** and the third person singular or plural of the verb, depending on whether the grammatical subject is singular or plural. The usual translation of the **se** construction in English is the passive voice.

Se terminó el proyecto.	*The project was finished.*
Se toman unas decisiones importantes.	*Important decisions are made.*
Se vendieron las computadoras viejas.	*The old computers were sold.*
Se va a construir una carretera.	*A highway is going to be built.*

For intransitive verbs, the verb is always third person singular in the **se** construction.

Se vive bien en esta ciudad.	*People live well in this city. / You live well in this city.*
¿Por dónde se sale?	*Where is the exit?*

When an intransitive infinitive is the subject of the **se** construction, the verb is third person singular.

Se puede salir por aquí.	*You can go out this way.*
Se debe manejar con cuidado.	*One should drive carefully.*

If the verb has a reflexive **se**, then the **se** construction cannot be used. **Uno** is used instead.

Uno se divierte mucho en Barcelona.	*People have a great time in Barcelona.*
Uno no se aburre en esta ciudad.	*People don't get bored in this city.*
Uno se debe cuidar bien.	*You should take good care of yourself.*

The agent phrase with **por** cannot be used in the **se** construction.

I   *Se* **construction.** Rewrite each sentence using the **se** construction + verb in the present tense. Follow the *modelos*.

MODELOS   Recorren el país.   Recorren los países.
      → Se recorre el país.   → Se recorren los países.

1. Visitan la zona histórica.
2. Sacas fotos.
3. Cultiva verduras.
4. Hago turismo.
5. Resolvemos el problema.
6. Oímos música.
7. Realizan el proyecto.
8. Produzco vinos.
9. Servimos platos vegetarianos.
10. Ves mariposas.

J   *Se* **construction with intransitive verbs.** Rewrite each sentence using the **se** construction + verb in the present tense. Follow the *modelo*.

MODELO   Entran por la puerta principal.
      → Se entra por la puerta principal.

1. Navegamos en la red.
2. Abren a las nueve y media.
3. Vivimos muy bien en nuestro país.
4. Hablamos por celular.
5. Trabajan de lunes a jueves.
6. Salimos para el centro.
7. Suben en el ascensor.
8. Llegan a la puerta de embarque.
9. Manejan con cuidado.
10. Bajamos en la escalera mecánica.

K   *Se* **construction.** Rewrite each of the following sentences, expanding each sentence with a **se** construction by adding the verb in parentheses. Follow the *modelo*.

MODELO   Se baja del avión. (necesitar)
      → Se necesita bajar del avión.

1. Se cambia el vuelo. (poder)
2. Se sube a la pirámide. (permitir)
3. No se come comida basura. (deber)
4. Se apaga el celular. (necesitar)
5. No se ve nada por la niebla. (poder)
6. No se fuma en este edificio. (permitir)
7. Se deja una propina. (deber)
8. Se pasa por el control de seguridad. (necesitar)

⏵ DIÁLOGO 4 · Las fotos del cafetal

Study the dialogue, then listen to the recording and repeat each line.

JOSÉ   ¿No ibas a enseñarme las fotos del cafetal?
ELENA   Naturalmente. Te las enseño ahora mismo.

Análisis

Check that you understand the linguistic breakdown of each speech from *Diálogo 4*.

¿No ibas a enseñarme las fotos del cafetal?	*Weren't you going to show me the photos of the coffee plantation?*
ibas	*you were going*
enseñar	*to show*
enseñarme	*to show me*
ibas a enseñarme	*you were going to show me*
la foto	*photo*
Naturalmente. Te las enseño ahora mismo.	*Of course. I'll show them to you right now.*
te las	*them to you*
te las enseño	*I'll show them to you*
ahora mismo	*right now*

⏵ Variantes

Listen, and repeat the same structures from *Diálogo 4*, now with new vocabulary.

¿Las fotos? Te las enseño.	*The photos? I'll show them to you.*
¿La foto? Te la enseño.	*The photo? I'll show it to you.*
¿El regalo? Te lo enseño.	*The gift? I'll show it to you.*
¿Los regalos? Te los enseño.	*The gifts? I'll show them to you.*
¿Ibas a enseñarme el cafetal?	*Were you going to show me the coffee plantation?*
Sí, quería enseñártelo antes, pero te fuiste.	*Yes, I was going to show it to you before, but you left.*

Estructura y Práctica

Double Object Pronouns

In standard English, direct and indirect object pronouns do not occur together. When a direct and indirect object are present in the same sentence, the indirect object must appear in a prepositional phrase.

*I give it **to him**.*

In this sentence, *it* is the direct object and *to him* is the indirect object in a prepositional phrase.

In Spanish, however, an indirect object pronoun and a direct object pronoun always appear together when they are dependent on the same verb. The indirect object pronoun precedes the direct object pronoun. Here are the possible combinations with a first or second person indirect object pronoun.

me lo, me la	*it to me*	**nos lo, nos la**	*it to us*
me los, me las	*them to me*	**nos los, nos las**	*them to us*
te lo, te la	*it to you*	**os lo, os la**	*it to you*
te los, te las	*them to you*	**os los, os las**	*them to you*

The indirect object pronouns of the third person, **le** and **les**, change to **se** before the direct object pronouns.

le/les + lo → se lo	le/les + la → se la
le/les + los → se los	le/les + las → se las

se lo, se la	*it to him / to her / to you / to them / to you* (plural)
se los, se las	*them to him / to her / to you / to them / to you* (plural)

If speakers need to focus on the person **se** refers to, they add a phrase beginning with the preposition **a**.

Se lo presté **a ella**, no **a él**.	*I lent it **to her**, not **to him**.*
Él se los pidió **a Ud.**	*He asked **you** for them.*

L **Double object pronouns.** Rewrite each sentence, changing the direct object noun to a pronoun. Make all necessary changes. Retain the original tense of the verb. Follow the *modelo*.

> MODELO   Le explicaba la idea.
> → Se la explicaba.

1. Les enseñábamos el cafetal.

2. Te consigo los billetes.

3. Le cuenta la historia.

4. Me trajeron las flores.

5. Le entregué el pasaporte.

6. Nos mostraban sus fotos.

7. Les mandabas los informes.

8. Les sirvió la torta.

9. No le presta el dinero.

10. Me enviaba las cartas.

The Reflexive Pronoun as Indirect Object

Certain reflexive verbs can appear with direct objects. Most of these verbs express actions that have an effect on articles of clothing or parts of the body. (For reflexive verbs, see Chapter 8.)

ponerse + *article of clothing*	*to put on*
probarse (**o** > **ue**) + *article of clothing*	*to try on*
quitarse + *article of clothing*	*to take off*
romperse + *article of clothing*	*to tear*
lavarse + *part of the body*	*to wash*
quemarse + *part of the body*	*to burn*
romperse + *part of the body*	*to break*

For these verbs, the reflexive pronoun **se** is an indirect object, not a direct object.

Remember that an indirect object pronoun and a direct object pronoun always appear together if they are dependent on the same verb. The indirect object pronoun precedes the direct object pronoun.

Me puse los zapatos.	*I put on my shoes.*
Me los puse.	*I put them on.*
Se lavó el pelo.	*She washed her hair.*
Se lo lavó.	*She washed it.*
Se quitaron la chaqueta.	*They took off their jackets.*
Se la quitaron.	*They took them off.*

In English, the equivalent of the indirect object reflexive pronoun is usually a possessive adjective.

Se lavó el pelo.	*She washed **her** hair.*

Spanish uses a singular noun for articles of clothing and parts of the body, even with plural subjects. It is assumed that each person has one item, unless the item comes in pairs like shoes or gloves, in which case Spanish uses a plural noun.

Se quitaron **la chaqueta**.	*They took off **their jackets**.*
Se quitaron **los guantes**.	*They took off **their gloves**.*

M **Double object pronouns and reflexive verbs.** Write a response to each question, changing the direct object noun to a pronoun. Make all necessary changes. Retain the tense of the question in your answer. Follow the *modelo*.

> MODELO ¿Pedro se lavaba las manos?
> → Sí, se las lavaba.

1. ¿Te pusiste la camisa nueva?

2. ¿Inés se prueba las botas?

3. ¿Los pasajeros se abrocharon el cinturón de seguridad?

4. ¿Alfonso se corta el pelo?

5. ¿Uds. se cepillaban los dientes?

6. ¿Tus amigas se maquillan la cara?

7. ¿El jugador se rompió el tobillo?

8. ¿Ud. se secó el pelo?

▶ DIÁLOGO 5 · Las pirámides

Study the dialogue, then listen to the recording and repeat each line.

JOSÉ   Las pirámides de San Juan de Teotihuacán fueron construidas por los aztecas, ¿verdad?

ELENA   No, chico, las pirámides ya estaban cuando los aztecas fundaron su imperio en Tenochtitlán, hoy Ciudad de México.

JOSÉ   Pues eso no lo sabía. ¿Quién las construyó entonces?

ELENA   Los toltecas.

Análisis

Check that you understand the linguistic breakdown of each speech from *Diálogo 5*.

Las pirámides de San Juan de Teotihuacán fueron construidas por los aztecas, ¿verdad?	*The pyramids in San Juan de Teotihuacán were built by the Aztecs, weren't they?*
la pirámide	*pyramid*
San Juan de Teotihuacán	*San Juan de Teotihuacán (town northeast of Mexico City where the Pyramid of the Sun and Pyramid of the Moon are located)*
construir	*to build*
fueron construidas	*they were built*
los aztecas	*Aztecs (the most advanced pre-Columbian culture in Mexico at the time of the Spanish conquest; Aztec empire overthrown by Hernán Cortés in 1520)*
No, chico, las pirámides ya estaban cuando los aztecas fundaron su imperio en Tenochtitlán, hoy Ciudad de México.	*Well, no, the pyramids were already there when the Aztecs founded their empire in Tenochtitlán, today (known as) Mexico City.*
chico	*boy (used as interjection)*
estar	*to be there, exist*
ya estaban	*they were already there*
fundar	*to found*
el imperio	*empire*
Pues eso no lo sabía. ¿Quién las construyó entonces?	*Well, I didn't know that. Then who built them?*
eso	*that (neuter demonstrative pronoun)*
sabía	*I knew*
construyó	*built*
Los toltecas.	*The Toltecs.*
los toltecas	*Toltecs (indigenous people of Mexico, in decline by the thirteenth century)*

▶ Variantes

Listen, and repeat the same structures from *Diálogo 5*, now with new vocabulary.

Me interesaban las pirámides.	***I was interested in** the pyramids.*
Me gustaban	*I liked*
Me encantaban	*I loved*
Me fascinaban	*I was fascinated by*
Me entusiasmaban	*I was enthusiastic about*
Las pirámides fueron construidas por los toltecas.	*The pyramids were built by the Toltecs.*
La Gran Muralla fue construida por los chinos.	*The Great Wall was built by the Chinese.*

El Coliseo fue construido por los romanos.	*The Coliseum was built by the Romans.*
Los Jardines Colgantes fueron construidos por los babilonios.	*The Hanging Gardens were built by the Babylonians.*

Estructura y Práctica

Imperfect vs. Preterit: Two Aspects of Past Time

The imperfect and the preterit are both past tenses. The difference between them is not a difference in time, but a difference in how past actions are viewed. The preterit views past actions as completed or as having happened once. The imperfect views past actions as ongoing processes in past time.

When Spanish speakers refer to a past action, they have to choose between these two tenses. In English this distinction is not mandatory.

Cuando yo era joven, **dormía** bien.	*When I was young, **I slept** well.*
Anoche **dormí** bien.	*Last night **I slept** well.*

The imperfect has several common translations in English, such as *used to do something* or *was/were doing something.*

Mauricio **trabajaba** en aquella empresa.	*Mauricio **used to work** at that firm.*
¿Sabes lo que **hacía** en México?	*Do you know what **he was doing** in Mexico?*

The imperfect is the tense most often selected to express repeated actions in the past.

Yo me levantaba temprano todos los días.	***I got up*** *early every day.*
Nosotros siempre **pasábamos** el verano allí.	***We** always **spent** the summer there.*

The imperfect expresses the background of events. The events themselves are in the preterit.

Eran las tres cuando **terminé** mi informe.	***It was*** *three o'clock when **I finished** my report.*
Hacía buen tiempo cuando **salieron**.	*The weather **was** good when **they left**.*
Empezó a llover mientras **nos paseábamos**.	***It began*** *to rain while **we were taking a walk**.*
No **fui** a la oficina porque **me sentía** mal.	***I didn't go*** *to the office because **I felt** sick.*
Yo **entraba** datos en la computadora cuando el jefe me **llamó**.	***I was entering*** *data on the computer when the boss **called** me.*

It is possible to have sentences with all verbs in the imperfect or all verbs in the preterit.

Leíamos mientas ellos **navegaban** en la red.	***We were reading*** *while **they were surfing** the web.*
Rita **se maquilló, se peinó** y **se vistió**.	*Rita **put on makeup, combed her hair,** and **got dressed**.*

N *¿Imperfecto o pretérito?* Write either the imperfect or the preterit form of each verb in parentheses to correctly complete each of the following sentences. Each sentence has two verbs, one of which will be in the imperfect and the other in the preterit. Follow the *modelo*.

MODELO   Carmen _estaba_ estresada hasta que _cambió_ su estilo de vida. (estar, cambiar)

1. Yo no _____ a nadie en la fiesta hasta que _____ mis amigos. (conocer, llegar)

2. Tú _____ veintiocho años cuando _____, ¿no? (tener, casarse)

3. Nosotros _____ la ciudad hasta que _____ a llover. (recorrer, empezar)

4. Julio _____ al médico porque le _____ la garganta. (ir, doler)

5. Margarita _____ mientras _____ música. (dormirse, escuchar)

6. Juan Pedro y yo _____ un taxi cuando _____ un accidente de tráfico. (buscar, ver)

7. _____ las once de la noche cuando ellos _____ del teatro. (Ser, regresar)

8. Cuando yo _____ niña, mis papás me _____ a Inglaterra. (ser, llevar)

9. _____ sol y calor cuando Uds. _____ del hotel, ¿verdad? (Hacer, salir)

10. Las pirámides ya _____ cuando los aztecas _____ su imperio. (estar, fundar)

11. Paula no _____ el problema hasta que Gabriel se lo

    _____. (comprender, explicar).

12. Ellos le _____ a Marcos que _____ darle una beca. (decir, pensar)

13. Nosotros _____ cola en la aduana hasta que los aduaneros nos

    _____ el pasaporte. (hacer, pedir)

14. Rafael no _____ jugar al fútbol porque _____ el pie. (poder, romperse)

15. Tú _____ en el lago hasta que ellos _____ la merienda campestre. (nadar, servir)

NEUTER PRONOUNS

In *Diálogo 5*, you saw the sentence **Pues eso no lo sabía**. **Eso** is a neuter demonstrative pronoun that refers to the information about the pyramids in the previous line of dialogue. The three neuter demonstrative pronouns in Spanish—**esto**, **eso**, and **aquello**—refer to situations or ideas, not to specific nouns.

Mi hijo consiguió una beca de investigación.	*My son got a research grant.*
¡**Eso** es estupendo!	*That's great!* (**eso** = *the fact that he got the grant*)
Miguel está resentido porque lo despidieron.	*Miguel is resentful because they fired him.*
Pero **aquello** fue hace mucho tiempo.	*But that was a long time ago.* (**aquello** = *the fact that he was fired*)

▶ DIÁLOGO 6 · El profesor explica sus ideas.

Study the dialogue, then listen to the recording and repeat each line.

JOSÉ   El profesor les iba a explicar a Uds. sus ideas sobre las civilizaciones precolombinas.

ELENA   En efecto. Creo que nos las va a explicar la semana entrante.

Análisis

Check that you understand the linguistic breakdown of each speech from *Diálogo 6*.

El profesor les iba a explicar a Uds. sus ideas sobre las civilizaciones precolombinas.	*The professor was going to explain his ideas about pre-Columbian civilizations to you.*
iba a + *infinitive*	*was going to (do something)*
la idea	*idea*
sobre	*about, on the topic of*
la civilización	*civilization*
precolombino	*pre-Columbian (before the arrival of Christopher Columbus)*
En efecto. Creo que nos las va a explicar la semana entrante.	*That's right. I think he's going to explain them to us next week.*
en efecto	*that's right, indeed*
creer	*to believe*
nos las	*them* (feminine) *to us*
nos las va a explicar	*he's going to explain them to us*
entrante	*next*
la semana entrante	*next week*

Variantes

Listen, and repeat the same structures from *Diálogo 6*, now with new vocabulary.

¿Les iba a explicar sus ideas a Uds.?
Sí, nos las iba a explicar.

Was he going to explain his ideas to you?
Yes, he was going to explain them to us.

¿Les iba a explicar sus ideas a ellos?
Sí, se las iba a explicar.

Was he going to explain his ideas to them?
Yes, he was going to explain them to them.

¿Le iba a explicar sus ideas a él?
Sí, se las iba a explicar.

Was he going to explain his ideas to him?
Yes, he was going to explain them to him.

¿Le iba a explicar sus ideas a ella?
Sí, se las iba a explicar.

Was he going to explain his ideas to her?
Yes, he was going to explain them to her.

Estructura y Práctica

Double Object Pronouns in Verb + Infinitive Constructions

Like single object pronouns, double object pronouns precede the conjugated verb. In verb + infinitive constructions, double object pronouns may either precede the conjugated verb or follow the infinitive. When they follow, they are attached to the infinitive in writing and an accent mark is added to the vowel before the **-r** of the infinitive.

¿**Me lo** vas a explicar? ⎱
¿Vas a explicár**melo**? ⎰　　　*Are you going to explain **it to me**?*

O　**Double object pronouns: expanded sentences.** Rewrite each of the following sentences to include either **ir a** or **acabar de** as indicated in parentheses. Make necessary changes to the verb and the object pronouns. Write each sentence in two ways. Follow the *modelo.*

MODELO　Se lo piden. (acabar de)
　　　　→ Acaban de pedírselo.
　　　　→ Se lo acaban de pedir.

1. Se la vendemos. (ir a)

2. Nos los regala. (acabar de)

3. Se lo digo. (ir a)

4. Te lo escribimos. (acabar de)

5. Me las llevan. (ir a)

6. Se la devuelves. (acabar de)

7. Se los hago. (ir a)

8. Nos lo dan. (acabar de)

P **Double object pronouns.** Write answers to each of the following questions, adding **ir a** to the original sentence to say that you didn't help the children do certain things, but you are going to help them soon. Write each answer expressing the **ir a** + infinitive construction in two ways. Follow the *modelo.*

MODELO   ¿Ya le lavaste la cabeza a Juanita?
→ No, pero se la voy a lavar pronto.
→ No, pero voy a lavársela pronto.

1. ¿Ya les abrochaste el abrigo a Carlitos y Tere?
2. ¿Ya le limpiaste los dientes a Fede?
3. ¿Ya le pusiste las medias a Carlita?
4. ¿Ya le ataste los zapatos a Luisito?
5. ¿Ya les secaste el pelo a las niñas?
6. ¿Ya le quitaste el pijama al bebé?
7. ¿Ya les cepillaste el pelo a los gemelos?
8. ¿Ya le cortaste el pelo al niño?

▶ DIÁLOGO 7 · Los abuelos

Study the dialogue, then listen to the recording and repeat each line.

ELENA   ¿Te acuerdas bien de tus abuelos? ¿Cómo eran?
JOSÉ   Eran muy simpáticos y cariñosos. Y los abuelos tuyos, ¿cómo eran?
ELENA   Por desgracia yo nunca los conocí.
JOSÉ   Qué triste. Yo quería mucho a mis abuelos. Ellos hacían un papel muy importante en mi vida.

Análisis

Check that you understand the linguistic breakdown of each speech from *Diálogo 7.*

¿Te acuerdas bien de tus abuelos? ¿Cómo eran?	*Do you remember your grandparents well? What were they like?*
acordarse de (**o** > **ue**)	*to remember*
los abuelos	*grandparents*
eran	*they were*
Eran muy simpáticos y cariñosos. Y los abuelos tuyos, ¿cómo eran?	*They were very nice and loving. What about your grandparents? What were they like?*
simpático	*nice, likeable*
cariñoso	*loving, affectionate*
los abuelos tuyos	*your grandparents*
Por desgracia yo nunca los conocí.	*Unfortunately, I never met them.*
por desgracia	*unfortunately*
conocí	*I met*
Qué triste. Yo quería mucho a mis abuelos. Ellos hacían un papel muy importante en mi vida.	*How sad. I loved my grandparents very much. They played a very important role in my life.*
qué triste	*how sad*
querer	*to love*
quería	*I loved*

hacían	*they did, they made*
hacer un papel	*to play a role*
ellos hacían un papel	*they played a role*
la vida	*life*
en mi vida	*in my life*

▶ Variantes

Listen, and repeat the same structures from *Diálogo 7*, now with new vocabulary.

¿Cómo eran los abuelos tuyos ?	*What were **your** grandparents like?*
suyos	*his, her, your, their*
Los abuelos míos eran muy cariñosos.	***My** grandparents were very loving.*
nuestros	*Our*

Estructura y Práctica

Verbs with Different Meanings in Imperfect and Preterit

Some Spanish verbs have very different translations in the imperfect and the preterit. English may even use different verbs to express the difference between the imperfect and the preterit of some Spanish verbs.

Yo **tenía** una idea.	*I **had** an idea.*
Yo **tuve** una idea.	*I **got** an idea.*
Sabía su nombre.	*He **knew** her name.*
Supe su nombre.	*He **found out** her name.*
Conocíamos a sus abuelos.	*We **knew** his grandparents.*
Conocimos a sus abuelos.	*We **met** his grandparents.*
No podían volver hasta las ocho.	*They **couldn't** return until eight o'clock. (It doesn't say whether they returned by eight or not.)*
No pudieron volver hasta las ocho.	*They **couldn't** return by eight o'clock. (They didn't return by eight.)*
No querías ir, ¿verdad?	*You **didn't want** to go, did you?*
No quisiste ir, ¿verdad?	*You **refused** to go, didn't you? (You didn't want to go, and you didn't.)*

Q *¿Imperfecto o pretérito?* Express the following sentences in Spanish, choosing either the imperfect or the preterit tense.

1. *We wanted to (and did) go sightseeing.*
2. *They found out their nationality.*
3. *The contract? She refused to give it to them.*
4. *I had (was in the process of having) a plan.*
5. *Did you (tú) meet those friends [masc.] of his?*
6. *He couldn't (and didn't) meet with me.*

▶ DIÁLOGO 8 · La historia de la familia

Study the dialogue, then listen to the recording and repeat each line.

JOSÉ   Me parece que Uds. saben mucho sobre la historia de su familia.
ELENA   Es que nuestros abuelos siempre nos contaban cosas de su vida.
JOSÉ   Entonces Uds. sabían mucho de su vida.
ELENA   Sí. Nos hablaban de su lucha, de sus sueños, de sus triunfos y desilusiones.

Análisis

Check that you understand the linguistic breakdown of each speech from *Diálogo 8*.

Me parece que Uds. saben mucho sobre la historia de su familia.	*I think that you know a lot about the history of your family.*
me parece que	*I think that, it seems to me that*
sobre	*about (on the topic of)*
la historia	*history, story*
la familia	*family*
Es que nuestros abuelos siempre nos contaban cosas de su vida.	*That's because our grandparents always told us things about their lives.*
es que	*that's because, the fact is that*
contar (**o** > **ue**)	*to tell, relate, narrate*
contaban	*they told*
la cosa	*thing*
cosas de su vida	*things about their lives*
Entonces Uds. sabían mucho de su vida.	*So you knew a lot about their lives.*
sabían	*you knew*
Sí. Nos hablaban de su lucha, de sus sueños, de sus triunfos y desilusiones.	*Yes. They spoke to us about their struggle, their dreams, their successes and disappointments.*
hablaban	*they spoke*
la lucha	*struggle*
el sueño	*dream*
el triunfo	*success, triumph*
la desilusión	*disappointment*

▶ Variantes

Listen, and repeat the same structures from *Diálogo 8*, now with new vocabulary.

¿Sus abuelos les contaban la historia de su familia?	*Did your grandparents tell you about your family history?*
Sí, les encantaba contárnosla.	*Yes, they loved to tell us about it.*
¿Quieres contarles la historia a los niños?	*Do you want to tell the story to the boys?*
Sí, quiero contársela.	*Yes, I want to tell it to them.*
¿Les quieres contar el cuento a las niñas?	*Do you want to tell the story to the girls?*
Sí, quiero contárselo.	*Yes, I want to tell it to them.*

⏵ DIÁLOGO 9 · Merienda al aire libre

Study the dialogue, then listen to the recording and repeat each line.

ELENA	Yo no pude ir a la merienda campestre. ¿Fue divertida?
JOSÉ	Mucho. Éramos como veinte personas. Hacía sol y calor. Era un día ideal.
ELENA	¿Nadaron en el lago y jugaron al béisbol y al vólibol?
JOSÉ	Ah sí. El ejercicio nos dio hambre. Comimos todo lo que había pero seguíamos con hambre.

Análisis

Check that you understand the linguistic breakdown of each speech from *Diálogo 9.*

Yo no pude ir a la merienda campestre. ¿Fue divertida?	*I couldn't go to the picnic. Was it fun?*
pude	*I could*
no pude ir	*I couldn't (and didn't) go*
la merienda campestre	*picnic*
fue	*it was*
divertido	*fun, amusing*
Mucho. Éramos como veinte personas. Hacía sol y calor. Era un día ideal.	*It really was. We were about twenty people. It was sunny and hot. It was a perfect day.*
mucho	*very much so* (from **muy divertido**, with **divertido** omitted)
éramos	*we were*
como	*about (approximately)*
hacía sol	*it was sunny*
hacía calor	*it was hot*
era	*it was*
ideal	*ideal, perfect*
¿Nadaron en el lago y jugaron al béisbol y al vólibol?	*Did you swim in the lake and play baseball and volleyball?*
nadar	*to swim*
el lago	*lake*
jugar (**u** > **ue**)	*to play*
jugar + a + *definite article* + *name of game*	*to play* + name of game
jugar al béisbol	*to play baseball*
jugar al vólibol	*to play volleyball*
Ah sí. El ejercicio nos dio hambre. Comimos todo lo que había pero seguíamos con hambre.	*Oh, yes. The exercise made us hungry. We ate all there was, but we were still hungry.*
el ejercicio	*exercise*
darle hambre a uno	*to make someone hungry*
nos dio hambre	*it made us hungry*
había	*there was, there were*
todo lo que había	*everything that there was*

seguir (**e** > **i**)	*to follow*
seguíamos	*we were following*
seguir con hambre	*to still be hungry*
seguíamos con hambre	*we were still hungry*

⏵ Variantes

Listen, and repeat the same structures from *Diálogo 9*, now with new vocabulary.

¿Qué tiempo hacía?	*What was the weather like?*
Hacía calor .	*It was **hot**.*
frío	*cold*
setenta grados	*seventy degrees*
viento	*windy*

| Estaba nublado . | *It was **cloudy**.* |
| despejado | *clear* |

| Llovía. | *It was raining.* |
| Nevaba. | *It was snowing.* |

Nos daba hambre .	*It was making us **hungry**.*
sed	*thirsty*
calor	*warm*
frío	*cold*
sueño	*sleepy*
miedo	*afraid / It was scaring us.*

Estructura y Práctica

Uses of the Imperfect: Describing the Weather

The imperfect is the tense used for description and expressing background in the past against which completed actions or events occur. For example, when weather expressions provide the background for an event that occurred in the past, the imperfect is used for the weather expression, and the preterit is used for the event or action that occurred in the past.

| **Hacía buen tiempo** cuando **fui** al centro comercial. | *It was nice weather when I went to the mall.* |

R **¿Qué tiempo hacía?** Express the following sentences in Spanish, using imperfect or preterit verb forms.

1. *It was very cloudy when we got to the beach.*

2. *When the tourists went to see the pyramids, it was very hot.*

3. *It was ninety degrees when he got back to the coffee plantation.*

4. *When the plane took off, it was very windy.*

5. *It was clear when the picnic began.*

6. *Was it raining when you (tú) left the theater?*

7. *It was snowing when she came by.*

8. *It was cold when they woke up.*

Uses of the Verb **seguir**

In *Diálogo 9*, the verb **seguir** is used with the preposition **con** in the expression **seguir con hambre** (*to still be hungry*).

Seguían con sed.	*They were still thirsty.*
¿Sigues con dolor?	*Do you still have pain?*

Seguir con can also mean *to continue / go on / carry on with*.

Los peloteros **siguieron con** el partido.	*The baseball players **went on with** the game.*

Seguir con la vista means *to keep in view, keep one's eye on, not take one's eye off*.

Seguía al tipo sospechoso **con la vista**.	*He kept his eye on the suspicious guy.*

Seguir means *to still be* before an adjective.

Seguían preocupados/enojados/molestos.	*They were still worried/angry/annoyed.*

Expressions with **dar**

Some idioms with **tener** can be constructed with **dar** + indirect object to express the idea of *to make someone feel something*. One such expression appeared in *Diálogo 9*. Here are some others.

darle envidia *to make someone feel envious*
darle celos a uno *to make someone jealous*
darle la razón a uno *to agree that someone is right*
darle ganas a uno *to make someone feel like doing something*
darle confianza a uno *to give someone confidence*
darle vergüenza a uno *to make someone feel ashamed*
darle dolor a uno *to make someone feel pain*

Le di la razón.	*I agreed that he was right.*
Eso les dio ganas de llorar.	*That (situation) made them feel like crying.*

(For idioms with **tener**, see Chapter 7.)

S *Tengo... → Me dio...* Rewrite each of the following sentences, replacing the **tener** + noun idiom with a **dar** + indirect object expression. Follow the *modelo*.

MODELO   Tenía frío.
　　　→ Le dio frío.

1. Teníamos hambre.
2. Ellos tenían miedo.
3. Tenías sueño.
4. Él tenía vergüenza.
5. Yo tenía confianza.
6. Ud. tenía calor.
7. Uds. tenían celos.
8. Ella tenía dolor.
9. Ellas tenían envidia.
10. Teníamos frío.

T Express the following sentences in Spanish, using a **dar** + indirect object expression. Use the imperfect of the verb **dar**.

1. *The boring film was making him sleepy.*

2. *The songs were making us feel like dancing.*

3. *Our support was giving them confidence.*

4. *Her handsome friend was making her boyfriend jealous.*

5. *The good aroma of the soup was making me feel hungry.*

6. *The behavior* (el comportamiento) *of their little boy was making his parents feel ashamed.*

7. *What was making you* (tú) *feel envious?*

8. *The rain was making us feel cold.*

▶ DIÁLOGO 10 · ¡Qué olvidadizos somos!

Study the dialogue, then listen to the recording and repeat each line.

PABLO   Uds. nos dijeron que iban a hacernos los sándwiches y las ensaladas
              para la merienda campestre, ¿verdad?

JULIA   Ay, ¡qué olvidadizos somos! Se los preparamos ahora.

Análisis

Check that you understand the linguistic breakdown of each speech from *Diálogo 10*.

Uds. nos dijeron que iban a hacernos los sándwiches y las ensaladas para la merienda campestre, ¿verdad?	*You told us that you were going to make the sandwiches and the salads for the picnic (for us), didn't you?*
nos dijeron que	*you told us that*
iban	*you were going*
iban a hacernos	*you were going to make for us*
el sándwich	*sandwich*
la ensalada	*salad*
la merienda campestre	*picnic*
Ay, ¡qué olvidadizos somos! Se los preparamos ahora.	*Oh, how forgetful we are! We'll prepare them for you now.*
olvidadizo	*forgetful*
se los	*them for you*
se los preparamos	*we'll prepare them for you*

▶ Variantes

Listen, and repeat the same structures from *Diálogo 10*, now with new vocabulary.

¿Debemos servirles la torta y el café ahora?	*Should we serve you the cake and coffee now?*
No, ahora no. ¿Por qué no nos los sirven más tarde?	*No, not now. Why don't you serve them to us later?*

DIÁLOGO 11 · Días universitarios

Study the dialogue, then listen to the recording and repeat each line.

JULIA	Yo asistí a una universidad privada. ¿Y tú?
PABLO	Yo no. La universidad mía era estatal. Costaba menos.
JULIA	Yo no tenía beca. Trabajaba en una librería para ganar dinero.
PABLO	Y yo trabajaba de mesero en un café cuando no tenía clases.

Análisis

Check that you understand the linguistic breakdown of each speech from *Diálogo 11*.

Yo asistí a una universidad privada.	*I attended a private university.*
¿Y tú?	*How about you?*
asistir a	*to attend*
la universidad	*university*
privado	*private*
Yo no. La universidad mía era estatal.	*Not me. My university was a state university.*
Costaba menos.	*It cost less.*
la universidad mía	*my university*
era	*it was*
costar (**o** > **ue**)	*to cost*
costaba menos	*it cost less*
Yo no tenía beca. Trabajaba en una	*I didn't have a scholarship. I worked in a*
librería para ganar dinero.	*bookstore to earn money.*
tenía	*I had*
la beca	*scholarship (monetary award)*
trabajaba	*I used to work*
la librería	*bookstore*
ganar	*to earn*
para ganar dinero	*in order to earn money*
Y yo trabajaba de mesero en un café	*And I worked as a waiter in a café*
cuando no tenía clases.	*when I didn't have classes.*
trabajar de	*to work as*
el mesero	*waiter*
trabajar de mesero	*to work as a waiter*
yo trabajaba de mesero	*I used to work as a waiter*
el café	*café*
la clase	*class*

Variantes

Listen, and repeat the same structures from *Diálogo 11*, now with new vocabulary.

La universidad mía era estatal.	**Mine** *was a state university.*
tuya	*Yours*
suya	*His, Hers, Yours, Theirs*
nuestra	*Ours*

Estructura y Práctica

U *Una narrativa.* Write the correct imperfect form of each of the following verbs in parentheses to create a narrative.

Habla Mercedes. Todos los días yo (1) _____ (despertarse) a las seis

y media de la mañana. Al levantarme, yo (2) _____ (cepillarse) los dientes,

(3) _____ (ducharse), (4) _____ (maquillarse) y

(5) _____ (vestirse). Después yo (6) _____ (desayunar)

con mis compañeras de cuarto y (7) _____ (salir) para la universidad.

Yo (8) _____ (asistir) a una universidad privada donde

(9) _____ (hacer) la carrera de economía. Al graduarme

(10) _____ (esperar) trabajar en finanzas. Aunque yo

(11) _____ (tener) beca me (12) _____ (faltar) dinero

así que (13) _____ (trabajar) de mesera en el café universitario.

▶ DIÁLOGO 12 · Se da una propina.

Study the dialogue, then listen to the recording and repeat each line.

JULIA Yo pagué la cuenta. ¿Por qué no le dejas tú la propina al mesero?
PABLO Mira. Ya se la dejé.
JULIA ¿Esta miserable propina? ¡Qué poco generoso eres! Se debe dejar el veinte
       por ciento de propina.
PABLO ¿Tanto? Bueno, tienes razón. Yo también fui mesero una vez.

Análisis

Check that you understand the linguistic breakdown of each speech from *Diálogo 12.*

Yo pagué la cuenta. ¿Por qué no le dejas tú la propina al mesero?	*I paid the check. Why don't you leave the tip for the waiter?*
la cuenta	bill, check (restaurant)
dejarle algo a uno	*to leave something for someone*
dejarle una propina al mesero	*to leave the waiter a tip*
Mira. Ya se la dejé.	*Look. I already left it for him.*
se la	*it for him*
se la dejé	*I left it for him*
¿Esta miserable propina? ¡Qué poco generoso eres! Se debe dejar el veinte por ciento de propina.	*This meager tip? How ungenerous you are! One should leave a tip of twenty percent.*
miserable	*miserable, meager*
generoso	*generous*
poco	*little, not much* (negates adjectives)
poco generoso	*stingy, ungenerous*

se debe dejar	*one should leave*
por ciento	*percent*
el veinte por ciento	*twenty percent*
de propina	*as a tip*

¿Tanto? Bueno, tienes razón. Yo también fui mesero una vez.	*That much? Well, you're right. I was also a waiter once.*
tanto	*so much*
bueno	*well*
tener razón	*to be right*
tienes razón	*you're right*
una vez	*once*

▶ Variantes

Listen, and repeat the same structures from *Diálogo 12*, now with new vocabulary.

| ¿Piensas dejarle una propina a la mesera? Mira. Acabo de dejársela. | *Do you intend to leave a tip for the waitress? Look. I've just left it for her.* |

Se debe hacer ejercicio.	*You should exercise.*
Se puede entrar por esa puerta.	*One can go in through that door.*
No se permite fumar en este edificio.	*Smoking is not allowed in this building.*
Se necesita hacer cola en la aduana.	*You have to stand in line at customs.*

▶ DIÁLOGO 13 · La beca fue suspendida.

Study the dialogue, then listen to the recording and repeat each line.

JULIA   Cien estudiantes iban a recibir esa beca. ¿Qué pasó?
PABLO   La beca fue suspendida porque no había suficiente dinero. Así que no se la dieron a nadie.

Análisis

Check that you understand the linguistic breakdown of each speech from *Diálogo 13*.

Cien estudiantes iban a recibir esa beca. ¿Qué pasó?	*One hundred students were going to receive that scholarship. What happened?*
iban a recibir	*they were going to receive*
¿Qué pasó?	*What happened?*

La beca fue suspendida porque no había suficiente dinero. Así que no se la dieron a nadie.	*The scholarship was discontinued because there wasn't enough money. So they didn't give it to anyone.*
suspender	*to discontinue, suspend*
fue suspendido	*it was discontinued, it was suspended*
suficiente	*enough*
se la	*it to him, it to her, it to you, it to them*
no se la dieron a nadie	*they didn't give it to anyone*

▶ Variantes

Listen, and repeat the same structures from *Diálogo 13*, now with new vocabulary.

¿Le dieron la beca a Jaime?	*Did Jaime get the scholarship?*
No, no se la dieron.	*No, they didn't give it to him.*
¿Le dieron el puesto a Susana?	*Did Susana get the position?*
No, no se lo dieron.	*No, they didn't give it to her.*
¿Le dieron la pasantía a Ud.?	*Did you get the internship?*
No, no me la dieron.	*No, they didn't give it to me.*
El proyecto fue suspendido.	*The project was postponed.*
La reunión fue suspendida.	*The meeting was adjourned.*
Los programas fueron suspendidos.	*The programs were discontinued.*
Las becas fueron suspendidas.	*The scholarships were discontinued.*

▶ DIÁLOGO 14 · Dificultades en la carretera

Study the dialogue, then listen to the recording and repeat each line.

PABLO   ¿Qué hora era cuando Uds. llegaron a casa?
JULIA   Eran las diez y media. Había mucho tráfico y no conocíamos la carretera. ¿Y Uds.?
PABLO   Era medianoche. Había tormenta y manejábamos muy lentamente. No se podía ver nada por la lluvia y la niebla.

Análisis

Check that you understand the linguistic breakdown of each speech from *Diálogo 14*.

¿Qué hora era cuando Uds. llegaron a casa?	*What time was it when you got home?*
¿Qué hora era?	*What time was it?*
llegar a casa	*to get home, arrive home*
Eran las diez y media. Había mucho tráfico y no conocíamos la carretera. ¿Y Uds.?	*It was ten thirty. There was a lot of traffic and we weren't familiar with the highway. How about you?*
eran las diez y media	*it was ten thirty*
había	*there was*
el tráfico	*traffic*
no conocíamos	*we were not familiar with, we didn't know*
la carretera	*the highway*
Era medianoche. Había tormenta y manejábamos muy lentamente. No se podía ver nada por la lluvia y la niebla.	*It was midnight. There was a storm and we were driving very slowly. You couldn't see anything because of the rain and the fog.*
la medianoche	*midnight*
era medianoche	*it was midnight*

había	*there was*
la tormenta	*storm*
había tormenta	*there was a storm*
manejar	*to drive*
manejábamos	*we were driving*
lento	*slow, slowly*
lentamente	*slowly*
podía	*was able*
no se podía ver nada	*you couldn't see anything*
por	*because of*
la lluvia	*rain*
la niebla	*fog*

▶ Variantes

Listen, and repeat the same structures from *Diálogo 14*, now with new vocabulary.

¿Qué hora era cuando regresaron?	*What time was it when you came back?*
Era la una.	*It was one o'clock.*
Era mediodía.	*It was noon.*
Eran las siete.	*It was seven o'clock.*
Era tarde.	*It was late.*

Había un embotellamiento.	*There was a traffic jam.*
Había tantos líos de tráfico.	*There were so many traffic jams.*
Había una gran cantidad de carros.	*There were loads of cars.*

No se podía ver por la nieve.	*We couldn't **see** because of the snow.*
manejar	*drive*
caminar	*walk*
aparcar	*park*

Manejaban muy lentamente .	*They were driving very **slowly**.*
rápidamente.	*fast*

¿Cuánto (tiempo) hacía que manejaban?	*How long had you been driving?*
Hacía tres horas que manejábamos.	*We had been driving for three hours.*
Manejábamos hacía tres horas.	*We had been driving for three hours.*

Estructura y Práctica

Uses of the Imperfect: Telling Time

The imperfect tense is used to tell what time it was in the past. The preterit is never used.

¿Qué hora **era**?	*What time **was** it?*
Eran las tres de la tarde.	*It **was** 3:00 P.M.*

V **¿Qué hora era?** Write sentences telling at what time certain things happened, using the elements given. The imperfect tense is used to tell the time, and the preterit is used to tell what happened. Follow the *modelo*.

MODELO   las dos de la tarde / ella / tomar el almuerzo
→ Eran las dos de la tarde cuando ella tomó el almuerzo.

1. las nueve de la noche / ellos / volver de las pirámides

2. las siete y media de la mañana / tú / levantarse

3. la una de la tarde / nosotros / ir a la merienda campestre

4. las tres cuarenta y cinco de la tarde / los directores de la empresa / reunirse

5. las cinco de la tarde / yo / empezar a jugar al tenis

6. las ocho menos veinte de la noche / Uds. / llegar a la finca

7. casi las once de la noche / Ud. / terminar de escribir su informe

8. las diez de la mañana / él / salir para el cafetal

⏵ DIÁLOGO 15 · Se realizaba un sueño.

Study the dialogue, then listen to the recording and repeat each line.

JULIA   En aquella época venían muchos inmigrantes a los Estados Unidos.
PABLO   En efecto. Había muchos italianos, irlandeses, alemanes y polacos.
JULIA   Soñaban con mejorar su vida.
PABLO   Y en este país muchos pudieron realizar su sueño.

Análisis

Check that you understand the linguistic breakdown of each speech from *Diálogo 15*.

En aquella época venían muchos inmigrantes a los Estados Unidos.	*At that time, many immigrants were coming to the United States.*
la época	*time, era, epoch, period of time*
en aquella época	*at that time, during that period*
venían	*they were coming*
el inmigrante	*immigrant*
los Estados Unidos	*United States*

En efecto. Había muchos italianos, irlandeses, alemanes y polacos.	*That's right. There were many Italians, Irish, Germans, and Poles.*
en efecto	*that's right, indeed*
había	*there was, there were* (imperfect of **hay**)
el italiano	*Italian*
el irlandés	*Irish*
el alemán	*German*
el polaco	*Pole*

Soñaban con mejorar su vida.	*They dreamed of improving their lives.*
soñar con	*to dream of*
mejorar	*to improve*
soñar con mejorar	*to dream of improving*
la vida	*life*
Y en este país muchos pudieron realizar su sueño.	*And in this country, many were able to realize their dream.*
en este país	*in this country*
pudieron	*they could, they were able*
realizar	*to achieve, realize*
el sueño	*dream*

▶ Variantes

Listen, and repeat the same structures from *Diálogo 15*, now with new vocabulary.

Soñaban con mejorar su vida .	*They used to dream about **making their lives better**.*
llevar una vida mejor	*leading a better life*
vivir mejor	*living better*
triunfar en la vida	*getting ahead, succeeding in life*
una vida mejor	*a better life*
¿Cuánto tiempo llevaban en los Estados Unidos?	*How long had they been in the United States?*
Llevaban diez años en el país.	*They had been living in the country for ten years.*

Estructura y Práctica

W *Una narrativa.* Write the correct imperfect form of each of the following verbs in parentheses to complete this paragraph about immigrants.

A principios del siglo veinte (*In the early twentieth century*) (1) _____ (llegar) mucha gente a los Estados Unidos de otros países. Muchos de esos inmigrantes (2) _____ (ser) pobres y (3) _____ (esperar) encontrar empleo. Ellos (4) _____ (soñar) con llevar una vida mejor y por lo tanto (5) _____ (tener) que aprender inglés para poder trabajar. Ellos (6) _____ (trabajar) en fábricas (*factories*) y tiendas pequeñas. La vida (7) _____ (ser) muy difícil para ellos pero (8) _____ (saber) que (9) _____ (vivir) en un país que les (10) _____ (dar) la oportunidad de realizar sus sueños y triunfar en la vida.

▶ DIÁLOGO 16 · Lo que hacíamos

Study the dialogue, then listen to the recording and repeat each line.

PABLO   ¿Qué hacían Uds.?

JULIA   Yo escribía unos correos electrónicos mientras Marisol leía una novela.
         ¿Y Uds.?

PABLO   Pues yo oía música en mi cuarto mientras Felipe veía televisión en la sala.

Análisis

Check that you understand the linguistic breakdown of each speech from *Diálogo 16*.

¿Qué hacían Uds.?	*What were you doing?*
hacían	*you were doing*
Yo escribía unos correos electrónicos	*I was writing some emails while Marisol*
mientras Marisol leía una novela.	*was reading a novel. How about you?*
¿Y Uds.?	
escribía	*I was writing*
unos	*some*
unos correos electrónicos	*some emails*
mientras	*while*
leía	*she was reading*
Pues yo oía música en mi cuarto	*Well, I was listening to music in my room*
mientras Felipe veía televisión en	*while Felipe was watching television in*
la sala.	*the living room.*
oía	*I was hearing, I was listening to*
veía	*he was seeing, he was watching*
ver televisión	*to watch television*
la sala	*living room*

▶ Variantes

Listen, and repeat the same structures from *Diálogo 16*, now with new vocabulary.

Ellos dormían la siesta mientras nosotros navegábamos en la red.	*They were taking a nap while we were surfing the web.*
¿Cuánto (tiempo) hacía que navegabas en la red?	*How long had you been surfing the web?*
Hacía una hora que navegaba en la red.	*I had been surfing the web for an hour.*
¿Desde cuándo navegabas en la red?	*Since when had you been surfing the web?*
Navegaba en la red desde las tres.	*I had been surfing the web since three o'clock.*

Estructura y Práctica

Hacía + Expression of Time + **que** + Verb in Imperfect Tense

Spanish uses the imperfect tense to refer to past actions that are seen as continuing at another point of time in the past. English uses a *had been doing something* construction for this function.

To tell how long something had been going on, the following constructions are used:

hacía + expression of time + **que** + verb in imperfect
Hacía dos años que vivía en Madrid.   *I had been living in Madrid for two years.*

OR

verb in imperfect + **hacía** + expression of time
Vivía en Madrid **hacía dos años.**   *I had been living in Madrid for two years.*

To ask a question about how long something had been going on, the following construction is used (the word **tiempo** is optional).

¿Cuánto (tiempo) hacía que + verb in the imperfect?
¿Cuánto tiempo hacía que vivías   *How long had you been living in Madrid?*
en Madrid?

Desde is used to specify the starting point of an action that began in the past and continues to another point in the past.

¿Desde cuándo trabajabas con ellos?   *Since when had you been working with them?*

Trabajaba con ellos **desde** enero.   *I had been working with them since January.*

(For equivalent time expressions in present tense, see Chapter 6.)

X *Diálogos. ¿Cuánto tiempo hacía que...?* Write questions using the construction **¿Cuánto tiempo hacía que...?** and answer them using the construction **hacía** + expression of time + **que** + verb in the imperfect. Follow the *modelo.*

MODELO   Ud. / estudiar español / viajar a Costa Rica (tres años)
→ —¿Cuánto tiempo hacía que Ud. estudiaba español cuando viajó a Costa Rica?
→ —Hacía tres años que estudiaba español.

1. tú / tocar el piano / ellos / darte una beca (ocho años)

2. ella / jugar al golf / comenzar a llover (dos horas)

3. Uds. / esperar / sus primos / ellos / llegar (media hora)

4. él / trabajar en Chile / su empresa / mandarlo al Perú (cinco meses)

Y Express the following sentences in Spanish, using the appropriate time expression and the imperfect tense.

1. *I had been looking for the dog for an hour.*

2. *Since when had the farmers been growing corn?*

3. *How long had you (tú) been interested in modern art?*

4. *Cars had been produced in this plant for fifty years.*

5. *We had been doing ecotourism since June.*

6. *They had been serving healthy food for many years.*

7. *How long had it been snowing?*

8. *He had been attending a state university since last year.*

▶ DIÁLOGO 17 · La dirección electrónica

Study the dialogue, then listen to the recording and repeat each line.

JULIA   Ud. nos dijo que iba a mandarnos la dirección electrónica de Franco.
PABLO   Se la mandé ayer.
JULIA   ¿De veras? Pero no la encontré en nuestro buzón.
PABLO   Se la voy a mandar otra vez. No entiendo por qué no la recibieron.

Análisis

Check that you understand the linguistic breakdown of each speech from *Diálogo 17*.

Ud. nos dijo que iba a mandarnos la dirección electrónica de Franco.	*You said that you would send us Franco's email address.*
iba a	*you were going to*
Se la mandé ayer.	*I sent it to you yesterday.*
se la	*it to you*
se la mandé	*I sent it to you*
¿De veras? Pero no la encontré en nuestro buzón.	*Really? But I didn't find it in our inbox.*
¿De veras?	*Really?*
encontrar (**o** > **ue**)	*to find*
el buzón	*mailbox, inbox*
Se la voy a mandar otra vez. No entiendo por qué no la recibieron.	*I'll send it to you again. I don't understand why you didn't get it.*
se la voy a mandar	*I'm going to send it to you*
otra vez	*again*
entender (**e** > **ie**)	*to understand*
recibir	*to receive, get*

▶ Variantes

Listen, and repeat the same structures from *Diálogo 17*, now with new vocabulary.

Ellos nos dijeron que iban a casarse.	*They **told** us they were going to get married.*
contaron	*told*
escribieron	*wrote*
informaron	*informed*
¿El número de teléfono? Se lo mandé ayer.	*The telephone number? I sent it to you yesterday.*
¿Las fechas? Se las voy a mandar esta tarde.	*The dates? I'm going to send them to you this afternoon.*

Estructura y Práctica

Preterit and Imperfect in Indirect Discourse (Reported Speech)

The imperfect tense is used in indirect discourse, or reported speech (reporting what someone said), after the preterit form of verbs such as **decir** and **escribir**.

¿Qué te dijo Mario?	*What did Mario tell you?*
Me **dijo** que **volvía** tarde.	*He **told** me he **was coming back** late.*
¿Le escribiste a Carmen?	*Did you write to Carmen?*
Sí, le **escribí** que **me mudaba**.	*Yes, I **wrote** her that I **was moving**.*

Z **Reported speech.** Write answers to the following questions, using the elements given, to show reported speech. Follow the *modelo*.

MODELO   ¿Qué te dijo Alonso? (venir a visitarme)
→ Me dijo que venía a visitarme.

1. ¿Qué le dijeron a Ud. sus tíos? (mi primo / casarse)

2. ¿Qué les escribió Anita a Uds.? (ella / ir al extranjero)

3. ¿Qué te escribieron tus papás? (disfrutar de sus vacaciones)

4. ¿Qué te texteó tu amigo? (estar en camino)

5. ¿Qué le dijiste a tu novia? (quererla mucho)

6. ¿Qué le preguntó Ud. a su colega? (si / trabajar todavía en la base de datos)

7. ¿Qué te contó tu hijo? (interesarle estudiar administración de empresas)

8. ¿Qué les informó a Uds. el jefe de producción? (él / hacer un estudio de mercado)

▶ DIÁLOGO 18 · ¿Quién tiene el iPod?

Study the dialogue, then listen to the recording and repeat each line.

PABLO   ¿Me prestas tu iPod, por favor?
JULIA   Se lo presté a Esteban la semana pasada. ¿Por qué no se lo pides a él?
PABLO   ¿Y todavía no te lo devolvió?
JULIA   No. Pero si él te lo da a ti, tú me lo puedes devolver.

Análisis

Check that you understand the linguistic breakdown of each speech from *Diálogo 18*.

¿Me prestas tu iPod, por favor?	*Can you lend me your iPod, please?*
prestarle algo a uno	*to lend something to someone*
Se lo presté a Esteban la semana pasada.	*I lent it to Esteban last week. Why don't you*
¿Por qué no se lo pides a él?	*ask him for it?*
se lo	*it to him*
se lo presté	*I lent it to him*
se lo presté a Esteban	*I lent it to Esteban*
pedirle algo a uno	*to ask someone for something*
pedírselo a él	*to ask him for it*
¿Y todavía no te lo devolvió?	*And he still hasn't returned it to you?*
devolverle algo a uno	*to return something to someone*
todavía	*still, yet*
No. Pero si él te lo da a ti, tú me lo	*No. But if he gives it to you, you can return*
puedes devolver.	*it to me.*
darle algo a uno	*to give something to someone*
te lo da a ti	*he gives it to you*

▶ Variantes

Listen, and repeat the same structures from *Diálogo 18*, now with new vocabulary.

¿Me prestas tu cámara, por favor?	*Will you lend me your camera, please?*
Claro. Pero tienes que devolvérmela	*Of course. But you have to return it to me*
para el fin de semana.	*by the weekend.*

Estructura y Práctica

AA   *Fue ayer.* Express the following sentences in Spanish, explaining that everything happened yesterday. Use double object pronouns. Follow the *modelo*.

> MODELO   *The suitcase? I lent it to Antonio yesterday.*
> → ¿La maleta? Se la presté a Antonio ayer.

1. *The folders? We returned them to her yesterday.*

2. *The contract? He sent it to the lawyers yesterday.*

3. *The ticket? They gave it to me yesterday.*

4. *The gardens? She showed them to us yesterday.*

5. *The package? They wrapped* (envolver) *it for you (Uds.) yesterday.*

6. *The money? You (Ud.) asked me for it yesterday.*

7. *The earrings? We gave them to her as a gift yesterday.*

8. *The wallet? I brought it to you (tú) yesterday.*

9. *The documents? I handed them to him yesterday.*

10. *The cookies? I made them for him yesterday.*

Un paso más

Are you ready to take your Spanish a step further? Here are exercises that will enhance your knowledge of the language and allow you to express yourself freely.

BB   *Preguntas personales.* Answer each question with a complete Spanish sentence.

1. Cuando eras niño/niña, ¿cómo eras?

2. ¿Qué hacías todos los días?

3. ¿Quiénes formaban parte de tu familia?

4. ¿Era muy unida (*close*) tu familia?

5. ¿Convivías con tus abuelos? ¿Cómo eran? ¿Hacían un papel importante en tu vida?

6. ¿Te reunías mucho con tus tíos y primos?

7. ¿Dónde vivías de niño/niña?

8. ¿Adónde ibas de vacaciones?

9. ¿Cuáles son los recuerdos más vivos de tu niñez?

CC   *Narrativas personales*

Narrativa personal 1. Write a paragraph about your family history. Use the following questions as a guide to discuss a relative or relatives who emigrated to the United States.

1. ¿Tus abuelos o bisabuelos (*great-grandparents*) eran inmigrantes a los Estados Unidos?

2. ¿De dónde eran?

3. ¿En qué año llegaron a los Estados Unidos?

4. ¿Por qué o para qué emigraron a los Estados Unidos?

5. Describe (*Describe*) su experiencia, sus sueños y su lucha. ¿Pudieron triunfar en la vida?

6. ¿Qué idioma(s) hablaban?

7. ¿Se habla el idioma en tu familia todavía?

Narrativa personal 2. Write a paragraph about your visit—either real or imaginary—to the *Museo Nacional de Antropología. Diálogo 5* of this chapter talks about pre-Columbian civilizations in Mexico—the Aztecs, the Toltecs, and the pyramids of San Juan de Teotihuacán. To learn more and view impressive artifacts, visit the *Museo Nacional de Antropología* in Mexico City via the website http://www.mna .inah.gob.mx/. Use information from the museum website and the following questions as a guide.

Cuando estaba en México, visité el Museo Nacional de Antropología...

1. ¿Por qué estabas en México?

2. ¿Cuándo hiciste el viaje?

3. ¿Cómo era el museo?

4. ¿Qué había en las salas *(rooms)*?

5. ¿Qué viste en las salas dedicadas a la cultura tolteca y la cultura azteca?

6. ¿Qué aprendiste de las culturas precolombinas?

7. ¿También conociste las pirámides de San Juan de Teotihuacán? ¿Cómo eran?

> ***Narrativa personal 3.*** Write a paragraph about your college experience, using the following questions as a guide.

Cuando yo era universitario/universitaria...

1. ¿Asistías a una universidad privada o estatal? ¿A cuál?

2. ¿Qué carrera hacías?

3. ¿Qué materias tomabas? ¿En qué te especializabas?

4. ¿Qué título(s) universitario(s) *(degree(s))* tienes?

5. ¿Tenías beca?

6. ¿Trabajabas mientras estudiabas? ¿Qué hacías?

7. ¿Vivías en un apartamento o en una residencia universitaria *(dormitory)*?

Health and Accidents

Communication Goals

- Talking about health, accidents, and unplanned events
- Describing a visit to the doctor
- Vocabulary: healthy lifestyle, illnesses, parts of the body

Grammar Topics

- The Imperfect and the Preterit: Two Aspects of Past Time
- Reflexive Verbs with Reciprocal Meaning
- Augmentatives
- Diminutives
- Reverse Construction Verbs: **doler** *to hurt, ache*
- Unplanned Occurrences (Use of the Indirect Object Pronoun)

DIÁLOGO 1 · En el centro comercial

Study the dialogue, then listen to the recording and repeat each line.

RAQUEL	Entonces, ¿viste a Gonzalo en el centro comercial?
MIGUEL	Sí, él me saludó cuando yo subía en la escalera mecánica.
RAQUEL	Pero cuando nosotros le dijimos que íbamos, él dijo que no podía acompañarnos.
MIGUEL	No sé qué decirte. A lo mejor cambió de idea.

Análisis

Check that you understand the linguistic breakdown of each speech from *Diálogo 1*.

Entonces, ¿viste a Gonzalo en el centro comercial?	*So you saw Gonzalo at the mall?*
viste	*you saw*

Sí, él me saludó cuando yo subía en la   *Yes, he said hello to me when I was going*
escalera mecánica.   *up the escalator.*
    saludar   *to say hello to, greet*
    saludó   *he said hello*
    subir   *to go up*
    subía   *I was going up*
    la escalera mecánica   *escalator*

Pero cuando nosotros le dijimos que   *But when we told him that we were going,*
íbamos, él dijo que no podía   *he told us that he couldn't go with us.*
acompañarnos.
    dijimos   *we said, we told*
    íbamos   *we were going*
    dijo   *he said, he told*
    no podía   *he couldn't*
    acompañar   *to accompany, go with*

No sé qué decirte. A lo mejor cambió   *I don't know what to say (to you). Maybe*
de idea.   *he changed his mind.*
    qué decirte   *what to say to you*
    a lo mejor   *maybe*
    cambiar   *to change*
    cambiar de idea   *to change one's mind*

▶ Variantes

Listen, and repeat the same structures from *Diálogo 1*, now with new vocabulary.

Él nos dijo que no podía acompañarnos.   *He **told** us he wasn't able to go with us.*
    contó   *told*
    escribió   *wrote*
    informó   *informed*

Él nos dijo que no podía acompañarnos.   *He told us he **wasn't able** to go with us.*
    no quería   *didn't want*
    no pensaba   *didn't intend*
    no esperaba   *didn't expect*
    no necesitaba   *didn't need*
    no tenía que   *didn't have*

Él me saludó cuando yo subía en la   *He **waved** to me when I was going up*
escalera mecánica.   *the escalator.*
    llamó   *called*
    gritó   *shouted*

Él me saludó cuando yo subía en la   *He waved to me when I **was going up***
escalera mecánica.   *the escalator.*
    bajaba   *was going down*

¿Subieron por las escaleras o por el ascensor?	Did they walk up or take the elevator?
Subieron a pie porque el ascensor no funcionaba.	They walked up because the elevator wasn't working.
Bajaron a pie porque el elevador estaba descompuesto.	They walked down because the elevator was broken.
Cuando llegué al tercer piso, no había nadie.	When I got to the third floor, nobody was there.

Estructura y Práctica

The Imperfect and the Preterit: Two Aspects of Past Time

In Chapter 10, you learned the imperfect tense and how it contrasts with the preterit. (See also Chapter 9.) This chapter provides a more extensive study of this complicated topic: imperfect and preterit as two aspects of past time.

A **Imperfect or preterit.** Write either the imperfect or the preterit for each verb in parentheses to correctly complete each of the following sentences. Each sentence has two verbs; one might be in the imperfect and the other in the preterit, or both might be in the same tense. Follow the *modelo*.

MODELO   Nosotros __*salíamos*__ (salir) de casa cuando __*sonó*__ (sonar) el teléfono.

1. Mercedes _____ (ir) a pie porque no _____ (poder) encontrar un taxi.

2. Ellos _____ (pensar) acompañarnos pero _____ (cambiar) de idea.

3. Felipe _____ (bajar) en la escalera mecánica mientras yo

   _____ (subir) en el ascensor.

4. Alonso _____ (entrar) en la oficina y nos _____ (saludar).

5. ¿Ud. les _____ (decir) que _____ (querer) trasladarse a otra oficina?

6. Yo _____ (almorzar) fuerte, pero _____ (seguir) con hambre toda la tarde.

7. Todos los años nosotros _____ (visitar) la finca donde

   _____ (montar) a caballo.

8. Hoy Uds. _____ (levantarse) a las siete y _____ (arreglarse) a las ocho.

9. Ayer yo _____ (despertarse) temprano porque

   _____ (tener) mucho que hacer.

▶ DIÁLOGO 2 · Un partido de béisbol

Study the dialogue, then listen to the recording and repeat each line.

MIGUEL   ¿Qué tal el partido de béisbol? ¿Ganó tu equipo?

RAQUEL   ¿No sabes qué pasó? Veíamos el partido y comíamos unos perros
         calientes cuando de repente hubo un tremendo aguacero.

MIGUEL   Entonces el partido fue suspendido por la lluvia.

RAQUEL   Esperábamos hasta que dejó de llover. ¡Siguió el partido, dos horas
         más tarde!

Análisis

Check that you understand the linguistic breakdown of each speech from *Diálogo 2*.

¿Qué tal el partido de béisbol? ¿Ganó tu equipo?
How was the baseball game? Did your team win?

el partido	*game, sports match*
el partido de béisbol	*baseball game*
ganó	*he won*
el equipo	*team*

¿No sabes qué pasó? Veíamos el partido y comíamos unos perros calientes cuando de repente hubo un tremendo aguacero.
Don't you know what happened? We were watching the game and eating hot dogs when suddenly there was a huge downpour.

pasó	*it happened*
veíamos	*we were watching*
comíamos	*we were eating*
de repente	*suddenly*
hubo	*there was, there were*
tremendo	*tremendous, huge, terrible*
el aguacero	*shower, downpour*

Entonces el partido fue suspendido por la lluvia.
So the game was suspended because of the rain.

suspender	*to suspend*
fue suspendido	*was suspended*
por	*because of*
por la lluvia	*because of the rain*

Esperábamos hasta que dejó de llover. ¡Siguió el partido, dos horas más tarde!
We waited until it stopped raining. The game went on, two hours later!

esperar	*to wait*
esperábamos	*we waited*
hasta que	*until*
dejar de + *infinitive*	*to stop (doing something)*
dejó de llover	*it stopped raining*
seguir	*to continue*
siguió el partido	*the game continued*
más tarde	*later*

Variantes

Listen, and repeat the same structures from *Diálogo 2*, now with new vocabulary.

Veíamos el partido cuando comenzó a llover.
   Oíamos
   Esperábamos

We were watching the game when it started to rain.
   We were listening to
   We were waiting for

Veíamos el partido cuando comenzó a llover.
   empezó a

We were watching the game when **it started to rain**.
   it began

Esperábamos hasta que dejó de llover .
   salió el sol

We waited until **it stopped raining**.
   the sun came out

Cenábamos cuando Paco pasó por la casa.

We were having dinner when Paco stopped by.

Estructura y Práctica

B **Imperfect or preterit.** Write either the imperfect or the preterit for each verb in parentheses to correctly complete each of the following sentences. Each sentence has two verbs; one might be in the imperfect and the other in the preterit, or both might be in the same tense. Follow the *modelo*.

MODELO   El lanzador (*pitcher*) _se hizo_ (hacerse) daño mientras se _jugaba_ (jugar) la quinta entrada (*inning*).

1. _____ (Llover) tanto que ellos _____ (tener) que suspender el partido.

2. Nosotros _____ (esperar) en el café hasta que

_____ (dejar) de nevar.

3. Yo _____ (comer) un perro caliente mientras Esteban

_____ (tomar) su cerveza.

4. _____ (Estar) despejado todo el día hasta que por fin

_____ (haber) un aguacero.

5. Cuando el jugador _____ (pegar (*to hit*)) un jonrón, los aficionados

_____ (ponerse) a gritar de alegría.

⏵ DIÁLOGO 3 · Al señor Reyes lo trasladaron.

Study the dialogue, then listen to the recording and repeat each line.

MIGUEL   Por favor, ¿está el señor Reyes?

RAQUEL   No, señor. José Reyes trabajaba en esta sucursal hasta que lo trasladaron en mayo.

MIGUEL   ¿Ud. sabe cómo puedo ponerme en contacto con él?

RAQUEL   Lo siento. El número de teléfono que yo tenía ya no sirve porque lo cambiaron.

Análisis

Check that you understand the linguistic breakdown of each speech from *Diálogo 3*.

Por favor, ¿está el señor Reyes?	*Excuse me, is Mr. Reyes in?*
por favor	*please; excuse me (to get someone's attention)*
estar	*to be in, be there*
No, señor. José Reyes trabajaba en esta sucursal hasta que lo trasladaron en mayo.	*No, sir. José Reyes worked at this branch until they transferred him in May.*
trabajaba	*he worked, he used to work*
la sucursal	*branch (of a company, etc.)*
hasta que	*until*
trasladar	*to transfer*
trasladaron	*they transferred*
¿Ud. sabe cómo puedo ponerme en contacto con él?	*Do you know how I can get in touch with him?*
el contacto	*contact*
ponerse en contacto con	*to get in touch with*
Lo siento. El número de teléfono que yo tenía ya no sirve porque lo cambiaron.	*I'm sorry. The telephone number I had is no good anymore because they changed it.*
lo siento	*I'm sorry*
el número de teléfono	*telephone number*
tenía	*I had*
ya no	*no longer, no more*
servir	*to be useful*
ya no sirve	*is no good, is not valid anymore*
cambiaron	*they changed*

⏵ Variantes

Listen, and repeat the same structures from *Diálogo 3*, now with new vocabulary.

Marta trabajaba aquí hasta que la trasladaron .	*Marta used to work here until she was **transferred**.*
despidieron	*fired*

Hasta que Juan se jubiló era gerente de sucursal.	*Until Juan retired, he was branch manager.*
El número de teléfono que yo tenía fue cambiado.	*The telephone number I had was changed.*

Estructura y Práctica

C **Translation.** Express the following sentences in Spanish, selecting either the imperfect or the preterit for each verb.

1. *I was secretary* [masc.] *to the CEO* (director ejecutivo) *until he got sick.*

2. *Elena and Mercedes stopped working at that branch.*

3. *The telephone number was changed so* (así que) *we couldn't call them.*

4. *Did the manager transfer or fire Joaquín?*

5. *Víctor didn't finish the report because there wasn't enough data.*

SERVIR (E > I)

You are familiar with the verb **servir** (**e** > **i**) meaning *to serve*. The verb has different meanings in different structures and contexts. For example, in this chapter, **servir** is used in the sentence **ya no sirve**, meaning *it's no good* or *it's not valid anymore*. Note these uses of **servir**.

No **sirve quejarse/llorar**.	*There's no use in complaining/crying.*
Eso **no sirve para nada**.	*That's no good at all. / It's useless.*
Tener una rabieta no **te sirve para nada.**	*It's no use for you to throw a tantrum.*
¿Para qué **sirve esperar**?	*What's the point in waiting?*
¿**Sirven de** algo estos documentos?	*Do these documents have a purpose?*
Juan Diego **nos servía de** traductor.	*Juan Diego was our translator.*
Ellos no **sirven para** esas cosas.	*They're not good at those things.*
Me sirvo más arroz.	*I'll help myself to more rice.*
Se servía de estos sitios web todos los días.	*He used these websites every day.*
¿**En qué puedo servirle**?	*What can I do for you? / May I help you?* (*in a store*)
Sírvete. / Sírvase Ud.	*Help yourself.* (*to food*)

DIÁLOGO 4 · Compañeros de clase

Study the dialogue, then listen to the recording and repeat each line.

RAQUEL ¿Cuánto tiempo hacía que conocías a Isabel cuando Uds. se casaron?
MIGUEL Casi seis años. Nos conocimos mientras los dos estudiábamos en el extranjero.
RAQUEL Eran compañeros de clase en la Universidad de Sevilla, ¿verdad?
MIGUEL Sí. Mientras tomábamos clases de español, comenzamos a salir juntos.

Análisis

Check that you understand the linguistic breakdown of each speech from *Diálogo 4*.

¿Cuánto tiempo hacía que conocías a Isabel cuando Uds. se casaron?	*How long had you known Isabel when you two got married?*
¿Cuánto tiempo?	*How long?*
conocías a Isabel	*you knew Isabel*
¿Cuánto tiempo hacía que (tú) + *imperfect*?	*How long had (you) been (doing something)?*
se casaron	*you got married*

Casi seis años. Nos conocimos mientras los dos estudiábamos en el extranjero.	*Almost six years. We met (each other) while we were both studying abroad.*
casi	*almost*
conocerse	*to meet each other*
nos conocimos	*we met*
mientras	*while*
estudiábamos	*we were studying*
extranjero	*foreign*
en el extranjero	*abroad*

Eran compañeros de clase en la Universidad de Sevilla, ¿verdad?	*You were classmates at the University of Seville, right?*
el compañero	*companion, friend*
el compañero de clase	*classmate*

Sí. Mientras tomábamos clases de español, comenzamos a salir juntos.	*Yes. While we were taking Spanish classes, we began to go out together.*
tomábamos	*we were taking*
comenzar a + *infinitive*	*to begin to (do something)*
comenzamos	*we began*
salir	*to go out*
juntos	*together*

▶ Variantes

Listen, and repeat the same structures from *Diálogo 4*, now with new vocabulary.

¿Cuánto tiempo hacía que conocías a Isabel cuando Uds. se casaron?	*How long had you known Isabel when you got married?*
Hacía tres años que yo conocía a Isabel cuando nos casamos.	*I had known Isabel for three years when we got married.*
Nos conocimos mientras estábamos en el extranjero.	**We met** *while we were abroad.*
Nos enamoramos	*We fell in love*
Nos comprometimos	*We got engaged*

Mientras estudiábamos , Raquel prendió la tele.	While **we were studying**, Raquel turned on the TV.
leíamos	we were reading
comíamos	we were eating
dormíamos	we were sleeping
Yo salí mientras tú navegabas en la red.	I **went out** while you were surfing the web.
regresé	came back
me fui	left
Yo salí mientras tú oías música.	I went out while **you were listening to** music.
descargabas	you were downloading
componías	you were composing

Estructura y Práctica

Reflexive Verbs with Reciprocal Meaning

You learned in Chapter 8 that the plural forms of reflexive verbs are used to express reciprocal action corresponding to the English phrase *each other*.

¿**Se escribían** todos los meses?	**Did you write to each other** every month?
¡Qué va! **Nos escribíamos** una vez al año.	Are you kidding! **We wrote to each other** once a year.

D **Translation.** Express the following sentences in Spanish, selecting either the imperfect or the preterit for each verb. Pay special attention to the reflexive verbs with reciprocal meaning.

1. *How long had you* (Uds.) *known each other when you got engaged?*

2. *We had been seeing each other for a week when we began to address each other as* tú.

3. *How long had we been helping each other with the project when you* (Ud.) *moved?*

4. *While Lola and Juan were hugging and kissing each other, Lola's little brother started to laugh.*

5. *They understood each other very well until something happened.*

6. *We met when we were working at a high tech company.*

DIÁLOGO 5 · Alguien se equivocó de número.

Study the dialogue, then listen to the recording and repeat each line.

RAQUEL   Chico, ¡qué ojeras tienes! ¿No dormiste anoche?

MIGUEL   Al contrario. Dormía profundamente cuando sonó el teléfono a las cinco de la mañana.

RAQUEL   Ay, te despertaste sobresaltado. ¿Quién fue?

MIGUEL   Alguien se equivocó de número. Yo estaba tan alterado que no pude volver a dormirme.

Análisis

Check that you understand the linguistic breakdown of each speech from *Diálogo 5*.

Chico, ¡qué ojeras tienes! ¿No dormiste anoche?	*Wow, what dark circles you have under your eyes! Didn't you sleep last night?*
chico	*wow* (interjection)
la ojera	*dark circle under the eye*
dormiste	*you slept*
anoche	*last night*
Al contrario. Dormía profundamente cuando sonó el teléfono a las cinco de la mañana.	*Just the opposite. I was in a deep sleep when the telephone rang at five o'clock in the morning.*
al contrario	*on the contrary, just the opposite*
dormía	*I was sleeping*
profundo	*deep*
profundamente	*deeply*
sonar (**o** > **ue**)	*to ring*
sonó	*it rang*
Ay, te despertaste sobresaltado. ¿Quién fue?	*Oh, you woke up startled. Who was it?*
despertarse (**e** > **ie**)	*to wake up*
te despertaste	*you woke up*
sobresaltado	*startled*
fue	*it was*
Alguien se equivocó de número. Yo estaba tan alterado que no pude volver a dormirme.	*Someone dialed the wrong number. I was so unnerved that I couldn't fall asleep again.*
equivocarse	*to be mistaken*
equivocarse de	*to get the wrong thing, do the wrong thing*
equivocarse de número	*to dial the wrong number*
se equivocó de número	*he dialed the wrong number*
estaba	*I was*
alterado	*unnerved, upset*
no pude	*I couldn't (and didn't)*
volver a hacer algo	*to do something again*
volver a dormirse	*to fall asleep again*
No pude volver a dormirme.	*I couldn't fall asleep again.*

▶ Variantes

Listen, and repeat the same structures from *Diálogo 5*, now with new vocabulary.

Dormía cuando sonó el teléfono.	***I was sleeping** when the phone rang.*
Me dormía	*I was falling asleep*
Me duchaba	*I was taking a shower*
Me lavaba la cabeza	*I was washing my hair*
Me relajaba	*I was relaxing*

Volví a dormirme .	*I **fell asleep** again.*
peinarme	*combed my hair*
ducharme	*showered*

Estructura y Práctica

E **Interruptions.** Write either the imperfect or the preterit for each verb in parentheses to correctly complete each of the following sentences, explaining how some people were interrupted from what they were doing. Follow the *modelo*.

MODELO   Rafael __*dormía*__ (dormir) la siesta cuando __*llamó*__ (llamar) su hermano.

1. Nosotros _____ (imprimir) unos papeles cuando la impresora

   _____ (dejar) de funcionar.

2. Mateo _____ (leer) una novela policíaca (*crime novel*) cuando

   _____ (oír) unos ruidos raros en la casa.

3. Yo _____ (ver) las noticias en la tele cuando mis amigos

   _____ (venir) a buscarme.

4. Laura _____ (preparar) la cena cuando alguien

   _____ (tocar) el timbre.

5. Los chicos _____ (jugar) al béisbol cuando su perro

   _____ (comenzar) a ladrar (*bark*).

▶ DIÁLOGO 6 · Un niño prodigio

Study the dialogue, then listen to the recording and repeat each line.

MIGUEL   Me dijeron que Julio era un niño prodigio.
RAQUEL   Es cierto. Tenía doce años cuando se graduó en la universidad.
MIGUEL   ¿Lo conociste cuando era niño? ¿Cómo era?
RAQUEL   Era un niño encantador, superdotado pero nada presumido.

Análisis

Check that you understand the linguistic breakdown of each speech from *Diálogo 6*.

Me dijeron que Julio era un niño prodigio.	*They told me that Julio was a child prodigy.*
dijeron	*they said, they told*
era	*he was*
prodigio	*wonder, prodigy*
el niño prodigio	*child prodigy*

Es cierto. Tenía doce años cuando se graduó en la universidad.	*It's true. He was twelve years old when he graduated from the university.*
tenía	*he had*
tenía doce años	*he was twelve years old*
graduarse en	*to graduate from*
graduarse en la universidad	*to graduate from college, graduate from the university*
se graduó	*he graduated*

¿Lo conociste cuando era niño?	*Did you meet him when he was a child?*
¿Cómo era?	*What was he like?*
conociste	*you met*
era	*he was*

Era un niño encantador, superdotado pero nada presumido.	*He was a delightful child, extremely gifted, but not at all conceited.*
era	*he was*
encantador	*delightful*
dotado	*gifted*
superdotado	*extremely gifted*
nada	*not at all* (when it precedes an adjective)
presumido	*conceited*
nada presumido	*not at all conceited*

▶ Variantes

Listen, and repeat the same structures from *Diálogo 6*, now with new vocabulary.

Me dijeron que Julio era un niño prodigio.	***They told me** Julio was a child prodigy.*
Me informaron	*They informed me*

Tenía veinticinco años cuando se graduó .	*He was twenty-five years old **when he graduated**.*
cuando se hizo ingeniero	*when he became an engineer*
cuando se recibió de ingeniero	*when he got his engineering degree*

¿Camila era estudiante cuando la conociste?	*Was Camila a student when you met her?*
No, ya era física cuando la conocí.	*No, she was already a physicist when I met her.*

Manolo era un niño mandón .	*Manolo was **a bossy child**.*
un niño llorón	*a crybaby*
un niño preguntón	*an inquisitive child, a nosey child*
un niño dormilón	*a sleepyhead*

¿Raúl nunca se casó?	*Raúl never married?*
No, es solterón.	*No, he's a confirmed bachelor.*

Sofía tiene mucho dinero, ¿no?   *Sofía has a lot of money, doesn't she?*
¡Muchísimo! Es una ricachona.   *Loads! She's a very rich woman.*

¡Qué niñito más adorable!   *What a cute **little boy**!*
    chiquita   *little girl*
    bebito   *little baby*

Estructura y Práctica

F **Translation.** Express the following sentences in Spanish, selecting either the imperfect or the preterit for each verb.

1. *They told me their daughter was going to graduate from college.*

2. *Alonso was a confirmed bachelor until he met and married Sofía.*

3. *Victoria became a lawyer when she was twenty-seven.*

4. *You (tú) were very young when you got your medical degree.*

5. *The twins [masc.] were very gifted and nice, but also somewhat conceited.*

Augmentatives

Augmentatives indicate largeness, but they also have other meanings, such as disparagement. The most common augmentative ending in Spanish is **-ón/-ona**. It is often added to nouns and adjectives.

el hombre	→ el hombrón	*big man*
la mujer	→ la mujerona	*big woman*
rico	→ ricachón	*very rich, loaded*
inocente	→ inocentón	*naïve, gullible*

When the suffixes **-ón/-ona** are added to a verb root, they denote *given to performing the action of the verb.*

preguntar	→ preguntón	*always asking questions, inquisitive, nosey*
comer	→ comilón	*big eater, gluttonous*

The suffixes **-ote/-ota** and **-azo** are also used to form augmentatives, sometimes with the added connotation of contempt.

el libro	→ el librote	*big book*
grande	→ grandote, grandota	*very big, enormous*

In addition, **-azo** added to a noun can denote a blow or a strike with the object (or body part) indicated by the noun.

el codo (*elbow*)	→ el codazo	*elbow jab*
la cabeza	→ el cabezazo	*head butt*
el puño	→ el puñetazo	*fist punch*

Sometimes the addition of an augmentative suffix creates a new word. There is usually no suggestion of size.

la palabra	→ la palabrota	*swear word*
el éxito	→ el exitazo	*smash hit*
el soltero	→ el solterón	*confirmed bachelor*
la cintura (*waist*)	→ el cinturón	*belt*
la caja	→ el cajón	*drawer*
la rata (*rat*)	→ el ratón	*mouse*

G **Aumentativos.** Rewrite each of the following words with the augmentative ending **-ón/-ona**.

1. la casa

5. mirar

2. contestar

6. la muchacha

3. fácil

7. matar

4. llorar

Rewrite each of the following words with the augmentative ending **-azo**.

8. el martillo (*hammer*)

11. los ojos

9. el perro

12. el catarro

10. el puño (*fist*)

▶ DIÁLOGO 7 · Paquito estaba enfermo.

Study the dialogue, then listen to the recording and repeat each line.

MIGUEL   Oye, ¿no me dijiste que Paquito estaba enfermo?
RAQUEL   Sí. Lo llevé al pediatra porque le dolía el oído y tenía fiebre.
MIGUEL   Pobrecito. ¿Qué dijo el pediatra?
RAQUEL   Me dijo que mi hijito tenía infección. Le recetó un antibiótico.

Análisis

Check that you understand the linguistic breakdown of each speech from *Diálogo 7*.

Oye, ¿no me dijiste que Paquito estaba enfermo?	*Say, didn't you tell me that Paquito was sick?*
oye	*say, hey* (attention-getting word, informal)
dijiste	*you said, you told*
estaba	*he was*
enfermo	*sick*
estar enfermo	*to be sick*

Sí. Lo llevé al pediatra porque le dolía el oído y tenía fiebre.	*Yes, I took him to the pediatrician because his ear hurt and he had a fever.*
llevar	*to take (someone somewhere)*
llevé	*I took*
el pediatra	*pediatrician*
doler (**o** > **ue**)	*to hurt* (patterns like **gustar**)
le dolía	*it hurt him*
le dolía el oído	*his ear hurt (him)*
tenía	*he had*
la fiebre	*fever*

Pobrecito. ¿Qué dijo el pediatra?	*Poor kid. What did the pediatrician say?*
pobrecito	*poor kid, poor guy*
dijo	*he said, he told*

Me dijo que mi hijito tenía infección. Le recetó un antibiótico.	*He told me that my son had an infection. He prescribed an antibiotic for him.*
me dijo	*he told me*
mi hijito	*my son*
tenía	*he had*
la infección	*infection*
recetar	*to prescribe*
recetarle algo a uno	*to prescribe something for someone*
le recetó	*he prescribed for him*
el antibiótico	*antibiotic*

⏵ Variantes

Listen, and repeat the same structures from *Diálogo 7*, now with new vocabulary.

Paquito estaba enfermo.	**Paquito** *was sick.*
Juanito	*Juanito*
Carlitos	*Carlitos*
Dieguito	*Dieguito*

A Paquita le dolía la cabeza.	**Paquita** *had a headache.*
Juanita	*Juanita*
Paulita	*Paulita*

A Carmencita le dolía la garganta.	**Carmencita** *had a sore throat.*
Lolita	*Lolita*
Rosita	*Rosita*

Al abuelito le duele la espalda .	*Grandpa's* **back** *hurts.*
el cuello	*neck*
la rodilla	*knee*
el tobillo	*ankle*

A la abuelita le duelen los ojos .	*Grandma's* **eyes** *hurt.*
las piernas	*legs*
los dedos	*fingers*

Su hermanito tenía dolor de estómago.	Their **little brother** had a stomachache.
nietecito	little grandson
sobrinito	little nephew
primito	little cousin

Su hermanita tenía dolor de cabeza.	Their **little sister** had a headache.
nietecita	little granddaughter
sobrinita	little niece
primita	little cousin

El jovencito tomaba aspirinas.	The young man took **aspirins**.
vitaminas	vitamins

Florecita tenía catarro.	Florecita had **a cold**.
resfriado	a cold
gripe	the flu
alergia	an allergy

¿Quieres tomar un cafecito?	Do you want to have a quick cup of coffee?
Ahora tengo cita con el médico.	I have a doctor's appointment now.
Quizás después.	Maybe afterwards.

Estructura y Práctica

Diminutives

Spanish makes wide use of diminutives. The most common diminutive ending in Spanish is **-ito/-ita**. Diminutive endings are most commonly added to nouns, but they may appear also with adjectives.

libro	librito
casa	casita
viejo	viejito

Diminutives in Spanish express a variety of meanings, not only small size. They can express affection, sarcasm, politeness, etc.

Tienen una casita en el campo.	They have a small house in the country.
El perrito de ellos es muy cariñoso.	Their dog is very affectionate.
Él es timidito.	He's somewhat shy.

Diminutives are very common with proper names. Notice that in writing, the letters **c** and **g** change to **qu** and **gu**, respectively, before the diminutive ending.

Luis	→ Luisito
Paco	→ Paquito
Elena	→ Elenita
Diego	→ Dieguito
Sara	→ Sarita

Several groups of words take the ending -**cito**: words that end in -**e**, -**n**, or -**r**; words that end in a stressed vowel; and words of one syllable.

pobre → pobrecito
tren → trencito
pan → pancito
dolor → dolorcito
papá → papacito

Two-syllable nouns that have a first syllable containing -**ie**- or -**ue**- and that end in -**o** or -**a** pattern differently. They drop the -**o** or -**a** and add -**ecito/-ecita**. The same is true of many one-syllable nouns ending in a consonant.

tienda → tiendecita
puerta → puertecita
flor → florecita

However, the rules vary from country to country, especially for words of one syllable. **Papito**, **trenecito**, and **panecito** are also current.

TICO

Tico, a colloquial term for a native of Costa Rica, derives from the prominent use of the diminutive ending -**ico** rather than -**ito** in Costa Rica. -**Ico** is also used in Cuba, the Dominican Republic, and other countries, but it appears most widely in Costa Rica.

H *Diminutivos.* Rewrite each of the following words as a diminutive ending in -**ito** or -**ita**.

1. la ropa
2. el dedo
3. la niña
4. el pájaro
5. la voz
6. el chico
7. fresco
8. el joven
9. la botella
10. el calor
11. la fiesta
12. Miguel
13. poco
14. la nieta
15. el abuelo
16. cerca
17. la cabeza
18. Rodrigo
19. mismo
20. el choque
21. el pez
22. la luz
23. la tos

Reverse Construction Verbs: **doler** *to hurt, ache*

In Chapter 9, you learned about reverse construction verbs. These verbs appear with an indirect object pronoun and pattern like **gustar** (*to like*). The verb **doler** (**o > ue**) fits into this pattern.

Me gusta este barrio.	*I like this neighborhood.*
Me gustan estos barrios.	*I like these neighborhoods.*
Le duele el pie.	*His foot hurts.*
Le duelen los pies.	*His feet hurt.*
Le duele una muela.	*She has a toothache.*

Doler also means *to distress*.

Nos duele verlo en una silla de ruedas.	*We're distressed to see him in a wheelchair. / It distresses us to see him in a wheelchair.*

I ¡**Ay, qué dolor!** Express the following sentences in Spanish, using either the present or the imperfect tense of the verb **doler** in your answers.

1. *Juanita has a stomachache.*

2. *Pedro had a backache.*

3. *Their knees are aching.*

4. *Our little niece has a sore throat.*

5. *You (tú) had a headache.*

6. *The player's ankles are painful.*

7. *Paco's little grandson had an earache.*

8. *Their eyes were hurting.*

▶ DIÁLOGO 8 · Un chequeo médico

Study the dialogue, then listen to the recording and repeat each line.

MIGUEL   Fui al médico porque me sentía mal y tenía mucho estrés.
RAQUEL   Entonces tuviste un chequeo. ¿Te hicieron un análisis de sangre?
MIGUEL   Sí. Parece que tengo el colesterol alto. Tengo que ponerme a dieta.
RAQUEL   Yo también tuve que bajar de peso porque tenía la presión sanguínea alta.

Análisis

Check that you understand the linguistic breakdown of each speech from *Diálogo 8*.

Fui al médico porque me sentía mal y tenía mucho estrés.	*I went to the doctor because I felt sick and I had a lot of stress.*
fui al médico	*I went to the doctor*
sentirse (**e > ie**)	*to feel*
me siento mal	*I feel sick*
me sentía mal	*I was feeling sick*
tenía	*I had*
el estrés	*stress*

Entonces tuviste un chequeo.	*So you had a checkup. Did they do a blood*
¿Te hicieron un análisis de sangre?	*test (on you)?*
tuviste	*you had*
el chequeo	*checkup*
hicieron	*they did*
el análisis	*analysis, study, test*
la sangre	*blood*
el análisis de sangre	*blood test*

Sí. Parece que tengo el colesterol alto.	*It seems that my cholesterol is high.*
Tengo que ponerme a dieta.	*I have to go on a diet.*
parece que	*it seems that*
el colesterol alto	*high cholesterol*
ponerse a dieta	*to go on a diet*

Yo también tuve que bajar de peso	*I also had to lose weight because I had high*
porque tenía la presión sanguínea alta.	*blood pressure.*
tuve que	*I had to*
el peso	*weight*
bajar de peso	*to lose weight*
tuve que bajar de peso	*I had to (and did) lose weight*
tenía	*I had*
la presión	*pressure*
sanguíneo	*blood* (adjective)
la presión sanguínea	*blood pressure*

▶ Variantes

Listen, and repeat the same structures from *Diálogo 8*, now with new vocabulary.

Empecé a comer sano porque me	***I started to eat healthy food*** *because*
sentía cansado.	*I was feeling tired.*
Cambié mi estilo de vida	*I changed my lifestyle*
Comencé a hacer ejercicio	*I started to exercise*
Dejé de comer tanta grasa	*I stopped eating so much fat*

¿Viste a Javier? Se puso gordo.	*Did you see Javier? He got fat.*
Sí, engordó mucho porque es comilón.	*Yes, he got very fat because he's a big eater.*

¿Viste a Rosa? Se puso delgada.	*Did you see Rosa? She got thin.*
Sí, adelgazó porque come como un	*Yes, she got thin because she eats like*
pajarito.	*a (little) bird.*

Tuve que bajar de peso porque la ropa	*I had to lose weight because my clothing*
me quedaba pequeña.	*didn't fit. (literally, my clothing was small*
	on me)

Tuve que aumentar de peso porque	*I had to gain weight because my clothing*
la ropa me quedaba grande.	*didn't fit. (literally, my clothing was big*
	on me)

▶ DIÁLOGO 9 · Los mosquitos le comían vivo.

Study the dialogue, then listen to the recording and repeat each line.

RAQUEL   Oye chico, ¿qué tienes en la piel? ¿Es un sarpullido?
MIGUEL   Son picaduras de mosquito. Los mosquitos me comían vivo cuando
              acampábamos la semana pasada.
RAQUEL   ¿No dormiste en una tienda de campaña?
MIGUEL   Claro, pero me olvidé de ponerme el repelente contra mosquitos.
              ¡Mira tú el resultado!

Análisis

Check that you understand the linguistic breakdown of each speech from *Diálogo 9*.

Oye chico, ¿qué tienes en la piel?	*Hey, what have you got on your skin?*
¿Es un sarpullido?	*Is it a rash?*
oye, chico	*hey (interjection) (literally, listen, guy;*
	addressed to a male)
la piel	*skin*
el sarpullido	*rash*
Son picaduras de mosquito.	*They're mosquito bites. The mosquitos*
Los mosquitos me comían vivo cuando	*were eating me alive when we went camping*
acampábamos la semana pasada.	*last week.*
la picadura	*bite*
el mosquito	*mosquito*
la picadura de mosquito	*mosquito bite*
comer vivo	*to eat (someone) alive*
me comían vivo	*they were eating me alive*
acampar	*to camp, go camping*
acampábamos	*we were camping*
¿No dormiste en una tienda de	*Didn't you sleep in a tent?*
campaña?	
dormiste	*you slept*
la tienda de campaña	*tent*
Claro, pero me olvidé de ponerme	*Of course, but I forgot to put on mosquito*
el repelente contra mosquitos. ¡Mira tú	*repellent. And look what happened!*
el resultado!	
olvidarse de hacer algo	*to forget to do something*
ponerse	*to put on*
el repelente	*repellent*
contra	*against*
el repelente contra mosquitos	*mosquito repellent*
el resultado	*the result*
¡Mira tú el resultado!	*Look what happened! (literally, Look at*
	the result!)

Variantes

Listen, and repeat the same structures from *Diálogo 9*, now with new vocabulary.

Me pica mucho la picadura de abeja.	*The bee sting itches a lot.*
Debes tratar de no rascártela.	*You should try not to scratch it.*
El champú me entró en los ojos.	*I got shampoo in my eyes.*
Están rojos. Te pican, ¿no?	*They look red. They sting, don't they?*
Tomaba el sol y ahora tengo quemadura de sol.	*I was sunbathing, and now I have a sunburn.*
¿Te olvidaste de ponerte el filtro solar?	*Did you forget to put sunblock on? /* *Did you forget to put sunscreen on?*
Uso lentes .	*I wear **glasses**.*
lentes de sol	*sunglasses*
lentes de contacto	*contact lenses*

Estructura y Práctica

Unplanned Occurrences (Use of the Indirect Object Pronoun)

In Spanish, unplanned occurrences—such as forgetting, breaking, losing, or dropping something—can be expressed by adding the indirect object pronoun to a **se** construction with certain verbs. These constructions focus on the object affected rather than on the person involved. These are high frequency structures heard in everyday speech.

acabársele
    Se les acabó el repelente contra mosquitos.   ***They ran out of** mosquito repellent.*

caérsele
    Se me cayeron los lentes de contacto.   ***I dropped** my contact lenses.*

rompérsele
    Se le rompió el meñique al beisbolista.   *The baseball player **broke** his pinky.*

olvidársele
    Se nos olvidó llevar el paraguas.   ***We forgot** to bring the umbrella.*

ocurrírsele
    ¿Por qué no **se te ocurrió** llevar el paraguas?   *Why **didn't you think of** taking an umbrella?*

Here are some other verbs used in this construction.

descomponérsele a uno *to have something break down*
perdérsele a uno *to lose*
quebrársele a uno *to break*
quedársele a uno *to leave something behind*

J *Sucesos inesperados* (**Unplanned occurrences**). Rewrite each of the following sentences, transforming the **se** construction into an unplanned occurrence structure. Use the correct indirect object pronoun, as indicated by the cue in parentheses. Follow the *modelo*.

MODELO   Se rompió la botella de champú. (á el)
             → Se le rompió la botella de champú.

1. Se acabó el filtro solar. (a ella)

2. Se olvidaron las toallas de playa (*beach towels*). (a nosotros)

3. ¿Se quedó el repelente contra mosquitos en casa? (a Uds.)

4. Se cayeron los lentes de sol. (a mí)

5. Se descompuso el carro. (a ellos)

6. Se perdieron las gafas oscuras. (a ti)

7. Se quebraron los platos. (a Ud.)

K Express the following sentences in Spanish.

1. *The mosquitos were eating us alive.*

2. *What a bite! You* (tú) *shouldn't scratch it.*

3. *Catalina was sunbathing until a bee stung her.* (picar (*to sting*))

4. *Pedro lost his sunglasses in the sand* (la arena).

5. *They left the tent at the campsite* (el campamento).

6. *Poor thing* [fem.]*! She got shampoo in her eyes.*

DIÁLOGO 10 · Aurora tuvo un niño.

Study the dialogue, then listen to the recording and repeat each line.

MIGUEL   ¿Sabes que Aurora tuvo un niño?
RAQUEL   ¿De veras? Yo ni sabía que estaba embarazada.
MIGUEL   Aurora me contó que su esposo regresaba de un viaje de negocios cuando ella dio a luz.
RAQUEL   ¡Ay, ese Santiago! ¡Hasta al nacimiento de su hijo llega tarde!

Análisis

Check that you understand the linguistic breakdown of each speech from *Diálogo 10*.

¿Sabes que Aurora tuvo un niño?	*Do you know that Aurora had a baby boy?*
tener un niño	*to have a child, to have a boy child*
tuvo un niño	*she had a baby boy*

¿De veras? Yo ni sabía que estaba
embarazada.
  ni
  sabía
  ni sabía
  estar embarazada

Really? I didn't even know that she was
pregnant.
  not even
  I knew
  I didn't even know
  to be pregnant

Aurora me contó que su esposo
regresaba de un viaje de negocios
cuando ella dio a luz.
  contar (**o** > **ue**)
  me contó que...
  regresar
  regresaba
  regresaba de un viaje de negocios
  dar a luz
  dio a luz

Aurora told me that her husband was
coming back from a business trip when
she gave birth.
  to tell, recount
  she told me that . . .
  to return, come/go back
  he was returning
  he was coming back from a business trip
  to give birth
  she gave birth

¡Ay, ese Santiago! ¡Hasta al nacimiento
de su hijo llega tarde!
  el nacimiento
  el nacimiento de su hijo

Oh, that Santiago! He even comes late
to the birth of his son!
  the birth
  the birth of his son

Variantes

Listen, and repeat the same structures from *Diálogo 10*, now with new vocabulary.

Nos contó que estaba embarazada .
  que iba al médico
  que tenía una enfermedad

*She told us **that she was pregnant**.*
  that she was going to the doctor
  that she had an illness

Estructura y Práctica

L **Imperfect or preterit.** Write either the imperfect or the preterit for each verb
in parentheses to correctly complete each of the following sentences.

1. Hace unos días yo _____ (saber) que Claudia _____ (estar)
   embarazada.

2. Los Arriaga nos _____ (decir) que su hija _____ (ir) a tener
   un hijo.

3. Nosotros _____ (esperar) en la sala de espera hasta que Matilde
   _____ (dar) a luz.

4. Cuando Jorge _____ (estar) en el consultorio del médico, la enfermera
   le _____ (hacer) un análisis de sangre.

5. Los papás de Fernandito lo _____ (llevar) al pediatra porque al niño
   le _____ (doler) el estómago y _____ (tener) fiebre.

▶ DIÁLOGO 11 · Falsa alarma

Study the dialogue, then listen to the recording and repeat each line.

RAQUEL   ¿No sabes? Mientras Mateo y yo subíamos en el ascensor, sonó la alarma.
MIGUEL   Dios mío, ¡qué susto! ¿Creían que había un incendio?
RAQUEL   Sí. Llegaron los bomberos y la policía. Por suerte fue una falsa alarma.

Análisis

Check that you understand the linguistic breakdown of each speech from *Diálogo 11*.

¿No sabes? Mientras Mateo y yo subíamos en el ascensor, sonó la alarma.	*You know? While Mateo and I were going up in the elevator, the alarm went off.*
subíamos	*we were going up*
el ascensor	*elevator*
sonó	*it sounded, it went off*
la alarma	*the alarm*

Dios mío, ¡qué susto! ¿Creían que había un incendio?	*My gosh, what a scare! Did you think there was a fire?*
Dios	*God*
Dios mío	*my gosh, my goodness*
el susto	*fright*
¿creían?	*did you think?*
había	*there was*
el incendio	*fire (accidental)*

Sí. Llegaron los bomberos y la policía. Por suerte fue una falsa alarma.	*Yes. The firefighters and the police arrived. Luckily, it was a false alarm.*
llegaron	*they arrived*
el bombero	*firefighter*
los bomberos	*firefighters*
la policía	*the police*
la suerte	*luck*
por suerte	*luckily*
fue	*it was*
una falsa alarma	*a false alarm*

▶ Variantes

Listen, and repeat the same structures from *Diálogo 11*, now with new vocabulary.

Mientras subíamos en el ascensor, sonó la alarma .	*While we were going up in the elevator,* **the alarm sounded**.
llegaron los bomberos	*the firefighters arrived*
Mientras estaban en el banco, hubo un atraco.	*While they were in the bank, there was a holdup.*
Mientras viajaban, estalló una guerra en su país.	*While they were traveling, a war broke out in their country.*
La policía atrapó al ladrón mientras él se escapaba.	*The police caught the thief while he was escaping.*

Estructura y Práctica

M **Imperfect or preterit.** Write either the imperfect or the preterit for each verb in parentheses to correctly complete each of the following sentences.

1. Mientras nosotros _____ (bajar) en la escalera mecánica,

   _____ (ver) un atraco (*mugging*) a un paseante (*passerby*).

2. Mientras la familia _____ (estar) de vacaciones,

   _____ (sonar) la alarma de su casa.

3. El incendio _____ (arder (*to burn*)) hasta que los bomberos lo

   _____ (apagar).

4. Su vida _____ (ser) tranquila hasta que _____ (estallar)
   la guerra.

DIÁLOGO 12 · Un choque de carros

Study the dialogue, then listen to the recording and repeat each line.

MIGUEL   Hoy, mientras yo retiraba dinero del cajero automático, hubo un choque
         de carros delante del banco.
RAQUEL   ¿Hubo heridos? ¿Llegó una ambulancia?
MIGUEL   Sí, dos paramédicos atendieron a las víctimas. Afortunadamente sólo
         tenían heridas leves.

Análisis

Check that you understand the linguistic breakdown of each speech from *Diálogo 12*.

Hoy, mientras yo retiraba dinero del cajero automático, hubo un choque de carros delante del banco.	*Today, while I was withdrawing money from the ATM, there was a car crash in front of the bank.*
retirar dinero	*to withdraw money*
retiraba	*I was withdrawing*
el cajero automático	*the ATM*
hubo	*there was, there were*
el choque	*collision*
un choque de carros	*a car crash*
delante de	*in front of*
delante del banco	*in front of the bank*
¿Hubo heridos? ¿Llegó una ambulancia?	*Were any people injured? Did an ambulance arrive?*
el herido	*injured or wounded person*
la ambulancia	*ambulance*

Sí, dos paramédicos atendieron a las
víctimas. Afortunadamente sólo tenían
heridas leves.

Yes, two paramedics tended to the victims.
Fortunately, they only had light injuries.

el paramédico	*paramedic*
atender a	*to tend to, look after*
la víctima	*victim* (always feminine in Spanish)
afortunadamente	*fortunately*
sólo	*only*
tenían	*they had*
la herida	*injury, wound*
leve	*light, slight*

Variantes

Listen, and repeat the same structures from *Diálogo 12*, now with new vocabulary.

Yo estaba en la esquina cuando
chocaron dos coches .

*I was at the corner when **two cars crashed**.*

vi un accidente de tráfico
un coche atropelló a un peatón

I saw a traffic accident
a car ran a pedestrian over

Todo el mundo miraba mientras los
paramédicos atendían a las víctimas .

Everyone was watching while the paramedics
***were tending to the victims**.*

daban primeros auxilios

were giving first aid

Estructura y Práctica

N *Una narrativa.* Write either the imperfect or the preterit for each of the following verbs in parentheses to create a narrative about an accident.

Samuel (1) _____ (ir) todas las semanas al banco para retirar dinero del cajero

automático. El miércoles pasado él (2) _____ (llegar) a la esquina donde

(3) _____ (quedar) el banco y (4) _____ (acercarse) al cajero

automático. De repente él (5) _____ (oír) el ruido de sirenas y una ambulancia

y (6) _____ (ver) a muchos policías y bomberos. Le (7) _____

(preguntar) a un policía qué (8) _____ (pasar). El policía le

(9) _____ (decir) que un peatón (*pedestrian*) (10) _____

(cruzar) la calle sin mirar y un taxi lo (11) _____ (atropellar). Los paramédicos

(12) _____ (atender) a la víctima que afortunadamente sólo

(13) _____ (tener) heridas leves.

Un paso más

Are you ready to take your Spanish a step further? Here are exercises that will enhance your knowledge of the language and allow you to express yourself freely.

Phrases, Expressions, and Filler Words

To make your Spanish sound more like a native speaker's in conversation, it is important to use words, phrases, and expressions that a Spanish speaker uses automatically and repeats often in speech. Among these are *fillers*—words, phrases or sounds that mark a pause or hesitation in speech. In everyday English conversation, we use fillers such as *ah, um,* and *er,* and words and phrases including *okay, well, hey, right?, y'know, that is, I mean, like, so, actually,* and *basically.*

Spanish also has phrases, expressions, and filler words (**muletillas**) that you would want to use to make your conversation more colloquial. These include **este** (like *um* or *er,* this is a delaying or hesitating technique); **bueno, pues, oye, mira, chico, entonces, ¿no sabes?, ¡ah sí!, ¡Dios mío!, vale, no me digas, menos mal, claro (que sí/que no), cómo no, ¡caramba!, ¡ni hablar!, ¡ya lo creo!, en realidad, o sea, ¿de veras?, fíjate, me imagino, ¿entiendes?, ¿me explico?**; tags like **¿verdad?, ¿no?,** and **¿no es cierto?**; **¡vaya!** (wow!); and exclamations such as **¡Qué bien!, ¡Qué maravilloso!, ¡Qué pena!,** and **¡Qué horror!**

O To make the following dialogues more authentic, rewrite the speeches, choosing phrases and fillers from the above list (or others you learned in previous chapters) and placing them anywhere in the sentences you think appropriate. Add punctuation and capital or lowercase letters as needed. You'll be surprised what a difference these little words and phrases make!

1. —¿Quieres ir conmigo al partido de béisbol mañana?
   —¡Van a jugar mis equipos favoritos!
   —Vamos a comer perros calientes y cacahuetes.
   —¡Y tomar unas cervecitas también!

2. —¡Qué sarpullido tienes en las piernas! ¿Qué te pasó?
   —Daba una caminata con unos amigos y pisamos hiedras venenosas (*poison ivy*).
   —Te pica mucho. Pero no debes rascarte.
   —La loción de calamina me alivia un poco la picazón.
   —Se ve feíto. ¡Por ahora debes usar un pantalón largo!

3. —Hubo un accidente en el centro comercial.
   —¿Qué pasó?
   —Parece que dos personas se cayeron en la escalera mecánica.
   —¿Tenían heridas graves?
   —No sé. Espero que no.

P *Preguntas personales.* Answer each question with a complete Spanish sentence.

1. ¿Ud. prefiere comprar ropa y otros artículos en una tienda o en línea? ¿Qué cosas compra en las tiendas? ¿Y por internet?

2. ¿Cuánto tiempo hacía que conocía a su prometido/prometida cuando se casaron?

3. ¿Cómo se conocieron?

4. ¿Cómo era de niño/niña? ¿Mandón/mandona, llorón/llorona, preguntón/preguntona?

5. ¿Tiene un hijo? ¿Es un niño / una niña prodigio? ¿Cómo es?

6. ¿Ud. va de campamento (*to go camping*)? ¿Adónde va? ¿Con quiénes va?

7. ¿Qué es lo que le gusta del camping?

8. ¿Cómo puede describir su "estilo de vida"?

Q Write a paragraph about a medical experience you had. Use the following questions as a guide.

1. ¿Ud. tuvo un accidente o sufría de una enfermedad?

2. ¿Tenía dolor? ¿Otros síntomas?

3. ¿Los paramédicos lo/la atendieron? ¿Le dieron primeros auxilios?

4. ¿Fue al médico o a una sala de emergencias?

5. ¿Fue al hospital en ambulancia?

6. ¿Le hicieron un análisis de sangre?

7. ¿Le tomaron la presión arterial?

8. ¿Cuál fue el diagnóstico?

9. ¿Qué le recomendaron?

10. ¿Le recetaron un medicamento?

11. ¿Va al médico por un chequeo todos los años?

12. ¿Qué hace para mantener la salud física y emocional?

R Write a paragraph about the medical personnel you and your family members see, choosing words from the following list. Most of these words are cognates of English words, and others are words you learned in previous chapters. You already know how to derive the feminine forms of the nouns, so you'll be able to talk about female counterparts.

el cardiólogo
el cirujano
el/la dentista
el dermatólogo
el enfermero practicante
el/la especialista
el gastroenterólogo
el ginecólogo
el médico asistente
el médico de cabecera, el médico de familia
el neurólogo

el/la obstetra
el oftalmólogo
el oncólogo
el/la osteópata
el otorrinolaringólogo
el/la pediatra
el/la periodontista
el/la psiquiatra
el reumatólogo
el urólogo

12

People: Character and Personality, Societal Problems

Communication Goals
- Comparing people and things
- Talking about character and personality
- Vocabulary: environmental pollution and other problems of society

Grammar Topics
- Comparative of Adjectives, Adverbs, and Nouns
- Adverbs of Manner
- Superlative of Adjectives: Absolute Superlative
- Nominalization of Adjectives (Adjectives Used as Nouns)
- Conjunctions: **y** *and,* **o** *or*
- Review: Prepositional Pronouns

DIÁLOGO 1 · ¿Quién es más terco?

Study the dialogue, then listen to the recording and repeat each line.

MANUEL ¿No te parece que Sofía es terca?
TERESA Ah sí, pero tú no conoces a su hermana Julia. Es más terca que ella.
MANUEL Y su hermano, ¿es tan terco como ellas?
TERESA ¿Pepe? Pepe les gana y con mucho. Él es el más terco de la familia.

Análisis

Check that you understand the linguistic breakdown of each speech from *Diálogo 1.*

¿No te parece que Sofía es terca?	*Don't you think that Sofía is stubborn?*
no te parece que	*don't you think that, doesn't it seem to you that*
terco	*stubborn*

339

Ah sí, pero tú no conoces a su hermana Julia. Es más terca que ella.	*Oh, yes, but you don't know her sister Julia. She is more stubborn than she is.*
más + *adjective* + que	*more* + adjective + *than*
Y su hermano, ¿es tan terco como ellas?	*And their brother? Is he as stubborn as they are?*
tan + *adjective* + como	*as* + adjective + *as*
¿Pepe? Pepe les gana y con mucho. Él es el más terco de la familia.	*Pepe? Pepe is the champ. He's the most stubborn one in the family.*
ganarle a uno	*to have someone beat*
les gana	*has them beat* (literally, *beats them all*)
con mucho	*by a lot*
el más terco	*the most stubborn one*
el más terco de la familia	*the most stubborn one in the family*

▶ Variantes

Listen, and repeat the same structures from *Diálogo 1*, now with new vocabulary.

Ella es más despistada que su hermana.	*She is **more absentminded than** her sister.*
más caprichosa que	*more unpredictable than*
más atractiva que	*more attractive than*
más entrometida que	*more meddlesome than*
más comprensiva que	*more understanding than*
más pesada que	*more annoying than*
más coqueta que	*more flirtatious than*
más cortés que	*more polite than*
Él es menos serio que su hermano.	*He is **not as serious as** his brother.*
menos presumido que	*not as conceited as*
menos maleducado que	*not as rude as*
menos tímido que	*not as shy as*
menos mentiroso que	*not as deceitful as*
menos egoísta que	*not as selfish as*
menos calculador que	*not as calculating as*
menos raro que	*not as strange as, not as weird as*
Ellos no son tan ambiciosos como Uds.	*They are not **as ambitious as** you are.*
tan optimistas como	*as optimistic as*
tan pesimistas como	*as pessimistic as*
tan realistas como	*as realistic as*
tan trabajadores como	*as hardworking as*
tan sensatos como	*as sensible as*
Yo estoy tan ocupada como tú.	*I'm **as busy as** you are.*
tan contenta como	*as happy as*
tan preocupada como	*as worried as*
tan aburrida como	*as bored as*
tan decepcionada como	*as disappointed as*
tan emocionada como	*as excited as*
tan estresada como	*as stressed as*

tan entusiasmada como	*as enthusiastic as*
tan deprimida como	*as depressed as*

José es el más gruñón de la familia.	*José is **the grouchiest one** in his family.*
el más amable	*the kindest one*
el más sincero	*the sincerest one*
el más considerado	*the most thoughtful one*
el más cascarrabias	*the most cantankerous one*

Carmen es la más alegre de la familia.	*Carmen is **the most cheerful one** in her family.*
la más sensible	*the most sensitive one*
la más ingenua	*the most naïve one*
la más falsa	*the most two-faced one*
la más perezosa	*the laziest one*

Esteban te gana y con mucho.	*Esteban beats **you** by a lot.*
me	*me*
nos	*us*
le	*him, her, you (Ud.)*
les	*them, you (Uds.)*

Estructura y Práctica

Comparative of Adjectives, Adverbs, and Nouns

Adjectives

The comparative of adjectives is relatively simple in Spanish. Here is the basic pattern for comparisons of inequality.

más + adjective + **que**
menos + adjective + **que**

Más + adjective is the equivalent of English *more* + adjective, or the adjective with the suffix *-er*.

más inteligente que	*more intelligent than*
más bonito que	*prettier than*

Menos means *less*, but it is usually translated as *not as*.

menos interesante que	*less interesting than, not as interesting as*

Spanish uses **tan** + adjective + **como** to express the comparison of equality.

tan terco como	*as stubborn as*
tan aburrido como	*as boring as*

The adjectives **bueno** and **malo** have irregular comparative forms.

mejor *better*
peor *worse*

Este hotel es **mejor** que el otro.	*This hotel is **better** than the other one.*
Su situación es **peor** que la nuestra.	*Their situation is **worse** than ours.*

Más bueno and **más malo** refer to moral qualities.

Ese chico es más bueno que el pan.	*That boy is as good as gold.* (literally, *better than bread*)
Aquella mujer es más mala que su hermana.	*That woman is worse than her sister.*

The comparatives **más grande** and **más pequeño** are replaced by **mayor and menor**, respectively, when referring to age.

Mi hermano es **mayor** que yo.	*My brother is **older** than I.*
Mi hermano es **más grande** que yo.	*My brother is **bigger** than I.*
Su esposa es **menor** que él.	*His wife is **younger** than he.*
Su esposa es **más pequeña** que él.	*His wife is **shorter** than he.*

Superlative of Adjectives

Spanish has no particular superlative form. Usually, the definite article (or possessive adjective) is used with the noun that the adjective modifies to imply a superlative.

Quiero hablar con una persona más comprensiva.	*I want to speak with a more understanding person.*
Julia es **la persona más comprensiva** que conozco.	*Julia is **the most understanding person** I know.*

After a superlative, *in* is translated as **de**.

Es la ciudad más importante **del** país.	*It's the most important city **in** the country.*
Miguel es el alumno más dotado **de la** clase.	*Miguel is the most gifted student **in** the class.*

Adverbs

Adverbs are compared in the same way as adjectives. Here is the pattern for the comparison of inequality.

más + adverb + **que**
menos + adverb + **que**

Se viaja **más cómodamente** en tren **que** en autobús.	*One travels **more comfortably** by train **than** by bus.*
Se viaja **menos cómodamente** en burro **que** en carro.	*One travels **less comfortably** by donkey **than** by car.*

Spanish uses **tan** + adverb + **como** to express the comparison of equality.

Se viaja **tan cómodamente** en tren **como** en avión.	*One travels **as comfortably** by train **as** by plane.*

Nouns

When nouns are the object of comparison, the patterns **más** + noun + **que** and **menos** + noun + **que** are used.

Él escribe **más informes que** yo.	*He writes **more reports than** I.*
Él escribe **menos informes que** yo.	*He writes **fewer reports than** I.*

For the comparison of equality, **tan** changes to **tanto** before a noun and agrees with the noun in gender and number.

Él escribe **tantos informes como** yo.   *He writes **as many reports as** I do.*

Verbs

Más que, **menos que**, and **tanto como** can also modify verbs.

Ella trabaja **más que** yo.   *She works **more than** I do.*
Ella trabaja **menos que** yo.   *She works **less than** I do.*
Ella trabaja **tanto como** yo.   *She works **as much as** I do.*

Note that in colloquial English, speakers often use an object pronoun after *than*, even when a subject pronoun would be required grammatically—for example, *She works more than me.* This usage is impossible in Spanish.

Comparisons with Numerals

In comparisons involving numbers, **que** is replaced by **de** before a numeral.

En esta oficina trabajan **más de cincuenta** personas.   ***More than fifty** people work in this office.*

However, if the meaning is *only* or *no more than*, **más que** is used. In this case, the verb is usually negative.

No cursa **más que dos** materias.   *He's **only** taking **two** subjects. (literally, He's not taking more than two subjects.)*

No me quedan **más que cuatro** dólares.   *I have **only four** dollars left. (literally, I don't have more than four dollars left.)*

Que (*Than*) + Negative Words

After **que** (*than*), Spanish uses negative words such as **nada**, **nadie**, and **nunca** after a comparative where English uses indefinite words such as *anything, anyone,* and *ever.*

La salud es más importante **que nada**.   *Health is more important **than anything**.*
Él estudia más **que nadie**.   *He studies more **than anyone**.*
Ahora la comida cuesta más **que nunca**.   *Now food costs more **than ever**.*

A **Comparisons of inequality and equality: Adjectives.** Write two new sentences that show comparisons of inequality by combining the two sentences given. Write one new sentence that shows a comparison using **más que** (*more than*) and a second sentence that shows a comparison using **menos que** (*less than*). Follow the *modelo*.

MODELO   Gonzalo es trabajador. / Diego es más trabajador.
          → Diego es más trabajador que Gonzalo.
          → Gonzalo es menos trabajador que Diego.

1. Aurora es presumida. / Consuelo es más presumida.

2. Jaime y Federico están entusiasmados. / Nosotros estamos más entusiasmados.

3. El profesor de física es exigente. / La profesora de química es más exigente.

4. Los pantalones son caros. / La chaqueta es más cara.

5. Tú eres optimista. / Yo soy más optimista.

6. La casa es moderna. / El condominio es más moderno.

7. Juan Manuel es cortés. / Uds. son más corteses.

8. Los tamales están ricos. / Los tacos están más ricos.

B **Comparisons of equality: Adjectives.** Write sentences from the elements given to show comparisons of equality. Follow the *modelo*.

> MODELO   Timoteo / amable / su hermano
> → Timoteo es tan amable como su hermano.

1. Elena / caprichosa / Victoria

2. Pedro / ingenuo / tú

3. ellos / egoístas / Rodrigo

4. Paquita / coqueta / su prima

5. los empleados / trabajadores / el director

6. Uds. / estresados / sus amigos

7. Ana María / calculadora / su cuñada

8. Bernardo / emocionado / Beatriz

9. nuestros hijos / ocupados / nosotros

10. tú / comprensiva / tus papás

Adverbs of Manner

As you learned in Chapter 8, most adverbs of manner in Spanish are formed by adding the suffix -**mente** to the feminine singular form of the adjective.

MASCULINE SINGULAR	FEMININE SINGULAR	ADVERB	MEANING
ingenuo	ingenua	ingenuamente	*naively*
caprichoso	caprichosa	caprichosamente	*unpredictably*
rígido	rígida	rígidamente	*rigidly*
estricto	estricta	estrictamente	*strictly*

If the adjective has only one form for the masculine and feminine singular, then the suffix -**mente** is added to that form.

SINGULAR	ADVERB	MEANING
amable	amablemente	*kindly*
inflexible	inflexiblemente	*inflexibly*
alegre	alegremente	*happily*
indulgente	indulgentemente	*leniently*

Adverbs ending in -**mente** have two stresses in speech, one on the original stressed syllable of the adjective and one on the first **e** of the suffix -**mente**.

If the adjective itself has a written accent mark, the accent mark is retained when the suffix -**mente** is added.

cortés	cortésmente
tímido	tímidamente
fácil	fácilmente

C **Comparisons of inequality and equality: Adverbs.** Write sentences from the elements given to show comparisons of inequality and equality using **más**, **menos**, and **tan**. Use the preterit tense. Follow the *modelo*.

MODELO   él / hablar / tímidamente / ella
          → Él habló más tímidamente que ella.
          → Ella habló menos tímidamente que él.
          → Él habló tan tímidamente como ella.

1. Guillermo / escuchar / atentamente / Josefa

2. Alberto / trabajar / ambiciosamente / Santiago

3. Uds. / ir de compras / frecuentemente / nosotros

4. la familia Suárez / vivir / cómodamente / la familia Morales

5. nosotros / manejar / lentamente / tú

6. Antonio / ofenderse / fácilmente / su hermano

7. Damián / correr / rápidamente / Uds.

8. tú / pensar / profundamente / yo

9. Blanca / contestar / amablemente / Pepe

10. Ud. / reaccionar / sensible / Daniela

D **Comparisons of inequality and equality: Nouns.** Write sentences from the elements given to show comparisons of inequality and equality using **más**, **menos**, and **tan**. Use the imperfect tense. Follow the *modelo*.

MODELO   Arturo / recibir / textos / Celeste
          → Arturo recibía más textos que Celeste.
          → Celeste recibía menos textos que Arturo.
          → Arturo recibía tantos textos como Celeste.

1. yo / cursar / materias / tú

2. el niño / tener / hambre / su hermanita

3. Uds. / comprar / libros de texto / los otros estudiantes

4. Eva / ver / películas / María Elena

5. tú / comer / comida chatarra / tus amigos

6. nosotros / leer / obras maestras / ellos

7. Sofía / recorrer / países / su marido

8. Ignacio / hacer / ejercicio / Mateo

E **¿Cómo son sus parientes?** Write sentences from the elements given to describe what these members of the Vargas family are like. Use the superlative of each adjective. Make all necessary changes. Follow the *modelo*.

> MODELO   la tía Olivia / ingenuo
> → La tía Olivia es la más ingenua.

1. la abuela Raquel / sensato

2. el tío Rodrigo / cascarrabias

3. los primos Laura y Martín / calculador

4. las nietas Teresita y Paquita / coqueta

5. la cuñada Lucía / entrometido

6. los sobrinos Ramón y Eugenia / terco

7. el yerno (*son-in-law*) Manolo / realista

8. la nuera (*daughter-in-law*) Montserrat / pesado

F   **Translation.** Express the following sentences in Spanish.

1. *Anita is more conceited than her sister.*

2. *Jorge is less rude than his friends.*

3. *Cristóbal was as stressed as you (tú) were.*

4. *My brother and sister are as thoughtful as I.*

5. *Matilde is the shyest person in her family.*

6. *Juanito is the strangest student in his class.*

DIÁLOGO 2 · La primera novela es la mejor de todas.

Study the dialogue, then listen to the recording and repeat each line.

TERESA   Dicen que la nueva novela de Fuentes es buenísima.
MANUEL   Es cierto. Yo la leí y creo que es mejor que su última novela.
TERESA   Pero no es tan buena como la primera que escribió, ¿verdad?
MANUEL   Claro que no. Ésa es una obra maestra. Es la mejor de todas.

Análisis

Check that you understand the linguistic breakdown of each speech from *Diálogo 2*.

Dicen que la nueva novela de Fuentes es buenísima.	*They say that Fuentes's new novel is very good.*
buenísimo	*very good*
Es cierto. Yo la leí y creo que es mejor que su última novela.	*It's true. I read it, and I think that it is better than his last novel.*
mejor que	*better than*
último	*last*

Pero no es tan buena como la primera que escribió, ¿verdad?	*But it's not as good as the first one he wrote, is it?*
la primera	*the first one*
no es tan buena como	*it's not as good as*
Claro que no. Ésa es una obra maestra. Es la mejor de todas.	*Of course not. That one is a masterpiece. It's the best one of all.*
claro que no	*of course not*
ésa	*that one*
la obra	*work (literary, musical, etc.)*
la obra maestra	*masterpiece*
la mejor	*the best one*

▶ Variantes

Listen, and repeat the same structures from *Diálogo 2*, now with new vocabulary.

El nuevo libro no es tan bueno como el último.	*The new book is not **as good as** the last one.*
tan interesante como	*as interesting as*
tan divertido como	*as entertaining as*
tan atractivo como	*as engaging as*
tan largo como	*as long as*
Su novela es buenísima .	*His novel is **very good**.*
interesantísima	*very interesting*
divertidísima	*very entertaining*
larguísima	*very long*
aburridísima	*very boring*
Este libro es el mejor de todos.	*This book is the best one of all.*
Paz es el mejor autor del mundo.	*Paz is the best author in the world.*

Estructura y Práctica

Superlative of Adjectives: Absolute Superlative

The absolute superlative is a term used for the suffix -**ísimo** in Spanish, a suffix that is the equivalent of *very*. The addition of the suffix -**ísimo** creates a new four-form adjective. The final vowel of the masculine singular form of the adjective is dropped before the -**ísimo** ending. If the masculine singular form of the adjective ends in a consonant, the suffix -**ísimo** is added directly to the adjective.

caro	→ carísimo	*very expensive*
contento	→ contentísimo	*very happy*
raro	→ rarísimo	*very strange*
tonto	→ tontísimo	*very silly*
inteligente	→ inteligentísimo	*very intelligent*
potente	→ potentísimo	*very powerful*
difícil	→ dificilísimo	*very difficult*

Adverbs can be formed by adding **-mente** to the feminine singular form of the absolute superlative.

rarísimamente	*very strangely*
tontísimamente	*very stupidly*

Adverbs of quantity also have absolute superlative forms.

mucho	→ muchísimo	*very much*
poco	→ poquísimo	*very little*

Adjectives or adverbs of quantity whose last consonant is **c** or **g** show a spelling change before adding the ending **-ísimo**: The **c** changes to **qu** and **g** changes to **gu** before the ending **-ísimo** is added.

poco	→ poquísimo	*very little*
simpático	→ simpatiquísimo	*very nice, very pleasant*
largo	→ larguísimo	*very long*

G **The absolute superlative.** Write the absolute superlative of the adjective in parentheses to correctly complete each of the following sentences. Follow the *modelo.*

MODELO   La clase de matemáticas es _dificilísima_. (difícil)

1. Carolina lleva ropa _____. (elegante)

2. Todos los platos que probamos estuvieron _____. (rico)

3. Los informes que escribieron son _____. (largo)

4. Este museo de arte es _____. (interesante)

5. Se presentaban unas obras de teatro _____. (bueno)

6. Los paisajes que vieron eran realmente _____. (hermoso)

7. Conocimos a unas personas _____. (simpático)

8. Estos exámenes son _____. (fácil)

9. El profesor dio una explicación _____. (claro)

10. Los programadores van a estar _____ todo el día. (ocupado)

H **Translation.** Express the following sentences in Spanish. Write all numbers as words.

1. *It's the best book in our library.*

2. *It's the most famous brand on the market.*

3. *We were working more than ever.*

4. *Enrique used to travel as frequently as we did.*

5. *Last year Perla earned more than 200,000 dollars.*

6. *Pablo has only 1,700 dollars left in his savings account* (la cuenta de ahorros).

7. *Our team beat the other team by a lot.*

8. *They bought as many pens and pencils as we.*

9. *Do you (Ud.) think this manager is more demanding than the former one?*

10. *Are you kidding? He's the most lenient manager in the company.*

11. *Health is more important than anything.*

12. *Raquel complains more than anyone.*

DIÁLOGO 3 · Busco una nueva computadora.

Study the dialogue, then listen to the recording and repeat each line.

MANUEL   Esta computadora es más potente que la mía.
TERESA   También es más cara que la tuya.
MANUEL   ¿Y aquélla? Es aún más cara que ésta.
TERESA   Me imagino que funciona mejor que ésta.

Análisis

Check that you understand the linguistic breakdown of each speech from *Diálogo 3*.

Esta computadora es más potente que la mía.	*This computer is more powerful than mine.*
potente	*powerful*
la mía (< la computadora mía)	*mine*
También es más cara que la tuya.	*It's also more expensive than yours.*
la tuya (< la computadora tuya)	*yours*
¿Y aquélla? Es aún más cara que ésta.	*And that one? It's even more expensive than this one.*
aquélla (< aquella computadora)	*that one*
aún más	*even more*
ésta (< esta computadora)	*this one*
Me imagino que funciona mejor que ésta.	*I imagine that it works better than this one.*
imaginarse	*to imagine*
funcionar	*to work, function*
mejor que	*better than*
ésta (< esta computadora)	*this one*

Variantes

Listen, and repeat the same structures from *Diálogo 3*, now with new vocabulary.

Esta computadora es más potente que la tuya .	*This computer is **more powerful than yours**.*
más potente que la suya	*more powerful than his/hers/yours (Ud., Uds.)/theirs*
más potente que la nuestra	*more powerful than ours*

Este teléfono celular es menos caro que el mío .	*This cell phone **isn't as expensive as mine.***
es menos caro que el tuyo	* isn't as expensive as yours*
es menos caro que el suyo	* isn't as expensive as his/hers/yours (Ud., Uds.)/theirs*
es menos caro que el nuestro	* isn't as expensive as ours*

Estos bolígrafos son tan baratos como ésos.	*These **pens** are as cheap as those.*
lápices	* pencils*
cuadernos	* notebooks*
disquetes	* diskettes*
cartuchos de tinta	* ink cartridges*

Esta marca es tan buena como ésa.	*This brand is as good as that one.*
Estas plumas son tan buenas como ésas.	*These pens are as good as those.*

¿Ese software es más fácil de usar que éste?	*Is that software more user friendly than this one?*
No, este software es tan fácil de usar como ése.	*No, this software is as user friendly as that one.*

Este iPod funciona mejor que aquél.	*This iPod works better than that one.*

Estructura y Práctica

Nominalization of Adjectives (Adjectives Used as Nouns)

Nominalization is the process by which a part of speech, such as an adjective, is made to function as a noun or pronoun. In English, there are several processes that accomplish this. In Spanish, however, there is only one: deletion of the noun. Nominalization takes place in several types of structures.

1 · A noun may be deleted from a phrase consisting of a determiner + noun + adjective. In this structure, the adjective plus the definite article (or other determiner) can function as a noun. The definite article is not stressed in the nominalized phrase, but the indefinite article is.

el modelo nuevo y el **modelo** antiguo → el modelo nuevo y **el antiguo**	*the new model and the old model* *the new model and **the old one***
las ciudades grandes y las **ciudades** pequeñas → las ciudades grandes y **las pequeñas**	*the big cities and the little cities* *the big cities and **the little ones***
una computadora barata y una **computadora** cara → una computadora barata y **una cara**	*a cheap computer and an expensive computer* *a cheap computer and **an expensive one***

2 · A noun may be deleted in a prepositional phrase beginning with **de**, including phrases expressing possession. In this structure, the definite article (or other determiner) becomes a pronoun and is stressed.

la casa de María y la **casa** de Juan	*María's house and John's house*
→ la casa de María y **la de Juan**	*María's house and **John's***
los zapatos de cuero y los **zapatos** de tela	*the leather shoes and the cloth shoes*
→ los zapatos de cuero y **los de tela**	*the leather shoes and **the cloth ones***

3 · A noun may be deleted after a demonstrative adjective. In this structure, an accent mark was traditionally added to the demonstrative adjective when the noun was deleted, but the accent mark is optional in current usage. The resultant structure is a demonstrative pronoun.

ese vuelo y este **vuelo**	*that flight and this flight*
→ ese vuelo y **éste/este**	*that flight and **this one***
estas dietas y esa **dieta**	*these diets and that diet*
→ estas dietas y **ésa/esa**	*these diets and **that one***
estos documentos y aquellos **documentos**	*these documents and those documents*
→ estos documentos y **aquéllos/aquellos**	*these documents and **those***
aquella sucursal y estas **sucursales**	*that branch and these branches*
→ aquella sucursal y **éstas/estas**	*that branch and **these***

4 · A noun may be deleted from a phrase containing a long-form possessive. The resultant structure is called a possessive pronoun.

el tráfico nuestro y el **tráfico** suyo	*our traffic and their traffic*
→ el tráfico nuestro y **el suyo**	*our traffic and **theirs***
la universidad tuya y la **universidad** mía	*your university and my university*
→ la universidad tuya y **la mía**	*your university and **mine***
los consejos suyos y los **consejos** tuyos	*his advice and your advice*
→ los consejos suyos y **los tuyos**	*his advice and **yours***
la pasantía mía y las **pasantías** de Uds.	*my internship and your internships*
→ la pasantía mía y **las de Uds.**	*my internship and **yours***

I ***¿Cuál te gusta más?*** Write a response to each of the following questions, eliminating the nouns that are being compared. Follow the *modelo*.

> MODELO   ¿Cuál te gusta más, la primera novela o la segunda novela?
> → Prefiero la primera, pero me gusta la segunda también.

1. ¿Cuál te gusta más, el abrigo marrón o el abrigo negro?

2. ¿Cuáles te gustan más, los libros de cuentos o los libros de poesía?

3. ¿Cuál te gusta más, la oficina de enfrente o la oficina de al lado?

4. ¿Cuáles te gustan más, los museos de arte o los museos de ciencias?

5. ¿Cuál te gusta más, el restaurante italiano o el restaurante mexicano?

6. ¿Cuáles te gustan más, los carros fabricados en los Estados Unidos o los carros fabricados en el extranjero?

7. ¿Cuál te gusta más, la mochila grande o la mochila pequeña?

8. ¿Cuáles te gustan más, las asignaturas obligatorias o las asignaturas optativas?

9. ¿Cuáles te gustan más, los sándwiches vegetarianos o los sándwiches de carne?

10. ¿Cuál te gusta más, el suéter de lana o el suéter de algodón?

J **Possessive pronouns used in comparisons.** Rewrite each sentence, replacing the underlined phrase with the corresponding possessive adjective. Follow the *modelo*.

MODELO   Mi casa es más grande que la casa de Fernanda.
              → Mi casa es más grande que la suya.

1. Nuestra calle es más tranquila que la calle de ellos.

2. Tu proyecto era tan interesante como mi proyecto.

3. Sus cursos son menos difíciles que nuestros cursos.

4. Nuestras empresas ganaron tanto dinero como las empresas de Ud.

5. Su equipo juega tan bien como tu equipo.

6. La novia de Ricardo es tan alegre como la novia de su hermano.

7. Este celular funcionaba mejor que el celular de Susana.

8. Tus profesores son tan exigentes como mis profesores.

K **Demonstrative pronouns.** Write a response to each of the following questions, using demonstrative pronouns to say that you like the first item better than the second. Follow the *modelo*.

MODELO   ¿Qué sopa le gusta más? ¿Esta sopa o esa sopa?
              → Me gusta ésta más que ésa.
              OR
              → Me gusta esta más que esa.

1. ¿Qué tienda de ropa le gusta más? ¿Esta tienda de ropa o aquella tienda de ropa?

2. ¿Qué hotel le gusta más? ¿Aquel hotel o este hotel?

3. ¿Qué cuadernos le gustan más? ¿Esos cuadernos o estos cuadernos?

4. ¿Qué camisas le gustan más? ¿Estas camisas o aquellas camisas?

5. ¿Qué libro de texto le gusta más? ¿Este libro de texto o aquel libro de texto?

6. ¿Qué lentes de sol te gustan más? ¿Estos lentes de sol o esos lentes de sol?

▶ DIÁLOGO 4 · ¿El traje negro o el gris?

Study the dialogue, then listen to the recording and repeat each line.

TERESA   Me parece que este traje negro es más fino que ese gris.
MANUEL   Pero fíjate que el gris cuesta tanto como el negro. ¿Cómo puede ser?
TERESA   Chico, a veces el precio engaña.

Análisis

Check that you understand the linguistic breakdown of each speech from *Diálogo 4*.

Me parece que este traje negro es más fino que ese gris.	*I think that this black suit is of better quality than that gray one.*
fino	*fine, of good quality*
más fino que	*of better quality than*
ese gris (< ese traje gris)	*that gray one*
Pero fíjate que el gris cuesta tanto como el negro. ¿Cómo puede ser?	*But notice that the gray one costs as much as the black one. How can that be?*
fijarse	*to notice*
fíjate que	*notice that*
el gris (< el traje gris)	*the gray one*
costar (**o** > **ue**)	*to cost*
tanto como	*as much as*
el negro (< el traje negro)	*the black one*
Chico, a veces el precio engaña.	*Well, sometimes the price doesn't tell you everything.*
chico	*well* (interjection)
a veces	*sometimes*
el precio	*the price*
engañar	*to deceive, fool*
el precio engaña	(literally) *the price fools you*

▶ Variantes

Listen, and repeat the same structures from *Diálogo 4*, now with new vocabulary.

Esta camisa blanca es más fina que esa azul.	*This white shirt is of better quality than that blue one.*
Aquellos suéteres de lana son más finos que éstos de algodón.	*Those wool sweaters are of better quality than these cotton ones.*
Los zapatos españoles no cuestan tanto como los italianos.	*The Spanish shoes cost less than the Italian ones.*

Estructura y Práctica

L **Translation.** Express each of the following sentences in Spanish. All sentences are in the present tense.

1. *These ink cartridges cost more than those.*

2. *The silk gloves are of better quality than the leather ones.*

3. *This red coat is longer than that navy blue one.*

4. *I think you (tú) got to know as many Latin American cities as we did.*

▶ DIÁLOGO 5 · La contaminación del ambiente

Study the dialogue, then listen to the recording and repeat each line.

MANUEL   Me pican los ojos. Creo que hay muchísima contaminación del ambiente aquí.

TERESA   Pues fíjate que yo no la noto. En realidad creo que hay menos polución en esta ciudad que en la nuestra.

Análisis

Check that you understand the linguistic breakdown of each speech from *Diálogo 5*.

Me pican los ojos. Creo que hay muchísima contaminación del ambiente aquí.	*My eyes are itching. I think there's an awful lot of environmental pollution here.*
picarle a uno	*to itch*
me pican los ojos	*my eyes itch*
muchísimo	*very much, an awful lot*
la contaminación	*pollution*
el ambiente	*environment*
la contaminación del ambiente	*environmental pollution*
Pues fíjate que yo no la noto. En realidad creo que hay menos polución en esta ciudad que en la nuestra.	*Can you imagine, I don't notice it. Actually, I think that there is less pollution in this city than in ours.*
fijarse	*to notice*
fíjate que	*notice that, imagine that, can you imagine*
notar	*to notice*
yo no la noto	*I don't notice it*
en realidad	*actually*
menos	*less*
la polución	*pollution*
menos polución que	*less pollution than*
la ciudad	*city*
la nuestra (< la ciudad nuestra)	*ours*

▶ Variantes

Listen, and repeat the same structures from *Diálogo 5*, now with new vocabulary.

Hay muchísimo ⟨ruido ambiental⟩ aquí.
   espíritu cívico
   reciclaje
	*There's an awful lot of **noise pollution** here.*
	   civic spirit
	   recycling

Hay muchísima ⟨basura⟩ aquí.
   drogadicción
   pobreza
	*There's an awful lot of **garbage** here.*
	   drug addiction
	   poverty

Hay poquísimo ⟨crimen⟩ aquí.
   abuso de drogas
	*There's very little **crime** here.*
	   drug abuse

Ésta es la ciudad más contaminada del país.	*This is the most polluted city in the country.*

Éste es el país más contaminado del
   mundo.
	This is the most polluted country in the
	   world.

Estructura y Práctica

M **Translation.** Express each of the following sentences in Spanish.

1. *There's more noise pollution than ever in our society.*

2. *This is the most polluted region in the state.*

3. *There are people who think that recycling is more important than anything.*

4. *There's less crime in our city than in yours* (Uds.).

5. *There was a great deal of civic spirit in the country during the fifties* (los años cincuenta).

6. *There's more drug addiction than ever.*

▶ DIÁLOGO 6 · Un nuevo puesto

Study the dialogue, then listen to the recording and repeat each line.

TERESA	Me gusta tu nueva oficina. Es más amplia que la anterior.
MANUEL	Sí, y entra más luz en ésta que en la que tenía.
TERESA	Entonces estás más contento aquí que en tu otro puesto.
MANUEL	No completamente. Mi nuevo jefe es mucho más exigente que el antiguo.

Análisis

Check that you understand the linguistic breakdown of each speech from *Diálogo 6*.

Me gusta tu nueva oficina. Es más
amplia que la anterior.
   amplio
   más amplio que
   anterior
   la anterior (< la oficina anterior)
	I like your new office. It's more spacious
	than your previous one.
	   spacious, broad, ample
	   more spacious than
	   previous
	   the former one

Sí, y entra más luz en ésta que en la que tenía.	*Yes, and this one is brighter than the one I had.*
entra luz	*it's bright* (literally, *light comes in*)
ésta (< esta oficina)	*this one*
entra más luz en ésta que	*it's brighter in this one than*
la que tenía (< la oficina que tenía)	*the one I had*
Entonces estás más contento aquí que en tu otro puesto.	*So you're happier here than in your other job.*
estar contento	*to be happy*
estás más contento aquí que	*you're happier here than*
tu otro puesto	*your other job*
No completamente. Mi nuevo jefe es mucho más exigente que el antiguo.	*Not entirely. My new boss is much more demanding than the former one.*
completamente	*completely, entirely*
mi nuevo jefe	*my new boss*
exigente	*demanding, strict*
más exigente que	*more demanding than*
mucho más exigente que	*much more demanding than*
antiguo	*former* (when it precedes a noun)
el antiguo (< el antiguo jefe)	*the former one*

▶ Variantes

Listen, and repeat the same structures from *Diálogo 6*, now with new vocabulary.

Tu nuevo apartamento es más amplio que el anterior.	*Your new apartment is more spacious than your previous one.*
Entra más luz en éste que en el que tenía.	*This one has more light than the one I had before.*
Éste tiene más dormitorios que el que tenía.	*This one has more bedrooms than the one I had before.*
cuartos de baño	*bathrooms*
armarios	*closets*
ventanas	*windows*
¿Estás más contento aquí que en tu puesto anterior?	*Are you happier here than in your former position?*
Ah sí, ¡estoy contentísimo!	*Oh, yes, I'm very happy!*
Me gusta tu nueva oficina.	*I like your new office.*
Entonces a ti te gusta más que a mí.	*Then you like it more than I do.*
Yo tengo más trabajo que Ud.	*I have **more** work than you do.*
menos	*less*
Uds. tenían tanto trabajo como yo.	*You had as much work as I had.*
Ellos escribieron tantos informes como nosotros.	*They wrote as many reports as we did.*

¿Navegas en la red tanto como yo?	*Do you surf the web as much as I do?*
No, yo navego más que tú.	*No, I surf **more** than you do.*
menos	*less*
¿Tu nueva jefa es tan exigente como el antiguo?	*Is your new boss as demanding as your old one?*
Es más exigente que él. Yo trabajo más que nunca.	*She's more demanding than he. I work harder than ever.*

Estructura y Práctica

N **Translation.** Express each of the following sentences in Spanish.

1. *This apartment is more spacious than the ones you (Ud.) saw previously.*

2. *That condominium is bigger and less expensive than mine.*

3. *This house has as many bedrooms as theirs, but it has fewer bathrooms than ours.*

4. *This computer is more powerful than the one I had.*

5. *The previous computer was more user friendly than the one I have now.*

DIÁLOGO 7 · Curso cinco asignaturas.

Study the dialogue, then listen to the recording and repeat each line.

MANUEL	Este semestre curso cinco asignaturas. Tengo más trabajo que nunca.
TERESA	¿Para cuál materia estudias más? ¿Para historia?
MANUEL	No, para química. La materia es dificilísima y estudio con el doctor Figueroa.
TERESA	¿Con Figueroa? Pobre de ti. Es el profesor más estricto e inflexible de la universidad.

Análisis

Check that you understand the linguistic breakdown of each speech from *Diálogo 7*.

Este semestre curso cinco asignaturas.	*This semester I'm taking five subjects.*
Tengo más trabajo que nunca.	*I have more work than ever.*
el semestre	*semester*
cursar	*to take (academic subjects)*
la asignatura	*(school) subject*
más trabajo que nunca	*more work than ever*
¿Para cuál materia estudias más?	*For which subject do you study the most?*
¿Para historia?	*For history?*
cuál	*which*
la materia	*(school) subject*
para cuál materia	*for which subject*
más	*more, the most*
la historia	*history*

No, para química. La materia es
dificilísima y estudio con el doctor
Figueroa.

    la química
    dificilísimo

*No, for chemistry. The subject is very difficult
and I'm studying with Dr. Figueroa.*

    chemistry
    very difficult

¿Con Figueroa? Pobre de ti. Es el
profesor más estricto e inflexible de
la universidad.

    pobre de ti
    estricto
    inflexible
    el profesor más estricto e inflexible
    de

*With Figueroa? Poor you. He's the strictest
and most rigid professor in the university.*

    poor you
    strict
    rigid, inflexible
    the strictest and most rigid professor
    in (when it follows a superlative)

Variantes

Listen, and repeat the same structures from *Diálogo 7*, now with new vocabulary.

Yo estudié más que nunca.
    más que nadie
    más que nada

*I studied **harder than ever**.*
    harder than anyone
    harder than anything

La materia es dificilísima.
    facilísima
    importantísima
    interesantísima

*The subject is **very difficult**.*
    very easy
    very important
    very interesting

Yo siempre cursaba más de cinco
asignaturas.
Siempre escribíamos más de dos
composiciones.
Yo no tomaba más que cuatro cursos.
No escribíamos más que dos
composiciones.

I always took more than five subjects.

*We always wrote more than two
compositions.*
I took only four courses.
We wrote only two compositions.

Las asignaturas obligatorias son las
más fáciles.
    Las asignaturas optativas

The required subjects *are the easiest ones.*

    The electives

Pobre de mí.
    ti
    Ud.
    él
    ella
    nosotros
    Uds.
    ellos/ellas

*Poor **me**.*
    you
    you
    guy
    girl
    us
    you
    guys

¿Vas a ir conmigo a la librería?
Claro que voy contigo.

Are you going to go to the bookstore with me?
Of course I'll go with you.

¿Tienes que comprar un libro de texto para la clase de filosofía?	*Do you have to buy a textbook for philosophy class?*
Sí, para ella y también para la de biología.	*Yes, for that class and also for biology.*

Es la profesora más indulgente de la universidad.
    popular
	*She's the most **lenient** professor in the university.*
	    popular

Los cursos de matemáticas son los más difíciles de la facultad de ciencias. Son más difíciles que los de física.	*The math courses are the most difficult ones in the (school of) sciences.* *They are harder than the physics (courses).*

Yo resolví el problema más fácilmente que tú.
    menos fácilmente que
	*I solved the problem **more easily than** you.*
	
	    less easily than

Ellos trabajan tan cuidadosamente como nosotros.	*They work as carefully as we do.*

Estructura y Práctica

Conjunctions: y and, o or

The conjunction **y** (*and*) is written and pronounced **e** when it immediately precedes a word that begins with the sound /i/: **guapos e inteligentes, padres e hijos**. There is no change when a word begins with a diphthong such as /ie/: **fuego y hielo** (*fire and ice*).

Similarly, **o** (*or*) is written and pronounced **u** when it immediately precedes a word that begins with the sound /o/: **siete u ocho, minutos u horas**.

O   **Conjunctions *y* and *o*.** Rewrite each of the following phrases, reversing the order of the two items and adding the correct form of the conjunction to each new phrase. Follow the *modelos*.

MODELOS   inglés y español   hoy o mañana
           → español e inglés   → mañana u hoy

1. idiomas y lingüística
2. Honduras o Costa Rica
3. ingenua y sensible
4. hombres o mujeres
5. optimista o pesimista
6. italianos y franceses
7. oeste o este
8. iglesias y sinagogas
9. hidrógeno y oxígeno
10. igualdad y libertad
11. hipopótamos y rinocerontes
12. holandés o escocés

Review: Prepositional Pronouns

In Chapter 6, you learned the special set of pronouns used after prepositions. These pronouns are identical with the subject pronouns except in the first and second persons singular.

para **mí**   para **nosotros/nosotras**
para **ti**   para **vosotros/vosotras**
para **él/ella**   para **ellos/ellas**
para **Ud.**   para **Uds.**

Note that after **con** there are three irregular forms.

con + mí → conmigo   *with me*
con + ti → contigo   *with you* (**tú**)
consigo   *with himself, with herself, with yourself*
                                 (**Ud.**), *with yourselves* (**Uds.**), *with themselves*

P   *Te equivocas.* Write a response to each of the following questions to tell your friend that he's wrong about who you were going to do things with or for. Use prepositional pronouns in your responses. Follow the *modelo*.

MODELO   Ibas a almorzar con Rosa, ¿verdad?
→ No, con ella, no.

1. Ibas a comprar un regalo para los Fernández, ¿verdad?

2. Ibas a pasar por nosotros, ¿verdad?

3. Ibas a jugar al tenis con tus amigas, ¿verdad?

4. Ibas a preparar unos platos para mí, ¿verdad?

5. Ibas a casarte con Juan Antonio, ¿verdad?

6. Ibas a hacer las investigaciones por tu jefa, ¿verdad?

7. Ibas a reunirte conmigo, ¿verdad?

8. Ibas a ver la obra de teatro conmigo, ¿verdad?

Un paso más

Are you ready to take your Spanish a step further? Here are exercises that will enhance your knowledge of the language and allow you to express yourself freely.

Q   *Preguntas personales.* Answer each question with a complete Spanish sentence.

1. ¿Cómo eres?

2. ¿Cómo son los miembros de tu familia?

3. Para ti, ¿quién es el mejor escritor / la mejor escritora (actor, actriz, dramaturgo/a, director(a) de cine)? ¿Por qué crees que son los mejores?

4. ¿Cuáles son los mejores libros que leíste? ¿Las mejores películas que viste? ¿Por qué crees que son los mejores?

5. ¿Qué asignaturas cursas/cursabas en la universidad? ¿Son/Eran obligatorias u optativas?

6. ¿Cómo son/eran tus profesores?

R Write a paragraph about American ideals and principles. You may want to include discussion of some issues in American society today. Resources to help you with this topic, including useful vocabulary, appear below. You will be able to read and understand much of the material because you are already familiar with it and many words are cognates of English words. Use the following questions as a guide.

1. ¿Cuáles son los principios e ideas fundamentales de los Estados Unidos de América reflejados (*reflected*) en sus documentos fundacionales?

2. ¿Hay mucho espíritu cívico en el país?

3. ¿Cuáles son algunos ejemplos del espíritu cívico en su ciudad o su pueblo?

4. ¿Cuáles son los problemas más graves de la sociedad estadounidense actualmente?

5. ¿Tú crees que se pueden resolver? ¿Cómo?

Resources

The Declaration of Independence
https://www.archives.gov/espanol/la-declaracion-de-independencia.html

The Constitution of the United States of America
https://www.archives.gov/espanol/constitucion

Vocabulario útil

el bien común *the common good, the public good*
el bienestar *general welfare*
la caridad *charity*
la ciudadanía *citizenship*
el ciudadano *citizen*
la Constitución de los Estados Unidos de América *Constitution of the United States of America*
la cultura política *political culture*
el deber *obligation*
la Declaración de Derechos *the Bill of Rights*
la Declaración de la Independencia *the Declaration of Independence*
la democracia *democracy*
el derecho *right*
los documentos fundacionales *founding documents*
la enmienda *amendment*

las diez primeras enmiendas a la Constitución de los Estados Unidos de América *the first ten amendments to the Constitution of the United States of America (the Bill of Rights)*
el estado de derecho *rule of law*
el gobierno *government*
   el gobierno estatal *state government*
   el gobierno federal *federal government*
   el gobierno municipal *city government*
la igualdad *equality*
los impuestos *taxes*
la justicia *justice*
la ley *law*
la libertad *freedom*
"Nosotros el Pueblo" *"We the People"*
el orgullo *pride*
la responsabilidad *responsibility, accountability*

Business and the Growth of Cities

(13)

Communication Goals

- Talking about things that have happened in the recent past
- Talking about things that had happened
- Describing a business plan and a budget
- Vocabulary: business and the economy, religious rites and traditions, urban growth

Grammar Topics

- Past Participle: Formation
- Past Participle: Uses
- Present Perfect
- Present Perfect: Position of Object Pronouns
- **Estar** + Past Participle: Expressing Positions of the Body
- Past Perfect (Pluperfect)
- The Progressive Tenses

DIÁLOGO 1 · Un día de mucho ajetreo

Study the dialogue, then listen to the recording and repeat each line.

MARÍA ¿Por qué no has contestado mi email? ¿No lo has recibido acaso?

FELIPE Hoy ha sido un día de mucho ajetreo. No he tenido ni un solo minuto para respirar.

Análisis

Check that you understand the linguistic breakdown of each speech from *Diálogo 1*.

¿Por qué no has contestado mi email? — *Why haven't you answered my email?*
¿No lo has recibido acaso? — *Maybe you didn't receive it?*
  has (< *auxiliary verb* **haber**) — *you have*
  contestar — *to answer*
  contestado — *answered*

362

has contestado	*you have answered*
el email	*email*
recibir	*to get, receive*
recibido	*received*
has recibido	*you have received*
lo has recibido	*you have received it*
acaso	*maybe, perhaps*

Hoy ha sido un día de mucho ajetreo.	*Today has been a very hectic day.*
No he tenido ni un solo minuto para respirar.	*I haven't had even a minute to breathe.*
ha (< *auxiliary verb* **haber**)	*it has*
ser	*to be*
sido	*been*
ha sido	*it has been*
el ajetreo	*intense activity, hustle and bustle*
de mucho ajetreo	*hectic*
he (< *auxiliary verb* **haber**)	*I have*
tener	*to have*
tenido	*had*
he tenido	*I have had*
ni	*not even*
solo	*alone, single*
ni un solo	*not even one single*
ni un solo minuto	*not even one (single) minute*
respirar	*to breathe*

▶ Variantes

Listen, and repeat the same structures from *Diálogo 1*, now with new vocabulary.

¿Por qué no has contestado el email?	*Why haven't you **answered** the email?*
escrito	*written*
leído	*read*
mandado	*sent*

No lo he recibido .	*I haven't **received** it.*
enviado	*sent*
abierto	*opened*
visto	*seen*

Ha sido un día difícil .	*It has been a **difficult** day.*
largo	*long*
corto	*short*
duro	*hard*
maravilloso	*wonderful*

Estructura y Práctica

Past Participle: Formation

The past participle in Spanish ends in **-do**. Some irregular verbs have past participles ending in **-to** or **-cho**.

The past participle consists of the following elements.

verb stem + the vowel **a** for **-ar** verbs / the vowel **i** for **-er** and **-ir** verbs + do

tomar → tom + a + do → **tomado**   *taken*
comer → com + i + do → **comido**   *eaten*
vivir → viv + i + do → **vivido**   *lived*

The past participles of **ir** and **ser** are regular.

ir → **ido**
ser → **sido**

The past participle of **haber** is **habido**. The present perfect of the irregular verb form **hay** (*there is, there are*) is **ha habido**.

Ha habido un gran cambio.   *There has been a great change.*
Ha habido unos problemas graves.   *There have been some serious problems.*

-Er and **-ir** verbs whose stems end in a vowel add an accent mark over the **i**.

caer → caído
creer → creído
leer → leído
oír → oído
traer → traído

The following verbs have irregular past participles.

abrir	**abierto**	morir	**muerto**
cubrir	**cubierto**	poner	**puesto**
decir	**dicho**	resolver	**resuelto**
escribir	**escrito**	romper	**roto**
hacer	**hecho**	ver	**visto**
imprimir	**impreso**	volver	**vuelto**

When a prefix is added to these verbs, the past participle of the new verb shows the same irregularities.

contradecir *to contradict*	**contradicho**
describir *to describe*	**descrito**
descubrir *to discover*	**descubierto**
devolver (**o** > **ue**) *to give back*	**devuelto**
prever *to foresee*	**previsto**
rehacer *to redo*	**rehecho**
suponer *to suppose*	**supuesto**

Past Participle: Uses

1 · The past participle is frequently used as an adjective. It may either follow a noun or a form of **estar** or **ser**. When used as an adjective, it agrees in gender and number with the noun it refers to.

un documento **roto**	a **torn** document
los mensajes **escritos**	the **written** messages
una reunión **aburrida**	a **boring** meeting
las puertas **cerradas**	the **closed** doors
El profesor está **enojado**.	The teacher is **angry**.
La cena está **servida**.	Dinner is **served**.
Los turistas están **cansados**.	The tourists are **tired**.
Las ventanas están **abiertas**.	The windows are **open**.

2 · The past participle is used with **estar** to express positions of the body such as sitting or standing. The past participle functions as an adjective, thereby agreeing in gender and number with the noun it refers to. (See also *Diálogo 10* in this chapter.)

Alicia **está sentada** en la mecedora.   Alicia **is sitting** in the rocking chair.

3 · The past participle is used with **ser** to form the passive voice. In the passive voice, the past participle agrees in gender and number with the noun it refers to. (For more on the passive voice, see Chapter 10.)

Mi sitio web **fue diseñado** por Carlos.	My website **was designed** by Carlos.
Los datos **fueron analizados** ayer.	The data **was analyzed** yesterday.

4 · The past participle is used with **haber** to form the present perfect, the past perfect, and the other perfect tenses. In the perfect tenses, the past participle is invariable—it does not agree in gender or number.

A **Past participle used as adjective.** Write the adjective form derived from the verb in parentheses to correctly complete each noun phrase. Follow the *modelo*.

MODELO   los datos _guardados_ (guardar)

1. el lavaplatos _____ (descomponer)

2. una lengua _____ (escribir)

3. unos soldados _____ (*fallen, dead*) (caer)

4. el suéter _____ (romper)

5. el sueldo _____ (aumentar)

6. la carne poco _____ (hacer)

7. unos paisajes _____ (ver)

8. las obras maestras más _____ (leer)

9. las hojas (*leaves*) _____ (morir)

10. unos proyectos _____ a cabo (llevar) (llevar a cabo (*to carry out, achieve*))

B Past participle as adjective with *estar*. Write sentences using **estar** and the elements given to describe the physical or emotional state of each person. Make all necessary changes. Follow the *modelo*.

MODELO   Federico / resfriado
→ Federico está resfriado.

1. Carmen / angustiado
2. Rodrigo y Diego / aburrido
3. nosotras / emocionado
4. tú [*fem.*] / estresado
5. Juanita / deprimido

6. Carlos y Mateo / entusiasmado
7. yo [*masc.*] / preocupado
8. Esteban y Vera / acatarrado
9. Ud. [*fem.*] / cansado
10. Fernando / confundido

Present Perfect

The present perfect tense in Spanish consists of the present tense of the auxiliary verb **haber** + the past participle. In the perfect tenses, the past participle is invariable—it does not agree in gender or number. The Spanish present perfect usually corresponds to the English present perfect, which consists of *have* + past participle.

SINGULAR
he comido   *I have eaten*
has comido   *you have eaten*
ha comido   *he/she has eaten,*
              you (Ud.) *have eaten*

PLURAL
hemos comido   *we have eaten*
habéis comido *you have eaten*
han comido   *they/you* (Uds.) *have eaten*

The negative word **no** precedes the form of **haber** in the perfect tenses.

Hoy **no** he visto a nadie.   *Today I haven't seen anyone.*
¿Por qué **no** han llamado?   *Why haven't they called?*

No words can be placed between the auxiliary verb and the past participle, including in questions. This is different from English usage.

¿Han terminado Uds.?   ***Have** you **finished**?*
¿Han llegado los invitados?   ***Have** the guests **arrived**?*
¿Ha leído el estudiante el libro? ***Has** the student **read** the book?*

C *Haber* or past participle? Write either a form of the auxiliary verb **haber** or the past participle to correctly complete each of the following phrases, using the cue in parentheses. Follow the *modelo*.

MODELO   has _escrito_ (escribir)

1. _____ contestado (yo)
2. han _____ (volver)
3. hemos _____ (oír)
4. _____ comprendido (Ud.)
5. ha _____ (decir)

6. _____ comido (Uds.)
7. he _____ (ver)
8. _____ subido (nosotros)
9. _____ ido (tú)
10. han _____ (dar)

D Rewrite each sentence, changing the verb from the present tense to the present perfect. Follow the *modelo.*

> MODELO Venden su casa.
> → Han vendido su casa.

1. Cursa dos asignaturas optativas.
2. Quieren visitarnos.
3. Ponemos la mesa.
4. Llueve todo el día.
5. Es difícil adelgazar.
6. Se incluyen los ingresos y los gastos.
7. Abro las ventanas.
8. No ves a nadie, ¿verdad?
9. Hay mucho ajetreo hoy.
10. Estamos tan emocionados como Uds.
11. Tienen que pagar el seguro de salud.
12. ¿Pides más vino?

E Write a sentence with the verb in present perfect, using the string of elements given. Then write a second sentence with **estar** + the past participle to show the resulting condition of the first sentence. Follow the *modelo.*

> MODELO él / terminar / el proyecto
> → Él ha terminado el proyecto.
> → El proyecto está terminado.

1. yo / escribir / los documentos
2. nosotros / hacer / el plan de negocios
3. ella / pagar / la hipoteca
4. Uds. / recibir / la invitación
5. ellos / abrir / las fábricas
6. tú / facturar / el equipaje
7. él / alquilar / el apartamento
8. ellas / poner / la mesa
9. Ud. / descargar / su canción favorita
10. ellos / construir / los rascacielos

DIÁLOGO 2 · Han empezado el proyecto.

Study the dialogue, then listen to the recording and repeat each line.

FELIPE ¿Uds. ya han elaborado el presupuesto?
MARÍA No todavía. Apenas hemos comenzado a recoger los datos.
FELIPE ¿Entonces no han podido seguir con el proyecto?
MARÍA Bueno, hemos hecho un plan de negocios, eso es todo hasta ahora.

Análisis

Check that you understand the linguistic breakdown of each speech from *Diálogo 2.*

¿Uds. ya han elaborado el presupuesto?	*Have you already drawn up the budget?*
han (< *auxiliary verb* **haber**)	*you (Uds.) have*
elaborar	*to draw up, develop*
elaborado	*drawn up, developed*
Uds. han elaborado	*you have drawn up, you have developed*
el presupuesto	*budget*

No todavía. Apenas hemos comenzado
a recoger los datos.

*Not yet. We've barely begun to collect
the data.*

todavía	*still, yet*
no todavía	*not yet*
apenas	*hardly, barely*
hemos (< *auxiliary verb* **haber**)	*we have*
comenzar (**e** > **ie**)	*to begin*
comenzado	*begun*
hemos comenzado	*we have begun*
recoger	*to collect, gather*
los datos	*data*

¿Entonces no han podido seguir con
el proyecto?

*So you haven't been able to go on with
the project?*

han (< *auxiliary verb* **haber**)	*you* (Uds.) *have*
poder (**o** > **ue**)	*to be able to, can*
podido	*been able to*
han podido	*have been able to*
seguir (**e** > **i**) con	*to go on with, continue* (*with*)
el proyecto	*the project*

Bueno, hemos hecho un plan de
negocios, eso es todo hasta ahora.

*Well, we have made a business plan,
that's all up to now.*

hemos (< *auxiliary verb* **haber**)	*we have*
hacer (*irreg.*)	*to do, make*
hecho	*done, made*
hemos hecho	*we have made*
el plan	*plan*
los negocios	*business*
el plan de negocios	*business plan*
eso	*that*
todo	*everything*
hasta	*until*
hasta ahora	*up to now, so far*

▶ Variantes

Listen, and repeat the same structures from *Diálogo 2*, now with new vocabulary.

Hemos comenzado a recoger los datos .

*We've begun **to collect the data**.*

entrar los datos	*to enter the data*
analizar los datos	*to analyze the data*
guardar los datos	*to save the data*

 Han podido seguir.

***You have been able to** continue.*

Han querido	*You have wanted to*
Han necesitado	*You have needed to*
Han preferido	*You have preferred to*
Han pensado	*You have intended to*
Han tenido que	*You have had to*

Hemos elaborado el presupuesto.	**We've drawn up** the budget.
Hemos estudiado	We've studied
Hemos cambiado	We've changed
Hemos mirado	We've looked at
¿Ud. ha incluido los ingresos ?	Have you included **income?**
los gastos	expenses
El presupuesto incluye su sueldo .	The budget includes **his salary**.
la hipoteca	the mortgage
el seguro de salud	health insurance
Lo han hecho .	**They have done** it.
han dicho	They have said
han visto	They have seen
han devuelto	They have returned
han roto	They have broken
han traído	They have brought
han leído	They have read

Estructura y Práctica

F   *Un proyecto.* Write a sentence using the string of elements given to tell what you and your colleagues have recently done on your project. Use the present perfect tense. Follow the *modelo.*

MODELO   todos nosotros / empezar / el proyecto
→ Todos nosotros hemos empezado el proyecto.

1. el equipo / hacer / el plan de negocios

2. Alejo y yo / elaborar / el presupuesto

3. los asesores / recoger / los datos

4. el artista gráfico / dibujar / el logo

5. yo / crear / diapositivas (*slides*) en PowerPoint

6. tú / mandar / los emails

7. Uds. / reunirse / en la sala de conferencias

8. Leonardo / diseñar / el folleto (*brochure*)

9. Claudia y su asistente / leer / todos los documentos

10. Ud. / imprimir / el volante (*flyer*)

🔊 DIÁLOGO 3 · Ha muerto Ramón Fernández.

Study the dialogue, then listen to the recording and repeat each line.

MARÍA   ¿Has oído la noticia? Ha muerto Ramón Fernández.
FELIPE   Sí, yo sé. He ido al velorio y le he dado el pésame a su viuda.
MARÍA   ¿Sabes cuándo va a ser el entierro?
FELIPE   Me han dicho que va a tener lugar el jueves.

Análisis

Check that you understand the linguistic breakdown of each speech from *Diálogo 3*.

¿Has oído la noticia? Ha muerto Ramón Fernández.	*Have you heard the news? Ramón Fernández has died.*
has (< *auxiliary verb* **haber**)	*you* (**tú**) *have*
oír	*to hear*
oído	*heard*
has oído	*you have heard*
la noticia	*(piece of) news*
ha (< *auxiliary verb* **haber**)	*he has*
morir	*to die*
muerto	*died*
ha muerto	*he has died*

Sí, yo sé. He ido al velorio y le he dado el pésame a su viuda.	*Yes, I know. I went to the wake and I paid my condolences to his widow.*
he (< *auxiliary verb* **haber**)	*I have*
ir	*to go*
ido	*gone*
he ido	*I have gone*
el velorio	*wake*
el pésame	*condolences*
dar el pésame	*to pay condolences*
he (< *auxiliary verb* **haber**)	*I have*
dar	*to give*
dado	*given*
he dado	*I have given*
le he dado el pésame	*I expressed my condolences to her*
la viuda	*widow*

¿Sabes cuándo va a ser el entierro?	*Do you know when the funeral will be?*
el entierro	*funeral, burial*

Me han dicho que va a tener lugar el jueves.	*I've been told that it will take place on Thursday.*
han (< *auxiliary verb* **haber**)	*they have*
decir	*to say, tell*
dicho	*said*
han dicho	*they have said, they have told*
el lugar	*place*
tener lugar	*to take place*

▶ Variantes

Listen, and repeat the same structures from *Diálogo 3*, now with new vocabulary.

He ido al velorio .	*I've gone* **to the wake**.
al entierro	*to the funeral*
al cementerio	*to the cemetery*
a la sinagoga	*to the synagogue*
a la iglesia	*to the church*

Le he dicho "mi más sentido pésame" al viudo.	*I said "you have my deepest sympathy" to the widower.*

¿Qué te han dicho?	*What have they told you?*
No me han dicho nada.	*They haven't told me anything.*

Estructura y Práctica

Present Perfect: Position of Object Pronouns

In the perfect tenses, direct and indirect object pronouns, as well as reflexive pronouns, precede the form of **haber**. The negative word **no** precedes the object pronouns.

Buscamos a Ana. ¿**No la has** visto?	*We're looking for Ana. Haven't you seen her?*
¿El iPod? **Se lo he** dado a Lorenzo.	*The iPod? I've given it to Lorenzo.*

G Write an answer to each of the following questions, using the present perfect of the verb from the question. Add object pronouns in your response as needed. Follow the *modelo*.

MODELO   ¿Vas a visitar a tus primos?
→ Ya los he visitado.

1. ¿Vas a regalarle unas flores a tu novia?

2. ¿Uds. van a pedirles un aumento de sueldo a los jefes?

3. ¿Su mamá va a leerle un cuento al niño?

4. ¿Ud. va a darles el pésame a los dolientes (*mourners*)?

5. ¿Vas a llevar a tus amigas a la universidad?

6. ¿Ellas van a decirles a Uds. lo que pasó?

7. ¿Tina va a prestarte la sartén?

8. ¿Uds. van a hacer el café?

▶ DIÁLOGO 4 · Son puros chismes.

Study the dialogue, then listen to the recording and repeat each line.

FELIPE   ¿Vas a decirle a Teresa lo que oíste?
MARÍA   Ya se lo he dicho.
FELIPE   ¿Cómo ha reaccionado?
MARÍA   Me ha asegurado que son puros chismes.

Análisis

Check that you understand the linguistic breakdown of each speech from *Diálogo 4*.

¿Vas a decirle a Teresa lo que oíste?	*Are you going to tell Teresa what you heard?*
decirle a Teresa	*to tell Teresa*
lo que	*what*
oíste	*you heard*

Ya se lo he dicho.	*I've already told (it to) her.*
ya	*already*
he (< *auxiliary verb* **haber**)	*I have*
decir (*irreg.*)	*to say, tell*
dicho	*said, told*
he dicho	*I have told*
se lo he dicho	*I have told it to her*

¿Cómo ha reaccionado?	*How did she react?*
ha (< *auxiliary verb* **haber**)	*she has*
reaccionar	*to react*
reaccionado	*reacted*
ha reaccionado	*she has reacted*

Me ha asegurado que son puros chismes.	*She (has) assured me that it's nothing more than gossip.*
ha (< *auxiliary verb* **haber**)	*she has*
asegurar	*to assure*
asegurado	*assured*
ha asegurado	*she has assured*
me ha asegurado	*she has assured me*
puro	*just, merely, only* (when it appears before a noun)
el chisme	*gossip*
puros chismes	*nothing more than gossip*

▶ Variantes

Listen, and repeat the same structures from *Diálogo 4*, now with new vocabulary.

Yo se lo he dicho.	*I've said it to her.*
Yo se lo he contado.	*I've told it to her.*
Yo se lo he asegurado.	*I've assured her of it.*

Me la ha dado .	*She **has given** it to me.*
ha entregado	*has handed*
ha mandado	*has sent*

Estructura y Práctica

H **Translation.** Express each of the following sentences in Spanish.

1. *She has already told them what she heard.*

2. *Have you (tú) already paid your condolences to Daniel's widow?*

3. *The budget? We've drawn it up for them.*

4. *The contract? They haven't explained it to us yet.*

5. *The coffee pot (la cafetera)? I haven't had time to return it to him.*

6. *The income and expenses? Have you (Ud.) shown them to the accountant [fem.]?*

7. *There has been a lot of hustle and bustle in the company.*

DIÁLOGO 5 · Antonio no tiene pelos en la lengua.

Study the dialogue, then listen to the recording and repeat each line.

FELIPE   ¡Qué barbaridad! ¿Antonio se ha atrevido a decir tal cosa?
MARÍA   Tú sabes cómo es. No tiene pelos en la lengua.
FELIPE   Es cierto. Siempre ha sido así.

Análisis

Check that you understand the linguistic breakdown of each speech from *Diálogo 5*.

¡Qué barbaridad! ¿Antonio se ha atrevido a decir tal cosa?	*How outrageous! Antonio dared to say something like that?*
la barbaridad	*outrageous thing*
¡Qué barbaridad!	*How outrageous! / How awful!*
ha (< *auxiliary verb* **haber**)	*he has*
atreverse a + *infinitive*	*to dare to (do something)*
atrevido	*dared*
se ha atrevido	*he has dared*
tal	*such a*
tal cosa	*such a thing, something like that*
Tú sabes cómo es. No tiene pelos en la lengua.	*You know what he's like. He doesn't mince his words.*
no tener pelos en la lengua	*not to mince one's words*
Es cierto. Siempre ha sido así.	*It's true. He's always been like that.*
siempre	*always*
ha (< *auxiliary verb* **haber**)	*he has*
ser	*to be*
sido	*been*
ha sido	*he has been*
así	*like that*

Variantes

Listen, and repeat the same structures from *Diálogo 5*, now with new vocabulary.

¿Ellos siempre han sido así?   *Have they always been like that?*
Ella, sí, siempre ha sido así. Él no.   *Yes, she has always been like that. But he*
                                            hasn't.

Estructura y Práctica

IDIOMS WITH **TENER**

In this chapter, you learned the idiom **no tener pelos en la lengua** (*to not mince one's words*), adding to the many idioms with **tener** that you learned in previous chapters. Here are idioms with the verb **tener** that use parts of the body.

tener en la punta de la lengua
¿La palabra? Este... La tengo   *The word? Um . . . It's on the tip of*
  en la punta de la lengua.   *my tongue.*
no tener pelo de tonto
Carlos no tiene pelo de tonto.   *Carlos is nobody's fool.*
no tener ni pies ni cabeza
Este plan no tiene ni pies ni   *This plan doesn't make any sense*
  cabeza.   *at all.*
tener pájaros en la cabeza
Ese tipo tenía pájaros en la   *That guy had crazy ideas, he acted*
  cabeza.   *so foolishly.*

Present Perfect of Reflexive Verbs

In the perfect tenses, all object pronouns, including reflexive pronouns, precede the form of **haber**. The negative word **no** precedes the object pronouns.

¿Vas a ponerte los zapatos?   *Are you going to put your shoes on?*
Ya me los he puesto.   *I've already put them on.*
No, no me los he puesto.   *No, I haven't put them on yet.*

(For more on reflexive pronouns, see Chapter 8.)

I *Ya ha pasado.* Write an answer to each of the following questions, using the present perfect of the reflexive verb in the question to explain that these things have already happened. Change direct object nouns to pronouns and make all necessary changes. Follow the *modelo*.

MODELO   ¿Cuándo va María a arreglarse?
            → Se ha arreglado ya.

1. ¿Cuándo van Uds. a matricularse?   4. ¿Cuándo van ellos a reunirse?

2. ¿Cuándo va Pedro a graduarse?   5. ¿Cuándo va Ud. a probarse las camisas?

3. ¿Cuándo vas a lavarte la cabeza?   6. ¿Cuándo van Camila y Samuel a casarse?

7. ¿Cuándo vas a comprometerte con Julián?

8. ¿Cuándo van Uds. a mudarse al nuevo condominio?

9. ¿Cuándo van los niños a cepillarse los dientes?

10. ¿Cuándo va Olivia a maquillarse la cara?

▶ DIÁLOGO 6 · No nos han invitado.

Study the dialogue, then listen to the recording and repeat each line.

FELIPE   ¿Uds. van a asistir al bautizo del bebé de Margarita y Leonardo?
MARÍA   No nos han invitado todavía. ¿Y Uds.?
FELIPE   Nosotros tampoco hemos recibido la invitación.

Análisis

Check that you understand the linguistic breakdown of each speech from *Diálogo* 6.

¿Uds. van a asistir al bautizo del bebé de Margarita y Leonardo?	*Are you going to attend the baptism of Margarita and Leonardo's baby?*
asistir a	*to attend*
el bautizo	*baptism*
asistir al bautizo	*to attend the baptism*
No nos han invitado todavía. ¿Y Uds.?	*They haven't invited us yet. How about you?*
han (< *auxiliary verb* **haber**)	*they have*
invitar	*to invite*
invitado	*invited*
han invitado	*they've invited*
no nos han invitado	*they haven't invited us*
Nosotros tampoco hemos recibido la invitación.	*We haven't received the invitation either.*
tampoco	*neither*
recibir	*to get, receive*
recibido	*received*
hemos recibido	*we have received*
tampoco hemos recibido la invitación	*we haven't received the invitation either*

▶ Variantes

Listen, and repeat the same structures from *Diálogo* 6, now with new vocabulary.

No nos han invitado .	*They **haven't invited** us.*
han preguntado	*haven't asked*
han contestado	*haven't answered*
han llamado	*haven't called*
han visitado	*haven't visited*
han comprendido	*haven't understood*
han creído	*haven't believed*

▶ DIÁLOGO 7 · La mesa está puesta.

Study the dialogue, then listen to the recording and repeat each line.

MARÍA   ¿Cuándo vas a poner la mesa? Pronto llegan los invitados.
FELIPE   Mira, ya está puesta.
MARÍA   Muy bien, pero faltan los vasos.
FELIPE   Los he sacado del lavaplatos. ¿Por qué no los colocas tú en la mesa?

Análisis

Check that you understand the linguistic breakdown of each speech from *Diálogo 7*.

¿Cuándo vas a poner la mesa?	*When are you going to set the table?*
Pronto llegan los invitados.	*The guests will be arriving soon.*
poner la mesa	*to set the table*
pronto	*soon*
pronto llegan	*they'll soon be arriving*
el invitado	*guest*
Mira, ya está puesta.	*Look, it's already set.*
puesto	*put; set (past participle of **poner**)*
estar puesta	*to be set (of the table)*
Muy bien, pero faltan los vasos.	*Great, but there are no glasses.*
faltar	*to be missing*
el vaso	*(drinking) glass*
faltan los vasos	*the glasses are missing, there are no glasses*
Los he sacado del lavaplatos. ¿Por qué no los colocas tú en la mesa?	*I have taken them out of the dishwasher. Why don't you put them on the table?*
he	*I have*
sacar	*to take out*
sacado	*taken out*
he sacado	*I have taken out*
los he sacado	*I have taken them out*
el lavaplatos	*dishwasher*
colocar	*to place, put*
tú los colocas	*you place them, you put them*

▶ Variantes

Listen, and repeat the same structures from *Diálogo 7*, now with new vocabulary.

El almuerzo está servido.	*Lunch is served.*
La cena está servida.	*Dinner is served.*
Los vasos están rotos.	*The glasses are broken.*
Las tazas están rotas.	*The cups are broken.*
He sacado las cucharas de la gaveta.	*I've taken **the spoons** out of the drawer.*
las cucharitas	*the teaspoons*
los tenedores	*the forks*
los cuchillos	*the knives*
las servilletas	*the napkins*

Estructura y Práctica

J *Ya está hecho.* Write answers to each of the following questions, explaining that these things have already been done. Use the past participle as an adjective in your responses. Make all necessary changes. Follow the *modelo*.

> MODELO   Rita, ¿cuándo vas a peinarte?
> → Ya estoy peinada.

1. ¿Cuándo va Gerardo a levantarse?

2. Gabriela, ¿cuándo vas a enamorarte?

3. ¿Cuándo van ellos a acostarse?

4. Nora y Clara, ¿cuándo van a vestirse?

5. Chicos, ¿cuándo van Uds. a bañarse?

6. Marta, ¿cuándo vas a arreglarte?

7. ¿Cuándo van los Rivera a instalarse en su nueva casa?

8. ¿Cuándo van Armando y Carolina a divorciarse?

DIÁLOGO 8 · Las ventanas están abiertas.

Study the dialogue, then listen to the recording and repeat each line.

> FELIPE   Me muero de calor. ¿Has abierto las ventanas?
> MARÍA   Sí, están abiertas.

Análisis

Check that you understand the linguistic breakdown of each speech from *Diálogo 8*.

Me muero de calor. ¿Has abierto las ventanas?	*I'm dying of the heat. Have you opened the windows?*
morirse de	*to die of, die from* (often figurative)
el calor	*heat*
morirse de calor	*to be dying of the heat*
has	*you have*
abrir	*to open*
abierto	*opened* (past participle of **abrir**)
has abierto	*you have opened*
Sí, están abiertas.	*Yes, they're open.*
estar abierto	*to be open*

Variantes

Listen, and repeat the same structures from *Diálogo 8*, now with new vocabulary.

¿Has cerrado la puerta?	*Have you closed the door?*
Sí, está cerrada.	*Yes, it's closed.*

▶ DIÁLOGO 9 · Los informes están impresos.

Study the dialogue, then listen to the recording and repeat each line.

MARÍA   Hay que imprimir los informes.
FELIPE   Ya están impresos.

Análisis

Check that you understand the linguistic breakdown of each speech from *Diálogo 9*.

Hay que imprimir los informes.	*It's necessary to print the reports.*
hay que + *infinitive*	*one must (do something), you have to (do something)*
el informe	*report*
Ya están impresos.	*They're already printed.*
impreso	*printed (past participle of **imprimir**)*
estar impreso	*to be printed*

▶ Variantes

Listen, and repeat the same structures from *Diálogo 9*, now with new vocabulary.

Hay que resolver este problema.	*It's necessary to solve this problem.*
Ya está resuelto.	*It's solved already.*

▶ DIÁLOGO 10 · Los niños no se han acostado.

Study the dialogue, then listen to the recording and repeat each line.

FELIPE   ¿Los niños se han acostado?
MARÍA   No, no están acostados todavía.

Análisis

Check that you understand the linguistic breakdown of each speech from *Diálogo 10*.

¿Los niños se han acostado?	*Have the children gone to bed?*
han	*they have*
acostarse (**o** > **ue**)	*to go to bed*
acostado	*gone to bed*
se han acostado	*they have gone to bed*
No, no están acostados todavía.	*No, they're not in bed yet.*
estar acostado	*to be in bed, be lying down*

▶ Variantes

Listen, and repeat the same structures from *Diálogo 10*, now with new vocabulary.

¿La niña se ha acostado?	*Has the little girl gone to bed?*
No, no está acostada.	*No, she's not in bed.*

¿El niño se ha levantado?	*Has the little boy gotten up?*
No, no está levantado.	*No, he's not up.*
¿Te aburres?	*Are you bored?*
No, no estoy aburrido.	*No, I'm not bored.*
¿Uds. se preocupan mucho?	*Do you worry a lot?*
Sí, siempre estamos preocupados.	*Yes, we're always worried.*
¿Ellas se enojan mucho?	*Do they get angry a lot?*
Sí, siempre están enojadas.	*Yes, they're always angry.*
Ellos están sentados en el sofá.	*They're sitting on the couch.*
Ellas están paradas en la cola.	*They're standing in line.*

Estructura y Práctica

Estar + Past Participle: Expressing Positions of the Body

As you learned in Chapter 4, **estar** is used with the past participle to express positions of the body such as sitting or standing. The past participle functions as an adjective, thereby agreeing in gender and number with the noun it refers to. English uses the *-ing* form for this purpose.

Raquel **está sentada** en el sillón.	*Raquel **is sitting** in the armchair.*
Los niños **estaban acostados**.	*The children **were lying down**.*

K **¿Sentado o parado?** Write the form of **estar** plus past participle that correctly completes each of the following sentences describing how these people are positioned. Use the verb cue in parentheses. Make all necessary changes. Follow the *modelo*.

MODELO   Eugenio _está sentado_ en el banquillo (*bench*). (sentarse)

1. Pedro _____ en la hamaca. (tumbarse)

2. La flautista y el pianista _____ ante el público. (inclinarse (*to bow*))

3. El bebé _____ en su cuna (*crib*). (dormir)

4. El receptor (*catcher*) _____ detrás del plato (*home plate*). (agacharse (*to crouch*))

5. Nosotros _____ en el autobús. (parar)

6. Camila _____ a caballo. (montar)

7. Los niños ya _____ de la cama. (levantarse)

8. El abuelo _____ en el sofá. (echarse)

⏵ DIÁLOGO 11 · ¡Cómo ha cambiado la ciudad!

Study the dialogue, then listen to the recording and repeat each line.

MARÍA   ¡Cómo ha cambiado la ciudad!
FELIPE   No cabe duda. Han construido tantos rascacielos en los últimos años.
MARÍA   Han convertido muchas fábricas en apartamentos de lujo.
FELIPE   Y han hecho maravillas con los barrios bajos también.

Análisis

Check that you understand the linguistic breakdown of each speech from *Diálogo 11*.

¡Cómo ha cambiado la ciudad!	*How the city has changed!*
ha	*it has*
cambiar	*to change*
cambiado	*changed*
ha cambiado	*it has changed*
la ciudad	*the city*
No cabe duda. Han construido tantos rascacielos en los últimos años.	*That's for sure. They have built so many skyscrapers in the last few years.*
no cabe duda	*that's for sure, there is no doubt*
han	*they have*
construir	*to build*
construido	*built*
han construido	*they have built*
el rascacielos	*skyscraper*
los rascacielos	*skyscrapers*
tantos rascacielos	*so many skyscrapers*
último	*last*
en los últimos años	*in the last few years*
Han convertido muchas fábricas en apartamentos de lujo.	*They have converted many factories into luxury apartments.*
han	*they have*
convertir (**e** > **ie**)	*to convert*
convertir algo en otra cosa	*to convert something into something else*
convertido	*converted*
han convertido	*they have converted*
la fábrica	*factory*
el apartamento	*apartment*
el lujo	*luxury*
el apartamento de lujo	*luxury apartment*
Y han hecho maravillas con los barrios bajos también.	*And they've done wonders with the poor neighborhoods, too.*
han	*they have*
hacer (*irreg.*)	*to do, make*
hacer maravillas	*to do wonders*
hecho	*done, made*

han hecho	*they have done, they have made*
el barrio bajo	*poor neighborhood*

Variantes

Listen, and repeat the same structures from *Diálogo 11*, now with new vocabulary.

¡Cómo ha cambiado la ciudad!	*How the city **has changed**!*
ha crecido	*has grown*
La ciudad está muy cambiada.	*The city is very changed.*

DIÁLOGO 12 · El costo de la vida

Study the dialogue, then listen to the recording and repeat each line.

FELIPE   Nuestra ciudad se ha convertido en una metrópoli muy importante.

MARÍA   Sí, la población ha aumentado muchísimo. Actualmente hay casi siete millones de habitantes.

FELIPE   El precio de las viviendas ha subido muchísimo. El costo de la vida ha subido tanto.

MARÍA   A veces tengo ganas de mudarme a una ciudad menos costosa.

Análisis

Check that you understand the linguistic breakdown of each speech from *Diálogo 12*.

Nuestra ciudad se ha convertido en una metrópoli muy importante.	*Our city has become a very important metropolis.*
ha	*it has*
convertirse en (**e** > **ie**)	*to become*
convertido	*become*
se ha convertido	*it has become*
la metrópoli	*metropolis, capital (city), major city*
importante	*important*

Sí, la población ha aumentado muchísimo. Actualmente hay casi siete millones de habitantes.	*Yes, the population has increased a great deal. At present, there are nearly seven million inhabitants.*
la población	*population*
ha	*it has*
aumentar	*to increase*
aumentado	*increased*
ha aumentado	*it has increased*
muchísimo	*greatly, a great deal*
actualmente	*at present*
un millón de + *noun*	*a million* + noun
siete millones de + *noun*	*seven million* + noun
el habitante	*inhabitant*
siete millones de habitantes	*seven million inhabitants*

El precio de las viviendas ha subido muchísimo. El costo de la vida ha subido tanto.	The price of housing has gone up tremendously. The cost of living has gone up so much.
el precio	price
la vivienda	housing, housing unit
ha	it has
subir	to go up, rise
subido	gone up, risen
ha subido	it has gone up, it has risen
el costo	cost
el costo de la vida	cost of living
A veces tengo ganas de mudarme a una ciudad menos costosa.	Sometimes I feel like moving to a less expensive city.
a veces	sometimes
tener ganas de + *infinitive*	to feel like (doing something)
mudarse	to move (change residence)
costoso	costly, expensive
menos costoso	less expensive

Variantes

Listen, and repeat the same structures from *Diálogo 12*, now with new vocabulary.

El pueblo se ha convertido en una ciudad.	The town has become a city.
El desempleo ha aumentado.	Unemployment has risen.
Los impuestos han aumentado.	Taxes have gone up.

Estructura y Práctica

L **Translation.** Express the following dialogue exchanges in Spanish.

1. *How much the city has grown in the last few years!*
   And the population has increased a lot. There are almost four million inhabitants.

2. *Our little town has become a big and important city.*
   Indeed. Many buildings have been built, and little by little there are fewer poor neighborhoods.

3. *They've done wonderful things! Our city is very changed.*
   It's true. But what overcrowding (la aglomeración)*! What traffic! What noise!*

DIÁLOGO 13 · ¡Cómo había cambiado la ciudad!

Study the dialogue, then listen to the recording and repeat each line.

MARÍA   Cuando yo llegué a la ciudad, ya se había convertido en una metrópoli muy importante.

FELIPE   Ah sí. Cuando yo me mudé aquí, el costo de la vida ya había subido muchísimo.

Análisis

Check that you understand the linguistic breakdown of each speech from *Diálogo 13*.

Cuando yo llegué a la ciudad, ya se había convertido en una metrópoli muy importante.	*When I arrived in this city, it had already become an important metropolis.*

había (< *auxiliary verb* **haber**)	*it had*
convertirse en (**e** > **ie**)	*to become*
convertido	*become*
se había convertido	*it had become*

Ah sí. Cuando yo me mudé aquí, el costo de la vida ya había subido muchísimo.	*Oh, yes. When I moved here, the cost of living had already risen tremendously.*

mudarse	*to move (change residence)*
había (< *auxiliary verb* **haber**)	*it had*
subir	*to go up, rise*
subido	*gone up, risen*
había subido	*it had gone up, it had risen*

▶ Variantes

Listen, and repeat the same structures from *Diálogo 13*, now with new vocabulary.

Cuando yo regresé, ellos ya se habían ido .	*When I came back, **they had already left**.*
ella ya había oído la noticia	*she had already heard the news*
tú ya te habías acostado	*you had already gone to bed*

Estructura y Práctica

Past Perfect (Pluperfect)

The past perfect tense (also known as the pluperfect) in Spanish consists of the imperfect tense of the auxiliary verb **haber** + the past participle. In the perfect tenses, the past participle is invariable—it does not agree in gender or number. The Spanish past perfect corresponds to the English past perfect *had* + past participle.

SINGULAR	había comido	*I had eaten*
	habías comido	*you had eaten*
	había comido	*he, she, you* (Ud.) *had eaten*
PLURAL	habíamos comido	*we had eaten*
	habíais comido	*you had eaten*
	habían comido	*they, you* (Uds.) *had eaten*

No habían regresado cuando yo llegué.	*They hadn't returned when I arrived.*
¿No había llamado todavía?	*Hadn't she called yet?*

Object pronouns, including reflexive pronouns, precede the form of **haber** in the perfect tenses. The negative word **no** precedes the object pronouns.

¿La cámara? **Se la hemos** devuelto.   *The camera? We've returned it to them.*
No me había probado el traje.   *I hadn't tried on the suit.*

M *Ya había pasado.* Write sentences from the strings of elements to say that certain things had already happened by the time something else occurred. Use the preterit in the dependent **cuando** clause and the past perfect in the main clause. Follow the *modelo.*

MODELO   nosotros / volver del teatro : Uds. / salir
         → Cuando nosotros volvimos del teatro, Uds. ya habían salido.

1. Ud. / comprar los cartuchos de tinta : Jorge / imprimir las invitaciones

2. los invitados / llegar para cenar : Pepita y Tomás / poner la mesa

3. despegar el avión : los pasajeros / abrocharse el cinturón de seguridad

4. nosotros / conocer a Nora : ella / hacerse ingeniera

5. Eduardo / comenzar a trabajar : sus colegas / leer los documentos

6. tú / llegar al cementerio : el entierro / tener lugar

7. sonar el teléfono : tú / despertarte

8. yo / ver a Antonio : su empresa / trasladarlo a otra sucursal

9. Uds. / darnos la noticia : nosotros / oírla del vecino

10. Nora / regresar a su pueblo natal (*hometown*) : el pueblo / ya convertirse en una ciudad grande

DIÁLOGO 14 · No habían hecho nada.

Study the dialogue, then listen to the recording and repeat each line.

MARÍA   Los analistas ya habían analizado los datos cuando yo llegué a la oficina.
FELIPE No me digas. Cuando yo los vi, todavía no habían hecho nada.

Análisis

Check that you understand the linguistic breakdown of each speech from *Diálogo 14.*

Los analistas ya habían analizado los   *The analysts had already analyzed the data*
datos cuando yo llegué a la oficina.   *when I arrived at the office.*
   había (< *auxiliary verb* **haber**)   *they had*
   analizar   *to analyze*
   analizado   *analyzed*
   habían analizado   *they had analyzed*

No me digas. Cuando yo los vi, todavía no habían hecho nada.

You don't say. When I saw them, they still hadn't done anything.

No me digas.	You don't say.
habían (< auxiliary verb **haber**)	they had
hacer (irreg.)	to do, make
hecho	done, made (past participle of **hacer**)
habían hecho	they had done, they had made
no habían hecho nada	they hadn't done anything

▶ Variantes

Listen, and repeat the same structures from *Diálogo 14*, now with new vocabulary.

Él ya había elaborado el presupuesto cuando yo llamé.

He had already drawn up the budget when I called.

Uds. ya habían resuelto el problema	You had already solved the problem
Ella ya había contestado el email	She had already answered the email

Cuando Esteban volvió, Pablo y Lidia ya se habían casado .

When Esteban returned, **Pablo and Lidia had already gotten married**.

su familia ya se había instalado en su nueva casa	his family had already moved into their new house
nosotros ya habíamos visto la película	we had already seen the film

Estructura y Práctica

N **Translation.** Express the following dialogue exchanges in Spanish.

1. *Have you (Ud.) drawn up the budget already?*
   Yes, I've included income and expenses.

2. *Is the table set?*
   Yes, and dinner is served.

3. *It has been a very difficult day.*
   Why is that? (literally, Why do you say it?) Have you (tú) had to do a lot of work?

4. *Was it snowing when you (Uds.) were returning home?*
   No, we had already returned home when it began to snow.

5. *When the airplane landed, the passengers had already turned on their cell phones.*
   I suppose they had also taken down their carry-on luggage.

6. *When we got to Mario's house, the party had already ended.*
   And nobody had told you (it) before? How outrageous!

The Progressive Tenses

The progressive tenses consist of the present, imperfect, preterit, future, and conditional forms of the verb **estar**, followed by the gerund. In this chapter, the progressive tenses are presented for recognition purposes only.

PRESENT PROGRESSIVE	**Estoy elaborando** el presupuesto.
	I'm drawing up the budget.
IMPERFECT PROGRESSIVE	**Estaba elaborando** el presupuesto.
	I was drawing up the budget.
PRETERIT PROGRESSIVE	**Estuve elaborando** el presupuesto hasta que llegaron.
	I was drawing up the budget until they arrived.
FUTURE PROGRESSIVE	**Estaré elaborando** el presupuesto todo el día.
	I'll be drawing up the budget all day.
CONDITIONAL PROGRESSIVE	**Estaría elaborando** el presupuesto.
	I'd be drawing up the budget.

(For a presentation of the future and conditional tenses, see Chapter 15.)

The gerund or **-ndo** form in Spanish corresponds to the *-ing* form or present participle in English. For **-ar** verbs, the ending of the gerund is **-ando**; for **-er** and **-ir** verbs, the ending is **-iendo**.

hablar	habl**ando**
esperar	esper**ando**
comer	com**iendo**
aprender	aprend**iendo**
escribir	escrib**iendo**
abrir	abr**iendo**

-Er and **-ir** verbs whose stems end in a vowel use **-yendo** and not **-iendo** to form the gerund.

caer	ca**yendo**
creer	cre**yendo**
leer	le**yendo**
oír	o**yendo**
traer	tra**yendo**

-Ir verbs whose preterit form has a change in the vowel of the stem in the third person show the same change in the gerund.

INFINITIVE	PRETERIT	GERUND
decir	dijo	**diciendo**
dormir	durmió	**durmiendo**
morir	murió	**muriendo**
pedir	pidió	**pidiendo**
repetir	repitió	**repitiendo**
sentir	sintió	**sintiendo**
servir	sirvió	**sirviendo**
venir	vino	**viniendo**

Poder and **ir** have irregular gerunds.

poder	**pudiendo**
ir	**yendo**

The gerunds of **estar**, **ir**, and **venir** are not commonly used.

For now, we will focus only on the present progressive. In Spanish, the present progressive is different from the corresponding simple present tense in that it emphasizes that the action is in progress. It may also suggest that the action is temporary, not habitual. The present progressive in Spanish can never refer to the future, as the present progressive in English does. To express future time, Spanish uses the simple present, the **ir a** +infinitive construction, or the future tense.

Salimos para el campo mañana.	*We are leaving for the country tomorrow.*
Vamos a salir para el campo mañana.	*We are going to leave for the country tomorrow.*
Saldremos para el campo mañana.	*We will leave for the country tomorrow.*

In the progressive tenses, object and reflexive pronouns may either precede the form of **estar** or be attached to the gerund in writing. In the latter case, a written accent is added over the vowel before the **-ndo** ending.

Nos estamos divirtiendo mucho. ⎫
Estamos divirtiéndo**nos** mucho. ⎬ *We're having a great time.*

Se lo están explicando. ⎫
Están explicándo**selo**. ⎬ *They're explaining it to them.*

NOTE   Be aware that English-speaking learners of Spanish tend to overuse the present progressive.

Un paso más

Are you ready to take your Spanish a step further? Here are exercises that will enhance your knowledge of the language and allow you to express yourself freely.

O *Preguntas personales.* Answer each question with a complete Spanish sentence.

1. ¿Ud. elabora un presupuesto personal para los gastos de la casa? Haga (*Make*) una lista de todos los puntos que incluye en el presupuesto. (Repase (*Review*) el vocabulario del capítulo.)

2. ¿Trabaja con las bases de datos empresariales (de una empresa)? ¿Cómo las organiza?

3. ¿Qué hace para asegurar la protección y la seguridad de los datos?

4. ¿Vive en una ciudad? ¿Qué cosas le agradan de la vida urbana? ¿Qué cosas encuentra desagradables?

5. ¿Se celebran ritos y tradiciones religiosos en su familia? ¿Cuáles son? (Repase los Diálogos 3 y 6 de este capítulo.)

¡Una cena fantástica! Write a brief description of the dinner party you gave last night. Review the vocabulary used in *Diálogo 7* to describe your table setting. Additional vocabulary is provided below. Tell what you served, who the guests were, and other details.

el azucarero (la azucarera) *sugar bowl*
la copa *wine glass*
el cubierto *cutlery, utensils; place setting*
el mantel *tablecloth*
el mantelito *place mat*

el pimentero *pepper mill*
el sopero *soup plate*
el salero *saltshaker*
la vajilla *set of dishes*
la vela *candle*

 La gentrificación. Write a paragraph expressing your thoughts on gentrification, using the words and phrases you learned in this chapter. (Review *Diálogos 11, 12,* and *13* in this chapter.) Use these questions as a guide.

1. ¿Cuáles son los objetivos de la gentrificación?

2. ¿Cuáles son sus ventajas (*advantages*) y sus desventajas (*disadvantages*)?

3. ¿Cómo transforma la gentrificación los espacios urbanos deteriorados?

4. ¿Hay barrios bajos donde Ud. vive? ¿Cómo son?

5. ¿Ud. conoce sectores de su comunidad que han sido gentrificados? ¿Cómo son?

6. ¿Cree que el urbanismo (*urban planning, city planning*) mejora la vida de los habitantes de las ciudades? ¿Cómo?

Directions, Air Travel, Recipes

Communication Goals

- Telling someone to do or not to do something
- Asking for and giving directions
- Giving instructions for a recipe
- Vocabulary: traffic signs and signals, at the airport, a doctor's advice, cooking, a hotel emergency

Grammar Topics

- The Imperative
- Imperative: Command Forms for **Ud.** and **Uds.**
- Imperative: Command Forms for **tú** and **vosotros**
- Irregular Command Forms: **tú**
- Object Pronouns in the Imperative: **tú**, **Ud.**, **Uds.**
- Imperative: Command Forms for **nosotros**
- Object Pronouns in the Imperative: **nosotros**
- Irregular Command Forms: **Ud.**, **Uds.**, **nosotros**
- Other Ways of Giving Commands

▶ DIÁLOGO 1 · Cómo se llega al museo

Study the dialogue, then listen to the recording and repeat each line.

INÉS   Perdone, señor, ¿cómo llego al museo de arte?

JAIME   Pues mire Ud., siga por esta avenida. Al llegar a la calle Castaño, doble a la derecha. Camine tres cuadras hasta llegar a una plaza. Cruce la plaza. Allí queda el museo.

INÉS   Muchas gracias, señor.

JAIME   De nada, señorita.

Análisis

Check that you understand the linguistic breakdown of each speech from *Diálogo 1*.

Perdone, señor, ¿cómo llego al museo de arte?	*Excuse me, sir. How can I get to the art museum?*
perdonar	*to forgive, pardon*
perdone	*excuse me*
¿cómo llego?	*how do I get to?*
el museo de arte	*art museum*

Pues mire Ud., siga por esta avenida. Al llegar a la calle Castaño, doble a la derecha. Camine tres cuadras hasta llegar a una plaza. Cruce la plaza. Allí queda el museo.	*Well, look, continue along this avenue. When you get to Castaño street, turn right. Walk three blocks until you get to a square. Cross the square. That's where the museum is.*
mirar	*to look at*
mire	*look*
seguir (**e** > **i**) por	*to continue along*
siga	*continue*
al llegar	*when you arrive*
la calle	*street*
doblar	*to turn*
doble	*turn*
a la derecha	*to the right*
caminar	*to walk*
camine	*walk*
la cuadra	*(city) block*
hasta	*until*
hasta llegar	*until you get to*
la plaza	*square (in a city)*
cruzar	*to cross*
cruce	*cross*
quedar	*to be (for location of inanimate nouns)*
allí queda	*that's where it is*

Muchas gracias, señor.	*Thank you very much, sir.*
De nada, señorita.	*You're welcome, miss.*

▶ Variantes

Listen, and repeat the same structures from *Diálogo 1*, now with new vocabulary.

Perdone , señor.	***Excuse me***, *sir.*
Dispense	*Excuse me*
Disculpe	*Excuse me*

Doble a la derecha .	*Turn* ***right***.
a la izquierda	*left*

Camine rápidamente.	***Walk*** *quickly.*
Corra	*Run*
Ande	*Walk*

Maneje con cuidado.	***Drive*** *carefully.*
Conduzca	*Drive*

Cruce la plaza .	*Cross **the square**.*
la calle	*the street*
el puente	*the bridge*
el río	*the river*

Estructura y Práctica

THE IMPERATIVE

The imperative is used to tell someone to do something or not to do something. There are imperative forms in Spanish for **tú**, **Ud.**, **nosotros**, **vosotros**, and **Uds.** (The imperative forms for **vosotros** (the plural form of **tú** in Spain) appear in some of the charts in this chapter, but they will not be practiced actively.)

Imperative: Command Forms for **Ud.** and **Uds.**

Most imperative forms involve a change in the vowel of the ending. In other words, the **a** in the endings of **-ar** verbs changes to **e**, and the **e** or **i** in the endings of **-er** and **-ir** verbs changes to **a**.

comprar	**Compre** (Ud.) esta calculadora.	***Buy*** *this calculator.*
	Compren (Uds.) esta calculadora.	***Buy*** *this calculator.*
leer	**Lea** (Ud.) la propuesta.	***Read*** *the proposal.*
	Lean (Uds.) la propuesta.	***Read*** *the proposal.*
añadir	**Añada** (Ud.) un comentario.	***Add*** *a comment.*
	Añadan (Uds.) un comentario.	***Add*** *a comment.*

The addition of the pronoun **Ud.** or **Uds.** to an imperative adds a polite tone to the command, much as *please* does in English.

To form the negative imperative for **Ud.** and **Uds.**, add **no** before the command form.

No compre (Ud.) esta calculadora.	***Don't buy*** *this calculator.*
No compren (Uds.) esta calculadora.	***Don't buy*** *this calculator.*
No lea (Ud.) la propuesta.	***Don't read*** *the proposal.*
No lean (Uds.) la propuesta.	***Don't read*** *the proposal.*
No añada (Ud.) un comentario.	***Don't add*** *a comment.*
No añadan (Uds.) un comentario.	***Don't add*** *a comment.*

Verbs whose present tense has an irregularity in the stem of the first person singular have the same irregular stem in the **Ud.** and **Uds.** forms of the imperative.

INFINITIVE	**yo** FORM	**Ud.** COMMAND	**Uds.** COMMAND
decir	digo	**diga**	**digan**
hacer	hago	**haga**	**hagan**
poner	pongo	**ponga**	**pongan**
tener	tengo	**tenga**	**tengan**
venir	vengo	**venga**	**vengan**
conocer	conozco	**conozca**	**conozcan**
ver	veo	**vea**	**vean**

If the present tense form of a verb has a change in the vowel of the stem, the command forms for **Ud.** and **Uds.** show that change as well. (For more on stem-changing verbs, see Chapter 6.)

INFINITIVE	**Ud., Uds.** FORMS	**Ud.** COMMAND	**Uds.** COMMAND
cerrar	cierra, cierran	**cierre**	**cierren**
mostrar	muestra, muestran	**muestre**	**muestren**
encender	enciende, encienden	**encienda**	**enciendan**
volver	vuelve, vuelven	**vuelva**	**vuelvan**
convertir	convierte, convierten	**convierta**	**conviertan**
pedir	pide, piden	**pida**	**pidan**
dormir	duerme, duermen	**duerma**	**duerman**

A Write an affirmative **Ud.** command for each item. Follow the *modelo*.

> MODELO   doblar a la derecha
>   → Doble a la derecha.

1. correr el maratón
2. manejar con cuidado
3. abrir las ventanas
4. asistir al concierto
5. cruzar la calle
6. subir al avión
7. comer con nosotros
8. seguir por el río
9. elaborar un presupuesto
10. leer este libro
11. diseñar el sitio web
12. volver para el viernes
13. pedir una disculpa (*to apologize*)
14. hacer un plan de negocios

B Write an affirmative **Uds.** command for each item. Follow the *modelo*.

> MODELO   caminar rápidamente
>   → Caminen rápidamente.

1. beber mucha agua
2. trabajar con el equipo
3. vivir felizmente
4. escribir el email
5. conducir con cuidado
6. aprender las fechas de memoria
7. tomar el tren
8. vestir a los niños
9. prender la televisión
10. analizar los datos
11. cobrar el cheque
12. compartir sus ideas
13. dormir la siesta
14. servir la comida

C **Please.** Express the following commands in Spanish, adding the pronoun **Ud.** or **Uds.** to add a polite tone. Follow the *modelos.*

MODELOS   *Please come back soon.* (Ud.)   *Please come back soon.* (Uds.)
    → Regrese Ud. pronto.   → Regresen Uds. pronto.

1. *Please arrive early.* (Uds.)   5. *Please look at the traffic sign.* (Ud.)

2. *Please serve dinner.* (Ud.)   6. *Please go up in the elevator.* (Uds.)

3. *Please open the window.* (Ud.)   7. *Please store the data.* (Ud.)

4. *Please cross the street carefully.* (Uds.)   8. *Please draw up a budget.* (Uds.)

Spelling Changes in the Imperative: **Ud. and Uds.**

In the command forms for **Ud.** and **Uds.**, the following spelling changes take place.

In **-ar** verbs ending in **-car**, **-gar**, **-zar**, the final consonants of the stem **c**, **g**, **z** change respectively to **qu**, **gu**, **c** before an ending beginning with **-e**.

INFINITIVE	**Ud.** COMMAND	**Uds.** COMMAND
sacar	sa**que**	sa**que**n
pagar	pa**gue**	pa**gue**n
almorzar	almuer**ce**	almuer**ce**n

-Er and **-ir** verbs whose stem ends in **-g-** change the **g** to **j** before an ending beginning with **-a**.

INFINITIVE	**Ud.** COMMAND	**Uds.** COMMAND
escoger	esco**ja**	esco**ja**n
elegir	eli**ja**	eli**ja**n

◉ DIÁLOGO 2 · No estacione en esta calle.

Study the dialogue, then listen to the recording and repeat each line.

JAIME   Dispense, señorita, ¿se permite estacionar en esta calle?
INÉS   No, señor, se prohíbe. Mire la señal. Le pueden poner una multa.
JAIME   Entonces dígame, por favor, ¿hay un estacionamiento por aquí?
INÉS   Bueno, siga derecho hasta el semáforo. En la esquina hay uno.

Análisis

Check that you understand the linguistic breakdown of each speech from *Diálogo 2.*

Dispense, señorita, ¿se permite estacionar en esta calle?	*Excuse me, miss, is parking allowed on this street?*
dispensar	*to excuse*
dispense	*excuse me*
permitir	*to permit, allow*
se permite	*it is allowed*
¿se permite estacionar?	*is parking allowed?*

No, señor, se prohíbe. Mire la señal.
Le pueden poner una multa.
  se prohíbe
  mirar
  mire
  la señal
  la multa
  ponerle una multa a uno
  Le pueden poner una multa.

No, sir, it's forbidden. Look at the sign.
They can fine you.
  it is forbidden
  to look at
  look at
  sign, road sign, traffic sign
  fine
  to fine someone
  They can fine you.

Entonces dígame, por favor, ¿hay un estacionamiento por aquí?
  decir
  diga
  dígame
  el estacionamiento
  por aquí

Then tell me, please, is there a parking garage around here?
  to say, tell
  tell
  tell me
  parking lot, parking garage
  around here

Bueno, siga derecho hasta el semáforo. En la esquina hay uno.
  seguir (e > i) por
  siga
  siga derecho
  hasta
  el semáforo
  la esquina

Well, keep going straight ahead until the traffic light. There's one on the corner.
  to continue along
  continue
  keep going straight ahead
  until, up to
  traffic light
  street corner

▶ Variantes

Listen, and repeat the same structures from *Diálogo 2*, now with new vocabulary.

No estacione en esta calle.
  No aparque

Don't park *on this street.*
  Don't park

Mire la señal de tráfico .
  la placa

*Look at **the traffic sign**.*
  the license plate

Dígame , por favor.
  Míreme
  Cuénteme
  Óigame

Tell me, *please.*
  Look at me
  Tell me
  Listen to me

El semáforo está en verde .
  en rojo
  en amarillo
  en naranja

*The light is **green**.*
  red
  yellow
  yellow

Estructura y Práctica

Negative Commands: **Ud.** and **Uds.**

To form the negative imperative for **Ud.** and **Uds.**, add **no** before the command form.

No firme (Ud.) el contrato.	***Don't sign*** *the contract.*
No firmen (Uds.) el contrato.	***Don't sign*** *the contract.*
No lo **crea** (Ud.).	***Don't believe*** *it.*
No lo **crean** (Uds.).	***Don't believe*** *it.*
No escriba (Ud.) otra carta.	***Don't write*** *another letter.*
No escriban (Uds.) otra carta.	***Don't write*** *another letter.*
No salga (Ud.) todavía.	***Don't leave*** *yet.*
No salgan (Uds.) todavía.	***Don't leave*** *yet.*

D Write an affirmative and a negative **Ud.** command for each item. Follow the *modelo*.

MODELO   asistir al evento
→ Asista al evento.
→ No asista al evento.

1. guardar los suéteres
2. ver el programa
3. estacionar en la plaza
4. añadir más sal
5. cerrar la puerta
6. imprimir los contratos
7. poner la mesa
8. probar ese plato
9. descargar el archivo
10. repetir las palabras

E Write an affirmative and a negative **Uds.** command for each item. Follow the *modelo*.

MODELO   asistir al evento
→ Asistan al evento.
→ No asistan al evento.

1. guardar los suéteres
2. ver el programa
3. estacionar en la plaza
4. añadir más sal
5. cerrar la puerta
6. imprimir los contratos
7. poner la mesa
8. probar ese plato
9. descargar el archivo
10. repetir las palabras

DIÁLOGO 3 · En el aeropuerto

Study the dialogue, then listen to the recording and repeat each line.

INÉS   Aquí hay un quiosco. Vamos a registrarnos.
JAIME   Sí, saquemos las tarjetas de embarque y facturemos el equipaje.
INÉS   Luego, vamos a ir a la puerta de embarque.
JAIME   Espera. Primero comamos algo. Yo me muero de hambre.

Análisis

Check that you understand the linguistic breakdown of each speech from *Diálogo 3*.

Aquí hay un quiosco. Vamos a registrarnos.	*There's a kiosk here. Let's check in.*
el quiosco	*automatic check-in kiosk*
vamos a + *infinitive*	*let's (do something)*
registrarse	*to check in, register*
vamos a registrarnos	*let's check in*

Sí, saquemos las tarjetas de embarque y facturemos el equipaje.	*Yes, let's get the boarding passes and check the luggage.*
sacar	*to take out, get*
sacamos	*we get*
saquemos	*let's get*
la tarjeta	*card*
el embarque	*boarding*
la tarjeta de embarque	*boarding pass*
facturar	*to check (luggage)*
facturamos	*we check*
facturemos	*let's check*
el equipaje	*luggage*

Luego, vamos a ir a la puerta de embarque.	*Then let's go to the departure gate.*
luego	*then*
vamos a + *infinitive*	*let's (do something)*
vamos a ir	*let's go*
la puerta	*gate*
la puerta de embarque	*departure gate*

Espera. Primero comamos algo. Yo me muero de hambre.	*Wait. Let's eat something first. I'm dying of hunger.*
espera	*wait* (**tú** command)
primero	*first*
comemos	*we eat*
comamos	*let's eat*
comamos algo	*let's eat something*
morirse (**o** > **ue**) de	*to be dying of* (often figurative)
me muero de hambre	*I'm dying of hunger. / I'm starving.*

▶ Variantes

Listen, and repeat the same structures from *Diálogo 3*, now with new vocabulary.

Vamos a registrarnos .	*Let's **check in**.*
irnos	*go, leave*
sacar las tarjetas de embarque	*get our boarding passes*
facturar el equipaje	*check the luggage*
comer algo	*eat something*

Registrémonos.	*Let's check in.*
Vámonos.	*Let's go.*
Sentémonos.	*Let's sit down.*
Reunámonos.	*Let's get together.*
Vistámonos.	*Let's get dressed.*
No comamos ahora.	***Let's not eat*** *now.*
No nos vayamos	*Let's not go*
No nos registremos	*Let's not check in*
No nos sentemos	*Let's not sit down*
No nos reunamos	*Let's not get together*
No nos vistamos	*Let's not get dressed*
Espera.	*Wait.*
Come.	*Eat.*
Sube.	*Go up.*
Vuelve.	*Come back.*
No esperes.	*Don't wait.*
No comas.	*Don't eat.*
No subas.	*Don't go up.*
No vuelvas.	*Don't come back.*
Ve.	*Go.*
Sal.	*Go out.*
Ven.	*Come.*
No vayas.	*Don't go.*
No salgas.	*Don't go out.*
No vengas.	*Don't come.*
Haz las maletas.	*Pack.* (literally, *Do the suitcases.*)
Hazlas.	*Pack them* (*the suitcases*).
No hagas las maletas.	*Don't pack.* (literally, *Don't do the suitcases.*)
No las hagas.	*Don't pack them* (*the suitcases*).
Saca la tarjeta de embarque.	*Get (out) your boarding pass.*
No saques la tarjeta de embarque.	*Don't get (out) your boarding pass.*
Sácala.	*Get it.*
No la saques.	*Don't get it.*

Estructura y Práctica

Imperative: Command Forms for **tú** and **vosotros**

Negative commands for **tú** and **vosotros** are formed just like the **Ud.** and **Uds.** commands—by switching the vowel of the ending. These negative **tú** and **vosotros** commands, as well as the command forms for **Ud.** and **Uds.**, all derive from the present subjunctive. (For a full presentation of the present subjunctive, see Chapter 16.)

INFINITIVE	tú PRESENT TENSE	tú COMMAND	vosotros PRESENT TENSE	vosotros COMMAND
comprar	no compras	**no compres**	no compráis	**no compréis**
leer	no lees	**no leas**	no leéis	**no leáis**
añadir	no añades	**no añadas**	no añadís	**no añadáis**
cerrar	no cierras	**no cierres**	no cerráis	**no cerréis**
mostrar	no muestras	**no muestres**	no mostráis	**no mostréis**
encender	no enciendes	**no enciendas**	no encendéis	**no encendáis**
volver	no vuelves	**no vuelvas**	no volvéis	**no volváis**

Irregularities that appear in the **Ud.** and **Uds.** commands also appear in the negative **tú** and **vosotros** commands.

INFINITIVE	NEGATIVE tú COMMAND	NEGATIVE vosotros COMMAND
decir	**no digas**	**no digáis**
hacer	**no hagas**	**no hagáis**
poner	**no pongas**	**no pongáis**
tener	**no tengas**	**no tengáis**
venir	**no vengas**	**no vengáis**
conocer	**no conozcas**	**no conozcáis**
ver	**no veas**	**no veáis**
ir	**no vayas**	**no vayáis**
saber	**no sepas**	**no sepáis**
ser	**no seas**	**no seáis**
dar	**no des**	**no deis**
estar	**no estés**	**no estéis**

Affirmative commands for **tú** and **vosotros** do not show a change in the vowel of the ending of the imperative. Affirmative commands for **tú** are formed by dropping the final **-s** of the **tú** form of the present tense. Affirmative commands for **vosotros** are formed by replacing the **-r** of the infinitive with **-d**.

INFINITIVE	tú PRESENT TENSE	tú COMMAND	vosotros PRESENT TENSE	vosotros COMMAND
comprar	compras	**compra**	compráis	**comprad**
comer	comes	**come**	coméis	**comed**
añadir	añades	**añade**	añadís	**añadid**
cerrar	cierras	**cierra**	cerráis	**cerrad**
encender	enciendes	**enciende**	encendéis	**encended**
convertir	conviertes	**convierte**	convertís	**convertid**
pedir	pides	**pide**	pedís	**pedid**
dormir	duermes	**duerme**	dormís	**dormid**
dar	das	**da**	dais	**dad**
estar	estás	**está**	estáis	**estad**

Irregular Command Forms: tú

Eight affirmative **tú** commands have irregular one-syllable forms. The corresponding **vosotros** commands are regular.

INFINITIVE	**tú** PRESENT TENSE	**tú** COMMAND	**vosotros** PRESENT TENSE	**vosotros** COMMAND
decir	dices	**di**	decís	decid
hacer	haces	**haz**	hacéis	haced
ir	vas	**ve**	vais	id
poner	pones	**pon**	ponéis	poned
salir	sales	**sal**	salís	salid
ser	eres	**sé**	sois	sed
tener	tienes	**ten**	tenéis	tened
venir	vienes	**ven**	venís	venid

Spelling Changes in the Imperative: Negative **tú** and **vosotros** Commands

In the command forms for the negative **tú** and **vosotros** commands, the following spelling changes take place.

In **-ar** verbs ending in **-car**, **-gar**, **-zar**, the final consonants of the stem **c**, **g**, **z** change respectively to **qu**, **gu**, **c** before an ending beginning with **-e**.

INFINITIVE	NEGATIVE **tú** COMMAND	NEGATIVE **vosotros** COMMAND
sacar	no sa**qu**es	no sa**qu**éis
pagar	no pa**gu**es	no pa**gu**éis
almorzar	no almuer**c**es	no almor**c**éis

-Er and **-ir** verbs whose stem ends in **-g-** change the **g** to **j** before an ending beginning with **-a**.

INFINITIVE	NEGATIVE **tú** COMMAND	NEGATIVE **vosotros** COMMAND
escoger	no esco**j**as	no esco**j**áis
elegir	no eli**j**as	no eli**j**áis

F   Write an affirmative and a negative **tú** command for each item. Follow the *modelo*.

> MODELO   doblar a la izquierda
> → Dobla a la izquierda.
> → No dobles a la izquierda.

1. vender el carro
2. navegar en la web
3. subir en el ascensor
4. seguir por esta calle
5. hacer la maleta
6. pensar en eso
7. venir el sábado
8. salir antes de las cuatro
9. tener prisa
10. jugar al golf

Object Pronouns in the Imperative: **tú, Ud., Uds.**

In all negative imperative forms, object pronouns are placed in their usual position before the verb. This includes reflexive pronouns.

No **te** metas en estos asuntos.	*Don't butt into these matters.*
Esta camisa está rota. No **te la** pongas.	*This shirt is torn. Don't put it on.*
No **me** diga que no puede venir.	*Don't tell me that you can't come.*
Él quiere dinero. No **se lo** preste Ud.	*He wants money. Don't lend it to him.*
No **se** vayan Uds.	*Don't go away.*
¿Las maletas? No **las** facturen.	*The suitcases? Don't check them.*

For affirmative command forms, object pronouns follow the verbs and are attached to them in writing. For **tú**, **Ud.**, and **Uds.** commands, an accent mark is added to the stem vowel when an object pronoun (or reflexive pronoun) is added, if the command form has more than one syllable.

Cuídate.	***Take care.***
Aquí tienes el informe. **Léelo.**	*Here's the report. **Read it.***
Ana tiene la calculadora. **Pídesela.**	*Ana has the calculator. **Ask her for it.***
Él quiere dinero. **Présteselo Ud.**	*He wants money. **Lend it to him.***
Necesito los documentos. **Tráigamelos Ud.**	*I need the documents. **Bring them to me.***
Váyanse Uds.	***Go away.***
Escúchenme bien.	***Listen to me*** *carefully.*

No accent mark is added to a one-syllable command form when a single object pronoun is added.

Esto es tu trabajo. **Hazlo.**	*This is your work. **Do it.***
Ponte el abrigo. Hace frío.	***Put on*** *your coat. It's cold outside.*
Dime si necesitas algo.	***Tell me*** *if you need anything.*

However, the command forms **dé**, **esté**, and **está** may keep their accents when a pronoun is added.

Déme un consejo.	***Give me*** *some advice.*
¡**Estáte** quieto!	***Stay*** *still! / Stop fidgeting! / Behave yourself!*

All command forms require a written accent when two object pronouns are added.

Busca tus guantes y **póntelos.**	*Get your gloves and **put them on.***
No entiendo su idea. **Explíquemela.**	*I don't understand your idea. **Explain it to me.***
Si terminaron el mensaje, **envíenselo.**	*If you finished the message, **send it to them.***

IMPERATIVE: **VOSOTROS** + OBJECT PRONOUNS

No accent mark is added to **vosotros** command forms when a single object pronoun is added.

¡Niños, **hacedme** caso!	*Children, pay attention to what I say!*
Mandadle un email.	*Send her an email.*

Vosotros command forms drop the final **-d** before the reflexive pronoun **os.**

Acostaos ahora mismo.	*Go to bed right now.*
Poneos en contacto con ella.	*Get in touch with her.*
¡Divertíos muchísimo!	*Have a great time!*

However, the **-d** is retained in **idos** (*go away*).

G Express each of the following affirmative and negative commands for **tú** in Spanish.

1. *Don't worry.*

2. *Go away.*

3. *The truth. Tell it to them.*

4. *You owe her money. Return it to her.*

5. *Don't be like that.*

6. *This tie is ugly. Don't put it on.*

7. *Don't be angry with me.*

8. *Dinner, please. Make it for us.*

9. *He needs the headphones. Give them to him.*

10. *Be patient.*

H Express each of the following affirmative and negative commands for **Ud.** and **Uds.** in Spanish. Pay special attention to all required spelling changes.

1. *The dog? Look at him. / Don't look at him.* (Uds.)

2. *The piano? Play it. / Don't play it.* (Ud.)

3. *The magazines? Hand them to me. / Don't hand them to me.* (Ud.)

4. *The gifts? / Choose them for her. / Don't choose them for her.* (Ud.)

5. *The keys? Look for them. / Don't look for them.* (Uds.)

6. *The news (item)? Tell* (contar) *it to them. / Don't tell it to them.* (Ud.)

7. *The idea? Explain it to him. / Don't explain it to him.* (Uds.)

8. *The orchestra* (la orquesta)*? Conduct* (dirigir) *it for us. / Don't conduct it for us.* (Ud.)

9. *The bill? Pay it for him. / Don't pay it for him.* (Uds.)

10. *The game? Start it. / Don't start it.* (Uds.)

I **Object pronouns with *Ud.* and *Uds.* commands.** Write both **Ud.** and **Uds.** commands for each of the following items, adding object pronouns (including reflexive pronouns) based on the English cues. Follow the *modelo.*

MODELO	mandar el paquete		
	Send it.	→ Mándelo.	Mándenlo.
	Send it to me.	→ Mándemelo.	Mándenmelo.

1. leer el cuento
   Read it.
   Read it to them.

2. traer las cucharitas
   Bring them.
   Bring them to him.

3. explicar su punto de vista (*point of view*)
   Explain it.
   Explain it to her.

4. decir el chisme
   Tell it.
   Tell it to us.

5. mostrar las pinturas
   Show them.
   Show them to them.

6. servir el postre
   Serve it.
   Serve it to us.

7. lavarse
   Wash up.
   Wash your hands.
   Wash them.

8. pedir los datos
   Ask for it (them).
   Ask her for it (them).

9. ponerse
   Put your jacket on.
   Put it on.

10. secarse
    Dry your hair.
    Dry it.

Imperative: Command Forms for **nosotros**

As you learned in *Diálogo 1*, most imperative forms involve a change in the vowel of the ending. In other words, the **a** in the endings of -**ar** verbs changes to **e**, and the **e** or **i** in the endings of -**er** and -**ir** verbs changes to **a**. Those vowel changes for -**ar**, -**er**, and -**ir** verbs occur in the command forms for **nosotros**.

Tomemos fotos.	*Let's take pictures.*
No **tomemos** fotos.	*Let's not take pictures.*
Comamos en este restaurante.	*Let's eat at this restaurant.*
No **comamos** en este restaurante.	*Let's not eat at this restaurant.*
Escribamos una propuesta.	*Let's write a proposal.*
No **escribamos** una propuesta.	*Let's not write a proposal.*

Note that since the present indicative **nosotros** forms of -**ar** and -**er** verbs have no stem change, the **nosotros** form of the imperative does not have a stem change either.

INFINITIVE	PRESENT TENSE	**nosotros** COMMAND
cerrar (**e** > **ie**)	cerramos	cerremos
mostrar (**o** > **ue**)	mostramos	mostremos
encender (**e** > **ie**)	encendemos	encendamos
volver (**o** > **ue**)	volvemos	volvamos

Verbs whose present tense has an irregularity in the stem of the first person singular have the same irregular stem in the **nosotros** forms of the imperative.

INFINITIVE	**yo** FORM	**nosotros** COMMAND
decir	digo	**digamos**
hacer	hago	**hagamos**
poner	pongo	**pongamos**
tener	tengo	**tengamos**
venir	vengo	**vengamos**
conocer	conozco	**conozcamos**
ver	**veo**	**veamos**

However, -**ir** verbs whose preterit form has a change in the vowel of the stem in the third person show the same change in the stem vowel in the **nosotros** form of the imperative. Thus, in the **nosotros** form of the imperative, the verb **pedir** has **i** as the stem vowel and the verb **dormir** has **u** as the stem vowel. Note that the **nosotros** forms of the present tense of these verbs do not have a stem change.

INFINITIVE	él/ella/Ud. PRETERIT	nosotros PRESENT TENSE	nosotros COMMAND
convertir	convirtió	convertimos	convirtamos
pedir	pidió	pedimos	pidamos
dormir	durmió	dormimos	durmamos

The **nosotros** imperative of the verb **ir** is most commonly **vamos** (*let's go*). The negative imperative, *let's not go*, is **no vayamos**.

Vamos al cine, ¿quieres?	*Let's go to the movies, would you like to?*
No, **no vayamos** al cine. **Vamos** al concierto.	*No, let's not go to the movies. Let's go to the concert.*

Spelling Changes in the Imperative: **nosotros**

In **nosotros** command forms, the following spelling changes take place.

In -**ar** verbs ending in -**car**, -**gar**, -**zar**, the final consonants of the stem **c**, **g**, **z** change respectively to **qu**, **gu**, **c** before an ending beginning with -**e**.

INFINITIVE	nosotros COMMAND
sacar	saquemos
pagar	paguemos
almorzar	almorcemos

-**Er** and -**ir** verbs whose stem ends in -**g**- change the **g** to **j** before an ending beginning with -**a**.

INFINITIVE	nosotros COMMAND
escoger	escojamos
elegir	elijamos

Object Pronouns in the Imperative: **nosotros**

In negative **nosotros** command forms, object pronouns, including reflexive pronouns, are placed in their usual position before the verb.

No **nos** mudemos a aquella ciudad.	*Let's not move to that city.*
¿El almuerzo? No **se lo** sirvamos todavía.	*Lunch? Let's not serve it to them yet.*

However, in affirmative command forms, object pronouns follow the verb and are attached to it in writing. When an object pronoun is added to the **nosotros** command form, a written accent is placed on the **a** or **e** of the ending.

Tenemos el informe. **Traigámoselo.**	*We have the report. **Let's bring it to her.***
Ellos están enfermos. **Ayudémoslos.**	*They're sick. **Let's help them.***

Nosotros command forms lose their final -**s** before the reflexive pronoun **nos** and before the pronoun **se**.

Levantémonos. (Levantemos + nos)	*Let's get up.*
Divirtámonos. (Divirtamos + nos)	*Let's have a good time.*

Vámonos. (Vamos + nos)   *Let's go.*
Pongámonoslo. (Pongamos + nos + lo)   *Let's put it on.*
Expliquémoselos. (Expliquemos + se + los)   *Let's explain them to him.*
Digámoselo. (Digamos + se + lo)   *Let's tell it to them.*

J Write an affirmative and a negative **nosotros** command for each item. Follow the *modelo*.

> MODELO   leer este artículo
> → Leamos este artículo.
> → No leamos este artículo.

1. llegar el domingo
2. hacer turismo
3. sacar el pasaporte
4. dar consejos
5. ir al teatro
6. dormir la siesta
7. salir esta noche
8. venir en tren
9. pensar en el futuro
10. pedir un café
11. sentarse en el sofá
12. quedarse unos días más

Vamos a + Infinitive

In everyday speech, the affirmative **nosotros** command is often replaced by **vamos a** + infinitive.

Compremos flores. → **Vamos a comprar** flores.
Hagamos turismo. → **Vamos a hacer** turismo.
Sirvamos la cena. → **Vamos a servir** la cena.

However, the negative **nosotros** commands cannot be replaced by **vamos a** + infinitive. Thus, **vamos a salir** can mean *let's go out* or *we're going to go out*. **No vamos a salir**, however, means only *we are not going to go out*. The phrase *let's not go out* has to be rendered as **no salgamos**.

K Write the affirmative **nosotros** command in response to each question. Express each command in two ways, as the **nosotros** command and as the **ir a** + infinitive construction. Change direct object nouns to pronouns in your answers. Follow the *modelo*.

> MODELO   ¿Quieres entrar los datos?
> → Sí, entrémoslos.
> → Sí, vamos a entrarlos.

1. ¿Quieres ver la telenovela?
2. ¿Quieres discutir estas ideas?
3. ¿Quieres conseguir los boletos?
4. ¿Quieres compartir los gastos?
5. ¿Quieres pedir vino tinto?
6. ¿Quieres visitar a la tía?
7. ¿Quieres aparcar el carro?
8. ¿Quieres traducir estas palabras?
9. ¿Quieres probarte estos abrigos?
10. ¿Quieres cortarte el pelo?

L Write the negative **nosotros** command in response to each question. Change direct object nouns to pronouns in your answers. Follow the *modelo*.

MODELO   ¿Quieres entrar los datos?
→ No, no los entremos.

1. ¿Quieres ver la telenovela?
2. ¿Quieres discutir estas ideas?
3. ¿Quieres conseguir los boletos?
4. ¿Quieres compartir los gastos?
5. ¿Quieres pedir vino tinto?
6. ¿Quieres visitar a la tía?
7. ¿Quieres aparcar el carro?
8. ¿Quieres traducir estas palabras al español?
9. ¿Quieres probarte estos abrigos?
10. ¿Quieres cortarte el pelo?

M *Nosotros* **commands with reflexive verbs.** Express the following pairs of sentences in Spanish. First, write an affirmative **nosotros** command, then write a negative **nosotros** command. Change direct object nouns to pronouns in your answers.

1. *Let's take a stroll in the park. / Let's not take a stroll in the park.*
2. *Let's get married in December. / Let's not get married in December.*
3. *Let's put them (our gloves) on. / Let's not put them on.*
4. *Let's get together on Sunday. / Let's not get together on Sunday.*
5. *Let's fasten them (our seatbelts; one per person). / Let's not fasten them.*
6. *Let's wake up early. / Let's not wake up early.*
7. *Let's wash them (our hands). / Let's not wash them.*
8. *Let's go now. / Let's not go now.*
9. *Let's dry it for them (the children's hair). / Let's not dry it for them.*
10. *Let's say goodbye to them. / Let's not say goodbye to them.*

▶ DIÁLOGO 4 · A bordo del avión

Study the dialogue, then listen to the recording and repeat each line.

JAIME   Por favor, señora, coloque Ud. su equipaje de mano arriba.
INÉS   Es que no hay lugar.
JAIME   Entonces colóquelo debajo de su asiento. Si no cabe, démelo y lo coloco en otra parte. Y abróchese Ud. el cinturón de seguridad, por favor.

Análisis

Check that you understand the linguistic breakdown of each speech from *Diálogo 4*.

Por favor, señora, coloque Ud. su equipaje de mano arriba.	*Please, ma'am, place your hand luggage above.*
colocar	*to place, put*
coloque	*place*
el equipaje de mano	*carry-on luggage, hand luggage*
arriba	*above*

Es que no hay lugar.	*But there's no room.*
es que	*the fact is that*
lugar	*place, room*
no hay lugar	*there's no room*

Entonces colóquelo debajo de su asiento. Si no cabe, démelo y lo coloco en otra parte. Y abróchese Ud. el cinturón de seguridad, por favor.	*Then place it under your seat. If it doesn't fit, give it to me and I will place it somewhere else. And fasten your seatbelt, please.*
colóquelo	*place it*
debajo de	*under*
el asiento	*seat*
debajo de su asiento	*under your seat*
caber (*irreg.*)	*to fit*
dar	*to give*
dé	*give*
démelo	*give it to me*
y lo coloco	*and I'll put it*
en otra parte	*somewhere else*
abrocharse	*to fasten*
abróchese	*fasten*
el cinturón	*belt*
la seguridad	*security, safety*
el cinturón de seguridad	*seatbelt*

▶ Variantes

Listen, and repeat the same structures from *Diálogo 4*, now with new vocabulary.

Búsquelo.	*Look for it.*
Sáquelo.	*Take it out.*
Entréguelo.	*Hand it in.*
Páguelo.	*Pay it.*
Comiéncelo.	*Begin it.*
Analícelo.	*Analyze it.*
No lo busque.	*Don't look for it.*
No lo saque.	*Don't take it out.*
No lo entregue.	*Don't hand it in.*
No lo pague.	*Don't pay it.*
No lo comience.	*Don't begin it.*
No lo analice.	*Don't analyze it.*
Démelo.	*Give it to me.*
Hágamelo.	*Do it for me.*
Dígamelo.	*Tell it to me.*
No me lo dé.	*Don't give it to me.*
No me lo haga.	*Don't do it for me.*
No me lo diga.	*Don't tell it to me.*

Abróchese el cinturón de seguridad. Desabróchese	**Fasten** *your seat belt.* *Unfasten*
Póngase el abrigo. Quítese	**Put on** *your coat.* *Take off*
¿El abrigo? Póngaselo. Quíteselo.	*Your coat?* **Put it on.** *Take it off.*
¿El abrigo? Póngaselo. Quíteselo.	*Her coat?* **Help her on with it.** *Help her off with it.*

Estructura y Práctica

Irregular Command Forms: **Ud., Uds., nosotros**

Several verbs have irregular command forms.

INFINITIVE	**Ud.** COMMAND	**Uds.** COMMAND	**nosotros** COMMAND
ir	**vaya**	**vayan**	**vamos / no vayamos**
saber	**sepa**	**sepan**	**sepamos**
ser	**sea**	**sean**	**seamos**

The verbs **dar** and **estar** have an accent mark in the **Ud.** command form. **Estar** also has an accent mark in the **Uds.** command form. The **nosotros** command forms of **dar** and **estar** are regular.

INFINITIVE	**Ud.** COMMAND	**Uds.** COMMAND	**nosotros** COMMAND
dar	**dé**	**den**	**demos**
estar	**esté**	**estén**	**estemos**

N *En la oficina.* Write an affirmative and a negative **Ud.** command in response to each of the following questions. Change direct object nouns to pronouns (**le** = *to him, to her*; **les** = *to them*). Make all necessary changes. Follow the *modelos*.

MODELOS   ¿Debo escribirle el email? (sí)   ¿Debo escribirle el email? (no)
   → Sí, escríbaselo.   → No, no se lo escriba.

1. ¿Debo entregarles los papeles? (sí)
   ¿Debo entregarles los papeles? (no)

2. ¿Debo mostrarles las diapositivas (*slides*)? (sí)
   ¿Debo mostrarles las diapositivas? (no)

3. ¿Debo pedirle el contrato? (sí)
   ¿Debo pedirle el contrato? (no)

4. ¿Debo darle el informe? (sí)
   ¿Debo darle el informe? (no)

5. ¿Debo calcularle los ingresos y gastos? (sí)
   ¿Debo calcularle los ingresos y gastos? (no)

6. ¿Debo hacerles la base de datos? (sí)
   ¿Debo hacerles la base de datos? (no)

7. ¿Debo describirles el plan de mercadeo? (sí)
   ¿Debo describirles el plan de mercadeo? (no)

8. ¿Debo traerles el correo (*mail*)? (sí)
   ¿Debo traerles el correo? (no)

▶ DIÁLOGO 5 · Durante el vuelo

Study the dialogue, then listen to the recording and repeat each line.

INÉS   Quiero oír música pero no tengo auriculares.
JAIME   Pídeselos al auxiliar de vuelo. Oye, ¿tú ves mi almohada?
INÉS   No. Pídesela al auxiliar de vuelo.

Análisis

Check that you understand the linguistic breakdown of each speech from *Diálogo 5*.

Quiero oír música pero no tengo auriculares.	*I want to listen to music, but I don't have headphones.*
oír (*irreg.*)	*to hear, listen to*
oír música	*to listen to music*
los auriculares	*headphones, headset*
Pídeselos al auxiliar de vuelo.	*Ask the flight attendant for them.*
Oye, ¿tú ves mi almohada?	*Say, do you see my pillow?*
pedir (**e** > **i**)	*to ask for*
pedirle algo a uno	*to ask someone for something*
pide	*ask*
pídeselos	*ask him for them*
el auxiliar de vuelo	*flight attendant*
Pídeselos al auxiliar de vuelo.	*Ask the flight attendant for them.*
la almohada	*pillow*
No. Pídesela al auxiliar de vuelo.	*No, ask the flight attendant for it.*
pídesela	*ask him for it*

▶ Variantes

Listen, and repeat the same structures from *Diálogo 5*, now with new vocabulary.

¿Los auriculares? Pídeselos.	*The headphones? Ask her for them.*
¿Las galletas? Pídeselas.	*The cookies? Ask her for them.*
¿El periódico? Pídeselo.	*The newspaper? Ask him for it.*
¿La revista? Pídesela.	*The magazine? Ask him for it.*
¿Debo pedírselo?	*Should I ask him for it?*
No, no se lo pidas.	*No, don't ask him for it.*

▶ DIÁLOGO 6 · Niños, a la cama.

Study the dialogue, then listen to the recording and repeat each line.

INÉS	Niños, acuéstense. Ya son las nueve.
JAIME	Pero mamá, por favor, queremos terminar este videojuego. Falta poco.
INÉS	Bueno, termínenlo y apaguen la computadora. Luego pónganse el pijama, cepíllense los dientes y a la cama.

Análisis

Check that you understand the linguistic breakdown of each speech from *Diálogo 6.*

Niños, acuéstense. Ya son las nueve.	*Children, go to bed. It's already nine o'clock.*
acostarse (**o > ue**)	*to go to bed*
acuéstense	*go to bed*
son las nueve	*it's nine o'clock*
Pero mamá, por favor, queremos terminar este videojuego. Falta poco.	*Please, mom. We want to finish this video game. It's almost over.*
terminar	*to finish*
queremos terminar	*we want to finish*
el videojuego	*video game*
faltar	*to be missing*
falta poco	*there is little (time) remaining, it's almost over*
Bueno, termínenlo y apaguen la computadora. Luego pónganse el pijama, cepíllense los dientes y a la cama.	*All right, finish it and shut off the computer. Then put on your pajamas, brush your teeth, and off to bed.*
terminar	*to finish*
terminen	*finish*
termínenlo	*finish it*
apagar	*to turn off, shut off, extinguish*
apaguen	*shut off*
ponerse (*irreg.*)	*to put on (article of clothing)*
pónganse	*put on*
pónganse el pijama	*put on your pajamas*
cepillarse (**o > ue**)	*to brush*
cepíllense	*brush*
cepíllense los dientes	*brush your teeth*
la cama	*bed*
a la cama	*(off) to bed*

▶ Variantes

Listen, and repeat the same structures from *Diálogo 6,* now with new vocabulary.

Niños, acuéstense .	*Children, **go to bed**.*
duérmanse	*go to sleep, fall asleep*
despiértense	*wake up*
levántense	*get up, get out of bed*
vístanse	*get dressed*

No se acuesten.	*Don't go to bed.*
No se duerman.	*Don't fall asleep.*
¿El pijama? Pónganselo.	*Your pajamas?* **Put them on.**
Quítenselo.	*Take them off.*
¿El pijama? No se lo pongan.	*Your pajamas?* **Don't put them on.**
No se lo quiten.	*Don't take them off.*
Límpiense los dientes.	*Brush your teeth.*
Lávense la cara.	*Wash your faces.*
Córtense el pelo.	*Cut your hair.*
¿La computadora? Apáguenla.	*The computer?* **Shut it off.**
Préndanla.	*Turn it on.*

▶ DIÁLOGO 7 · En la consulta de médico

Study the dialogue, then listen to the recording and repeat each line.

JAIME	Doctora, ¿qué hago para perder peso?
DOCTORA REYES	Bueno, señor Díaz, póngase a dieta. Coma granos integrales y deje de comer tanta grasa.
JAIME	¿Ud. me va a recetar unas pastillas para adelgazar?
DOCTORA REYES	De ningún modo. Haga Ud. ejercicio y cambie su manera de comer.

Análisis

Check that you understand the linguistic breakdown of each speech from *Diálogo 7*.

Doctora, ¿qué hago para perder peso?	*Doctor, what shall I do to lose weight?*
¿qué hago?	*what shall I do?*
el peso	*weight*
perder (**e** > **ie**)	*to lose*
perder peso	*to lose weight*
Bueno, señor Díaz, póngase a dieta. Coma granos integrales y deje de comer tanta grasa.	*Well, Mr. Díaz, go on a diet. Eat whole grains and stop eating so much fat.*
ponerse	*to put on (article of clothing)*
póngase	*put yourself on*
póngase a dieta	*put yourself on a diet, go on a diet*
comer	*to eat*
coma	*eat*
el grano	*grain*
el grano integral	*whole grain*

dejar	*to leave, let*
dejar de + *infinitive*	*to stop (doing something)*
deje de comer	*stop eating*
la grasa	*fat*
tanta grasa	*so much fat*

¿Ud. me va a recetar unas pastillas para adelgazar?	*Are you going to prescribe some pills for me to lose weight?*
recetarle algo a uno	*to prescribe something for someone*
recetarle pastillas a uno	*to prescribe pills for someone*
adelgazar	*to get thinner, lose weight*
para adelgazar	*in order to lose weight*

De ningún modo. Haga Ud. ejercicio y cambie su manera de comer.	*Absolutely not. Start exercising and change your way of eating.*
de ningún modo	*absolutely not, no way*
hacer	*to do, make*
haga	*do*
haga ejercicio	*do exercise, start exercising*
cambiar	*to change*
cambie	*change*
la manera	*way*
la manera de comer	*way of eating*

Variantes

Listen, and repeat the same structures from *Diálogo 7*, now with new vocabulary.

Beba mucha agua.	*Drink a lot of water.*
No beba refrescos.	*Don't drink soft drinks.*

Viva la vida plenamente.	*Live life to its fullest.*
Baje de peso.	*Lose weight.*
Pierda peso.	*Lose weight.*
Adelgace.	*Lose weight.*
Aumente de peso.	*Gain weight.*
Engorde.	*Gain weight.*

Ponte a dieta.	*Go on a diet.*
Pierde peso.	*Lose weight.*
Cambia tu manera de comer.	*Change your way of eating.*
Haz ejercicio.	*Exercise.*
No seas comilón.	*Don't overeat. / Don't be a glutton.*
No comas comida basura.	*Don't eat junk food.*
No tomes refrescos.	*Don't drink soft drinks.*

EATING AND DRINKING

Diálogo 7 deals with diet and the food we eat. Here are some expressions that are related to how and what we eat.

comer como un rey	*to eat like a king*
comer como un pajarito	*to eat like a bird*
tener afición a los dulces, ser goloso	*to have a sweet tooth*
repetir (**e** > **i**)	*to have a second helping*
Come y bebe que la vida es breve.	*Eat and drink, because life is short.*
La vida es demasiado corta para beber mal vino.	*Life is too short to drink bad wine.*
Todo lo bueno o es pecado o engorda.	*Everything that's good is either a sin or makes you fat.*
Uvas y queso, saben a beso.	*Grapes and cheese, they taste like a kiss.*

Estructura y Práctica

O *¿Ud. o tú?* **Affirmative commands.** Answer each question with an affirmative command for **Ud.** or **tú**, based on the question. Change direct object nouns to pronouns and make all necessary changes. Follow the *modelos*.

MODELOS   ¿Le enseño las fotos?   ¿Te enseño las fotos?
              → Sí, enséñemelas.   → Sí, enséñamelas.

1. ¿Le muestro los cuadros?   6. ¿Le doy las tarjetas de crédito?

2. ¿Le explico mi idea?   7. ¿Te presto el paraguas?

3. ¿Te pongo el abrigo?   8. ¿Le envío la copia de seguridad?

4. ¿Te hago la merienda?   9. ¿Te digo lo que pasó?

5. ¿Le entrego los cartuchos de tinta?   10. ¿Te sirvo las tapas?

P *¿Ud. o tú?* **Negative commands.** Answer each question with a negative command for **Ud.** or **tú**, based on the question. Change direct object nouns to pronouns and make all necessary changes. Follow the *modelos*.

MODELOS   ¿Le enseño las fotos?   ¿Te enseño las fotos?
              → No, no me las enseñe.   → No, no me las enseñes.

1. ¿Le muestro los cuadros?   6. ¿Le doy las tarjetas de crédito?

2. ¿Le explico mi idea?   7. ¿Te presto el paraguas?

3. ¿Te pongo el abrigo?   8. ¿Le envío la copia de seguridad?

4. ¿Te hago la merienda?   9. ¿Te digo lo que pasó?

5. ¿Le entrego los cartuchos de tinta?   10. ¿Te sirvo las tapas?

▶ DIÁLOGO 8 · En la playa

Study the dialogue, then listen to the recording and repeat each line.

JAIME   Oye chica, te vas a quemar. Ponte más filtro solar.
INÉS   Mírame, ya estoy bronceada. No me hace falta.
JAIME   No seas tonta. El sol daña la piel. Cuídate de él.

Análisis

Check that you understand the linguistic breakdown of each speech from *Diálogo 8*.

Oye chica, te vas a quemar. Ponte más filtro solar.	*Listen, you're going to get burned. Put on more sunscreen.*
quemarse	*to get burned, get sunburned*
poner (*irreg.*)	*to put*
pon	*put*
ponerse	*to put on oneself*
ponte	*put on*
el filtro solar	*sunscreen*
ponte más filtro solar	*put on more sunscreen*
Mírame, ya estoy bronceada. No me hace falta.	*Look at me, I'm already tan. I don't need it.*
mirar	*to look at*
mira	*look*
mírame	*look at me*
bronceado	*tanned, suntanned*
estar bronceado	*to be tanned*
hacerle falta a uno	*to need*
no me hace falta	*I don't need it*
No seas tonta. El sol daña la piel. Cuídate de él.	*Don't be silly. The sun damages the skin. Protect yourself from it.*
ser	*to be*
no seas	*don't be*
tonto	*silly, stupid*
no seas tonta	*don't be silly, don't be stupid*
el sol	*the sun*
dañar	*to harm, damage*
la piel	*skin*
cuidarse de	*to take care of, protect/guard oneself from*
cuídate	*protect yourself, take care*
cuídate de él	*protect yourself from it*

▶ Variantes

Listen, and repeat the same structures from *Diálogo 8*, now with new vocabulary.

Ponte el filtro solar.	*Put on sunscreen.*
Póntelo.	*Put it on.*
No te lo pongas.	*Don't put it on.*

Cuídate.   *Take care of yourself.*
No te quemes.   *Don't burn.*

▶ DIÁLOGO 9 · Una receta de cocina

Study the dialogue, then listen to the recording and repeat each line.

INÉS   Y ahora, ¿qué hago? ¿Bato los huevos?
JAIME   Primero calienta un poco de aceite de oliva en la sartén. Luego, bate los
          huevos y añádelos a la sartén. Fríelos a fuego lento.
INÉS   ¿Echo sal a los huevos?
JAIME   Sí, pero no les pongas demasiada sal.

Análisis

Check that you understand the linguistic breakdown of each speech from *Diálogo 9*.

Y ahora, ¿qué hago? ¿Bato los huevos?	*And now what shall I do? Should I beat the eggs?*
¿qué hago?	*what shall I do?*
el huevo	*egg*
batir	*to beat*
batir los huevos	*to beat the eggs*
¿Bato los huevos?	*Do I beat the eggs?*

Primero calienta un poco de aceite de oliva en la sartén. Luego, bate los huevos y añádelos a la sartén. Fríelos a fuego lento.	*First, heat a little olive oil in the frying pan. Then beat the eggs and add them to the frying pan. Fry them over low heat.*
calentar (**e** > **ie**)	*to heat, warm up*
calienta	*heat*
el aceite	*oil*
el aceite de oliva	*olive oil*
la sartén (also, **el sartén**)	*frying pan*
batir	*to beat*
bate	*beat*
añadir	*to add*
añade	*add*
añádelos	*add them*
freír (**e** > **i**)	*to fry*
fríe	*fry*
fríelos	*fry them*
el fuego	*fire*
lento	*slow*
a fuego lento	*on a low flame, over low heat*

¿Echo sal a los huevos?	*Should I put salt on the eggs?*
la sal	*salt*
echar	*to throw*
echar sal	*to salt*
¿echo sal?	*shall I put salt?*

Sí, pero no les pongas demasiada sal.   *Yes, but don't put too much salt on them.*
  poner   *to put*
  no pongas   *don't put*
  no les pongas   *don't put (on them)*
  demasiada sal   *too much salt*

▶ Variantes

Listen, and repeat the same structures from *Diálogo 9*, now with new vocabulary.

No batas los huevos.   ***Don't beat*** *the eggs.*
  No calientes   *Don't warm*
  No añadas   *Don't add*
  No frías   *Don't fry*
  No sirvas   *Don't serve*
  No cocines   *Don't cook*
  No hagas   *Don't make*

Estructura y Práctica

LA COCINA: SABORES (*TASTES*) Y OLORES (*SMELLS*)

saber *to taste*
  Este plato **sabe** bien/mal.   *This dish tastes good/bad.*
  Sabe un poco dulce/amargo.   *It tastes rather sweet/bitter.*

saber a *to taste of*
  ¿**A** qué **sabe** el guacamole?   *What does the guacamole taste of?*
  El guacamole **sabe a** ajo.   *The guacamole tastes of garlic.*

saborear *to taste, savor, relish, enjoy* (also figuratively)
  ¡**Saborea** este chocolate negro   *Taste this dark artisanal chocolate!*
    artesanal!
  ¡**Saboreemos** el éxito de nuestro   *Let's enjoy the success of our book!*
    libro!

el sabor *taste*
  Me gusta **el sabor** de la miel.   *I love the taste of honey.*
  Tiene buen/mal **sabor**.   *It tastes good/bad.*

oler (huele) *to smell*
  El arroz con pollo **huele** bien/mal.   *The chicken and rice smells good/ bad.*

oler a *to smell of*
  La torta **huele a** canela.   *The cake smells of cinnamon.*
  El vino **huele a** cerezas.   *The wine smells of cherries.*

el olor *smell*
  El pan tiene **un olor** a quemado.   *The bread smells burned.*
  Tiene buen/mal **olor**.   *It smells good/bad.*

Q *¡Casi listos para la cena!* Write a response to each of the following questions about how to prepare for your dinner party. Use affirmative and negative **tú** commands, based on the cue in parentheses. Change direct object nouns to pronouns in your answers. Follow the *modelos*.

MODELOS   ¿Tengo que lavar las uvas? (sí)   ¿Tengo que lavar las uvas? (no)
          → Sí, lávalas.   → No, no las laves todavía.

1. ¿Necesito leer la receta de cocina? (sí)
2. ¿Debo poner la mesa ahora? (no)
3. ¿Tengo que sacar los tenedores de la gaveta? (sí)
4. ¿Debo calentar el aceite de oliva? (no)
5. ¿Necesito batir las yemas de huevo (*egg yolks*)? (sí)
6. ¿Tengo que echar sal y pimienta? (sí)
7. ¿Debo añadir este queso? (no)
8. ¿Necesito freír las papas? (sí)
9. ¿Debo servir los espárragos? (no)
10. ¿Tengo que preparar el postre? (sí)

R *¡Cálmate!* Write an affirmative or negative **tú** command for each item to tell your excited and nervous friend to relax and enjoy the party. Follow the *modelos*.

MODELOS   calmarse   angustiarse
          → Cálmate.   → No te angusties.

1. tranquilizarse
2. no preocuparse
3. volverse loca (*to go crazy*)
4. no morderse (**o** > **ue**) las uñas (morderse las uñas (*to bite one's nails*))
5. no ser tonta
6. ir a la fiesta sin cuidado
7. no ponerse nerviosa
8. no alterarse (*to be upset*)
9. ser feliz
10. relajarse
11. disfrutar de las festividades
12. divertirse mucho

DIÁLOGO 10 · ¡Suena la alarma!

Study the dialogue, then listen to the recording and repeat each line.

JAIME   ¡Suena la alarma! Salgan Uds. del hotel inmediatamente.
INÉS   Sí, señor, pero primero vamos por nuestras cosas. Bajamos en seguida.
JAIME   Señores, no suban a su habitación por nada. Puede haber un incendio.

Análisis

Check that you understand the linguistic breakdown of each speech from *Diálogo 10*.

¡Suena la alarma! Salgan Uds. del hotel inmediatamente.	*The alarm is sounding! Please leave the hotel immediately.*
sonar (**o** > **ue**)	*to sound*
la alarma	*alarm*
salir	*to go out*
salgan	*leave, go out*
salgan Uds.	*please leave*
salir de + *place*	*to leave* + place
salir del hotel	*to leave the hotel*
salgan Uds. del hotel	*please leave the hotel*
inmediatamente	*immediately*
Sí, señor, pero primero vamos por nuestras cosas. Bajamos en seguida.	*Yes, sir, but first we'll go get our things. We'll come down right away.*
ir por algo	*to go to get something*
vamos por nuestras cosas	*we'll go to get our things*
bajar	*to come down*
en seguida	*immediately, right away*
Señores, no suban a su habitación por nada. Puede haber un incendio.	*Excuse me, don't go up to your room for any reason. There may be a fire.*
subir	*to go up, go upstairs*
no suban	*don't go up*
la habitación	*room (especially in a hotel, dormitory, etc.)*
por nada	*for any reason*
puede haber	*there may be*
el incendio	*fire (accidental)*

▶ Variantes

Listen, and repeat the same structures from *Diálogo 10*, now with new vocabulary.

Vayan Uds. al hotel.	**Go** *to the hotel.*
Vuelvan	*Go back*
Vengan	*Come*
Caminen	*Walk*
Regresen	*Go back*
Puede haber un encendio .	*There may be* **a fire**.
un huracán	*a hurricane*
un terremoto	*an earthquake*
un sismo	*an earthquake*
un atentado terrorista	*a terrorist attack*
un ataque terrorista	*a terrorist attack*
una emergencia	*an emergency*

Estructura y Práctica

Other Ways of Giving Commands

Commands Using the Infinitive

Another way of giving commands is to use the infinitive instead of the command form. This type of command is mostly used in formal written language. Examples are newspaper ads for employment, recipes, instructions on product labels, and public service announcements. They are depersonalized commands, that is, not directed at a specific person.

Interesados **mandar** curriculum vitae.	*Interested persons, **send** your curriculum vitae.*
Interesados **llamar** al teléfono...	*Interested persons, **call** . . .*
Pelar y **cortar** las zanahorias.	***Peel** and **cut** the carrots.*
Masajear suavemente el cuero cabelludo.	***Massage** the scalp gently.*
Hacer clic en el enlace.	***Click** on the link.*
No fumar.	***No smoking.***

S Change the **Uds.** commands to commands with infinitives. Follow the *modelo*.

MODELO   Conecten la cámara a la computadora.
          → Conectar la cámara a la computadora.

1. Sigan las instrucciones.

2. No pisen el césped (*grass, lawn*).

3. ¡Pintura fresca, no toquen!

4. Agreguen una pizca (*pinch*) de sal.

5. Laven y sequen las hojas de lechuga.

6. Pulsen (*Press*) el botón.

7. Enjuaguen (*Rinse*) bien el pelo.

8. Introduzcan la contraseña (*password*).

▶ DIÁLOGO 11 · Trabajen en el proyecto.

Study the dialogue, then listen to the recording and repeat each line.

JAIME	Hemos recogido y guardado los datos. ¿Qué hacemos ahora?
INÉS	Por favor, analicen los datos y entréguenme su análisis.
JAIME	También hemos elaborado el presupuesto. ¿Quiere Ud. verlo?
INÉS	Sí, por favor. Enséñenmelo lo antes posible.

Análisis

Check that you understand the linguistic breakdown of each speech from *Diálogo 11*.

Hemos recogido y guardado los datos.	*We have collected and stored the data.*
¿Qué hacemos ahora?	*What shall we do now?*
recoger	*to collect, gather*
hemos recogido	*we have collected, we have gathered*
guardar	*to store*
los datos	*the data*
¿Qué hacemos ahora?	*What shall we do now?*

Por favor, analicen los datos y entréguenme su análisis.	*Analyze the data, please, and submit your analysis to me.*
analizar	*to analyze*
analicen	*analyze*
entregar	*to submit, hand in*
entreguen	*submit*
entréguenme	*hand in to me, submit to me*
el análisis	*analysis*
También hemos elaborado el presupuesto. ¿Quiere Ud. verlo?	*We have also drawn up the budget. Do you want to see it?*
hemos elaborado	*we have drawn up*
el presupuesto	*budget*
Sí, por favor. Enséñenmelo lo antes posible.	*Yes, please. Show it to me as soon as possible.*
enseñar	*to show*
enseñen	*show*
enséñenmelo	*show it to me*
antes	*before*
lo antes posible	*as soon as possible*

▶ Variantes

Listen, and repeat the same structures from *Diálogo 11*, now with new vocabulary.

Enséñenmelo.	*Show it to me.*
Tráiganmelo.	*Bring it to me.*
Dénmelo.	*Give it to me.*
Muéstrenmelo.	*Show it to me.*
Entréguenmelo.	*Hand it to me.*
Explíquenmelo.	*Explain it to me.*
Háganmelo.	*Do it for me.*
No me lo enseñen.	*Don't show it to me.*
No me lo traigan.	*Don't bring it to me.*
No me lo den.	*Don't give it to me.*
No me lo muestren.	*Don't show it to me.*
No me lo entreguen.	*Don't hand it to me.*
No me lo expliquen.	*Don't explain it to me.*
No me lo hagan.	*Don't do it for me.*
Favor de enseñármelas.	*Please show them to me.*
Haga el favor de	*Please*
Tenga la bondad de	*Please*
Favor de firmar los papeles.	*Please sign the papers.*
Hagan el favor de	*Please*
Tengan la bondad de	*Please*

Commands Using the Infinitive + Expressions of Formality

The infinitive rather than the command form is also used with expressions that convey formality and politeness. They are the English equivalent of asking something with *please* and may be used in written or spoken language.

Favor de entrar.	*Please come in.*
Haga el favor de sentarse.	*Please sit down.*
Hágame el favor de llegar a las siete en punto.	*Please arrive at seven o'clock sharp.*
Tenga la bondad de pasar al comedor.	*Please go into the dining room.*

You will remember that in *Diálogo 1* of this chapter, you learned that the addition of the pronoun **Ud.** or **Uds.** to an imperative adds a polite tone to the command, much as *please* does in English.

Siéntese Ud.	*Please sit down.*
Pasen Uds. a la sala de reuniones.	*Please go into the meeting room.*

T **Polite commands.** For each of the following sentences, change the command form for **Ud.** to the infinitive, and add the expression in parentheses. Follow the *modelo.*

MODELO   Mándeme el informe. (favor de)
→ Favor de mandarme el informe.

1. Présteme los auriculares. (tenga la bondad de)

2. Cuénteme lo ocurrido (*what happened*). (haga el favor de)

3. Explíquenoslo. (favor de)

4. Haga una copia de seguridad (*backup*). (favor de)

5. Dígamelo. (tenga la bondad de)

6. Ayúdeme con el abrigo. (favor de)

7. Llámeme lo antes posible. (haga el favor de)

8. Envíemelas para la semana entrante. (tenga la bondad de)

Un paso más

Are you ready to take your Spanish a step further? Here are exercises that will enhance your knowledge of the language and allow you to express yourself freely.

U *Preguntas personales.* Answer each question with a complete Spanish sentence.

1. ¿Cómo llega Ud. de su casa a su lugar de trabajo? (*Give a friend directions.*)

2. ¿Cómo es el tráfico donde vive? ¿Se permite o se prohíbe estacionar en su calle?

3. Cuando viaja en avión, ¿qué le pide al auxiliar de vuelo?

Miguel de Cervantes Saavedra (1547–1616) fue un gran novelista, poeta y dramaturgo. Es el escritor más famoso de la literatura española y universalmente conocido por ser el autor de El Ingenioso Hidalgo Don Quijote de la Mancha, *una de las obras más importantes de la literatura universal. La primera parte de* El Quijote *fue publicada en 1605 y la segunda en 1615.*

Escriba una explicación en español de lo que significa la siguiente cita de El Quijote. *Se trata de un consejo que le da don Quijote a su escudero Sancho Panza.*

"Come poco y cena más poco que la salud de todo el cuerpo se fragua en la oficina del estómago."

la cita *quote*	el hidalgo *nobleman (lower nobility)* (Spain)
comer *to have a heavy lunch* (la comida) (Spain)	ingenioso *ingenious, clever*
el dramaturgo *playwright*	más poco *even less* (archaic)
el escudero *squire*	la oficina *workshop*
se fragua *is forged*	se trata de *it's about, it deals with*
	significar *to mean*

 ¡Buen provecho! **(Enjoy your meal!)** Express the cooking instructions below in Spanish, using the **Ud.** command form of these verbs. Use the vocabulary terms below as a resource.

agregar *to add*	guisar *to stew*
asar *to roast*	hervir (**e > ie, e > i**) *to boil*
asar a la parrilla *to grill, broil*	hornear *to bake*
condimentar *to season*	mezclar *to mix*
cortar *to cut*	pelar *to peel*
cortar en trocitos (el trozo) *to cut in small pieces*	picar *to chop, dice*
descongelar *to defrost*	remover (**o > ue**) *to stir*
enfriar *to chill*	sazonar *to season*

1. *Grill the meat.*

2. *Stir the soup.*

3. *Mix the fruits and chocolate chips (las chispas de chocolate).*

4. *Add lemon juice to the fish.*

5. *Chill the wine.*

6. *Season with salt and pepper.*

7. *Bake the bread.*

8. *Chop the onions.*

X *Conversaciones.* Write short conversations in Spanish about the following situations, using the appropriate command forms (**Ud., Uds., tú, nosotros**) in your exchanges. Draw upon the theme-related vocabulary you learned in this chapter.

1. En la ciudad: *A tourist stops you on the street to ask directions to* _____.

2. En la oficina: *You are a project manager addressing your team about the tasks they must carry out.*

3. En la playa: *You and your children are having a conversation while at the beach.*

4. En el avión: *You and your husband (wife, friend), passengers on an airplane, are speaking with a flight attendant.*

5. En la consulta del médico: *You are a doctor giving advice to a patient about how to treat his/her medical problem.*

Holidays and Celebrations, Planning for the Future

▶ DIÁLOGO 1 · Planes para el futuro

Study the dialogue, then listen to the recording and repeat each line.

PEDRO   Bueno chica, nos graduaremos en junio. ¿Sabes qué harás después?

EVA   Haré un viaje a Israel con mi familia. Luego trabajaré en la empresa de mi papá. ¿Y tú?

PEDRO   Comenzaré mis estudios de administración de empresas. Tendré la maestría en dos años.

EVA   Yo también cursaré el MBA. Solicitaré una beca el año que viene.

Análisis

Check that you understand the linguistic breakdown of each speech from *Diálogo 1*.

Bueno chica, nos graduaremos en junio.	*Well, my friend, we'll graduate in June.*
¿Sabes qué harás después?	*Do you know what you'll do afterwards?*
graduarse	*to graduate*
nos graduaremos	*we'll graduate*
harás	*you'll do*
después	*after, afterwards*

Haré un viaje a Israel con mi familia.	*I'll take a trip to Israel with my family.*
Luego trabajaré en la empresa de mi	*Then I'll work in my father's company.*
papá. ¿Y tú?	*How about you?*
haré	*I will do, I will make*
haré un viaje	*I'll take a trip*
Israel	*Israel*
trabajaré	*I'll work*
la empresa	*firm, company*

Comenzaré mis estudios de	*I'll begin studying business administration.*
administración de empresas. Tendré	*I'll have a master's degree in two years.*
la maestría en dos años.	
comenzaré	*I'll begin*
comenzar sus estudios de + *subject*	*to begin studying* + subject
tendré	*I will have*
la maestría	*master's degree*

Yo también cursaré el MBA. Solicitaré	*I'll also study for the MBA. I'll apply for*
una beca el año que viene.	*a scholarship next year.*
cursar + *subject*	*to study* + subject
cursaré	*I'll study for*
el MBA	*MBA*
solicitar algo	*to apply for something*
solicitaré	*I'll apply for*
una beca	*a scholarship*

▶ Variantes

Listen, and repeat the same structures from *Diálogo 1*, now with new vocabulary.

Nos graduaremos en junio.	**We will graduate** in June.
Nos matricularemos	*We will register*
Nos mudaremos	*We will move*
Nos instalaremos	*We will move in*
Nos comprometeremos	*We will get engaged*
Nos casaremos	*We will get married*

¿Qué harás ?	*What* **will you do?**
dirás	*will you say*
querrás	*will you want*

Trabajaré.	I will work.
Comeré.	I will eat.
Leeré.	I will read.
Escribiré.	I will write.
Subiré.	I will go up.

Tendré una beca el año que viene.	I will have a scholarship next year.
Solicitaré	I will apply for
Recibiré	I will receive
Necesitaré	I will need

Estructura y Práctica

The Future Tense

The future tense in Spanish, used to express future time, is formed by adding a specific set of endings to the infinitive of the verb. All verbs, regular, irregular, and stem-changing, form the future tense in this way.

Estudiaré español en Madrid.	I'll study Spanish in Madrid.
Comeremos al aire libre.	We'll eat outside.
Subirán a la azotea.	They'll go up to the rooftop terrace.
¿Harás un descanso pronto?	Will you take a break soon?
Uds. vendrán a vernos, ¿no?	You'll come to see us, won't you?

trabajar *to work*

Trabajaré con el equipo.	I'll work with the team.
Trabajarás con el equipo.	You'll work with the team.
Trabajará con el equipo.	He'll/She'll/You'll work with the team.
Trabajaremos con el equipo.	We'll work with the team.
Trabajaréis con el equipo.	You'll work with the team.
Trabajarán con el equipo.	They'll/You'll work with the team.

comer *to eat*

Comeré al aire libre.	I'll eat outside.
Comerás al aire libre.	You'll eat outside.
Comerá al aire libre.	He'll/She'll/You'll eat outside.
Comeremos al aire libre.	We'll eat outside.
Comeréis al aire libre.	You'll eat outside.
Comerán al aire libre.	They'll/You'll eat outside.

discutir *to discuss*

Discutiré el asunto.	I'll discuss the matter.
Discutirás el asunto.	You'll discuss the matter.
Discutirá el asunto.	He'll/She'll/You'll discuss the matter.
Discutiremos el asunto.	We'll discuss the matter.
Discutiréis el asunto.	You'll discuss the matter.
Discutirán el asunto.	They'll/You'll discuss the matter.

A ***Del presente al futuro.*** Rewrite each of the following sentences, changing the verb from the present tense to the future tense. Follow the *modelo.*

> MODELO   Viaja la semana entrante.
> → Viajará la semana entrante.

1. Entrego el informe.
2. Vende su casa.
3. No discuten ese asunto.
4. Te diviertes mucho.
5. Duerme la siesta.
6. Juego al tenis.
7. Diseñamos el sitio web.
8. Elijo un nuevo celular.
9. ¿No comes nada más?
10. Se reúnen en la sala de conferencias.
11. Consigo una beca.
12. Hace ochenta grados.

▶ DIÁLOGO 2 · Estarán muy contentos.

Study the dialogue, then listen to the recording and repeat each line.

> PEDRO   ¿Sabes que Rodrigo ganó una beca? Ahora podrá terminar su maestría en computación.
> EVA   Estará contentísimo.
> PEDRO   ¡Y sus papás aún más, porque no tendrán que pagar la matrícula!

Análisis

Check that you understand the linguistic breakdown of each speech from *Diálogo 2.*

¿Sabes que Rodrigo ganó una beca? Ahora podrá terminar su maestría en computación.	*Do you know that Rodrigo won a scholarship? Now he will be able to finish his master's in computer science.*
ganar una beca	*to win a scholarship*
podrá	*he will be able to*
la maestría	*master's degree*
terminar la maestría	*finish one's master's degree*
la computación	*computer science*
Estará contentísimo.	*He must be very happy.*
estará	*he must be, he is probably*
contentísimo	*very happy*
¡Y sus papás aún más, porque no tendrán que pagar la matrícula!	*And his parents even more so, because they won't have to pay the tuition!*
aún	*even*
aún más	*even more*
tendrán	*they will have*
no tendrán que	*they won't have to*
la matrícula	*tuition*

Variantes

Listen, and repeat the same structures from *Diálogo 2*, now with new vocabulary.

Podrá terminar su maestría.   **He will be able to** *finish his master's degree.*
  Querrá   *He will want to*
  Tendrá que   *He will have to*

Estará contentísimo .   *He must be **very happy**.*
  ocupadísimo   *very busy*
  aburridísimo   *very bored*

No tendrán que pagar la matrícula.   **They won't have** *to pay the tuition.*
  No podrán   *They won't be able*
  No querrán   *They won't want*

Estructura y Práctica

The Future Tense: Verbs with a Modified Infinitive

There are 12 verbs that have modified infinitive forms in the future. These verbs have the same endings as the verbs in the charts that appear in the section "The Future Tense" earlier in this chapter. The **yo** form is shown as a model for the entire conjugation.

INFINITIVE	FUTURE
poner	**pondré**
salir	**saldré**
tener	**tendré**
valer	**valdré**
venir	**vendré**
caber	**cabré**
poder	**podré**
querer	**querré**
saber	**sabré**
decir	**diré**
hacer	**haré**
haber	**habré**

Compounds of verbs that have modified infinitives in the future have the same shortened infinitives when conjugated in the future: **componer** → **compondré, mantener** → **mantendré, convenir** → **convendré, rehacer** → **reharé**.

The future of **hay**, derived from **haber**, is **habrá** (*there will be*).

-Ir verbs that have an accent mark in the infinitive, such as **oír** (*to hear*), **freír** (*to fry*), and **reír** (*to laugh*), lose that accent mark in the future tense: **freiré, oiré, reiré**.

B   **The future: verbs with modified infinitives.** Write the future form of the verb in parentheses that correctly completes each of the following sentences. Follow the *modelo*.

> MODELO   No _*cabrá*_ nadie más en el taxi. (caber)

1. Yo les _____ lo que pasó. (decir)

2. El libro _____ a fines del mes. (salir)

3. Tú _____ solicitar una beca, ¿verdad? (querer)

4. Camila y yo _____ en contacto. (ponerse)

5. ¿A qué hora _____ los invitados? (venir)

6. Las reuniones _____ lugar en esa oficina. (tener)

7. _____ mucho frío esta noche. (hacer)

8. Nosotros no _____ nada hasta la semana próxima. (saber)

9. ¿Ud. no _____ acompañarnos? (poder)

10. _____ gangas en las tiendas por departamentos en enero. (haber)

The Future Used to Express Probability or Conjecture

One of the most common uses of the future tense is to express probability or conjecture about the present. Speakers use the future of probability when wondering about things that are going on in the present. The English equivalents of the future of probability (*I wonder, it's probably, it might,* etc.) are usually unlike the Spanish structures. The verbs most commonly used to express this are **estar, haber, ser,** and **tener**.

¿Qué hora **será**?	*I **wonder** what time **it is**.*
Serán las nueve.	*It's **probably** nine o'clock.*
Habrá un atasco de tráfico.	*There's **probably** a traffic jam.*
¿Cuántos años **tendrá** Carlitos?	*I **wonder** how old Carlitos **is**.*
Tendrá cinco años.	*He **must be** five years old.*
¿Qué **querrá** para su cumpleaños?	*I **wonder** what **she wants** for her birthday.*
Estarán de vacaciones todavía.	*They're **probably** still on vacation.*

Context will determine whether a verb in the future tense refers to a future time or to probability or conjecture in present time. For example, **¿Qué pasará?** means *What will happen?* as well as *I wonder what's happening.*

C   *Probabilidad en el presente.* Rewrite each sentence using the future tense to express probability in present time. Remove the word or words that express probability or conjecture in the original sentence. Follow the *modelo*.

> MODELO   Probablemente no entiende nada.
>   → No entenderá nada.

1. Supongo que los gemelos tienen siete u ocho años.

2. Me imagino que sabes su número de teléfono.

3. Probablemente son las once.

4. Supongo que Camila quiere ver esta obra de teatro.

5. Me imagino que su casa cuesta una fortuna.

6. Probablemente están acatarrados.

7. Me imagino que Cristóbal se hace ingeniero.

8. Supongo que este anillo vale miles de dólares.

9. Probablemente hay muchos documentos sobre este tema.

10. Probablemente cabe el equipaje en el maletero del coche.

D **Translation.** Express the following sentences in Spanish, using the future of probability.

1. *I wonder how old Mr. Durán is.*

2. *He must be fifty years old.*

3. *I wonder what time it is.*

4. *It's probably four o'clock.*

5. *What an elegant suit! It must cost a lot of money.*

6. *I can't find my credit card. I wonder where it is.*

7. *I imagine it will snow tomorrow.*

8. *They probably know what happened.*

▶ DIÁLOGO 3 · El organizador de bodas

Study the dialogue, then listen to the recording and repeat each line.

JORGE   Como organizador de bodas, yo me encargaré de todo—las invitaciones,
        la ceremonia, la música, la comida, el pastel, las flores, la fotografía.
LUCÍA   ¡Magnífico! Felipe y yo no podríamos hacer todo esto sin ti. Ni sabemos
        dónde será la ceremonia.
JORGE   Bueno, mañana los llevaré a conocer el jardín de una hermosa hacienda
        y unos elegantes salones de hotel. Uds. escogerán el lugar.

Análisis

Check that you understand the linguistic breakdown of each speech from *Diálogo 3*.

Como organizador de bodas, yo me encargaré de todo—las invitaciones, la ceremonia, la música, la comida, el pastel, las flores, la fotografía.	*As a wedding planner, I'll take care of everything—the invitations, the ceremony, the music, the food, the cake, the flowers, the photography.*
encargarse de	*to take care of*
yo me encargaré de	*I'll take care of*
yo me encargaré de todo	*I'll take care of everything*
la invitación	*invitation*
la ceremonia	*ceremony*
la música	*music*
la comida	*food*

el pastel	*cake, pie*
la flor	*flower*
la fotografía	*photography*

¡Magnífico! Felipe y yo no podríamos hacer todo esto sin ti. Ni sabemos dónde será la ceremonia.	*Terrific! Felipe and I wouldn't be able to do all of this without you. We don't even know where the ceremony will be.*
podríamos	*we would be able to*
ni	*not even*
ni sabemos	*we don't even know*
será	*it will be*
dónde será la ceremonia	*where the ceremony will be*

Bueno, mañana los llevaré a conocer el jardín de una hermosa hacienda y unos elegantes salones de hotel. Uds. escogerán el lugar.	*Well, tomorrow I will take you to see the garden of a lovely estate and some elegant hotel ballrooms. You will pick the place.*
llevaré	*I will take*
los llevaré	*I will take you*
conocer	*to get to know, see*
el jardín	*garden*
hermoso	*beautiful*
la hacienda	*estate; farm, ranch*
el salón	*large public room*
escoger	*to choose*
escogerán	*you will choose*
el lugar	*the place*

▶ Variantes

Listen, and repeat the same structures from *Diálogo 3*, now with new vocabulary.

La ceremonia será en una hacienda.	*The wedding **will be** at an estate.*
tendrá lugar	*will take place*
se realizará	*will take place*

Los novios llegarán a las cuatro.	*The bride and groom **will arrive** at four o'clock.*
vendrán	*will come*
saldrán	*will leave*

No podríamos hacerlo.	***We wouldn't be able** to do it.*
No tendríamos que	*We wouldn't have*
No querríamos	*We wouldn't want*
No necesitaríamos	*We wouldn't need*

Los llevaré .	***I'll take** you.*
llamaré	*I'll call*
veré	*I'll see*
comprenderé	*I'll understand*
ayudaré	*I'll help*
buscaré	*I'll look for*

Uds. escogerán el lugar.	*You'll choose the place.*
elegirán	*You'll choose*
encontrarán	*You'll find*
conocerán	*You'll be familiar with*

Estructura y Práctica

The Conditional Tense

The conditional tense is formed by adding the imperfect tense endings of -**er** and -**ir** verbs to the infinitive. All verbs, including -**ar** verbs, use these endings in the conditional.

¿Qué **haría** Ud.?	*What **would** you **do**?*
Yo no **diría** nada.	*I **wouldn't say** anything.*
¡Con una prometida como la tuya, yo no **me casaría** nunca!	*With a fiancée like yours, I **would** never **get married**!*

trabajar *to work*

Trabajar**ía** con el equipo.	*I'd work with the team.*
Trabajar**ías** con el equipo.	*You'd work with the team.*
Trabajar**ía** con el equipo.	*He'd/She'd/You'd work with the team.*
Trabajar**íamos** con el equipo.	*We'd work with the team.*
Trabajar**íais** con el equipo.	*You'd work with the team.*
Trabajar**ían** con el equipo.	*They'd/You'd work with the team.*

comer *to eat*

Comer**ía** al aire libre.	*I'd eat outside.*
Comer**ías** al aire libre.	*You'd eat outside.*
Comer**ía** al aire libre.	*He'd/She'd/You'd eat outside.*
Comer**íamos** al aire libre.	*We'd eat outside.*
Comer**íais** al aire libre.	*You'd eat outside.*
Comer**ían** al aire libre.	*They'd/You'd eat outside.*

discutir *to discuss*

Discutir**ía** el asunto.	*I'd discuss the matter.*
Discutir**ías** el asunto.	*You'd discuss the matter.*
Discutir**ía** el asunto.	*He'd/She'd/You'd discuss the matter.*
Discutir**íamos** el asunto.	*We'd discuss the matter.*
Discutir**íais** el asunto.	*You'd discuss the matter.*
Discutir**ían** el asunto.	*They'd/You'd discuss the matter.*

The same 12 verbs that have modified infinitive forms in the future have them in the conditional. These verbs have the same endings as the verbs in the charts above. The **yo** form is shown as a model for the entire conjugation.

INFINITIVE	CONDITIONAL
poner	**pondría**
salir	**saldría**
tener	**tendría**

INFINITIVE	CONDITIONAL
valer	**valdría**
venir	**vendría**
caber	**cabría**
poder	**podría**
querer	**querría**
saber	**sabría**
decir	**diría**
hacer	**haría**
haber	**habría**

Compounds of verbs that have modified infinitives in the conditional have the same shortened infinitives when conjugated in the conditional: **componer** → **compondría, mantener** → **mantendría, convenir** → **convendría, rehacer** → **reharía**.

The conditional of **hay**, derived from **haber**, is **habría** (*there would be*).

-Ir verbs that have an accent mark in the infinitive, such as **oír** (*to hear*), **freír** (*to fry*), and **reír** (*to laugh*), lose that accent mark in the conditional tense: **freiría, oiría, reiría**.

E *¿Qué harían?* Write sentences using the strings of elements given to tell what would or would not happen. Use the correct conditional form of the verb. Follow the *modelo*.

MODELO los empleados / llegar / a las nueve
→ Los empleados llegarían a las nueve.

1. Daniel y yo / elaborar / el presupuesto
2. Uds. / aprender / español / en Bogotá
3. tú / tener / suerte
4. yo / no / decírselo / a nadie
5. la cocinera / querer / añadir / más sal
6. nosotros / hacer escala / en Miami
7. mis colegas / compartir / los gastos
8. sus suegros / no poder / visitarlos
9. tú / salir / más tarde
10. Ud. / mudarse / a ese barrio

The Conditional Used to Express Probability or Conjecture

The conditional in Spanish is also used to express probability or conjecture in past time. The verbs most commonly used to express this are **estar**, **haber**, **ser**, and **tener**. Context will determine whether a verb in the conditional refers to the conditional or to probability in past time.

¿Dónde **estaría** Blanca?	*I wonder where Blanca was.*
Habría un atasco de tráfico.	*There was probably a traffic jam.*
Serían las seis.	*It was probably six o'clock.*
Tendrían mucho éxito.	*I imagine they were very successful.*

F *Probabilidad en el pasado.* Express the following short dialogues in Spanish, using the conditional to express probability.

1. *I wonder how old María Elena was when she finished her master's.*
2. *She was probably twenty-three when she finished it.*

3. *I wonder what time it was when Mr. and Mrs. Fernández arrived at the seaside resort* (el balneario).

4. *It was probably noon.*

5. *I wonder who was to blame for the crime.*

6. *I suppose it was the butler* (el mayordomo).

7. *I wonder where you* (Uds.) *were when we called you.*

8. *We were probably still at the office.*

9. *I wonder what (there) was in the package.*

10. *I suppose there were toys for the children.*

REVIEW: USE OF **SER**

As you learned in Chapter 4, the verb **ser** is used to indicate where an event takes place.

Note this sentence from *Diálogo 3* of this chapter:

Ni sabemos dónde **será** la ceremonia.	*We don't even know where the ceremony **will be**.*

Estar cannot be used for this purpose.

▶ DIÁLOGO 4 · Celebraremos la Pascua.

Study the dialogue, then listen to the recording and repeat each line.

LUIS   ¿Cómo celebrarán Uds. la Pascua?

BLANCA   Habrá una comida grande con todos nuestros parientes, como de costumbre.

LUIS   ¿Tú harás la comida o será en casa de tus papás?

BLANCA   Nos tocará a nosotros tenerla en nuestra casa. Mi esposo, mis hijos y yo prepararemos la comida y usaremos las recetas de las abuelas.

Análisis

Check that you understand the linguistic breakdown of each speech from *Diálogo 4*.

¿Cómo celebrarán Uds. la Pascua?	*How will you celebrate Easter?*
celebrar	*to celebrate*
celebrarán	*you will celebrate*
la Pascua	*Easter*
Habrá una comida grande con todos nuestros parientes, como de costumbre.	*There will be a big dinner with all our relatives, as usual.*
habrá	*there will be*
una comida	*dinner*
los parientes	*relatives*
de costumbre	*as usual*
como de costumbre	*as usual, as we usually do*

¿Tú harás la comida o será en casa de tus papás?

Will you make the meal or will it be at your parents' house?

    harás

        you will do, you will make

    será

        it will be

    tus papás

        your parents (especially in Spanish America)

Nos tocará a nosotros tenerla en nuestra casa. Mi esposo, mis hijos y yo prepararemos la comida y usaremos las recetas de las abuelas.

It will be our turn to have it at our house. My husband, my children, and I will prepare the meal, and we will use our grandmothers' recipes.

    tocarle a uno (*rev. constr.*)

        to be someone's turn

    nos tocará a nosotros

        it will be our turn

    prepararemos

        we will prepare

    usaremos

        we will use

    la receta

        recipe

▶ Variantes

Listen, and repeat the same structures from *Diálogo 4*, now with new vocabulary.

¿Cómo celebrarán Uds. la Pascua ?

*How will you celebrate **Easter?***

    la Pascua judía — *Passover*

    la Navidad — *Christmas*

    Jánuca — *Hanukkah*

    el Año Nuevo — *New Year's*

    la Noche Vieja — *New Year's Eve*

    el Día de la Independencia — *Independence Day*

    el Día de los Enamorados — *Valentine's Day*

    su aniversario — *your anniversary*

    el Ramadán — *Ramadan*

Habrá una comida grande .

*There will be **a big dinner**.*

    mucha gente — *many people*

    una orquesta — *an orchestra*

    un desfile — *a parade*

    champaña — *champagne*

    un brindis — *a toast*

Nos tocará a nosotros. — *It will be our turn.*

Me tocará a mí. — *It will be my turn.*

Te tocará a ti. — *It will be your turn.*

Le tocara a él. — *It will be his turn.*

Le tocará a ella. — *It will be her turn.*

Les tocará a Uds. — *It will be your turn.*

Les tocará a ellos. — *It will be their turn.*

Les tocará a ellas. — *It will be their turn.*

Prepararemos la comida.	**We will prepare** the meal.
Cocinaremos	We will cook
Haremos	We will make
Pediremos	We will order
Serviremos	We will serve
Disfrutaremos (de)	We will enjoy

Estructura y Práctica

FIESTAS Y CELEBRACIONES

Many of the holidays celebrated in the United States are also celebrated in Spanish-speaking countries, for example, Independence Day—**el Día de la Independencia** (a different date in each country), Mother's Day—**el Día de la Madre**, Father's Day—**el Día del Padre**, and New Year's Eve—**la Noche Vieja (el Fin de Año)**. Columbus Day is celebrated in Spain as **el Día de la Hispanidad** and in many Spanish American countries as **el Día de la Raza**.

Christmas holidays are also celebrated in some countries, such as Mexico, where the **Posadas (posada** (*room at the inn*)) last for nine days leading up to Christmas Eve. In most Spanish-speaking countries, children traditionally receive holiday gifts on January 6, **El Día de los Reyes Magos (la Epifanía)**— Three Kings' Day (Epiphany).

In many countries of Spanish America, a young woman's fifteenth birthday is celebrated with a special event known as the **Fiesta de quinceañera (Fiesta de quince)**. The young woman is the **quinceañera**. This event, ranging from informal festivities at home, sometimes of a religious nature, to an extravagant party in a hotel, is also widely celebrated in the Spanish-speaking community of the United States and is reminiscent of the traditional sweet sixteen coming-of-age party.

Review: Reverse Construction Verbs

You learned about reverse construction verbs in Chapter 9. These are verbs that pattern like **gustar**: **Me gusta el libro.** (*I like the book.*)

Note the use of **tocar** as a reverse construction verb in this sentence from *Diálogo 4*:

Nos tocará a nosotros tenerla en nuestra casa.	**It will be our turn** to have it (*the dinner*) at our house.

The infinitive **tener** is the subject of **tocar**, which is therefore in third person singular: **tocará**. To focus on the person involved in sentences with reverse construction verbs, a phrase consisting of the preposition **a** + a prepositional pronoun is used. In this sentence, **a nosotros** focuses on the people whose turn it is to have the dinner.

G Express the following sentences in Spanish, using reverse construction verbs in the future tense. Use the correct **a** + prepositional pronoun with each reverse construction verb.

1. *You (Uds.) will like this Mexican food.*

2. *She'll be excited to meet our friends.*

3. *You (tú) will be interested in this project.*

4. *I'll still have two exams left.*

5. *They'll be short of money.*

6. *We'll need more information.*

7. *It will be good for you (Ud.) to be in charge of the office.*

8. *Nothing will matter to him. (He won't care about anything.)*

DIÁLOGO 5 · El fin de semana

Study the dialogue, then listen to the recording and repeat each line.

ANTONIO   Mis primos estarán de visita este fin de semana. ¿Adónde los llevaremos?

VICTORIA   Dicen que el sábado hará buen tiempo así que podremos enseñarles la ciudad.

ANTONIO   Creo que el domingo lloverá así que podremos ir a un museo.

VICTORIA   Y querremos llevarlos a cenar a nuestros restaurantes favoritos.

Análisis

Check that you understand the linguistic breakdown of each speech from *Diálogo 5*.

Mis primos estarán de visita este fin de semana. ¿Adónde los llevaremos?	*My cousins will be visiting (us) this weekend. Where shall we take them?*
los primos	*cousins*
estarán	*they will be*
estar de visita	*to be visiting*
el fin de semana	*weekend*
llevaremos	*we will take*
Dicen que el sábado hará buen tiempo así que podremos enseñarles la ciudad.	*They say that Saturday the weather will be nice, so we can show them the city.*
el sábado	*Saturday, on Saturday*
hará	*it will do, it will make*
hará buen tiempo	*the weather will be nice*
así que	*so*
podremos	*we will be able to*
enseñarles	*to show them*
Creo que el domingo lloverá así que podremos ir a un museo.	*I think that it will rain on Sunday, so we will be able to go to a museum.*
el domingo	*Sunday, on Sunday*
lloverá	*it will rain*
podremos	*we will be able to*
el museo	*museum*

Y querremos llevarlos a cenar a nuestros restaurantes favoritos.	*And we'll want to take them to have dinner at our favorite restaurants.*
querremos	*we will want to*
llevarlos a cenar	*to take them to have dinner*

▶ Variantes

Listen, and repeat the same structures from *Diálogo 5*, now with new vocabulary.

Dicen que hará buen tiempo .	*They say **the weather will be nice**.*
lloverá	*it will rain*
nevará	*it will snow*
estará nublado	*it will be cloudy*
hará ochenta grados	*it will be eighty degrees*
hará sol	*it will be sunny*
habrá sol	*it will be sunny*
Podremos enseñarles la ciudad.	***We will be able** to show them the city.*
Querremos	*We will want*
Preferiremos	*We will prefer*
Tendremos que	*We will have*
Si ellos salen a cenar, nosotros saldremos a cenar también.	*If they go out for dinner, we will go out for dinner, too.*
Nosotros saldremos a cenar si ellos salen a cenar.	*We will go out for dinner if they go out for dinner.*

Estructura y Práctica

The Future Tense: Usage

In spoken Spanish, the **ir a** + infinitive construction and the present tense are used more frequently than the future tense to express future events.

Los **veremos** el sábado.	***We'll see** them on Saturday.*
Vamos a verlos el sábado.	***We're going to see** them on Saturday.*
Los **vemos** el sábado.	***We're seeing** them on Saturday.*

H *Ir a* **+ infinitive.** Rewrite each sentence, changing the future tense of the verb to the **ir a** + infinitive construction to tell what's going to happen. Follow the *modelo*.

MODELO   Comerán comida japonesa.
          → Van a comer comida japonesa.

1. Asistiremos al concierto.

2. Saldré para la hacienda.

3. Uds. se irán pasado mañana.

4. ¿Podrás acompañarme a la boda?

5. Habrá una fiesta de quinceañera para Inés.

6. La fiesta será en el Hotel Palacio.

7. Ellos tendrán que trabajar.

8. Manuel querrá esquiar.

The Future Tense in Conditional Sentences

The future tense is commonly used in the main clause of a conditional sentence when the **si**-clause (*if*-clause) has the verb in the present tense. Note that the order of the clauses can be reversed, with the **si**-clause following the main clause.

Si tú **vas** al concierto, yo **iré** también.   *If you go to the concert, I'll go, too.*
Yo **iré** al concierto si **vas** tú.   *I'll go to the concert if you go.*

I **Future tense in sentences with a *si*-clause.** Write the forms of each verb in parentheses that correctly complete each of the following sentences. The main clause has the verb in future tense, and the **si**-clause has the verb in present tense. Follow the *modelos.*

MODELOS   Si tú _pruebas_ este plato, yo lo _probaré_ también. (probar)

Yo _probaré_ este plato si lo _pruebas_ tú.

1. Si Uds. _____ a la fiesta, nosotros _____ a la fiesta también. (ir)

2. Ella _____ ejercicio si sus amigas _____ ejercicio también. (hacer)

3. Si él _____ postre, yo lo _____ también. (pedir)

4. Si nosotros _____ el lunes, Ud. _____ el lunes también. (volver)

5. Ud. _____ el tren si ella _____ el tren también. (tomar)

6. Si yo _____ por la mañana, tú _____ por la mañana también. (pasearse)

7. Nosotros _____ en el centro si Uds. _____ en el centro también. (almorzar)

8. Si tú _____ con el gerente, yo _____ con el gerente también. (reunirse)

The Future Tense in Subordinate Clauses

The future is used commonly in subordinate (dependent) clauses after main verbs of communication (**decir**) and verbs of knowledge or belief (**saber**, **creer**).

Osvaldo **dice** que **saldrá**.   *Osvaldo says he'll go out.*
Creo que **hará** mucho calor.   *I think it will be very hot.*

J ***Creen que...*** Write the future tense form of the verb in parentheses that correctly completes each of the following sentences to find out what people say, know, or believe will happen. Follow the *modelo.*

MODELO   Pablo dice que nos _llamará_. (llamar)

1. Ana dice que _____ toda la semana. (llover)

2. Miguel sabe que nosotros _____ tarde. (llegar)

3. Laura está segura de que _____ en contacto con nosotros. (ponerse)

4. Juan Carlos nos escribe que _____ en la universidad estatal. (matricularse)

5. Me aseguran que _____ el informe para la semana próxima. (entregar)

6. Alicia cree que sus papás _____ su condominio. (vender)

7. Sé que tú _____ instalarte en el apartamento lo antes posible. (querer)

8. Parece que Uds. _____ de hacer los trámites. (encargarse)

▶ DIÁLOGO 6 · ¿Adónde irán Uds.?

Study the dialogue, then listen to the recording and repeat each line.

DIEGO   ¿Cómo pasarán tú y Jaime las vacaciones?
ALICIA Creo que iremos a la sierra para esquiar. ¿Y tú y Carlota? ¿Viajarán o se quedarán en casa?
DIEGO   Vendrán mis suegros. Nos dijeron que les gustaría pasar unos días en la playa.

Análisis

Check that you understand the linguistic breakdown of each speech from *Diálogo 6*.

¿Cómo pasarán tú y Jaime las vacaciones? | *How will you and Jaime spend your vacation?*
  pasarán | *you will spend*
  las vacaciones | *vacation, your vacation*

Creo que iremos a la sierra para esquiar. ¿Y tú y Carlota? ¿Viajarán o se quedarán en casa? | *I think we'll go to the mountains to ski. How about you and Carlota? Will you travel, or will you stay home?*
  iremos | *we will go*
  la sierra | *the mountains*
  para | *in order to*
  esquiar | *to ski*
  viajarán | *you will travel*
  se quedarán | *you will stay*
  se quedarán en casa | *you will stay home*

Vendrán mis suegros. Nos dijeron que les gustaría pasar unos días en la playa. | *My in-laws will come. They told us that they would like to spend a few days at the beach.*
  vendrán | *they will come*
  los suegros | *in-laws (mother-in-law and father-in-law)*
  les gustaría | *they would like*

▶ Variantes

Listen, and repeat the same structures from *Diálogo 6*, now with new vocabulary.

Vendrán mis suegros. | *My in-laws **will come**.*
  Se irán | *will leave*
  Se quedarán | *will stay*

Llegarán	*will arrive*
Volverán	*will come back*
Regresarán	*will come back*
Se pasearán	*will go for a walk*

Dijeron que haría buen tiempo .	*They said **the weather would be nice**.*
llovería	*it would rain*
nevaría	*it would snow*
estaría nublado	*it would be cloudy*
haría ochenta grados	*it would be eighty degrees*
haría sol	*it would be sunny*
habría sol	*it would be sunny*

¿A Uds. les gustaría ir a la playa?	*Would you like to go to the beach?*
Sí, nos encantaría.	*Yes, we'd love to.*

¿Te gustaría reunirte con nosotros mañana?	*Would you like to meet with us tomorrow?*
En realidad, no me convendría esta semana.	*Actually, it wouldn't work for me this week.*

¿Le interesaría jugar al ajedrez?	*Would you be interested in playing chess?*
Me interesaría mucho.	*I'd be very interested.*

Estructura y Práctica

The Conditional Tense in Subordinate Clauses

The conditional tense is used commonly in subordinate (dependent) clauses after main verbs of communication (**decir**) and verbs of knowledge or belief (**saber**, **creer**) when the main verb is in one of the past tenses.

This correspondence of tenses occurs in both Spanish and English: The present tense in the main clause is used with the future tense in a subordinate clause; a past tense in the main clause is used with the conditional tense in a subordinate clause.

Consuelo **dice** que **volverá** el viernes.	*Consuelo **says she'll be back** on Friday.*
Consuelo **dijo** que **volvería** el viernes.	*Consuelo **said she would be back** on Friday.*

Sabemos que nos **visitarán**.	*We **know they'll visit** us.*
Sabíamos que nos **visitarían**.	*We **knew they'd visit** us.*

K *Dijeron que...* Write the conditional form of the verb in parentheses that correctly completes each of the following sentences to find out what people said, knew, or believed would happen. Follow the *modelo*.

MODELO   Marta me dijo que _*estaría*_ en casa toda la tarde. (estar)

1. Eugenia me escribió que _____ el miércoles. (regresar)

2. Rafael y María anunciaron que _____ en la primavera. (casarse)

3. ¿Sabías lo que _____? (pasar)

4. Creíamos que el asesor nos _____ buenos consejos. (dar)

5. Yo les pregunté si _____ pasar por mí. (poder)

6. Te aseguraron que no _____ ninguna dificultad. (haber)

7. Me dijeron que a sus hijos les _____ los regalos. (encantar)

8. Creías que nosotros nos _____ más a menudo. (ver)

L Express the following sentences in Spanish, using reverse construction verbs in the conditional tense.

1. *I would like to learn to ski.*

2. *The children would be excited to open their presents.*

3. *You* (tú) *would be very interested in these museums.*

4. *We'd love to have a glass* (una copa) *of champagne!*

5. *Carlos wouldn't care about anything.*

6. *You* (Ud.) *would need your passport.*

7. *It would be Julia's turn in the board game* (el juego de mesa).

8. *It would be best* (most convenient) *for you* (Uds.) *to take a nonstop flight.*

DIÁLOGO 7 · Buscaremos un regalo.

Study the dialogue, then listen to the recording and repeat each line.

PEDRO   Susana cumplirá veintiocho años el sábado. Tendré que comprarle
             un regalo.
EVA   ¡Caramba! Me olvidé de su cumpleaños. ¿Qué le regalarás?
PEDRO   No tengo la menor idea. ¿Qué querrá?
EVA   No sabría decirte. Vamos al centro comercial. Estoy segura de que
             encontraremos algo.

Análisis

Check that you understand the linguistic breakdown of each speech from *Diálogo 7*.

Susana cumplirá veintiocho años el sábado. Tendré que comprarle un regalo.	*Susana will be twenty-eight on Saturday. I'll have to buy her a gift.*
cumplir años	*to have a birthday, get to be ___ years old*
cumplirá	*she will be/turn*
cumplirá veintiocho años	*she will be twenty-eight*
tendré	*I will have*
Tendré que comprarle un regalo.	*I'll have to buy her a gift.*

¡Caramba! Me olvidé de su cumpleaños. ¿Qué le regalarás? — *Gosh! I forgot her birthday. What will you give her?*

¡Caramba! — *Gosh!*
olvidarse de algo — *to forget something*
el cumpleaños — *birthday*
Me olvidé de su cumpleaños. — *I forgot her birthday.*
regalarle algo a uno — *to give someone something (as a gift)*
regalarás — *you will give (as a gift)*

No tengo la menor idea. ¿Qué querrá? — *I haven't the slightest idea. What might she want?*

la idea — *idea*
menor — *least*
la menor idea — *the slightest idea*
querrá — *she might want*

No sabría decirte. Vamos al centro comercial. Estoy segura de que encontraremos algo. — *I couldn't tell you. Let's go to the shopping center. I'm sure that we will find something (there).*

sabría — *I would know*
No sabría decirte. — *I couldn't tell you. / I wouldn't know what to tell you.*
estar seguro de que — *to be sure that*
encontraremos — *we will find*

▶ Variantes

Listen, and repeat the same structures from *Diálogo 7*, now with new vocabulary.

¿Qué le regalarás ? — *What **will you give** her?*
darás — *will you give*
ofrecerás — *will you offer*
traerás — *will you bring*
prestarás — *will you lend*
entregarás — *will you hand*

¿Qué querrá para su cumpleaños? — *I wonder what she wants for her birthday.*
Querrá unos aretes. — *She probably wants earrings.*
Probablemente quiere unos aretes. — *She probably wants earrings.*

Isaac y Valeria estarán cansados después de su vuelo. — *Isaac and Valeria must be tired after their flight.*
Y tendrán mucha hambre también. — *And they must be very hungry, too.*
Supongo que tienen mucha hambre también. — *I suppose they're very hungry, too.*

¿ Lloverá mañana? — ***Do you think it may rain** tomorrow?*
Nevará — *Do you think it may snow*
Hará frío — *Do you think it will be cold*
Estará nublado — *Do you think it will be cloudy*
Habrá sol — *Do you think it will be sunny*

Estructura y Práctica

 Conjeturas. **Nobody understands María Dolores!** Express the following questions in Spanish, using the future of probability, to ask what María Dolores might be thinking. Follow the *modelo.*

MODELO   *What might María Dolores want?*
→ ¿Qué querrá?

1. *What might she say?*

2. *What might she know?*

3. *What might she think?*

4. *What might she understand?*

5. *What might she imagine?*

6. *What might she suppose?*

7. *What might she wonder* (preguntarse)*?*

8. *What might she conjecture* (conjeturar)*?*

DIÁLOGO 8 · En la sala de recepción

Study the dialogue, then listen to the recording and repeat each line.

ELADIO   Buenas tardes, señorita. Me gustaría ver al señor Torres. Soy Eladio Díaz. Tengo cita con él a las tres.

MARTA   Mucho gusto, señor. Yo le diré al director que Ud. está. Él no tardará en llegar. Siéntese, por favor.

Análisis

Check that you understand the linguistic breakdown of each speech from *Diálogo 8.*

Buenas tardes, señorita. Me gustaría ver al señor Torres. Soy Eladio Díaz. Tengo cita con él a las tres.	*Good afternoon, miss. I would like to see Mr. Torres. I'm Eladio Díaz. I have an appointment with him at three.*
me gustaría	*I'd like*
la cita	*appointment*
tener cita con	*to have an appointment with*
Mucho gusto, señor. Yo le diré al director que Ud. está. Él no tardará en llegar. Siéntese, por favor.	*Pleased to meet you, sir. I'll tell the director you are here. He won't be long (in arriving). Please sit down.*
diré	*I will tell*
le diré al director	*I'll tell the director*
Ud. está	*you are here*
tardar en + *infinitive*	*to be long in (doing something)*
tardará	*he will be long*
no tardará en llegar	*he won't be long in arriving*
siéntese	*sit down*

▶ Variantes

Listen, and repeat the same structures from *Diálogo 8*, now with new vocabulary.

Me gustaría verlos.	***I would like** to see them.*
Me encantaría	*I would love*
¿No te importaría su actitud?	*Wouldn't you care about his attitude?*
Sí, pero me importarían más sus valores.	*Yes, but I would care more about his values.*

Estructura y Práctica

N ***Eladio Díaz y la entrevista de trabajo.*** Imagine that Eladio Díaz has an appointment with Mr. Torres for a job interview. Express the following dialogue between Eladio Díaz and Mr. Torres in Spanish. Helpful vocabulary is included below. Pay special attention to the use of the future and conditional tenses.

La entrevista de trabajo

el/la aspirante *applicant*
la autoconfianza *self-confidence*
el candidato / la candidata *applicant*
la carta de motivación *cover letter*
la confianza en sí mismo/a *self-confidence*
los conocimientos de informática
   computer skills
cumplir con fechas límites / con los plazos
   establecidos *to meet deadlines*
el currículum vitae *curriculum vitae, CV*
la entrevista de trabajo/empleo *job interview*
entrevistar *to interview*
la experiencia profesional *professional*
   experience
la fecha límite *deadline*
la formación *background*
las habilidades comunicativas
   communication skills

las habilidades requeridas *skill set*
llevar a cabo múltiples tareas *to multitask*
mostrar (**o** > **ue**) iniciativa *to show initiative*
el nivel educativo / de formación
   level of education
la oferta de trabajo/empleo *job offer*
el plazo establecido *deadline*
el puesto disponible *available position*
resolver (**o** > **ue**) problemas *to solve*
   problems
el/la solicitante *applicant*
solicitar un empleo *to apply for a job*
la solicitud *application*
solucionar problemas *to solve problems*
el trabajo en equipo *teamwork*

1. SEÑOR TORRES *Good afternoon, Mr. Díaz. You are one of the few candidates for this position.*

2. ELADIO DÍAZ *Pleased to meet you, sir. Thank you very much.*

3. SEÑOR TORRES *We liked your cover letter, and your CV is impressive. Please tell me more about your professional experience.*

4. ELADIO DÍAZ *I had been working for my former company for fifteen years. I have the skill set and very good communication skills. And I always meet deadlines.*

5. SEÑOR TORRES *You would have to solve difficult problems and show initiative.*

6. ELADIO DÍAZ *I'm sure I would be able to. As manager and project manager, I was successful in all my projects and got along very well with my team.*

7. SEÑOR TORRES *I'm glad to know it. Teamwork is very important for our company. Thank you, Mr. Díaz. We'll be in touch with you.*

8. ELADIO DÍAZ *Thank you very much, Mr. Torres. I would be very glad to work with you.*

▶ DIÁLOGO 9 · Habrá reunión a las dos.

Study the dialogue, then listen to the recording and repeat each line.

EVA   Acaban de anunciar que habrá reunión a las dos. Podrás asistir, ¿no?
ELADIO   Yo sí, pero es una reunión imprevista. No sé si los otros miembros
           del equipo podrán.

Análisis

Check that you understand the linguistic breakdown of each speech from *Diálogo 9*.

Acaban de anunciar que habrá reunión a las dos. Podrás asistir, ¿no?	*They've just announced that there will be a meeting at two. You'll be able to attend, won't you?*
acabar de + *infinitive*	*to have just (done something)*
habrá	*there will be*
la reunión	*meeting*
podrás	*you will be able to*
asistir a + *event*	*to attend* + event
Yo sí, pero es una reunión imprevista. No sé si los otros miembros del equipo podrán.	*I will, but it's an unexpected meeting. I don't know if the other members of the team will be able to.*
yo sí	*I will (be able to)*
imprevisto	*unexpected, unscheduled, unforeseen*
el miembro	*member*
el equipo	*team*
podrán	*they will be able to*

▶ Variantes

Listen, and repeat the same structures from *Diálogo 9*, now with new vocabulary.

Acaban de anunciar que habrá reunión hoy.	***They have just announced that*** *there will be a meeting today.*
Dicen que	*They say that*
Creen que	*They think that*
Saben que	*They know that*
Escriben que	*They write that*
Están seguros de que	*They are sure that*
Yo no sé si estarán en la oficina .	*I don't know **if they will be in the office**.*
si habrá reunión	*if there will be a meeting*
si podré asistir	*if I will be able to attend*
si nuestros colegas tendrán otra cita	*if our colleagues will have another appointment*
si la reunión será a las dos	*if the meeting will be at 2:00*
si nos reuniremos en la sala de conferencias	*if we'll meet in the conference room*

Si mis colegas van, yo iré también.	*If my colleagues go, I'll go too.*
Yo iré si mis colegas van.	*I will go if my colleagues go.*

Estructura y Práctica

O *Eladio Díaz consiguió el puesto.* Eladio has joined the company and is talking with a team member about what they'll discuss at the meeting. Express the following dialogue between Eladio and Eva in Spanish, using additional vocabulary included below. Pay special attention to the use of the future and conditional tenses.

El marketing

la agencia de publicidad / publicitaria *advertising agency*	los medios sociales *social media*
	el mercadeo de redes *network marketing*
el anuncio *ad*	el mercado *market*
la campaña publicitaria *publicity campaign*	la muestra *sample*
fomentar *to promote*	poner a prueba *to test*
lanzar un nuevo producto *to launch a new product*	el producto *product*
	la promoción *advertising*
el lema *motto, slogan*	promocionar *to promote*
el logo *logo*	promover (**o** > **ue**) *to promote*
la marca *brand*	la publicidad *advertising*

1. ELADIO *Eva, do you know if Carmen, Daniel, and Federico will attend the meeting?*

2. EVA *Carmen and Federico will certainly be here, but Daniel told me he would have to see a client in the afternoon. He didn't know there would be a meeting today.*

3. ELADIO *Mr. Torres wants to launch a publicity campaign to announce the new product, so we'll have a lot to do.*

4. EVA *Eladio, you and I will draw up the budget. Federico will discuss network marketing, and Carmen will explain her ideas about social media.*

5. ELADIO *Mr. Torres will have samples of the product and will want to create a logo and a slogan.*

6. EVA *I think the designers will be in charge of graphic design. Look. Mr. Torres has just come in. The meeting will begin.*

▶ DIÁLOGO 10 · Serán las cuatro.

Study the dialogue, then listen to the recording and repeat each line.

PEDRO	¿Qué hora es? No tengo mi reloj.
EVA	Serán las cuatro.

Análisis

Check that you understand the linguistic breakdown of each speech from *Diálogo 10*.

¿Qué hora es? No tengo mi reloj.	*What time is it? I don't have my watch.*
el reloj	*watch*

Serán las cuatro.	*It's probably about four.*
serán	*it must be, it's probably*
serán las cuatro	*it must be four, I guess it's four,*
	it's probably four

Variantes

Listen, and repeat the same structures from *Diálogo 10*, now with new vocabulary.

¿Qué hora será?	*I wonder what time it is.*
Serán las diez.	*It's probably ten o'clock.*
Probablemente son las diez.	*It's probably ten o'clock.*

¿Tomaremos el tren de las ocho?	*Will we take the eight o'clock train?*
Será demasiado tarde ya.	*It's probably too late already.*
Me imagino que es demasiado tarde ya.	*I imagine it's too late already.*

DIÁLOGO 11 · ¿Dónde estará el anillo?

Study the dialogue, then listen to the recording and repeat each line.

LUCÍA   ¡Qué horror! No puedo encontrar mi anillo de boda. ¿Dónde estará?
JORGE   Me imagino que lo encontrarás. Valdrá mucho dinero.
LUCÍA   Muchísimo. Pero yo no podría calcular su valor sentimental.

Análisis

Check that you understand the linguistic breakdown of each speech from *Diálogo 11.*

¡Qué horror! No puedo encontrar mi anillo de boda. ¿Dónde estará?	*How awful! I can't find my wedding ring. Where could it be?*
el horror	*horror*
¡Qué horror!	*How awful!*
el anillo	*ring*
la boda	*wedding*
el anillo de boda	*wedding ring*
estará	*it will be*
¿Dónde estará?	*Where could it be?*

Me imagino que lo encontrarás. Valdrá mucho dinero.	*I imagine that you will find it. It must be worth a lot of money.*
imaginarse	*to imagine*
me imagino que	*I imagine that*
encontrarás	*you will find*
valer	*to be worth*
valdrá	*it will be worth, it's probably worth*
Valdrá mucho dinero.	*It must be worth a lot of money.*

Muchísimo. Pero yo no podría calcular su valor sentimental.	*An awful lot. But I couldn't calculate its sentimental value.*
muchísimo	*very much*
podría	*I would be able to*
calcular	*to calculate, figure out*
el valor	*value*
sentimental	*sentimental*

Variantes

Listen, and repeat the same structures from *Diálogo 11*, now with new vocabulary.

¿Dónde estará Mauricio?	*I wonder **where** Mauricio is.*
Cómo	*how*
Con quién	*with whom*

Tendrá gran valor sentimental.	*It probably has great sentimental value.*
Probablemente tiene gran valor sentimental.	*It probably has great sentimental value.*

DIÁLOGO 12 · ¿Cuántos años tendrá?

Study the dialogue, then listen to the recording and repeat each line.

ANTONIO   Juan Carlos está muy grande. ¿Cuántos años tendrá?
VICTORIA   No sé exactamente. Tendrá catorce o quince. Preguntémoselo
            a su mamá. ¡Ella sí lo sabrá!

Análisis

Check that you understand the linguistic breakdown of each speech from *Diálogo 12*.

Juan Carlos está muy grande. ¿Cuántos años tendrá?	*Juan Carlos has gotten very big. I wonder how old he is.*
está muy grande	*has gotten very big*
tendrá	*he must have, I wonder if he has*
¿Cuántos años tendrá?	*I wonder how old he is.*

No sé exactamente. Tendrá catorce o quince. Preguntémoselo a su mamá. ¡Ella sí lo sabrá!	*I don't know exactly. He must be fourteen or fifteen. Let's ask his mother. She will certainly know!*
exactamente	*exactly*
tendrá	*he must have, he probably has*
preguntémoselo	*let's ask her (it)*
sabrá	*she will know, she probably knows*
sí	*(emphatic particle)*
sí lo sabrá	*she will certainly know*

Variantes

Listen, and repeat the same structures from *Diálogo 12*, now with new vocabulary.

¿Cuántos meses tendrán los gemelos?	*How many months old are the twins?*
Tendrán casi tres meses.	*They must be almost three months old.*
Probablemente tienen casi tres meses.	*They're probably almost three months old.*
¡Ella sí lo sabrá !	*She'll certainly **know!***
dirá	* tell*

Estructura y Práctica

P   *¡Sí reaccionarán así!* Express the following sentences in Spanish, using the future tense and the emphatic particle **sí** to stress that people will certainly react in a certain way when they hear the gossip. Follow the *modelo*.

> MODELO   *Juan will certainly be annoyed!*
>   → ¡Juan sí se molestará!

1. *Isabel will certainly worry!*

2. *My parents will certainly understand!*

3. *You (tú) will certainly complain!*

4. *I will certainly tell everyone (it)!*

5. *You (Ud.) will certainly get offended!*

6. *Rodrigo and I will certainly be surprised (sorprenderse)!*

7. *You (Uds.) will certainly get angry!*

8. *Alfredo will certainly be to blame!*

DIÁLOGO 13 · No se podrá hacer la ensalada.

Study the dialogue, then listen to the recording and repeat each line.

VICTORIA	Me dice Ester que no podrá hacer la ensalada de frutas porque no tiene duraznos.
ANTONIO	Dile que yo iré al supermercado para comprarlos. ¿Qué más necesitará?
VICTORIA	Bueno, querrá añadir manzanas y fresas, que tampoco tiene.

Análisis

Check that you understand the linguistic breakdown of each speech from *Diálogo 13*.

Me dice Ester que no podrá hacer la ensalada de frutas porque no tiene duraznos.	*Ester tells me that she won't be able to make the fruit salad because she doesn't have any peaches.*
no podrá	* she won't be able to*
la fruta	* fruit*
la ensalada de frutas	* fruit salad*
el durazno	* peach*

Dile que yo iré al supermercado para comprarlos. ¿Qué más necesitará?	*Tell her that I will go to the supermarket to buy them. What else might she need?*
dile	* tell her*
necesitará	* she might need, she must need*
Bueno, querrá añadir manzanas y fresas, que tampoco tiene.	*Well, she will probably want to add apples and strawberries, which she also doesn't have.*
querrá	* she may want*
añadir	* to add*
la manzana	* apple*
la fresa	* strawberry*
tampoco	* neither*

▶ Variantes

Listen, and repeat the same structures from *Diálogo 13*, now with new vocabulary.

Querrá comprar uvas .	*She probably wants to buy **grapes**.*
cerezas	* cherries*
peras	* pears*
mangos	* mangos*
papayas	* papayas*
cebollas	* onions*
aceitunas	* olives*
aguacates	* avocados*
tomates	* tomatoes*
ajo	* garlic*
azúcar	* sugar*

▶ DIÁLOGO 14 · ¿Te interesaría ver el partido de béisbol?

Study the dialogue, then listen to the recording and repeat each line.

ANTONIO   ¿Te interesaría ver el partido de béisbol hoy?

VICTORIA   Me encantaría. ¿Cómo podríamos sacar boletos una hora antes del partido?

ANTONIO   Andrés me dijo que él nos vendería los suyos. Parece que él y su hermano no pueden ir.

Análisis

Check that you understand the linguistic breakdown of each speech from *Diálogo 14*.

¿Te interesaría ver el partido de béisbol hoy?	*Would you be interested in seeing the baseball game today?*
te interesaría	* would you be interested in*
el partido	* game*

Me encantaría. ¿Cómo podríamos sacar boletos una hora antes del partido?	*I would love to. How could we get tickets an hour before the game?*
me encantaría	*I'd love to*
podríamos	*we'd be able to*
sacar boletos	*to get tickets, buy tickets*
antes de	*before*

Andrés me dijo que él nos vendería los suyos. Parece que él y su hermano no pueden ir.	*Andrés told me that he would sell us his. It seems that he and his brother can't go.*
vender	*to sell*
vendería	*he would sell*
los suyos	*his*

▶ Variantes

Listen, and repeat the same structures from *Diálogo 14*, now with new vocabulary.

¿Les interesaría asistir a este concierto?	*Would you be interested in attending this concert?*
Claro, nos encantaría.	*Of course, we'd love to.*
¿Cómo podríamos llegar a tiempo?	*How would we be able to arrive on time?*
Ya te dije que no podríamos.	*I told you that we wouldn't be able to.*
Él me dijo que iría .	*He told me that **he would go.***
saldría	*he would go out*
vendría	*he would come*
regresaría	*he would come back*

▶ DIÁLOGO 15 · A la comisaría

Study the dialogue, then listen to the recording and repeat each line.

POLICÍA   Señorita, Ud. rebasó la velocidad de sesenta y cinco millas. Su licencia de manejar, por favor.
MARTA   ¿Dónde estará? Señor policía, lo siento. Creo que la dejé en casa.
POLICÍA   Bueno, Ud. tendrá que acompañarme a la comisaría. Tendrán que chequear su licencia de manejar en la base de datos.

Análisis

Check that you understand the linguistic breakdown of each speech from *Diálogo 15*.

Señorita, Ud. rebasó la velocidad de sesenta y cinco millas. Su licencia de manejar, por favor.	*Miss, you went above the sixty-five mile an hour speed limit. Your driver's license, please.*
rebasar	*to pass, exceed*
la velocidad	*speed*
la milla	*mile*
la licencia de manejar	*driver's license*

¿Dónde estará? Señor policía, lo siento. Creo que la dejé en casa.	*Where could it be? Officer, I'm sorry. I think I left it at home.*
estará	*it will be, it may be*
creer	*to believe*
creo que	*I think that*
dejar	*to leave (something somewhere)*

Bueno, Ud. tendrá que acompañarme a la comisaría. Tendrán que chequear su licencia de manejar en la base de datos.	*Well, you'll have to come with me to the police station. They will have to check your driver's license in the database.*
tendrá	*you will have*
tendrá que	*you will have to*
acompañar	*to accompany*
la comisaría	*police station*
tendrán	*they will have*
tendrán que	*they will have to*
chequear	*to check*
la base de datos	*database*

▶ Variantes

Listen, and repeat the same structures from *Diálogo 15*, now with new vocabulary.

Mi pasaporte . ¿Dónde estará?	**My passport**. *I wonder where it is.*
Mi tarjeta de embarque	*My boarding pass*
Mi cartera	*My wallet*

Mis llaves . ¿Dónde estarán?	**My keys**. *Where can they be?*
Mis papeles	*My papers*
Mis tarjetas de crédito	*My credit cards*

Un paso más

Are you ready to take your Spanish a step further? Here are exercises that will enhance your knowledge of the language and allow you to express yourself freely.

Ⓠ **Preguntas personales.** *Contesta las siguientes preguntas con oraciones completas en español.*

1. Si estudias en la universidad, ¿cuándo te graduarás? ¿Cuál es tu especialidad?

2. ¿Harás estudios de posgrado? ¿Querrás obtener la maestría o el doctorado? ¿En qué te especializarás?

3. ¿Cuándo irás de vacaciones? ¿Adónde irás? ¿Qué países y ciudades te gustaría conocer?

4. ¿Rebasaste la velocidad máxima en la carretera alguna vez? ¿Un(a) policía te paró? Explica qué pasó.

5. ¿Contrataste un organizador / una organizadora para tu boda u otra celebración? ¿De qué se encargó? ¿Estuviste contento/a con su trabajo?

6. ¿Se te perdió algo de valor alguna vez? ¿Qué fue? ¿Lograste encontrarlo? ¿Dónde y cómo lo encontraste?

R *En mis ratos libres.* (**In my free time.**) *Expresa en español lo que te gustaría hacer en tus ratos libres.*

1. Me gustaría...

2. Me interesaría...

3. Me encantaría...

S *Fiestas y celebraciones.* *En este capítulo aprendiste los nombres de unas fiestas en español, por ejemplo,* **la Pascua, la Pascua judía, la Navidad, el Día de la Independencia, la Fiesta de Quinceañera, el Día de la Madre,** *y* **el Día del Padre.** *Escribe un párrafo* (paragraph) *en español en el que hablas de las fiestas más importantes que celebras y de su significado* (meaning) *para ti.*

T **Translation.** *Lee las siguientes citas* (quotes) *y tradúcelas al inglés. Fíjate en el uso del tiempo futuro y el imperativo. Después, explica lo que significan* (they mean) *en español. Una pista* (hint)*: Tienen que ver con* (they have to do with) *el matrimonio.* (See the Answer Key for translations.)

1. "Ten tus ojos bien abiertos antes del matrimonio y medio cerrados después de él."
   — *Benjamin Franklin*

2. "Cásate con un arqueólogo. Cuánto más vieja te hagas, más encantadora te encontrará."
   — *Agatha Christie*

3. "Casarse por segunda vez es el triunfo de la esperanza sobre la experiencia."
   — *Samuel Johnson*

The
Ultimate Spanish
201

Family Relations and Careers

Communication Goals

- Expressing emotions, doubt, value judgments, imposition of will, and denial
- Vocabulary: the classroom, family relations, choosing a career

Grammar Topics

- The Present Subjunctive
- Use of the Present Subjunctive in Noun Clauses
- Formation of the Present Subjunctive of Regular Verbs
- Formation of the Present Subjunctive of Irregular Verbs
- Spelling Changes in the Present Subjunctive

▶ DIÁLOGO 1 · La maestra y sus alumnos

Study the dialogue, then listen to the recording and repeat each line.

SEÑORITA RIVERA	Chicos, quiero que estudien los capítulos siete y ocho para mañana. Será útil que tomen apuntes porque habrá una prueba el viernes.
RAFAEL	Señorita Rivera, ¿es necesario que aprendamos las fechas de memoria?
SEÑORITA RIVERA	Claro que sí, Rafael. Es muy importante que sepas las fechas de los acontecimientos históricos más importantes.

Análisis

Check that you understand the linguistic breakdown of each speech from *Diálogo 1*.

Chicos, quiero que estudien los capítulos siete y ocho para mañana. Será útil que tomen apuntes porque habrá una prueba el viernes.

Kids, I want you to study chapters seven and eight for tomorrow. It will be useful for you to take notes, since there will be a test on Friday.

estudian	*you study*
que estudien (*subjunctive*)	*you study*
quiero que + *subjunctive*	*I want (someone to do something)*
quiero que estudien	*I want you to study*
el capítulo	*chapter*
será útil	*it will be useful*
tomar apuntes	*to take notes*
toman	*you take*
que tomen (*subjunctive*)	*you take*
es útil que + *subjunctive*	*it's useful for (someone to do something)*
será útil que tomen apuntes	*it will be useful for you to take notes*
habrá	*there will be*
la prueba	*quiz, test*

Señorita Rivera, ¿es necesario que aprendamos las fechas de memoria?

Miss Rivera, is it necessary for us to memorize the dates?

aprender	*to learn*
aprendemos	*we learn*
que aprendamos (*subjunctive*)	*we learn*
es necesario que + *subjunctive*	*it is necessary for (someone to do something)*
es necesario que aprendamos	*it is necessary for us to learn*
aprender de memoria	*to memorize*
aprender las fechas de memoria	*to memorize the dates*

Claro que sí, Rafael. Es muy importante que sepas las fechas de los acontecimientos históricos más importantes.

Yes, of course, Rafael. It's very important for you to know the dates of the most important historical events.

Claro que sí.	*Yes, of course.*
sabes	*you know*
que sepas (*subjunctive*)	*you know*
es muy importante que + *subjunctive*	*it's very important for (someone to do something)*
es muy importante que sepas	*it's very important for you to know*
el acontecimiento	*event*
el acontecimiento histórico	*historical event*

▶ Variantes

Listen, and repeat the same structures from *Diálogo 1*, now with new vocabulary.

Quiero que estudien el libro.	***I want you to study*** the book.
Quiero que lean	*I want you to read*
Quiero que abran	*I want you to open*
Quiero que compren	*I want you to buy*
Quiero estudiar el libro.	***I want to study*** the book.
Quiero leer	*I want to read*
Quiero abrir	*I want to open*
Quiero comprar	*I want to buy*
Es útil que tomen apuntes .	*It's useful **for you to take notes**.*
que lean este capítulo	*for you to read this chapter*
que miren el mapa	*for you to look at the map*
que escriban una composición	*for you to write a composition*
Es útil tomar apuntes .	*It's useful **to take notes**.*
leer este capítulo	*to read this chapter*
mirar el mapa	*to look at the map*
escribir una composición	*to write a composition*
Es necesario que aprendamos las fechas de memoria.	***It's necessary*** *for us to memorize the dates.*
Es imprescindible	*It's crucial*
Es bueno	*It's good*
Es preciso	*It's necessary*
Es necesario aprender las fechas de memoria.	***It's necessary*** *to memorize the dates.*
Es imprescindible	*It's crucial*
Es bueno	*It's good*
Es preciso	*It's necessary*
Es importante que sepas las fechas .	*It's important **that you know the dates**.*
que saques buenas notas	*that you get good grades*
que vayas a la sala de clase	*that you go to the classroom*
que seas aplicado	*that you be studious*
que te prepares para la prueba	*that you prepare for the test*
que traigas la calculadora de bolsillo	*that you bring your pocket calculator*
que hagas la tarea	*that you do the homework*
Es importante saber las fechas .	*It's important **to know the dates**.*
sacar buenas notas	*to get good grades*
ir a la sala de clase	*to go to the classroom*
ser aplicado	*to be studious*
prepararse para la prueba	*to prepare for the test*
traer la calculadora de bolsillo	*to bring your pocket calculator*
hacer la tarea	*to do the homework*

Estructura y Práctica

THE PRESENT SUBJUNCTIVE

The Spanish tenses studied in previous chapters belong to the indicative mood. Verbs in the indicative mood express events or states that are considered factual, definite, or part of the speaker's experienced reality. Verbs that are in the subjunctive mood express an action that is not yet part of reality and/or the speaker's experience.

Use of the Present Subjunctive in Noun Clauses

The following examples have subordinate (dependent) noun clauses in the indicative. They show events perceived as part of reality, because they are the objects of verbs in the main clause: **saber, ver, oír, parecer.**

Sé que **llegan** mañana.	*I know that **they're arriving** tomorrow.*
¿No **ves** que **llueve?**	*Don't **you see it's raining?***
Oímos que **tienen** problemas todavía.	*We hear they're still **having** problems.*
Parece que no **hay** vuelo directo.	*It seems there's no direct flight.*

There are verbs that appear in the main clause that require the use of the subjunctive in the subordinate (dependent) clause. These can be in the present, present perfect, or future tenses, or the imperative. Here is a list of such verbs categorized by meaning.

1 · Imposition of will: **querer que, desear que, esperar que, necesitar que, preferir que.** The negative of these verbs is also followed by a clause in the present subjunctive.

Queremos que **te quedes** un poco más.	*We want you to stay a little longer.*
Espero que **puedan** venir.	*I hope they'll be able to come.*
No necesitamos que nos **ayudes.**	*We don't need you to help us.*

2 · Getting someone to do something: **aconsejarle a uno que, exigirle a uno que, pedirle a uno que, mandarle a uno que, proponerle a uno que, recomendarle a uno que, insistir en que.** The indirect object may be omitted when a subjunctive clause follows.

Te aconsejo que le **hagas** caso.	*I advise you to pay attention to what he says.*
Me exigen que **trabaje** los fines de semana.	*They demand that I work on weekends.*
Siempre nos pide que le **prestemos** dinero.	*He always asks us to lend him money.*
Les propongo que **salgan** antes de la una.	*I suggest they leave before one o'clock.*
Insisto en que Ud. **coma** con nosotros.	*I insist that you eat with us.*

An infinitive clause is also possible with **aconsejar, exigir, pedir, mandar, proponer, recomendar** (e > ie), **permitir, prohibir** (**prohíbo** (*to forbid*)).

Te aconsejo **hacerle** caso.	*I advise you to pay attention to what he says.*

3 · Doubt, uncertainty: **dudar que**, **no creer que**, **no pensar que**

Dudo que ella lo **sepa**.	*I doubt she knows it.*
No creen que **seamos** capaces de hacerlo.	*They don't think we're capable of doing it.*

Note that the negative of **dudar** and the affirmative of **creer** and **pensar** are followed by the indicative, not the subjunctive.

No dudamos que te **ama**.	*We don't doubt that he loves you.*
Pienso que **es** una tienda muy cara.	*I think it's a very expensive store.*

4 · Emotions and subjective value judgments: **alegrarse de que**, **sentir que**, **(no) gustarle a uno que**, **(no) parecerle a uno bien/mal que**, **es una lástima que**

Me alegro de que me **comprendas**.	*I'm glad you understand me.*
Sentimos que él **esté** enojado.	*We're sorry that he's angry.*
No les gusta que su hija **salga** con Álvaro.	*They don't like that their daughter is going out with Álvaro.*
Me parece bien que **tengamos** vacaciones.	*I think it's good that we'll have a vacation.*
Es una lástima que no **se lleven** bien.	*It's a pity they don't get along well.*

Expressions consisting of **es** + adjective + **que** (impersonal expressions) that have meanings similar to the verbs listed in these categories (imposition of will, getting someone to do something, doubt, emotions and subjective value judgments) are also followed by the subjunctive.

Es necesario que **vengas**.	*It's necessary for you to come.*
Es importante que ella **hable** con su esposo.	*It's important for her to talk with her husband.*
Es poco probable que me **conozcan**.	*It's unlikely that they will know me.*
Es triste que no **encuentren** empleo.	*It's sad that they can't find work.*
Es mejor que las **llamemos** mañana.	*It's better for us to call them tomorrow.*

The following impersonal expressions are followed by the subjunctive only when negative: **no es cierto que**, **no es verdad que**, **no es evidente que**, **no estoy seguro (de) que**.

No es verdad que él **sea** médico.	*It's not true that he's a doctor.*
No estoy seguro de que **quieran** salir.	*I'm not sure they want to go out.*

When these expressions are affirmative, they are followed by the indicative.

Es verdad que él **es** médico.	*It's true that he's a doctor.*
Es evidente que tú la **amas**.	*It's evident that you love her.*

The expression **es dudoso que** is followed by the subjunctive when affirmative, but by the indicative when negative.

Es dudoso que se **pueda** terminar este proyecto.	*It's doubtful that this project can be completed.*
No es dudoso que se **puede** terminar este proyecto.	*It's not doubtful that this project can be completed.*

The English equivalent of a subjunctive clause is often an infinitive clause rather than a subordinate clause beginning with *that*.

Quiero **que ellos vayan**.   *I want **them to go**.*

If, however, there is no change of subject, the subjunctive is not used in Spanish. The infinitive, not the subjunctive, is used in Spanish when the subject is the same in both clauses of the sentence.

Verb in Main Clause + Subordinate Clause in Subjunctive
(two clauses: two different subjects)

Quiero que Uds. **estudien** español.   *I want you to study Spanish.*
Esperamos que **regreses** pronto.   *We hope you'll come back soon.*
Prefieren que **vivamos** en el centro.   *They prefer that we live downtown.*

Verb in Main Clause + Infinitive
(both clauses of the sentence have the same subject)

Quiero estudiar español.   *I want to study Spanish.*
Esperamos regresar pronto.   *We hope to come back soon.*
Prefieren vivir en el centro.   *They prefer to live downtown.*

The expressions **tal vez** (*perhaps*) and **quizás** (*perhaps*) can be followed either by the indicative or the subjunctive.

Tal vez nieve esta noche.   *Perhaps it will snow tonight.*
Quizás juegan al golf mañana.   *Perhaps they'll play golf tomorrow.*

Formation of the Present Subjunctive of Regular Verbs

The present subjunctive is formed by switching the characteristic vowels of the conjugations. -**Ar** verbs change the **a** of the present indicative to **e**, while -**er** and -**ir** verbs change the vowels **e** and **i** of the present indicative to **a** in the subjunctive. Regular -**er** and -**ir** verbs have identical endings in all persons of the subjunctive.

trabajar *to work*

Quiere que trabaj**e** con él.   *He wants me to work with him.*
Quiere que trabaj**es** con él.   *He wants you to work with him.*
Quiere que trabaj**e** con él.   *He wants her to work with him.*
Quiere que trabaj**emos** con él.   *He wants us to work with him.*
Quiere que trabaj**éis** con él.   *He wants you to work with him.*
Quiere que trabaj**en** con él.   *He wants them to work with him.*

aprender *to learn*

Espera que aprend**a** español.   *She hopes I'll learn Spanish.*
Espera que aprend**as** español.   *She hopes you'll learn Spanish.*
Espera que aprend**a** español.   *She hopes he'll learn Spanish.*
Espera que aprend**amos** español.   *She hopes we'll learn Spanish.*
Espera que aprend**áis** español.   *She hopes you'll learn Spanish.*
Espera que aprend**an** español.   *She hopes they'll learn Spanish.*

escribir *to write*

Prefieren que les escrib**a** un email.	*They prefer that I write them an email.*
Prefieren que les escrib**as** un email.	*They prefer that you write them an email.*
Prefieren que les escrib**a** un email.	*They prefer that he write them an email.*
Prefieren que les escrib**amos** un email.	*They prefer that we write them an email.*
Prefieren que les escrib**áis** un email.	*They prefer that you write them an email.*
Prefieren que les escrib**an** un email.	*They prefer that they write them an email.*

Note that in the present subjunctive, the **yo** form and the **él/ella/Ud.** form are identical.

-Ar and **-er** verbs that have changes in the vowel of the stem in the present indicative have these same changes in the present subjunctive.

Quiero que ci**e**rres la puerta.	*I want you to close the door.*
Quieren que c**e**rremos la puerta.	*They want us to close the door.*
Prefiero que Uds. no vu**e**lvan muy tarde.	*I prefer that you don't come back very late.*
¿A qué hora quieres que v**o**lvamos?	*What time do you want us to come back?*

-Ir verbs that have the change **e > ie** or **e > i** in the present indicative also have these changes in the present subjunctive. These verbs also change the **e** of the stem to **i** in the **nosotros** and **vosotros** forms of the present subjunctive.

sentir (i > ie) *to feel*		**pedir (e > i)** *to ask for*	
si**e**nta	sintamos	pida	pidamos
si**e**ntas	sintáis	pidas	pidáis
si**e**nta	si**e**ntan	pida	pidan

Dormir and **morir** change **o** to **u** in the stem of the **nosotros** and **vosotros** forms.

dormir (o > ue) *to sleep*		**morir (o > ue)** *to die*	
d**ue**rma	d**u**rmamos	m**ue**ra	m**u**ramos
d**ue**rmas	d**u**rmáis	m**ue**ras	m**u**ráis
d**ue**rma	d**ue**rman	m**ue**ra	m**ue**ran

Verbs ending in **-iar** or **-uar** that have an accent mark on the **i** (**í**) or the **u** (**ú**) in the singular and third person plural of the present tense also have the accent mark in the same four persons of the present subjunctive. The **nosotros** and **vosotros** forms do not have an accent over the **i** or the **u** of the stem.

enviar	envíe, envíes, envíe, enviemos, enviéis, envíen
continuar	continúe, continúes, continúe, continuemos, continuéis, continúen

Formation of the Present Subjunctive of Irregular Verbs

Verbs that have an irregularity such as **-g-** or **-zc-** in the **yo** form of the present indicative have that irregularity in all persons of the present subjunctive. These irregularities occur only in **-er** and **-ir** verbs; therefore, all of these verbs have present subjunctive endings with **-a-**.

SUBJUNCTIVE						
PRESENT INDICATIVE	yo	tú	él, ella, Ud.	nosotros	vosotros	ellos, ellas, Uds.
caber						
quepo	quepa	quepas	quepa	quepamos	quepáis	quepan
caer						
caigo	caiga	caigas	caiga	caigamos	caigáis	caigan
conocer						
conozco	conozca	conozcas	conozca	conozcamos	conozcáis	conozcan
construir						
construyo	construya	construyas	construya	construyamos	construyáis	construyan
decir						
digo	diga	digas	diga	digamos	digáis	digan
hacer						
hago	haga	hagas	haga	hagamos	hagáis	hagan
oír						
oigo	oiga	oigas	oiga	oigamos	oigáis	oigan
poner						
pongo	ponga	pongas	ponga	pongamos	pongáis	pongan
salir						
salgo	salga	salgas	salga	salgamos	salgáis	salgan
tener						
tengo	tenga	tengas	tenga	tengamos	tengáis	tengan
traer						
traigo	traiga	traigas	traiga	traigamos	traigáis	traigan
venir						
vengo	venga	vengas	venga	vengamos	vengáis	vengan
ver						
veo	vea	veas	vea	veamos	veáis	vean

Other irregular verbs in the present subjunctive are some of the most commonly used verbs.

	yo	tú	él, ella, Ud.	nosotros	vosotros	ellos, ellas, Uds.
dar	dé	des	dé	demos	deis	den
estar	esté	estés	esté	estemos	estéis	estén
haber	haya	hayas	haya	hayamos	hayáis	hayan
ir	vaya	vayas	vaya	vayamos	vayáis	vayan
saber	sepa	sepas	sepa	sepamos	sepáis	sepan
ser	sea	seas	sea	seamos	seáis	sean

Spelling Changes in the Present Subjunctive

Spelling changes in the present subjunctive are similar to those that you learned for the **yo** form of the preterit. (For a review of the preterit, see Chapter 9).

Verbs with stems ending in the letters **c**, **g**, **z**, and **j** have spelling changes in the present subjunctive.

According to Spanish spelling conventions, the sounds /k/, /g/, /s/ (written **z**, not **s**), and /x/ are written differently before **e** and **i** than before **a**, **o**, and **u**.

/k/	/g/	/s/	/x/
ca	ga	za	ja
que	**gue**	**ce**	**ge**
qui	**gui**	**ci**	**gi**
co	go	zo	jo
cu	gu	zu	ju

PRESENT TENSE	SUBJUNCTIVE
Lo bus**c**o.	Quieren que lo bus**qu**e.
Lle**g**an en tren.	Prefiero que lle**gu**en en tren.
Empie**z**a a llorar.	Tememos que empie**c**e a llorar.
Esco**g**es algo.	Desean que esco**j**as algo.
Si**gu**e esta ruta.	Esperas que si**g**a esta ruta.

The spelling change **g** > **j** also occurs in the **yo** form of the present tense of verbs with infinitives that end in **-ger** and **-gir**: **escojo, finjo**. It occurs in all persons of the present subjunctive: **que yo escoja/finja, que tú escojas/finjas, que él escoja/finja, que nosotros escojamos/finjamos, que vosotros escojáis/finjáis, que ellos escojan/finjan.**

A **Present subjunctive.** Write the present subjunctive form of the verb in parentheses that correctly completes each of the following sentences. Follow the *modelo*.

MODELO   Quieren que Ud. *imprima* los documentos. (imprimir)

1. Prefiero que ellos _____ para las ocho. (llegar)

2. Es necesario que tú _____ el cinturón de seguridad. (abrocharse)

3. Siente que ellos no le _____ una beca. (dar)

4. Es muy importante que _____ reunión hoy. (haber)

5. Esperamos que nuestros hijos _____ sanos y felices. (ser)

6. Es preciso que Ud. nos _____ toda la verdad. (decir)

7. Es bueno que nadie _____. (enfermarse)

8. Desean que nosotros _____ los gastos. (compartir)

B   **Present subjunctive or present indicative?** Write either the present subjunctive or the present indicative of the verb in parentheses to correctly complete each of the following sentences. Follow the *modelos*.

MODELOS   Creo que él _*manda*_ un email. (mandar)

Necesito que él _*mande*_ un email. (mandar)

1. Sabemos que ellos _____ la semana entrante. (volver)

2. Espero que tú _____ buenas notas. (sacar)

3. Prefieren que ella _____ la tarea ahora mismo. (hacer)

4. Han oído que _____ un buen club de jazz. (ser)

5. Desean que nosotros _____ la cuenta. (pagar)

6. Vemos que tú _____ muy estresado. (estar)

7. Quieren que yo _____ un rato más. (quedarse)

8. Me parece que ella no _____ pelos en la lengua. (tener)

9. Siento que no les _____ mi regalo. (gustar)

10. Tememos que Uds. _____ el tren. (perder)

C   *En la sala de clase.* Write sentences that express how Mr. Arenas responds to his students when he insists that they do what they don't want to do. Use the cue in parentheses in the main clause of your answer; use the present subjunctive of the verb (from the student's statement) in the subordinate clause. Change direct object nouns to pronouns. Follow the *modelo*.

MODELO   MARCOS Yo no quiero mirar el mapa. (insistir en)
   → SEÑOR ARENAS Marcos, yo insisto en que lo mires.

1. PILAR Yo no quiero sacar mi computadora. (es necesario)

2. ALONSO Yo no quiero tomar apuntes. (es importante)

3. ANDRÉS Yo no quiero traer mi libro de texto. (es útil)

4. SILVIA Yo no quiero aprender las fechas de memoria. (insistir en)

5. GILBERTO Yo no quiero hacer la tarea. (es imprescindible)

6. FLOR Yo no quiero empezar a escribir la composición. (es preciso)

D   **Translation.** Express the following sentences in Spanish. Write either a sentence with two clauses and two different subjects (which will require a verb in present subjunctive) or a sentence with a verb in the main clause + an infinitive.

1. *I want to go out.*

2. *We hope she'll be studious.*

3. *It's necessary to take notes.*

4. *It's important that they read a lot.*

5. *Do you (tú) prefer to buy the tickets online?*

6. *It will be crucial for us to learn all the dates.*

7. *They want to have a great time!*

8. *It's good that you (Uds.) are graduating this year.*

DIÁLOGO 2 · Relaciones familiares: Rosario y su papá

Study the dialogue, then listen to the recording and repeat each line.

ROSARIO	Papá, quiero que conozcas a mi novio. Jaime es muy buena gente.
PAPÁ	Hija, tu mamá y yo preferimos que salgas con Antonio Maldonado. Es que nosotros somos íntimos amigos de sus papás.
ROSARIO	Ay papi, no creo que eso tenga importancia. Es más importante que Jaime y yo nos queramos.
PAPÁ	Bueno, Rosario, te aconsejo que pienses mucho en lo que haces. Antes que te cases mira lo que haces.

Análisis

Check that you understand the linguistic breakdown of each speech from *Diálogo 2*.

Papá, quiero que conozcas a mi novio.
Jaime es muy buena gente.
   conoces
   que conozcas (*subjunctive*)
   quiero que conozcas
   ser buena gente

Dad, I want you to meet my boyfriend.
Jaime is a wonderful person.
   you know, get to know
   you know
   I want you to meet
   to be a nice person

Hija, tu mamá y yo preferimos que
salgas con Antonio Maldonado. Es que
nosotros somos íntimos amigos de sus
papás.
   sales
   que salgas (*subjunctive*)
   preferir que + *subjunctive*
   preferimos que salgas
   es que
   íntimo
   íntimos amigos

Well, your mother and I prefer that you go
out with Antonio Maldonado. The fact is that
we are close friends of his parents.

   you go out
   you go out
   to prefer that (someone do something)
   we prefer that you go out
   the fact is that, because
   intimate, close
   close friends

Ay papi, no creo que eso tenga
importancia. Es más importante que
Jaime y yo nos queramos.
   tiene importancia
   que tenga (*subjunctive*)
   que tenga importancia
   no creo que + *subjunctive*
   no creo que eso tenga importancia
   quererse
   nos queremos
   que nos queramos (*subjunctive*)
   es más importante que + *subjunctive*
   es más importante que nos queramos

Oh, Dad, I don't think that that is important.
It's more important that Jaime and I love
each other.
   it's important
   it has
   it's important
   I don't think that . . .
   I don't think that that's important
   to love each other
   we love each other
   we love each other
   it's more important that . . .
   it's more important that we love each other

Bueno, Rosario, te aconsejo que pienses mucho en lo que haces. Antes que te cases mira lo que haces.	*Well, Rosario, I advise you to think carefully about what you are doing. Look before you leap.*
pensar en	*to think about*
piensas	*you think*
que pienses (*subjunctive*)	*you think*
aconsejarle a uno que + *subjunctive*	*to advise someone to (do something)*
te aconsejo que pienses mucho	*I advise you to think carefully*
lo que	*what*
antes que + *subjunctive*	*before (doing something)*
antes que te cases	*before you get married*
mira	*look; examine*
mira lo que haces	*look at what you are doing*
Antes que te cases mira lo que haces.	*Look before you leap. (literally, before you get married, look at what you're doing)*

▶ Variantes

Listen, and repeat the same structures from *Diálogo 2*, now with new vocabulary.

Quiero que lo conozcas .	*I want **you to meet** him.*
conozcan	*them to meet*
conozca	*her to meet*
conozcamos	*us to meet*
conozca	*you* (Ud.) *to meet*
conozcan	*you* (Uds.) *to meet*
conozca	*him to meet*

Quiero conocerlo.	*I want to know him.*
Quiere	*She wants*
Queremos	*We want*
Quieren	*They want*

Preferimos que salgas con él.	*We prefer you go out with him.*
Queremos que salgas	*We want you to go out*
Esperamos que salgas	*We hope you'll go out*
Deseamos que salgas	*We want you to go out*
Insistimos en que salgas	*We insist that you go out*

Queremos salir con él.	*We want to go out with him.*
Esperamos salir	*We hope to go out*
Deseamos salir	*We want to go out*
Insistimos en salir	*We insist on going out*

No creo que tenga importancia.	*I don't think it's important.*
No pienso que	*I don't think*
No me parece que	*I don't think*
Dudo que	*I doubt*

Es importante que se lleven bien.	*It's important that they get along well.*
Es necesario que	*It's necessary that*
Es bueno que	*It's good that*
Es imprescindible que	*It's crucial that*
Es posible que	*It's possible that*
Es probable que	*It's probable that*
Es dudoso que	*It's doubtful that*
Te aconsejo que pienses mucho.	*I advise you to think hard.*
Te digo que	*I'm telling you*
Les recomiendo que esperen.	*I recommend that they wait.*
Les pido que	*I ask that*
Les exijo que	*I demand that*
Les ruego que	*I request that*
Les propongo que	*I propose that*

Estructura y Práctica

E *Les aconsejo que...* Write a sentence from the elements given to advise people how they can live healthier lives. Use the present subjunctive. Follow the *modelo*.

MODELO   Le aconsejo a Bernardo... / comer sano
    → Le aconsejo a Bernardo que coma sano.

1. Le aconsejo a Marta... / beber mucha agua

2. Les recomiendo a mis amigos... / dormir ocho horas diarias (*daily*)

3. Le propongo a Pablo... / ponerse a dieta

4. Le digo a Inés... / tomar vitaminas

5. Le exijo a mi primo... / perder peso

6. Les pido a mis papás... / hacer ejercicio

7. Le ruego a mi abuelito... / dejar de comer comida basura

8. Insisto en que mis colegas... / alimentarse bien

F *Problemas de familia.* Express the following sentences in Spanish to find out some of this family's problems. Use the present subjunctive.

1. *Dad, I don't think that you (tú) understand the problem.*

2. *We hope that Marta succeeds in catching a husband (pescar un marido; pescar (to fish)).*

3. *It's doubtful that Antonio and Victoria love each other.*

4. *Blanca doesn't think her parents know her boyfriend.*

5. *It's bad that the relatives don't get along well.*

6. *The grandparents tell their grandchildren to visit them.*

7. *Mario demands that his brother-in-law return the money to him.*

8. *Cristina insists that her father-in-law pay for the wedding.*

▶ DIÁLOGO 3 · Relaciones familiares: Jaime y su mamá

Study the dialogue, then listen to the recording and repeat each line.

MAMÁ Jaime, me alegro de que estés contento pero te aconsejo que pienses mucho antes de comprometerte.

JAIME Mamá, a ti y a papá les cae bien Rosario, ¿verdad? Entonces, ¿por qué no quieren que yo me case con ella?

MAMÁ Es que nosotros no conocemos a los padres de Rosario. Preferimos que te comprometas con Aurora Elizondo porque somos íntimos amigos de sus papás.

JAIME Pero mamá, yo no quiero a Aurora. Y no dudo que te van a caer muy bien los papás de Rosario.

Análisis

Check that you understand the linguistic breakdown of each speech from *Diálogo 3*.

Jaime, me alegro de que estés contento pero te aconsejo que pienses mucho antes de comprometerte.	*Jaime, I'm glad you are happy, but I advise you to think carefully before getting engaged.*
alegrarse de que + *subjunctive*	*to be glad about (something)*
que estés (*subjunctive*)	*you are*
me alegro de que estés contento	*I'm glad you are happy*
aconsejarle a uno que + *subjunctive*	*to advise someone to (do something)*
te aconsejo que pienses mucho	*I advise you to think carefully*
antes de + *infinitive*	*before (doing something)*
comprometerse	*to get engaged*
antes de comprometerte	*before getting engaged*

Mamá, a ti y a papá les cae bien Rosario, ¿verdad? Entonces, ¿por qué no quieren que yo me case con ella?	*Mom, you and Dad like Rosario, don't you? So then why don't you want me to marry her?*
caerle bien a uno	*to like someone*
les cae bien Rosario	*you like Rosario*
no quieren que + *subjunctive*	*you don't want (someone to do something)*
casarse con uno	*to marry someone*
no quieren que yo me case	*you don't want me to marry*

Es que nosotros no conocemos a los padres de Rosario. Preferimos que te comprometas con Aurora Elizondo porque somos íntimos amigos de sus papás.	*Because we don't know Rosario's parents. We prefer that you get engaged to Aurora Elizondo, because we are close friends of her parents.*
comprometerse con	*to get engaged to*
te comprometes	*you get engaged*
que te comprometas (*subjunctive*)	*you get engaged*
preferir que + *subjunctive*	*to prefer that (someone do something)*
preferimos que te comprometas	*we prefer that you get engaged*

Pero mamá, yo no quiero a Aurora.	*But Mom, I don't love Aurora. And I don't*
Y no dudo que te van a caer muy bien	*doubt that you are going to like Rosario's*
los papás de Rosario.	*parents very much.*
querer a uno	*to love someone*
yo no quiero a Aurora	*I don't love Aurora*
no dudar que + *indicative*	*not to doubt that . . .*
no dudo que te van a caer muy bien	*I don't doubt that you are going to like*
	them very much

▶ Variantes

Listen, and repeat the same structures from *Diálogo 3*, now with new vocabulary.

Se alegra de que se vayan.	***She's glad*** *they're leaving.*
Siente que	*She's sorry*
Tiene miedo de que	*She's afraid*
Teme que	*She fears*
Le sorprende que	*She's surprised*
¿No quieren que me case ?	*Don't you want* ***me to get married****?*
se case	*him to get married*
nos casemos	*us to get married*
se case	*her to get married*
se casen	*them to get married*
Es que somos íntimos amigos.	***The fact is that*** *we're close friends.*
Es verdad que	*It's true that*
Es cierto que	*It's true that*
Está seguro que	*He's sure that*
No es que seamos íntimos amigos.	***It's not that*** *we're close friends.*
No es verdad que	*It's not true that*
No es cierto que	*It's not true that*
No está seguro que	*He's not sure that*
Prefieren que vengamos en taxi.	***They prefer that we come*** *by taxi.*
Les gusta que vengamos	*They like us to come*
Les sorprende que vengamos	*They're surprised that we come*
No dudo que te van a caer bien.	***I don't doubt that*** *you'll like them.*
No es dudoso que	*It's not doubtful that*

Estructura y Práctica

G **Impersonal expressions.** Write a sentence from the elements given, using the correct present subjunctive or present indicative form of the verb in parentheses. Follow the *modelos.*

MODELOS   es verdad / ellos / casarse en tres meses
                → Es verdad que ellos se casan en tres meses.

                    no es verdad / ellos / casarse en tres meses
                → No es verdad que ellos se casen en tres meses.

1. es que / nosotros / ser íntimos amigos

2. no estoy seguro / ella / ir a la fiesta

3. es dudoso / hacer buen tiempo mañana

4. es cierto / mis primos / estar de vacaciones

5. no es evidente / la empresa / tener problemas económicos

6. no es que / tú y yo / verse todos los días

7. es evidente / Uds. / no ponerse de acuerdo

8. estamos seguros / él / poder diseñar el sitio web

H **Translation.** Express the following sentences in Spanish, using the correct present subjunctive form of the verb.

1. *They're glad we're staying with them.*

2. *She's surprised the museum is closed.*

3. *We're afraid that they spend too much money.*

4. *I'm sorry you're* (tú) *feeling sick.*

5. *We fear the airplane is not taking off now.*

6. *They like us to stay in touch with them.*

▶ DIÁLOGO 4 · Quieren que me haga médico.

Study the dialogue, then listen to the recording and repeat each line.

RICARDO   Sara, me dicen que te has inscrito en la facultad de bellas artes.

SARA   Sí, pero mis padres se oponen. Ellos prefieren que yo curse medicina.

RICARDO   Los míos también quieren que yo me haga médico. Pero yo sé que
                me van a apoyar de todas formas.

Análisis

Check that you understand the linguistic breakdown of each speech from *Diálogo 4*.

Sara, me dicen que te has inscrito en la facultad de bellas artes.	*Sara, I'm told you have registered in the School of Fine Arts.*
inscribirse en	*to register in, register at, register for*
te has inscrito	*you have registered*
el arte	*art* (masculine in the singular)
las artes	*arts* (feminine in the plural)
las bellas artes	*fine arts*
la facultad	*school within a university*
la facultad de bellas artes	*School of Fine Arts*
Sí, pero mis padres se oponen. Ellos prefieren que yo curse medicina.	*Yes, but my parents are against it. They prefer that I study medicine.*
oponerse	*to oppose (it), be against (it)* (conjugated like **poner**)
cursar	*to take (courses, a major)*
que curse (*subjunctive*)	*I take*
preferir que + *subjunctive*	*to prefer (someone do something)*
prefieren que curse	*they prefer that I study*
Los míos también quieren que yo me haga médico. Pero yo sé que me van a apoyar de todas formas.	*My parents also want me to become a doctor. But I know that they will support me in any case.*
hacerse + *profession*	*to become* + profession
me hago médico	*I become a doctor*
que me haga médico (*subjunctive*)	*I become a doctor*
quieren que + *subjunctive*	*they want (someone to do something)*
quieren que yo me haga médico	*they want me to become a doctor*
apoyar a uno	*to support someone (morally, etc.), support someone's choice*
de todas formas	*anyway, in any case*

▶ Variantes

Listen, and repeat the same structures from *Diálogo 4*, now with new vocabulary.

Él me dice que se ha inscrito al curso.	*He tells me he has signed up for the course.*
Él me dice que me inscriba al curso.	*He tells me to sign up for the course.*
Les digo que se van pronto.	*I'm telling them that they're leaving soon.*
Les digo que se vayan pronto.	*I'm telling them to leave soon.*
Le digo que curso medicina.	*I tell her I'm studying medicine.*
Le digo que curse medicina.	*I tell her to study medicine.*

Prefieren que yo me haga médico.	**They prefer that I** become a doctor.
Esperan que yo	They hope that I
Quieren que yo	They want me to
Exigen que yo	They demand that I
Me aconsejan que	They advise me to
Insisten en que yo	They insist that I
Me piden que	They ask that I
Me recomiendan que	They recommend that I
Me proponen que	They propose that I

Saben que me hago médico.	**They know that** I'm becoming a doctor.
Piensan que	They think that
Dicen que	They say that
Comprenden que	They understand that
Han oído que	They've heard that
Les parece que	They think that
Ven que	They see that

Estructura y Práctica

I **Getting someone to do something.** Write a sentence from the elements given, using the correct present subjunctive form of the verb. Follow the *modelo*.

MODELO le aconsejo a Roberto / terminar el plan de negocios
→ Le aconsejo a Roberto que termine el plan de negocios.

1. le pido a Juan / elaborar el presupuesto

2. le exijo a Enrique / crear una base de datos

3. les digo a mis asistentes / trabajar en equipo

4. le mando a Nora / dedicarse a los medios sociales

5. insisto en que Catalina / encargarse de lanzar el nuevo producto

6. les digo a los asesores / resolver el problema del servicio al cliente

7. le aconsejo a Lorena / comenzar la campaña publicitaria

8. les propongo a mis colegas / realizar un plan de investigación global de mercado

J Write the present subjunctive or present indicative form of the verb in parentheses to correctly complete each of the following sentences. Follow the *modelo*.

MODELO Sé que Octavio _quiere_ estudiar medicina. (querer)

1. He oído que Vicente _____ de vuelta. (estar)

2. Nos piden que los _____. (apoyar)

3. Creo que Uds. _____ una prueba de matemáticas hoy. (tener)

4. Te recomiendo que _____ al perro en el jardín. (buscar)

5. Veo que estos alumnos _____ muy aplicados. (ser)

6. Los jugadores me proponen que _____ al béisbol con ellos. (jugar)

7. Le aconsejamos a Raquel que _____ con su novio. (romper)

8. Les exijo a los maestros que _____ más paciencia. (tener)

K **Translation.** Express each of the following sentences in Spanish. Write sentences in two ways where indicated by (2).

1. *The teacher tells us to read chapter seven.*

2. *I advise you (Ud.) to write the report.* (2)

3. *They recommend that I bring my pocket calculator.* (2)

4. *Eduardo tells me that he and Lorenzo don't get along well.*

5. *I insist that you (tú) stop smoking.*

6. *I ask them to come to our house.* (2)

7. *The boss demands that I hand in the report by Tuesday.* (2)

8. *I suggest that you (Uds.) attend the meeting.* (2)

▶ DIÁLOGO 5 · Ojalá que ella cambie de idea.

Study the dialogue, then listen to the recording and repeat each line.

JUDITH   Ay Lorenzo, siento que Sara no nos haga caso. Ya se ha inscrito en la facultad de bellas artes.

LORENZO   Judith, no podemos permitir que estudie arte. ¿Cómo se ganará la vida?

JUDITH   Ojalá que ella cambie de idea. Pero si no, de todas formas la vamos a apoyar.

Análisis

Check that you understand the linguistic breakdown of each speech from *Diálogo 5*.

Ay Lorenzo, siento que Sara no nos haga caso. Ya se ha inscrito en la facultad de bellas artes.	*Oh, Lorenzo, I regret that Sara is not listening to us. She has already registered at the School of Fine Arts.*
hacerle caso a uno	*to pay attention to someone, listen to someone*
no nos hace caso	*she doesn't listen to us, she doesn't pay attention to us*
que no nos haga caso (*subjunctive*)	*she doesn't listen to us, she doesn't pay attention to us*
sentir (**e** > **ie**)	*to regret, be sorry*
siento que + *subjunctive*	*to be sorry that (something is happening)*
siento que no nos haga caso	*I'm sorry that she doesn't listen to us*

Judith, no podemos permitir que	Judith, we can't allow her to study art.
estudie arte. ¿Cómo se ganará la vida?	How will she make a living?
permitir que + *subjunctive*	to permit (someone to do something),
	allow (someone to do something)
permitir que estudie arte	to allow her to study art
ganarse la vida	to earn one's living
Ojalá que ella cambie de idea. Pero	I hope that she changes her mind. But
si no, de todas formas la vamos a apoyar.	if she doesn't, we'll support her anyway.
ojalá que + *subjunctive*	I hope that . . .
cambiar de idea	to change one's mind
que cambie de idea (*subjunctive*)	she changes her mind
ojalá que cambie de idea	I hope she changes her mind
si no	if she doesn't
la vamos a apoyar	we'll support her (choice)

▶ Variantes

Listen, and repeat the same structures from *Diálogo 5*, now with new vocabulary.

Siento que ella estudie arte.	*I'm sorry that* she's studying art.
Dudo que	*I doubt that*
Me alegro de que	*I'm glad that*
Me gusta que	*I like that*
Me sorprende que	*I'm surprised that*
No permitimos que estudie arte.	*We don't allow her* to study art.
No le mandamos que	*We don't order her*
No le prohibimos que	*We don't forbid her*
No le permitimos estudiar arte.	*We don't allow her* to study art.
No le mandamos	*We don't order her*
No le prohibimos	*We don't forbid her*
Dejamos que él estudie arte.	*We let him* study art.
Hacemos que él	*We make him*
La dejamos estudiar arte.	*We let her* study art.
La hacemos	*We make her*
Ojalá que tenga éxito.	*I hope he'll be successful.*
Ojalá no se pierdan.	*I hope they don't get lost.*

Estructura y Práctica

L   *La familia Gómez.* Write sentences from the elements given to find out about the Gómez family. Use the correct present subjunctive form of the verb. Follow the *modelo*.

MODELO   ojalá / todos los miembros de la familia Gómez / salir adelante
          → Ojalá que todos los miembros de la familia Gómez salgan adelante.

1. a sus papás les gusta / Leonor / hacerse actriz

2. el abuelo se alegra de que / Ramón / seguir la carrera de ingeniería

3. la abuela prohíbe / su nieta / salir con ese tipo

4. los tíos / dejan / su hija / ir al extranjero para estudiar inglés

5. Miguel le aconseja / a su hermano / no comprometerse con Lola

6. los papás les dicen / a sus hijos / ser corteses y amables

7. los cuñados hacen / sus hijos / inscribirse en la universidad

8. la familia Gómez espera / que todos ellos / lograr tener salud, felicidad y éxito

---

EXPRESSIONS WITH **HACER**

hacerle caso a uno *to pay attention to someone, listen to someone*
hacerse + *profession* *to become* + profession
hacer las paces *to make up* (la paz (*peace*))
hacerse tarde *to become late, get late*
hacer juego (con) *to match*
hacer el ridículo *to make a fool of oneself; to look foolish*
hacer un alto *to take a break*
hacer un papel *to play a role, play a part*

M *Expresiones con hacer.* Express the following sentences in Spanish, using idioms and expressions with **hacer** from the box above. All answers require the present subjunctive.

1. *It's bad that Luisito doesn't pay attention to his parents.*

2. *It's possible Fernanda will become an archaeologist.*

3. *Aunt Sara wants Juan and Blanca to make up once and for all* (de una vez).

4. *Let's leave before it gets late* (antes (de) que + *subjunctive*).

5. *I don't think this blouse matches the skirt.*

6. *They tell Arturo to stop making a fool of himself.*

7. *We advise you* (tú) *to take a break.*

8. *We hope Lorenzo Olivo will play the role of Hamlet in this production* (la producción).

DIÁLOGO 6 · Es necesario ahorrar más.

Study the dialogue, then listen to the recording and repeat each line.

ÁLVARO Es una lástima que no podamos salir de vacaciones este año.
JIMENA ¿Por qué? ¿Problemas de dinero?
ÁLVARO Pues sí. Con los tiempos que corren es mejor que no gastemos tanto dinero en un viaje a Europa.
JIMENA Yo le entiendo. Es necesario que todos tratemos de ahorrar más y gastar menos.

Análisis

Check that you understand the linguistic breakdown of each speech from *Diálogo 6*.

Es una lástima que no podamos salir de vacaciones este año.	*It's a shame that we can't go on vacation this year.*
la lástima	*pity, shame*
es una lástima que + *subjunctive*	*it's a shame that . . .*
podemos	*we can*
que podamos (*subjunctive*)	*we can*
es una lástima que no podamos	*it's a shame that we can't*
salir de vacaciones	*go on vacation, leave on vacation*
¿Por qué? ¿Problemas de dinero?	*Why? Money problems?*
Pues sí. Con los tiempos que corren es mejor que no gastemos tanto dinero en un viaje a Europa.	*Well, yes. In these times, it's better that we don't spend so much money on a trip to Europe.*
correr	*to run*
los tiempos que corren	*these times*
gastamos	*we spend*
que gastemos (*subjunctive*)	*we spend*
es mejor que + *subjunctive*	*it's better that . . .*
es mejor que no gastemos tanto dinero	*it's better that we don't spend so much money*
Yo le entiendo. Es necesario que todos tratemos de ahorrar más y gastar menos.	*I understand you. It's necessary for all of us to try to save more and spend less.*
entender (**e** > **ie**)	*to understand*
es necesario que + *subjunctive*	*it's necessary for (someone to do something)*
tratar de + *infinitive*	*to try to (do something)*
tratamos de	*we try to*
que tratemos de (*subjunctive*)	*we try to*
es necesario que tratemos	*it's necessary for us to try*
ahorrar	*to save*
gastar	*to spend*

▶ Variantes

Listen, and repeat the same structures from *Diálogo 6*, now with new vocabulary.

Es una lástima que Uds. se vayan .	*It's a pity **that you're going away**.*
que Uds. salgan	*that you're going out*
que Uds. vuelvan	*that you're going back*
que Uds. se muden	*that you're moving away*

Es mejor que gastemos menos dinero.	***It's better** that we spend less money.*
Es necesario	*It's necessary*
Es importante	*It's important*
Es imprescindible	*It's crucial*
Es preciso	*It's necessary*
Es bueno	*It's good*
Es urgente	*It's urgent*

Es mejor gastar menos.	***It's better** to spend less.*
Es necesario	*It's necessary*
Es importante	*It's important*
Es imprescindible	*It's crucial*
Es preciso	*It's necessary*
Es bueno	*It's good*
Es urgente	*It's urgent*

Hace falta que ahorremos más.	***It's necessary that** we save more.*
Más vale que	*It's better that*
Urge que	*It's urgent that*

Hace falta ahorrar más.	***It's necessary** to save more.*
Más vale	*It's better*
Urge	*It's urgent*

Estructura y Práctica

N ***Expresiones impersonales.*** Rewrite each of the following sentences, conjugating the verb in the subordinate clause with the subject shown in parentheses. Follow the *modelo.*

MODELO Es necesario ganarse la vida. (tú)
→ Es necesario que tú te ganes la vida.

1. Es bueno ahorrar dinero. (Ud.)

2. Es imprescindible ponerse el repelente contra mosquitos. (ellos)

3. Es urgente salir para el aeropuerto. (yo)

4. Es preciso promocionar la marca. (Uds.)

5. Es mejor jugar al tenis por la mañana. (tú)

6. Es importante comer granos integrales. (todos nosotros)

7. Urge ir al medico. (él)

8. Más vale viajar en tren. (Ud.)

9. Hace falta aprender las fechas de memoria. (ella)

10. Es útil actualizar los datos. (yo)

▶ DIÁLOGO 7 · Es poco probable que yo pueda ir.

Study the dialogue, then listen to the recording and repeat each line.

JIMENA	Mañana vamos a reunirnos en mi casa para ver una película. Vienes, ¿no?
RICARDO	Es poco probable que yo pueda ir.
JIMENA	¿Por qué? ¿Tienes un compromiso?
RICARDO	Sí, mi hermana se muda y me ha pedido que la ayude.

Análisis

Check that you understand the linguistic breakdown of each speech from *Diálogo 7*.

Mañana vamos a reunirnos en mi casa para ver una película. Vienes, ¿no?	*Tomorrow we are going to get together at my house to see a movie. You'll come, won't you?*
reunirse	*to get together*
vamos a reunirnos	*we're going to get together*
Es poco probable que yo pueda ir.	*It's improbable that I'll be able to come.*
probable	*probable*
poco probable	*improbable, not likely, unlikely*
es poco probable que + *subjunctive*	*it's improbable that . . .*
es poco probable que yo pueda ir	*it's improbable that I can come*
¿Por qué? ¿Tienes un compromiso?	*Why? Do you have an appointment?*
el compromiso	*appointment, engagement, commitment*
Sí, mi hermana se muda y me ha pedido que la ayude.	*Yes, my sister is moving and has asked me to help her.*
mudarse	*to move (change residence)*
pedirle a uno que + *subjunctive*	*to ask someone to (do something)*
la ayudo	*I help her*
que la ayude (*subjunctive*)	*I help her*
me ha pedido que la ayude	*she has asked me to help her*

▶ Variantes

Listen, and repeat the same structures from *Diálogo 7*, now with new vocabulary.

Es poco probable que yo vaya.	***It's improbable** that I'll go.*
Es posible	*It's possible*
Es dudoso	*It's doubtful*
Tal vez haya una prueba esta semana.	***Perhaps** there will be a quiz this week.*
Quizás	*Perhaps*
Tal vez hay una prueba esta semana.	***Perhaps** there will be a quiz this week.*
Quizás	*Perhaps*
Me ha pedido que la ayude.	***She has asked me** to help her.*
Me ha dicho	*She has told me*
Me ha mandado	*She has ordered me*

Él niega que hable mal de Uds.   *He denies that he speaks badly about you.*
Él no niega que habla mal de Uds.   *He doesn't deny that he speaks badly about you.*

No me parece que entiendan el asunto.   *I don't think they understand the issue.*
Me parece que entienden el asunto.   *I think they understand the issue.*

Estructura y Práctica

O   *Imperativo y presente de subjuntivo.* Express each of the following **tú** commands as a sentence using the present subjunctive. Use the cues in parentheses. (To review the imperative, see Chapter 14.) Follow the *modelo*.

MODELO   Vive la vida plenamente. (Espero que)
       → Espero que vivas la vida plenamente.

1. Cuídate mucho. (Te aconsejo que)

2. Sal con nosotros al teatro. (Quiero que)

3. Córtate el pelo. (Es necesario que)

4. Apaga la computadora. (Hace falta que)

5. Ven a vernos hoy. (Es mejor que)

6. Hazme caso. (Insisto en que)

7. Ten paciencia. (Más vale que)

8. Diviértete mucho. (Me alegro de que)

9. Pruébate el abrigo azul marino. (Te recomiendo que)

10. Aprovéchate de las ofertas de enero. (Urge que)

P   Express the following sentences in Spanish, using the present subjunctive form of the verb.

1. *It's improbable that Pedro will get the position.*

2. *It's crucial that we support our friends.*

3. *Perhaps these foreign students [masc.] are of English descent.*

4. *It's a pity that Lupe can't find her earrings.*

5. *Laura and Sergio deny they're getting a divorce.*

6. *I've told the children to wash their hands.*

7. *It's better that you (tú) do your homework now.*

8. *It's bad that they don't get in touch with us more often.*

Un paso más

Are you ready to take your Spanish a step further? Here are exercises that will enhance your knowledge of the language and encourage you to express yourself freely.

Q *Más vale...* The impersonal expression **más vale** appears in many Spanish sayings and aphorisms. Express the following sayings in English, then write an explanation of the meaning in Spanish. Note that in these sayings, **más vale** is not followed by a verb in present subjunctive, but rather by an infinitive, a noun, or an adverb. (See the Answer Key for meanings.)

1. Más vale tarde que nunca.

2. Más vale estar solo que mal acompañado.

3. Más vale dar que recibir.

4. Más vale pájaro en mano que ciento volando. (volar (**o** > **ue**) (*to fly*))

5. Más vale arrepentirse de lo que se hizo que de lo que no se hizo.

6. Más vale prevenir que curar.

7. Más vale lo malo conocido que lo bueno por conocer.

8. Más vale la salud que el dinero.

R *Preguntas personales.* *Contesta las siguientes preguntas con oraciones completas en español.*

1. ¿Qué esperas lograr en tu vida personal y profesional?

2. ¿Qué quieres que tus hijos logren en su vida personal y profesional?

3. ¿Qué les aconsejas a tus amigos? ¿A tus padres e hijos?

4. ¿Qué te aconsejan tus amigos? ¿Tus familiares?

5. ¿Tienes una alma gemela (una media naranja) (*soulmate*)? ¿Quién es? ¿Cómo es?

6. ¿Crees que es importante tener una alma gemela? ¿Por qué?

7. ¿Te caen bien tus familiares políticos (*relatives by marriage*)? ¿Quiénes son?

8. En los diálogos 2 y 3 del capítulo 16, leíste conversaciones sobre las relaciones familiares. ¿Qué te parecen las ideas de los papás y las de sus hijos, Rosario y Jaime, con respecto al matrimonio? Compara sus ideas con las tuyas y con las de la sociedad norteamericana.

S *Mis sentimientos y pensamientos.* Complete each of the following phrases, using the present subjunctive to express your feelings and thoughts in Spanish.

1. Yo quiero que...

2. Yo espero que...

3. Yo necesito que...

4. Me alegro de que...

5. Siento que...

6. Dudo que...

7. Es importante que...

8. Es posible que...

9. Es bueno que...

10. Es imprescindible que...

11. Es una lástima que...

12. Ojalá...

Family and Friends

Communication Goals

- Talking about things that are happening or were happening
- Talking about the past and the more distant past
- Expressing a shift in focus from one part of the sentence to another
- Expressing to whom, for whom, from whom something is done, including the "interested bystander"
- Describing unplanned or unexpected occurrences
- Vocabulary: family relationships, an interactive museum, friends, celebrations, a day in the country

Grammar Topics

- The Progressive Tenses: Review and Expansion
- The Gerund
- Forms of the Progressive Tenses
- Uses of the Progressive Tenses
- The Perfect Tenses: Review and Expansion
- The Present Perfect
- The Past Perfect (Pluperfect)
- The Future Perfect and the Conditional Perfect
- The Passive Voice
- Other Ways of De-emphasizing the Performer of the Action
- The Indirect Object
- **Se me** Construction
- Indirect Commands

▶ DIÁLOGO 1 · ¡Al socorro!

Study the dialogue, then listen to the recording and repeat each line.

MIGUEL   Hermanita, ¿por qué estás levantando estas cajas tan pesadas tú sola?
          ¿No hay nadie para ayudarte?

SOFÍA   Pues tu cuñado está durmiendo la siesta. Me da pena despertarlo.

MIGUEL   Y mis sobrinos, ¿qué están haciendo? ¿Descansando también?

SOFÍA   ¡Qué va! Pablo está jugando al fútbol y Diego está haciendo una
          videollamada con su novia. Y Laura, hace un rato estaba estudiando
          para un examen.

LAURA   (*Entra repentinamente.*) No te preocupes, mamita, yo te ayudo.
          ¡El tío Miguel y yo al socorro!

Análisis

Check that you understand the linguistic breakdown of each speech from *Diálogo 1.*

¡Al socorro!	*To the rescue!*
Hermanita, ¿por qué estás levantando estas cajas tan pesadas tú sola? ¿No hay nadie para ayudarte?	*My dear sister, why are you lifting these heavy boxes all by yourself? Is there nobody to help you?*
hermanita (*diminutive*)	*my dear sister* (literally, *little sister*)
¿por qué?	*why?*
estás	*you are*
levantando (*gerund*)	*lifting*
estás levantando	*you are lifting*
la caja	*box*
pesado	*heavy*
solo	*alone*
Pues tu cuñado está durmiendo la siesta. Me da pena despertarlo.	*Well, your brother-in-law is taking a nap. It's a pity to wake him up.*
el cuñado	*brother-in-law*
está	*he is*
dormir la siesta	*to take a nap*
durmiendo (*gerund*)	*sleeping*
está durmiendo	*he's sleeping*
la siesta	*nap*
está durmiendo la siesta	*he's napping, he's taking a nap*
la pena	*sorrow, pity*
dar pena	*to make (someone) feel sad/sorry*
despertarlo	*to wake him up*
me da pena despertarlo	*it's a pity/shame to wake him up*
Y mis sobrinos, ¿qué están haciendo? ¿Descansando también?	*And my nephews and niece? What are they doing? Also resting?*
el sobrino	*nephew*
los sobrinos	*nephews, nephew(s) and niece(s)*
haciendo (*gerund*)	*doing*

están haciendo	*they are doing*
descansando (*gerund*)	*resting*

¡Qué va! Pablo está jugando al fútbol y Diego está haciendo una videollamada con su novia. Y Laura, hace un rato estaba estudiando para un examen.	*You must be joking! Pablo is playing soccer and Diego is videochatting with his girlfriend. And Laura, a little while ago she was studying for an exam.*
¡Qué va!	*You must be joking! / No way!*
jugando (*gerund*)	*playing*
jugar al fútbol	*to play soccer*
está jugando al fútbol	*he's playing soccer*
la videollamada	*videochat*
está haciendo una videollamada	*he's videochatting*
la novia	*girlfriend*
hace un rato	*a little while ago*
estaba	*she was*
estudiando (*gerund*)	*studying*
el examen	*exam*

(*Entra repentinamente.*) No te preocupes, mamita, yo te ayudo. ¡El tío Miguel y yo al socorro!	(She enters suddenly.) *Don't worry, mommy, I'll help you. Uncle Miguel and I to the rescue!*
entra	*she enters*
repentinamente	*suddenly*
entra repentinamente	*she enters suddenly, she bursts in*
preocuparse	*to worry*
No te preocupes.	*Don't worry.*
mamita (*diminutive*)	*dearest mom* (term of endearment)
ayudo	*I'll help*
yo te ayudo	*I'll help you*
el tío	*uncle*
el socorro	*help, aid*
¡al socorro!	*to the rescue!*

⏵ Variantes

Listen, and repeat the same structures from *Diálogo 1*, now with new vocabulary.

¿Qué están haciendo ?	*What are they **doing**?*
mandando	*sending*
enviando	*sending*
comiendo	*eating*
aprendiendo	*learning*
escribiendo	*writing*
mirando	*looking at*
diciendo	*saying*
trayendo	*bringing*
construyendo	*building*
sirviendo	*serving*
pidiendo	*asking for*

Estaba **estudiando diseño de web** .   He was **studying web design**.
    trabajando en equipo   working on a team
    creando una base de datos   creating a database
    analizando el presupuesto   analyzing the budget
    leyendo el contrato   reading the contract
    desarrollando software   developing software
    imprimiendo los documentos   printing the documents
    buscando una tienda de cómputo   looking for a computer store
    escuchando las noticias   listening to the news

Me da pena verla tan decaída.   **I'm sorry** to see her so down.
    Le da pena (a él)   He's sorry
    Nos da pena   We're sorry
    Te da pena   You're sorry
    Les da pena   They're sorry
    Le da pena (a Ud.)   You're sorry
    Les da pena (a Uds.)   You're sorry
    Le da pena (a ella)   She's sorry

IDIOMS AND EXPRESSIONS WITH **LA PENA** (*SORROW, PITY*)

¡Qué pena! *What a shame! / What a pity!*

valer la pena, merecer la pena *to be worth the trouble, be worth the effort*
    No vale la pena discutir este   *It's not worth the trouble to discuss this*
        asunto más.   *matter anymore.*

a duras penas *with difficulty, hardly, barely*
    Lograron terminar la tarea   *They barely managed to finish the task.*
        a duras penas.

sin pena ni gloria *uneventful, unremarkable, unnoticed*
    El año pasó sin pena ni gloria.   *It was an uneventful year.*

tener una pena *to be sad*
    La pobre mujer tiene una pena   *The poor woman is very sad.*
        muy grande.

Estructura y Práctica

THE PROGRESSIVE TENSES: REVIEW AND EXPANSION

In this chapter, you will review and practice the progressive tenses, which were intro-duced for recognition purposes only in Chapter 13. Like the perfect tenses, the progres-sive tenses are also compound tenses because they consist of two parts: an auxiliary verb and the present participle.

The Gerund

The gerund in Spanish is the form of the verb that ends in **-ndo**, corresponding to the *-ing* form in English: **hablando** (*talking*). The Spanish gerund, in contrast to the English *-ing* form, cannot be used as a noun. (Compare English *smoking is bad for your health* with Spanish **fumar es malo para la salud**.) It functions rather as the English present participle. Thus, the most frequent use of the gerund in Spanish is to form the progressive tenses with the verb **estar**.

When the Spanish gerund stands alone (that is, it is not part of a progressive construction), it is usually equivalent to an English clause or gerund phrase beginning with *by*, *while*, *if*, *when*, or *because*.

Siguiendo una dieta sana, tendrás más energía.	***By following*** *a healthy diet, you'll have more energy.*
Mario se quebró el dedo **jugando** al tenis.	*Mario broke his finger **while playing** tennis.*

With verbs of perception, such as **ver**, **mirar**, **oír**, and **escuchar**, either the infinitive or the gerund can be used, as in English.

La vimos regar las flores. ⎫
La vimos regando las flores. ⎭   *We saw her water/watering the flowers.*

A Write sentences from the elements given, using the verb of perception in the preterit. Write two sentences for each item—one using the gerund, the other using the infinitive. Follow the *modelo*.

MODELO   ella / ver trotar / a Diego
→ Ella lo vio trotando.
→ Ella lo vio trotar.

1. él / oír ladrar / al perro

2. yo / observar cocinar / a la jefa de cocina

3. ellos / escuchar cantar / a las cantantes

4. Uds. / oír reír / a esos jóvenes

5. nosotros / mirar actuar / a los actores

6. tú / ver correr / a la atleta

7. Ud. / observar sonreír / a las niñas

8. ella / escuchar gritar con alegría / a los aficionados

9. yo / mirar dormir / al bebé

10. tú y yo / oír estornudar (*to sneeze*) / a nuestra hermana

Forms of the Progressive Tenses

The progressive tenses consist of the present, imperfect, preterit, future, and conditional forms of the verb **estar**, followed by the gerund (present participle).

PRESENT PROGRESSIVE   **Estoy trabajando** en el proyecto a distancia.
I'm working on the project remotely.

IMPERFECT PROGRESSIVE   **Estaba trabajando** en el proyecto a distancia.
I was working on the project remotely.

PRETERIT PROGRESSIVE	**Estuve trabajando** en el proyecto a distancia hasta la medianoche.
	I was working on the project remotely until midnight.
FUTURE PROGRESSIVE	**Estaré trabajando** en el proyecto a distancia.
	I'll be working on the project remotely.
CONDITIONAL PROGRESSIVE	**Estaría trabajando** en el proyecto a distancia.
	I'd be working on the project remotely.

Uses of the Progressive Tenses

The present, imperfect, future, and conditional progressive tenses emphasize that the action *is, was, will be,* or *would be* in progress. The preterit progressive, a less frequently used tense, usually appears in a sentence where the end of the action is specified and, like all preterits, implies a completed action. It conveys the idea of an action going on in the past, but ended.

Estuve haciendo cola hasta que abrieron la taquilla.	*I was standing in line until the box office opened.*
Estuvo poniendo la mesa hasta que llegaron los invitados.	*She was setting the table until the guests arrived.*

The present, imperfect, and future progressive tenses may indicate that an action is temporary or that it represents a change from the usual pattern.

—Siempre se quejan de que la comida del Café Dulce es pésima.	*They always complain that Café Dulce's food is awful.*
—¿Ah sí? ¡Pues están cenando allí en este momento!	*Oh, really? Well, they're having dinner there right now!*

The present progressive in Spanish can never refer to the future, as the present progressive in English does. To express future time, Spanish uses the simple present, the **ir a** + infinitive construction, or the future tense. Be aware that English-speaking learners of Spanish tend to overuse the present progressive, a tense that in Spanish is reserved for actions going on at the moment of speech.

Su equipo **comienza** el proyecto la semana que viene.	*Their team **is starting** the project next week.*
Su equipo **va a comenzar** el proyecto la semana que viene.	*Their team **is going to start** the project next week.*
Su equipo **comenzará** el proyecto la semana que viene.	*Their team **will start** the project next week.*

The sentence **El equipo está comenzando el proyecto** can only mean *The team is starting the project (right now).*

The simple imperfect is used to convey both a habitual action in the past and a continuing action in the past. The imperfect progressive, however, cannot be used for a habitual action, only for a continuing one.

Mireia tocaba el piano.	*Mireia used to play the piano.* (every day or at a particular time in the past)
Mireia estaba tocando el piano.	*Mireia was playing the piano.* (at a particular time in the past)

B Rewrite each of the following sentences, changing the verb from the present indicative to the present progressive. Follow the *modelo*.

MODELO   Paga las cuentas.
         → Está pagando las cuentas.

1. Paseamos al perro.

2. Corre el maratón.

3. Discuten por nada.

4. Leo una novela distópica.

5. ¿Pruebas la sopa de ajo (*garlic*)?

6. Salgo de la oficina.

7. Siente muchas emociones.

8. Envuelve el regalo de cumpleaños.

9. Abrimos una cuenta de ahorros.

10. ¿Empiezan a grabar la película?

11. Llueve muy fuerte.

12. Oigo un ruido.

C *En el preescolar* (In preschool). Rewrite each of the following sentences, in which Miguelito describes what he and his friends were doing at school. Change the verb from the imperfect to the imperfect progressive. Follow the *modelo*.

MODELO   Los niños practicaban ortografía (*spelling*).
         → Los niños estaban practicando ortografía.

1. Yo hacía unos carritos de plastilina (*playdough*).

2. Uds. saltaban a la cuerda. (saltar a la cuerda (*to jump rope*))

3. Carlitos aprendía el alfabeto.

4. Tú armabas un rompecabezas (*jigsaw puzzle*).

5. Clarita vestía a su oso de peluche (*teddy bear*).

6. Paquito y yo construíamos un castillo medieval de cubos (*blocks*).

7. Marisol leía unos cuentos de hadas (*fairy tales*).

8. Todos nosotros jugábamos al escondite (*hide-and-seek*).

▶ DIÁLOGO 2 · Una visita al museo interactivo (1)

Study the dialogue, then listen to the recording and repeat each line.

RAQUEL   ¡Estoy rendida! Juanito sigue corriendo por las salas. Estoy volviéndome
         loca andando en pos de él.

JAIME   ¡Y sigue haciendo travesuras! Un guardia hasta tuvo que regañarlo.

RAQUEL   El niño va de una exposición interactiva a otra. Juanito, ¡ven acá!

JUANITO Pero mami, me encanta pulsar los botones y tocar la pantalla táctil.
         ¡Es muy divertido!

Análisis

Check that you understand the linguistic breakdown of each speech from *Diálogo 2*.

Una visita al museo interactivo	*A visit to the interactive museum*
¡Estoy rendida! Juanito sigue corriendo por las salas. Estoy volviéndome loca andando en pos de él.	*I'm worn out! Juanito keeps on running through the rooms. I'm going crazy chasing after him.*
rendido	*exhausted, worn-out*
sigue	*he continues*
corriendo (*gerund*)	*running*
sigue corriendo	*he keeps on running*
la sala	*room (museum)*
volverse (**o** > **ue**) + *adjective*	*to go/become + adjective*
loco	*crazy*
volviéndome (*gerund*)	*(I'm) going, (I'm) becoming*
estoy volviéndome loca	*I'm going crazy*
andando (*gerund*) en pos de él	*chasing/running after him*
¡Y sigue haciendo travesuras! Un guardia hasta tuvo que regañarlo.	*And he keeps on making mischief! A guard even had to scold him.*
haciendo (*gerund*)	*making, doing*
las travesuras	*pranks, mischief*
haciendo travesuras	*making mischief, being mischievous*
el guardia	*guard*
hasta	*even*
tuvo	*he had (preterit of **tener**)*
tener que + *infinitive*	*he had to + verb*
regañar	*to scold*
hasta tuvo que regañarlo	*he even had to scold him*
El niño va de una exposición interactiva a otra. Juanito, ¡ven acá!	*The child goes from one interactive exhibit to another. Juanito, come here!*
va	*he goes (**ir**)*
la exposición	*exhibit*
interactivo	*interactive*
de una exposición interactiva a otra	*from one interactive exhibit to another*
ven	*come (**tú** command form of **venir**)*

acá	*here*
¡ven acá!	*come here!*

Pero mami, me encanta pulsar los botones y tocar la pantalla táctil. ¡Es muy divertido!	*But mommy, I love to press the buttons and touch the touch screen. It's a lot of fun!*
mami	*mommy*
me encanta	*I love it*
pulsar	*to press*
los botones (el botón)	*buttons*
tocar	*to touch*
la pantalla	*screen*
táctil	*touch* (adjective)
la pantalla táctil	*touch screen*
me encanta pulsar los botones	*I love to press the buttons*
me encanta tocar la pantalla táctil	*I love to touch the touch screen*
divertido	*fun, entertaining*
es muy divertido	*it's a lot of fun*

Variantes

Listen, and repeat the same structures from *Diálogo 2*, now with new vocabulary.

Sigue corriendo .	*He keeps on **running**.*
saltando	*jumping*
riendo (riéndose)	*laughing*
hablando	*speaking*
soñando	*dreaming*
llorando	*crying*
bromeando	*joking around*
bostezando	*yawning*
estornudando	*sneezing*
tosiendo	*coughing*
roncando	*snoring*
chismeando	*gossiping*
mintiendo	*lying*

Estoy volviéndome loca .	*I'm **going crazy**.*
emocionándome	*getting excited*
divirtiéndome	*having fun*
relajándome	*relaxing*
enojándome	*getting angry*
enfadándome	*getting angry*
aburriéndome	*getting bored*
tranquilizándome	*calming down*
calmándome	*calming down*
animándome	*cheering up*
preocupándome	*getting worried*

Me estoy volviendo loca .	*I'm **going crazy**.*
emocionando	*getting excited*
divirtiendo	*having fun*
relajando	*relaxing*
enojando	*getting angry*
enfadando	*getting angry*
aburriendo	*getting bored*
tranquilizando	*calming down*
calmando	*calming down*
animando	*cheering up*
preocupando	*getting worried*

▶ DIÁLOGO 3 · Una visita al museo interactivo (2)

Study the dialogue, then listen to the recording and repeat each line.

JAIME   Raquel, ¿te fijas en lo corto que es el período de atención de Juanito?

RAQUEL   Sí, no dura más de dos minutos. ¿Qué le estará pasando a ese muchacho?

JAIME   Nuestro hijo estará sufriendo de un exceso de interactividad.

RAQUEL   La próxima vez lo llevaremos a un museo donde tenga que leer más
          y jugar menos.

Análisis

Check that you understand the linguistic breakdown of each speech from *Diálogo 3*.

Raquel, ¿te fijas en lo corto que es el período de atención de Juanito?	*Raquel, do you notice how short Juanito's attention span is?*
te fijas	*you notice*
fijarse en	*to notice*
lo corto	*how short*
¿te fijas en lo corto?	*do you notice how short?*
el período de atención	*attention span*

Sí, no dura más de dos minutos. ¿Qué le estará pasando a ese muchacho?	*Yes, it doesn't last more than two minutes. What can be wrong with that boy?*
durar	*to last*
más de + *number*	*more than* + number
el minuto	*minute*
más de dos minutos	*more than two minutes*
pasando (*gerund*)	*happening*
estará (*future of probability or conjecture*)	*it will be, it's probably*
le estará pasando	*it's probably happening to him*
¿Qué le estará pasando?	*What might be happening to him? / What can be wrong with him?*

Nuestro hijo estará sufriendo de un exceso de interactividad.	*Our son is probably suffering from too much interactivity.*
nuestro hijo	*our son*
sufriendo (*gerund*)	*suffering*

estará sufriendo de	*he's probably suffering from*
el exceso	*excess*
la interactividad	*interactivity*
un exceso de interactividad	*too much interactivity*

La próxima vez lo llevaremos a un museo donde tenga que leer más y jugar menos.	*Next time we'll take him to a museum where he has to read more and play less.*
la vez	*time, occasion*
próximo	*next*
la próxima vez	*next time*
lo llevaremos	*we'll take him*
el museo	*museum*
tenga que (*subjunctive*)	*he has to (**tener**)*
leer	*to read*
donde tenga que leer	*where he has to read*
jugar (**u** > **ue**)	*to play*
donde tenga que leer más y jugar menos	*where he has to read more and play less*

▶ Variantes

Listen, and repeat the same structures from *Diálogo 3*, now with new vocabulary.

¿Qué estarán haciendo ?	*What might they be **doing**?*
creyendo	*thinking*
pensando	*thinking*
planeando	*planning*
exigiendo	*demanding*
sugiriendo	*suggesting*
proponiendo	*proposing*
llevando	*carrying, wearing*
celebrando	*celebrating*

¿Qué le estará pasando a ese niño?	*What can be wrong with that little boy?*
Es un niño mimado .	*He's **a spoiled brat**.*
un niño consentido	*a spoiled brat*
un niño engreído	*a spoiled brat*
un niño malcriado	*a spoiled brat*
un mocoso	*a brat*
un escuincle	*a brat* (Mexico)
un niño maleducado	*a rude little boy*

¿Qué le estará pasando a esa niña?	*What can be wrong with that little girl?*
Es una niña mimada .	*She's **a spoiled brat**.*
una niña consentida	*a spoiled brat*
una niña engreída	*a spoiled brat*
una niña malcriada	*a spoiled brat*
una mocosa	*a brat*
una escuincla	*a brat* (México)
una niña maleducada	*a rude little girl*

IDIOMS AND EXPRESSIONS WITH HACER

hacer pedazos *to break to pieces*
¡Qué niño más travieso!	*What a mischievous child!*
El pobre robot, lo ha hecho pedazos.	*The poor robot, he's broken it to pieces.*

hacerle gracia a alguien *to find something amusing; to like*
Para ser sincero, su actitud no me hace ninguna gracia.	*To tell the truth, I don't like their attitude.*

hacérsele agua la boca *to make someone's mouth water*
El rico aroma del guiso me está haciendo agua la boca.	*The delicious aroma of the stew is making my mouth water.*

hacer la vista gorda *to turn a blind eye; to pretend not to notice*
¿Cómo se puede hacer la vista gorda a los efectos negativos de las redes sociales?	*How can people turn a blind eye to the negative effects of social media?*

hacerse el sordo *to turn a deaf ear; to ignore or refuse to listen to what someone says*
Se hace el sordo cada vez que le damos consejos.	*He turns a deaf ear every time we give him advice.*

hacerse a la idea *to accept the idea, fact, or situation as it is*
Tienes que hacerte a la idea de que nunca podrás volver a tu patria.	*You have to accept the idea that you'll never be able to go back to your home country.*

Estructura y Práctica

Using the Future Progressive and the Conditional Progressive to Express Probability or Conjecture

The future and conditional progressive tenses may be used to express probability or conjecture. As with the simple future and conditional of probability, the future progressive expresses probability or conjecture about the present, the conditional progressive about the past. (See also Chapter 15.)

¿Por qué estarán llamando?	*I wonder why they're calling.*
—Mateo no pudo asistir a la boda.	*Mateo couldn't attend the wedding.*
—Estaría haciendo un viaje de negocios.	*He was probably on a business trip. / He was probably traveling on business.*

In the progressive tenses, object pronouns and reflexive pronouns may either precede the form of **estar** or follow the gerund. They are attached to the gerund in writing, in which case an accent mark is written over the **a** or **e** of the -**ndo** ending.

Te están buscando. Están buscándote.	*They're looking for you.*
¿El email? Se lo estoy escribiendo. ¿El email? Estoy escribiéndoselo.	*The email? I'm writing it to him.*

Nos estábamos divirtiendo mucho. ⎫
Estábamos divirtiéndonos mucho. ⎭   *We were having a great time.*

Se estarán mudando para esas fechas. ⎫
Estarán mudándose para esas fechas. ⎭   *They'll be moving by then.*

D Write sentences from the elements given, using either the present progressive or the imperfect progressive as indicated in parentheses. Change direct object nouns to pronouns and make all necessary changes. Write each sentence in two ways, according to the *modelos*.

> MODELOS   tú / mandarme el paquete (*present*)
>   → Tú estás mandándomelo.
>   → Tú me lo estás mandando.
>
>   él / pasearse (*imperfect*)
>   → Él estaba paseándose.
>   → Él se estaba paseando.

1. yo / abrir los paquetes (*present*)

2. Uds. / ¿esperar al programador? (*imperfect*)

3. nosotros / servirles la comida (*present*)

4. ella / quejarse de todo (*imperfect*)

5. yo / ponerme la chaqueta (*present*)

6. Ud. / ¿leerles el cuento? (*imperfect*)

7. ellos / tranquilizarse (*present*)

8. tú / decirle la verdad (*imperfect*)

9. él / probarse los zapatos (*present*)

10. Uds. / lavarse las manos (*imperfect*)

E **Probability or conjecture.** Express each of the following sentences in Spanish, using the future progressive to express probability or conjecture. Follow the *modelo*.

> MODELO   *What could be happening to them?*
>   → ¿Qué les estará pasando?

1. *They could be getting sick.*

2. *José is probably walking the dog.*

3. *Luz could be planning the birthday party.*

4. *They are probably having a lot of fun.*

5. *What could you* (tú) *be thinking about?*

6. *He's probably taking a nap.*

7. *What books might you* (Ud.) *be reading?*

8. *It's probably raining already.*

9. *The team is probably finishing the project.*

10. *The kids could be going crazy!*

Estructura y Práctica

Other Verbs Used in Progressive Constructions

Verbs other than **estar** are used in progressive constructions. The verb **seguir** is used with the gerund to mean *to be still doing something, keep on doing something*. **Ir** is used with the gerund to mean *to be doing something gradually* or *to be doing something little by little*. **Andar** is used with the gerund to convey the idea of *going around doing something* and may suggest aimlessness.

Seguimos pasando los veranos en la sierra.	*We still spend our summers in the mountains.*
¡Sigues fastidiando a tu hermanito!	*You keep on teasing your little brother!*
Los casos de gripe iban disminuyendo.	*The cases of flu were gradually decreasing.*
El tipo andaba metiéndose en líos.	*The guy went around getting into trouble.*

The **llevar** + **-ndo** (gerund) construction expresses actions that began in the past and are continuing into the present. It is the equivalent of **hace** + time expression + **que** + verb in the present tense and **desde hace** + time expression. (See Chapter 6.)

Llevan dos años trabajando en el extranjero.
Hace dos años que trabajan en el extranjero. } *They've been working abroad for two*
Trabajan en el extranjero desde hace dos años. *years.*

Note that the gerund of **estar** is not used in the **llevar** + gerund construction. **Llevar** is used by itself to express *to have been*.

Llevan mucho tiempo en este país.	*They've been in this country for a long time.*

Other verbs of motion such as **salir**, **entrar**, **llegar**, **subir**, and **bajar** can be used with the gerund to specify how the motion was performed. English usually distinguishes the different types of motion with an adverbial complement such as *out*, *in*, *into*, *up*, or *down*.

El ladrón **salió corriendo**.	*The thief ran out.*
Los bomberos **entraron corriendo**.	*The firefighters ran in.*
Las niñas **subieron corriendo**.	*The girls ran up the stairs.*
Su perro **bajó la escalera corriendo**.	*His dog ran down the stairs.*

F   *Todo sigue igual.* Answer each of the following questions using **seguir** + the gerund to say that things are continuing as before. Change direct object nouns to pronouns. Write each answer in two ways, according to the *modelo*.

MODELO   Y Uds., ¿todavía estudian japonés?
      → Sí, seguimos estudiándolo.
      → Sí, lo seguimos estudiando.

1. Y tú, ¿todavía lees novelas de misterio?

2. Y Diego, ¿todavía corre el maratón?

3. Y Uds., ¿todavía pintan pinturas con acuarelas (*watercolors*)?

4. Y Ud., ¿todavía enseña microbiología?

5. Y Olivia, ¿todavía ayuda a los discapacitados (*disabled*)?

6. Y los gerentes, ¿todavía escriben planes de negocios?

7. Y tú, ¿todavía resuelves problemas estratégicos?

8. Y Uds., ¿todavía toman clases a distancia?

🅓 DIÁLOGO 4 · ¡Vivan las gangas!

Study the dialogue, then listen to the recording and repeat each line.

CAMILA	Está lloviendo a cántaros. ¿Seguimos caminando o tomamos un taxi?
SARA	Nos estamos mojando hasta los huesos. Vamos a buscar un taxi.
CAMILA	Yo no veo ninguno desocupado. Mira, las bolsas de las tiendas por departamentos están empapadas.
SARA	El paraguas no nos está protegiendo del aguacero.
CAMILA	¿Por qué no entramos en el café que está en la esquina? Podemos tomar un té y esperar hasta que deje de llover.
SARA	Excelente idea. Y vamos a echar un vistazo a la linda ropa que compramos a precios rebajados.
CAMILA Y SARA	(*Gritan juntas.*) ¡Vivan las gangas!

Análisis

Check that you understand the linguistic breakdown of each speech from *Diálogo 4*.

¡Vivan las gangas!	*Hooray for bargains!*
Está lloviendo a cántaros. ¿Seguimos caminando o tomamos un taxi?	*It's pouring. Should we keep on walking or take a taxi?*
llover (**o** > **ue**)	*to rain*
está lloviendo	*it's raining*
el cántaro	*pitcher, jug*
está lloviendo a cántaros	*it's pouring, it's raining cats and dogs*
seguir (**e** > **i**)	*to follow; to continue*
seguimos	*we continue*
caminando (*gerund*)	*walking*
seguimos caminando	*we keep on walking*
tomamos un taxi	*we take a taxi*
Nos estamos mojando hasta los huesos. Vamos a buscar un taxi.	*We're getting soaked to the bone. Let's look for a taxi.*
mojarse	*to get wet*
nos estamos mojando	*we're getting wet*
el hueso	*bone*
nos estamos mojando hasta los huesos	*we're getting soaked to the bone, we're getting drenched*
buscar	*to look for*

Yo no veo ninguno desocupado.	*I don't see a single empty taxi.*
Mira, las bolsas de las tiendas por departamentos están empapadas.	*Look, the bags from the department stores are soaked.*
desocupado	*empty*
mira	*look* (**tú** command form of **mirar**)
la bolsa	*bag*
la tienda por departamentos	*department store*
empapado	*soaked*

El paraguas no nos está protegiendo del aguacero.	*Our umbrella isn't protecting us from the downpour.*
el paraguas	*umbrella*
proteger (yo protejo)	*to protect, shield*
protegiendo (*gerund*)	*protecting*
no nos está protegiendo	*it's not protecting*
el aguacero	*downpour*

¿Por qué no entramos en el café que está en la esquina? Podemos tomar un té y esperar hasta que deje de llover.	*Why don't we go into the café on the corner? We can have a cup of tea and wait until it stops raining.*
entramos en	*we enter, we go in*
la esquina	*corner*
el té	*tea*
dejar de + *infinitive*	*to stop (doing something)*
dejar de llover	*to stop raining*
hasta que deje de llover	*until it stops raining*

Excelente idea. Y vamos a echar un vistazo a la linda ropa que compramos a precios rebajados.	*Excellent idea. And let's peek at the lovely clothing we bought at reduced prices.*
(*Gritan juntas.*) ¡Vivan las gangas!	(*They shout together.*) *Hooray for bargains!*

▶ Variantes

Listen, and repeat the same structures from *Diálogo 4*, now with new vocabulary.

Está lloviendo .	*It's **raining**.*
nevando	*snowing*
lloviznando	*drizzling*
haciendo sol	*sunny*
haciendo calor	*hot*
haciendo mucho frío	*very cold*
haciendo viento	*windy*
haciendo buen tiempo	*nice weather*
haciendo mal tiempo	*bad weather*

Nos estamos mojando .	We're **getting wet**.
lavando	*washing up*
duchando	*showering*
bañando	*bathing*
secando	*getting dry, drying off*
peinando	*combing our hair*
vistiendo	*getting dressed*
acostando	*going to bed*
durmiendo	*falling asleep*
despertando	*waking up*
levantando	*getting up*
Estamos mojándonos .	We're **getting wet**.
lavándonos	*washing up*
duchándonos	*showering*
bañándonos	*bathing*
secándonos	*getting dry, drying off*
peinándonos	*combing our hair*
vistiéndonos	*getting dressed*
acostándonos	*going to bed*
durmiéndonos	*falling asleep*
despertándonos	*waking up*
levantándonos	*getting up*
¿Seguimos caminando ?	*Should we keep on **walking**?*
andando	*walking*
manejando	*driving*
conduciendo	*driving*

▶ DIÁLOGO 5 · Una historia de éxito

Study the dialogue, then listen to the recording and repeat each line.

MATEO   Yo estaba trotando en el parque ayer y ¿a que no sabes con quién me encontré? ¡Jaime Vega!

ISABEL   ¡No me digas! Si no recuerdo mal, Jaime estaba trabajando de consultor cuando lo conocimos. ¿Sigue trabajando para la misma empresa?

MATEO   Ya no. Renunció a su puesto y lleva tres años dirigiendo su propia consultoría. Va teniendo mucho éxito.

ISABEL   Estará trabajando como un burro.

MATEO   Ya lo creo. ¡Y estará ganando una fortuna!

Análisis

Check that you understand the linguistic breakdown of each speech from *Diálogo 5*.

Una historia de éxito	*A success story*

Yo estaba trotando en el parque ayer y ¿a que no sabes con quién me encontré? ¡Jaime Vega!	*I was jogging in the park yesterday and I bet you don't know whom I ran into. Jaime Vega!*
trotando (*gerund*)	*jogging*
estaba trotando	*I was jogging*
el parque	*park*
ayer	*yesterday*
a que no sabes	*I bet you don't know*
con quién	*with whom*
encontrarse (**o** > **ue**) con	*to run into*
me encontré con	*I ran into*

¡No me digas! Si no recuerdo mal, Jaime estaba trabajando de consultor cuando lo conocimos. ¿Sigue trabajando para la misma empresa?	*You don't say! If I remember correctly, Jaime was working as a consultant when we met him. Is he still working for the same firm?*
¡No me digas!	*You don't say!*
recordar (**o** > **ue**)	*to remember*
recuerdo	*I remember*
si no recuerdo mal	*if I remember correctly*
trabajando (*gerund*)	*working*
estaba trabajando	*he was working*
el consultor	*consultant*
trabajar de + *profession*	*to work as a* + profession
estaba trabajando de consultor	*he was working as a consultant*
conocimos	*we met*
cuando lo conocimos	*when we met him*
seguir (**e** > **i**)	*to follow; to continue*
sigue	*he continues*
sigue trabajando	*he's still working*
la empresa	*firm, company*
para la misma empresa	*for the same firm*

Ya no. Renunció a su puesto y lleva tres años dirigiendo su propia consultoría. Va teniendo mucho éxito.	*Not anymore. He quit his job and has been running his own consulting firm for three years. He's becoming very successful.*
ya no	*no longer, not anymore*
renunció	*he quit, he resigned*
el puesto	*job, position*
renunció a su puesto	*he quit his job*
dirigiendo (*gerund*)	*running* (a business) (**dirigir**)
lleva tres años dirigiendo	*he has been running* (a business) *for three years*
la consultoría	*consulting firm, consultancy*

su propia consultoría	his own consulting firm
tener mucho éxito	to be very successful
va teniendo (**ir** + *gerund*)	he's becoming
va teniendo mucho éxito	he's becoming very successful

Estará trabajando como un burro.	He's probably working like a dog.
estará trabajando	he's probably working
trabajar como un burro	to work like a dog

Ya lo creo. ¡Y estará ganando una fortuna!	You bet. And he's probably making a fortune!
ya lo creo	you bet
ganando (*gerund*)	earning
estará ganando	he's probably earning
la fortuna	fortune
ganar una fortuna	to make a fortune
estará ganando una fortuna	he's probably making a fortune

▶ Variantes

Listen, and repeat the same structures from *Diálogo 5*, now with new vocabulary.

¿Sigue trabajando de consultor ?	Is he still **working as a consultant**?
dirigiendo la empresa	running the company
encargándose de las inversiones	in charge of investments
ocupándose de la ciberseguridad	responsible for cybersecurity
solicitando un empleo	applying for a job
lanzando una campaña publicitaria	launching a publicity campaign
elaborando soluciones innovadoras	coming up with innovative solutions, coming up with cutting-edge solutions

Estábamos trotando en el parque.	We were **jogging** in the park.
dando un paseo	walking, strolling
paseándonos	walking, strolling
montando en bicicleta	taking a bicycle ride
montando a caballo	horseback riding
jugando al fútbol	playing soccer
patinando sobre ruedas	roller-skating
observando pájaros	bird-watching

Lleva una hora haciendo llamadas .	She has been **making phone calls** for an hour.
leyendo su email	reading her email
creando archivos	creating files
redactando documentos	editing documents
almacenando datos	storing data
recuperando datos	retrieving data
haciendo copias de seguridad	making backup copies
organizando carpetas	organizing folders
llevando a cabo múltiples tareas	multitasking

Va teniendo éxito .	*He's gradually **becoming successful**.*
alcanzando sus objetivos	*achieving his goals*
promoviendo el nuevo producto	*promoting the new product*
abriendo sucursales	*opening branch offices*
explotando los medios sociales	*making use of social media*
contratando a más gerentes de proyecto	*hiring more product managers*
aumentando los sueldos	*raising salaries*
haciendo crecer la compañía	*growing the company*

G *Del pasado al presente.* Answer each of the following questions, using the **llevar** + **-ndo** (gerund) construction instead of the **cuánto hace** + time expression + **que** + verb construction of the question. Use the time cues in parentheses. Change direct object nouns to pronouns. Follow the *modelo*.

MODELO   ¿Cuánto tiempo hace que estudias español? (dos años)
         → Llevo dos años estudiándolo.

1. ¿Cuánto tiempo hace que Uds. viven en Panamá? (cinco años)

2. ¿Cuánto tiempo hace que Rafael trabaja de jefe de cocina (*head chef*)? (siete años)

3. ¿Cuánto tiempo hace que haces videollamadas? (cuatro meses)

4. ¿Cuánto tiempo hace que Elena y Mario juegan al tenis? (una hora)

5. ¿Cuánto tiempo hace que el maestro Leonardo Ámbar dirige su orquesta? (dieciocho años)

6. ¿Cuánto tiempo hace que Ud. cocina platos vegetarianos? (ocho meses)

7. ¿Cuánto tiempo hace que elaboras el presupuesto? (tres días)

8. ¿Cuánto tiempo hace que Uds. imprimen los informes? (cuarenta minutos)

H **Translation.** Express each of the following sentences in Spanish, using progressive constructions in your answers.

1. *It was snowing when we arrived.*

2. *Jorge is still working like a dog.*

3. *What a downpour! I'm getting soaked to the bone.*

4. *You (tú) have been trying on shoes for two hours!*

5. *The little girl is learning to count little by little.*

6. *Are they still waiting for us?*

7. *These students are gradually mastering Spanish.*

8. *What might our friends be doing?*

9. *They're probably attending a concert.*

10. *We were getting together to discuss the project.*

Estructura y Práctica

THE PERFECT TENSES: REVIEW AND EXPANSION

The Present Perfect

Both Spanish and English have a series of compound tenses called the perfect tenses. They are called compound tenses because they consist of two parts: an auxiliary verb and the past participle.

In Chapter 13, you learned the present perfect tense, a tense that consists of the present tense of the auxiliary verb **haber** + the past participle. The present perfect expresses a completed action in the past that is seen as having a connection with or an effect on the present moment.

—No hay nada que comer en la nevera.	*There's nothing to eat in the refrigerator.*
—Lo siento. No **he hecho** la compra.	*I'm sorry. I haven't done the shopping.*
—**¿Has visto** a los Morales hoy?	*Have you seen the Morales today?*
—No. Creo que **han salido** de viaje.	*No. I think they've left on a trip.*
—La casa es un desastre.	*The house is a mess.*
—¡Caramba! ¿Qué **ha sucedido**?	*Oh, no! What's happened?*

In all the perfect tenses, object pronouns and reflexive pronouns precede the forms of the auxiliary verb.

—¿Van a ver esta película?	*Are you going to see this film?*
—No. Ya **la hemos visto**.	*No. We've already seen it.*
—¿Vas a lavarte el pelo?	*Are you going to wash your hair?*
—Ya **me lo he lavado**.	*I've already washed it.*
—Los niños deben ponerse los zapatos.	*The children should put on their shoes.*
—Míralos. Ya **se los han puesto**.	*Look at them. They've already put them on.*
—Hace frío en la casa, ¿verdad?	*It's cold in the house, isn't it?*
—Sí. Creo que **se ha descompuesto** la calefacción.	*Yes. I think the heating system has broken down.*
—Uds. deben enseñarles sus pinturas.	*You should show them your paintings.*
—Ya **se las hemos enseñado**.	*We've already shown them to them.*
—Eva dice que ya tiene copia del informe.	*Eva says she already has a copy of the report.*
—Es que yo **se la había enviado**.	*Yes, that's because I had sent it to her.*

▶ DIÁLOGO 6 · Un malentendido familiar

Study the dialogue, then listen to the recording and repeat each line.

MARTA	(*Con voz triste*) He entendido que en esta familia yo estoy pintada en la pared.
CARMEN	Pero, tía, ¿cómo se te ocurre?
MARTA	Pues nadie se había tomado la molestia de invitarme a la reunión familiar el domingo.
CARMEN	¿Qué reunión? Que yo sepa no hay reunión el domingo.
MARTA	Hija, tú sabes que nos reunimos todos los domingos en casa de la abuela.
CARMEN	Ay, tía, el domingo los abuelos van a estar fuera. No hemos planeado ninguna reunión.
MARTA	¡Qué alivio! ¡Entonces no se han olvidado de invitarme!

Análisis

Check that you understand the linguistic breakdown of each speech from *Diálogo 6*.

Un malentendido familiar	*A family misunderstanding*
(*Con voz triste*) He entendido que en esta familia yo estoy pintada en la pared.	(With a sad voice) *I have realized that in this family I count for nothing.*
la voz	*voice*
voz triste	*sad voice*
entender (**e** > **ie**)	*to understand*
he entendido que	*I have understood that, now I understand that*
la familia	*family*
pintar	*to paint*
pintado	*painted*
estar pintado en la pared	*to count for nothing* (literally, *to be painted on the wall*)
Pero, tía, ¿cómo se te ocurre?	*But, Aunt, how can you think such a thing?*
ocurrírsele a uno	*to think something*
¿cómo se te ocurre?	*How can you think such a thing?*
Pues nadie se había tomado la molestia de invitarme a la reunión familiar el domingo.	*Well, no one had bothered to invite me to the family get-together this Sunday.*
pues	*well, well then*
la molestia	*bother*
tomarse la molestia de + *infinitive*	*to bother to (do something), take the trouble to (do something)*
había tomado	*had taken* (past perfect)
nadie se había tomado la molestia de invitarme	*no one had taken the trouble to invite me*

familiar	*family* (adjective)
la reunión	*get-together, gathering, meeting*

¿Qué reunión? Que yo sepa no hay reunión el domingo.	*What get-together? As far as I know, there's no get-together on Sunday.*
que yo sepa (*subjunctive*)	*as far as I know* (**saber**), *to my knowledge*
no hay reunión	*there's no get-together*

Hija, tú sabes que nos reunimos todos los domingos en casa de la abuela.	*Dear, you know that we get together every Sunday at Grandma's house.*
la hija	*dear* (literally, *daughter*)
reunirse	*to get together*
nos reunimos	*we get together*
todos los domingos	*every Sunday*
en casa de la abuela	*at Grandma's house*

Ay, tía, el domingo los abuelos van a estar fuera. No hemos planeado ninguna reunión.	*Why, Aunt, on Sunday my grandparents are going to be away. We haven't planned a get-together.*
estar fuera	*to be out, be away*
planear	*to plan*
no hemos planeado	*we haven't planned*

¡Qué alivio! ¡Entonces no se han olvidado de invitarme!	*What a relief! Then they haven't forgotten to invite me!*
el alivio	*relief*
¡Qué alivio!	*What a relief!*
Entonces	*then*
olvidarse de + *infinitive*	*to forget to (do something)*
se han olvidado	*they have forgotten*
no se han olvidado de invitarme	*they haven't forgotten to invite me*

▶ Variantes

Listen, and repeat the same structures from *Diálogo 6*, now with new vocabulary.

He entendido todo eso.	*I've **understood** all of that.*
comprendido	*understood*
hecho	*done*
visto	*seen*
leído	*read*
aprendido	*learned*
explicado	*explained*
experimentado	*experienced*
oído	*heard*
creído	*believed*

No se han olvidado .	*They haven't* **forgotten**.
acordado	*remembered*
molestado	*gotten annoyed*
sorprendido	*been surprised*
decidido	*made up their minds*
asustado	*gotten scared*
enterado	*found out*
animado	*cheered up*
entusiasmado	*gotten excited*
No habíamos planeado ninguna reunión.	*We hadn't* **planned** *a get-together.*
organizado	*organized*
arreglado	*arranged*
asistido a	*attended*
oído hablar de	*heard any talk about*

▶ DIÁLOGO 7 · Planeando una quinceañera (1)

Study the dialogue, then listen to the recording and repeat each line.

RAMÓN	Buenas tardes, señores Arroyo. Yo he elaborado el presupuesto para la fiesta de quince años de su hija. Aquí lo tienen.
CARLOS	¡Veinte mil dólares para la quinceañera! ¡No puede ser! Hemos acordado en una cifra mucho más baja.
RAMÓN	Pues estoy dispuesto a revisar el presupuesto.
CARLOS	Por favor, tenemos que reducir los gastos.

Análisis

Check that you understand the linguistic breakdown of each speech from *Diálogo 7*.

Buenas tardes, señores Arroyo. Yo he elaborado el presupuesto para la fiesta de quince años de su hija. Aquí lo tienen.	*Good afternoon, Mr. and Mrs. Arroyo. I've drawn up the estimate for your daughter's fifteenth birthday party. Here it is.*
elaborar	*to draw up*
he elaborado	*I've drawn up*
el presupuesto	*estimate*
la fiesta de quince años	*fifteenth birthday party*
Aquí lo tienen.	*Here it is.* (literally, *Here you have it.*)
¡Veinte mil dólares por la quinceañera! ¡No puede ser! Hemos acordado en una cifra mucho más baja.	*Twenty thousand dollars for the* quinceañera *party! It can't be! We agreed on a much lower figure.*
veinte mil dólares	*twenty thousand dollars*
la quinceañera	*girl's sweet 15 party; also, the 15-year-old girl*

¡No puede ser!	*It can't be!*
acordar (**o** > **ue**) en	*to agree on*
la cifra	*figure*
mucho más baja	*much lower*

Pues estoy dispuesto a revisar el presupuesto.	*Well, I'm willing to look over the estimate.*
estar dispuesto a	*to be willing to, ready to*
revisar	*to look over, check, review*
el presupuesto	*estimate*

Por favor, tenemos que reducir los gastos.	*Please, we have to reduce costs.*
reducir (yo reduzco)	*to reduce*
los gastos	*costs, expenses*

Variantes

Listen, and repeat the same structures from *Diálogo 7*, now with new vocabulary.

Yo he elaborado el presupuesto.	*I've **drawn up** the estimate.*
redactado	*drawn up, written up*
revisado	*checked*
finalizado	*finalized, completed*
analizado	*analyzed*
cambiado	*changed*

La quinceañera se ha lavado la cara.	*The sweet-fifteen birthday girl **washed her face**.*
se ha limpiado los dientes	*brushed her teeth*
se ha lavado la cabeza	*washed her hair*
se ha secado el pelo	*dried her hair*
se ha cepillado el cabello	*brushed her hair*
se ha maquillado	*put on makeup*
se ha pintado los labios	*put on lipstick (lips)*
se ha puesto el vestido de fiesta	*put on her gown*

Hemos organizado una fiesta de cumpleaños.	*We've given **a birthday party**.*
una despedida de soltero	*a bachelor party*
una despedida de soltera	*a bachelorette party*
un cóctel	*a cocktail party*
una fiesta de disfraces (el disfraz (*costume*))	*a costume party*

To learn more about the **fiesta de quince años**, see Chapter 15.

▷ DIÁLOGO 8 · Planeando una quinceañera (2)

Study the dialogue, then listen to the recording and repeat each line.

PAULA Carlos, habíamos añadido unos platos más elaborados incluso los
       entremeses favoritos de Alicia. ¿No te acuerdas?

CARLOS Es cierto. Me había olvidado hasta ahora.

PAULA A fin de cuentas, queremos que nuestra quinceañera tenga una fiesta
       inolvidable.

CARLOS Ramón, confío plenamente en su talento de proveedor. ¡Que vengan
        los entremeses!

Análisis

Check that you understand the linguistic breakdown of each speech from *Diálogo 8*.

Carlos, habíamos añadido unos platos más elaborados incluso los entremeses favoritos de Alicia. ¿No te acuerdas?	*Carlos, we had added some fancier dishes, including Alicia's favorite hors d'oeuvres. Don't you remember?*
añadir	*to add*
habíamos añadido	*we had added*
el plato	*dish*
elaborado	*fancy*
los entremeses	*hors d'oeuvres*
acordarse (**o** > **ue**)	*to remember*
te acuerdas	*you remember*
Es cierto. Me había olvidado hasta ahora.	*That's right. I had forgotten until now.*
me había olvidado	*I had forgotten*
A fin de cuentas, queremos que nuestra quinceañera tenga una fiesta inolvidable.	*After all, we want our fifteen-year-old to have an unforgettable party.*
a fin de cuentas	*after all*
la quinceañera	*fifteen-year-old girl*
queremos que tenga (*subjunctive*)	*we want her to have*
inolvidable	*unforgettable*
Ramón, confío plenamente en su talento de proveedor. ¡Que vengan los entremeses!	*Ramón, I'm completely confident in your talent as a caterer. Bring on the hors d'oeuvres!*
confiar en	*to have confidence in, trust*
plenamente	*completely, totally*
el talento	*talent*
el proveedor	*caterer*
que vengan (*subjunctive*)	*have them come, let them come*
¡Que vengan los entremeses!	*Bring on the hors d'oeuvres!*

▶ Variantes

Listen, and repeat the same structures from *Diálogo 8*, now with new vocabulary.

Confío plenamente en su talento.	*I'm completely confident in your **talent**.*
inteligencia	*intelligence*
experiencia	*experience*
conocimiento	*knowledge*
entereza	*integrity*
responsabilidad	*responsibility*
ingenio	*ingenuity, resourcefulness*
habilidad	*ability*
honradez	*honesty, integrity*
lealtad	*loyalty*
¡Que vengan los entremeses!	*Bring on the hors d'oeuvres!*
¡Que preparen los tacos!	*Let them prepare the tacos!*
¡Que pidan las quesadillas!	*Have them order the quesadillas!*
¡Que entreguen las enchiladas!	*Let them deliver the enchiladas!*

I *¡Feliz cumpleaños, Aurorita!* Write sentences from the elements given, using the verb in present perfect, to describe Aurora's 12th birthday party. Follow the *modelo*.

MODELO mis papás / organizar / esta linda fiesta
→ Mis papás han organizado esta linda fiesta.

1. mi hermano / encargarse de crear invitaciones en línea

2. mis hermanas / hacer decoraciones con globos (*balloons*) y manualidades (*arts and crafts*)

3. mi papá / colgar la piñata

4. mi mamá / preparar una rica torta de chocolate

5. yo / pedir un deseo (*to make a wish*)

6. yo / soplar las velas (*to blow out the candles*)

7. los invitados / regalarme unas cosas muy bonitas

8. ¡todos nosotros / divertirse muchísimo!

J *Ya ha pasado.* Answer each of the following questions, using the present perfect of the verb in the original sentence to explain that these things have already happened. Change direct object nouns to pronouns and make all necessary changes. Follow the *modelo*.

MODELO ¿Cuándo va Ud. a elaborar el presupuesto?
→ Ya lo he elaborado.

1. ¿Cuándo va Felipe a leer estos cuentos?

2. ¿Cuándo van Uds. a reunirse?

3. ¿Cuándo vas a ver a la quinceañera?

4. ¿Cuándo van los meseros a servir los entremeses?

5. ¿Cuándo vas a probarte el traje?

6. ¿Cuándo van los estudiantes a matricularse?

7. ¿Cuándo va Ud. a abrir la cuenta de ahorros?

8. ¿Cuándo van Uds. a pasearse?

Estructura y Práctica

The Past Perfect (Pluperfect)

The past perfect tense in Spanish consists of the imperfect of the auxiliary verb **haber** + the past participle. It is the equivalent of the English past perfect, which consists of the auxiliary *had* + past participle. In a sentence with two past actions, the past perfect labels the action that happened first—the action that was completed before the other action took place. (See Chapter 13.)

Cuando yo **salí**, todavía no **habían llegado**.	*When I left, they still hadn't arrived.*
Creía que la secretaria te lo **había dicho**.	*I thought the secretary had told you.*
—¿Cómo es que no **sabías** lo que **pasó**?	*How come you didn't know what happened?*
—No **había visto** las noticias.	*I hadn't seen the news.*

The Future Perfect and the Conditional Perfect

The future perfect consists of the future of the auxiliary verb **haber** + the past participle. The basic function of the future perfect is to label an action that will be completed in the future before another future action or before a specified time in the future. Note that in all the perfect tenses, the past participle is invariable.

Habremos terminado el trabajo antes del viernes.	*We will have finished the work before Friday.*
Habrán regresado antes de llegar nosotros.	*They will have returned before we arrive.*
Habré entregado el informe para fines del mes.	*I will have handed in the report by the end of the month.*

The conditional perfect consists of the conditional of the auxiliary verb **haber** + the past participle. The conditional perfect tells what would have happened if an implied or stated condition were fulfilled.

—Ellos decidieron no ir a la playa ayer.	*They decided not to go to the beach yesterday.*
—Nosotros sí **habríamos ido**.	*We certainly would have gone.*

We will return to the future perfect and the conditional perfect in Chapter 19.

DIÁLOGO 9 · ¡La fuga o la boda cursi! (1)

Study the dialogue, then listen to the recording and repeat each line.

ROBERTO	¡Andrés! ¿Tú aquí? Creía que tú ya te habías fugado con tu novia.
ANDRÉS	Sí. Habíamos pensado casarnos en el extranjero.
ROBERTO	Y habías reservado el vuelo y el hotel, ¿verdad?
ANDRÉS	Claro. Pues, acabamos muy decepcionados.
ROBERTO	Cuéntame, ¿qué pasó?

Análisis

Check that you understand the linguistic breakdown of each speech from *Diálogo 9*.

¡La fuga o la boda cursi!	*Elopement or a tacky wedding!*
¡Andrés! ¿Tú aquí? Creía que tú ya te habías fugado con tu novia.	*Andrés! What are you doing here? I thought that you had already eloped with your fiancée.*
¿Tú aquí?	*What are you doing here?*
fugarse	*to run away; to elope*
te habías fugado	*you had eloped* (past perfect)
la novia	*fiancée*
Sí. Habíamos pensado casarnos en el extranjero.	*Yes, we had intended to get married abroad.*
pensar + *infinitive*	*to intend to (do something)*
habíamos pensado	*we had intended* (past perfect)
casarse	*to get married*
habíamos pensado casarnos	*we had intended to get married*
en el extranjero	*abroad*
Y habías reservado el vuelo y el hotel, ¿verdad?	*And you had booked the flight and hotel, hadn't you?*
reservar	*to reserve, book*
el vuelo	*flight*
habías reservado el vuelo	*you had booked the flight*
el hotel	*hotel*
Claro. Pues, acabamos muy decepcionados.	*Of course. Well, we ended up very disappointed.*
claro	*of course*
pues	*well*
acabar	*to end, finish*
decepcionado	*disappointed*
acabamos muy decepcionados	*we ended up very disappointed*
Cuéntame, ¿qué pasó?	*Tell me what happened.*
contar (**o** > **ue**)	*to tell*
cuenta	*tell* (**tú** command form of **contar**)
cuéntame	*tell me*
¿qué pasó?	*what happened?*

Variantes

Listen, and repeat the same structures from *Diálogo 9*, now with new vocabulary.

Habíamos pensado fugarnos.	We had **intended** to elope.
querido	wanted
deseado	wanted
esperado	hoped
podido	been able
preferido	preferred
intentado	tried
tratado de	tried

Ya se habían fugado .	They had already **eloped**.
comprometido	gotten engaged
casado	gotten married
ido de luna de miel	gone on their honeymoon

Acabamos muy decepcionados .	We ended up very **disappointed**.
desilusionados	disappointed
preocupados	worried
inquietos	worried
angustiados	distressed
estresados	stressed
confundidos	confused
fastidiados	annoyed

DIÁLOGO 10 · ¡La fuga o la boda cursi! (2)

Study the dialogue, then listen to the recording and repeat each line.

ANDRÉS   Bueno, los padres de Clara se enteraron de nuestra fuga.
ROBERTO   Y pusieron el grito en el cielo, me imagino.
ANDRÉS   Al contrario. Sus padres se pusieron al mando del asunto.
ROBERTO   Entonces, ¿Clara no rompió contigo? ¿Habrá boda?
ANDRÉS   Sí, una boda grande y cursi. ¡Es de eso precisamente que huíamos!
ROBERTO   Hombre, ánimo. Ve el lado positivo. ¡Yo voy a ser tu padrino de boda!

Análisis

Check that you understand the linguistic breakdown of each speech from *Diálogo 10*.

Bueno, los padres de Clara se enteraron de nuestra fuga.	Well, Clara's parents found out about our elopement.
enterarse de algo	to find out about something
la fuga	elopement
se enteraron de nuestra fuga	they found out about our elopement

Y pusieron el grito en el cielo, me imagino.	And they raised the roof, I imagine.
poner el grito en el cielo	to raise the roof, hit the ceiling
imaginarse	to imagine

Al contrario. Sus padres se pusieron al mando del asunto.

On the contrary. Her parents took control of the situation.

al contrario	*on the contrary*
el mando	*control, direction*
al mando	*in control, in charge*
ponerse al mando de algo	*to take control of something*
el asunto	*matter*
se pusieron al mando del asunto	*they took control of the situation*

Entonces, ¿Clara no rompió contigo? ¿Habrá boda?

So, Clara didn't break up with you? Will there be a wedding?

romper con alguien	*to break up with someone*
rompió contigo	*she broke up with you*
habrá	*there will be* (future of **hay**)
una boda	*a wedding*

Sí, una boda grande y cursi. ¡Es de eso precisamente que huíamos!

Yes, a big, tacky wedding. That's exactly what we were running away from!

cursi	*tacky, tasteless*
una boda grande y cursi	*a big, tacky wedding*
huir de algo	*to flee from, run away from*
eso	*that*
de eso huíamos	*that's what we were running away from*
precisamente	*exactly, precisely*

Hombre, ánimo. Ve el lado positivo. ¡Yo voy a ser tu padrino de boda!

My friend, cheer up. Look at the positive side. I'm going to be your best man!

hombre	*my friend* (interjection)
el ánimo	*spirit, encouragement*
ánimo	*cheer up, come on*
ve	*see* (**tú** command form of **ver**)
el lado	*the side*
positivo	*positive*
el padrino	*godfather*
el padrino de boda	*best man*

▶ Variantes

Listen, and repeat the same structures from *Diálogo 10*, now with new vocabulary.

Nos habremos fugado antes de marzo.

*We will have **eloped** before March.*

comprometido	*gotten engaged*
casado	*gotten married*

Nos habríamos fugado antes de marzo.

*We would have **eloped** before March.*

comprometido	*gotten engaged*
casado	*gotten married*

El padrino de boda brindó por los novios.	***The best man*** *toasted the bride and groom.*
La dama de honor	*The bridesmaid*
El invitado	*The guest*
La invitada	*The guest*
El rabino	*The rabbi*
La rabina	*The rabbi*
El cura	*The priest*
El sacerdote	*The priest*
El pastor	*The minister/pastor*
La pastora	*The minister/pastor*

K *¿Es cierto que había pasado?* **(Is it true that it had happened?)** Write questions from the elements given to inquire whether these things had happened. Use the past perfect tense of the verb. Follow the *modelo*.

MODELO   Jaime y Juana / casarse
     → ¿Es cierto que Jaime y Juana se habían casado?

1. los recién casados (*newlyweds*) / volver de la luna de miel (*honeymoon*)

2. Mario / ponerse en contacto contigo

3. nosotros / olvidarse del cumpleaños del primo

4. Isabel / dejar plantado (*to jilt*) a su novio de tres años

5. el pueblo entero / huir del huracán

6. tú / enterarse de la fuga

7. Uds. / ver el estreno de la película

8. nadie / darles la buena noticia a Uds.

Estructura y Práctica
THE PASSIVE VOICE

English *to be* and Spanish **ser** are used with the past participle to form the passive voice. The passive voice can be used to de-emphasize the performer of the action and shift the focus of the sentence to the action itself and to its object. The participle functions as an adjective and agrees with the subject in gender and number. The performer of the action—the agent—can be added in a prepositional phrase beginning with **por**.

In English, the passive voice is one of the most common ways of de-emphasizing the performer of the action. In Spanish, however, the passive voice is used more in formal written language than in everyday speech.

Below, active sentences are followed by their passive counterparts.

Una empresa constructora líder **construyó** muchos rascacielos en el centro.	*A leading construction company built many skyscrapers downtown.*
Muchos rascacielos **fueron construidos** en el centro por una empresa constructora líder.	*Many skyscrapers were built downtown by a leading construction company.*
El profesor **va a suspender** las clases.	*The professor is going to cancel the classes.*
Las clases **van a ser suspendidas** por el profesor.	*The classes are going to be canceled by the professor.*
Los epidemiólogos **estudiaron** estas enfermedades.	*The epidemiologists studied these diseases.*
Estas enfermedades **fueron estudiadas** por los epidemiólogos.	*These diseases were studied by the epidemiologists.*
El médico **trató** a los enfermos.	*The doctor treated the sick people.*
Los enfermos **fueron tratados** por el médico.	*The sick people were treated by the doctor.*
Los mediadores **han resuelto** el conflicto.	*The mediators have resolved the conflict.*
El conflicto **ha sido resuelto** por los mediadores.	*The conflict has been resolved by the mediators.*

L Rewrite each of the following sentences, changing its active construction to the passive construction. Use a prepositional phrase beginning with **por** to express the performer of the action. Follow the *modelo*.

> MODELO   Mis papás compraron la casa.
> → La casa fue comprada por mis papás.

1. Mi hermano llevó las cajas a la buhardilla (*attic*).

2. Los señores Ayala pidieron el préstamo.

3. Estos asistentes hicieron las copias de seguridad.

4. La jefa de cocina preparó los entremeses.

5. Un pintor francés pintó este cuadro.

6. La quinceañera invitó a las chicas del colegio.

7. Octavio y José abrieron la consultoría.

8. Aquellas directoras montaron la exposición interactiva.

Other Ways of De-emphasizing the Performer of the Action

The passive voice is a way of shifting the focus of the sentence to the action of the verb or to the direct object of the verb. In Spanish, there are several ways to de-emphasize the performer of the action. Note that some of these grammatical patterns have parallels in English, and others do not.

1 · Spanish and English both use the third person plural of the verb. In Spanish, the verb is used without a subject; in English, the verb is used with an unstressed *they* as subject.

Abren muchos restaurantes nuevos por aquí.	*They're opening a lot of new restaurants around here.*
Dicen que esta película es estupenda.	*They say this movie is terrific.*
Hoy en día **necesitan** más peritos en seguridad.	*Nowadays they need more security experts.*

2 · Spanish and English both use a nonspecific subject. Where Spanish uses **tú**, English often uses unstressed *you*.

Si **trabajas** mucho en la vida, **tendrás** éxito.	*If you work hard in life, you'll be successful.*
Necesitas un abogado cuando **compras** casa.	*You need a lawyer when you buy a house.*
Debes ser cortés con la gente.	*You should be courteous to people.*

3 · Spanish and English use **la gente** and *people*, respectively, as a non-specific subject. Note that **la gente** always takes a third person singular verb in Spanish, but English *people* takes a plural verb.

La gente espera gozar de buena salud.	*People hope to enjoy good health.*
La gente quiere un gobierno honesto y responsable.	*People want an honest and accountable government.*
La gente exige el derecho a la libertad de expresión.	*People demand the right to free speech.*

4 · Both Spanish **uno** and English *one* are used. Spanish **uno** (and **una** if the reference is to a woman) can be used in both formal and informal contexts. English *one*, however, is limited to formal contexts.

Uno debe ser un buen ciudadano.	*One should be a good citizen.*
Uno no debe decir tal cosa.	*One shouldn't say such a thing.*

Note that reflexive verbs in Spanish only use **uno** or **una** with a third person singular verb to show the de-emphasized subject.

Uno se divierte mucho con los amigos íntimos.	*One has a great time with close friends.*
Uno debe cepillarse los dientes dos o tres veces al día.	*One should brush one's teeth two or three times a day.*

5 · In Spanish, the most common construction with passive meaning consists of the reflexive pronoun **se** + third person singular or third person plural of the verb. The **se** construction with passive meaning does not use an agent phrase (**por** + the performer of the action).

Se escribe un informe detallado.	*A detailed report is being written.*
Se organiza una exposición de arte.	*An art exhibition is being organized.*
Aquí **se sirve** comida muy rica.	*Very good food is served here.*

The noun that follows the **se** construction is the grammatical subject of the sentence. Therefore, if that noun is plural, the verb must also be plural.

Se apagan las luces a las nueve.	*Lights are turned off at nine o'clock.*
Se venden artículos de lujo en esa tienda.	*Luxury goods are sold in that store.*
Se alquilan apartamentos al mes.	*Apartments are rented by the month.*

This construction can be used in all tenses.

Se construyó un edificio muy moderno.	*A very modern building was built.*
Se ha perdido mucho tiempo en tonterías.	*A lot of time was wasted on nonsense.*
No sé cuándo **se terminará** el proyecto.	*I don't know when the project will be finished.*

The **se** construction can be used with intransitive verbs (verbs that do not take a direct object). Such sentences do not have a grammatical subject and the verb is always third person singular. The English equivalents of these sentences have many possible translations.

Se entra por aquí.	*One goes in this way.*
¿Por dónde **se sube**?	*How does one get upstairs?*
Se sale antes de las horas punta.	*You leave before rush hour.*
Se debe entrar por aquí.	*One should go in this way.*
¿Por dónde **se puede subir**?	*How can one get upstairs?*
Se necesita salir antes de las horas punta.	*You need to leave before rush hour.*
Se tiene que tomar esta clase a distancia.	*You have to take this class remotely.*

M Rewrite each of the following sentences using the **se** construction. Retain the tense of the original sentence. Follow the *modelo*.

MODELO   Terminan el proyecto.
   → Se termina el proyecto.

1. Envío los paquetes.

2. Buscábamos ingenieros.

3. Prepararon el arroz con pollo.

4. Debemos conocer el museo interactivo.

5. Elaboraron el presupuesto.

6. Vivían bien en esta ciudad.

7. Tendrás que llegar para las nueve.

8. Han abierto sucursales (sucursal (*branch*)) en el extranjero.

9. Entro a la galería por aquella puerta.

10. No podríamos trabajar los viernes.

The Indirect Object

In English, the indirect object labels *to whom* or *for whom* something is done—in other words, either the recipient or the beneficiary of the action. These functions have parallels in Spanish.

A Juana le di el mensaje. (Juana is the recipient.)	*I gave Juana the message.*
Su padre **le** pagó la multa **a Raúl**. (Raúl is the beneficiary.)	*Raul's father paid the fine for Raúl.*

In Spanish, the indirect object covers a wider range of functions than in English. With certain verbs, the indirect object in Spanish can also label the person *from whom* something was taken or gotten.

Me compraron ese coche viejo.	*They bought that old car from me.*
José **le** quitó la novia **a Alberto**.	*José took Alberto's girlfriend away from him.*
Nos han robado una fortuna.	*They've stolen a fortune from us.*

Notice that the first of the above sentences is ambiguous out of context. It can also mean *They bought that old car for me*.

In Spanish, the indirect object pronouns can be added to certain impersonal expressions.

Es importante leer mucho.	*It's important to read a lot.*
Les es importante leer mucho.	*It's important for them to read a lot.*
Es necesario triunfar en la vida.	*It's necessary to succeed in life.*
Nos es necesario triunfar en la vida.	*It's necessary for us to succeed in life.*
Es muy útil saber hablar español.	*It's very useful to know how to speak Spanish.*
Me es muy útil saber hablar español.	*It's very useful for me to know how to speak Spanish.*
¿Es fácil aprender las cosas de memoria?	*Is it easy to learn things by heart?*
¿Te es fácil aprender las cosas de memoria?	*Is it easy for you to learn things by heart?*

The "Interested Bystander"

The Spanish indirect object may refer to someone who was interested in or affected by the action of the verb in some way: the "interested bystander." This function can sometimes be expressed in English by a prepositional phrase beginning with "on."

Se nos fue el tiempo.	*The time ran out on us.*
Se me murió el gato.	*The cat died on me.*
Mi primo **se nos instaló**.	*My cousin moved in on us.*
Se les escapó el perro.	*Their dog ran away (on them).*

The use of the indirect object referring to the interested bystander is sometimes difficult to express in English, as in the following example:

Mi vecino me gritó a mis hijos.	*My neighbor yelled at my children.*

This use of the indirect object lends a colloquial and personal tone to the sentence. A translation that might better convey this tone in English would be *Can you imagine? My neighbor yelled at my children.*

Se me Construction

In the **se me** construction, an indirect object pronoun is added to an impersonal **se** construction, which consists of a third person singular or third person plural verb preceded by **se**. The indirect object pronoun is inserted after **se** and before the verb.

Se le quedó el celular en casa.	*He left his cell phone at home.*
Se me acabó la gasolina.	*I ran out of gas.*

The indirect object as interested bystander is most commonly used in the **se me** construction. To focus on the interested bystander, a phrase consisting of the preposition **a** + proper noun or the preposition **a** + prepositional pronoun is used.

A Juan se le quedó el celular en casa.	*Juan left his cell phone at home.*
A mí se me acabó la gasolina.	*I ran out of gas.*

The **se me** construction is also used to express unplanned or unexpected occurrences.

Se me rompió la camisa.	*I tore my shirt. / My shirt tore.*
Se te cayó la bandeja.	*You dropped the tray.*
Se nos han perdido los documentos.	*We lost the documents.*
Se te va a acabar la gasolina.	*You're going to run out of gas.*
Se me olvidó decirte.	*I forgot to tell you.*

Verbs often used in the **se me** construction appear in vocabulary lists in the following format. The phrase **a uno** represents the indirect object.

acabársele a uno *to run out of something*
caérsele a uno *to drop something*
descomponérsele a uno *to break down* (of machines)
ocurrírsele a uno *to think of something, have something dawn on someone*
olvidársele a uno *to forget something*
perdérsele a uno *to lose something*
quebrársele a uno *to break* (*part of the body*)
quedársele a uno *to leave something behind*
rompérsele a uno *to tear* (*article of clothing*); *to break* (*part of the body*)

⏵ DIÁLOGO 11 · ¡Un día inolvidable en el campo! (1)

Study the dialogue, then listen to the recording and repeat each line.

ALBERTO	¡Qué mal nos ha salido el día en el campo!, ¿verdad, cariño?
REBECA	En efecto. Primero, la comida. Se me olvidó comprar fiambres para hacer los sándwiches.
ALBERTO	Y a mí se me quedaron las ensaladas en la nevera.
REBECA	Por añadidura los niños se pusieron quejumbrosos. A Ricardito se le había quedado el balón de fútbol en casa.

Análisis

Check that you understand the linguistic breakdown of each speech from *Diálogo 11*.

¡Un día inolvidable en el campo!	*An unforgettable day in the country!*
¡Qué mal nos ha salido el día en el campo!, ¿verdad, cariño?	*How awful our day in the country has turned out, hasn't it, honey?*
nos ha salido mal	*it has turned out badly for us*
el campo	*country, countryside*
el cariño	*love, affection*
cariño	*honey* (term of endearment)
En efecto. Primero, la comida. Se me olvidó comprar fiambres para hacer los sándwiches.	*Indeed. First, the food. I forgot to buy cold cuts to make the sandwiches.*
se me olvidó comprar	*I forgot to buy*
los fiambres	*cold cuts*
el sándwich	*sandwich*
Y a mí se me quedaron las ensaladas en la nevera.	*And I left the salads in the refrigerator.*
se me quedaron	*I left them*
la ensalada	*salad*
la nevera	*refrigerator, fridge*
Por añadidura los niños se pusieron quejumbrosos. Y a Ricardito se le había quedado el balón de fútbol en casa.	*To top it all off, the children got whiny. And Ricardito had left his soccer ball at home.*
por añadidura	*to top it all off*
los niños	*children*
ponerse + *adjective*	*to get/become* + adjective
se pusieron	*they got, they became*
quejumbroso	*whiny*
se pusieron quejumbrosos	*they got whiny*
el balón de fútbol	*soccer ball*

▶ Variantes

Listen, and repeat the same structures from *Diálogo 11*, now with new vocabulary.

¡Qué mal nos ha salido el día!	*How awful **our** day has turned out!*
me	*my*
te	*your* (informal)
le	*your* (formal)
le	*his*
le	*her*
les	*your* (plural)
les	*their*

Se me olvidó comprar el vino.	*I forgot **to buy** the wine.*
enfriar (yo enfrío)	*to chill*
verter (**e** > **ie**)	*to pour*
servir (**e** > **i**)	*to serve*
probar (**o** > **ue**)	*to try, to taste*
tomar	*to drink*

Se le quedaron las gafas oscuras en alguna parte.	***She left** her sunglasses somewhere.*
Se le olvidaron	*She forgot*
Se le perdieron	*She lost*
Se le cayeron	*She dropped*
Se le rompieron	*She broke*

Se les acabó el pan .	*They ran out of **bread**.*
la mantequilla	*butter*
el aceite de oliva	*olive oil*
el arroz	*rice*
la miel	*honey*

¿Se te acabaron los huevos ?	*Did you run out of **eggs**?*
las cebollas	*onions*
los quesos	*cheeses*
las uvas	*grapes*
las galletas	*cookies*

DIÁLOGO 12 · ¡Un día inolvidable en el campo! (2)

Study the dialogue, then listen to the recording and repeat each line.

ALBERTO	Y a Lucía se le había roto su muñeca favorita.
REBECA	Empezó a llover y en camino a casa se nos acabó la gasolina.
ALBERTO	Nos perdimos tomando un atajo a la gasolinera.
REBECA	Y si eso no fuera poco, se te perdió la cartera.
ALBERTO	(*Rebeca y Alberto riéndose*) Un día realmente inolvidable.
	¡Qué tontos somos! ¡¿Cómo se nos ocurrió ir al campo hoy?!

Análisis

Check that you understand the linguistic breakdown of each speech from *Diálogo 12*.

Y a Lucía se le había roto su muñeca favorita.	*And Lucía had broken her favorite doll.*
se le había roto	*she had broken it*
la muñeca	*doll*
favorita	*favorite*

Empezó a llover y en camino a casa se nos acabó la gasolina.	*It began to rain and on the way home we ran out of gas.*
empezar (**e** > **ie**)	*to begin*
empezó	*it began*

llover (**o** > **ue**)	*to rain*
empezó a llover	*it began to rain*
el camino	*way, road*
en camino a casa	*on the way home*
la gasolina	*gas*
se nos acabó	*we ran out of it*

Nos perdimos tomando un atajo a la gasolinera.	*We got lost taking a shortcut to the gas station.*
perderse (**e** > **ie**)	*to get lost*
nos perdimos	*we got lost*
el atajo	*shortcut*
tomar un atajo	*to take a shortcut*
la gasolinera	*gas station*

Y si eso no fuera poco, se te perdió la cartera.	*And as if that weren't enough, you lost your wallet.*
si eso no fuera poco	*as if that weren't enough*
se te perdió	*you lost it*
la cartera	*wallet*
se te perdió la cartera	*you lost your wallet*

(*Rebeca y Alberto riéndose*) Un día realmente inolvidable. ¡Qué tontos somos! ¡¿Cómo se nos ocurrió ir al campo hoy?!	(*Rebeca and Alberto laughing*) *A truly unforgettable day. How silly of us! How did we ever come up with the idea of going to the country today?!*
reírse (**e** > **i**)	*to laugh*
riéndose	*laughing*
realmente	*really, truly*
inolvidable	*unforgettable*
tonto	*silly, foolish, stupid*
¡Qué tontos somos!	*How foolish we are! / How silly of us!*
se nos ocurrió	*we thought of (something)*
ir al campo	*to go to the country*

▶ Variantes

Listen, and repeat the same structures from *Diálogo 12*, now with new vocabulary.

Se le perdió la cartera , ¿no?	*You lost your **wallet**, didn't you?*
la billetera	*wallet*
el bolso	*handbag*
la licencia de manejar	*driver's license*
la licencia de conducir	*driver's license*
la chequera	*checkbook*
el celular	*cell phone*

Se le perdieron las llaves del carro , ¿no?	*You lost your **car keys**, didn't you?*
los anteojos	*eyeglasses*
los audífonos	*hearing aids*

las tarjetas de crédito	*credit cards*
los documentos	*documents, papers*

Se nos había descompuesto el televisor . *Our **television set** had broken.*

la máquina de lavar	*washing machine*
la lavadora	*washing machine*
la secadora	*dryer*
el lavaplatos	*dishwasher*
la nevera	*refrigerator*
la aspiradora	*vacuum cleaner*
el microondas	*microwave*
la cafetera	*coffee maker*
la batidora eléctrica	*electric mixer*

N *Lo inesperado* **(The unexpected).** Write sentences from the elements given, using the **se me** construction in the preterit, to tell what unexpected things happened to these people. Use the cue in parentheses. Follow the *modelo*.

MODELO   (Paula) olvidársele / la cita
        → A Paula se le olvidó la cita.

1. (Marcelo) perdérsele / la bicicleta

2. (la señorita Ortiz) quedársele en el coche / los paquetes

3. (Ud.) acabársele / la paciencia

4. (ti) rompérsele / las medias

5. (mesero) caérsele / los platos

6. (mis amigos) descomponérsele / la videocámara

7. (mí) ocurrírsele / una idea genial

8. (el beisbolista) quebrársele / el meñique (*pinky, little finger*)

9. (nosotros) perdérsele / las mochilas

10. (Uds.) olvidársele / la contraseña (*password*)

Estructura y Práctica

Indirect Commands

Indirect commands (sometimes referred to as third person commands) express instructions or wishes referring to a third person—someone who is neither the speaker nor the person spoken to. Indirect commands may also express a hope about something that may happen in the future.

Spanish indirect commands consist of the conjunction **que** + the present subjunctive of the verb. English equivalents of these structures often involve phrases such as *let him/her/it/them do something, have him/her/it/them do something,* or *I hope he/she/it does / they do something.*

—Marta está acatarrada.	*Marta has a cold.*
—Que no salga entonces.	*Don't let her go out then.*
—Pablito ha sacado muy malas notas.	*Pablito has gotten very bad grades.*
—Que estudie más y juegue menos.	*Have him study more and play less.*
—Pronto va a comenzar el partido de fútbol.	*Soon the soccer match is going to start.*
—¡Que no empiece a llover!	*I hope it doesn't start to rain!*

Commands with the **Se me** Construction

The grammatical subject of a sentence using the **se me** construction becomes the subject of the indirect command. Thus, to tell someone carrying a tray "don't drop the tray," we begin with the present tense sentence **No se te cae la charola**. **La charola** is the subject of the sentence, so the indirect command is expressed as follows.

Que no se te caiga la charola.	*Don't drop the tray.*

If the subject is plural, the verb of the indirect command is also plural.

Que no se te pierdan los sobres.	*Don't lose the envelopes.*

With some verbs in the **se me** construction, the idea of a wish or hope is more appropriate in the English translation.

Que no se nos descomponga el coche.	*I hope our car doesn't break down.*
Que no se te ocurra gastar esa plata.	*Don't even think about spending that money.*

O *Que lo haga otro.* **(Have somebody else do it.)** Write sentences using an indirect command to say that the people named in parentheses should do the things that you don't want to do. Change direct object nouns to pronouns and make all necessary changes. Follow the *modelo*.

MODELO   No quieres invitar a los amigos, ¿verdad? (Carmen)
→ No, que los invite Carmen.

1. No quieres organizar la boda, ¿verdad? (la planeadora)

2. No puedes elaborar el presupuesto, ¿verdad? (nuestro colega)

3. No debes servirles la cena, ¿verdad? (la mesera)

4. No vas a crear una base de datos, ¿verdad? (los analistas)

5. No piensas enviarle los emails, ¿verdad? (el secretario)

6. No puedes resolver el conflicto, ¿verdad? (los mediadores (*mediators*))

7. No tienes que empezar el proyecto, ¿verdad? (el gerente)

8. No necesitas entregarles los contratos, ¿verdad? (las abogadas)

P *Dando consejos* **(Giving advice).** Write sentences using indirect commands to suggest what these people can do to remedy their situations. Use the cues in parentheses. Follow the *modelo*.

MODELO   Leonardo dice que tiene sueño. (dormir la siesta)
→ Que duerma la siesta entonces.

1. Daniel cree que le han robado la bicicleta. (llamar a la policía)

2. A Fernanda le duele la cabeza. (tomar unas aspirinas)

3. Mi primo tiene problemas digestivos. (seguir una dieta más sana)

4. Josefa dice que su novio es imbécil. (romper el noviazgo (*engagement*))

5. Alicia dice que tiene frío. (ponerse el suéter)

6. A los Reyes les falta dinero para comprar una casa. (pedir un préstamo)

7. Lupe y su hija se están mojando hasta los huesos. (abrir el paraguas)

8. Paco está rendido trabajando como un burro. (ir de vacaciones)

Q *¡Chiquillos, que tengan cuidado!* **(Boys and girls, be careful!)** Rewrite each of the following sentences, changing the **ir a** + infinitive construction to an indirect command using the **se me** construction. Follow the *modelo*.

MODELO   Pablito, ¡cuidado! Se te va a romper el pantalón.
→ Pablito, ¡que no se te rompa el pantalón!

1. Carmencita, ¡cuidado! Se te va a caer ese vaso.

2. Luisito, ¡cuidado! Se te van a romper los anteojos.

3. Cecilia, ¡cuidado! Se te va a acabar el papel.

4. Martín, ¡cuidado! Se te va a perder la mochila.

5. Adelita, ¡cuidado! Se te van a quedar los mitones (el mitón (*mitten*)) en la sala de clase.

6. Marco, ¡cuidado! Se te va a quebrar la pierna.

7. Miguelito, ¡cuidado! Se te va a ocurrir decir tonterías.

8. Rita, ¡cuidado! Se te van a descomponer esos juguetes electrónicos.

Un paso más

Are you ready to take your Spanish a step further? Here are exercises that will enhance your knowledge of the language and encourage you to express yourself freely.

R *Diálogos.* Express the following dialogues in Spanish. They contain tenses presented in this chapter (progressive, present perfect, past perfect), the passive voice, the **se me** construction, and indirect commands.

1. *Are you (Ud.) writing the reports?*

2. *No, I've already written them. Now I'm reading them.*

3. *Why were you (tú) getting annoyed?*

4. *It's that Timoteo was being mischievous.*

5. *We're going to have dinner very soon. Have Diego wash his hands.*

6. *I saw him washing them. Let dinner be served!*

7. *It's pouring, and we don't have an umbrella.*

8. *We're getting soaked to the bone.*

9. *What's the name of the architecture firm that designed this apartment building?*

10. *It was designed and built by Serrano and Associates.* (el asociado (*associate, partner*))

11. *What a pity! We've run out of olive oil.*

12. *And I forgot to buy it.*

S *Preguntas personales.* *Contesta las siguientes preguntas con oraciones completas en español.*

1. ¿Qué estás haciendo en este momento?

2. ¿Qué estabas haciendo antes?

3. ¿Se te perdió algo importante alguna vez? ¿Qué fue? ¿Por qué te fue importante? ¿Pudiste recuperarlo?

4. ¿Se te olvidó algo importante alguna vez? ¿Qué fue? ¿La pérdida tuvo consecuencias graves para ti?

5. ¿Cuál es tu profesión? ¿Trabajas para una empresa o por cuenta propia (*self-employed*)? ¿Diriges tu propio negocio? ¿En qué consiste tu trabajo?

6. ¿Se organizan reuniones familiares en tu familia? ¿Quiénes asisten a las reuniones? ¿Con qué frecuencia las hay? ¿Cómo son?

7. ¿Conoces unos museos interactivos? ¿Cómo son? ¿Qué te parecen?

T *Anécdotas personales.* Escribe unas anécdotas personales sobre los siguientes temas que se tratan en los diálogos del capítulo 17. Usa palabras y expresiones de los diálogos pertinentes al tema que escojas.

1. Mi familia

2. Mis amigos

3. Una fiesta o un evento especial

4. Un suceso o incidente inesperado

U *Expresiones y modismos.* Explica en español lo que significan estas expresiones que se presentan en el capítulo 17.

1. trabajar como un burro

2. estar pintado en la pared

3. mojarse hasta los huesos

4. poner el grito en el cielo

5. ponerse al mando del asunto

V *Citas* **(Quotations).** Lee las siguientes citas y tradúcelas al inglés. Después, explica lo que significan en español. Tienen que ver con la familia y los amigos.

1. "Los momentos más felices de mi vida son los pocos que he pasado en casa en el seno (*bosom*) de mi familia."
   —*Thomas Jefferson*

2. "La cultura se transmite a través de la familia y cuando esta institución deja de funcionar de manera adecuada el resultado es el deterioro (*decline, breaking down*) de la cultura."
   —*Mario Vargas Llosa*

3. "Cuando yo tenía catorce años, mi padre era tan ignorante que no podía soportarlo. Pero cuando cumplí los veintiuno, me parecía increíble lo mucho que mi padre había aprendido en siete años."
   —*Mark Twain*

4. "Un verdadero amigo es quien te toma de la mano y te toca el corazón."
   —*Gabriel García Márquez*

5. "No hay mayor placer que el de encontrar un viejo amigo, salvo el de hacer uno nuevo."
   —*Rudyard Kipling*

Education and Health

▶ DIÁLOGO 1 · ¿Estudiar medicina o ingeniería aeroespacial? (1)

Study the dialogue, then listen to the recording and repeat each line.

ABUELA ¿Qué dices, Jacobo? ¿No te interesa estudiar medicina? Tu papá siempre quería que fueras médico como él y tu abuelo.

JACOBO Abue, mi papá es un gran cardiólogo pero no quiero seguir sus pasos. Quiero estudiar física, matemáticas y astronomía y obtener el doctorado en ingeniería aeroespacial.

ABUELA   (*Riéndose entre dientes*) Y después, ¿te vas a hacer astronauta y viajar
         a Marte en una nave espacial?

JACOBO   Quizás algún día, con suerte. Pero antes de eso me gustaría diseñar
         y desarrollar naves espaciales. ¡Ojalá pudiera colocarme en la
         NASA/SpaceX!

Análisis

Check that you understand the linguistic breakdown of each speech from *Diálogo 1.*

¿Qué dices, Jacobo? ¿No te interesa
estudiar medicina? Tu papá siempre
quería que fueras médico como él
y tu abuelo.

    te interesa
    ¿No te interesa estudiar?
    la medicina
    quería que fueras (*imperfect
      subjunctive*)
    Quería que fueras médico.

*What are you saying, Jacobo? Aren't you
interested in studying medicine? Your dad
always wanted you to be a doctor like him
and your grandfather.*
    you're interested in it
    Aren't you interested in studying?
    medicine
    he wanted you to be (**ser**)

    He wanted you to be a doctor.

Abue, mi papá es un gran cardiólogo
pero no quiero seguir sus pasos.
Quiero estudiar física, matemáticas y
astronomía y obtener el doctorado en
ingeniería aeroespacial.

    abue (< abuela)
    el cardiólogo
    el paso
    seguir sus pasos
    el doctorado
    la ingeniería aeroespacial

*Dearest Grandma, my dad is a great
cardiologist, but I don't want to follow in
his footsteps. I want to study physics, math,
and astronomy and get a doctorate in
aerospace engineering.*
    Grandma (term of endearment)
    cardiologist
    step
    to follow in his footsteps
    doctorate (PhD)
    aerospace engineering

(*Riéndose entre dientes*) Y después,
¿te vas a hacer astronauta y viajar a
Marte en una nave espacial?

    riéndose
    el diente
    entre dientes
    riéndose entre dientes
    hacerse + *profession*
    el/la astronauta
    la nave especial
    Marte

(Chuckling) *And afterwards, are you going
to become an astronaut and travel to Mars
in a spacecraft?*
    laughing (present participle of **reírse**)
    tooth
    through one's teeth
    chuckling
    to become a + profession
    astronaut
    spacecraft, spaceship
    Mars

Quizás algún día, con suerte. Pero antes de eso me gustaría diseñar y desarrollar naves espaciales. ¡Ojalá pudiera colocarme en la NASA/SpaceX!	*Maybe someday, if I'm lucky. But before that I would like to design and develop spacecraft. I wish I could get a position with NASA/SpaceX!*
diseñar	*to design*
desarrollar	*to develop*
Ojalá + *imperfect subjunctive*	*I wish* + verb
Ojalá pudiera (*imperfect subjunctive*)	*I wish I could* (**poder**)
colocarse	*to get a job/position*
Ojalá pudiera colocarme	*I wish I could get a position*
la NASA (la ANAE (Administración Nacional de Aeronáutica y el Espacio))	*NASA (National Aeronautics and Space Administration)*

To learn more about NASA in Spanish, see https://www.youtube.com/NASA_ES and https://ciencia.nasa.gov.

 ## Variantes

Listen, and repeat the same structures from *Diálogo 1*, now with new vocabulary.

Tu papá quería que fueras cardiólogo.	*Your dad wanted you **to be a doctor**.*
estudiaras medicina	*to study medicine*
siguieras sus pasos	*to follow in his footsteps*
trabajaras con él en su consulta	*to work with him in his medical office*
Mi padre es un gran cardiólogo.	*My father is a great **cardiologist**.*
médico de familia	*family doctor*
pediatra	*pediatrician*
cirujano	*surgeon*
veterinario	*veterinarian*
Mi madre es una gran neuróloga.	*My mother is a great **neurologist**.*
médica de familia	*family doctor*
pediatra	*pediatrician*
cirujana	*surgeon*
veterinaria	*veterinarian*
Los primeros intervinientes le salvaron la vida a la niña.	***The first responders** saved the little girl's life.*
Los técnicos médicos de emergencia	*The emergency medical technicians (EMTs)*
Los paramédicos	*The paramedics*
El policía le salvó la vida al niño.	***The police officer** saved the little boy's life.*
La policía	*The police officer, The policewoman*
El bombero	*The firefighter, The fireman*
La bombera	*The firefighter, The firewoman*
El rescatador	*The rescuer*
La rescatadora	*The rescuer*
El socorrista	*The rescuer*
La socorrista	*The rescuer*

DIÁLOGO 2 · ¿Estudiar medicina o ingeniería aeroespacial? (2)

Study the dialogue, then listen to the recording and repeat each line.

ABUELA   Hijo, desde pequeño te fascinaban los libros sobre el espacio exterior. Jugabas al lanzamiento de la nave espacial a la luna. Hasta dormías con tus gemelos. Nunca me imaginaba que tu pasión juvenil se convirtiera en tu profesión.

JACOBO   Abue, quiero dedicarme a la investigación de mundos más allá de nuestras fronteras. ¡Quiero ver la Tierra desde Marte! ¡Quiero conocer los orígenes del universo!

ABUELA   (*Riéndose felizmente*) De tal palo tal astilla. Tu papá también tiene una curiosidad insaciable. Él busca la verdad adentrándose en el corazón. Y tú, en galaxias más allá de nuestros sueños más preciados. Jacobo, estoy tan orgullosa de ti.

JACOBO   Abuela, eres tan comprensiva y de mente abierta. ¡Eres lo máximo! ¡Ven conmigo y te enseño las estrellas!

ABUELA   ¡Sí, mi vida, voy con tal que veamos la Tierra desde Marte!

Análisis

Check that you understand the linguistic breakdown of each speech from *Diálogo 2*.

Hijo, desde pequeño te fascinaban los libros sobre el espacio exterior. Jugabas al lanzamiento de la nave espacial a la luna. Hasta dormiste con tus gemelos. Nunca me imaginaba que tu pasión juvenil se convirtiera en tu profesión.	*My son, from the time you were small you loved books about outer space. You played spaceship launch to the moon. You even slept with your binoculars. I never imagined your childhood passion would become your profession.*

desde pequeño	*from the time you were small*
te fascinaban los libros	*you loved books*
el espacio exterior	*outer space*
el lanzamiento	*launch (**lanzar**)*
la nave espacial	*spacecraft, spaceship*
la luna	*moon*
los gemelos	*binoculars*
imaginarse	*to imagine, expect*
nunca me imaginaba	*I never imagined*
juvenil	*childhood (adjective), of early years*
la pasión juvenil	*childhood passion*
convertirse en (**e > ie**)	*to become*
que se convirtiera (*imperfect subjunctive*)	*that it would become*
nunca me imaginaba que se convirtiera	*I never imagined it would become*

Abue, quiero dedicarme a la investigación de mundos más allá de nuestras fronteras. ¡Quiero ver la Tierra desde Marte! ¡Quiero conocer los orígenes del universo!

Dearest Grandma, I want to devote my life to researching worlds beyond our frontiers. I want to see the Earth from Mars! I want to learn the origins of the universe!

dedicarse a	to devote oneself to
la investigación	research
el mundo	world
más allá	beyond
la frontera	frontier, border
más allá de nuestras fronteras	beyond our frontiers
la Tierra	Earth
Marte	Mars
los orígenes (el origen)	origins
el universo	universe

(*Riéndose felizmente*) De tal palo tal astilla. Tu papá también tiene una curiosidad insaciable. Él busca la verdad adentrándose en el corazón. Y tú, en galaxias más allá de nuestros sueños más preciados. Jacobo, estoy tan orgullosa de ti.

De tal palo tal astilla.

(Laughing happily) *Like father, like son. Your dad also has an insatiable curiosity. He seeks truth in the depths of the heart. And you, in galaxies beyond our wildest dreams. Jacobo, I'm so proud of you.*

Like father, like son. / The apple doesn't fall far from the tree.

la curiosidad	curiosity
insaciable	insatiable
adentrarse en	to go into
el corazón	heart
la galaxia	galaxy
el sueño	dream
más allá de nuestros sueños más preciados	beyond our wildest dreams
orgulloso	proud

Abuela, eres tan comprensiva y de mente abierta. ¡Eres lo máximo! ¡Ven conmigo y te enseño las estrellas!

Grandma, you are so understanding and open-minded. You are the best! Come with me and I'll show you the stars!

comprensivo	understanding
de mente abierta	open-minded
lo máximo	the best, the greatest, the top
ven	come (**tú** command form of **venir**)
ven conmigo	come with me
te enseño	I'll show you
la estrella	star

¡Sí, mi vida, voy con tal que veamos la Tierra desde Marte!	*Yes, my dear boy, I'll go, provided that we see the Earth from Mars!*
la vida	*life*
mi vida	*my dear boy* (literally, *my life* (term of endearment))
con tal que + *subjunctive*	*provided that* + verb
veamos (*present subjunctive*)	*we see* (**ver**)
con tal que veamos	*provided that we see*

Variantes

Listen, and repeat the same structures from *Diálogo 2*, now with new vocabulary.

La profesora les dijo a los estudiantes que leyeran el libro sobre los planetas .	*The teacher told the students to read the book about **the planets**.*
Mercurio	*Mercury*
Venus	*Venus*
Tierra	*Earth*
Marte	*Mars*
Júpiter	*Jupiter*
Saturno	*Saturn*
Urano	*Uranus*
Neptuno	*Neptune*
Plutón, un planeta enano	*Pluto, a dwarf planet*
el sistema solar	*the Solar System*
el sol	*the sun*
la luna	*the moon*
los asteroides	*asteroids*
La Vía Láctea	*the Milky Way*
Los estudiantes le pidieron a la astronauta que les explicara cómo es la gravedad .	*The students asked the astronaut to explain what **gravity** is like.*
un transbordador espacial	*a space shuttle*
la Estación Espacial Internacional	*the International Space Station*

Estructura y Práctica

THE SUBJUNCTIVE

You learned in Chapter 16 that the subjunctive is not a tense, but a "mood," which in grammar signifies a category of verbal forms that express the speaker's attitude toward the action of the verb. The subjunctive, like the indicative, has different tenses, although many fewer than the indicative. So far, you have learned only the present subjunctive. In this chapter, you will learn the imperfect subjunctive.

The Imperfect Subjunctive

To form the imperfect subjunctive of all verbs, start with the third person plural of the preterit. Delete the **-ron** ending and replace it with the appropriate imperfect subjunctive ending.

(yo) **-ra**, (tú) **-ras**, (él, ella, Ud.) **-ra**
(nosotros) **-ramos**, (vosotros) **-rais**, (ellos, ellas, Uds.) **-ran**

	entrar	volver	subir
3RD-PERSON PLURAL PRETERIT	entraron	volvieron	subieron
Querían que			
-ra	entrara	volviera	subiera
-ras	entraras	volvieras	subieras
-ra	entrara	volviera	subiera
-ramos	entráramos	volviéramos	subiéramos
-rais	entrarais	volvierais	subierais
-ran	entraran	volvieran	subieran

Note that the first person singular (**yo**) form and the third person singular (**él, ella, Ud.**) form are identical. The first person plural (**nosotros**) form has a written accent mark over the vowel before the **r** of the ending: **entráramos, volviéramos, subiéramos.**

Here are some examples of the imperfect subjunctive of regular verbs.

Querían que entrara.	*They wanted me to go in.*
Querían que volvieras.	*They wanted you to come back.*
Querían que subiéramos.	*They wanted us to go upstairs.*

There is an alternate form of the imperfect subjunctive, also formed from the third person singular of the preterit, that has endings in **-se** instead of **-ra**. In function, these two sets of forms are interchangeable. However, in most Spanish-speaking countries, the **-se** forms convey a more formal tone.

	entrar	volver	subir
3RD-PERSON PLURAL PRETERIT	entraron	volvieron	subieron
Querían que			
-se	entrase	volviese	subiese
-ses	entrases	volvieses	subieses
-se	entrase	volviese	subiese
-semos	entrásemos	volviésemos	subiésemos
-seis	entraseis	volvieseis	subieseis
-sen	entrasen	volviesen	subiesen

Any irregularity present in the third person plural of the preterit will appear in all persons of the imperfect subjunctive.

	ir/ser	hacer	querer	poder	poner
3RD-PERSON PLURAL PRETERIT	**fueron**	**hicieron**	**quisieron**	**pudieron**	**pusieron**
	fuera	hiciera	quisiera	pudiera	pusiera
	fueras	hicieras	quisieras	pudieras	pusieras
	fuera	hiciera	quisiera	pudiera	pusiera
	fuéramos	hiciéramos	quisiéramos	pudiéramos	pusiéramos
	fuerais	hicierais	quisierais	pudierais	pusierais
	fueran	hicieran	quisieran	pudieran	pusieran

	ver	saber	pedir	dormir
3RD-PERSON PLURAL PRETERIT	**vieron**	**supieron**	**pidieron**	**durmieron**
	viera	supiera	pidiera	durmiera
	vieras	supieras	pidieras	durmieras
	viera	supiera	pidiera	durmiera
	viéramos	supiéramos	pidiéramos	durmiéramos
	vierais	supierais	pidierais	durmierais
	vieran	supieran	pidieran	durmieran

	servir	seguir	tener	venir
3RD-PERSON PLURAL PRETERIT	**sirvieron**	**siguieron**	**tuvieron**	**vinieron**
	sirviera	siguiera	tuviera	viniera
	sirvieras	siguieras	tuvieras	vinieras
	sirviera	siguiera	tuviera	viniera
	sirviéramos	siguiéramos	tuviéramos	viniéramos
	sirvierais	siguierais	tuvierais	vinierais
	sirvieran	siguieran	tuvieran	vinieran

	construir	producir	traer	decir
3RD-PERSON PLURAL PRETERIT	**construyeron**	**produjeron**	**trajeron**	**dijeron**
	construyera	produjera	trajera	dijera
	construyeras	produjeras	trajeras	dijeras
	construyera	produjera	trajera	dijera
	construyéramos	produjéramos	trajéramos	dijéramos
	construyerais	produjerais	trajerais	dijerais
	construyeran	produjeran	trajeran	dijeran

The addition of a prefix to a verb does not change the way the imperfect subjunctive is formed.

hacer	deshacer	deshicieron	deshiciera, *etc.*
seguir	conseguir	consiguieron	consiguiera, *etc.*
pedir	impedir	impidieron	impidiera, *etc.*
poner	proponer	propusieron	propusiera, *etc.*
venir	convenir	convinieron	conviniera, *etc.*

When a verb in a past tense requires the subjunctive in a dependent clause, use the imperfect subjunctive rather than the present subjunctive. Compare the following pairs of sentences.

Esperan que les **escribamos**.	*They hope that we'll write to them.*
Esperaban que les **escribiéramos**.	*They hoped that we'd write to them.*
Quiero que Uds. **hagan** copias del informe.	*I want you to make copies of the report.*
Quería que Uds. **hicieran** copias del informe.	*I wanted you to make copies of the report.*
No **creemos** que **vuelvan** hoy.	*We don't think they're coming back today.*
No **creíamos** que **volvieran** hoy.	*We didn't think they were coming back today.*
Es necesario que Ud. **lea** más.	*It's necessary that you read more.*
Fue necesario que Ud. **leyera** más.	*It was necessary that you read more.*
Me **pide** que la **acompañe**.	*She asks me to go with her.*
Me **pidió** que la **acompañara**.	*She asked me to go with her.*
Buscamos médicos de familia que **tengan** mucha experiencia.	*We're looking for family doctors who have a lot of experience.*
Buscábamos médicos de familia que **tuvieran** mucha experiencia.	*We were looking for family doctors who had a lot of experience.*
Necesitan una casa que **quede** en el centro.	*They need a house that's in the downtown area.*
Necesitaban una casa que **quedara** en el centro.	*They needed a house that was in the downtown area.*
No **hay** película que le **guste**.	*There's no film he likes.*
No **había** película que le **gustara**.	*There was no film he liked.*
¿**Hay** alguien que **conozca** a ese tipo?	*Is there anyone who knows that guy?*
¿**Había** alguien que **conociera** a ese tipo?	*Was there anyone who knew that guy?*

Note that in each of the above pairs of sentences, the first sentence has the verb of the main clause in the present tense and the verb of the dependent clause in the present subjunctive. In the second sentence of each pair, the verb of the main clause is in a past tense and the verb of the dependent clause is in the imperfect subjunctive. This automatic change in the tense of the verb of the dependent clause is one aspect of a set of rules in Spanish called the sequence of tenses.

A **Imperfect subjunctive.** Write the imperfect subjunctive form of the verb in parentheses that correctly completes each of the following sentences. Follow the *modelo*.

MODELO Querían que Ud. *estudiara* medicina. (estudiar)

1. Prefería que nosotros no se lo _____ todavía. (decir)

2. Era bueno que él _____ su propia empresa. (dirigir)

3. Dudaban que ella _____ pediatra. (hacerse)

4. ¿Era posible que ellos ya lo _____? (saber)

5. Sentían que Ud. _____ con todo el mundo. (discutir)

6. Nos alegramos de que Uds. _____ mucho éxito. (tener)

7. Ojalá que nosotros _____ asistir a la fiesta de quince. (poder)

8. Tenían miedo de que _____ una pandemia. (haber)

9. No queríamos que Ud. _____ decepcionado. (estar)

10. Era importante que tú _____ el artículo. (leer)

11. Les aconsejé que _____ una dieta equilibrada (*balanced*). (seguir)

12. Me pidieron que _____ con ellos. (ir)

13. Esperábamos que los primeros intervinientes _____ rápido. (llegar)

14. ¿Te gustaba que nosotros _____ el miércoles? (reunirse)

15. Era necesario que tú _____ el traje antes de comprarlo. (probarse)

16. No creía que ellos _____ en mayo. (graduarse)

⏵ DIÁLOGO 3 · El tiempo vuela

Study the dialogue, then listen to the recording and repeat each line.

SAMUEL   Mira, Elena, nuestros gemelos están subiendo al autobús escolar. ¡Qué orgullosos están! Imagínate que ya están en primer grado.

ELENA   El tiempo vuela, ¿verdad? Este año dejé que los chiquillos escogieran sus propios útiles escolares.

SAMUEL   Cada uno con su mochila llena de cuadernos, lápices, bolígrafos, reglas y la lonchera.

ELENA   No me es fácil verlos tan grandes ya. La casa no será igual con ellos en la escuela todo el día.

Análisis

Check that you understand the linguistic breakdown of each speech from *Diálogo 3*.

Mira, Elena, nuestros gemelos están subiendo al autobús escolar. ¡Qué orgullosos están! Imagínate que ya están en primer grado.

Look, Elena, our twins are getting on the school bus. How proud they are! Imagine, they're already in first grade.

mira	*look (**tú** command form of **mirar**)*
el gemelo	*twin*
están subiendo	*they're getting on*
escolar	*school (adjective)*
el autobús escolar	*school bus*
orgulloso	*proud*
imagínate	*imagine (**tú** command form of **imaginarse**)*
el grado	*grade*
primer grado	*first grade*

El tiempo vuela, ¿verdad? Este año dejé que los chiquillos escogieran sus propios útiles escolares.

Time flies, doesn't it? This year I let the kids choose their own school supplies.

El tiempo vuela.	*Time flies.*
el chiquillo (< chico)	*little boy, kid*
los chiquillos	*little boys, little boys and girls, children, kids*
escogieran (*imperfect subjunctive*)	*choose (**escoger**)*
dejé que los chiquillos escogieran	*I let the little boys choose, I let the kids choose*
los útiles escolares	*school supplies*

Cada uno con su mochila llena de cuadernos, lápices, bolígrafos, reglas y la lonchera.

Each one with his backpack full of notebooks, pencils, pens, rulers, and his lunch box.

la mochila	*backpack*
los lápices (el lápiz)	*pencils*
el bolígrafo	*pen*
la regla	*ruler*
la lonchera	*lunch box*

No me es fácil verlos tan grandes ya. La casa no será igual con ellos en la escuela todo el día.

It's not easy for me to see them so grown up already. Our house won't be the same with them in school all day.

no es fácil	*it's not easy*
no me es fácil	*it's not easy for me*
no me es fácil verlos	*it's not easy for me to see them*
tan grandes	*so grown up (literally, so big)*
no será	*it won't be*
igual	*the same*
la escuela	*school*

▶ Variantes

Listen, and repeat the same structures *from Diálogo 3,* now with new vocabulary.

¿Los chiquillos escogieron sus útiles escolares?	*Did the children choose their school supplies?*
No, querían que los escogiera yo.	*No, they wanted me to choose them.*
Pero yo preferí que los chiquillos los escogieran.	*But I preferred that the kids choose them.*
¿Qué útiles escolares compraron?	*What school supplies did they buy?*

Compraron lápices .	*They bought **pencils**.*
un estuche para lápices	*a pencil case*
lápices de colores	*colored pencils*
marcadores (el marcador)	*markers*
una caja de crayones (el crayón)	*a box of crayons*
un sacapuntas	*a sharpener*
un compás	*a compass*
un protractor	*a protractor*
unas tijeras	*a pair of scissors*
un paquete de papel (el papel)	*a packet of paper*
cuadernos de papel rayado	*lined notebooks*
un rollo de cinta adhesiva	*a roll of tape*

B   **Present subjunctive → imperfect subjunctive.** Rewrite each of the following sentences, changing the verb of the main clause according to the cue in parentheses. The verb in the dependent clause will then change from present subjunctive to imperfect subjunctive. Follow the *modelo.*

MODELO   Desea que todo les salga bien. (Deseaba)
          → Deseaba que todo les saliera bien.

1. Te pido que vengas a vernos más a menudo. (pedí)

2. Sentimos que el profesor de física renuncie a su puesto. (Sentíamos)

3. Se alegran de que yo dé una conferencia. (alegraron)

4. Es probable que la empresa abra otras sucursales (la sucursal (*branch*)). (Era)

5. ¿Les exige que empiecen el proyecto esta semana? (exigió)

6. Espera que Uds. se diviertan mucho en la boda. (Esperaba)

7. Le recomiendan que haga ejercicio para adelgazar. (recomendaron)

8. Te digo que no te enojes por cada cosa. (dije)

9. No nos gusta que sigan contando chismes. (gustaba)

10. Les aconseja que tomen las cosas con calma. (aconsejó)

⏵ DIÁLOGO 4 · Cursando la licenciatura en línea

Study the dialogue, then listen to the recording and repeat each line.

BEATRIZ   Manolo, ¡estoy muy emocionada! Gané una beca para estudiar en la universidad en línea.

MANOLO   ¡Felicidades, chica! ¿Vas a cursar la licenciatura en enfermería?

BEATRIZ   Sí, quería empezar antes de que pasara más tiempo. Puedo seguir trabajando mientras estudio.

MANOLO   ¡Qué maravillosa noticia, de verdad! Yo sé que tu familia esperaba que siguieras estudiando.

Análisis

Check that you understand the linguistic breakdown of each speech from *Diálogo 4*.

Cursando la licenciatura en línea	*Studying for the bachelor's degree online*
Manolo, ¡estoy muy emocionada! Gané una beca para estudiar en la universidad en línea.	*Manolo, I'm very excited! I won a scholarship to study at the university online.*
emocionado	*excited*
estoy muy emocionada	*I'm very excited*
la beca	*scholarship*
gané una beca	*I won a scholarship*
en línea	*online*
¡Felicidades, chica! ¿Vas a cursar la licenciatura en enfermería?	*Congratulations, my friend! Are you going to study for your bachelor's in nursing?*
felicidades	*congratulations*
cursar	*to study, take courses*
la licenciatura	*bachelor's degree*
la enfermería	*nursing*
Sí, quería empezar antes de que pasara más tiempo. Puedo seguir trabajando mientras estudio.	*Yes, I wanted to begin before more time passed. I can keep on working while I study.*
antes de que pasara más tiempo	*before more time passed*
puedo seguir trabajando	*I can keep on working, I can continue working*
mientras estudio	*while I study*
¡Qué maravillosa noticia, de verdad! Yo sé que tu familia esperaba que siguieras estudiando.	*What wonderful news, really! I know that your family was hoping that you would keep on studying.*
maravilloso	*wonderful*
¡Qué maravillosa noticia!	*What wonderful news!*
de verdad	*really*
seguir + -**ndo** form (*gerund*)	*to keep on (doing something), continue (doing something)*
esperaba que siguieras estudiando	*was hoping that you would keep on studying*

Variantes

Listen, and repeat the same structures from *Diálogo 4*, now with new vocabulary.

Esperaban que siguieras estudiando.	**They hoped that** you would keep on studying.
Dudaban que	They doubted that
No creían que	They didn't think that
Les gustaba que	They liked that
Era bueno que	It was good that
Era preciso que	It was necessary that
Era importante que	It was important that

Curso la licenciatura en enfermería.	I'm studying for my bachelor's degree **in nursing**.
en economía	in economics
en historia	in history
en química	in chemistry
en computación	in computer science
en física	in physics
en filosofía	in philosophy

Son egresados de la facultad de administración de empresas.	They're graduates of **the business school**.
la facultad de derecho	the law school
la facultad de ingeniería	the engineering school
la facultad de medicina	the medical school
la facultad de ciencias políticas y sociales	the political and social sciences school
la facultad de filosofía y letras	the humanities school (literally, *the school of philosophy and letters*)
la facultad de música	the music school
la facultad de odontología	the dental school

¿Ud. va a matricularse en el programa de posgrado?	Are you going to register in **the postgraduate program?**
el programa de licenciatura	the bachelor's (degree) program

No, voy a inscribirme en el programa de maestría.	No, I'm going to enroll in **the master's (degree) program**.
el programa de doctorado	the doctoral (degree) program, the PhD program

Era útil que viéramos el plan de estudios.	It was useful for us to see **the curriculum**.
el currículo	the curriculum
el sílabo	the syllabus

C   Express each of the following sentences in Spanish. Many of the sentences require the use of the imperfect subjunctive.

1. *She hoped her daughter would follow in her footsteps.*

2. *They advised him to become an engineer.*

3. *I was glad to register in the master's degree program.*

4. *Did you (Ud.) ask them to update (actualizar) the database?*

5. *It was good that you (Uds.) were applying for (solicitar (to apply for)) a scholarship.*

6. *His parents were very understanding.*

7. *Is she a graduate of the law school?*

8. *It was important that we see the curriculum.*

9. *The graduates of the engineering school found good jobs after graduating.*

10. *We think he's going to study for the bachelor's degree in chemistry.*

▶ DIÁLOGO 5 · La vacunación: las ventajas y las desventajas (1)

Study the dialogue, then listen to the recording and repeat each line.

DOCTORA RUBIO	Señora, a su hija le toca la vacunación contra el sarampión, las paperas y la rubéola. Hagan Uds. el favor de pasar a mi consulta.
SEÑORA MOLINA	Doctora Rubio, mi abuela se oponía a que la vacunáramos. Tenía miedo de que la vacuna le hiciera daño.
DOCTORA RUBIO	Señora, ésa es una idea muy anticuada. Siempre hay un riesgo mínimo pero las vacunas han prevenido muchas enfermedades mortales.

Análisis

Check that you understand the linguistic breakdown of each speech from *Diálogo 5*.

La vacunación: las ventajas y las desventajas	*Vaccination: pros and cons*
Señora, a su hija le toca la vacunación contra el sarampión, las paperas y la rubéola. Hagan Uds. el favor de pasar a mi consulta.	*Mrs. Molina, it's time for your daughter to have the measles, mumps, and rubella vaccination. Please go to my office.*
le toca	*it's time, it's her turn*
la vacunación	*vaccination*
el sarampión	*measles*
las paperas	*mumps*
la rubéola	*rubella (German measles)*
hagan Uds. el favor de + *infinitive*	*please (do something) (formal)*
la consulta	*doctor's office*

Doctora Rubio, mi abuela se oponía a que la vacunáramos. Tenía miedo de que la vacuna le hiciera daño.

> se oponía a
> se oponía a que la vacunáramos
> la vacuna
> tenía miedo de que + *subjunctive*
> tenía miedo de que le hiciera daño

Doctor Rubio, my grandmother was against our vaccinating her. She was afraid that the vaccine would harm her.

> *she was against, she opposed*
> *she was against our vaccinating her*
> *vaccine*
> *she was afraid* + verb
> *she was afraid it would harm her*

Señora, ésa es una idea muy anticuada. Siempre hay un riesgo mínimo pero las vacunas han prevenido muchas enfermedades mortales.

> ésa es una idea
> anticuado
> el riesgo
> mínimo
> prevenir
> la enfermedad
> mortal

Mrs. Molina, that's a very old-fashioned idea. There's always a very small risk, but vaccines have prevented many deadly diseases.

> *that is an idea*
> *old-fashioned, outdated, antiquated*
> *risk*
> *minimal, very small*
> *to prevent* (conjugated like **venir**)
> *illness, disease*
> *deadly*

▶ Variantes

Listen, and repeat the same structures from *Diálogo 5*, now with new vocabulary.

Tenía miedo de que la vacuna contra la gripe le hiciera daño.

> la influenza
> el coronavirus
> el Covid-19
> la varicela
> la poliomielitis
> la neumonía
> la pulmonía
> la hepatitis
> la (fiebre) tifoidea
> la tuberculosis
> la difteria
> la viruela

*He was afraid the **flu** vaccine would harm her.*

> *influenza*
> *coronavirus*
> *Covid-19*
> *chicken pox*
> *polio*
> *pneumonia*
> *pneumonia*
> *hepatitis*
> *typhoid fever*
> *tuberculosis*
> *diphtheria*
> *smallpox*

¿Cómo se propaga el Covid-19?

> se contagia
> se previene
> se cura
> se trata

*How is Covid-19 **spread**?*

> *caught, spread*
> *prevented*
> *treated, cured*
> *treated*

Por favor, vaya Ud. a la consulta .	*Please go to **the doctor's office**.*
la sala de espera	*the waiting room*
la sala de emergencias	*the emergency room*
la sala de urgencias	*the emergency room*
la unidad de cuidados intensivos (UCI)	*the intensive care unit (ICU)*
la habitación de hospital	*the hospital room*
la estación de enfermería	*the nurses' station*
la estación de enfermeros	*the nurses' station*
la clínica	*the clinic*

El médico admitió al paciente.	*The doctor **admitted** the patient.*
dio de alta	*discharged*

Es paciente ambulatorio.	*He is an outpatient.*

▶ DIÁLOGO 6 · La vacunación: las ventajas y las desventajas (2)

Study the dialogue, then listen to the recording and repeat each line.

SEÑORA MOLINA   Doctora, yo no quería que mi abuela se ofendiera, pero le dije que es mi deber proteger a mi hija. Por favor, quisiera que le aplique la vacuna a mi niñita para que nunca sufra de estas terribles enfermedades.

DOCTORA RUBIO   Haces lo correcto, señora. Imagínese si hubieran tenido una vacuna contra la influenza durante la pandemia de 1918, no habrían muerto cincuenta millones o más de personas.

Análisis

Check that you understand the linguistic breakdown of each speech from *Diálogo 6*.

Doctora, yo no quería que mi abuela se ofendiera, pero le dije que es mi deber proteger a mi hija. Por favor, quisiera que le aplique la vacuna a mi niñita para que nunca sufra de estas terribles enfermedades.	*Doctor, I didn't want my grandmother to feel hurt, but I told her that it's my duty to protect my daughter. Please, I'd like you to give my little girl the shot so that she'll never have these dreadful diseases.*
ofenderse	*to get offended, be insulted, feel hurt*
no quería que se ofendiera	*I didn't want her to feel hurt*
el deber	*duty*
proteger (yo protejo)	*to protect*
quisiera (*imperfect subjunctive*)	*I would like* (to soften a request)
aplicar	*to apply, give* (an injection)
quisiera que le aplique	*I'd like you to give her*
la vacuna	*vaccine*
la niñita	*little girl*
sufrir de	*to have; to suffer from*
para que nunca sufra de	*so that she'll never have*
terrible	*dreadful*

Haces lo correcto, señora. Imagínese si hubieran tenido una vacuna contra la influenza durante la pandemia de 1918, no habrían muerto cincuenta millones o más de personas.	*You're doing the right thing, Mrs. Molina. Imagine if they had had a vaccine against influenza during the pandemic of 1918, fifty million or more people would not have died.*
hacer lo correcto	*to do the right thing*
imagínese	*imagine (**Ud.** command form of **imaginarse**)*
si hubieran tenido (*pluperfect subjunctive*)	*if they had had*
contra la influenza	*against influenza/flu*
la pandemia	*pandemic*
mil novecientos dieciocho	*1918*
no habrían muerto (*conditional perfect*)	*they wouldn't have died*
cincuenta millones o más de personas	*50 million or more people*

Variantes

Listen, and repeat the same structures from *Diálogo 6*, now with new vocabulary.

Yo no quería que mi abuela se ofendiera .	*I didn't want my grandmother **to feel hurt**.*
se enojara	*to get angry*
se enfadara	*to get angry*
se preocupara	*to worry*
se alterara	*to get upset*
se afligiera	*to get upset*
se molestara	*to get annoyed*
se asustara	*to get scared*
se desesperara	*to despair, to lose hope*

Era necesario que el médico le hiciera un chequeo de rutina .	*It was necessary that the doctor **give him a routine checkup**.*
le tomara la tensión	*take his blood pressure*
le examinara la garganta y los oídos	*examine his throat and ears*
le tomara el peso	*weigh him*
lo pusiera a dieta	*put him on a diet*
lo pusiera a régimen	*put him on a diet*
le recetara un medicamento	*prescribe a medicine for him*
le aplicara la vacuna contra el tétanos	*give him a tetanus shot*
lo mandara al laboratorio	*send him to the lab*
le hiciera un análisis de sangre	*give him a blood test*
le hiciera una radiografía torácica	*take a chest X-ray*
le diera estrategias para dejar de fumar	*give him strategies to stop smoking*

Era posible que Uds. tuvieran gripe por los síntomas .	It was possible that you had the flu because of **the symptoms**.
los estornudos	the sneezing (literally, sneezes)
la tos	the cough
la fatiga	the fatigue
el malestar general	the malaise, the unwell feeling
la fiebre	the fever
el dolor de cabeza	the headache
el dolor de estómago	the stomachache
los dolores musculares	the muscle aches

Nos sentíamos tristes que él sufriera de una enfermedad grave .	We felt sad that he had **a serious disease**.
de diabetes	diabetes
de cáncer	cancer
de una enfermedad cardiovascular	cardiovascular disease
de la artritis	arthritis
de la enfermedad de Alzheimer	Alzheimer's disease
del síndrome de inmunodeficiencia adquirida (el SIDA)	acquired immunodeficiency syndrome (AIDS)

Doctora, yo quisiera que le aplique la vacuna .	Doctor, I'd like you to give her **the vaccine**.
la segunda dosis	the second dose
la inyección	the injection

D Express each of the following sentences in Spanish.

1. *It's time for our children's routine checkup.*
2. *There was no vaccine to prevent influenza in 1918.*
3. *Doctor Jonas Salk developed a vaccine to prevent polio.*
4. *We were afraid that Covid-19 would spread throughout the whole country.*
5. *Their family doctor told them not to worry.*
6. *The patients* [masc.] *were gradually getting better* (mejorarse (*to get better*)).
7. *The nurse* [fem.] *took the patient's* [masc.] *blood pressure and gave him a flu shot.*
8. *It was necessary for the doctor* [fem.] *to put her obese* (obeso) *patients on a diet.*
9. *The cardiologist advised his patients to exercise and stop smoking.*
10. *Although she had no symptoms, it was possible that she was a carrier* (el portador / la portadora) *of the virus.*

Estructura y Práctica

Softening Requests and Suggestions with the Imperfect Subjunctive

Spanish uses the imperfect subjunctive in main clauses to add a polite tone to the conversation. Note the difference in tone between these sentences, where the first sentence is more direct than the second.

Quiero hablar con usted.	*I want to speak with you.*
Quisiera hablar con usted.	*I would like to speak with you.*

The verbs **querer** and **poder** are frequently used in the imperfect subjunctive to soften a request, and **deber** in the imperfect subjunctive serves to soften a suggestion.

Quiero pedirle un favor.	*I want to ask you a favor.*
Quisiera pedirle un favor	*I'd like to ask you a favor.*
¿**Puedes** ayudarme?	*Can you help me?*
¿**Pudieras** ayudarme?	*Could you help me?*
Uds. **deben** ser más amables.	*You must be kinder.*
Uds. **debieran** ser más amables.	*You ought to be kinder.*

The conditional of these verbs (as well as others) may also be used to soften requests and suggestions. English uses *would* in a similar way.

¿Me **prestaría** Ud. veinte dólares?	*Would you lend me twenty dollars?*
¿Me **darías** su número de teléfono?	*Would you give me his phone number?*

IDIOMS AND EXPRESSIONS: **LA SANGRE** (*BLOOD*)

de sangre caliente *warm-blooded* / de sangre fría *cold-blooded*

Casi todos los mamíferos y las aves son animales de sangre caliente.	*Almost all mammals and birds are warm-blooded animals.*
La víbora, la rana, la tortuga y los peces son animals de sangre fría.	*The snake, frog, turtle, and fish are cold-blooded animals.*

llevar algo en la sangre *to have something in one's blood*

Lleva la música y el baile en la sangre.	*She has music and dance in her blood.*

sudar sangre *to make a great effort, work hard doing something* (literally, *to sweat blood*)

Están sudando sangre porque la fecha tope es mañana.	*They're working hard because the deadline is tomorrow.*

hervirle la sangre a alguien *to make someone's blood boil*

Tanta polémica le hierve la sangre.	*So much controversy makes her blood boil.*

tener mala sangre *to have bad intentions, be evil* (literally, *to have bad blood*)

Ese tipo tiene mala sangre así que no debes confiar en él.	*That guy has bad intentions so you shouldn't trust him.*

no tener sangre en las venas *to be coldhearted, be a cold fish*

Esa mujer a quien le falta empatía no tiene sangre en las venas.	*That woman, who's lacking empathy, is coldhearted.*
"No tengo nada que ofrecer más que sangre, esfuerzo, lágrimas y sudor." —Winston Churchill	*"I have nothing to offer but blood, toil, tears, and sweat."*

Relative Pronouns

In both Spanish and English, relative pronouns introduce a dependent clause that is part of a larger sentence.

In Spanish, the most common relative pronoun is **que**. **Que** can refer to both people and things, and it can function either as the subject or object of the verb in its clause.

- **Que** functioning as subject

el libro **que** me gusta (**que** is the subject of the verb **gusta**)	the book (**that**) I like
el profesor **que** nos enseña español (**que** is the subject of the verb **enseña**)	the professor **who** teaches us Spanish

- **Que** functioning as object

el libro **que** leímos (**que** is the object of the verb **leímos**)	the book (**that**) we read
el profesor **que** todo el mundo admira (**que** is the object of the verb **admira**)	the professor **that** everyone admires

When **que** refers to a person and is the object of the verb in its clause, it can be replaced by **a quien / a quienes**.

el profesor **a quien** todo el mundo admira	the professor (**whom**) everyone admires
los médicos **a quienes** todo el mundo consulta	the doctors (**whom**) everyone consults

The relative pronoun **que** is used after the prepositions **a**, **de**, **con**, and **en**. The sequence **en que** is especially common when referring to time.

el año **en que** nací	the year **in which** I was born

It is also used to refer to imprecise locations or when figurative meanings of **en** are implied.

la ciudad **en que** vivimos	the city we live in
el método **en que** insisten	the method they insist on

After all prepositions other than **a**, **de**, and **con** and after **en** when **en** indicates physical location inside an object, **que** is replaced by **el que, la que, los que, las que** or by **el cual, la cual, los cuales, las cuales**. These two sets of relative pronouns can refer to either people or things. They can also replace **que** after **a**, **de**, and **con** for greater precision. Note that they agree in gender and number with the antecedent.

Abrí la caja **en la que** estaba el regalo.	I opened the box that the gift was in.
el procedimiento **según el que / el cual** se han organizado las elecciones	the procedure according to which the election was organized
la epidemia **durante la que / la cual** murieron tantas personas	the epidemic during which so many people died

The relative pronouns **quien/quienes** can replace **el que, la que, los que, las que** or **el cual, la cual, los cuales, las cuales** when these relative pronouns refer to people.

los empresarios para **quienes / los que /** **los cuales** hemos trabajado	*the businesspeople for whom we have worked*

El cual, la cual, los cuales, and **las cuales** are especially common after compound prepositions, such as **cerca de, delante de, al frente de, encima de, antes de, después de, a causa de**.

los árboles **cerca de los cuales** acampamos	*the trees near which we camped*
el edificio **encima del cual** hay un restaurante giratorio	*the building on top of which there's a revolving restaurant*
la construcción **a causa de la cual** nos retrasamos	*the construction because of which we were late*

The relative pronouns **lo que** and **lo cual** refer to a preceding clause or idea, and they occur only in clauses set off by commas (nonrestrictive clauses).

Mis vecinos hacen mucho ruido, **lo que / lo cual** me molesta mucho.	*My neighbors make a lot of noise, which bothers me a lot.*
El zoólogo habló de la fauna sudamericana, **lo que / lo cual** fue muy interesante.	*The zoologist spoke about South American fauna, which was very interesting.*

E Write the dependent clause that correctly completes each of the following sentences. Write each clause in two ways, using the correct relative pronouns. Follow the *modelo*.

MODELO   Hay agua de lluvia debajo de esos tejados (*roofs*).

→ Son esos tejados *debajo de los cuales* hay agua de lluvia.

→ Son esos tejados *debajo de los que* hay agua de lluvia.

1. Hay un cine enfrente de ese restaurante.

   Es ese restaurante _____ hay un cine.

2. Siempre encuentro buenos libros en esa librería.

   Esa es la librería _____ siempre encuentro buenos libros.

3. Compramos regalos para esos niños.

   Esos son los niños _____ compramos regalos.

4. Se pueden alquilar barcos al otro lado de este lago.

   Este es el lago _____ se pueden alquilar barcos.

5. Hay una fuente en medio de la plaza.

   Es la plaza _____ hay una fuente.

6. Vivimos cerca de la calle comercial.

   Ven a ver la calle comercial _____ vivimos.

7. Jaime tuvo que dejar de trabajar a causa de sus problemas de salud.

   Te voy a decir cuáles son los problemas de salud _____ Jaime tuvo que dejar de trabajar.

8. Se ha fijado (fijarse (*to fix*)) su sueldo según estos criterios (*criteria*).

   Estos son los criterios _____ se ha fijado su sueldo.

9. Yo regresaré después de algunas palabras del jefe de nuestro equipo.

   Primero, algunas palabras del jefe de nuestro equipo _____ yo regresaré.

10. Se presentaron varias canciones nuevas durante ese festival.

    Asistimos al festival _____ se presentaron varias canciones nuevas.

F   Express each of the following phrases in Spanish.

1. *the river toward which we are going*

2. *an illness against which we need a vaccine*

3. *the date before which we have to pay*

4. *the documents about which I need more information*

5. *the school opposite which there is a computer store*

6. *a neighborhood in the middle of which there is a park*

7. *a skyscraper on top of which there's a restaurant*

8. *the art museum in front of which there are two statues*

TYPES OF CLAUSES

A clause is a group of words containing a subject and a predicate. There are two basic types of clauses: independent clauses and dependent clauses.

An independent clause, also called a main clause, can stand on its own.

    Los Miranda compraron una casa.   *The Mirandas bought a house.*

A dependent clause, also called a subordinate clause or an embedded clause, cannot stand on its own. A sentence containing both an independent clause and a dependent clause is called a complex sentence. A dependent clause is embedded in a complex sentence by means of a conjunction or a relative pronoun.

    Los Miranda compraron una casa   *The Mirandas bought a house*
      que queda cerca del parque.   ***that is near the park***.

Note that in the above sentences, the highlighted words are dependent clauses introduced by conjunctions: Spanish **que** or English *that*. In Spanish, the word **que** must introduce such dependent clauses. In English, the conjunction *that* is often omitted.

Noun Clauses

The subjunctive is a verbal category that occurs almost exclusively in dependent clauses. Most of the examples of the subjunctive studied so far have occurred in noun clauses. A noun clause is a dependent clause that functions the way a noun does: It can be either the subject or the object of the verb of the main clause.

- Noun clause as the subject of the verb

Que no quieras quedarte es malo.	*It's bad that you don't want to stay.*
Es increíble que él no lo sepa.	*It's unbelievable that he doesn't know it.*
Nos preocupa que no nos llamen.	*It worries us that they don't call us.*

- Noun clause as the object of the verb

Prefieren que ella regrese mañana.	*They prefer that she return tomorrow.*
No quiero que los niños se enfermen.	*I don't want the children to get sick.*
No creemos que conozcas a nuestro primo.	*We don't believe that you know our cousin.*

Adjective Clauses

An adjective clause is a dependent clause that functions as an adjective in the sentence. It adds information about a noun.

el carro nuevo	*the new car*
el carro que compré	*the car that I bought*

Both the adjective **nuevo** and the dependent clause **que compré** modify the noun **carro** in the same way. Adjective clauses are also known as relative clauses.

In the phrase **el carro que compré**, the word **que** is the relative pronoun—the word that introduces the adjective clause and embeds it in the larger sentence. The word **carro** is the antecedent, that is, the word that the relative pronoun refers to. (See Chapter 5.)

In Spanish, the verb of a dependent clause is in the subjunctive if the antecedent is indefinite, not yet identified, or negated.

Buscamos empleados **que hablen** **español**.	*We're looking for employees who speak Spanish.*
Quiero un carro **que funcione bien**.	*I want a car that works well.*

In the above sentences, the antecedents **empleados** and **un carro** have not yet been identified by the speaker, because he or she is still seeking them. Therefore, the verb of the dependent clause is in the subjunctive. Antecedents that are the objects of verbs such as **buscar** and **querer** and that are not preceded by the definite article or a demonstrative adjective are followed by dependent clauses with a verb in the subjunctive.

No hay vecino que **quiera** mudarse.	*There is no neighbor who wants to move.*
No hay ningún celular que me **guste**.	*There is no cell phone that I like.*
No hay nadie aquí que nos **comprenda**.	*There is no one here who understands us.*

In the above sentences, the existence of the antecedent is negated, and therefore the verb of the adjective clause that modifies it is in the subjunctive.

When words like **alguien**, **alguno**, and **uno** are used in questions and followed by a dependent clause, the verb in that clause is often in the subjunctive.

¿Hay **algún médico que** te **pueda** atender?	*Is there any doctor who can see / tend to you?*
¿Hay **alguien** aquí **que sepa** química?	*Is there anyone here who knows chemistry?*
¿Tienen Uds. **un amigo que** los **quiera** acompañar?	*Do you have a friend who wants to go with you?*

G *Se necesitan empleados.* Express each of the following adjective clauses in Spanish to tell what kind of employees this business needs. Follow the *modelo*.

MODELO   La empresa necesita empleados __que quieran trabajar__.
          (who want to work)

La empresa necesita empleados _____.

1. *who are serious and reliable*

2. *who have a lot of experience*

3. *who want to learn*

4. *who get along with their colleagues*

5. *who don't complain about every little thing*

6. *who don't waste time*

7. *who don't arrive late*

8. *who are polite*

Words Ending in *-ever*: the Indicative vs. the Subjunctive

Compare two possible answers to the following question.

¿Qué película debemos ver?	*What film should we see?*
La película que tú **quieres** ver.	*The film that you want to see.*
OR	
La película que tú **quieras** ver.	*Whichever film you want to see.*

In the first answer, the verb is in the indicative because the person speaking is implying that he or she knows which film the other person wants to see: The antecedent **la película** has been identified. In the second answer, the verb is in the subjunctive because the speaker does not yet know which film the other person wants to see: The antecedent **la película** has not yet been identified. In English, this "not yet identified" function is communicated by words ending in *-ever*: *whichever, whatever, whoever, whomever, wherever, whenever, however.*

Here are some additional examples.

¿Qué día quieres viajar?	*What day do you want to travel?*
El día que **dices**.	*The day you say.*
OR	
El día que **digas**.	*Whichever day you say.*

¿Qué debemos comprar para comer?	*What should we buy to eat?*
Lo que at ti te **gusta** comer.	*What you like to eat.*
OR	
Lo que a ti te **guste** comer.	*Whatever you like to eat.*
¿Adónde quieres ir para acampar?	*Where do you want to go camping?*
Donde tú **prefieres**.	*Where you prefer.*
OR	
Donde tú **prefieras**.	*Wherever you prefer.*

H *Como quieran.* Express each of the following phrases in Spanish to tell your friends your preferences for dinner. Use the present subjunctive to say it's up to them. Follow the *modelo.*

MODELO   Vamos a cenar ___*cuando Uds. tengan hambre*___ . *(whenever you're hungry)*

Vamos a cenar _____.

1. *wherever you choose*

2. *whenever you say*

3. *in whatever restaurant you like*

4. *whatever you desire*

5. *at whatever time you want*

6. *with whomever you prefer*

DIÁLOGO 7 · La vida en los tiempos del coronavirus

Study the dialogue, then listen to the recording and repeat each line.

TERESA	Gabriel, vi a nuestro hijo con sus amigos ayer, sin la mascarilla.
GABRIEL	Ay, ese muchacho. Y con el Covid-19 que sigue propagándose. ¿No le insististe en que se pusiera la mascarilla?
TERESA	¡No sabes cuántas veces! Ojalá nos hiciera caso. Él nos oye como quien oye llover.
GABRIEL	Pues, de ahora en adelante le prohibimos salir sin que se ponga la mascarilla. Tan pronto como Fernando llegue a casa, voy a decirle cuatro verdades.
TERESA	De acuerdo. Es para protegerlo y también a nosotros en estos tiempos tan espantosos.

Análisis

Check that you understand the linguistic breakdown of each speech from *Diálogo 7.*

Gabriel, vi a nuestro hijo con sus amigos ayer, sin la mascarilla.	*Gabriel, I saw our son with his friends yesterday, without his mask.*
la mascarilla	*mask, surgical mask*

Ay, ese muchacho. Y con el Covid-19 que sigue propagándose. ¿No le insististe en que se pusiera la mascarilla?

Oh, that boy. And with Covid-19 that keeps on spreading. Didn't you insist that he put his mask on?

propagar	*to spread*
sigue propagándose	*it keeps on spreading*
insistir en	*to insist on*
le insististe en que se pusiera	*you insisted that he put on*

¡No sabes cuántas veces! Ojalá nos hiciera caso. Él nos oye como quien oye llover.

You don't know how many times! I wish he would listen to us. It goes in one ear and out the other.

cuántas veces	*how many times*
hacerle caso a alguien	*to listen to someone, pay attention to someone*
Ojalá nos hiciera caso.	*I wish he would listen to us.*
Nos oye como quien oye llover.	*It goes in one ear and out the other.*

Pues, de ahora en adelante le prohibimos salir sin que se ponga la mascarilla. Tan pronto como Fernando llegue a casa, voy a decirle cuatro verdades.

Well, from now on we'll forbid him to go out without putting his mask on. As soon as Fernando comes home, I'm going to give him a piece of my mind.

de ahora en adelante	*from now on*
prohibir (yo prohíbo)	*to forbid*
sin que se ponga	*without his putting on*
le prohibimos salir sin que se ponga la mascarilla	*we'll forbid him to go out without putting on his mask*
tan pronto como llegue	*as soon as he arrives*
decirle cuatro verdades	*to give someone a piece of your mind*

De acuerdo. Es para protegerlo y también a nosotros en estos tiempos tan espantosos.

Okay. It's to protect him and us, too, in these dreadful times.

de acuerdo	*okay, right, agreed*
proteger (yo protejo)	*to protect*
para protegerlo y también a nosotros	*to protect him and us, too*
espantoso	*frightening, dreadful*
estos tiempo espantosos	*these dreadful times*

▶ Variantes

Listen, and repeat the same structures from *Diálogo 7*, now with new vocabulary.

Te prohíbo salir sin que te pongas la mascarilla .

*I forbid you to go out without putting on your **mask**.*

las botas impermeables	*waterproof boots*
el anorak	*anorak*
la parka	*parka*
la chaqueta con capucha	*hooded jacket*
el mono de nieve	*snowsuit*
los pantalones de nieve	*snow pants*

Lo haremos antes de que se enteren.	*We'll do it **before** they find out.*
a menos que	*unless*
en caso de que	*in case*
a condición de que	*on condition that*
a fin de que	*so that*
para que	*so that*

Llevaba una mascarilla quirúrgica para no contagiarse del coronavirus.	***She wore a surgical mask*** *so she wouldn't catch coronavirus.*
Mantenía una distancia segura de los demás	*She kept a safe distance from other people*
Se lavaba las manos muy a menudo	*She washed her hands very often*
Usaba desinfectante de manos	*She used hand sanitizer*
Evitaba tocarse la cara con las manos	*She avoided touching her face with her hands*
Saludaba a la gente sin un apretón de manos	*She greeted people without a handshake*
Evitaba lugares mal ventilados	*She avoided badly ventilated places*
Desinfectaba las superficies con peróxido de hidrógeno	*She disinfected surfaces with hydrogen peroxide*

Estructura y Práctica

Adverb Clauses

Adverb clauses modify a verb in the same way that an adverb does. Adverb clauses are embedded in a complex sentence by means of a conjunction.

Lo hice **correctamente**.	*I did it **correctly**.*
Lo hice **como tú me habías dicho**.	*I did it **as you had told me**.*
Prefiero estudiar **en la biblioteca**.	*I prefer to study **in the library**.*
Prefiero estudiar **donde no hay ruido**.	*I prefer to study **where there's no noise**.*

In the above examples, **como** and **donde** are conjunctions.

The following conjunctions introduce adverb clauses in which the verb must be in the subjunctive: **a condición de que** (*on (the) condition that*), **a fin de que** (*in order that, so that*), **a menos que** (*unless*), **antes (de) que** (*before*), **con tal (de) que** (*provided that*), **en caso de que** (*in case*), **para que** (*in order that, so that*), and **sin que** (*without*).

Note that in the pairs of examples below, when the verb of the main clause is in a past tense, the verb of the dependent clause is in the imperfect subjunctive.

Volveré **antes de que** salgan.	*I'll return **before** they leave.*
Volví **antes de que** salieran.	*I returned **before** they left.*
Te lo explico **para que** lo comprendas.	*I'm explaining it to you **so that** you'll understand it.*
Te lo expliqué **para que** lo comprendieras.	*I explained it to you **so that** you'd understand it.*

> Abramos el archivo **sin que** nadie lo sepa.
>
> *Let's open the file **without** anyone knowing (it).*
>
> Abrimos el archivo **sin que** nadie lo supiera.
>
> *We opened the file **without** anyone knowing (it).*

I   ***Sin que…*** Express each of the following phrases in Spanish to tell how these friends planned a surprise party. Remember that the conjunction **sin que** introduces adverb clauses that require the subjunctive, in this case, the imperfect subjunctive. Follow the *modelo*.

MODELO   Hicimos los preparativos __*sin que nadie supiera nada*__.
               (*without anyone finding out anything*)

Hicimos los preparativos _____.

1. *without anyone seeing us*

2. *without anyone asking us anything*

3. *without anyone bothering us*

4. *without anyone helping us*

5. *without anyone looking for us*

6. *without anyone noticing us*

J   ***Con tal (de) que.*** Express each of the following phrases in Spanish to tell what has to happen for the virus not to spread. Remember that the conjunction **con tal (de) que** introduces adverb clauses that require the subjunctive, in this case, the present subjunctive. Follow the *modelo*.

MODELO   El virus no se propagará __*con tal (de) que nos pongamos la*__

         __*mascarilla*__. (*as long as we put on our masks*)

El virus no se propagará _____.

1. *as long as we take care*

2. *as long as we use disinfectant*

3. *as long as we avoid badly ventilated places*

4. *as long as we wash our hands often*

5. *as long as we keep a safe distance between people*

6. *as long as we don't touch our faces*

Adverb Clauses of Time: the Indicative vs. the Subjunctive

Some conjunctions of time can be followed by either the conditional or the subjunctive. The conjunctions **después (de) que** (*after*), **cuando** (*when*), **hasta que** (*until*), **tan pronto (como)** (*as soon as*), and **en cuanto a** (*as soon as*) are followed by a verb in the indicative tense when the main verb is in the present tense or a past tense.

Siempre espero hasta que **llega** mi padre.	*I always wait until my father arrives.*
Me alegro cuando mis hijos **están** contentos.	*I'm glad when my children are happy.*
Salí en cuanto me **avisaron**.	*I left as soon as they let me know.*

If, however, the verb of the main clause is in the future, or if it has a command form, the verb of the dependent clause is in the subjunctive.

Esperaré hasta que **llegue** mi padre.	*I'll wait until my father arrives.*
Me alegraré cuando mis hijos **estén** contentos.	*I'll be glad when my children are happy.*
Salgan Uds. en cuanto los **avisen**.	*Leave as soon as they let you know.*

K Write either the preterit indicative or the present subjunctive of the verb in parentheses to correctly complete each of the following sentences.

1. Lo inscribiré en cuanto nosotros _____ la solicitud (*application form*). (recibir)

2. Marco, no voy a dejarte salir hasta que _____ tu tarea. (terminar)

3. Seguí llamando hasta que ellos me _____. (contestar)

4. Avísame tan pronto como ellos te _____ el paquete. (entregar)

5. ¿Te matricularás en el programa de maestría a menos que ellos no te _____ una beca? (ofrecer)

6. Se sirvió la comida después de que los invitados _____ a la mesa. (sentarse)

7. ¡Qué contento se puso el perro cuando nos _____! (ver)

8. Leonor y Hugo se casaron tan pronto como los dos _____ médicos. (hacerse)

▶ DIÁLOGO 8 · ¿La escuela pública tradicional o la escuela pública subvencionada? (1)

Study the dialogue, then listen to the recording and repeat each line.

ANITA	¿Sabes? Gonzalo y yo no estamos nada satisfechos con la escuela pública.
MARIO	Carmen y yo tampoco. La disciplina es pésima.
ANITA	Nos gustaría que nuestra hija asistiera a la nueva escuela pública subvencionada.
MARIO	Nuestro hijo también es muy inteligente y se aburre en la escuela.
ANITA	El nivel académico es bajísimo.
MARIO	Carmen y yo estamos hartos de quejarnos al director.

Análisis

Check that you understand the linguistic breakdown of each speech from *Diálogo 8*.

¿Sabes? Gonzalo y yo no estamos nada satisfechos con la escuela pública.	*You know? Gonzalo and I are not at all satisfied with the public school.*
nada satisfechos	*not at all satisfied*
la escuela pública	*public school*

Carmen y yo tampoco. La disciplina es pésima.	Carmen and I aren't either. The discipline is awful.
la disciplina	discipline
pésimo	awful, dreadful

Nos gustaría que nuestra hija asistiera a la nueva escuela pública subvencionada.	We'd like our daughter to attend the new charter school.
asistir a	to attend
subvencionado	subsidized
la escuela pública subvencionada	charter school

Nuestro hijo también es muy inteligente y se aburre en la escuela.	Our son is very intelligent, too, and gets bored in school.
se aburre	he gets bored, he's bored (**aburrirse**)

El nivel académico es bajísimo.	The academic level is very low.
el nivel	level
académico	academic
bajísimo (< bajo)	very low

Carmen y yo estamos hartos de quejarnos al director.	Carmen and I are sick and tired of complaining to the principal.
estar harto de	to be sick of (something), be fed up with (something)
quejarse	to complain
el director	principal (of school)

▶ Variantes

Listen, and repeat the same structures from *Diálogo 8*, now with new vocabulary.

Nos gustaría que nuestra hija asistiera a una escuela privada.	We would like our daughter to attend a private school.
Nos encantaría que	We would love
Querríamos que	We would want
Desearíamos que	We would want

Queríamos que nuestros hijos asistieran a una escuela excelente .	We wanted our children to attend an excellent school.
asistieran a una escuela particular	to attend a private school
estudiaran con maestros excepcionales	to study with outstanding teachers
siguieran clases académicas rigurosas	to take rigorous academic courses
leyeran las obras maestras de la literatura universal	to read the masterpieces of world literature
estuvieran motivados	to be motivated
aprendieran mucho	to learn a lot
se graduaran con conocimientos profundos de las materias	to graduate with in-depth knowledge of the subjects
pensaran por sí mismos	to think for themselves
tuvieran un amor por el aprendizaje de toda la vida	to have a lifelong love of learning

Esperaban que hubiera	They hoped that there would be
una reforma escolar comprensiva .	**comprehensive school reform**.
elección de escuela para todos	*school choice for all children*
los niños	

ⓓ DIÁLOGO 9 · ¿La escuela pública tradicional o la escuela pública subvencionada? (2)

Study the dialogue, then listen to the recording and repeat each line.

ANITA   ¿Cómo hacemos para que admitan a nuestros hijos?
MARIO   He leído que la admisión es por solicitud.
ANITA   El sitio web de la escuela tendrá toda la información.
MARIO   ¡Vamos! No hay tiempo que perder.
ANITA   Tienes razón. Habrá miles de padres que piensan igual que nosotros.
MARIO   Inscribamos a nuestros hijos en cuanto podamos.

Análisis

Check that you understand the linguistic breakdown of each speech from *Diálogo 9.*

¿Cómo hacemos para que admitan a nuestros hijos?	How do we go about getting them to admit our children?
¿cómo hacemos?	*how do we go about?*
admitir	*to admit*
para que admitan	*so that they admit*
¿cómo hacemos para que admitan?	*how do we go about getting them to admit?*

He leído que la admisión es por solicitud.	I've read that admission is by application.
la admisión	*admission*
la solicitud	*application*
por solicitud	*by application*

El sitio web de la escuela tendrá toda la información.	The school website probably has all the information.
el sitio web	*website*
tendrá (*future of probability*)	*probably has* (**tener**)
toda la información	*all the information*

¡Vamos! No hay tiempo que perder.	Let's go! There's no time to lose.
¡Vamos!	*Let's go! / Come on!*
perder (**e > ie**)	*to lose*
no hay tiempo que perder	*there's no time to lose*

Tienes razón. Habrá miles de padres que piensan igual que nosotros.	You're right. There must be thousands of parents who think just like us.
habrá (*future of probability*)	*there must be* (**haber**)
miles de padres	*thousands of parents*
igual	*like, the same*
piensan igual que nosotros	*they think just like us, they think as we do*

Inscribamos a nuestros hijos en cuanto podamos.	*Let's enroll our children as soon as we can.*
inscribir	*to enroll*
inscribamos	*let's enroll*
inscribamos a nuestros hijos	*let's enroll our children*
en cuanto podamos	*as soon as we can*

▶ Variantes

Listen, and repeat the same structures from *Diálogo 9*, now with new vocabulary.

Estos padres piensan igual que nosotros.	*These parents **think** just like us.*
hacen las cosas	*do things*
crían a sus hijos	*raise their children*
quieren lo mejor para sus hijos	*want the best for their children*
buscan las mejores escuelas	*look for the best schools*
exigen normas académicas rigurosas	*demand high academic standards*

Los inscribiremos en cuanto podamos.	*We'll enroll them as soon as we can.*
Los inscribimos en cuanto pudimos.	*We enrolled them as soon as we could.*

Pagarán la matrícula tan pronto como la escuela admita a su hijo.	*They'll pay the tuition as soon as the school admits their son.*
Pagaron la matrícula tan pronto como la escuela admitió a su hijo.	*They paid the tuition as soon as the school admitted their son.*

¿Qué hacen Uds. para que sus hijos estudien más ?	*What do you do so that your children **study more**?*
lean más	*read more*
aprendan mucho	*learn a lot*
saquen buenas notas	*get good grades*
pasen menos tiempo pegados a los dispositivos electrónicos	*spend less time glued to their electronic devices*

L **Para que...** Express each of the following phrases in Spanish to give the reasons why Roberto's parents sent him to a private school. Remember that the conjunction **para que** introduces adverb clauses that require the subjunctive, in this case, the imperfect subjunctive. Follow the *modelo*.

MODELO   Mandaron a Roberto a un colegio privado _para que estudiara más_.
                      (*so that he would study more*)

Mandaron a Roberto a un colegio privado _____.

1. *so that he would learn a lot*

2. *so that he would not be bored*

3. *so that he would be able to take more rigorous courses*

4. *so that he would have better teachers*

5. *so that they would give him more homework*

6. *so that he would be motivated*

M **Translation.** Express each of the following sentences in Spanish, using the imperfect subjunctive as needed.

1. *Regina hoped that her children wouldn't be bored in school.*

2. *I told them to complain to the principal.*

3. *Did he advise you (Uds.) to submit* (presentar) *the application online?*

4. *We were sure that Benjamín was going to attend that charter school.*

5. *They would like us to see their website.*

6. *It was important that the academic level was very high.*

7. *What did they do so that their daughter would get good grades?*

8. *We didn't doubt that the parents wanted the best for their children.*

ⓘ DIÁLOGO 10 · Dos amigas hablan de la educación en casa. (1)

Study the dialogue, then listen to the recording and repeat each line.

SUSANA   Juli, ¿no sabes? Mis papás quieren que me eduque en casa como tú.
Eso me pone muy nerviosa.

JULIANA   Es cierto que la enseñanza en casa no les conviene a todos. Susi,
yo sé que vas a sacar mucho provecho de este plan de estudios.

SUSANA   ¿Qué asignaturas tomas? ¿Álgebra, biología, historia, literatura,
idiomas extranjeros?

JULIANA   Sí. Son cursos de nivel superior y de preparación universitaria.

Análisis

Check that you understand the linguistic breakdown of each speech from *Diálogo 10*.

Juli, ¿no sabes? Mis papás quieren que me eduque en casa como tú. Eso me pone muy nerviosa.	*Juli, you know what? My parents want me to be homeschooled, like you. That makes me very nervous.*
Juli	(nickname for *Juliana*)
¿no sabes?	*do you know what?*
educar en casa	*to homeschool*
educarse	*to be educated*
quieren que me eduque en casa	*they want me to be homeschooled*
me pone muy nerviosa	*it makes me very nervous*

Es cierto que la enseñanza en casa no les conviene a todos. Susi, yo sé que vas a sacar mucho provecho de este plan de estudios.	*It's true that homeschooling isn't good for everyone. Susi, I know that you're going to get a lot out of this curriculum.*
la enseñanza	*teaching*
la enseñanza en casa	*homeschooling*
convenirle a alguien	*to be suitable for someone, be good for someone*
Susi	(nickname for *Susana*)
sacar provecho de	*to benefit from*
sacar mucho provecho de	*to get a lot out of, benefit a lot from*
el plan de estudios	*curriculum*

¿Qué asignaturas tomas? ¿Álgebra, biología, historia, literatura, idiomas extranjeros?	*What subjects are you taking? Algebra, biology, history, literature, foreign languages?*
la asignatura	*subject*
el álgebra	*algebra*
la biología	*biology*
la historia	*history*
la literatura	*literature*
el idioma extranjero	*foreign language*

Sí. Son cursos de nivel superior y de preparación universitaria.	*Yes. They're AP and college prep courses.*
el curso	*course*
el nivel	*level*
superior	*advanced*
el curso de nivel superior	*advanced placement course (AP course)*
universitario	*university* (adjective)
la preparación universitaria	*college prep*
el curso de preparación universitaria	*college prep course*

▶ Variantes

Listen, and repeat the same structures from *Diálogo 10*, now with new vocabulary.

Eso me pone nerviosa .	*That makes me **nervous**.*
feliz	*happy*
contenta	*glad*
triste	*sad*
inquieta	*anxious, worried*
incómoda	*uncomfortable*
enojada	*angry*
enfadada	*angry*
furiosa	*furious*

Era obvio que eso le puso nerviosa.	*It was obvious that that made her nervous.*
Era lamentable que eso le pusiera nerviosa.	*It was unfortunate that that made her nervous.*

Era verdad que la enseñanza en casa no les convenía a todos.	*It was true that homeschooling wasn't suitable for everyone.*
Era posible que la enseñanza en casa no les conviniera a todos.	*It was possible that homeschooling wasn't suitable for everyone.*
Era cierto que sacaban provecho de este plan de estudios.	*It was certain that they got a lot out of this curriculum.*
Era probable que sacaran provecho de este plan de estudios.	*It was probable that they got a lot out of this curriculum.*

DIÁLOGO 11 · Dos amigas hablan de la educación en casa. (2)

Study the dialogue, then listen to the recording and repeat each line.

SUSANA   ¿Es difícil acostumbrarte a tomar clases en línea?

JULIANA   No, de ninguna manera. Se usan libros y apps. Ven, yo te enseño.

SUSANA   Juli, dime, ¿no extrañas a tus amigos? Temo sentirme sola.

JULIANA   Susi, no te preocupes. Nuestros horarios coinciden así que podemos vernos cuando nos dé la gana.

Análisis

Check that you understand the linguistic breakdown of each speech from *Diálogo 11*.

¿Es difícil acostumbrarte a tomar clases en línea?	*Is it difficult to get used to taking classes online?*
acostumbrarse a	*to get used to*
tomar (clases) en línea	*to take (classes) online*
la clase en línea	*online class*
No, de ninguna manera. Se usan libros y apps. Ven, yo te enseño.	*No, not at all. We use books and apps. Come, I'll show you.*
de ninguna manera	*not at all*
se usan	*they're used, you/we use*
el/la app (< la aplicación)	*app*
se usan libros y apps	*we use books and apps*
ven	*come (**tú** command form of **venir**)*
enseñar	*to show, teach*
te enseño	*I'll show you*
Juli, dime, ¿no extrañas a tus amigos? Temo sentirme sola.	*Juli, tell me, don't you miss your friends? I'm afraid of feeling lonely.*
dime	*tell me (**tú** command form of **decir**)*
extrañar a	*to miss (someone)*
extrañas a tus amigos	*you miss your friends*
Susi, no te preocupes. Nuestros horarios coinciden así que podemos vernos cuando nos dé la gana.	*Susi, don't worry. Our schedules match up so we can see each other whenever we want.*

Variantes

Listen, and repeat the same structures from *Diálogo 11*, now with new vocabulary.

Yo iba a ver a mis amigos con tal que todos tuviéramos tiempo .	*I was going to see my friends provided that* ***we all had time.***
nuestros horarios coincidieran	*our schedules matched up*
no se hiciera tarde	*it didn't get late*
termináramos la tarea primero	*we finished our homework first*
mis papás me dejaran	*my parents let me*
¿Había alguna clase que te interesara?	*Was there a class (that) you were interested in?*
No, no había ninguna clase que me interesara.	*No, there was no class (that) I was interested in.*
¿Había algún maestro que enseñara clases de español a un nivel superior?	*Was there a teacher who taught Spanish classes at an advanced level?*
No, no había ningún maestro que las enseñara.	*No, there was no teacher who taught them.*
Buscaban una secundaria que tuviera clases de formación profesional.	*They were looking for a high school that had vocational training classes.*
Querían inscribirse en una secundaria que ofreciera clases de formación profesional.	*They wanted to enroll in a high school that offered vocational training classes.*

N Write sentences from the elements given, using the imperfect subjunctive. Follow the *modelo*.

MODELO   Daniel / querer : sus padres / pagar la matricula
→ Daniel quería que sus padres pagaran la matrícula.

1. Lupe y Ricardo / insistir en : sus hijos / asistir a una escuela privada

2. tú / recomendarle a tu amigo : seguir una clase de español en línea

3. era bueno : la profesora de Lucía / ser un buen modelo a seguir (*role model*)

4. Isabel / preferir : sus papás / educarla en casa

5. Moisés y yo / esperar : nuestro hijo / tomar clases de nivel superior

6. Uds. / dudar : convenirle a Ignacio / ese plan de estudios

7. yo / alegrarse de : los estudiantes / estar tan motivados

8. era necesario : la secundaria / ofrecer cursos de preparación universitaria

Un paso más

Are you ready to take your Spanish a step further? Here are exercises that will enhance your knowledge of the language and encourage you to express yourself freely.

O *Mis pensamientos y sentimientos.* Complete each of the following sentences, using the imperfect subjunctive to express your thoughts and feelings in Spanish.

1. Yo quería que...

2. Yo esperaba que...

3. Me gustó que...

4. Me alegré de que...

5. Yo dudaba que...

6. Necesitaba que...

7. Sentía que...

Complete each of the following sentences, using the imperfect subjunctive to tell what you and another person (**nosotros**) told other people to do and what they told you (**Uds.**) to do.

8. Les aconsejamos que...

9. Nos pidieron que...

10. Les mandamos que...

11. Nos recomendaron que...

12. Les exigimos que...

13. Nos propusieron que...

14. Les dijimos que...

P *Preguntas personales. Contesta las siguientes preguntas con oraciones completas en español.*

1. ¿Asististe a una escuela pública tradicional / una escuela pública subvencionada / una escuela o secundaria privada? ¿Cómo fue tu experiencia?

2. ¿Tus padres te educaron en casa? ¿Por qué lo hicieron?

3. ¿Qué clases tomaste cuando cursaste la licenciatura?

4. ¿Qué querían tus padres que fueras? ¿Cuál es tu profesión?

5. ¿Hiciste una maestría? ¿Un doctorado? ¿Cuál fue tu especialidad?

6. ¿Es importante tener un modelo a seguir? ¿Tuviste uno? ¿Quién fue?

7. ¿Seguiste los pasos de tus papás o de otra persona? ¿Quién fue?

8. ¿Te interesa el espacio exterior? ¿Te gusta ver los lanzamientos espaciales? ¿Te gustaría ver la Tierra desde Marte?

9. ¿Conoces a unos primeros intervinientes? ¿Cómo ayudan a las personas afectadas por una catástrofe? (Por ejemplo, piensa en la pandemia del Covid-19 o los atentados/ataques terroristas de 9/11/2001.)

10. ¿Cómo les ha afectado a ti y a tu familia la pandemia del Covid-19?

Q *Unos ensayos. En este capítulo leíste unos diálogos sobre la educación y otros sobre la salud. Escribe dos ensayos en español, uno sobre algún aspecto de la educación y otro sobre algún aspecto de la salud. Usa los diálogos como punto de partida* (point of departure), *aportándoles* (bringing to them) *tus propias ideas.*

R *Citas. Lee las siguientes citas y tradúcelas al inglés. Después, explica lo que significan en español. Tienen que ver con los temas del capítulo 18, la educación y la salud.*

1. "El trabajo del maestro no consiste tanto en enseñar todo lo aprendible (*what can be learned*), como en producir en el alumno amor y estima por el conocimiento."
—*John Locke*

2. "El problema no es que Johnny no sepa leer. El problema no es que Johnny no pueda pensar. El problema es que Johnny no sabe qué es pensar; lo confunde con sentir."
—*Thomas Sowell*

3. "El futuro de los niños es siempre hoy. Mañana será tarde."
—*Gabriela Mistral*

4. "No se puede enseñar nada a un hombre; sólo se le puede ayudar a encontrar la respuesta dentro de sí mismo."
—*Galileo Galilei*

5. "Espero que algún día la práctica de contagiar la viruela bovina (*cowpox*) a los seres humanos se extienda por el mundo—cuando llegue ese día, ya no habrá más viruela."
—*Edward Jenner*

6. "Los mejores médicos del mundo son el doctor dieta, el doctor reposo y el doctor alegría."
—*Jonathan Swift*

Theater, Teleworking, and Shopping Online

Communication Goals

- Talking about things that will have happened
- Talking about things that would have happened
- Expressing probability or conjecture about an activity in the present, an activity in the past, or an ongoing activity
- Vocabulary: theater, teleworking, sports, shopping online, finding a job, films

Grammar Topics

- The Future Perfect
- The Conditional Perfect
- Expression of Probability and Conjecture
- The Future and the Conditional
- The Future Perfect and the Conditional Perfect
- The Progressive Tenses
- The Neuter Article **lo**
- The Present Perfect Subjunctive
- **Ojalá** *I hope, I wish* (Part 1)

▶ DIÁLOGO 1 · ¡Bien está lo que bien acaba!

Study the dialogue, then listen to the recording and repeat each line.

FEDERICA Apúrate, Esteban. Odio llegar tarde al teatro. Me muero por ver
esta obra.
ESTEBAN Pierde cuidado, Fede. Veo un taxi libre. Lo voy a parar.
FEDERICA Pero ya son casi las ocho. Habrán bajado ya las luces.
ESTEBAN No creo. Siempre retrasan un poco la función para los impuntuales.
FEDERICA ¡Ojalá! ¡Habrán empezado a levantar el telón!
ESTEBAN Mira, ya hemos llegado. Entremos y la acomodadora nos llevará
a nuestros asientos.
FEDERICA ¡Menos mal! Tengo los nervios de punta.
ESTEBAN (Riéndose) ¿Ves? Confía en mí, Fede. Nunca me he perdido una
función.

Análisis

Check that you understand the linguistic breakdown of each speech from *Diálogo 1*.

¡Bien está lo que bien acaba! · *All's well that ends well!*

Apúrate, Esteban. Odio llegar tarde al teatro. Me muero por ver esta obra. · *Hurry up, Esteban. I hate to arrive at the theater late. I'm dying to see this play.*
  apúrate · *hurry up (**tú** command form of **apurarse**)*
  odio · *I hate (**odiar**)*
  morirse (**o > ue**) · *to die*
  me muero · *I'm dying*
  me muero por ver · *I'm dying to see*
  la obra · *play*

Pierde cuidado, Fede. Veo un taxi libre. Lo voy a parar. · *Don't worry, Fede. I see an empty taxi. I'm going to hail it.*
  el cuidado · *care*
  perder (**e > ie**) · *to lose*
  pierde cuidado · *don't worry*
  Fede · *(nickname for Federica)*
  un taxi libre · *an empty taxi*
  parar · *to hail (literally, to stop)*

Pero ya son casi las ocho. Habrán bajado ya las luces. · *But it's almost eight o'clock. They have probably dimmed the lights.*
  habrán bajado (*future perfect of probability or conjecture*) · *they have probably dimmed/lowered*
  las luces (la luz) · *lights*

No creo. Siempre retrasan un poco la función para los impuntuales. · *I don't think so. They always delay the performance a little for the latecomers.*
  retrasar · *to delay*
  el impuntual · *latecomer*

¡Ojalá! ¡Habrán empezado a levantar el telón!

I hope so! The curtain must be going up!

> ojalá — *I hope so*
> habrán empezado (*future perfect of probability or conjecture*) — *they have probably begun*
> el telón (del teatro) — *(theater) curtain*
> levantar el telón — *to raise the curtain*

Mira, ya hemos llegado. Entremos y la acomodadora nos llevará a nuestros asientos.

Look, we're here already. Let's go in and the usher will show us to our seats.

> hemos llegado — *we've arrived*
> entremos — *let's go in*
> la acomodadora — *usher*
> nos llevará — *she will take us*
> el asiento — *seat*

¡Menos mal! Tengo los nervios de punta.

Thank goodness! I'm a nervous wreck.

> menos mal — *thank goodness*
> los nervios — *nerves*
> de punta — *on edge*
> tener los nervios de punta — *to be a nervous wreck*

(*Riéndose*) ¿Ves? Confía en mí, Fede. Nunca me he perdido una función.

(Laughing) You see? Trust me, Fede. I've never missed a performance.

> confiar en — *to trust in*
> confía en mí — *trust me (**tú** command form of **confiar**)*
> perderse — *to miss (an event)*
> la función — *performance*

⏵ Variantes

Listen, and repeat the same structures from *Diálogo 1*, now with new vocabulary.

Habrán bajado las luces .

*They probably have **dimmed the lights**.*

> subido el telón — *raised the curtain*
> terminado el ensayo — *finished the rehearsal*
> salido a escena — *come on stage*
> oído muchos aplausos del público — *heard loud applause from the audience*

La orquesta habrá empezado a tocar *la Obertura Guillermo Tell de Rossini* .

The orchestra probably has begun to play **Rossini's *William Tell* Overture**.

> la Sinfonía No. 2 de Brahms — *Brahms's Symphony No. 2*
> el Concierto para Piano No. 2 de Rachmaninoff — *Rachmaninoff's Piano Concerto No. 2*

Nunca me he perdido una función .	*I've never missed **a performance**.*
una obra de teatro	*a play*
un espectáculo	*a show*
un drama	*a drama*
un musical	*a musical*
una comedia	*a comedy*
una tragedia	*a tragedy*
una ópera	*an opera*
una telenovela	*a TV serial, a soap opera*
un concierto	*a concert*
una reunión	*a meeting*
una junta	*a meeting*
un evento	*an event*

Habrán perdido el vuelo .	*I bet they missed **the flight**.*
el tren	*the train*
una gran oportunidad	*a great opportunity*
una semana de trabajo	*a week of work*
su objetivo	*their objective*
la fecha límite	*the deadline*

IDIOMS AND EXPRESSIONS: LA PUNTA (*TIP*)

tener los nervios de punta *to be on edge, be a nervous wreck*
    Parece tener los nervios de punta.   *She seems to be on edge.*

ponerle los pelos de punta *to make someone's hair stand on end*

Algo terrible les puso los pelos de punta.	*Something dreadful made their hair stand on end.*
Sácale la punta al lápiz.	*Sharpen the pencil.*
Por favor, córteme el pelo, solamente las puntas.	*Please cut my hair, just the ends.*
Gibraltar es una importante punta estratégica para Europa.	*Gibraltar is an important strategic point for Europe.*

las horas punta del tráfico *rush hour traffic*
la tecnología de punta *high tech, leading-edge technology*
la punta de los dedos *fingertips*
la punta de la lengua *tip of the tongue*
la punta del pan *end of the bread*
la otra punta de la ciudad *other side of the city*
la punta de la mesa *end of the table*
la punta del iceberg *tip of the iceberg*

ⓓ DIÁLOGO 2 · El teletrabajo, ¡eso es!

Study the dialogue, then listen to the recording and repeat each line.

FELIPE	Oye, Aarón, ¿te habrá sido difícil acostumbrarte al teletrabajo?
AARÓN	Al principio sí, pero las ventajas compensan con mucho los aspectos negativos.
FELIPE	¿Es cierto que hasta las juntas se llevan a cabo de manera remota?
AARÓN	Por supuesto. Y con la funcionalidad de compartir pantalla podemos hacer presentaciones también.
FELIPE	Aarón, ¿no te es difícil trabajar en casa con los niños?
AARÓN	Al contrario. Para Inés y para mí, trabajando en casa pasamos más tiempo con ellos. Yo diría que así estamos aún más motivados.
FELIPE	También ahorrarás el tiempo de viajar al trabajo.
AARÓN	En efecto. Ahorro dos horas al día de viajes a la oficina.
FELIPE	Aarón, me has convencido. ¡La semana entrante empiezo a trabajar a distancia!

Análisis

Check that you understand the linguistic breakdown of each speech from *Diálogo 2*.

El teletrabajo, ¡eso es!	*Teleworking, way to go!*
Oye, Aarón, ¿te habrá sido difícil acostumbrarte al teletrabajo?	*Say, Aaron, I'll bet it was hard for you to get used to working from home.*
te habrá sido difícil (*future perfect of probability or conjecture*)	*it must have been hard for you, I'll bet it was hard for you*
acostumbrarse a algo	*to get used to something*
Al principio sí, pero las ventajas compensan con mucho los aspectos negativos.	*At the beginning it was, but the advantages far outweigh the disadvantages.*
el principio	*beginning*
al principio	*at the beginning*
la ventaja	*advantage*
compensar	*to make up for*
con mucho	*to a large degree*
el aspecto negativo	*disadvantage, negative aspect*
¿Es cierto que hasta las juntas se llevan a cabo de manera remota?	*Is it true that even meetings are conducted online?*
¿es cierto?	*is it true?*
hasta	*even*
la junta	*meeting*
llevar a cabo	*to conduct, carry out*
de manera remota	*remotely, online*

Por supuesto. Y con la funcionalidad de compartir pantalla podemos hacer presentaciones también.

Of course. And with the screen sharing feature, we can do presentations, too.

por supuesto	*of course*
la funcionalidad	*function, feature*
compartir	*to share*
la pantalla	*screen*
la funcionalidad de compartir pantalla	*screen sharing feature*
la presentación	*presentation*

Aarón, ¿no te es difícil trabajar en casa con los niños?

Aarón, isn't it hard for you to work at home with the children?

te es difícil	*it's hard for you*
te es difícil trabajar	*it's hard for you to work*

Al contrario. Para Inés y para mí, trabajando en casa pasamos más tiempo con ellos. Yo diría que así estamos aún más motivados.

Just the opposite. For Inés and me, by working at home we spend more time with them. I would say that this way we are even more motivated.

al contrario	*on the contrary, just the opposite*
pasar tiempo	*to spend time*
pasar más tiempo con	*to spend more time with*
yo diría	*I would say*
aún más	*even more*
motivado	*motivated*

También ahorrarás el tiempo de viajar al trabajo.

You probably save the time of commuting to work, too.

ahorrarás (*future of probability*)	*you probably save*
viajar	*to travel*
viajar al trabajo	*to travel to work, commute*

En efecto. Ahorro dos horas al día de viajes a la oficina.

I surely do. I save two hours a day commuting to the office.

dos horas al día	*two hours a day*
el viaje	*trip, commute*
de viajes	*in traveling, in commuting*

Aarón, me has convencido. ¡La semana entrante empiezo a trabajar a distancia!

Aarón, you have convinced me. Next week I'll begin to work remotely!

convencer	*to convince*
me has convencido	*you have convinced me*
entrante	*coming, next*
la semana entrante	*next week*
a distancia	*remotely, online*

Variantes

Listen, and repeat the same structures from *Diálogo 2*, now with new vocabulary.

¿Te habrá sido difícil acostumbrarte al teletrabajo?	*I'll bet it was hard for you **to get used to** working at home.*
adaptarse al	*to adapt to*
acomodarse al	*to adjust to*
hacerse a la idea del	*to get used to the idea of*
¿Cómo se llevan a cabo las juntas?	*How are the meetings **conducted**?*
se realizan	*conducted*
Estamos aún más motivados .	*We're even more **motivated**.*
animados	*inspired*
enérgicos	*energetic*
dinámicos	*dynamic*
Te habrá sido difícil hacerlo.	*I'll bet it was **hard** for you to do it.*
fácil	*easy*
complicado	*complicated*
desafiante	*challenging*

Estructura y Práctica

The Future Perfect

The perfect tenses in Spanish consist of the auxiliary verb **haber** + the past participle. You have learned the present perfect tense, a tense that consists of the present tense of **haber** + the past participle. You have also learned the past perfect (pluperfect) tense, a tense that consists of the imperfect tense of **haber** + the past participle. In all the perfect tenses, **haber** changes to show person and tense, while the past participle remains invariable, that is, it does not change for gender or number.

The future perfect tense consists of the future tense of **haber** + the past participle. The English equivalent is *will have done, will have gone, will have seen*, etc. Study the conjugation of **haber** in the future perfect.

habré vuelto	*I will have returned*
habrás vuelto	*you will have returned*
habrá vuelto	*he/she/you will have returned*
habremos vuelto	*we will have returned*
habréis vuelto	*you will have returned*
habrán vuelto	*they/you will have returned*

As in English, the future perfect labels an event that will be completed in the future before another event occurs or that will be completed before some point in the future.

Todos **habrán regresado** antes de la junta.	*Everyone will have come back before the meeting.*
Para septiembre, la empresa **habrá abierto** dos sucursales nuevas.	*By September, the company will have opened two new branches.*

    Habremos terminado el ensayo para las   *We will have finished the rehearsal by*
      cinco.   *five o'clock.*

A future event often appears as an adverb clause in the subjunctive.

    Cuando **él llegue** al concierto, yo ya **habré**   *When he gets to the concert, I will have*
      comprado las entradas.   *already bought the tickets.*
    ¿Les **habrá avisado** Ud. **antes de que**   *Will you have notified them before they*
      salgan para el aeropuerto?   *leave for the airport?*

A   *Cuando vuelva Lorenzo...* Write sentences from the elements given, using the future perfect to tell what people will have done by the time Lorenzo gets back. Follow the *modelo*.

    MODELO   su familia / tomar la cena
              → Su familia ya habrá tomado la cena.

1. sus hermanas / prepararse para un examen

2. nosotros / salir a ver una obra de teatro

3. su mamá / ver su telenovela favorita

4. tú / visitar con los abuelos por videollamada

5. su papá / teletrabajar con sus colegas

6. yo / leer un mamotreto (*hefty book*)

7. Uds. / echar un vistazo a (*to take a quick look at*) unas tiendas virtuales

8. Ud. / disfrutar de happy hour con sus amigos

B   *Una reunión en línea.* Write sentences from the elements given, using the future perfect to tell what each of these people will have done either before or at the opening of the online meeting. Follow the *modelo*.

    MODELO   el secretario / invitar a los empleados a la junta en línea
              → El secretario habrá invitado a los empleados a la junta en línea.

1. el director ejecutivo (*CEO*) / preparar el orden del día (*agenda*)

2. el asistente administrativo / enviarles el enlace (*link*) a los empleados

3. nosotros / decidir nuestra estrategia

4. tú / leer los documentos pertinentes

5. algunos empleados / ya hacer el login

6. los gerentes / unirse a la reunión

7. Ud. / darles la bienvenida (*to welcome*) a todos

8. yo / abrir la sesión (*to call the meeting to order*)

C **Translation.** Express each of the following sentences in Spanish.

1. *What will they have done?*

2. *I think that Ana will have bought tickets.*

3. *Carlos and Raúl will have attended the online meeting.*

4. *By that date, Felipe and Susana will have begun to work remotely.*

5. *We will already have gotten used to taking online classes.*

6. *You (tú) will have missed a great opportunity.*

7. *We will all have learned to use the screen sharing function.*

8. *Many theaters will have closed their doors.*

D Select the correct word or phrase that has the same or nearly the same meaning as the given word or phrase. Write the word or phrase that you have selected.

1. apurarse
   a. darse prisa
   b. retrasarse

2. Me muero por verlo.
   a. Tengo mucho miedo de verlo.
   b. Tengo muchas ganas de verlo.

3. un taxi libre
   a. un taxi que no cuesta
   b. un taxi sin pasajeros

4. la acomodadora
   a. persona que nos indica los asientos
   b. algo que está muy cómodo

5. lo que pasa cuando el telón baja
   a. empieza la obra
   b. habrá terminado la obra

6. Debes perder cuidado.
   a. Debes cuidarte más.
   b. No tienes por qué preocuparte.

7. Confía en mí.
   a. No te preocupes.
   b. Ten confianza en ti mismo.

8. Ella perdió el vuelo.
   a. Por eso subió al avión.
   b. Por eso no viaja.

9. No puedo hacerme a la idea de trabajar en casa.
   a. No puedo acostumbrarme al teletrabajo.
   b. No puedo acostumbrarme al trabajo en la oficina.

10. Tengo los nervios de punta.
    a. Es que tuve un sueño intranquilo.
    b. Es que dormí profundamente.

▶ DIÁLOGO 3 · Unos aficionados al fútbol decepcionados

Study the dialogue, then listen to the recording and repeat each line.

BLANCA   ¡Qué pena! Habríamos querido ver este partido de fútbol pero no conseguimos entradas. Verás, se habrán agotado.

ARTURO   No seas pesimista, Blanquita. Vamos a la taquilla. Es posible que haya alguien delante del estadio que quiera vender sus entradas.

BLANCA   ¿Un revendedor? ¡Ni hablar! Las entradas te costarán un ojo de la cara.

ARTURO   Pues habríamos hecho bien en comprar las entradas hace unos meses.

BLANCA   Arturo, lo hecho, hecho está. No nos queda más remedio que ver el partido en la pantalla grande.

Análisis

Check that you understand the linguistic breakdown of each speech from *Diálogo 3*.

Unos aficionados al fútbol decepcionados	*Some disappointed soccer fans*
¡Qué pena! Habríamos querido ver este partido de fútbol pero no conseguimos entradas. Verás, se habrán agotado.	*What a shame! We would have wanted to see this soccer game, but we didn't get tickets. You'll see, they're probably sold out.*
¡Qué pena!	*What a shame! / What a pity!*
habríamos querido	*we would have wanted* (conditional perfect)
el partido de fútbol	*soccer game/match*
conseguir	*to get* (conjugated like **seguir**)
la entrada	*ticket*
verás	*you'll see* (future of **ver**)
agotarse	*to sell out*
se habrán agotado	*they're probably sold out*
No seas pesimista, Blanquita. Vamos a la taquilla. Es posible que haya alguien delante del estadio que quiera vender sus entradas.	*Don't be pessimistic, Blanquita. Let's go to the box office. It's possible that there is someone in front of the stadium who wants to sell his tickets.*
no seas	*don't be* (**tú** negative command form of **ser**)
pesimista	*pessimistic*
Blanquita (*diminutive*)	*(nickname for Blanca)*
la taquilla	*box office*
haya (*present subjunctive of* **hay**)	*there is*
haya alguien	*there is someone*
alguien que quiera vender (*present subjunctive*)	*someone who wants to sell*
el estadio	*stadium*
delante del estadio	*in front of the stadium*

¿Un revendedor? ¡Ni hablar! Las entradas te costarán un ojo de la cara.	*A scalper? No way! The tickets will cost you an arm and a leg.*
el revendedor	*scalper*
¡Ni hablar!	*No way! / You must be kidding!*
costar (**o** > **ue**)	*to cost*
te costarán	*they'll cost you*
el ojo	*eye*
la cara	*face*
te costarán un ojo de la cara	*they'll cost you an arm and a leg* (literally, *they'll cost you an eye from your face*)
Pues habríamos hecho bien en comprar las entradas hace unos meses.	*Well, we would have done well to buy tickets a few months ago.*
habríamos hecho	*we would have done* (conditional perfect)
habríamos hecho bien	*we would have done well, we should have*
hace unos meses	*a few months ago*
Arturo, lo hecho, hecho está. No nos queda más remedio que ver el partido en la pantalla grande.	*Arturo, what's done is done. We have no choice but to watch the game on the big screen.*
lo hecho, hecho está	*what's done is done, what's done can't be undone*
no nos queda más remedio	*we have no choice*
la pantalla grande	*the big screen*

▶ Variantes

Listen, and repeat the same structures from *Diálogo 3*, now with new vocabulary.

Habríamos querido ver este partido.	*We would have **wanted** to see this match.*
esperado	*hoped*
pensado	*intended*
podido	*been able*
preferido	*preferred*
logrado	*managed*
tratado de	*tried*
Habrá conseguido las entradas .	*He will have **gotten the tickets**.*
ido al campo de fútbol	*gone to the soccer field*
marcado un gol	*scored a goal*
robado el balón	*stolen the (soccer) ball*
driblado el balón	*dribbled the ball*
animado a su equipo	*cheered for his team*
visto un partido emocionante	*seen an exciting game*

Estructura y Práctica

The Conditional Perfect

The conditional perfect consists of the conditional of **haber** + the past participle. The English equivalent is *would have done, would have gone, would have seen*, etc. Study the conjugation of **haber** in the conditional perfect.

habría salido	*I would have left*
habrías salido	*you would have left*
habría salido	*he/she/you would have left*
habríamos salido	*we would have left*
habríais salido	*you would have left*
habrían salido	*they/you would have left*

The conditional perfect is used when there is an expressed or implied condition.

Tú **lo habrías hecho** mucho mejor.	*You would have done it much better.*
En ese caso **yo no me habría quedado**.	*In that case, I wouldn't have stayed.*
Nadie **lo habría creído**.	*No one would have believed it.*
Con la inflación que hay, **nosotros no habríamos comprado una casa**.	*With the current inflation, we would not have bought a house.*

E *Todo lo contrario.* Write sentences using the conditional perfect to say that each person mentioned in parentheses would have done the opposite of what everyone else did. Change object nouns to pronouns. Follow the *modelos*.

MODELOS María compró una casa vieja. (yo)
→ Yo no la habría comprado.

Pablo no llamó a nuestros amigos. (Claudio)
→ Claudio los habría llamado.

1. Laura no estudió para el examen. (Carlos)
2. Tú perdiste el vuelo. (yo)
3. Él se acostumbró al teletrabajo. (su esposa)
4. Yo paré el taxi. (tú)
5. Paco y Leo no pasearon al perro. (nosotros)
6. Maite no vio la telenovela ayer. (sus hermanas)
7. Yo le regalé mis billetes a Juana. (Uds.)
8. Luis no fue a ver la obra. (yo)

F Translation. Express the following sentences in Spanish, using the conditional perfect.

1. *Why would he have given so much money to a scalper?*
2. *We would have gone to the game with you* (tú).
3. *I would have liked to see the championship.*
4. *Who would you* (tú) *have invited to the party?*

5. *I would have invited all our friends.*

6. *They would have been more motivated.*

7. *Who would have believed it?*

8. *I would have preferred to see an opera.*

ⓓ DIÁLOGO 4 · Haciendo las compras en línea (1)

Study the dialogue, then listen to the recording and repeat each line.

SERGIO	¿Qué haces, Nadia? ¿Todavía pegada a la pantalla de tu computadora?
NADIA	Que lo creas o no, estoy haciendo compras en línea.
SERGIO	¿No íbamos a salir?
NADIA	Cuando yo haya terminado, podremos salir.
SERGIO	Habrás gastado una fortuna.
NADIA	¡Qué va! También en línea hay grandes rebajas.
SERGIO	¿Y todo te lo entregan a domicilio?
NADIA	Sí, dentro de cuarenta y ocho horas habrá llegado mi compra entera.

Análisis

Check that you understand the linguistic breakdown of each speech from *Diálogo 4*.

¿Qué haces, Nadia? ¿Todavía pegada a la pantalla de tu computadora?	*What are you doing, Nadia? Still glued to your computer screen?*
pegado	*glued, stuck* (**pegar**)
pegado a	*glued to, stuck to*
la pantalla	*screen*
pegada a la pantalla	*glued to the screen*
Que lo creas o no, estoy haciendo compras en línea.	*Believe it or not, I'm shopping online.*
que lo creas o no	*whether you believe it or not*
hacer compras	*to shop*
estoy haciendo compras	*I'm shopping*
en línea	*online*
¿No íbamos a salir?	*Weren't we going to go out?*
Cuando yo haya terminado, podremos salir.	*When I have finished, we can go out.*
haya terminado (*present perfect subjunctive*)	*(I) have finished*
cuando yo haya terminado	*when I have finished*
Habrás gastado una fortuna.	*I'll bet you have spent a fortune.*
habrás gastado (*future perfect of probability or conjecture*)	*I'll bet you have spent*
una fortuna	*a fortune*

¡Qué va! También en línea hay grandes rebajas.	You must be kidding! Online there are great sales, too.
¡Qué va!	You must be kidding! / No way!
la rebaja	discount, sale

¿Y todo te lo entregan a domicilio?	And they deliver everything to your home?
el domicilio	home
entregar a domicilio	to deliver to one's home

Sí, dentro de cuarenta y ocho horas habrá llegado mi compra entera.	Yes, within forty-eight hours my entire purchase will have arrived.
dentro de + *expression of time*	*within* + time
habrá llegado	it will have arrived (future perfect)
la compra	purchase
entero	whole, entire

▶ Variantes

Listen, and repeat the same structures from *Diálogo 4*, now with new vocabulary.

Cuando yo haya terminado , podremos salir.	When **I've finished**, we can go out.
yo haya comido	I've eaten
yo haya vuelto	I've come back
yo haya escrito los emails	I've written the emails
yo haya hecho el pedido	I've placed the order
yo me haya arreglado	I've gotten ready
yo me haya vestido	I've gotten dressed
yo le haya dado de comer al perro	I've fed the dog

Habrás gastado una fortuna.	I'll bet you have **spent** a fortune.
ganado	earned
perdido	lost
regalado	given away
invertido	invested

▶ DIÁLOGO 5 · Haciendo las compras en línea (2)

Study the dialogue, then listen to the recording and repeat each line.

SERGIO Y ¿qué pasa si algo no te gusta? ¿Las devoluciones son fáciles?

NADIA Claro. Existen puntos de retiro y de entrega por toda la ciudad donde puedes devolver la mercancía.

SERGIO Veo en la pantalla que tienen de todo. No lo habría creído.

NADIA Ah sí. Moda, electrónica, alimentación, no hay categoría que falte.

SERGIO ¿Sabes? Yo necesito comprar herramientas. A ver lo que tienen.

NADIA Mira. Aquí ofrecen un maletín de herramientas.

SERGIO ¡Guau! Tiene martillos, destornilladores, llaves, una llave inglesa, un alicate, clavos y tornillos. Todo para el bricolaje.

NADIA ¡Creo que esta tienda virtual ya tiene un cliente nuevo!

Análisis

Check that you understand the linguistic breakdown of each speech from *Diálogo 5*.

Y ¿qué pasa si algo no te gusta? ¿Las devoluciones son fáciles?	*And what happens if you don't like something? Are returns easy?*
la devolución	*return (of merchandise)* (**devolver**)
Claro. Existen puntos de retiro y de entrega por toda la ciudad donde puedes devolver la mercancía.	*There are pickup and drop-off points all over the city where you can return the merchandise.*
existen	*there are* (**existir**)
el punto de retiro	*pickup point*
el punto de entrega	*drop-off point*
por toda la ciudad	*all over the city*
devolver	*to give (something) back*
devolver la mercancía	*to return merchandise*
Veo en la pantalla que tienen de todo. No lo habría creído.	*I see on your screen that they have everything. I wouldn't have believed it.*
tienen de todo	*they have everything*
no lo habría creído	*I wouldn't have believed it* (conditional perfect)
Ah sí. Moda, electrónica, alimentación— no hay categoría que falte.	*Oh, yes. Fashion, electronics, food— there's no category they don't have.*
la moda	*fashion, clothing*
la electrónica	*electronics*
la alimentación	*food, groceries, foodstuffs*
la categoría	*category, line of merchandise*
faltar	*to lack, be missing*
¿Sabes? Yo necesito comprar herramientas. A ver lo que tienen.	*You know? I need to buy tools. Let's see what they have.*
la herramienta	*tool*
a ver	*let's see*
lo que	*what*
Mira. Aquí ofrecen un maletín de herramientas.	*Look. Here they are featuring a tool kit.*
ofrecer (yo ofrezco)	*to feature, offer*
el maletín	*case, kit, satchel*
el maletín de herramientas	*tool kit, tool box*

¡Guau! Tiene martillos, destornilladores, llaves, una llave inglesa, un alicate, clavos y tornillos. Todo para el bricolaje.	*Wow! It has hammers, screwdrivers, wrenches, a monkey wrench, pliers, nails, and screws. Everything for do-it-yourself.*
¡Guau!	*Wow! / Terrific!*
el martillo	*hammer*
el destornillador	*screwdriver*
la llave	*wrench*
la llave inglesa	*monkey wrench*
el alicate	*pliers*
el clavo	*nail*
el tornillo	*screw*
el bricolaje	*do-it-yourself (DIY); (< bricoler (French) (to tinker, do odd jobs around the house))*
¡Creo que esta tienda virtual ya tiene un cliente nuevo!	*I think this online store has a new customer now!*
virtual	*virtual, online*
el cliente	*customer*

Variantes

Listen, and repeat the same structures from *Diálogo 5*, now with new vocabulary.

No lo habría creído .	*I wouldn't **have believed** it.*
habría pensado	*have thought*
habría comprendido	*have understood*
habría sugerido	*have suggested*
habría recomendado	*have recommended*
habría permitido	*have allowed*
habría prometido	*have promised*
Habremos hecho un bricolaje .	*We will have done **a do-it-yourself project**.*
un bricolaje	*a home improvement project*
una remodelación	*a remodeling*
un trabajo de albañilería	*masonry work*
un trabajo de mampostería	*masonry work*
un trabajo de plomería	*plumbing work*
un trabajo de electricidad	*electrical work*
un trabajo de pintura	*a paint job*

Estructura y Práctica

EXPRESSION OF PROBABILITY AND CONJECTURE

The Future and the Conditional

You learned in Chapter 15 that the future and conditional can be used to express probability and conjecture. The future expresses probability or conjecture about an event in the present.

Ese carro **será** muy caro.	*That car must be very expensive.*
¿Cuántos años **tendrá** ese tipo?	*How old could that guy be?*

The conditional expresses probability or conjecture about an event in the past, especially with the verbs **estar, haber, ser,** and **tener**. These clauses in the conditional are the equivalent of the imperfect tense + an expression of probability or conjecture.

¿Cuántos años **tendría** cuando se casó? ¿Cuántos años crees que **tenía** cuando se casó?	*How old do you think she was when she got married?*
Llegaron tarde. **Habría** obras en la carretera. Llegaron tarde. Probablemente **había** obras en la carretera.	*They got here late. There was probably construction on the highway.*

G **Translation.** Express the following sentences in Spanish, using the future of probability or the conditional of probability.

1. *I wonder what time it is.*
2. *It's probably three o'clock.*
3. *I wonder how old Carlitos is.*
4. *He's probably nine or ten.*
5. *It's probably raining now.*
6. *I wonder where my umbrella is.*
7. *I wonder what time it was.*
8. *It was probably eight o'clock.*
9. *They didn't answer the phone. I wonder where they were.*
10. *It's possible they were out* (estar fuera *(to be out/away)*).
11. *Or it could be they were busy.*
12. *I guess they had a lot to do.*

The Future Perfect and the Conditional Perfect

The future perfect and the conditional perfect are also used to express probability about past events. The future perfect is especially common in this function. It is the equivalent of the preterit or the present perfect + an expression of probability or conjecture.

Ese señor **habrá perdido** su trabajo. Ese señor probablemente **perdió** su trabajo.	*That man probably lost his job.*
Los obreros **habrán salido** en huelga. Me parece que los obreros **han salido** en huelga.	*The workers probably went on strike.*
La reunión **habrá sido** aquí. La reunión **fue** probablemente aquí.	*The meeting was probably here.*
¿Por qué **se habrán ido** del país? Me pregunto por qué **se fueron** del país.	*I wonder why they left the country.*

The conditional perfect is the equivalent of a past tense + an expression of probability or conjecture.

¿No lo **habrían llamado**?
¿No lo **habían llamado**? ¿Cómo puede ser? } *Could it be that they didn't call him?*

El director le **habría entregado** el guión a la primera actriz.
El director probablemente le **entregó** el guión a la primera actriz. } *The director must have handed the script to the leading actress.*

H **Future perfect of probability.** Rewrite each of the following sentences, removing the expression of probability and changing the verb to the future perfect. Follow the *modelo*.

MODELO   Probablemente ya ha comido.
          → Ya habrá comido.

1. Creo que no terminaron su trabajo.

2. Me parece que han abierto las puertas del teatro.

3. Seguro que ya te han entregado la mercancía.

4. Probablemente Diego se ha comprado un maletín de herramientas.

5. Me pregunto si has encontrado el punto de retiro.

6. La devolución del artículo fue fácil, creo.

7. A lo mejor los billetes costaron mucho dinero.

8. Probablemente te fue difícil conseguir este trabajo.

I **Future perfect of probability.** Write sentences using the future perfect to express a possible cause for each of these situations. Use the cues in parentheses. Follow the *modelo*.

MODELO   En casa de los Durán no contestan el teléfono. (salir)
          → Habrán salido.

1. Luisa sacó cien en el examen de física. (estudiar mucho)

2. La obra de teatro no ha comenzado todavía. (los gerentes / retrasar la función)

3. No hay luz en casa de los Meléndez. (acostarse)

4. Juan dice que no tiene su cartera. (perdérsele)

5. No hay más leche en la nevera. (acabársenos)

6. Paula dice que no puede ir al cine con nosotros. (no hacer la tarea)

7. El profesor está furioso. (los estudiantes / portarse mal (*to misbehave*))

8. Sara y Pablo no vinieron a la fiesta. (decidir quedarse en casa)

The Progressive Tenses

You learned the formation of the progressive tenses, which consist of **estar** + the gerund, in Chapters 13 and 17. The future progressive is commonly used to express probability and conjecture about ongoing activities.

—¡Tanto ruido arriba! ¿Qué **estarán haciendo?**
So much noise upstairs! What can they be doing?

—**Estarán reorganizando** los muebles.
They must be rearranging the furniture.

—¡Pepe Reyes ha ganado otro torneo!
Pepe Reyes has won another tournament!

—**Estará celebrando** en grande.
He's probably celebrating in a big way.

—Delia ha comprado unas maletas nuevas.
Delia has bought new suitcases.

—**Estará planeando** un viaje.
She must be planning a trip.

The conditional progressive is used to express probability or conjecture about ongoing activities in the past.

—¡Tanto ruido arriba ayer! ¿Qué **estarían haciendo?**
So much noise upstairs yesterday! What do you think they were doing?

—**Estarían reorganizando** los muebles.
They were probably rearranging the furniture.

Esos jóvenes **estarían tramando** algo.
Those young men may have been plotting something.

¿Qué **estaría planeando** ese grupo político?
What do you think that political group was planning?

—¿Qué **estarían haciendo** aquí esos policías?
What might those policemen have been doing here?

—**Estarían** buscando pruebas.
They were probably looking for evidence.

J **Probability and conjecture: Future progressive.** Write questions from the elements given to express Natalia's thoughts about what members of her family and people in her neighborhood are doing now. Use the future progressive of probability and conjecture. Follow the *modelo*.

MODELO   mis amigas / qué / hacer
→ ¿Qué estarán haciendo mis amigas?

1. mi esposo / en qué / trabajar

2. mis padres / qué / pensar

3. mis hijos / con quiénes / jugar

4. la vecina / por qué / llamarnos

5. el perro de los Huerta / por qué / ladrar (*to bark*) tanto

6. esos obreros / qué / construir en la esquina

7. mi primo / por dónde / trotar

8. los niños de al lado / qué / ver en línea

The Neuter Article **lo**

The Spanish neuter article **lo** + an adjective is used as a noun to express an abstract idea or a certain quality. The form **lo** is invariable, but the adjective following **lo** can be either masculine or feminine, singular or plural. **Lo** + adjective + **que** expresses *how* + adjective. **Lo** is also used with adverbs and adverbial phrases.

lo bueno	*the good part, what's good*
lo difícil	*the difficult part, what's hard*
lo impresionante	*the impressive part, what's impressive*
Te habrás fijado en **lo hermosa** que es ella.	*You've probably noticed how beautiful she is.*
Claro. ¡Y **lo guapo** que es él!	*Of course. And how handsome he is!*
¿Ves **lo malhumorados** / **lo malhumoradas** que están?	*Do you see how moody they are?*
¡**Lo feliz** que he sido!	*How happy I have been!*
Es muy inteligente, ¡pero **lo olvidadiza** que es!	*She's very intelligent, but how forgetful she is!*

Lo + **de** means *the matter concerning.*

lo del director ejecutivo	*the matter concerning the CEO*
lo de las entradas de teatro	*the business about the theater tickets*

Lo is used in the following phrases.

lo más posible	*as much as possible*
lo menos posible	*as little as possible*
lo antes posible	*as soon as possible*
lo más pronto posible	*as soon as possible*

K **Translation.** Express the following sentences in Spanish, using the neuter article **lo**.

1. *The wonderful part of the dinner is the dessert!*
2. *You (tú) are not going to believe how happy we are!*
3. *We would have told you (tú) as soon as possible.*
4. *The business about social media* (los medios sociales) *is disgraceful* (vergonzoso).
5. *What's interesting about the show is the music.*
6. *He would have wanted to spend as little as possible.*
7. *The most exciting part of the book is the ending* (el desenlace).
8. *We will have seen the good, the bad, and the ugly of the situation.*

DIÁLOGO 6 · Mariana consigue un puesto (1)

Study the dialogue, then listen to the recording and repeat each line.

JUAN JOSÉ	Hola, Mari. ¿Cómo van las cosas? Ya habrás conseguido trabajo, ¿no?
MARIANA	Sí, te iba a llamar. No sabes lo afortunada que he sido.
JUAN JOSÉ	Es bueno que te hayas colocado tan rápido. Cuéntame, chica. ¿Dónde vas a trabajar?
MARIANA	¿Conoces MundoRed? ¿La empresa proveedora de servicios de internet?
JUAN JOSÉ	Cómo no. Es una gran empresa de vanguardia.
MARIANA	En efecto. Es un líder en ayudar a empresarios a montar sistemas telemáticos en sus empresas.
JUAN JOSÉ	Mari, espero que te hayan contratado para hacer mercadeo. Eres perita en este campo.

Análisis

Check that you understand the linguistic breakdown of each speech from *Diálogo 6*.

Hola, Mari. ¿Cómo van las cosas? Ya habrás conseguido trabajo, ¿no?	*Hi, Mari. How are things? You've already gotten a job, haven't you?*
Mari	(nickname for *Mariana*)
¿Cómo van las cosas?	*How are things?*
habrás conseguido	*you've gotten*
conseguir trabajo	*to get a job*
habrás conseguido trabajo	*you've gotten a job*
Sí, te iba a llamar. No sabes lo afortunada que he sido.	*Yes, I was going to call you. You can't imagine how fortunate I've been.*
afortunado	*fortunate, lucky*
lo afortunado que	*how fortunate*
Es bueno que te hayas colocado tan rápido. Cuéntame, chica. ¿Dónde vas a trabajar?	*It's good that you got a job so quickly. Tell me about it. Where are you going to work?*
colocarse	*to get a job/position*
te hayas colocado (*present perfect subjunctive*)	*you found a job*
es bueno que te hayas colocado	*it's good that you found a job*
contar (**o > ue**)	*to tell*
cuéntame	*tell me (about it)* (**tú** command form of **contar**)
¿Conoces MundoRed? ¿La empresa proveedora de servicios de internet?	*Are you familiar with MundoRed? The internet services provider?*
la empresa	*business, company*
el proveedor, la proveedora	*provider*
proveedor	*providing* (adjective)
los servicios de internet	*internet services*

Cómo no. Es una gran empresa de vanguardia.	*Of course. It's a great leading-edge company.*
cómo no	*of course*
de vanguardia	*leading-edge, innovative*
la empresa de vanguardia	*leading-edge company*

En efecto. Es un líder en ayudar a empresarios a montar sistemas telemáticos en sus empresas.	*Exactly. It's a leader in helping businesspeople set up telematic systems in their businesses.*
en efecto	*exactly, indeed*
el líder	*leader*
el empresario	*entrepreneur, businessperson*
montar	*to set up*
el sistema	*system*
telemático	*telematic*
el sistema telemático	*telematic system (joining of telecommunications and informatics (information science))*

Mari, espero que te hayan contratado para hacer mercadeo. Eres perita en este campo.	*Mari, I hope they hired you to do marketing. You're an expert in this field.*
contratar	*to hire*
te hayan contratado (*present perfect subjunctive*)	*they hired you*
espero que te hayan contratado	*I hope they hired you*
el mercadeo	*marketing*
el perito	*expert*
el campo	*field*

▶ Variantes

Listen, and repeat the same structures from *Diálogo 6*, now with new vocabulary.

Es bueno que te hayas colocado .	*It's good that **you got a job**.*
hayas trabajado en alta tecnología	*you worked in high tech*
hayas logrado ser la directora de sistemas de información	*you became the chief information officer (CIO)*
hayas tenido mucho éxito	*you were very successful*

⏵ DIÁLOGO 7 · Mariana consigue un puesto (2)

Study the dialogue, then listen to the recording and repeat each line.

MARIANA	Bueno, MundoRed piensa expandir su mercado internacional y la directora de mercadeo quiere que yo forme parte de su equipo.
JUAN JOSÉ	¡Qué suerte que hayas solicitado empleo precisamente en este momento! ¿Cuáles países les interesan?
MARIANA	Los Estados Unidos y Canadá—Quebec, principalmente.
JUAN JOSÉ	El hecho de que tú sepas inglés y francés habrá sido un punto a tu favor.
MARIANA	Pepe, no cabe la menor duda. Y les gusta mucho que yo haya conocido los dos países.
JUAN JOSÉ	Amiga, ¡felicidades y suerte!

Análisis

Check that you understand the linguistic breakdown of each speech from *Diálogo 7*.

Bueno, MundoRed piensa expandir su mercado internacional y la directora de mercadeo quiere que yo forme parte de su equipo.	*Well, MundoRed intends to expand its international market, and the marketing director wants me to be part of their team.*
expandir	*to expand*
piensa expandir	*intends to expand*
el mercado	*market*
la directora de mercadeo	*marketing director*
formar parte	*to be a part*
quiere que yo forme parte	*wants me to be a part*
el equipo	*team*
¡Qué suerte que hayas solicitado empleo precisamente en este momento! ¿Cuáles países les interesan?	*How lucky that you applied for a position exactly at this time! Which countries are they interested in?*
la suerte	*luck*
qué suerte	*how lucky, what luck*
solicitar empleo	*to apply for a job/position*
hayas solicitado (*present perfect subjunctive*)	*you applied for*
qué suerte que hayas solicitado empleo	*how lucky that you applied for a position*
precisamente	*precisely, exactly*
en este momento	*at this time*
les interesan (*rev. constr.*)	*they interest them, they are interested in them*
¿Cuáles países les interesan?	*Which countries are they interested in?*

Los Estados Unidos y Canadá— / *The United States and Canada—mainly*
Quebec, principalmente. / *Quebec.*
  principalmente /   *mainly*

El hecho de que tú sepas inglés y / *The fact that you know English and French*
francés habrá sido un punto a tu favor. / *was probably to your advantage.*
  el hecho /   *fact*
  tú sepas (*subjunctive*) /   *you know* (**saber**)
  el hecho de que tú sepas /   *that fact that you know*
  habrá sido (*future perfect of* /   *was probably, must have been*
    probability or conjecture)
  un punto a tu favor /   *a point in your favor, to your advantage*

Pepe, no cabe la menor duda. Y les / *Pepe, there's no doubt about it. And they*
gusta mucho que yo haya conocido los / *really like that I'm quite familiar with the*
dos países. / *two countries.*
  Pepe /   *(nickname for José)*
  caber /   *to fit*
  la duda /   *doubt*
  no cabe la menor duda /   *there's no doubt about it*
  que yo haya conocido (*present* /   *that I've come to know, that I'm familiar*
    perfect subjunctive) /   *with*

Amiga, ¡felicidades y suerte! / *My friend, congratulations and good luck!*

▶ Variantes

Listen, and repeat the same structures from *Diálogo 7*, now with new vocabulary.

¡Qué suerte que te hayan contratado! / *How lucky they hired you!*

¡Qué bueno que te hayan dado un / *How good they gave you a promotion!*
ascenso!

¡Qué estupendo que te hayan / *How great they raised your salary!*
aumentado el sueldo!

¡Qué desafortunado que te hayan / *How unfortunate they fired you!*
despedido!

Les gusta que yo haya elaborado un / *They like **that I've drawn up a budget**.*
presupuesto .

  que yo haya hecho un plan de /   *that I've made a business plan*
    negocios

  que yo haya sabido ejecutar /   *that I've known how to multitask*
    múltiples tareas

  que yo me haya encargado de la /   *that I've been in charge of accounting*
    contabilidad

  que yo haya hecho crecer la /   *that I've grown the company*
    empresa

  que yo haya demostrado liderazgo /   *that I've shown leadership*

Estructura y Práctica

The Present Perfect Subjunctive

The present perfect subjunctive consists of the present subjunctive of the auxiliary verb **haber** + the past participle. Like most subjunctive forms, it usually occurs in a clause beginning with **que**. Study the present perfect subjunctive forms of the verbs **salir** and **equivocarse**.

que yo haya salido	que yo me haya equivocado
que tú hayas salido	que tú te hayas equivocado
que él/ella/Ud. haya salido	que él/ella/Ud. se haya equivocado
que nosotros hayamos salido	que nosotros nos hayamos equivocado
que vosotros hayáis salido	que vosotros os hayáis equivocado
que ellos/ellas/Uds. hayan salido	que ellos/ellas/Uds. se hayan equivocado

The present perfect subjunctive is used in the same types of dependent clauses that require the present subjunctive, but conveys the idea that the action of the dependent clause happens before the action of the main clause. Compare the following pairs of sentences.

Me alegro de que vengan.	*I'm glad that they're coming.*
Me alegro de que hayan venido.	*I'm glad that they came.*
No creo que puedan quedarse.	*I don't think they can stay.*
No creo que hayan podido quedarse.	*I don't think they were able to stay.*
¿No hay nadie que te ayude?	*Isn't there anyone who helps you?*
¿No hay nadie que te haya ayudado?	*Isn't there anyone who helped you?*
Espero que me comprendas.	*I hope that you understand me.*
Espero que me hayas comprendido.	*I hope that you have understood me.*
Es poco probable que viajen hoy.	*It's not likely that they'll travel today.*
Es poco probable que hayan viajado ayer.	*It's not likely that they traveled yesterday.*

L **Present perfect subjunctive.** Rewrite each of the following sentences, using the cue in parentheses as the main clause and changing the verb from the preterit to the present perfect subjunctive for the dependent clause. Follow the *modelo*.

MODELO   Ella vio la nueva obra de teatro. (es bueno)
    → Es bueno que ella haya visto la nueva obra de teatro.

1. El abogado escribió los contratos. (no creemos)

2. Conocieron muchos países europeos. (es importante)

3. Te acostumbraste al teletrabajo. (no piensan)

4. La directora de mercadeo perdió esta oportunidad. (es una lástima)

5. Su equipo no ganó el campeonato. (sienten)

6. Los estudiantes estuvieron más motivados. (me alegro)

7. Devolviste la mercancía que compraste en línea. (es mejor)

8. Las entradas para el espectáculo costaron una fortuna. (no les gusta)

M **Translation.** Express the following sentences in Spanish, using the present perfect subjunctive.

1. *I'm glad that they invited us to go to the theater with them.*

2. *We hope that the leading-edge company hired him.*

3. *Are you (Ud.) surprised that some employees missed the meeting?*

4. *Isn't there anyone who heard what happened?*

5. *It's possible that she bought a tool kit for her brother.*

6. *It's good that you (tú) saved three hours commuting to the office.*

7. *She's sorry that you (Uds.) didn't trust her.*

8. *They doubt that we missed the deadline.*

DIÁLOGO 8 · ¡Nieve, una película y tapas!

Study the dialogue, then listen to the recording and repeat each line.

ANTONIO   ¡Qué mal tiempo está haciendo! ¡Es una impresionante tormenta de nieve!

CATALINA   ¡Y nosotros que pensábamos ir al cine! Están dando una nueva película de Bollywood. ¡Me encanta el cine indio!

ANTONIO   Cata, acuérdate que estamos abonados a Telefilm. Podemos escoger entre un montón de películas de muchos países incluso de la India.

CATALINA   Es cierto. ¿Por qué no invitamos a Olivia y a Daniel a acompañarnos? Ellos tampoco habrán salido.

ANTONIO   ¡Excelente idea! No creo que ellos se hayan abonado a Telefilm. Les interesará conocer esta plataforma.

CATALINA   Ojalá puedan venir. Toni, aun si no hay película que nos guste a todos, vamos a pasar una tarde divertidísima picando tapas y tomando una copa de vino.

Análisis

Check that you understand the linguistic breakdown of each speech from *Diálogo 8*.

¡Qué mal tiempo está haciendo!	*What terrible weather we're having!*
¡Es una impresionante tormenta de nieve!	*It's an impressive snowstorm!*
impresionante	*impressive*
la tormenta de nieve	*snowstorm*

¡Y nosotros que pensábamos ir al cine! Están dando una nueva película de Bollywood. ¡Me encanta el cine indio!

> *And here we planned to go to the movies! They're showing a new Bollywood film. I love Indian cinema!*

pensábamos ir	*we intended to go*
el cine	*cinema, the movies*
dar una película	*to show a film*
están dando una película	*they're showing a film*
Bollywood	*Indian film industry*
me encanta	*I love it*
indio	*Indian (from India) (adjective)*
el cine indio	*Indian cinema*

Cata, acuérdate que estamos abonados a Telefilm. Podemos escoger entre un montón de películas de muchos países incluso de la India.

> *Cata, remember that we subscribe to Telefilm. We can choose from lots of films from many countries, including India.*

Cata	*(nickname for Catalina)*
acordarse (**o > ue**)	*to remember*
acuérdate	*remember (**tú** command form of **acordarse**)*
estamos abonados a	*we subscribe to*
podemos escoger	*we can choose*
un montón de	*lots of, loads of*
incluso	*including*
la India	*India*

Es cierto. ¿Por qué no invitamos a Olivia y a Daniel a acompañarnos? Ellos tampoco habrán salido.

> *It's true. Why don't we invite Olivia and Daniel to join us? I bet they haven't gone out either.*

es cierto	*it's true*
invitar	*to invite*
acompañar	*to accompany, go with, join*
invitamos a acompañarnos	*we invite (them) to join us*
no habrán salido (*future perfect of probability or conjecture*)	*they probably haven't gone out*
ellos tampoco habrán salido	*they probably haven't gone out either*

¡Excelente idea! No creo que ellos se hayan abonado a Telefilm. Les interesará conocer esta plataforma.

> *Excellent idea! I don't think they've subscribed to Telefilm. They'll probably be interested in getting to know this platform.*

abonarse	*to subscribe*
abonado a	*subscribed to*
no creo que se hayan abonado (*present perfect subjunctive*)	*I don't think they've subscribed*
les interesará (*future of probability*)	*they'll probably be interested*
la plataforma	*platform*

Ojalá puedan venir. Toni, aun si no hay película que nos guste a todos, vamos a pasar una tarde divertidísima picando tapas y tomando una copa de vino.	*I hope they can come. Toni, even if there's no film we all like, we're going to spend a really fun afternoon snacking on tapas and having a glass of wine.*
ojalá + *subjunctive*	*I hope* + verb, *I wish* + verb
Ojalá puedan venir.	*I hope they can come.*
Toni	*(nickname for Antonio)*
aun si	*even if*
nos guste (*present subjunctive*)	*we like*
no hay película que nos guste	*there's no film that we like*
divertido	*amusing, entertaining, funny*
divertidísimo (< divertido)	*very entertaining/amusing (absolute superlative)*
una tarde divertidísima	*a really fun afternoon*
picando (*gerund*)	*snacking on (**picar**)*
las tapas	*appetizers, snacks of savory hot or cold foods served in small dishes*
la copa	*glass, goblet, drink*
el vino	*wine*
tomando una copa de vino	*having a glass of wine*

▶ Variantes

Listen, and repeat the same structures from *Diálogo 8*, now with new vocabulary.

Habrán salido .	*They must have **gone out**.*
vuelto	*come back (past participle of **volver**)*
entrado	*gone in*
subido	*gone upstairs*
bajado	*gone downstairs*
Ojalá que ella se abone a Telefilm .	*I hope she'll **subscribe to Telefilm**.*
vea el estreno de la película	*see the premiere of the film*
sirva tapas en el cóctel	*serve tapas at the cocktail party*
disfrute de happy hour con nosotros	*enjoy happy hour with us*
asista al concierto	*attend the concert*
conozca al dramaturgo	*meet the playwright*
Ojalá que ella se haya abonado a Telefilm .	*I hope she **subscribed to Telefilm**.*
haya visto el estreno de la película	*saw the premiere of the film*
haya servido tapas en el cóctel	*served tapas at the cocktail party*
haya disfrutado de happy hour con nosotros	*enjoyed happy hour with us*
haya asistido al concierto	*attended the concert*
haya conocido al dramaturgo	*met the playwright*

Ojalá que Uds. se abonaran a Telefilm .	*We wish you would **subscribe to Telefilm.***
vieran el estreno de la película	*see the premiere of the film*
sirvieran tapas en el cóctel	*serve tapas at the cocktail party*
disfrutaran de happy hour con nosotros	*enjoy happy hour with us*
asistieran al concierto	*attend the concert*
conocieran al dramaturgo	*meet the playwright*

Estructura y Práctica

Ojalá *I hope, I wish* (Part 1)

Ojalá is a word frequently used in Spanish to introduce the expression of a wish. Derived from Arabic **inshallah** (*would to God*), it has become an everyday word in Spanish, and a very characteristic one.

When followed by the present subjunctive or the present perfect subjunctive, the best English equivalent of **ojalá** is *I hope, we hope, let's hope.*

Ojalá no nos perdamos la obra.	*I hope we don't miss the play.*
Ojalá que podamos parar un taxi.	*Let's hope we can hail a cab.*
Ojalá que no vuelvas tarde.	*I hope you won't return late.*
Ojalá que nuestro equipo llegue al campeonato.	*Let's hope that our team makes it into the championship.*
Ojalá hayan conseguido entradas.	*We hope they got tickets.*
Ojalá que no hayan levantado el telón.	*We hope they haven't raised the curtain.*

When **ojalá** is followed by the imperfect subjunctive, the best English equivalent of **ojalá** is *I wish, we wish.*

Ojalá que los chicos pudieran asistir a una buena escuela.	*I wish the kids could attend a good school.*
Ojalá que vinieran nuestros parientes.	*We wish our relatives were coming.*
Ojalá comprendieran el español.	*I wish they understood Spanish.*
Ojalá tú tomaras clases en línea.	*We wish you would take classes online.*

Note that the conjunction **que** may be omitted after **ojalá.**

N   **Translation.** Express the following sentences in Spanish, using **ojalá** and the present subjunctive, the present perfect subjunctive, or the imperfect subjunctive.

1. *I hope you* (Uds.) *like this Indian film.*

2. *We hope they hired her as marketing director.*

3. *I hope you* (tú) *didn't miss the concert.*

4. *We hope they expanded their international market.*

5. *I wish our team would win the soccer match.*

6. *We wish the film were dubbed* (doblar (*to dub*)).

7. *I wish we could attend the premiere of the play.*

8. *We hope their leading-edge business will be very successful.*

Un paso más

Are you ready to take your Spanish a step further? Here are exercises that will enhance your knowledge of the language and encourage you to express yourself freely.

O Complete each of the following sentences in Spanish, using the present perfect subjunctive to express your thoughts and feelings about something that happened in the past.

1. Me alegro de que...

2. Es bueno que...

3. Ojalá...

4. Espero...

5. Es posible que...

6. No creo que...

7. Siento que...

8. Dudo que...

P *Preguntas personales.* Contesta las siguientes preguntas con oraciones completas en español.

1. ¿Te gusta ir al teatro? ¿Qué género (*genre*) teatral te gusta más?

2. ¿Te has perdido un evento importante alguna vez? ¿Cuál fue? Describe la situación.

3. ¿A veces tienes los nervios de punta? ¿Cuál es la causa? ¿Qué o quién te pone los nervios de punta?

4. ¿En que industria o campo trabajas? ¿La empresa es de vanguardia? ¿Eres perito/perita en tu campo? Explica lo que haces.

5. ¿Trabajas en casa o en un lugar de trabajo fuera de casa? ¿Cuáles son las ventajas y las desventajas del teletrabajo?

6. ¿Eres aficionado/aficionada al fútbol o a otro deporte? ¿Prefieres ver los partidos en el estadio o en vivo por internet? ¿Le compraste billetes a un revendedor alguna vez?

7. ¿Cuáles son las ventajas y las desventajas de hacer las compras en línea? ¿Qué compras en las tiendas virtuales? ¿Vas a un punto de retiro y de entrega para devolver la mercancía? ¿Gastas más o menos dinero comprando en línea?

Q *¿Qué opinas?* Escribe unos ensayos en español sobre los siguientes temas que se tratan en los diálogos del capítulo 19.

1. El ocio (*leisure*): Lo que me gusta hacer en mi tiempo libre

2. Conciertos, obras de teatro y películas

3. El teletrabajo: Cómo me ha cambiado la vida

4. Haciendo las compras en línea

5. Las últimas tendencias (*latest trends*) en la sociedad

R ***Expresiones y modismos.*** *Explica en español lo que significan estas expresiones que se presentan en el capítulo 19.*

1. costar un ojo de la cara

2. ¡Bien está lo que bien acaba!

3. Lo hecho, hecho está.

S ***Citas.*** *Lee las siguientes citas y tradúcelas al inglés. Después, explica lo que significan en español. Tienen que ver con los dos temas del capítulo 19: el trabajo y el ocio.*

1. "Nunca he hecho un día de trabajo en mi vida. Todo fue diversión."
—*Thomas Edison*

2. "La recompensa del trabajo bien hecho es la oportunidad de hacer más trabajo bien hecho."
—*Jonas Salk*

3. "Nadie puede llegar a la cima (*to get to the top*) armado sólo de talento. Dios da el talento; el trabajo transforma el talento en genio."
—*Anna Pavlova*

4. "Para empezar un negocio requiere dos cosas: innovar un gran producto y tener un equipo detrás lleno de determinación e ilusión."
—*Elon Musk*

5. "La música puede dar nombre a lo innombrable y comunicar lo incognoscible."
—*Leonard Bernstein*

6. "El teatro no puede desaparecer porque es el único arte donde la humanidad se enfrenta a sí misma."
—*Arthur Miller*

7. "Las películas tocan el corazón, despiertan la visión y cambian nuestra forma de ver las cosas. Nos llevan a otros lugares. Nos abren las puertas y la mente. Las películas son los recuerdos de nuestra vida."
—*Martin Scorsese*

The Economy and Politics

Communication Goals

- Expressing the relative time of past actions
- Expressing conditional situations
- Wishing for something remotely possible
- Vocabulary: freedom of speech at the university, bankruptcy caused by a pandemic, a demonstration, the aqueduct of Segovia, the environment

Grammar Topics

- The Pluperfect Subjunctive
- Sequence of Tenses
- Conditional Sentences
- Sentences Expressing Possibility
- Contrary to Present Fact Conditional
- Contrary to Past Fact Conditional
- **Ojalá** *I hope, I wish* (Part 2)

DIÁLOGO 1 · La universidad y la libertad de expresión (1)

Study the dialogue, then listen to the recording and repeat each line.

JULIÁN   Hola, Livi, ¿Sabes lo que pasó? La universidad acaba de cerrar el periódico estudiantil en línea.

OLIVIA   No puede ser. No creo que Uds. hayan escrito nada tan ofensivo. ¿De qué se trata?

JULIÁN   Yo y otros colaboradores publicamos unos artículos de opinión criticando a la administración de la universidad por no apoyar diferencias de opinión política.

OLIVIA   Eso es censura. ¿Y muchas personas leyeron los artículos?

JULIÁN   Sí, miles. Muchos estudiantes los compartieron en las redes sociales.

Análisis

Check that you understand the linguistic breakdown of each speech from *Diálogo 1*.

Hola, Livi, ¿Sabes lo que pasó? La universidad acaba de cerrar el periódico estudiantil en línea.	*Hi, Livi. Do you know what happened? The university has just shut down the online student newspaper.*
Livi	(nickname for *Olivia*)
cerrar (**e** > **ie**)	*to close, shut down*
estudiantil	*student* (adjective)
el periódico estudiantil	*the student newspaper*
No puede ser. No creo que Uds. hayan escrito nada tan ofensivo. ¿De qué se trata?	*It can't be. I don't believe that you've written anything so offensive. What's this about?*
no puede ser	*it can't be, it's impossible*
que Uds. hayan escrito (*present perfect subjunctive*)	*that you have written*
ofensivo	*offensive*
nada tan ofensivo	*nothing so offensive*
tratarse de	*to be about, be at issue*
Yo y otros colaboradores publicamos unos artículos de opinión criticando a la administración de la universidad por no apoyar diferencias de opinión política.	*I and other contributors published some opinion pieces criticizing the university administration for not supporting differences of political opinion.*
el colaborador	*co-worker, contributor*
publicar	*to publish*
el artículo de opinión	*opinion piece*
criticar	*to criticize*
la administración	*administration*
la administración de la universidad	*university administration*
Eso es censura. ¿Y muchas personas leyeron los artículos?	*That's censorship. And did many people read the articles?*
la censura	*censorship*
Sí, miles. Muchos estudiantes los compartieron en las redes sociales.	*Yes, thousands. Many students shared them on social media.*
mil	*a thousand*
miles	*thousands*
compartir	*to share*
la red	*network*
las redes sociales	*social media*

Variantes

Listen, and repeat the same structures from *Diálogo 1*, now with new vocabulary.

Acaban de cerrar el periódico estudiantil.	*They have just **closed down** the student newspaper.*
clausurar	*closed down*
eliminar	*eliminated*
prohibir	*banned*

No creo que hayan publicado el editorial .	*I don't think they published **the editorial**.*
el artículo de opinión	*the opinion piece / op-ed*
el artículo de fondo	*the feature article*
el artículo de invitado	*the guest article*
las noticias de economía	*the financial news*
las noticias de política	*the political news*
el artículo de blog	*the blog post*
la entrada de blog	*the blog post*

La Constitución de los Estados Unidos garantiza la libertad de expresión .	*The Constitution of the United States guarantees **freedom of speech**.*
la libertad de prensa	*freedom of the press*
la libertad de culto	*freedom of religion*
la libertad de asociación	*freedom of assembly*
la libertad de petición	*freedom of petition*

La vacunación es un tema controvertido .	*Vaccination is **a controversial** issue.*
actual	*a current*
importante	*an important*
muy discutido	*a much discussed*
candente	*a hot/hot-button*
polémico	*a contentious*
polarizador	*a polarizing*

To learn more about the Constitution of the United States of America, see Chapter 12 (*Un paso más*).

DIÁLOGO 2 · La universidad y la libertad de expresión (2)

Study the dialogue, then listen to the recording and repeat each line.

OLIVIA   ¿Y la libertad de expresión garantizada por la Constitución? ¿No se extiende a la universidad?

JULIÁN   Sí, con tal que no postees nada que arroje una luz negativa sobre la administración universitaria.

OLIVIA   Julián, si tú no hubieras tocado un tema controvertido, te habrían dejado en paz.

JULIÁN   Yo no soy la única víctima de esta estrechez de miras. Por eso mañana se organiza una manifestación por los derechos civiles.

OLIVIA   Vamos los dos. Hay que protestar contra la erosión de nuestra libertad de expresión.

Análisis

Check that you understand the linguistic breakdown of each speech from *Diálogo 2*.

¿Y la libertad de expresión garantizada por la Constitución? ¿No se extiende a la universidad?

	And the freedom of speech guaranteed by the Constitution? Doesn't it extend to the university?
la libertad	*freedom, liberty*
la expresión	*expression, self-expression, speech*
la libertad de expresión	*freedom of speech*
garantizar	*to guarantee*
la constitución	*constitution*
extenderse (**e** > **ie**) a	*to extend to, cover*

Sí, con tal que no postees nada que arroje una luz negativa sobre la administración universitaria.

	Yes, as long as you don't post something that sheds a negative light on the university administration.
con tal (de) que	*as long as, provided that*
postear	*to post*
arrojar	*to throw*
la luz	*light*
una luz negativa	*a negative light*
arrojar una luz negativa sobre	*to shed a negative light on*
universitario	*university* (adjective)
la administración universitaria	*the university administration*

Julián, si tú no hubieras tocado un tema controvertido, te habrían dejado en paz.

	Julián, if you hadn't brought up a controversial topic, they would have left you alone.
tocar un tema	*to bring up a subject*
controvertido	*controversial*
hubieras tocado (*pluperfect subjunctive*)	*you had brought up*
la paz	*peace*
dejar a uno en paz	*to leave someone alone*
te habrían dejado en paz	*they would have left you alone*

Yo no soy la única víctima de esta estrechez de miras. Por eso mañana se organiza una manifestación por los derechos civiles.

	I am not the only victim of this narrow-mindedness. That's why tomorrow they're organizing a civil rights demonstration.
la víctima	*victim* (male or female)
la única víctima	*the only victim*
estrecho	*narrow*
la estrechez	*narrowness*
la mira	*view, sight*
estrecho de miras	*narrow-minded*
la estrechez de miras	*narrow-mindedness*
se organiza	*is being organized, they're organizing*
la manifestación	*demonstration*
el derecho	*right*
los derechos civiles	*civil rights*

Vamos los dos. Hay que protestar contra la erosión de nuestra libertad de expresión.	*Both of us will go. We must protest against the erosion of our freedom of speech.*

 ## Variantes

Listen, and repeat the same structures from *Diálogo 2*, now with new vocabulary.

Esperaba que hubieran defendido la libertad de expresión .	*I hoped that **they would have defended freedom of speech**.*
hubieran protestado contra la censura	*they would have protested against censorship*
hubieran exigido elecciones libres y transparentes	*they would have demanded free and transparent elections*
hubieran escrito un artículo poderoso	*they would have written a powerful article*
hubieran organizado una manifestación	*they would have organized a demonstration*
hubieran tenido el apoyo del estudiantado	*they would have had the support of the student body*
hubieran consultado con los profesores de la facultad de derecho	*they would have consulted with the law school professors*

Estructura y Práctica

The Pluperfect Subjunctive

The pluperfect (past perfect) subjunctive consists of the imperfect subjunctive of the auxiliary verb **haber** + the past participle. Study the forms of the pluperfect subjunctive of **venir** and **irse**.

que yo hubiera venido	que yo me hubiera ido
que tú hubieras venido	que tú te hubieras ido
que él/ella/Ud. hubiera venido	que él/ella/Ud. se hubiera ido
que nosotros hubiéramos venido	que nosotros nos hubiéramos ido
que vosotros hubierais venido	que vosotros os hubierais ido
que ellos/ellas/Uds. hubieran venido	que ellos/ellas/Uds. se hubieran ido

As with the imperfect subjunctive, there is an alternate form of the pluperfect subjunctive that has endings in **-se** instead of **-ra**. The auxiliary verb **haber** of the pluperfect subjunctive shows these alternate forms: **yo hubiese venido, tú hubieses venido, él/ella/Ud. hubiese venido, nosotros hubiésemos venido, vosotros hubieseis venido, ellos/ellas/ Uds. hubiesen venido**.

The pluperfect subjunctive replaces the imperfect subjunctive to convey the idea that the action of the dependent clause happened before the action or emotion of the main clause. Compare the following pairs of sentences.

Era poco probable que **cambiaran** el día de la junta.	*It was unlikely that they would change the day of the meeting.*
Era poco probable que **hubieran cambiado** el día de la junta.	*It was unlikely that they would have changed the day of the meeting.*

Esperaba que **escribieran** un artículo.	*I hoped that they would write an article.*
Esperaba que **hubieran escrito** un artículo.	*I hoped that they would have written an article.*
No creía que **pudieran** hacerlo.	*I didn't think that they could do it.*
No creía que **hubieran podido** hacerlo.	*I didn't think that they could have done it.*
Él negaba que **vinieran**.	*He denied that they were coming.*
Él negaba que **hubieran venido**.	*He denied that they had come.*
Dudábamos que te **cayera** bien.	*We doubted that you liked her.*
Dudábamos que te **hubiera caído** bien.	*We doubted that you had liked her.*

Now compare the use of all four subjunctive tenses: present subjunctive, present perfect subjunctive, imperfect subjunctive, pluperfect (past perfect) subjunctive. Note the English tenses that convey the meaning of the Spanish subjunctive clauses.

No creo que su proyecto resulte.	*I don't think his plan will work out.*
No creo que su proyecto haya resultado.	*I don't think his plan has worked out.*
No creía que su proyecto resultara.	*I didn't think his plan would work out.*
No creía que su proyecto hubiera resultado.	*I didn't think his plan had worked out.*
Es dudoso que termine el informe.	*It's doubtful that he will finish the report.*
Es dudoso que haya terminado el informe.	*It's doubtful that he has finished the report.*
Era dudoso que terminara el informe.	*It was doubtful that he would finish the report.*
Era dudoso que hubiera terminado el informe.	*It was doubtful that he had finished the report.*

A **Pluperfect subjunctive.** Write the pluperfect subjunctive form of the verb in parentheses that correctly completes each of the following sentences. Follow the *modelo*.

MODELO   No pude creer que la profesora __*hubiera dicho*__ tal cosa. (decir)

1. No me pareció bien que los niños _____ eso. (hacer)

2. Era una lástima que la policía _____ cerrar la playa. (decidir)

3. Era una pena que los médicos no _____ atención a estas investigaciones. (prestar)

4. No me gustó que los organizadores no _____ a ningún representante extranjero. (invitar)

5. Él no creía que nosotros lo _____ todo. (entender)

6. ¿Cómo fue posible que tú _____ hasta el puerto? (caminar)

7. Ellos dudaban que yo _____ de ayudarlos. (tratar)

8. Todos esperábamos que Uds. _____ antes. (llegar)

Estructura y Práctica
Sequence of Tenses

The patterns of tense selection for the subjunctive are called the sequence of tenses. These are rules of standard Spanish and characterize the written language of all Spanish-speaking countries. In spoken Spanish, there is some dialectal variation in the application of the sequence of tenses rules, but the rules presented here enable the learner to form sentences that are acceptable to all Spanish speakers.

A summary of rules for the sequencing of the subjunctive tenses follows.

1 · If the expression requiring the subjunctive is in the present tense, present perfect tense, or future tense, then it is followed by the present subjunctive.

me alegro de
me he alegrado de $\Big\}$ que me visites
me alegraré de

2 · If the expression requiring the subjunctive is in the preterit, imperfect, pluperfect (past perfect), or conditional tense, then it is followed by the imperfect subjunctive.

me alegré de
me alegraba de
me había alegrado de $\Big\}$ que me visitaras
me alegraría de

3 · If the speaker sees that the action of the dependent clause happened before the action or emotion of the verb in the main clause requiring the subjunctive, then one of the perfect subjunctives—either the present perfect subjunctive or the pluperfect subjunctive—is used in the dependent clause.

me alegro de
me he alegrado de $\Big\}$ que me hayas visitado
me alegraré de

me alegré de
me alegraba de
me había alegrado de $\Big\}$ que me hubieras visitado
me alegraría de

B **Present subjunctive → imperfect subjunctive.** Rewrite each of the following sentences according to the rules of the sequence of tenses. Change the verb in the main clause, using the cue in parentheses, and make all necessary changes. Then translate your sentence into English. Follow the *modelo*.

MODELO   Siento mucho que no quieras participar. (Sentía)
→ Sentía mucho que no quisieras participar.
→ *I was very sorry that you didn't want to participate.*

1. Tenemos miedo de que clausuren el periódico. (Teníamos)

2. Espero que publiquen mi artículo. (Esperaba)

3. No creo que asistan a la junta. (No creía)

4. Es bueno que se organice una protesta. (Fue)

5. Te aconsejo que no toques ese tema. (Te aconsejé)

6. Preferimos que nos dejen en paz. (Preferíamos)

7. Los estudiantes temen que prohíban la reunión. (temían)

8. Nadie quiere que perdamos la libertad de expresión. (quería)

C **Present perfect subjunctive → pluperfect subjunctive.** Rewrite each of the following sentences according to the rules of the sequence of tenses. Change the verb in the main clause, using the cue in parentheses, and make all necessary changes. Then, translate your sentence into English. Follow the *modelo*.

MODELO No creemos que hayan salido. (No creíamos)
→ No creíamos que hubieran salido.
→ *We didn't think they had gone out.*

1. Es posible que hayan criticado al gobierno. (Era)

2. Temo que hayan compartido estos artículos. (Temía)

3. Espero que no hayas posteado nada ofensivo. (Esperaba)

4. Es dudoso que ella haya leído ese periódico. (Era)

5. Es bueno que hayamos puesto el periódico estudiantil en línea. (Era)

6. No me gusta que la administración haya tenido esta estrechez de miras. (No me gustó)

D *Modo subjuntivo* **(Subjunctive mood).** Express each of the following sentences in Spanish, using the appropriate present, present perfect, imperfect, or pluperfect subjunctive verb form.

1. a. *I don't believe he's taking a business trip.*

   b. *I don't believe he has taken a business trip.*

   c. *I didn't believe that he was taking a business trip.*

   d. *I didn't believe that he had taken a business trip.*

2. a. *We are glad that you* (tú) *are studying music.*

   b. *We are glad that you* (tú) *have studied music.*

   c. *We were glad that you* (tú) *were studying music.*

   d. *We were glad that you* (tú) *had studied music.*

3. a. *It's probable that the students know this teacher* [masc.].

   b. *It's probable that the students have met this teacher* [masc.].

   c. *It was probable that the students knew this teacher* [masc.].

   d. *It was probable that the students had met this teacher* [masc.].

4. a. *They hope that we can finish the article.*

    b. *They hope that we have been able to finish the article.*

    c. *They hoped that we were able to finish the article.*

    d. *They hoped that we had been able to finish the article.*

Estructura y Práctica

CONDITIONAL SENTENCES

A conditional sentence is used to express conditions that could be either fulfilled or left unfulfilled. Conditional sentences consist of two clauses: the conditional clause, or *if*-clause, and the main clause.

Sentences Expressing Possibility

Some conditional sentences express possibility. When the result of the condition expressed in the *if*-clause is possible, Spanish uses the present tense, present progressive, or present perfect in the conditional clause, and the future tense or an imperative is used in the main clause. The future tense in the main clause can also be expressed by the **ir a** + infinitive construction. Spanish and English follow the same patterns for verb tenses used in these clauses.

Si no te cuidas, te enfermarás.	*If you don't take care, you'll get sick.*
Si no te has cuidado, te vas a enfermar.	*If you haven't taken care, you're going to get sick.*

Either the *if*-clause or the main clause can appear first in the sentence.

Si te enfermas, llama al médico.	*If you get sick, call the doctor.*
Llama al médico si te enfermas.	*Call the doctor if you get sick.*
Si siguen estudiando, sacarán buenas notas.	*If they keep on studying, they'll get good grades.*
Sacarán buenas notas si siguen estudiando.	*They'll get good grades if they keep on studying.*

Contrary to Present Fact Conditional

A conditional sentence can also be used to explain why things did not happen. This type of conditional sentence is called a contrary to fact conditional. Here are sentences expressing facts in present time, followed by a restatement of those facts as a contrary to present fact conditional sentence.

FACTS

Este restaurante no sirve buena comida. Pierde su clientela.	*This restaurant doesn't serve good food. It's losing its customers.*

RESTATEMENT AS A CONTRARY TO PRESENT FACT CONDITIONAL SENTENCE

Si este restaurante sirviera buena comida, no perdería a su clientela.	*If this restaurant served good food, it wouldn't lose its customers.*

FACTS

Él no es un estudiante aplicado. Saca malas notas.	*He's not a diligent student. He gets bad grades.*

RESTATEMENT AS A CONTRARY TO PRESENT FACT CONDITIONAL SENTENCE

Si él fuera un estudiante aplicado, no sacaría malas notas.	*If he were a diligent student, he wouldn't get bad grades.*

In Spanish, contrary to present fact conditional sentences use the imperfect subjunctive in the *if*-clause and the conditional in the main clause.

E **Contrary to present fact.** Rewrite each of the following sentences as a contrary to fact conditional sentence. Change it from a sentence that states present facts as cause and effect to a conditional sentence with an *if*-clause. Follow the *modelos*.

MODELOS   Él no lo hace porque no puede.
              → Si él pudiera, lo haría.

              Cierran el restaurante porque no hay clientes.
              → Si hubiera clientes, no cerrarían el restaurante.

1. Ella no consigue un buen trabajo porque no tiene un título universitario.

2. Los estudiantes se organizan porque la universidad no respeta la libertad de prensa.

3. Nosotros protestamos porque el gobierno no permite diferencias de opinión.

4. La administración te critica porque posteas temas controvertidos.

5. El director está enojado porque ellos comparten artículos ofensivos en las redes sociales.

6. Sabemos lo que él piensa porque escribe artículos de blog.

Como si...

The conjunction **como si** (*as if*) is a variant of the conditional conjunction **si** (*if*). In Spanish, when the verb in the main clause is in the present tense, **como si** is followed by the imperfect subjunctive if the action of the **como si** clause is seen as happening at the same time as the action or feeling of the main clause.

Él habla como si comprendiera el asunto.	*He talks as if he understood the matter.*
Ella da consejos sobre la salud como si fuera médica.	*She gives health advice as if she were a doctor.*
Él escribe artículos como si no tuviera miedo.	*He writes articles as if he were not afraid.*

When the verb in the main clause is in the preterit or the imperfect, **como si** is followed by the pluperfect subjunctive if the action of the **como si** clause is seen as having happened before the action or feeling of the main clause.

Parecía como si se hubiera hecho daño.	*It seemed as if he had been hurt.*
Fue como si el problema nunca hubiera existido.	*It was as if the problem had never existed.*
Me sentí como si hubieran escuchado nuestra conversación.	*I felt as if they had heard our conversation.*

Note also the phrase **hacer como si** (*to make it look as though*; *to pretend as if*), where **hacer como si** is followed by the imperfect subjunctive.

Él hace como si no me recordara.	*He acts as if he doesn't remember me.*
Deberíamos hacer como si pudiéramos lograr algo.	*We should act as if we could achieve something.*

F **Como si...** Express each of the following sentences in Spanish, using the conjunction **como si** followed by the appropriate subjunctive tense.

1. *We will go on as if there were no problem.*

2. *He asks as if he were interested.*

3. *Don't pretend (tú) as if you don't know.*

4. *Why are you (Ud.) walking as if you were in pain* (tener dolor)?

5. *They answered as if they hadn't understood.*

6. *It seemed as if she hadn't had a good time.*

7. *Let's act as if today were the last time.*

8. *You are working (Uds.) as if you didn't want to finish the project.*

⏵ DIÁLOGO 3 · Un restaurante al borde de la quiebra (1)

Study the dialogue, then listen to the recording and repeat each line.

BENJAMÍN	Paloma, me he enterado de que tu restaurante Girasol está al borde de la quiebra.
PALOMA	Paco y yo estamos destrozados, Benjamín. Llevamos tantos años en esta ciudad.
BENJAMÍN	Si el gobierno no hubiera dictado la orden de confinamiento, a lo mejor Girasol no hubiera llegado a este punto.
PALOMA	Tienes razón. Aun si pusiéramos dos mesas afuera en la acera, nos castigarían con una fuerte multa. Mesas distanciadas, mascarillas e higiene reforzada, pero nada basta para el gobierno.
BENJAMÍN	Sé que el gobierno temía que si no tomara esas medidas, el Covid-19 se propagaría aún más.

Análisis

Check that you understand the linguistic breakdown of each speech from *Diálogo 3*.

Un restaurante al borde de la quiebra	*A restaurant on the verge of bankruptcy*
Paloma, me he enterado de que tu restaurante Girasol está al borde de la quiebra.	*Paloma, I've learned that your Girasol restaurant is on the verge of bankruptcy.*
enterarse de algo	*to find out about something*
me he enterado	*I've learned*
el girasol	*sunflower*

el borde	*edge*
al borde de	*on the edge of*
estar al borde de	*to be on the verge of*
la quiebra	*bankruptcy*
estar al borde de la quiebra	*to be on the verge of bankruptcy*

Paco y yo estamos destrozados, Benjamín. Llevamos tantos años en esta ciudad.	*Paco and I are devastated, Benjamín. We've been in this city for so many years.*
destrozado	*devastated, heartbroken*
llevar + *amount of time*	*to be (somewhere)* + amount of time
llevamos tantos años en esta ciudad	*we've been in this city for so many years*

Si el gobierno no hubiera dictado la orden de confinamiento, a lo mejor Girasol no hubiera llegado a este punto.	*If the government had not issued the lockdown order, maybe Girasol would not have gotten to this point.*
la orden	*order, command*
dictar una orden	*to issue an order*
no hubiera dictado la orden (*pluperfect subjunctive*)	*would not have issued the order, had not issued the order*
el confinamiento	*lockdown, confinement*
a lo mejor	*maybe*
no hubiera llegado (*pluperfect subjunctive*)	*would not have arrived, would not have gotten to*
el punto	*point*
a este punto	*to this point*
llegar a este punto	*to get to this point*

Tienes razón. Aun si pusiéramos dos mesas afuera en la acera, nos castigarían con una fuerte multa. Mesas distanciadas, mascarillas e higiene reforzada, pero nada basta para el gobierno.	*You're right. Even if we were to put two tables outside on the sidewalk, they would punish us with a hefty fine. Tables set far apart, masks, and stricter hygiene, but nothing is enough for the government.*
aun si	*even if*
aun si pusiéramos	*even if we put*
afuera	*outside*
la acera	*sidewalk*
castigar	*to punish*
castigar a alguien con	*to punish someone with*
nos castigarían	*they'd punish us*
la multa	*fine*
con una fuerte multa	*with a hefty fine*
distanciar	*to put at a distance, keep away from*
mesas distanciadas	*tables set far apart*
la mascarilla	*mask, surgical mask*
reforzar (**o** > **ue**)	*to strengthen, reinforce*
la higiene	*hygiene, cleanliness*
la higiene reforzada	*stricter hygiene (practices)*
bastar	*to be enough*
nada basta	*nothing is enough*

Sé que el gobierno temía que si no tomara esas medidas, el Covid-19 se propagaría aún más.	*I know that the government feared that if it didn't take those steps, Covid-19 would spread even more.*
temer que	*to fear that*
la medida	*measure, step*
tomar medidas	*to take measures, take steps*
si no tomara (*imperfect subjunctive*)	*if it didn't take*
temía que si no tomara esas medidas	*it feared that if it didn't take those steps/ measures*
propagarse	*to spread (disease)*
se propagaría	*it would spread*
aún más	*even more*

▶ Variantes

Listen, and repeat the same structures from *Diálogo 3*, now with new vocabulary.

Están al borde de la quiebra .	*They're on the verge of **bankruptcy**.*
una crisis	*a crisis*
un descubrimiento	*a discovery*
un avance científico	*a scientific breakthrough*
la anarquía	*anarchy*
la guerra	*war*

Es necesario dictar una orden .	*It's necessary **to issue an order**.*
dictar medidas	*to impose measures*
dictar leyes	*to make laws, enact laws*
dictar una clase	*to teach a class*
dictar una conferencia	*to give a lecture*
dictar una charla	*to give a talk/lecture*

▶ DIÁLOGO 4 · Un restaurante al borde de la quiebra (2)

Study the dialogue, then listen to the recording and repeat each line.

PALOMA	Benja, comprendo eso, pero me pregunto qué van a hacer los treinta empleados de Girasol que hemos tenido que despedir. Son como familia para nosotros. Me parte el alma.
BENJAMÍN	Es una tragedia. Y el desempleo está en aumento por toda la ciudad.
PALOMA	Todos esperamos que con la vacuna la epidemia disminuya y desaparezca.
BENJAMÍN	Ojalá, y antes de que tú y Paco tengan que cerrar las puertas de Girasol definitivamente.
PALOMA	Eso queda por ver, amigo.

Análisis

Check that you understand the linguistic breakdown of each speech from *Diálogo 4.*

Benja, comprendo eso, pero me pregunto qué van a hacer los treinta empleados de Girasol que hemos tenido que despedir. Son como familia para nosotros. Me parte el alma.

Benja, I understand that, but I wonder what the thirty Girasol employees whom we've had to lay off are going to do. They're like family to us. It breaks my heart.

Benja	(nickname for *Benjamín*)
preguntarse	*to wonder*
me pregunto qué van a hacer	*I wonder what they are going to do*
el empleado	*employee*
los treinta empleados de Girasol	*the thirty Girasol employees*
despedir (**e > i**)	*to fire, dismiss, lay off*
hemos tenido que despedir	*we've had to lay off*
son como familia para nosotros	*they're like family to us*
partir el alma	*to break one's heart*
me parte el alma	*it breaks my heart*

Es una tragedia. Y el desempleo está en aumento por toda la ciudad.

It's very sad. And unemployment is increasing all over the city.

una tragedia	*a tragedy, something very sad*
el desempleo	*unemployment*
el aumento	*increase*
estar en aumento	*to be increasing, be rising, be on the rise*
por toda la ciudad	*all over the city*

Todos esperamos que con la vacuna la epidemia disminuya y desaparezca.

We all hope that with the vaccine, the epidemic will decrease and disappear.

todos esperamos	*we all hope*
la vacuna	*the vaccine*
la epidemia	*the epidemic*
disminuir (yo disminuyo)	*to decrease, decline*
desaparecer (yo desaparezco)	*to disappear*
todos esperamos que disminuya y desaparezca	*we all hope it will decrease and disappear*

Ojalá, y antes de que tú y Paco tengan que cerrar las puertas de Girasol definitivamente.

I hope so, and before you and Paco have to close the doors of Girasol for good.

ojalá	*I hope so*
cerrar (**e > ie**)	*to close*
antes de que tengan que cerrar	*before you have to close*
definitivamente	*for good, permanently*

Eso queda por ver, amigo.

That remains to be seen, my friend.

▶ Variantes

Listen, and repeat the same structures from *Diálogo 4*, now with new vocabulary.

La tasa de desempleo está en aumento.	***The unemployment rate** is on the rise.*
La tasa de empleo	*The employment rate*
La confianza del consumidor	*Consumer confidence*
El poder adquisitivo	*Purchasing power*
La inflación	*Inflation*

Eso queda por ver .	*That remains **to be seen**.*
por hacer	*to be done*
por probar	*to be proven*
por descubrir	*to be discovered*
por comprobar	*to be proven, be verified*

G *Oraciones idiomáticas* (Idiomatic sentences). Express each of the following idiomatic sentences in Spanish.

1. *There's a lot that remains to be done.*

2. *The city has to take important steps.*

3. *Unemployment is on the rise all over the country.*

4. *It breaks my heart that we have [subjunctive] to fire them.*

5. *We are on the verge of a great scientific breakthrough.*

6. *I like to read the opinion pieces and the guest articles.*

7. *Are they organizing a demonstration? What's this about?*

8. *The Constitution of the United States of America guarantees freedom of the press and freedom of assembly.*

▶ DIÁLOGO 5 · Una manifestación contra el alza de los precios

Study the dialogue, then listen to the recording and repeat each line.

JORGE   ¿Has oído? Ayer hubo una manifestación enorme en el centro.

DIEGO   Sí, frente al ayuntamiento. Protestaban contra el alza de los precios y exigían responsabilidad de parte del gobierno.

JORGE   No es para menos. Este año se disparó la inflación.

DIEGO   Por lo cual ha bajado mucho el poder adquisitivo de la gente.

JORGE   Si el gobierno lograra frenar la inflación, habría más estabilidad económica.

DIEGO   ¿Bromeas? Si el gobierno no se hubiera endeudado tanto, no habría tenido que imprimir tanto dinero.

JORGE   Lo de siempre. ¡Políticos sedientos de poder! Su incompetencia y su codicia han llevado a estos disturbios sociales.

DIEGO   ¿Hubo enfrentamientos entre los manifestantes y la policía?

JORGE   Cuatro manifestantes y tres policías tuvieron que ser llevados al hospital.

Análisis

Check that you understand the linguistic breakdown of each speech from *Diálogo 5*.

¿Has oído? Ayer hubo una manifestación enorme en el centro.	*Have you heard? Yesterday there was a huge demonstration downtown.*
la manifestación	*demonstration*
enorme	*huge, enormous*
en el centro	*downtown*

Sí, frente al ayuntamiento. Protestaban contra el alza de los precios y exigían responsabilidad de parte del gobierno.	*Yes, in front of City Hall. They were protesting the rise in prices and demanding accountability from the government.*
el ayuntamiento	*city hall*
frente al ayuntamiento	*in front of City Hall*
protestar contra	*to protest against*
el alza	*rise*
exigir (yo exijo)	*to demand*
la responsabilidad	*accountability, responsibility*
de parte de	*on the part of, from*
de parte del gobierno	*on the part of government, from the government*

No es para menos. Este año se disparó la inflación.	*It's no wonder. This year inflation skyrocketed.*
no es para menos	*it's no wonder*
disparar	*to shoot*
dispararse	*to go off* (of a gun); *to skyrocket* (of prices)

Por lo cual ha bajado mucho el poder adquisitivo de la gente.	*For that very reason, people's purchasing power has diminished.*
por lo cual	*for that very reason, which is why*
bajar	*to decrease, diminish*
el poder	*power*
el poder adquisitivo	*purchasing power*

Si el gobierno lograra frenar la inflación, habría más estabilidad económica.	*If the government succeeded in stopping inflation, there would be more economic stability.*
lograr + *infinitive*	*to succeed in (doing something)*
si el gobierno lograra (*pluperfect subjunctive*)	*if the government succeeded*
frenar	*to stop, restrain* (literally, *to brake*)
habría	*there would be*
la estabilidad	*stability*
la estabilidad económica	*economic stability*

¿Bromeas? Si el gobierno no se hubiera endeudado tanto, no habría tenido que imprimir tanto dinero.

Are you joking? If the government hadn't gone so much into debt, it wouldn't have had to print so much money.

la broma	*joke*
bromear	*to joke*
la deuda	*debt*
endeudarse	*to go into debt*
si no se hubiera endeudado (*pluperfect subjunctive*)	*if it hadn't gone into debt*
no habría tenido que	*it wouldn't have had to*
imprimir	*to print*

Lo de siempre. ¡Políticos sedientos de poder! Su incompetencia y su codicia han llevado a estos disturbios sociales.

Business as usual. Power-hungry politicians! Their incompetence and greed have led to this social unrest.

lo de siempre	*the usual, the same old thing*
el político	*politician*
sediento	*thirsty*
sediento de poder	*power-hungry* (literally, *thirsty of/ for power*)
la incompetencia	*incompetence*
la codicia	*greed*
llevar a	*to lead to*
el disturbio	*disturbance*
los disturbios	*unrest*
los disturbios sociales	*social unrest*

¿Hubo enfrentamientos entre los manifestantes y la policía?

Were there clashes between the demonstrators and the police?

el enfrentamiento	*clash*
entre	*between*
el/la manifestante	*demonstrator, protester*

Cuatro manifestantes y tres policías tuvieron que ser llevados al hospital.

Four demonstrators and three policemen had to be taken to the hospital.

llevar a alguien al hospital	*to take someone to the hospital*
ser llevado al hospital	*to be taken to the hospital*

▶ Variantes

Listen, and repeat the same structures from *Diálogo 5*, now with new vocabulary.

Ayer hubo una manifestación pacífica .

*Yesterday there was **a peaceful demonstration**.*

una manifestación violenta	*a violent demonstration*
un disturbio	*a riot*
un asalto	*a mugging*
un atraco	*a mugging*
una violación	*a rape*
un robo	*a robbery*
un asesinato	*a murder*

un crimen	*a crime*
un delito	*a crime*
un fuego	*a fire*
un incendio	*a fire*
un incendio provocado	*a case of arson*
saqueo de tiendas	*looting of stores*

Se disparó el costo de la vida .	**The cost of living** *skyrocketed.*
el costo de la construcción	*Construction costs*
el precio de la gasolina	*The price of gas*
el valor de la tierra	*The value of land*
su influencia	*Their influence*
su popularidad	*Their popularity*

Los crímenes fueron cometidos por el cartel de narcotráfico .	*The crimes were committed by* **the drug cartel**.
los terroristas	*the terrorists*
los secuestradores	*the kidnappers*

Contrary to Past Fact Conditional

Conditional sentences are also used to comment on facts in the past, using a separate sequence of tenses. Here are sentences expressing facts in past time, followed by a restatement of those facts as a contrary to past fact conditional sentence.

FACTS

| Ella no puso atención. Ella no comprendió. | *She didn't pay attention. She didn't understand.* |

RESTATEMENT AS A CONTRARY TO PAST FACT CONDITIONAL SENTENCE

| Si ella hubiera puesto atención, habría comprendido. | *If she had paid attention, she would have understood.* |

FACTS

| Invertimos dinero en la empresa. Ganamos tanto dinero. | *We invested money in the business. We made so much money.* |

RESTATEMENT AS A CONTRARY TO PAST FACT CONDITIONAL SENTENCE

| Si no hubiéramos invertido dinero en la empresa, no habríamos ganado tanto dinero. | *If we hadn't invested money in the business, we wouldn't have made so much money.* |

In Spanish, contrary to past fact conditional sentences use the pluperfect subjunctive in the *if*-clause and the conditional perfect in the main clause.

However, the pluperfect subjunctive may sometimes replace the conditional perfect in the main clause, thus forming a contrary to past fact conditional sentence with the pluperfect subjunctive in both clauses. Here we repeat the two example sentences above, using the pluperfect subjunctive in both clauses.

Si ella hubiera puesto atención, hubiera comprendido.
Si no hubiéramos invertido dinero en la empresa, no hubiéramos ganado tanto dinero.

H *Si lo hubiera sabido...* Complete each of the following sentences about what people would have done if only they had known certain things. Use the correct form of the pluperfect subjunctive in the **si**-clause and the conditional perfect or the pluperfect subjunctive in the main clause. Complete each sentence in two ways, using the cues in parentheses. Follow the *modelos.*

MODELOS   Si yo lo _hubiera sabido_ (saber), te _habría llamado_ (llamar).

Si yo lo _hubiera sabido_ (saber), te _hubiera llamado_ (llamar).

1. Si tú me lo _____ (decir), yo _____ (asistir) a la conferencia.

2. Si nosotros _____ (leer) el informe, _____ (comprender) de qué se trata.

3. Yo los _____ (conocer) si _____ (pasar) mis vacaciones en Puerto Rico.

4. Si Raquel _____ (casarse) con Francisco, _____ (tener) una vida más fácil.

5. _____ (Haber) menos heridos si la manifestación no _____ (volverse) tan violenta.

6. Si Ud. nos _____ (avisar), nosotros _____ (poder) participar también.

7. Yo _____ (estar) tan contenta si los chicos me _____ (visitar).

8. ¿Qué _____ tú (hacer) si (ellos) te _____ (prohibir) publicar tu artículo?

I *Oraciones condicionales* (**Conditional sentences**). Complete each of the following conditional sentences with the correct form of the verb in parentheses. Follow the *modelo.*

MODELO   Si hubiera menos delincuencia, la gente _tendría_ menos miedo. (tener)

1. Si el gobierno _____ la libertad de expresión de los ciudadanos, no habría tantas protestas. (respetar)

2. No _____ la inflación si el país no se hubiera endeudado. (dispararse)

3. Si ese profesor dicta una charla mañana, todos los estudiantes _____. (asistir)

4. Si no frenan el desempleo, el país _____ momentos difíciles. (vivir)

5. Los ciudadanos no se habrían enojado tanto si el costo de la vida no _____ tanto en un solo año. (subir)

6. Los periodistas no escribirían estas cosas si _____ la verdad. (saber)

7. Si no hubiera llegado la policía, la manifestación pacífica _____ en un disturbio. (convertirse)

8. Mucha gente _____ sin trabajo si cerraran esta fábrica. (quedar)

J *Más oraciones condicionales.* Express each of the following sentences in Spanish. Follow the *modelos*.

MODELOS *If he comes, we'll see him.*
→ Si viene, lo veremos.

If he came, we'd see him.
→ Si viniera, lo veríamos.

If he had come, we would have seen him.
→ Si hubiera venido, lo habríamos/hubiéramos visto.

1. a. *If the city doesn't issue lockdown orders, a lot of people will get sick.*

   b. *If the city didn't issue lockdown orders, a lot of people would get sick.*

   c. *If the city hadn't issued lockdown orders, a lot of people would have gotten sick.*

2. a. *If the newspaper doesn't criticize the government, the government won't shut it down.*

   b. *If the newspaper didn't criticize the government, the government wouldn't shut it down.*

   c. *If the newspaper hadn't criticized the government, the government wouldn't have shut it down.*

3. a. *If prices don't go up, there won't be a demonstration.*

   b. *If prices didn't go up, there wouldn't be a demonstration.*

   c. *If prices hadn't gone up, there wouldn't have been a demonstration.*

4. a. *If you (tú) share your article on social media, many people will read it.*

   b. *If you (tú) shared your article on social media, many people would read it.*

   c. *If you (tú) had shared your article on social media, many people would have read it.*

5. a. *If all the restaurants close, it will be a big problem for the city.*

   b. *If all the restaurants closed, it would be a big problem for the city.*

   c. *If all the restaurants had closed, it would have been a big problem for the city.*

Estructura y Práctica

Ojalá *I hope, I wish* (Part 2)

You learned several uses of **ojalá** in Chapter 19. When **ojalá** is followed by the present subjunctive, it expresses a hope for something that is possible.

Ojalá que la contraten.	*I hope they hire her.*
Ojalá pueda trabajar en mi campo.	*I hope I can work in my field.*

When **ojalá** is followed by the present perfect subjunctive, it expresses a hope that something that influences the current state of things either happened or did not happen.

Ojalá que su influencia en la empresa haya crecido.	*I hope her influence on the business has grown.*
Ojalá hayan puesto más mesas y sillas en el patio.	*We hope they've put more tables and chairs on the patio.*

When **ojalá** is followed by the imperfect subjunctive, it expresses a wish for something remotely possible.

Ojalá consiguieras un puesto mejor.	*I wish you'd get a better job.*
Ojalá no se declararan en quiebra.	*I wish they wouldn't declare bankruptcy.*
Ojalá él ganara las elecciones.	*We wish he'd win the election.*
Ojalá pensaran en el medio ambiente.	*I wish they would think about the environment.*

When **ojalá** is followed by the pluperfect subjunctive, it expresses a wish that things were not the way they are. This is a counter-to-fact wish.

Ojalá que Martín no hubiera perdido su trabajo.	*I wish Martín hadn't lost his job.*
Ojalá me hubieran ofrecido un sueldo mejor.	*I wish they would have offered me a better salary.*

Notice the parallels with *if*-clauses in conditional sentences. **Si** + imperfect subjunctive expresses something possible but not necessarily probable.

Si vinieras, nos veríamos.	*If you came, we'd see each other.*

Si + pluperfect subjunctive expresses something counter to the reality of the past.

Si hubieras venido, nos habríamos visto.	*If you had come, we'd have seen each other.*

K *Ojalá.* Express the following sentences in Spanish, using **ojalá** with the appropriate tense.

1. *I hope it will be a peaceful demonstration.*

2. *I wish we would have more purchasing power.*

3. *We wish he would not have brought up such a controversial topic.*

4. *We hope all citizens will understand the importance of the Constitution.*

5. *I wish the kids wouldn't have spent so much time on social media.*

6. *We wish the professor* [fem.] *would give a lecture on economic policy* (la política económica).

7. *I hope the schools won't close because of the epidemic.*

8. *We hope you* (Uds.) *have read the student newspaper.*

▶ DIÁLOGO 6 · Una visita al acueducto de Segovia (1)

Study the dialogue, then listen to the recording and repeat each line.

ALEJANDRO	¡Qué imponente es Segovia! Ya hemos visto el Alcázar y las murallas y ahora el célebre acueducto.
VICTORIA	Es asombroso que los romanos hayan construido el acueducto sin usar argamasa. Y funciona hasta hoy en día.
ALEJANDRO	¡Ojalá todas las obras públicas se construyeran para durar por los siglos!
VICTORIA	Sin embargo es normal que haya deterioro debido a la contaminación medioambiental. Mira, se ve la erosión de las grandes piedras de granito.
ALEJANDRO	Supongo que el denso tráfico por el acueducto tiene mucho que ver. El policía me dijo que los muchos conciertos realizados alrededor del acueducto también son responsables.

Análisis

Check that you understand the linguistic breakdown of each speech from *Diálogo 6.*

¡Qué imponente es Segovia! Ya hemos visto el Alcázar y las murallas y ahora el célebre acueducto.

Segovia is so impressive! We've already seen the Alcázar and the walls, and now the famous aqueduct.

imponente	*impressive, stunning*
el Alcázar (< Arabic)	*fortress, royal palace*
la muralla	*wall* (outside), *rampart*
célebre	*famous*
el acueducto	*aqueduct*

Es asombroso que los romanos hayan construido el acueducto sin usar argamasa. Y funciona hasta hoy en día.

It's amazing that the Romans built the aqueduct without using mortar. And it works to this day.

asombroso	*amazing*
los romanos	*Romans*
es asombroso que hayan construido	*it's amazing that they built*
usar	*to use*
la argamasa	*mortar*
funcionar	*to function, work*
hasta hoy en día	*to this day*

¡Ojalá todas las obras públicas se construyeran para durar por los siglos!

I wish all public works were built to last through the centuries!

ojalá	*I wish*
la obra	*work*
público	*public*
las obras públicas	*public works*
ojalá se construyeran	*I wish they were built*
durar	*to last*
el siglo	*century*

Sin embargo es normal que haya deterioro debido a la contaminación medioambiental. Mira, se ve la erosión de las grandes piedras de granito.

Still, it's not unusual that there's damage due to environmental pollution. Look, you can see the erosion of the large granite stones.

sin embargo	*nevertheless, however, still*
normal	*normal, not unusual*
es normal que haya	*it's normal that there is*
el deterioro	*damage*
debido a	*due to*
la contaminación	*pollution*
medioambiental	*environmental*
el medio ambiente	*environment*
mira	*look*
se ve	*you can see, it can be seen*
la erosión	*erosion*
la piedra	*stone*
el granito	*granite*

Supongo que el denso tráfico por el acueducto tiene mucho que ver. El policía me dijo que los muchos conciertos realizados alrededor del acueducto también son responsables.

I suppose that the dense traffic around the aqueduct has a lot to do with it. The policeman told me that the many concerts performed around the aqueduct are also responsible.

supongo	*I suppose (**suponer**)*
denso	*dense*
el tráfico	*traffic*
tiene mucho que ver	*it has a lot to do with it*
el policía	*policeman*
el concierto	*concert*
realizar	*to perform*
los muchos conciertos realizados	*the many concerts performed*
alrededor de	*around*
alrededor del acueducto	*around the aqueduct*
responsable	*responsible*

▶ Variantes

Listen, and repeat the same structures from *Diálogo 6*, now with new vocabulary.

Ojalá visites Segovia .

*I hope **you'll visit Segovia**.*

hagas una visita guiada del acueducto	*you'll take a guided tour of the aqueduct*
entres en el Alcázar	*you'll go into the Alcázar*
trepes la muralla que rodea la ciudad	*you'll climb the wall surrounding the city*
recorras el casco viejo	*you'll walk around the old quarter*
veas la catedral	*you'll see the cathedral*
vayas al barrio judío	*you'll go to the Jewish quarter*
te pasees por la Plaza Mayor	*you'll stroll around the main square*

Ojalá hubieran visitado Segovia .	*We wish **they had visited Segovia**.*
hubieran hecho una visita guiada del acueducto	*they had taken a guided tour of the aqueduct*
hubieran entrado en el Alcázar	*they had gone into the Alcázar*
hubieran trepado la muralla que rodea la ciudad	*they had climbed the wall surrounding the city*
hubieran recorrido el casco viejo	*they had walked around the old quarter*
hubieran visto la catedral	*they had seen the cathedral*
hubieran ido al barrio judío	*they had gone to the Jewish quarter*
se hubieran paseado por la Plaza Mayor	*they had strolled around the main square*

▶ DIÁLOGO 7 · Una visita al acueducto de Segovia (2)

Study the dialogue, then listen to the recording and repeat each line.

VICTORIA	O sea, la música a todo volumen produce vibraciones que dañan las piedras de los arcos. ¿Qué harán entonces? Estos eventos fomentan el turismo.
ALEJANDRO	Es cierto. También me enteré que van a emprender otra restauración del acueducto.
VICTORIA	Alejo, Segovia es un sueño hecho realidad. Y ahora, ¿por qué no conocemos otra maravilla segoviana, su cocina tradicional auténtica?
ALEJANDRO	Vale. Todo esto me abre el apetito. Hay un restaurante en la plaza cuya especialidad es el lechazo asado. Pidámoslo con un vino tinto de la región.
VICTORIA	Encantada. ¡Hagamos un brindis por nosotros, el acueducto y Segovia!
ALEJANDRO Y VICTORIA	(*Los dos juntos*) ¡Salud!

Análisis

Check that you understand the linguistic breakdown of each speech from *Diálogo 7*.

O sea, la música a todo volumen produce vibraciones que dañan las piedras de los arcos. ¿Qué harán entonces? Estos eventos fomentan el turismo.	*That is, the blaring music produces vibrations that damage the stones of the arches. Then what will they do? These events boost tourism.*
o sea	*that is*
la música	*music*
a todo volumen	*blaring, loudest*
produce	*it produces* (**producir**)
las vibraciones	*vibrations*

dañar	*damage*
el arco	*arch*
harán	*they will do* (**hacer**)
el evento	*event*
fomentar	*to promote, boost*
el turismo	*tourism*

Es cierto. También me enteré que van a emprender otra restauración del acueducto.

It's true. I also found out that they're going to undertake another restoration of the aqueduct.

es cierto	*it's true*
me enteré	*I found out* (**enterarse**)
emprender	*to undertake*
la restauración	*restoration*

Alejo, Segovia es un sueño hecho realidad. Y ahora, ¿por qué no conocemos otra maravilla segoviana, su cocina tradicional auténtica?

Alejo, Segovia is a dream come true. And now, why don't we get to know another wonder of Segovia, its authentic traditional cuisine?

Alejo	(nickname for *Alejandro* (*Alexander*))
el sueño	*dream*
hecho	*made* (past participle of **hacer**)
la realidad	*reality*
un sueño hecho realidad	*a dream come true*
la maravilla	*wonder*
segoviano	*of/from Segovia*
la cocina	*cuisine; kitchen*
tradicional	*traditional*
auténtico	*authentic*

Vale. Todo esto me abre el apetito. Hay un restaurante en la plaza cuya especialidad es el lechazo asado. Pidámoslo con un vino tinto de la región.

Okay. All of this is whetting my appetite. There's a restaurant on the square whose specialty is roast lamb. Let's order it with a red wine from the region.

vale	*okay*
todo esto	*all of this*
me abre el apetito	*it's whetting my appetite* (literally, *it's opening my appetite*)
cuyo	*whose* (relative pronoun)
la especialidad	*specialty, special dish*
cuya especialidad	*whose specialty*
el lechazo	*suckling lamb*
asado	*roasted*

el lechazo asado	*roast lamb*
pedir (**e > i**)	*to order*
pidamos	*let's order* (**nosotros** command form of **pedir**)
pidámoslo (lo = el lechazo)	*let's order it*
el vino tinto	*red wine*
la región	*region*

Encantada. ¡Hagamos un brindis por nosotros, el acueducto y Segovia!	*Delighted. Let's make a toast to us, the aqueduct, and Segovia!*
encantada	*delighted, thrilled*
hagamos	*let's do, let's make* (**nosotros** command form of **hacer**)
el brindis	*toast*
hacer un brindis	*to make a toast*
hagamos un brindis	*let's toast, let's make a toast*
por nosotros, el acueducto y Segovia	*for us, the aqueduct, and Segovia*

(*Los dos juntos*) ¡Salud!	(The two together) *Cheers!* (literally, *Health!*)

▶ Variantes

Listen, and repeat the same structures from *Diálogo 7*, now with new vocabulary.

Ojalá pudiéramos probar el lechazo asado .	*I wish we could try **the roast lamb**.*
las truchas a la segoviana	*trout Segovia style*
el cochinillo asado	*roast suckling pig*
patatas guisadas con chorizo	*stewed potatoes with sausage*
setas a la segoviana	*mushrooms Segovia style*
el ponche segoviano (bizcocho)	*Segovian punch (sponge cake)*

¡Se me hace agua la boca!	*It makes my mouth water!*

Ojalá que Uds. hayan conocido las ruinas romanas más espectaculares de España .	*I hope you've seen **the most spectacular Roman ruins in Spain**.*
el teatro de Mérida	*the theater in Merida*
el anfiteatro de Itálica	*the amphitheater in Itálica (in Sevilla)*
el arco de triunfo de Medinaceli	*the triumphal arch in Medinaceli (in Soria)*
el foro de Tarraco	*the forum in Tarraco (in Tarragona)*
el circo romano de Tarragona	*the Roman circus in Tarragona*
el templo de Diana de Mérida	*the temple of Diana in Mérida*
la presa de Prosperina de Mérida	*the reservoir of Prosperina in Mérida*

LA CONTAMINACIÓN MEDIOAMBIENTAL (*ENVIRONMENTAL POLLUTION*)

---

el aire limpio/sucio *clean/dirty air*
los animales en peligro de extinción *endangered animals*
el calentamiento global *global warming*
el cambio climático *climate change*
el dióxido de carbono *carbon dioxide*
la huella de carbono *carbon footprint*
el plástico reciclable *recyclable plastic*
los productos ecológicos *eco-friendly products*
el reciclaje *recycling*
la sostenibilidad *sustainability*
la sustentabilidad *sustainability*

L *Un viaje a Segovia.* Express each of the following sentences in Spanish.

1. *We hope the concerts will promote tourism.*

2. *These Segovian dishes are whetting my appetite.*

3. *This city is a dream come true!*

4. *If they had taken a trip to Spain, they would have gotten to know Segovia.*

5. *Let's make a toast with this red wine from the region.*

6. *I wish you (tú) had spent at least a month in Spain.*

7. *It's amazing that the Romans built the aqueduct without using mortar.*

8. *If there weren't dense traffic and blaring music, there would be less environmental pollution.*

Un paso más

Are you ready to take your Spanish a step further? Here are exercises that will enhance your knowledge of the language and encourage you to express yourself freely.

M *Si fuera posible, yo...* Write sentences in Spanish, telling what you would do if something were possible. Use the imperfect subjunctive and the conditional in contrary to present fact conditional sentences.

N *Si yo hubiera...* Write sentences in Spanish, explaining that if you had done something, another person would have done something in response. Use the pluperfect (past perfect) subjunctive in contrary to past fact conditional sentences.

O ***Preguntas personales.*** *Contesta las siguientes preguntas con oraciones completas en español.*

1. ¿Escribiste un artículo para un periódico estudiantil alguna vez? ¿Cuál fue el tema? ¿Fue controvertido? ¿Cómo reaccionó la administración?

2. Durante la epidemia del Covid-19, ¿cómo les afectó a ti y a tu familia el confinamiento? ¿Tuvieron dificultades económicas?

3. ¿Participaste en una manifestación alguna vez? ¿Contra qué protestaron tú y los otros manifestantes? ¿Cuál fue el resultado?

4. ¿Hiciste un viaje a España alguna vez? ¿Qué ciudades conociste?

P ***¿Qué opinas?*** *Escribe unos ensayos* (essays) *en español sobre los siguientes temas que se tratan en los diálogos del capítulo 20. Usa vocabulario y expresiones pertinentes al tema.*

1. La erosión de la libertad de expresión (o de otra libertad)

2. Un viaje a Segovia (real o imaginario)

3. Una manifestación política

4. La quiebra: un efecto devastador (*devastating*) del Covid-19

5. Unas consecuencias de la contaminación medioambiental

Q ***Citas*** **(Quotations).** *Lee las siguientes citas y tradúcelas al inglés. Después, explica lo que significan en español. Tienen que ver con los temas del capítulo 20: la economía y la política.*

1. "Cuando los gobiernos temen a la gente, hay libertad. Cuando la gente teme al gobierno, hay tiranía."
   —*Thomas Jefferson*

2. "La política es casi tan emocionante como la guerra y no menos peligrosa. En la guerra nos pueden matar una sola vez; en política, muchas veces."
   —*Winston Churchill*

3. "Lo que más me asombra de los Estados Unidos no es tanto la maravillosa grandeza de algunas empresas como la multitud de empresas pequeñas."
   —*Alexis de Tocqueville*

4. "Se puede medir la salud democrática de un país evaluando la diversidad de opiniones, la libertad de expresión y el espíritu crítico de sus diversos medios de comunicación."
   —*Mario Vargas Llosa*

5. "En tiempos de engaño universal, decir la verdad se convierte en un acto revolucionario."
   —*George Orwell*

6. "Mucha gente quiere que el gobierno proteja al consumidor. Un problema mucho más urgente es proteger al consumidor del gobierno."
   —*Milton Friedman*

Building Spanish Vocabulary

Word Formation

- Forming Nouns from Verbs
- Forming Nouns from Nouns
- Forming Adjectives from Verbs
- Forming Nouns from Adjectives
- Forming Adjectives from Nouns
- Forming Adjectives from Adjectives and Nouns
- Compound Nouns
- Forming the Names of Trees

"La higuera" by Juana de Ibarbourou

Felicidades on successfully working through the 20 chapters of *The Complete Ultimate Spanish* comprehensive first- and second-year course! You have built confidence in speaking and understanding Spanish through the audio program of *Diálogos* and *Variantes*, the exercises, and the culminating section of each chapter, *Un paso más*, which has taken you a step further in enhancing your knowledge and use of the Spanish language.

At this stage in your study of Spanish, an effective way to enhance your mastery of the language is to read and listen to authentic Spanish produced by native speakers for native speakers. For reading, the Spanish language press from all Spanish-speaking countries is available online. For listening to Spanish spoken by native speakers, streaming services provide a vast variety of films, television programs, and telenovelas in Spanish, most of which are available with English subtitles. To facilitate your transition to authentic materials, we devote this final chapter of *The Complete Ultimate Spanish* to vocabulary building through word formation.

The main problem posed by vocabulary in a foreign language is that native speakers of any language may have anywhere from 20,000 to 80,000 words at their disposal. How does a language learner deal with this wealth of material? In most languages, words are built from basic elements—roots, prefixes, and suffixes. It is therefore important that learners of a foreign language study how words are formed in that language so that they can make intelligent guesses about the meaning of new words they encounter.

Imagine learners of English who come across the word "irreplaceable." They will know how to make an informed guess at its meaning if they know how the word is constructed. Its root is the verb *to place*. To that root, the prefix *re-* is added, forming the new verb *replace*. To this new verb, the suffix *-able* is added, forming the adjective *replaceable*. To the adjective *replaceable*, the negative prefix *-in* is added. However, the *n* of that prefix changes to *r* before another *r*: *-ir*. Our newly constructed adjective, *irreplaceable*, means "which cannot be replaced or substituted for."

In this chapter, you will learn some of the ways in which Spanish transforms, for example, verbs into nouns, nouns into adjectives, and adjectives into nouns. You will practice these processes with productive exercises. The exercises provided with the analyses of word formation should equip you with the necessary tools to expand your Spanish vocabulary exponentially, tools that will serve you well in reading and writing as well as in speaking and understanding Spanish.

Forming Nouns from Verbs

1 · Many nouns derived from verbs consist of the verb stem + **-o** or **-a**.

almorzar (**o** > **ue**) *to have lunch*	> el almuerzo *lunch*
archivar *to file*	> el archivo *file*
cenar *to have dinner*	> la cena *dinner*
comprar *to buy*	> la compra *purchase*
contar (**o** > **ue**) *to tell, recount*	> el cuento *story*
contar (**o** > **ue**) *to count*	> la cuenta *bill*
desayunar *to have breakfast*	> el desayuno *breakfast*
esperar *to wait*	> la espera *wait, waiting*
practicar *to practice*	> la práctica *practice*
trabajar *to work*	> el trabajo *work*
volar (**o** > **ue**) *to fly*	> el vuelo *flight*

A   Write the verb from which each of the following nouns is derived.

1. el juego

2. la ayuda

3. el ensayo

4. el empleo

5. el consejo

6. el gobierno

7. el camino

8. el daño

9. la vuelta

10. el desarrollo

11. la firma

12. el apoyo

2 · Nouns are formed from the past participle of verbs. They consist of the verb stem + the suffix **-ada** (for **-ar** verbs) or **-ido/-ida** (for **-er** and **-ir** verbs).

caer *to fall*	> la caída *fall*
comer *to eat*	> la comida *meal, food*
entrar *to enter*	> la entrada *entrance*

ir *to go*	>	la ida *going (somewhere), one-way ticket*
llamar *to call*	>	la llamada *call*
llegar *to arrive*	>	la llegada *arrival*
mirar *to look (at)*	>	la mirada *look, glance*
pedir *to ask for, order*	>	el pedido *order, request*
salir *to go out*	>	la salida *exit*
sentir *to feel*	>	el sentido *sense*

B Write the verb from which each of the following nouns is derived.

1. la bebida

2. el contenido

3. la parada

4. el oído

5. la partida

6. la subida

7. la corrida

8. la herida

9. la medida

10. el cuidado

11. la bajada

12. la cruzada

3 · Many nouns are formed with the suffixes **-ción** and **-sión**. Most of these nouns have English cognates ending in *-tion* and *-sion*, respectively.

contaminar *to pollute*	>	la contaminación *pollution*
declarar *to declare*	>	la declaración *declaration*
elaborar *to draw up*	>	la elaboración *elaboration*
exportar *to export*	>	la exportación *exportation*
organizar *to organize*	>	la organización *organization*
presentar *to present*	>	la presentación *presentation*
restaurar *to restore*	>	la restauración *restoration*
concluir *to conclude*	>	la conclusión *conclusion*
dividir *to divide*	>	la división *division*
expresar *to express*	>	la expresión *expression*
impresionar *to impress*	>	la impresión *impression*
poseer *to possess, own*	>	la posesión *possession*

C Write the verb from which each of the following nouns is derived.

1. la inspiración

2. la computación

3. la vacunación

4. la decisión

5. la televisión

6. la función

7. la descripción

8. la modernización

9. la revisión

10. la erosión

11. la profesión

12. la construcción

4 · The suffixes **-ancia** and **-encia** are used to form nouns from verbs. Many of the nouns have English cognates ending in *-ance* and *-ence*, respectively.

ganar *to earn*	> la ganancia *earnings*
importar *to matter, be important*	> la importancia *importance*
asistir (a) *to attend*	> la asistencia *attendance, assistance*
coincidir *to coincide*	> la coincidencia *coincidence*
creer *to believe*	> la creencia *belief*
exigir *to demand*	> la exigencia *demand*
existir *to exist*	> la existencia *existence*
heredar *to inherit*	> la herencia *inheritance*
preferir *to prefer*	> la preferencia *preference*

D Write the verb from which each of the following nouns is derived.

1. la resonancia

2. la perseverancia

3. la estancia

4. la sugerencia

5. la convivencia

6. la influencia

7. la referencia

8. la ignorancia

9. la conferencia

10. la dependencia

5 · The suffix **-miento** is widely used to form nouns from verbs. **-Ar** verbs have the vowel **a** before this suffix; **-er** and **-ir** verbs have the vowel **i** before the suffix. Many of the nouns have English cognates ending in *-ment*.

agotar *to exhaust*	> el agotamiento *exhaustion*
aplazar *to postpone*	> el aplazamiento *postponement*
establecer *to establish*	> el establecimiento *establishment*
lanzar *to launch, throw*	> el lanzamiento *launch*
mover *to move*	> el movimiento *movement*
nacer *to be born*	> el nacimiento *birth*
nombrar *to name, appoint*	> el nombramiento *appointment*
sufrir *to suffer*	> el sufrimiento *suffering*

E Write the verb from which each of the following nouns is derived.

1. el agradecimiento

2. el conocimiento

3. el pensamiento

4. el estacionamiento

5. el crecimiento

6. el tratamiento

7. el entendimiento

8. el sentimiento

9. el descubrimiento

10. el envejecimiento

6 · Nouns that take the suffix -**eo** are derived from verbs that end in -**ear**.

blanquear *to whiten, bleach*   > el blanqueo *whitening, bleaching*
deletrear *to spell*   > el deletreo *spelling* (la letra (*letter*) (alphabet))
recrear *to amuse, entertain*   > el recreo *recreation, recess, playtime*
rodear *to encircle, round up*   > el rodeo *circumlocution, roundabout way, rodeo*
sondear *to sound out, poll, probe* > el sondeo *sounding, poll*
teclear *to type, key in*   > el tecleo *typing, keying in* (la tecla (*key*), el teclado (*keyboard*))

F Write the noun ending in -**eo** (including its definite article) that is derived from each of the following verbs.

1. pasear   6. bombardear

2. boxear   7. escanear

3. emplear   8. formatear

4. bloquear   9. fildear

5. zapatear   10. batear

Note that when technology and baseball were adopted by Spanish-speaking societies, English words from these two fields were borrowed into Spanish and changed according to Spanish pronunciation and grammar. These neologisms (new words) include verbs in the -**ar** conjugation, most with the -**ear** suffix; in some cases, their derivative nouns take the suffix -**eo**. Social media's impact has also led to the borrowing of English verbs in Spanish, such as **textear** (*to text, send a text message*) and **tuitear** (*to tweet*).

Forming Nouns from Nouns

7 · The suffix -**ero**/-**era** indicates the container for or place of something. (See sections 12, 13, and 16 for other word formations with the suffix -**ero**/-**era**.)

G Write the root noun for each of the following nouns. Then write the English meaning of each noun given.

1. la sopera   6. la pecera

2. el monedero   7. el llavero

3. la perrera   8. el billetero

4. el salero   9. el arenero

5. la pajarera   10. la papelera

Forming Adjectives from Verbs

8 · Adjectives with the suffixes -**ante** and -**ente** are formed from verbs. Adjectives ending in -**ante** are formed from -**ar** verbs and those ending in -**ente** from -**er** and -**ir** verbs. Most of the adjectives have English cognates ending in *-ing*.

colgar *to hang*	> colgante *hanging, pending*
interesar *to interest*	> interesante *interesting*
penetrar *to penetrate*	> penetrante *penetrating*
vacilar *to hesitate*	> vacilante *hesitating*
deprimir *to depress*	> deprimente *depressing*
equivaler *to be equivalent to*	> equivalente *equivalent*
referir *to refer*	> referente *referring, relating*
sobrevivir *to survive*	> sobreviviente *surviving*

H Write the verb from which each of the following adjectives is derived.

1. existente
2. durmiente
3. fascinante
4. atrayente
5. riente
6. creyente
7. contribuyente
8. naciente
9. corriente
10. siguiente
11. brillante
12. perteneciente

9 · When the suffixes -**dizo**/-**diza** are added to a verb root, they denote having a propensity to do the action of the verb or doing that action frequently.

resbalarse *to slip, slide* > resbaladizo *slippery*

I Complete each of the following sentences with the correct form of the appropriate adjective from the list below.

asustadizo   enamoradizo   enojadizo   movedizo   olvidadizo   quebradizo

1. Ese muchacho no se acuerda de nada. Es muy _____.

2. Mi gato tiene miedo de todo. Es muy _____.

3. Ten cuidado y no pises (*step on*) esa arena (*sand*). No es tierra sólida. Es arena

   _____.

4. Alberto me dice que ha conocido a una chica que es el amor de su vida. Cada mes

   hay otra. ¡Qué _____ es ese muchacho!

5. Estas galletas son muy duras. Cuidado al ponerles mantequilla. Son muy

   _____.

6. El jefe nuestro siempre está furioso y es muy difícil trabajar bajo una persona tan

   _____.

J Write the adjective ending in **-dizo/-diza** that correctly completes each of the following phrases. Use a verb from the vocabulary list below as the verb root for your answer.

anegar *to flood, inundate*   llover *to rain*
correr *to run, slip, side*   mudar *to change (opinion or mood)*
desmoronarse *to crumble*   pegar *to catch, catch on, stick*
huir *to flee*   plegar *to fold*
levar *to raise (anchor)*

1. *a drawbridge*   un puente _____

2. *a rickety house*   una casa _____

3. *a catchy song*   una canción _____

4. *a sliding door*   una puerta _____

5. *rainwater*   el agua _____

6. *a floodplain*   un terreno _____

7. *a fickle person*   una persona _____

8. *an elusive goal*   un objetivo _____

9. *a folding door*   una puerta _____

10 · The suffix **-ón/-ona** added to a verb root suggests performing the action of the verb repeatedly. For instance, from the verb **criticar**, you can form the adjective **criticón** (*hypercritical, faultfinding*). These adjectives have four forms. The accent mark in the masculine singular does not appear in the other forms.

un hombre criticón, una mujer criticona
hombres criticones, mujeres criticonas

These adjectives in **-ón/-ona** are frequently used as nouns.

el criticón *faultfinder, carping person*

Two of these adjectives have a slightly irregular derivation.

comer   >   un comilón *a big eater, a glutton*
dormir   >   un dormilón *a sleepyhead*

K Complete each of the following sentences with the correct form of the appropriate word from the list below.

abusón   contestón   destrozón   gritón   mandón   preguntón

1. Ese muchacho rompe todo lo que toca. Es un verdadero _____.

2. A esa mujer le gusta decirles a los demás lo que deben hacer. ¡Qué _____!

3. ¡Qué niño! Todo lo que le digo que haga, protesta y discute. Es muy _____.

4. Tomás es muy cruel con los otros niños. Es un _____.

5. Mi vecina quiere saberlo todo. Es muy curiosa y _____.

6. Ese hombre habla tan fuerte que me lastima los oídos. Es tan _____.

L Write the adjective or noun ending in **-ón/-ona** that correctly completes each of the following phrases. Use a verb from the vocabulary list below as the verb root for your answer.

adular *to flatter, fawn over*
bailar *to dance*
dormir *to sleep*
gruñir *to grunt, snarl*
jugar (**u** > **ue**) *to play*
llorar *to cry*

mandar *to order, command*
pelear *to fight*
refunfuñar *to grumble, grouse*
regañar *to scold*
responder *to answer*
saltar *to jump*

1. *a dancing dog*   un perro _____

2. *a scrappy kid, a brawler*   un muchacho _____

3. *a mean, stern teacher*   un profesor _____

4. *a playful friend*   una amiga _____

5. *a jumping bean*   un frijolito _____

6. *a grouchy neighbor*   una vecina _____

7. *a cantankerous colleague* un colega _____

8. *a crybaby*   una niña _____

9. *a bossy director*   una directora _____

10. *an obsequious man*   un hombre _____

11. *a sleepyhead*   un _____

12. *someone who talks back* un _____

Forming Nouns from Adjectives

11 · Many Spanish nouns with the suffix **-ez/-eza** are derived from their related adjective.

ávido *eager, avid*	> la avidez *eagerness*
bello *beautiful*	> la belleza *beauty*
limpio *clean*	> la limpieza *cleanliness*
maduro *mature*	> la madurez *maturity*
pequeño *small*	> la pequeñez *smallness*
puro *pure*	> la pureza *purity*
rápido *quick, speedy*	> la rapidez *quickness, speed*
torpe *clumsy, awkward*	> la torpeza *clumsiness, awkwardness*

M Write the noun (including its definite article) that is formed from each of the following adjectives. Accent marks that appear in the adjective are not in the noun form.

1. pálido
2. sencillo
3. natural
4. tímido
5. cierto
6. escaso

7. franco
8. lindo
9. rico
10. viejo
11. estúpido
12. sutil

Forming Adjectives from Nouns

12 · The suffix **-ero/-era** added to a noun root forms an adjective that refers to properties of the base noun. (See sections 7, 13, and 16 for other word formations with the suffix **-ero/-era**.)

la guerra *war*	> guerrero *warlike*
la verdad *truth*	> verdadero *true*
la aduana *customs*	> aduanero
el campo *country, countryside*	> campero
la oveja *sheep*	> ovejero

N Write the form of the adjective listed below that correctly completes each of the following sentences.

azucarero	bananero	banquero	callejero	faldero	llevadero
mañanero	pasajero	petrolero	playero	ranchero	traicionero

1. Pablo se despierta muy temprano todo los días. Es un chico _____.

2. A pesar de su enfermedad, Rita lleva una vida _____.

3. Dudan que el problema económico siga por mucho tiempo. Será _____.

4. Esta planta se especializa en procesar la remolacha (*beet*) _____.

5. El presidente engañó al pueblo y por lo tanto perdió su confianza. Era un político

   _____.

6. Houston es una de las principales ciudades _____ de los Estados Unidos.

7. Hay muchas instituciones financieras en la zona _____.

8. Javier Solís fue un célebre cantante de la música _____.

9. Los Álvarez siempre pasan el mes de julio en un centro turístico _____.

10. Las plantaciones _____ quedaron en ruinas por el huracán.

11. Esos músicos _____ que siempre oigo tocar en la esquina son muy talentosos.

12. Su perro _____ es amistoso, juguetón y se lleva bien con los niños.

13 · The suffix **-ero/-era** can also designate a profession having to do with the root noun. (See sections 7, 12, and 16 for other word formations with the suffix -**ero/** -**era**.)

O What are the professions of these people? Write the root noun from which each of the following nouns of profession is derived. Then write the English translation of the noun of profession. Note that some of the words refer to animals.

1. el zapatero

2. el carnicero

3. el cochero

4. el ovejero

5. la costurera

6. el verdulero

7. el camionero

8. la niñera

9. el mensajero

10. el librero

11. el banquero

12. el hotelero

Forming Adjectives from Adjectives and Nouns

14 · The suffix **-izo/-iza** in Spanish is used to derive new adjectives from other adjectives as well as from nouns. In both cases, -**izo/-iza** expresses a similarity to or an approximation to the meaning of the root.

blanco *white*	> blanquizo *whitish*
el cal *lime* (chemical substance)	> calizo *containing lime, limelike*
casto *pure, chaste*	> castizo *pure, untainted*
el cobre *copper*	> cobrizo *copper-colored*
enfermo *sick*	> enfermizo *sickly*
entero *whole, entire*	> enterizo *one-piece*
la frontera *border*	> fronterizo *border*
la paja *straw*	> pajizo *straw-colored*
el plomo *lead* (mineral)	> plomizo *leaden, gray*
primero *first*	> primerizo *first-time*
puesto *put, put on, added*	> postizo *artificial*
rojo *red*	> rojizo *reddish*

P Express each of the following phrases in English.

1. un pueblo fronterizo

2. una muchacha de pelo cobrizo

3. un cielo triste y plomizo

4. el bebé lleva una prenda enteriza

5. la prosa castiza

6. la piedra caliza

Q Write the form of the adjective listed below that correctly completes each of the following phrases.

enfermizo   pajizo   postizo   primerizo   rojizo

1. *a sickly child*   un niño _____

2. *a first-time visitor*   un visitante _____

3. *a false tooth*   un diente _____

4. *straw-colored hair*   el pelo _____

5. *reddish brown* (of hair) castaño _____

Compound Nouns

15 · Spanish and English both combine nouns and verbs to form new nouns. In English, these compound nouns put the noun first and the verb second. Spanish, however, uses the opposite word order, with the verb first and the noun second.

Compare English *dishwasher* with Spanish **lavaplatos** (**lavar** + **platos**), English *can opener* with Spanish **abrelatas** (**abrir** + **latas**). These Spanish compound nouns are typically masculine, and the noun usually appears in the plural. The compound noun is singular even though it ends in -**s**. No additional -**s** is added in the plural: **el lavaplatos/los lavaplatos, el abrelatas/los abrelatas**.

R Write the Spanish compound noun listed below that correctly expresses each of the following English words. Include its definite article. Vocabulary terms are provided as a resource.

el corcho *cork*   parar *to stop, ward off, protect from*
escurrir *to drain*   portar *to carry, bear*
guardar *to keep, store*   quitar *to take off, remove*
la ola *wave* (of the sea)   el rayo *lightning bolt*

el abrecartas	el cuentakilómetros	el escurreplatos	el espantapájaros
el guardarropas	el lavacoches	el lavadientes	el limpiapipas
el parabrisas	el paracaídas	el parachoques	el paraguas
el pararrayos	el portaviones	el quitanieves	el rompecabezas
el rompeolas	el sacacorchos	el sacapuntas	el salvavidas

1. *puzzle*   8. *car wash*   15. *letter opener*

2. *mouthwash*   9. *life jacket*   16. *lightning rod*

3. *breakwater*   10. *clothes closet* 17. *aircraft carrier*

4. *pipe cleaner*   11. *dish drainer*   18. *pencil sharpener*

5. *odometer*   12. *umbrella*   19. *bumper* (car)

6. *scarecrow*   13. *windshield*   20. *parachute*

7. *snowplow*   14. *corkscrew*

Forming the Names of Trees

16 · In Spanish, the names of many fruits, nuts, and spices are feminine and end in **-a**. To form the name of the tree or bush on which many of these grow, the noun becomes masculine in gender and its ending changes from **-a** to **-o**.

la oliva (la aceituna) *olive*   el olivo *olive tree*

S Write the missing elements in the chart below. Follow the *modelo*.

	MODELO	la manzana	*apple*	<u>el manzano</u>	*apple tree*
1.	la banana	*banana*	_____	*banana tree*
2.	la naranja	*orange*	_____	*orange tree*
3.	_____	*plum*	el ciruelo	*plum tree*
4.	la avellana	*hazelnut*	_____	*hazelnut tree*
5.	la canela	*cinnamon*	_____	*cinnamon tree*
6.	_____	*chestnut*	el castaño	*chestnut tree*
7.	_____	*almond*	el almendro	*almond tree*
8.	la cereza	*cherry*	_____	*cherry tree*
9.	_____	*raspberry*	el frambueso	*raspberry bush*
10.	la granada	*pomegranate*	_____	*pomegranate tree*

The names of other trees are formed by adding the suffix **-ero/-era** to the name of the fruit or nut that grows on it. (See sections 7, 12, and 13 for other word formations with the suffix **-ero/-era**.)

el albaricoque *apricot* > el albaricoquero *apricot tree*
el coco *coconut*   > el cocotero *coconut palm/tree*
el durazno *peach*   > el duraznero *peach tree*
el higo *fig*   > la higuera *fig tree*
el limón *lemon*   > el limonero *lemon tree*
el melocotón *peach*   > el melocotonero *peach tree*

Note that the Spanish word for *peach* varies by region: **El durazno** is more common in Latin America, but in Spain, **el melocotón** is more commonly used.

The names of other fruits also vary from country to country. In Spain and Mexico, the *banana* is called **el plátano**; in some South American and Central American countries, it is called **la banana**, **el banana**, **el plátano**, or **el guineo**. In Venezuela, it is called **el cambur**.

The Spanish word for *grapefruit* is **la toronja** throughout most of Spanish America, but it's called **el pomelo** in Spain and a few Spanish American countries.

The *pineapple* is widely known as **la piña** throughout Spanish America, although some countries use **el ananás** (or **el ananá**).

In Spain and most Spanish American countries, the *avocado* is **el aguacate**. However, in Argentina, Bolivia, Chile, Perú, and Uruguay, the *avocado* is known as **la palta**.

The suffixes **-ar** and **-al** are used to express the orchard, grove, or patch where a particular tree or fruit grows. Also commonly used is **la huerta / el huerto** (*orchard*): **la huerta de manzanas** (*apple orchard*).

la fresa *strawberry*   > el fresal *strawberry patch*
la calabaza *pumpkin* > el calabazar *pumpkin patch*

Note also the variation for **el cafetal** (*coffee plantation*) from **el café** (*coffee*), along with **el cafeto** (*coffee tree*).

T Express each of the following phrases in Spanish, using the **-al** suffix.

1. *fig orchard*

2. *orange grove*

3. *cherry orchard*

4. *banana grove*

5. *peach orchard* (Latin America)

   Express each of the following phrases in Spanish, using the **-ar** suffix.

6. *apple orchard*

7. *olive grove*

8. *lemon grove*

Fruits whose tree or bush is formed with the suffix **-al** form the noun for the grove or orchard in which they grow with the suffix **-eda**.

la pera *pear*   > el peral   > la peraleda
la mora *blackberry* > el moral > la moraleda

The suffix **-eda** is also used with the noun **el álamo** (*poplar tree*) to form **la alameda** (*poplar grove*), which can also refer to a boulevard or park surrounded by poplars or other trees.

SOBRE LOS ÁRBOLES Y LAS UVAS (*OF TREES AND GRAPES*)

Los árboles (*Trees*)

el abedul *birch tree*
el abeto *fir tree*
el árbol conífero *coniferous tree* (*conifer, tree producing cones*)
el arce *maple tree*
el cedro *cedar tree*
el ciprés *cypress tree*
el cocotero *coconut tree*
el nogal *walnut tree*
el olmo *elm tree*
la palmera *palm tree*
la palmera datilera *date palm tree* (el dátil (*date*))
la palmera de coco *coconut palm tree*
el pino *pine tree*
el roble *oak tree*
el sauce llorón *weeping willow tree*
la secuoya *sequoia tree*
el sicomoro (el sicómoro) *sycamore tree*

El cultivo de la uva (*Grape cultivation*)

la parra *grapevine*
la uva *grape*
la vid *grapevine*
la viña, el viñedo *vineyard*

vinícola *wine* (adjective)
   la industria vinícola *wine industry*
   las regiones vinícolas *wine-growing / wine-producing regions*
   el turismo vinícola *wine tourism*
la viticultura *vine-growing, viticulture*

De todo hay en la viña del Señor. *It takes all kinds to make a world.* (PROVERB)

Un paso más

Are you ready to take your Spanish a step further? Here are exercises that will enhance your knowledge of the language and encourage you to express yourself freely.

The focus of this section is *"La higuera"* ("The Fig Tree"), a beautiful and inspiring poem by Juana de Ibarbourou, one of the most important women poets of Uruguayan and Spanish American literature of the 20th century.

"La higuera" por Juana de Ibarbourou

Juana de Ibarbourou (1892–1979) nació en Uruguay. Fue una de las poetas más distinguidas e innovadoras de la literatura uruguaya e hispanoamericana del siglo XX. Publicó libros de cuentos y de teatro, pero se le conoce principalmente por su poesía. En 1929, fue proclamada "Juana de América". Consiguió el Gran Premio Nacional de Literatura de Uruguay en 1959, año en que también fue propuesta para el Premio Nobel de Literatura. La exquisita poesía lírica de Juana de Ibarbourou se basa en sus profundos sentimientos sobre la naturaleza, el amor, la belleza, el gozo de vivir y el papel de la mujer en la sociedad. "La higuera", impresionante poema temprano, fue publicado en su libro *Raíz salvaje* en 1922.

Para más información, ve https://es.wikipedia.org/wiki/Juana_de_Ibarbourou .

Vocabulario útil: *Las partes del árbol*

el brote *bud, shoot*	la hoja *leaf*
el capullo *bud*	el nido *nest*
el cono de pino *pine cone*	la raíz (las raíces) *root*
la copa *treetop, crown*	la rama *branch*
la corteza *bark*	la semilla *seed*
la flor *flower*	el tallo *stem, stalk*
el gajo *section* (here, *branch, bough*)	el tronco *trunk*

 # La higuera
Juana de Ibarbourou

Porque es áspera y fea,
porque todas sus ramas son grises,
yo le tengo piedad a la higuera.

En mi quinta hay cien árboles bellos,
ciruelos redondos,
limoneros rectos
y naranjos de brotes lustrosos.

En las primaveras,
todos ellos se cubren de flores
en torno a la higuera.

Y la pobre parece tan triste
con sus gajos torcidos que nunca
de apretados capullos se viste...

Por eso,
cada vez que yo paso a su lado,
digo, procurando
hacer dulce y alegre mi acento:
«Es la higuera el más bello
de los árboles todos del huerto».

Si ella escucha,
si comprende el idioma en que hablo,
¡qué dulzura tan honda hará nido
en su alma sensible de árbol!

Y tal vez, a la noche,
cuando el viento abanique su copa,
embriagada de gozo le cuente:
¡Hoy a mí me dijeron hermosa!

The Fig Tree
Juana de Ibarbourou

Because she is rough and ugly,
because all of her branches are gray,
I feel sorry for the fig tree.

At my country house there are a hundred beautiful trees,
round plum trees,
straight lemon trees
and orange trees with shiny buds.

In springtime,
they are all covered with flowers
surrounding the fig tree.

And the poor thing seems so sad,
that with her twisted branches, she is never
dressed with overflowing buds.

That's why,
each time I walk by her,
I say, trying
to make my voice sweet and happy:
"The fig tree is the most beautiful
of all the trees in the orchard."

If she's listening,
if she understands the language I'm speaking,
what a profound sweetness will nest
in her sensitive arboreal soul!

And perhaps, at night,
when the wind is fanning her crown,
inebriated with joy she tells him:

"Today someone told me I am beautiful!"

U *Preguntas. Al contestar las preguntas, cita versos de "La higuera" para justificar tus respuestas.*

1. La poeta usa la personificación para atribuirle rasgos (*traits*) humanos a la higuera.
   a. ¿Cuáles son los rasgos físicos y de personalidad de la higuera?
   b. ¿Cómo cambia la percepción que tiene la higuera de sí misma y su estado de ánimo a lo largo del poema?
   c. ¿A qué se deben estos cambios?

2. En todo poema, el/la poeta crea una voz poética, es decir, el/la hablante que narra las palabras del poema y transmite las ideas y las emociones. Es el narrador / la narradora, no necesariamente el/la poeta, la voz que habla en el poema.
   a. ¿Quién será el/la hablante de "La higuera"? ¿Es mujer u hombre? ¿Por qué lo crees?
   b. ¿Cómo es el/la hablante?
   c. ¿Cuál es la relación que existe entre el/la hablante y la higuera?

3. ¿Cuál es el tema (o los temas) de "La higuera"? (Considera la belleza física y la interior, la autoestima, la naturaleza, la compasión, la empatía, el amor.)

4. Explica la importancia del último verso del poema: *¡Hoy a mí me dijeron hermosa!*

5. Describe el tono del poema. Es decir, ¿cómo te hace sentir "La higuera"?

Verb Charts

Regular Verbs

-ar verbs

cantar *to sing*

INDICATIVE MOOD

PRESENT	canto, cantas, canta · cantamos, cantáis, cantan
IMPERFECT	cantaba, cantabas, cantaba · cantábamos, cantabais, cantaban
PRETERIT	canté, cantaste, cantó · cantamos, cantasteis, cantaron
FUTURE	cantaré, cantarás, cantará · cantaremos, cantaréis, cantarán
CONDITIONAL	cantaría, cantarías, cantaría · cantaríamos, cantaríais, cantarían
PRESENT PERFECT	he, has, ha · hemos, habéis, han
PLUPERFECT	había, habías, había · habíamos, habíais, habían
PRETERIT PERFECT	hube, hubiste, hubo · hubimos, hubisteis, hubieron
FUTURE PERFECT	habré, habrás, habrá · habremos, habréis, habrán
CONDITIONAL PERFECT	habría, habrías, habría · habríamos, habríais, habrían

} cantado

SUBJUNCTIVE MOOD

PRESENT	cante, cantes, cante · cantemos, cantéis, canten
IMPERFECT	cantara, cantaras, cantara · cantáramos, cantarais, cantaran
	cantase, cantases, cantase · cantásemos, cantaseis, cantasen
PRESENT PERFECT	haya, hayas, haya · hayamos, hayáis, hayan
PLUPERFECT	hubiera/hubiese, hubieras/hubieses, hubiera/hubiese · hubiéramos/hubiésemos, hubierais/hubieseis, hubieran/hubiesen

} cantado

PROGRESSIVE TENSES

PRESENT	estoy, estás, está · estamos, estáis, están
IMPERFECT	estaba, estabas, estaba · estábamos, estabais, estaban
PRETERIT	estuve, estuviste, estuvo · estuvimos, estuvisteis, estuvieron
FUTURE	estaré, estarás, estará · estaremos, estaréis, estarán
CONDITIONAL	estaría, estarías, estaría · estaríamos, estaríais, estarían
SUBJUNCTIVE	que + *corresponding subjunctive tense of* estar

} cantando

IMPERATIVE MOOD

canta / no cantes (tú), cante (Ud.) ·
   cantemos (nosotros), cantad / no cantéis (vosotros), canten (Uds.)

-er verbs

comer *to eat*

INDICATIVE MOOD

PRESENT	como, comes, come · comemos, coméis, comen
IMPERFECT	comía, comías, comía · comíamos, comíais, comían
PRETERIT	comí, comiste, comió · comimos, comisteis, comieron
FUTURE	comeré, comerás, comerá · comeremos, comeréis, comerán
CONDITIONAL	comería, comerías, comería · comeríamos, comeríais, comerían
PRESENT PERFECT	he, has, ha · hemos, habéis, han
PLUPERFECT	había, habías, había · habíamos, habíais, habían
PRETERIT PERFECT	hube, hubiste, hubo · hubimos, hubisteis, hubieron } comido
FUTURE PERFECT	habré, habrás, habrá · habremos, habréis, habrán
CONDITIONAL PERFECT	habría, habrías, habría · habríamos, habríais, habrían

SUBJUNCTIVE MOOD

PRESENT	coma, comas, coma · comamos, comáis, coman
IMPERFECT	comiera, comieras, comiera · comiéramos, comierais, comieran
	comiese, comieses, comiese · comiésemos, comieseis, comiesen
PRESENT PERFECT	haya, hayas, haya · hayamos, hayáis, hayan
PLUPERFECT	hubiera/hubiese, hubieras/hubieses, hubiera/hubiese · } comido
	hubiéramos/hubiésemos, hubierais/hubieseis,
	hubieran/hubiesen

PROGRESSIVE TENSES

PRESENT	estoy, estás, está · estamos, estáis, están
IMPERFECT	estaba, estabas, estaba · estábamos, estabais, estaban
PRETERIT	estuve, estuviste, estuvo · estuvimos, estuvisteis, estuvieron
FUTURE	estaré, estarás, estará · estaremos, estaréis, estarán } comiendo
CONDITIONAL	estaría, estarías, estaría · estaríamos, estaríais, estarían
SUBJUNCTIVE	que + *corresponding subjunctive tense of* estar

IMPERATIVE MOOD

come / no comas (tú), coma (Ud.) ·
    comamos (nosotros), comed / no comáis (vosotros), coman (Uds.)

-ir verbs

vivir *to live*

INDICATIVE MOOD

PRESENT	vivo, vives, vive · vivimos, vivís, viven
IMPERFECT	vivía, vivías, vivía · vivíamos, vivíais, vivían
PRETERIT	viví, viviste, vivió · vivimos, vivisteis, vivieron
FUTURE	viviré, vivirás, vivirá · viviremos, viviréis, vivirán
CONDITIONAL	viviría, vivirías, viviría · viviríamos, viviríais, vivirían
PRESENT PERFECT	he, has, ha · hemos, habéis, han
PLUPERFECT	había, habías, había · habíamos, habíais, habían
PRETERIT PERFECT	hube, hubiste, hubo · hubimos, hubisteis, hubieron
FUTURE PERFECT	habré, habrás, habrá · habremos, habréis, habrán
CONDITIONAL PERFECT	habría, habrías, habría · habríamos, habríais, habrían

} vivido

SUBJUNCTIVE MOOD

PRESENT	viva, vivas, viva · vivamos, viváis, vivan
IMPERFECT	viviera, vivieras, viviera · viviéramos, vivierais, vivieran
	viviese, vivieses, viviese · viviésemos, vivieseis, viviesen
PRESENT PERFECT	haya, hayas, haya · hayamos, hayáis, hayan
PLUPERFECT	hubiera/hubiese, hubieras/hubieses, hubiera/hubiese · hubiéramos/hubiésemos, hubierais/hubieseis, hubieran/hubiesen

} vivido

PROGRESSIVE TENSES

PRESENT	estoy, estás, está · estamos, estáis, están
IMPERFECT	estaba, estabas, estaba · estábamos, estabais, estaban
PRETERIT	estuve, estuviste, estuvo · estuvimos, estuvisteis, estuvieron
FUTURE	estaré, estarás, estará · estaremos, estaréis, estarán
CONDITIONAL	estaría, estarías, estaría · estaríamos, estaríais, estarían
SUBJUNCTIVE	que + *corresponding subjunctive tense of* estar

} viviendo

IMPERATIVE MOOD

vive / no vivas (tú), viva (Ud.) ·
     vivamos (nosotros), vivid / no viváis (vosotros), vivan (Uds.)

Verbs with Changes in the Vowel of the Stem

pensar (e > ie) *to think*

PRESENT INDICATIVE	pienso, piensas, piensa · pensamos, pensáis, piensan
PRESENT SUBJUNCTIVE	piense, pienses, piense · pensemos, penséis, piensen
IMPERATIVE	piensa / no pienses, piense · pensemos, pensad / no penséis, piensen

Other tenses and forms have no changes in the vowel of the stem.

entender (e > ie) *to understand*

PRESENT INDICATIVE	entiendo, entiendes, entiende · entendemos, entendéis, entienden
PRESENT SUBJUNCTIVE	entienda, entiendas, entienda · entendamos, entendáis, entiendan
IMPERATIVE	entiende / no entiendas, entienda ·
	entendamos, entended / no entendáis, entiendan

Other tenses and forms have no changes in the vowel of the stem.

recordar (o > ue) *to remember*

PRESENT INDICATIVE	recuerdo, recuerdas, recuerda · recordamos, recordáis, recuerdan
PRESENT SUBJUNCTIVE	recuerde, recuerdes, recuerde · recordemos, recordéis, recuerden
IMPERATIVE	recuerda / no recuerdes, recuerde ·
	recordemos, recordad / no recordéis, recuerden

Other tenses and forms have no changes in the vowel of the stem.

volver (o > ue) *to return*

PRESENT INDICATIVE	vuelvo, vuelves, vuelve · volvemos, volvéis, vuelven
PRESENT SUBJUNCTIVE	vuelva, vuelvas, vuelva · volvamos, volváis, vuelvan
IMPERATIVE	vuelve / no vuelvas, vuelva · volvamos, volved / no volváis, vuelvan

Other tenses and forms have no changes in the vowel of the stem.

Stem-changing **-ir** verbs have three types of possible changes in the vowel of the stem: **e > ie, e > i, o > ue**. In addition to the expected changes in the present subjunctive and imperative, verbs having the change **e > ie** and **e > i** have **i** as the stem vowel and verbs having the change **o > ue** have **u** as the stem vowel in the following forms:

- The **nosotros** and **vosotros** forms of the present subjunctive
- The **nosotros** command and the negative **vosotros** commands
- The third person singular and third person plural forms of the preterit
- All persons of the imperfect subjunctive (both **-ra** and **-se** forms)
- The present participle

Sample Conjugations

sentir (e > ie) *to feel, regret*

PRESENT INDICATIVE	siento, sientes, siente · sentimos, sentís, sienten
PRESENT SUBJUNCTIVE	sienta, sientas, sienta · sintamos, sintáis, sientan
IMPERATIVE	siente / no sientas, sienta · sintamos, sentid / no sintáis, sientan
PRETERIT	sentí, sentiste, sintió · sentimos, sentisteis, sintieron
IMPERFECT SUBJUNCTIVE	sintiera, sintieras, sintiera · sintiéramos, sintierais, sintieran
	sintiese, sintieses, sintiese · sintiésemos, sintieseis, sintiesen
PRESENT PARTICIPLE	sintiendo

Other tenses and forms have no changes in the vowel of the stem.

pedir (e > i) *to ask for*

PRESENT INDICATIVE	pido, pides, pide · pedimos, pedís, piden
PRESENT SUBJUNCTIVE	pida, pidas, pida · pidamos, pidáis, pidan
IMPERATIVE	pide / no pidas, pida · pidamos, pedid / no pidáis, pidan
PRETERIT	pedí, pediste, pidió · pedimos, pedisteis, pidieron
IMPERFECT SUBJUNCTIVE	pidiera, pidieras, pidiera · pidiéramos, pidierais, pidieran
	pidiese, pidieses, pidiese · pidiésemos, pidieseis, pidiesen
PRESENT PARTICIPLE	pidiendo

Other tenses and forms have no changes in the vowel of the stem.

dormir (o > ue) *to sleep*

PRESENT INDICATIVE	duermo, duermes, duerme · dormimos, dormís, duermen
PRESENT SUBJUNCTIVE	duerma, duermas, duerma · durmamos, durmáis, duerman
IMPERATIVE	duerme / no duermas, duerma · durmamos, dormid / no durmáis, duerman
PRETERIT	dormí, dormiste, durmió · dormimos, dormisteis, durmieron
IMPERFECT SUBJUNCTIVE	durmiera, durmieras, durmiera · durmiéramos, durmierais, durmieran
	durmiese, durmieses, durmiese · durmiésemos, durmieseis, durmiesen
PRESENT PARTICIPLE	durmiendo

Other tenses and forms have no changes in the vowel of the stem.

Verbs with Spelling Changes

These changes occur in the first person singular of the preterit, in all persons of the present subjunctive, and in imperative forms derived from the present subjunctive.

Verbs Ending in -car (c > **qu** before -e)

tocar *to play an instrument; to touch*

PRETERIT	toqué, tocaste, tocó · tocamos, tocasteis, tocaron
PRESENT SUBJUNCTIVE	toque, toques, toque · toquemos, toquéis, toquen
IMPERATIVE	toca / no toques, toque · toquemos, tocad / no toquéis, toquen

Verbs Ending in **-gar** (**g** > **gu** before **-e**)

llegar *to arrive*

PRETERIT	llegué, llegaste, llegó · llegamos, llegasteis, llegaron
PRESENT SUBJUNCTIVE	llegue, llegues, llegue · lleguemos, lleguéis, lleguen
IMPERATIVE	llega / no llegues, llegue · lleguemos, llegad / no lleguéis, lleguen

Verbs Ending in **-zar** (**z** > **c** before **-e**)

cruzar *to cross*

PRETERIT	crucé, cruzaste, cruzó · cruzamos, cruzasteis, cruzaron
PRESENT SUBJUNCTIVE	cruce, cruces, cruce · crucemos, crucéis, crucen
IMPERATIVE	cruza / no cruces, cruce · crucemos, cruzad / no crucéis, crucen

Verbs Ending in **-ger** and **-gir** (**g** > **j** before **-a** and **-o**)

recoger *to pick up*

PRESENT INDICATIVE	recojo, recoges, recoge · recogemos, recogéis, recogen
PRESENT SUBJUNCTIVE	recoja, recojas, recoja · recojamos, recojáis, recojan
IMPERATIVE	recoge / no recojas, recoja · recojamos, recoged / no recojáis, recojan

exigir *to demand*

PRESENT INDICATIVE	exijo, exiges, exige · exigimos, exigís, exigen
PRESENT SUBJUNCTIVE	exija, exijas, exija · exijamos, exijáis, exijan
IMPERATIVE	exige / no exijas, exija · exijamos, exigid / no exijáis, exijan

Verbs Ending in **-guir** (**gu** > **g** before **-a** and **-o**)

seguir *to follow*

PRESENT INDICATIVE	sigo, sigues, sigue · seguimos, seguís, siguen
PRESENT SUBJUNCTIVE	siga, sigas, siga · sigamos, sigáis, sigan
PRESENT PARTICIPLE	siguiendo
IMPERATIVE	sigue / no sigas, siga · sigamos, seguid / no sigáis, sigan

Verbs Ending in a Consonant + **-cer**, **-cir** (**c** > **z** before **-a** and **-o**)

convencer *to convince*

PRESENT INDICATIVE	convenzo, convences, convence · convencemos, convencéis, convencen
PRESENT SUBJUNCTIVE	convenza, convenzas, convenza · convenzamos, convenzáis, convenzan
IMPERATIVE	convence / no convenzas, convenza · convenzamos, convenced / no convenzáis, convenzan

-Er Verbs Having Stems Ending in a Vowel

These verbs change the **i** of the preterit endings **-ió** and **-ieron** and the **i** of the present participle ending **-iendo** to **y**. The **y** appears in all persons of the imperfect subjunctive. These verbs also add written accents to the endings of the second person singular and the first and second person plural forms of the preterit and the past participle.

creer *to believe*

PRETERIT	creí, creíste, creyó · creímos, creísteis, creyeron
IMPERFECT SUBJUNCTIVE	creyera (creyese), creyeras, creyera · creyéramos, creyerais, creyeran
PRESENT PARTICIPLE	creyendo
PAST PARTICIPLE	creído

-Ar Verbs Having Stems Ending in Syllabic -i or -u (Not as Part of a Diphthong)

These verbs have an accent mark over the **i** or **u** in all persons of the singular and in the third person plural of the present indicative and present subjunctive, and in all imperative forms except **nosotros** and **vosotros**.

enviar *to send*

PRESENT	envío, envías, envía · enviamos, enviáis, envían
PRESENT SUBJUNCTIVE	envíe, envíes, envíe · enviemos, enviéis, envíen
IMPERATIVE	envía / no envíes, envíe · enviemos, enviad / no enviéis, envíen

continuar *to continue*

PRESENT	continúo, continúas, continúa · continuamos, continuáis, continúan
PRESENT SUBJUNCTIVE	continúe, continúes, continúe · continuemos, continuéis, continúen
IMPERATIVE	continúa / no continúes, continúe · continuemos, continuad / no continuéis, continúen

Irregular Verbs

Only tenses with irregular forms are shown.

Verbs Ending in a Vowel + -cer or -ucir

These verbs change the final **-c** of the stem to **-zc** before **-a** and **-o**. The **-zc** appears in the first person singular of the present indicative, in all persons of the present subjunctive, and in imperative forms derived from the present subjunctive.

The verb **mecer** (*to rock/cradle a child*) is conjugated like **convencer**, and not like **conocer**: present **mezo, meces**, etc.; present subjunctive **meza, mezas**, etc. The verb **cocer** (*to cook, boil, bake*) is also conjugated like **convencer** and, in addition, has the stem change **o > ue**: present **cuezo, cueces**, etc.; present subjunctive **cueza, cuezas**, etc.

conocer *to know*

PRESENT INDICATIVE	conozco, conoces, conoce · conocemos, conocéis, conocen
PRESENT SUBJUNCTIVE	conozca, conozcas, conozca · conozcamos, conozcáis, conozcan
IMPERATIVE	conoce / no conozcas, conozca ·
	conozcamos, conoced / no conozcáis, conozcan

conducir *to drive*

PRESENT INDICATIVE	conduzco, conduces, conduce · conducimos, conducís, conducen
PRESENT SUBJUNCTIVE	conduzca, conduzcas, conduzca ·
	conduzcamos, conduzcáis, conduzcan
IMPERATIVE	conduce / no conduzcas, conduzca ·
	conduzcamos, conducid / no conduzcáis, conduzcan

Verbs Ending in -uir (Not Including Those Ending in -guir)

These verbs add **y** before a vowel other than **i** and change the unaccented **i** between vowels to **y**. The **y** appears in all singular forms and in the third person plural of the present, in the third person singular and plural of the preterit, in all persons of the present and imperfect subjunctive, and in all imperative forms except the affirmative **vosotros** command.

construir *to build*

PRESENT INDICATIVE	construyo, construyes, construye · construimos, construís, construyen
PRETERIT	construí, construiste, construyó ·
	construimos, construisteis, construyeron
IMPERATIVE	construye / no construyas, construya ·
	construyamos, construid / no construyáis, construyan
PRESENT SUBJUNCTIVE	construya, construyas, construya ·
	construyamos, construyáis, construyan
IMPERFECT SUBJUNCTIVE	construyera (construyese), construyeras, construyera ·
	construyéramos, construyerais, construyeran
PRESENT PARTICIPLE	construyendo

Other Irregular Verbs

Only tenses with irregular forms are shown.

andar *to walk*

PRETERIT	anduve, anduviste, anduvo · anduvimos, anduvisteis, anduvieron
IMPERFECT SUBJUNCTIVE	anduviera (anduviese), anduvieras, anduviera ·
	anduviéramos, anduvierais, anduvieran

caber *to fit*

PRESENT INDICATIVE	quepo, cabes, cabe · cabemos, cabéis, caben
PRETERIT	cupe, cupiste, cupo · cupimos, cupisteis, cupieron
FUTURE	cabré, cabrás, cabrá · cabremos, cabréis, cabrán
CONDITIONAL	cabría, cabrías, cabría · cabríamos, cabríais, cabrían
IMPERATIVE	cabe / no quepas, quepa · quepamos, cabed / no quepáis, quepan
PRESENT SUBJUNCTIVE	quepa, quepas, quepa · quepamos, quepáis, quepan
IMPERFECT SUBJUNCTIVE	cupiera (cupiese), cupieras, cupiera · cupiéramos, cupierais, cupieran

caer *to fall*

PRESENT INDICATIVE	caigo, caes, cae · caemos, caéis, caen
PRETERIT	caí, caíste, cayó · caímos, caísteis, cayeron
IMPERATIVE	cae / no caigas, caiga · caigamos, caed / no caigáis, caigan
PRESENT SUBJUNCTIVE	caiga, caigas, caiga · caigamos, caigáis, caigan
IMPERFECT SUBJUNCTIVE	cayera (cayese), cayeras, cayera · cayéramos, cayerais, cayeran
PRESENT PARTICIPLE	cayendo
PAST PARTICIPLE	caído

dar *to give*

PRESENT INDICATIVE	doy, das, da · damos, dais, dan
PRETERIT	di, diste, dio · dimos, disteis, dieron
IMPERATIVE	da / no des, dé · demos, dad / no deis, den
PRESENT SUBJUNCTIVE	dé, des, dé · demos, deis, den
IMPERFECT SUBJUNCTIVE	diera (diese), dieras, diera · diéramos, dierais, dieran

decir *to say, tell*

PRESENT INDICATIVE	digo, dices, dice · decimos, decís, dicen
PRETERIT	dije, dijiste, dijo · dijimos, dijisteis, dijeron
FUTURE	diré, dirás, dirá · diremos, diréis, dirán
CONDITIONAL	diría, dirías, diría · diríamos, diríais, dirían
IMPERATIVE	di / no digas, diga · digamos, decid / no digáis, digan
PRESENT SUBJUNCTIVE	diga, digas, diga · digamos, digáis, digan
IMPERFECT SUBJUNCTIVE	dijera (dijese), dijeras, dijera · dijéramos, dijerais, dijeran
PRESENT PARTICIPLE	diciendo
PAST PARTICIPLE	dicho

estar *to be*

PRESENT INDICATIVE	estoy, estás, está · estamos, estáis, están
PRETERIT	estuve, estuviste, estuvo · estuvimos, estuvisteis, estuvieron
IMPERATIVE	está / no estés, esté · estemos, estad / no estéis, estén
PRESENT SUBJUNCTIVE	esté, estés, esté · estemos, estéis, estén
IMPERFECT SUBJUNCTIVE	estuviera (estuviese), estuvieras, estuviera · estuviéramos, estuvierais, estuvieran

haber *to have* (auxiliary verb)

PRESENT INDICATIVE	he, has, ha · hemos, habéis, han
PRETERIT	hube, hubiste, hubo · hubimos, hubisteis, hubieron
FUTURE	habré, habrás, habrá · habremos, habréis, habrán
CONDITIONAL	habría, habrías, habría · habríamos, habríais, habrían
PRESENT SUBJUNCTIVE	haya, hayas, haya · hayamos, hayáis, hayan
IMPERFECT SUBJUNCTIVE	hubiera (hubiese), hubieras, hubiera · hubiéramos, hubierais, hubieran

hacer *to do, make*

PRESENT INDICATIVE	hago, haces, hace · hacemos, hacéis, hacen
PRETERIT	hice, hiciste, hizo · hicimos, hiciste, hicieron
FUTURE	haré, harás, hará · haremos, haréis, harán
CONDITIONAL	haría, harías, haría · haríamos, haríais, harían
IMPERATIVE	haz / no hagas, haga · hagamos, haced / no hagáis, hagan
PRESENT SUBJUNCTIVE	haga, hagas, haga · hagamos, hagáis, hagan
IMPERFECT SUBJUNCTIVE	hiciera (hiciese), hicieras, hiciera · hiciéramos, hicierais, hicieran
PAST PARTICIPLE	hecho

ir *to go*

PRESENT INDICATIVE	voy, vas, va · vamos, vais, van
IMPERFECT	iba, ibas, iba · íbamos, ibais, iban
PRETERIT	fui, fuiste, fue · fuimos, fuisteis, fueron
IMPERATIVE	ve / no vayas, vaya · vamos / no vayamos, id / no vayáis, vayan
PRESENT SUBJUNCTIVE	vaya, vayas, vaya · vayamos, vayáis, vayan
IMPERFECT SUBJUNCTIVE	fuera (fuese), fueras, fuera · fuéramos, fuerais, fueran
PRESENT PARTICIPLE	yendo

oír *to hear*

PRESENT INDICATIVE	oigo, oyes, oye · oímos, oís, oyen
PRETERIT	oí, oíste, oyó · oímos, oísteis, oyeron
IMPERATIVE	oye / no oigas, oiga · oigamos, oíd / no oigáis, oigan
PRESENT SUBJUNCTIVE	oiga, oigas, oiga · oigamos, oigáis, oigan
IMPERFECT SUBJUNCTIVE	oyera (oyese), oyeras, oyera · oyéramos, oyerais, oyeran
PRESENT PARTICIPLE	oyendo
PAST PARTICIPLE	oído

poder *to be able, can*

PRESENT INDICATIVE	puedo, puedes, puede · podemos, podéis, pueden
PRETERIT	pude, pudiste, pudo · pudimos, pudisteis, pudieron
FUTURE	podré, podrás, podrá · podremos, podréis, podrán
CONDITIONAL	podría, podrías, podría · podríamos, podríais, podrían
PRESENT SUBJUNCTIVE	pueda, puedas, pueda · podamos, podáis, puedan
IMPERFECT SUBJUNCTIVE	pudiera (pudiese), pudieras, pudiera · pudiéramos, pudierais, pudieran
PRESENT PARTICIPLE	pudiendo

poner *to put*

PRESENT INDICATIVE	pongo, pones, pone · ponemos, ponéis, ponen
PRETERIT	puse, pusiste, puso · pusimos, pusisteis, pusieron
FUTURE	pondré, pondrás, pondrá · pondremos, pondréis, pondrán
CONDITIONAL	pondría, pondrías, pondría · pondríamos, pondríais, pondrían
IMPERATIVE	pon / no pongas, ponga · pongamos, poned / no pongáis, pongan
PRESENT SUBJUNCTIVE	ponga, pongas, ponga · pongamos, pongáis, pongan
IMPERFECT SUBJUNCTIVE	pusiera (pusiese), pusieras, pusiera · pusiéramos, pusierais, pusieran
PAST PARTICIPLE	puesto

producir *to produce*

PRESENT INDICATIVE	produzco, produces, produce · producimos, producís, producen
PRETERIT	produje, produjiste, produjo · produjimos, produjisteis, produjeron
IMPERATIVE	produce / no produzcas, produzca ·
	produzcamos, producid / no produzcáis, produzcan
PRESENT SUBJUNCTIVE	produzca, produzcas, produzca · produzcamos, produzcáis, produzcan
IMPERFECT SUBJUNCTIVE	produjera (produjese), produjeras, produjera ·
	produjéramos, produjerais, produjeran

querer *to want*

PRESENT INDICATIVE	quiero, quieres, quiere · queremos, queréis, quieren
PRETERIT	quise, quisiste, quiso · quisimos, quisisteis, quisieron
FUTURE	querré, querrás, querrá · querremos, querréis, querrán
CONDITIONAL	querría, querrías, querría · querríamos, querríais, querrían
IMPERATIVE	quiere / no quieras, quiera · queramos, quered / no queráis, quieran
PRESENT SUBJUNCTIVE	quiera, quieras, quiera · queramos, queráis, quieran
IMPERFECT SUBJUNCTIVE	quisiera (quisiese), quisieras, quisiera ·
	quisiéramos, quisierais, quisieran

saber *to know*

PRESENT INDICATIVE	sé, sabes, sabe · sabemos, sabéis, saben
PRETERIT	supe, supiste, supo · supimos, supisteis, supieron
FUTURE	sabré, sabrás, sabrá · sabremos, sabréis, sabrán
CONDITIONAL	sabría, sabrías, sabría · sabríamos, sabríais, sabrían
IMPERATIVE	sabe / no sepas, sepa · sepamos, sabed / no sepáis, sepan
PRESENT SUBJUNCTIVE	sepa, sepas, sepa · sepamos, sepáis, sepan
IMPERFECT SUBJUNCTIVE	supiera (supiese), supieras, supiera · supiéramos, supierais, supieran

salir *to go out*

PRESENT INDICATIVE	salgo, sales, sale · salimos, salís, salen
FUTURE	saldré, saldrás, saldrá · saldremos, saldréis, saldrán
CONDITIONAL	saldría, saldrías, saldría · saldríamos, saldríais, saldrían
IMPERATIVE	sal / no salgas, salga · salgamos, salid / no salgáis, salgan
PRESENT SUBJUNCTIVE	salga, salgas, salga · salgamos, salgáis, salgan

ser *to be*

PRESENT INDICATIVE	soy, eres, es · somos, sois, son
IMPERFECT	era, eras, era · éramos, erais, eran
PRETERIT	fui, fuiste, fue · fuimos, fuisteis, fueron
IMPERATIVE	sé / no seas, sea · seamos, sed / no seáis, sean
PRESENT SUBJUNCTIVE	sea, seas, sea · seamos, seáis, sean
IMPERFECT SUBJUNCTIVE	fuera (fuese), fueras, fuera · fuéramos, fuerais, fueran

tener *to have*

PRESENT INDICATIVE	tengo, tienes, tiene · tenemos, tenéis, tienen
PRETERIT	tuve, tuviste, tuvo · tuvimos, tuvisteis, tuvieron
FUTURE	tendré, tendrás, tendrá · tendremos, tendréis, tendrán
CONDITIONAL	tendría, tendrías, tendría · tendríamos, tendríais, tendrían
IMPERATIVE	ten / no tengas, tenga · tengamos, tened / no tengáis, tengan
PRESENT SUBJUNCTIVE	tenga, tengas, tenga · tengamos, tengáis, tengan
IMPERFECT SUBJUNCTIVE	tuviera (tuviese), tuvieras, tuviera · tuviéramos, tuvierais, tuvieran

traer *to bring*

PRESENT INDICATIVE	traigo, traes, trae · traemos, traéis, traen
PRETERIT	traje, trajiste, trajo · trajimos, trajisteis, trajeron
IMPERATIVE	trae / no traigas, traiga · traigamos, traed / no traigáis, traigan
PRESENT SUBJUNCTIVE	traiga, traigas, traiga · traigamos, traigáis, traigan
IMPERFECT SUBJUNCTIVE	trajera (trajese), trajeras, trajera · trajéramos, trajerais, trajeran
PRESENT PARTICIPLE	trayendo
PAST PARTICIPLE	traído

valer *to be worth*

PRESENT INDICATIVE	valgo, vales, vale · valemos, valéis, valen
FUTURE	valdré, valdrás, valdrá · valdremos, valdréis, valdrán
CONDITIONAL	valdría, valdrías, valdría · valdríamos, valdríais, valdrían
IMPERATIVE	vale / no valgas, valga · valgamos, valed / no valgáis, valgan
PRESENT SUBJUNCTIVE	valga, valgas, valga · valgamos, valgáis, valgan

venir *to come*

PRESENT INDICATIVE	vengo, vienes, viene · venimos, venís, vienen
PRETERIT	vine, viniste, vino · vinimos, vinisteis, vinieron
FUTURE	vendré, vendrás, vendrá · vendremos, vendréis, vendrán
CONDITIONAL	vendría, vendrías, vendría · vendríamos, vendríais, vendrían
IMPERATIVE	ven / no vengas, venga · vengamos, venid / no vengáis, vengan
PRESENT SUBJUNCTIVE	venga, vengas, venga · vengamos, vengáis, vengan
IMPERFECT SUBJUNCTIVE	viniera (viniese), vinieras, viniera · viniéramos, vinierais, vinieran
PRESENT PARTICIPLE	viniendo

ver *to see*

PRESENT INDICATIVE	veo, ves, ve · vemos, veis, ven
IMPERFECT	veía, veías, veía · veíamos, veíais, veían
PRETERIT	vi, viste, vio · vimos, visteis, vieron
IMPERATIVE	ve / no veas, vea · veamos, ved / no veáis, vean
PRESENT SUBJUNCTIVE	vea, veas, vea · veamos, veáis, vean
IMPERFECT SUBJUNCTIVE	viera (viese), vieras, viera · viéramos, vierais, vieran
PAST PARTICIPLE	visto

Answer Key

THE ULTIMATE SPANISH 101

 Getting Around Town— Where Is It?

A

1. ¿Qué hay en el cartapacio? / Hay un teléfono celular en el cartapacio.   2. ¿Hay carpetas en la gaveta? / Sí, las hay.   3. ¿Qué hay en el estante? / Hay libros en el estante.   4. ¿Hay CDs (cedés) en el paquete? / Sí, los hay.   5. ¿Hay una computadora en la mochila? / No, hay una cámara.

B

1. Es un billetero.   2. Es una cartera.   3. Es un reloj.   4. Es una agenda electrónica.   5. Es un bolso.   6. Es una cámara.   7. Es un iPod.   8. Es un cartapacio.

C

1. El billetero no es para José. Es para Juan.
2. La cartera no es para Matilde. Es para Julia.
3. El reloj no es para Jorge. Es para Alberto.
4. La agenda electrónica no es para Lorenzo. Es para Nora.   5. El bolso no es para Rosa. Es para Margarita.   6. La cámara no es para Luz. Es para Daniel.   7. El iPod no es para Susana. Es para Guillermo.   8. El cartapacio no es para Carlos. Es para Roberto.

D

1. la / una   2. el / un   3. el / un   4. la / una   5. el / un   6. la / una   7. la / una   8. la / una   9. la / una   10. el / un   11. el / un   12. la / una   13. el / un   14. la / una   15. el / un   16. el / un

E

1. el mes   2. la gente   3. la mochila   4. el carro   5. el regalo   6. la maleta   7. la clase   8. la computadora   9. el libro   10. el reloj

F

1. teléfono   2. cartera   3. el cibercafé   4. hay   5. en   6. pulsera   7. las   8. cartapacio

G

1. ¿Qué hay en el armario?   2. ¿Es un regalo?   3. ¿Es cómodo el hotel?   4. ¿Qué flores hay?   5. ¿Qué cafés hay en la ciudad?   6. ¿Hay unos papeles en la mochila?   7. ¿Que libros hay en los estantes?   8. ¿El juguete es para Juanito?

H

1. La cámara no es un regalo.   2. No hay una computadora en el armario.   3. No es un iPod.   4. El paquete no es para Miguel.   5. No hay un cibercafé por aquí.   6. No hay maletas en el carro.   7. No es una oficina cómoda.   8. No hay dinero en el billetero.

I

1. No, no es una agenda electrónica.   2. No, no hay libros en el estante.   3. No, el reloj no es para Carlos.   4. No, no hay un supermercado por aquí.   5. No, no es un regalo para Julieta.   6. No, no hay ropa en la maleta.   7. No, no hay un cartapacio en la oficina.   8. No, no es un problema.

J

1. las maletas / unas maletas   2. los cines / unos cines   3. los relojes / unos relojes   4. las librerías / unas librerías   5. los problemas / unos problemas   6. las oficinas / unas oficinas   7. los teatros / unos teatros   8. los restaurantes / unos restaurantes   9. los papeles / unos papeles   10. las ciudades / unas ciudades   11. los teléfonos / unos teléfonos   12. las flores / unas flores   13. los meses / unos meses   14. las calles / unas calles   15. los maletines / unos maletines   16. las luces / unas luces

K

1. el libro / un libro   2. la bolsa / una bolsa   3. la clase / una clase   4. el lugar / un lugar   5. el hotel / un hotel   6. la llave / una llave   7. el tren / un tren   8. el animal / un animal   9. la cosa / una cosa   10. la vez / una vez   11. la pulsera / una pulsera   12. la cámara / una cámara   13. el mapa / un mapa   14. el tema / un tema   15. el café / un café   16. el hospital / un hospital

L

1. —Perdón, señor. ¿Hay un banco por aquí?
—Sí, señorita, hay uno en la esquina.
—Gracias, señor. —De nada. Adiós.
2. —Por favor, señorita. ¿Dónde hay una peluquería? —Hay una en la esquina, señora.
—Muchas gracias, señorita. —De nada, señora.

M

1. la tienda de ropa / las tiendas de ropa
2. la tienda de cómputo / las tiendas de cómputo
3. la tienda de zapatos / las tiendas de zapatos
4. la tienda de electrodomésticos / las tiendas de electrodomésticos   5. la tienda de deportes / las tiendas de deportes   6. la tienda por departamentos / las tiendas por departamentos

N

1. el libro de texto / los libros de texto   2. la base de datos / las bases de datos   3. el museo de arte / los museos de arte   4. la tarjeta de crédito / las tarjetas de crédito   5. la oficina de turismo / las oficinas de turismo   6. el salón de belleza / los salones de belleza

O

1. una computadora   2. dos ciudades
3. tres relojes   4. cuatro cosas   5. cinco cines
6. seis tiendas de ropa   7. siete hoteles   8. ocho regalos   9. nueve cámaras   10. diez heladerías
11. once cajas   12. doce cibercafés   13. trece mochilas   14. catorce teléfonos   15. quince días
16. dieciséis supermercados   17. diecisiete fotos
18. dieciocho tiendas por departamentos
19. diecinueve paquetes   20. veinte deportes

P

1. ¿Cómo? ¿Cuántos?   2. ¿Cómo? ¿Cuántos?
3. ¿Cómo? ¿Cuántas?   4. ¿Cómo? ¿Cuántos?
5. ¿Cómo? ¿Cuántas?   6. ¿Cómo? ¿Cuántos?
7. ¿Cómo? ¿Cuántas?   8. ¿Cómo? ¿Cuántas?
9. ¿Cómo? ¿Cuántos?   10. ¿Cómo? ¿Cuántas?

Q

1. un museo de arte   2. seis meses   3. la tienda por departamentos   4. una tarjeta de crédito
5. el centro comercial   6. once tiendas de cómputo
7. veinte paquetes   8. unas ciudades

R

1. la cámara   2. el documento   3. el sistema
4. el teléfono   5. la computadora   6. el análisis
7. el turismo   8. el arte   9. el teatro   10. el crédito
11. la farmacia   12. el museo   13. el texto
14. el supermercado   15. el problema
16. el departamento   17. el mapa   18. el banco

S

Answers will vary.

2   Describing Places and Things

A

1. El condominio es nuevo también.   2. La zona es comercial también.   3. La catedral es maravillosa también.   4. El café es animado también.
5. La tienda por departamentos es grande también.
6. El cartapacio es pequeño también.   7. El celular es útil también.   8. La habitación es oscura también.   9. La cámara es vieja también.
10. La calle es bonita también.

B

1. Los exámenes son difíciles también.
2. Las cajas son chiquitas también.   3. Los relojes son hermosos también.   4. Las tiendas de deportes son modernas también.   5. Las películas son interesantes también.   6. Las joyas son caras también.   7. Las farmacias son grandes también.
8. Los cartapacios son buenos también.
9. Las computadoras son útiles también.
10. Los restaurantes son malos también.

C

1. buen   2. tercera   3. algunos   4. primer
5. malas   6. gran   7. ningún   8. algún

D

1. la primera semana   2. algunas avenidas animadas   3. ciertas calles transitadas   4. bastantes zonas peatonales   5. cualquier periódico importante   6. varias revistas pesadas   7. ninguna computadora vieja   8. muchos problemas difíciles
9. ningún coche ruidoso   10. poca ropa barata

E

1. Son unas niñas grandes.   2. Es el mismo perro.
3. Hay algunas personas pobres.   4. Es su única oportunidad.   5. Es una civilización antigua.
6. Es medio americano.   7. Es un gran científico.
8. Hay ciertas cosas.

F

1. La avenida es animada y muy transitada.
2. Las casas son hermosas y muy caras.
3. Las calles son comerciales y muy ruidosas.
4. La biblioteca es vieja y muy importante.
5. La tienda por departamentos es nueva y muy grande.   6. Los condominios son pequeños y muy baratos.   7. La zona es tranquila y muy bonita.
8. Los garajes son oscuros y muy feos.   9. El salón de belleza es lindo y muy bueno.   10. Los jardines son peatonales y muy interesantes.

G

1. ¿Hay mucho ruido en el barrio? / No, la zona no es muy ruidosa. 2. ¿Cómo es la casa? / Es moderna y hermosa. / Y los cuartos, ¿cómo son? / Son claros y pequeños. 3. Los regalos son para Raquel. / ¿Qué hay en esta caja bonita? / Es una pulsera. 4. ¿Hay un centro comercial por aquí? / Sí, hay veinte tiendas. / No es muy grande. / No, pero las tiendas son muy buenas. 5. El jardín es lindo y hay muchas flores. / ¿No son hermosas? / El jardín es muy tranquilo. / Sí, es un lugar maravilloso.

H

1. los estantes de la librería 2. el maletín del director 3. el cibercafé de la esquina 4. los temas del documento 5. el supermercado del barrio 6. el condominio de la señorita 7. los teatros del centro 8. las computadoras de la oficina 9. el mapa de la ciudad 10. la luz del día 11. los coches de los garajes 12. los electrodomésticos de las casas 13. los datos del libro 14. el ruido del carro 15. los problemas de los museos 16. las cámaras del banco

I

1. la farmacia de la esquina 2. la oficina del director 3. las llaves del apartamento 4. los juguetes de la juguetería 5. las flores del jardín 6. los armarios de la habitación 7. los relojes de la joyería 8. el cine del barrio 9. las tiendas de la zona comercial 10. los datos de la agenda electrónica

J

1. su clase 2. mis libros 3. nuestro barrio 4. su dinero 5. sus perros 6. sus maletas 7. tu billetero (cartera) 8. mi teléfono celular 9. sus problemas 10. sus tarjetas de crédito 11. nuestras carpetas 12. su calle 13. tus zapatos 14. nuestra ciudad 15. su hotel 16. nuestros juguetes 17. sus tiendas de cómputo 18. sus tarjetas de embarque

K

1. su / Su 2. su / su 3. su / nuestra 4. sus / sus 5. sus / Sus 6. su / mi 7. sus / Mis 8. sus / nuestros

L

1. la ropa negra y blanca 2. unos carros azules 3. mi cuarto verde 4. muchas flores rojas y amarillas 5. sus maletas grises 6. tu mochila morada (violeta) 7. unas carteras marrones 8. su camiseta azul claro 9. los abrigos azul oscuro 10. unos bolsos beige

M

1. ¿Cómo es su casa? 2. ¿Cuántas tarjetas de crédito hay en su billetero? / ¿Qué hay en su billetero? 3. ¿De qué color es tu (su) carro? 4. ¿Qué hay en la caja? 5. ¿Dónde queda el restaurante mexicano? / ¿Qué queda en la esquina? 6. ¿Cómo son las revistas? 7. ¿Para quién son los regalos? 8. ¿Dónde queda el museo de arte? 9. ¿Cuántos estudiantes hay en la clase? 10. ¿Qué es? 11. ¿Qué son? 12. ¿De qué color es el interior de su casa? 13. ¿Qué tiendas hay en esta avenida? 14. ¿Cómo es su jardín?

N

1. ¿Son útiles los teléfonos celulares? 2. ¿Es caro su reloj? 3. ¿Son muy transitados los paseos? 4. ¿Es vieja la catedral? 5. ¿Son difíciles las preguntas? 6. ¿Son inteligentes Ana y Fernando? 7. ¿Es bueno el hotel? 8. ¿Es muy ruidosa esta calle? 9. ¿Son hermosas las flores? 10. ¿Es aburrido el profesor?

O

1. Mi clase de historia es muy interesante. 2. Las casas son tan hermosas. 3. El libro de arte es realmente maravilloso. 4. Es una ciudad bastante grande. 5. ¿Son demasiado largos los informes? 6. Nuestra empresa es relativamente nueva. 7. Unas calles son poco transitadas. 8. Sus hijos son sumamente inteligentes. 9. ¿Es verdaderamente tranquilo tu barrio? 10. ¿No son suficientemente modernas las oficinas?

P

1. quince folletos largos 2. unas avenidas animadas 3. en el maletín 4. mi examen de química 5. muchas flores amarillas 6. veinte habitaciones modernas 7. para nuestros amigos 8. el carro rojo 9. sus clases de matemáticas. 10. en los paseos transitados

Q

1. ¿Es animado tu barrio? / No, mi barrio es bastante tranquilo. 2. ¿Son interesantes sus libros de biología? / No, nuestros libros de biología son aburridos. 3. ¿Es nueva su empresa? / Sí, su empresa es nueva y muy importante. 4. ¿Son negras sus maletas? / No, sus maletas son marrones. 5. ¿Son difíciles sus artículos? / No, sus artículos son fáciles.

R

1. importante   2. difícil   3. ruidoso   4. tranquilo
5. comercial   6. nuevo   7. claro   8. interesante
9. hermoso   10. fácil   11. anaranjado   12. grande
13. transitado   14. oscuro   15. bueno   16. útil
17. cómodo   18. moderno   19. peatonal
20. animado   21. viejo   22. malo   23. verdadero

S

Answers will vary.

3 Nationalities, Professions, Food, and Films

A

1. Ud., él   2. nosotros   3. Uds., ellas   4. yo
5. Ud., ella   6. Uds., ellos, ellas   7. tú   8. nosotras

B

1. Eres de México.   2. Son de México.   3. Soy de
México.   4. Son de México.   5. Es de México.
6. Somos de México.   7. Es de México.   8. Son de
México.

C

1. De España, no. Son de los Estados Unidos.
2. De China, no. Es de los Estados Unidos.
3. De Australia, no. Soy de los Estados Unidos.
4. De Colombia, no. Es de los Estados Unidos.
5. De Alemania, no. Somos de los Estados Unidos.
6. De Irlanda, no. Son de los Estados Unidos.
7. De Corea del Sur, no. Soy de los Estados Unidos.
8. De Perú, no. Son de los Estados Unidos.

D

1. Sí, es escocés.   2. Sí, son tailandeses.
3. Sí, es vietnamita.   4. Sí, somos costarricenses.
5. Sí, son israelíes.   6. Sí, es sueca.   7. Sí, es belga.
8. Sí, son taiwanesas.   9. Sí, es iraní.   10. Sí, son
egipcios.

E

Raquel es ecuatoriana, pero de origen alemán.
2. Los señores Fuentes son brasileños, pero de
origen danés.   3. Yo soy escocés, pero de origen
austríaco.   4. María y Catalina son salvadoreñas,
pero de origen libanés.   5. Tú eres belga, pero
de origen iraní.   6. Regina y Mauricio son
uruguayos, pero de origen ucranio (ucraniano).
7. Uds. son francesas, pero de origen paquistaní.
8. La señorita Rivas es israelí, pero de origen
polaco.   9. Victoria y yo somos ingleses, pero
de origen marroquí.   10. Ignacio y Alberto son
nicaragüenses, pero de origen vietnamita.

F

1. el sueco   2. el portugués   3. el ruso
4. el finlandés   5. el francés   6. el alemán
7. el japonés   8. el italiano   9. el vietnamita
10. el holandés   11. el chino   12. el árabe
13. el alemán   14. el español   15. el coreano
16. el tailandés

G

1. ¡Qué hoteles más modernos!   2. ¡Qué comida
tan sabrosa!   3. ¡Qué libro más interesante!
4. ¡Qué señoras tan simpáticas!   5. ¡Qué ciudad
más animada!   6. ¡Qué temas tan importantes!
7. ¡Qué informe más aburrido!   8. ¡Qué calles
tan ruidosas!   9. ¡Qué jardín más tranquilo!
10. ¡Qué estudiantes tan inteligentes!

H

1. ¡Qué día!   2. ¡Qué maravilloso!   3. ¡Qué postre!
4. ¡Qué feo!   5. ¡Qué fácil!   6. ¡Qué músico!
7. ¡Qué auténtico!   8. ¡Qué pintora!

I

1. ¿De dónde es Ud.? / Soy norteamericano,
de Los Ángeles. / ¡Qué casualidad! Yo también soy
de California, de San Francisco.   2. Mi esposo
(marido) y yo somos ingleses, de Londres. /
¿De veras? Mi esposa (mujer) y yo también somos
de Londres. ¿De qué parte de la ciudad?
3. ¿De qué origen eres? / Soy de origen irlandés.
¿Y tú? / Mi familia es de origen escocés.
4. ¿De quién es la tarjeta de embarque? / Es del
señor Aguilar.   5. ¿Para quién es el regalo? /
Es para mi novia.

J

1. ¿Es peruano el marido de Anita?
2. ¿Es hondureña Pilar?   3. ¿Son guatemaltecos
los esposos?   4. ¿Es chilena su (tu) mujer?
5. ¿Es ecuatoriano Rafael?   6. ¿Son costarricenses
los novios?   7. ¿Son brasileños su marido y Ud.?
(¿Son brasileños tu marido y tú?)   8. ¿Son
panameñas Blanca y Consuelo?

K

1. No, Jaime no es de Venezuela.   2. No, no soy
de origen europeo.   3. No, Manuel no es el esposo
de Carolina.   4. No, sus estudiantes no son
hindúes.   5. No, la profesora Arriaga no es griega.
6. No, Santiago y Emilia no son novios.   7. No, no
somos de la capital.   8. No, nuestra familia no es
de Marruecos.

L

1. ningún queso suizo   2. varios jamones ingleses
3. bastante torta italiana   4. pocas uvas chilenas
5. algunas nueces españolas   6. suficiente aceite de
oliva griego   7. algún pescado japonés   8. varias
manzanas estadounidenses

M

1. carnes y aves   2. lácteos   3. frutas   4. postres
5. legumbres   6. carnes y aves   7. legumbres
8. postres   9. lácteos   10. frutas   11. lácteos
12. carnes y aves   13. frutas   14. postres
15. legumbres   16. frutas   17. legumbres
18. postres   19. carnes y aves   20. lácteos

N

1. en   2. Para / de / para / con / para   3. de / de
4. en   5. de   6. de / en   7. con / en / por   8. De
9. con OR en   10. de / para   11. Por / por / en
12. del   13. De / de / en   14. De   15. con / en
16. de / con / en

O

1. esta / esa / aquella   2. este / ese / aquel   3. estos /
esos / aquellos   4. estas / esas / aquellas   5. esta /
esa / aquella   6. este / ese / aquel   7. estas / esas /
aquellas   8. estos / esos / aquellos   9. este / ese /
aquel   10. esta / esa / aquella

P

1. Estas programadoras son buenas.   2. Este asesor
es muy inteligente.   3. Estos dentistas son viejos.
4. Esta cocinera es italiana.   5. Este escritor
es famoso.   6. Estos músicos son de Cuba.
7. Este cantante es brasileño.   8. Esta abogada es
trabajadora.   9. Estas bailarinas son maravillosas.
10. Estos médicos son hindúes.

Q

1. toda la ciudad   2. todas las películas   3. todos los
vinos   4. todo el centro   5. todo el país   6. todo el
mes   7. toda la semana   8. todas las comidas
9. todo el barrio   10. todas las actrices

R

1. la desarrolladora de programas
2. la desarrolladora de web   3. la administradora
de bases de datos   4. la arquitecta de red
5. la analista de seguridad de (la) información
6. la enfermera practicante   7. la médico (médica)
asistente   8. la gerente (gerenta) de marketing
(mercadeo)   9. la gerente (gerenta) de ventas
10. la diseñadora de videojuegos

S

1. hotel manager / la hotelera   2. electrician /
la electricista   3. policeman / la policía
4. taxi driver / la taxista   5. Uber driver / la uberista
6. waiter / la mesera   7. florist / la florista
8. gardener / la jardinera   9. baker / la panadera
10. mechanic / la mecánico (mecánica)
11. carpenter / la carpintera   12. plumber /
la plomera   13. journalist / la periodista
14. bookseller / la librera   15. secretary /
la secretaria   16. receptionist / la recepcionista
17. banker / la banquera   18. hairstylist / la estilista
19. office worker / la oficinista   20. butcher /
la carnicera   21. pharmacist / la farmacéutica
22. jeweler / la joyera

T

Answers will vary.

4 Describing People, Emotions, and Health

A

1. está   2. están   3. estoy   4. estás   5. está
6. estamos   7. están   8. están

B

1. Mi mamá está entusiasmada.   2. Mis hijos están
emocionados.   3. Yo estoy contenta.   4. Los tíos
están tristes.   5. La cuñada está estresada.
6. Tú estás preocupada.   7. La tía está deprimida.
8. Mis hermanos y yo estamos molestos.
9. Los abuelos están inquietos.   10. Mi papá
está nervioso.   11. Mis nietas están alegres.
12. Las sobrinas están angustiadas.

C

1. está   2. es   3. está   4. es   5. está   6. está
7. está   8. es   9. está   10. está   11. es   12. está

D

1. Está a nueve millas del centro.   2. Queda detrás
de la iglesia.   3. Está debajo de la mesa.   4. Están
cerca de la zona comercial.   5. Está en la esquina.
6. Están encima del estante.   7. Queda a una cuadra
del cibercafé.   8. Queda lejos de la ciudad.
9. Están por aquí.   10. Está a la derecha de nuestra
oficina.   11. Queda al lado de un restaurante
italiano.   12. Está delante de mi casa.   13. Queda
enfrente del hospital.   14. Están detrás del sofá.
15. Están al fondo del armario.   16. Queda a la
izquierda de la plaza.

E

1. son   2. soy   3. eres   4. es   5. somos   6. es
7. son   8. es   9. son   10. es

F

1. Son las siete.   2. Es la una.   3. Son las nueve y media. / Son las nueve y treinta.   4. Son las dos y cuarto. / Son las dos y quince.   5. Son las cinco menos cuarto. / Son las cuatro (y) cuarenta y cinco. / Faltan quince para las cinco.   6. Son las diez y veinte.   7. Son las cuatro menos diez. / Son las tres (y) cincuenta. / Faltan diez para las cuatro.   8. Son las seis de la mañana.   9. Son las cinco y veinticinco de la tarde.   10. Son las once y diez de la noche.   11. Son las ocho y cinco de la mañana.   12. Son las doce del día. (Es mediodía.) / Son las doce de la noche. (Es medianoche.)

G

1. ¿Dónde es la reunión? / Es en la sala de conferencias. / ¿A qué hora? / Es a las once y media de la mañana.   2. ¿Dónde es la fiesta de cumpleaños? / Es en la casa de Bernardo y Josefa. / ¿A qué hora? / Es a las siete de la tarde.   3. ¿Dónde es el partido de fútbol? / Es en el campo de fútbol. / ¿A qué hora? / Es a la una y media de la tarde.   4. ¿Dónde es la boda? / Es en la iglesia. / ¿A qué hora? / Es a las cuatro de la tarde.   5. ¿Dónde es la comida? / Es en el hotel. ¿A qué hora? / Es a las diez de la noche. /   6. ¿Dónde es el examen de historia? / Es en el salón de clase. / ¿A qué hora? / Es a las nueve y cuarto de la mañana.

H

1. Hay un partido de fútbol el sábado.   2. ¿Qué día es hoy?   3. Los museos están cerrados los lunes.   4. Su boda es el domingo.   5. Esta tienda por departamentos está abierta todos los días.   6. El señor Paz está en la oficina de lunes a jueves.   7. Hay conferencias en la universidad los miércoles.   8. Estamos reunidos todo el día.

I

1. es   2. es   3. están   4. Es / estoy   5. es   6. está   7. es / está   8. están   9. es   10. está   11. son   12. está   13. es   14. está

J

1. Tu impresora está descompuesta, ¿no?   2. Esta salsa está muy picante, ¿verdad?   3. Esos hombres de negocios son costarricenses, ¿no es cierto?   4. La carretera no queda lejos de aquí, ¿verdad?   5. La clase de economía es a las tres, ¿no es verdad?   6. El partido de béisbol es el sábado, ¿no?   7. No estás de mal humor, ¿verdad?   8. El domingo es tu día libre, ¿no es cierto?

K

1. Julio y Laura están sentados en la sala de conferencias.   2. Las hermanas están tumbadas en la cama.   3. El bebé está dormido.   4. Los jardineros están arrodillados.   5. Algunos pasajeros están parados en el autobús.   6. Virginia está echada en el sofá.   7. El receptor está agachado.

L

1. Estoy seguro que Marta está ocupada con su sitio web.   2. Estoy seguro que los señores Martínez están de vacaciones.   3. Estoy seguro que Paco está tumbado en la playa como de costumbre.   4. Estoy seguro que mis amigas están sentadas frente a la televisión.   5. Estoy seguro que los chicos están de viaje.   6. Estoy seguro que Lorenzo está acostado.   7. Estoy seguro que tu computadora está descompuesta.   8. Estoy seguro que están en la oficina todo el día.

M

1. Mis sobrinos son rubios y bajos.   2. Mis papás son inteligentes y simpáticos.   3. Mi hermano es alto y moreno.   4. Mis hijos son guapos y encantadores.   5. Mis cuñadas son antipáticas y arrogantes.   6. Mi hermana es emprendedora y rica.   7. Mis nietos son morenos y delgados.   8. Mi tía es flaca y linda.   9. Mi esposa es honrada y amable.   10. Mis primas son alegres y atentas.   11. Mis abuelos son trabajadores y divertidos.   12. Mi cuñado es gordo y feo.

N

1. ¿De quién es este libro? / Es del profesor.   2. Estos zapatos. ¿De quién son? / Son de ella.   3. ¿De quién es esa cartera (ese billetero)? / Es del doctor Lara.   4. Estas medias. ¿De quién son? / Son de ella.   5. ¿De quiénes es el coche (carro)? / Es de ellos.

O

1. Es de seda.   2. Son de cuero.   3. Son de poliéster.   4. Es de lino.   5. Son de pana.   6. Es de algodón.

P

1. ¿De quién es esta maleta? / Es de él.   2. ¿De qué son esos trajes? / Son de lana.   3. ¿Por favor, señorita, ¿dónde están las corbatas de seda? / Están al lado de las camisas.   4. ¿De quiénes son esos abrigos? / Son de ellos.   5. ¿Cuál es su nacionalidad? / Somos peruanos.   6. ¿Cuál es su profesión? / Soy abogada. / ¿Cuál es su nacionalidad? / Soy panameña. / ¿Y su origen? / Soy de origen inglés.

Q

1. ¿Dónde están los señores Arriaga?   2. ¿Cuál es su profesión?   3. ¿Cómo están las chicas? 4. ¿Qué hora es?   5. ¿De qué son las camisetas? 6. ¿Cuál es la capital de Chile?   7. ¿Cómo es la novia de Arturo?   8. ¿Qué día es hoy?   9. ¿Dónde es la reunión?   10. ¿A qué hora es la fiesta? 11. ¿De quién son los zapatos?   12. ¿Para quién es la pulsera?   13. ¿Cómo están estos platos? 14. ¿Cuál es tu (su) estado civil?   15. ¿Cuál es la dirección?   16. ¿Cuál es su religión?

R

1. ¿Están abiertas las tiendas por departamentos? 2. ¿Es aburrido su trabajo?   3. ¿Están emocionados sus hijos?   4. ¿Es atenta la novia de Juan Antonio? 5. ¿Están asustados los niños?   6. ¿Está muy ocupado este contador?   7. ¿Son simpáticos sus papás?   8. ¿Está descompuesto tu coche?   9. ¿Son impresionantes esos museos?   10. ¿Son casados Lola y Diego?   11. ¿Es emprendedor su hermano? 12. ¿Están muy adelantados estos países?

S

1. aburrido   2. acatarrado   3. adelantado   4. alegre 5. angustiado   6. asustado   7. reunido   8. cansado 9. emocionado   10. enfermo   11. entusiasmado 12. estresado   13. inquieto   14. molesto 15. nervioso   16. preocupado   17. atrasado 18. triste   19. divorciado   20. gracioso

T

Answers will vary.

U

Answers will vary.

5   Work and Leisure

A

1. Tú montas en bicicleta.   2. Uds. nadan. 3. Yo patino sobre hielo.   4. Mis amigos y yo montamos a caballo.   5. Ud. camina ocho millas diarias.   6. Marta y Simón trotan.   7. Nicolás levanta pesas.   8. Diana patina sobre ruedas.

B

1. hacen   2. hago   3. hace   4. hacen   5. hace 6. haces   7. hacemos   8. hace

C

1. Yo nado dos veces por semana.   2. ¿Montamos en bicicleta hoy?   3. Yo hago ejercicio mañana. 4. ¿Por qué no vamos al gimnasio juntos?   5. Mis amigos no hacen deportes.   6. Vamos a caminar a la cancha de baloncesto.

D

1. Felipe y yo vamos al campo.   2. Uds. van a la cancha de tenis.   3. Mercedes va a la piscina. 4. Los señores Vargas van a la playa.   5. Yo voy al concierto.   6. Tú vas al bar.   7. Mauricio va al bosque nacional.   8. Ud. va a la galería de arte.

E

1. Uds. van a tomar una copa.   2. Mario va a descargar música brasileña.   3. Yo voy a hacer las tapas.   4. Manuel y Leticia van a bailar el tango. 5. Tú vas a hablar con los invitados.   6. Alicia y yo vamos a tocar el piano.   7. Clara va a grabar un video.   8. ¡Nosotros vamos a disfrutar de una fiesta muy divertida!

F

1. ¿Uds. van a ir al mar mañana? / Sí, vamos a ir a la playa mañana en la tarde.   2. ¿Vas al gimnasio? / No, voy al club.   3. ¿Ud. camina a la tienda de cómputo? / Sí, pero primero voy a la heladería. 4. ¿Tus amigos van a la universidad? / No, van al campo de fútbol.   5. La reunión es a las dos, ¿verdad? / No, es a la una.   6. El teatro está a una cuadra de aquí, ¿no? / Ah sí. Queda al lado de una galería de arte.

G

1. Voy a tomar el almuerzo.   2. Vamos al museo. 3. ¿De qué hablan Uds.?   4. Hablamos del espectáculo.   5. ¿Qué escuchas?   6. Descargo música española.   7. ¿Por qué no patinamos sobre hielo?

H

1. X   2. ¿Vas a visitar a tus primos?   3. X 4. Voy a llamar a mis suegros.   5. X   6. ¿A quién miras?   7. Vamos a ayudar al asesor.   8. X 9. Buscan a su perro.   10. Armando lleva a su esposa al centro.   11. X   12. ¿Esperas a alguien?

I

1. Pedro es mi amigo que toca el saxofón. 2. Rebeca y Nora son mis amigas que estudian física.   3. Lorenzo es mi amigo que diseña sitios web.   4. Elena es mi amiga que cocina muy bien. 5. Antonio y Matilde son mis amigos que trabajan en mi oficina.   6. Ricardo es mi amigo que hace programación.

J

1. El museo que está abierto los lunes.   2. Las mujeres de negocios que ganan mucho dinero. 3. El asesor que habla tres idiomas.   4. El coche negro que está descompuesto.   5. Los estudiantes que hacen deportes.   6. La cancha de tenis que queda enfrente de la piscina.   7. Los profesores que

enseñan administración de empresas.   8. Los trajes que son de lana.

K

1. No, no esperamos a nadie.   2. No, Roberto no va a bailar salsa nunca.   3. No, los cocineros no preparan ningún plato de pollo (ninguno de pollo). 4. No, Leonor no habla ruso tampoco.   5. No, no estudio en la biblioteca nunca.   6. No, ya no patino sobre hielo.   7. No, Julio no busca ni a su perro ni a su gato.   8. No, ninguna abogada trabaja los sábados.

L

1. el lavaplatos / dishwasher   2. el rascacielos / skyscraper   3. el cortauñas / nail clippers   4. el cubrecama / bedcover   5. el paracaídas / parachute 6. el abrelatas / can opener   7. el cortacésped / lawn mower   8. el sacacorchos / corkscrew

M

1. preparan las maletas   2. viajan en avión 3. visitan varios museos   4. llegan al aeropuerto 5. sacan las tarjetas de embarque   6. hacen turismo 7. bailan salsa   8. nadan en la piscina

N

1. Vamos a hacer turismo mañana.   2. Hago las maletas ahora mismo.   3. Siempre ayudo a mis papás.   4. ¿Hacemos un viaje en el verano? 5. ¿Por qué no cenamos fuera el viernes?   6. ¿Uds. van al bosque nacional temprano?   7. Sí, vamos a ir a las siete de la mañana.   8. Emilia visita a su hermano pasado mañana.   9. Los diseñadores de web van a trabajar juntos muy pronto.   10. Vamos a llevar a los niños a la tienda de zapatos más tarde.

O

1. navega   2. escucho   3. tomas   4. hacen 5. observa   6. montan   7. diseña   8. disfrutamos

P

1. work / trabajar   2. song / cantar   3. wait / esperar   4. invitation / invitar   5. look / mirar 6. help / ayudar   7. visit / visitar   8. development / desarrollar   9. practice / practicar   10. celebration / celebrar   11. drawing, sketch / dibujar   12. arrival / llegar   13. preparation / preparar   14. purchase / comprar   15. cuisine, kitchen / cocinar 16. saving / ahorrar   17. expense / gastar 18. surfing / navegar   19. payment / pagar 20. recording / grabar   21. call / llamar 22. design / diseñar

Q

Answers will vary.

6   The Weather, Foreign Languages, and Sports

A

1. corren   2. vivimos   3. rompe   4. creo   5. subes 6. comparte   7. venden   8. resiste

B

1. Mario escribe un informe.   2. Nosotros leemos en la biblioteca.   3. Yo asisto a una conferencia. 4. Uds. abren los libros de texto.   5. Tú comprendes las teorías de la física.   6. María Elena imprime un artículo.   7. Rodrigo y Mateo suben unos archivos. 8. Ud. sale para el laboratorio.

C

1. ¿Cuánto tiempo hace que esperas a tus amigos? / Hace quince minutos que espero a mis amigos. / Espero a mis amigos hace quince minutos. 2. ¿Cuánto tiempo hace que los niños buscan a su perro? / Hace dos días que buscan a su perro. / Buscan a su perro hace dos días.   3. ¿Cuánto tiempo hace que Uds. viven en este barrio? / Hace dieciséis años que vivimos en este barrio. / Vivimos en este barrio hace dieciséis años.   4. ¿Cuánto tiempo hace que Pedro toma clases a distancia? / Hace un año que toma clases a distancia. / Toma clases a distancia hace un año.   5. ¿Cuánto tiempo hace que Uds. hacen deportes? / Hace cuatro meses que hacemos deportes. / Hacemos deportes hace cuatro meses.   6. ¿Cuánto tiempo hace que Susana y Fernando buscan casa? / Hace varios meses que buscan casa. / Buscan casa hace varios meses.   7. ¿Cuánto tiempo hace que nosotros asistimos a estos conciertos? / Hace mucho tiempo que asistimos a estos conciertos. / Asistimos a estos conciertos hace mucho tiempo.   8. ¿Cuánto tiempo hace que Ud. manda emails? / Hace una hora que mando emails. / Mando emails hace una hora.

D

1. comienza   2. vuelven   3. quiero   4. encuentras 5. piden   6. piensa   7. cuestan   8. prefiere 9. prueba   10. duerme   11. empiezan 12. entendemos   13. almuerzo   14. sirven 15. juegas   16. merendamos

E

1. Hace calor en Miami.   2. Llueve en Seattle. 3. Hace fresco en Philadelphia.   4. Hace buen tiempo en San Diego.   5. Hace mucho viento en Chicago.   6. Nieva en Boston.   7. Hace mucho frío en Anchorage.   8. Hace setenta y cinco grados en Washington, D.C.   9. Truena en Nueva York. 10. Hace sol en Dallas.   11. Hace mal tiempo en Baton Rouge.

F

1. X 2. a 3. X 4. a 5. X 6. que 7. de 8. X
9. de 10. a 11. X 12. a 13. que 14. X 15. X
16. de 17. X 18. X

G

1. Quiere ser experto en su campo. 2. ¿No puedes
encontrar tus gafas? 3. ¿Tienes que escribir el
informe en español? 4. Acabo de conocer a los
asesores chilenos. 5. Empieza a entender el inglés
muy bien. 6. Sé hacer programación. 7. El niño
aprende a contar hasta cien. 8. Esperan tener
mucho éxito con su empresa. 9. Piensan volver
de México la semana entrante. 10. Va a probar
las tapas, ¿no? 11. Prefieren jugar al fútbol.
12. Tratan de resistir a la tentación.

H

1. para 2. por 3. para 4. por 5. para 6. para
7. por 8. por 9. para 10. para / para 11. por /
por

I

1. sabe 2. sabes 3. conozco 4. saben 5. conoce
6. sé / conoces 7. sabe OR conoce 8. conocemos /
sabemos 9. sabe 10. conocen 11. sabes
12. conozco

J

1. Sí, lo leen. 2. No, no lo conozco. 3. Sí, lo llamo.
4. No, no lo servimos. 5. Sí, lo visita. 6. No, no
lo busca. 7. Sí, lo ayudo. 8. Sí, lo empezamos.
9. No, no lo cuenta. 10. No, no lo encontramos.

K

1. sirve 2. pedimos 3. sirven 4. pides 5. pido
6. servimos 7. sirves 8. pide 9. sirvo 10. piden

L

1. para ella 2. contigo 3. de él 4. para mí
5. con nosotros 6. de Uds. 7. por mí 8. conmigo
9. a ti 10. para ti 11. por Ud. 12. a mí 13. por ti
14. en él 15. de ti 16. en ellos

M

1. cuarenta y un 2. ochenta y cuatro 3. cien
4. setecientas treinta y una 5. novecientos setenta
y seis 6. mil 7. mil cuatrocientas noventa y cinco
8. tres mil quinientos ochenta y un 9. diez mil
setecientas veintinueve 10. doscientos sesenta y
cinco mil 11. un millón de 12. noventa y dos
millones de

N

1. Uds. siguen por la autopista. 2. Sigues la
conversación. 3. El perro sigue a los niños.
4. ¿Ud. sigue un curso de inglés a distancia?
5. Sigo los consejos de mis padres. 6. Seguimos

por una avenida bajo construcción. 7. Sigue las
órdenes del médico. 8. Siguen el ejemplo de su
abuelo.

O

1. Joaquín y yo jugamos al ajedrez. 2. Estos dos
equipos juegan en la Serie Mundial. 3. Nunca
juego al tenis de mesa. 4. Carlitos juega a los
videojuegos. 5. ¿Juegas a las cartas? 6. Ud. juega
al vólibol, ¿no? 7. Uds. juegan al dominó.
8. Blanca juega un juego de sociedad.

P

Synonyms 1. comenzar 2. regresar 3. descargar
4. beber 5. cargar 6. desear 7. comprender
Antonyms 1. triste 2. atrasado 3. cerrado
4. tranquilo 5. gordo 6. barato 7. aburrido
8. viejo 9. hermoso 10. pobre 11. claro
12. antipático

Q

1. Hace mal tiempo. Hace frío y viento.
2. Y empieza a llover. 3. Hace veintiún años que
Benjamín trabaja en este campo. 4. Él conoce
el mercado muy bien. 5. Los estudiantes piensan
tomar un curso de español por internet. 6. Saben
que tienen que practicar mucho para dominar el
idioma hablado. 7. Este restaurante sirve los
mejores postres de la ciudad. 8. Por eso pido dos.
¡No puedo resistir a la tentación! 9. ¿Sabes jugar
al tenis? 10. No, pero quiero aprender a jugar.
11. Tengo ganas de ir a la playa. ¿Quieres ir
conmigo? 12. Acabo de volver del mar. Prefiero
ir al campo.

R

Answers will vary.

7 Entertaining at Home

A

1. Hace / cae 2. trae / traigo 3. es / salgo
4. oyen / oímos 5. vienes / vengo 6. ponen / dice
7. ves / veo 8. hago / voy 9. cabemos / quepo
10. dice / decimos 11. eres / Soy 12. están /
estoy / está

B

1. Tienen mucha hambre. 2. ¿Tienes poca sed?
3. Tenemos razón. 4. Tiene mucha suerte.
5. ¿Por qué tiene tanta vergüenza? 6. No tengo
prisa. 7. ¿Tienen demasiado frío? 8. Tiene
demasiado cuidado. 9. ¿Por qué tienen tanto
sueño? 10. Tenemos muchas ganas de verlo.
11. Espero tener éxito. 12. ¿No tienes mucho
calor?

C

1. el agua potable   2. las aguas destiladas
3. el hambre extrema   4. el ave negra   5. las aves
rapaces   6. el alma divina   7. las almas humanas
8. el área grande   9. las áreas protegidas
10. el haba blanca   11. las habas frescas
12. el hacha afilada

D

1. veo   2. ve   3. ven   4. ve   5. ves   6. ve   7. vemos
8. ven

E

1. Sí, la pone.   2. No, no la venden.   3. Sí, las
servimos.   4. No, no los sube.   5. No, no la
comprendo.   6. Sí, los conozco.   7. Sí los
preferimos.   8. No, no la sé.   9. Sí, lo oímos.
10. Sí, lo entiendo.   11. No, no las llevo.
12. Sí, la comienza.

F

1. pone   2. ponen   3. pongo   4. pone   5. pone
6. pones   7. ponen   8. ponemos

G

1. No, señora, no la conozco.   2. No, señores,
no los busco.   3. No, señoras, no las llamo.
4. No, señorita, no la comprendo.   5. No, señor,
no lo ayudo.   6. No, señoritas, no las conozco.
7. No, señor, no lo quiero visitar. / No, señor, no
quiero visitarlo.   8. No, señores, no los pienso
invitar. / No, señores, no pienso invitarlos.
9. No, señora, no la voy a llevar. / No señora, no
voy a llevarla.   10. No, señor, no los necesito ver. /
No, señor, no necesito verlos.

H

1. Yo la veo.   2. Él me llama.   3. Nosotros vamos
a llevarlas. / Nosotros las vamos a llevar.   4. ¿Tú lo
buscas?   5. ¿Uds. quieren esperarnos? /¿Uds. nos
quieren esperar?   6. Ella espera conocerte. / Ella te
espera conocer.   7. ¿Ud. piensa ayudarlos? /¿Ud. los
piensa ayudar?   8. Ellas no pueden comprenderla. /
Ellas no la pueden comprender.   9. Yo deseo
invitarlos. / Yo los deseo invitar.   10. Yo no la voy
a visitar. / Yo no voy a visitarla.

I

1. Antonio y yo nunca damos consejos.   2. Juan
nunca da consejos.   3. María y Susana nunca dan
consejos.   4. Yo nunca doy consejos.   5. Tú nunca
das consejos.   6. La hermana de Pablo nunca da
consejos.   7. Uds. nunca dan consejos.

J

1. Tú no dices nada.   2. Nuestros amigos no dicen
nada.   3. Raúl no dice nada.   4. Ud. no dice nada.
5. Yo no digo nada.   6. Camila no dice nada.
7. Uds. no dicen nada.   8. Ana María y yo no
decimos nada.

K

1. Nosotros salimos a las seis y media.   2. Roberto
sale dentro de unos minutos.   3. Yo salgo en
veinte minutos.   4. Ud. sale muy pronto.   5. Los
empleados salen ahora mismo.   6. Tú sales un poco
tarde.   7. Uds. salen a la hora de cenar.   8. Timoteo
y Rebeca salen temprano.

L

1. Más vale salir al mediodía.   2. Más vale discutir
los problemas.   3. Más vale no ir.   4. Más vale
compartir la información.

M

1. Hay que dominar un idioma.   2. Hay que tener
suerte.   3. A veces hay que resistir a la tentación.
4. Hay que tener paciencia.

N

1. Debes devolverla. / La debes devolver.   2. ¿Uds.
no quieren probarlas? / ¿Uds. no las quieren
probar?   3. Empiezan a tenerlo. / Lo empiezan
a tener.   4. No puedo traducirlos. / No los puedo
traducir.   5. Esperamos verlos. / Los esperamos ver.
6. Voy a traerlas. / Las voy a traer.   7. Tenemos que
ayudarlos. / Los tenemos que ayudar.   8. Ud. logra
dominarlo. / Ud. lo logra dominar.   9. Alicia sabe
diseñarlas. / Alicia las sabe diseñar.   10. ¿Ud.
piensa llamarla? / ¿Ud. la piensa llamar?   11. Trato
de entenderlo. / Lo trato de entender.   12. Acaba
de encontrarla. / La acaba de encontrar.

O

1. Marta y yo oímos el timbre.   2. Ud. oye música.
3. Ellos oyen unos sonidos.   4. Yo oigo voces.
5. Tú oyes gritos.   6. Uds. oyen el teléfono.
7. Leonor oye una conversación.

P

1. Los chicos vienen en la tarde.   2. Ud. viene
el jueves.   3. Yo vengo a las ocho.   4. Uds. vienen
por la mañana.   5. Anita y yo venimos esta noche.
6. Tú vienes el miércoles.   7. Javier viene a la una y
media.

Q

1. No, los traen Lucas y Laura.   2. No, lo traigo yo.
3. No, las traen Uds.   4. No, la trae Guillermo.
5. No, los traes tú.   6. No, la traemos nosotros.
7. No, las traen Uds.

R

1. La reunión tiene lugar en la oficina del director. 2. Hay que poner las cartas sobre la mesa. 3. Clara ya no tiene novio. Ojos que no ven, corazón que no siente. 4. ¿Un trabajo excelente? Vale la pena esperarlo. 5. Juanito siempre da guerra. Y su hermana da lata. 6. Su plan no tiene pies ni cabeza. 7. No debemos decir nada. Las paredes oyen. 8. Nadie tiene la culpa de eso. 9. Diego, ¿estás enfermo? Tienes mala cara. 10. Doy una vuelta en el parque. ¿Vienes conmigo?

S

Answers will vary.

T

1. Es hora de almorzar. ¿Tienes hambre? / No, no tengo hambre pero tengo mucha sed. 2. Señor, por favor, ¿me puede ayudar con mi computadora? / Claro que sí, señora, la ayudo en seguida. 3. Nuestros amigos dicen que la película que dan en ese cine es estupenda. Tengo muchas ganas de verla. / Tienen razón. Acabo de verla. 4. Hace veinticinco grados y hace mucho viento. Tengo frío. / Sí, hace frío y la nieve cae pero no tengo mucho frío. 5. Quiero ver el programa de detectives. / Yo lo quiero ver también. 6. ¿Ud. conoce a los hombres de negocios que vienen esta tarde? / No, no los conozco pero pienso conocerlos. 7. Va a haber mucha gente en el teatro. / Yo sé. Vamos a tener que hacer cola. ¡Y yo no tengo paciencia! 8. ¿Cómo se dice *advice* en español? / Se dice "consejos".

8 The Daily Routine

A

1. Julio se molesta. 2. Uds. se aburren. 3. Victoria y yo nos entusiasmamos. 4. Tú te ríes. 5. Alfonso y Edit se asustan. 6. Ud. se emociona. 7. Yo me divierto. 8. Consuelo y Javier se ofenden. 9. María Elena se enoja. 10. Juan Carlos y yo nos animamos.

B

1. Yo me aburro. ¿Y tú? / ¡Qué va! Me divierto mucho. 2. ¿Él se ofende fácilmente? / Sí, y se molesta a menudo. 3. Los niños se entusiasman. / Sí, se ríen mucho. 4. ¿Por qué se enojan (se enfadan)? / No nos enojamos (nos enfadamos) pero sí nos exasperamos.

C

1. aburre 2. se enojan 3. nos emocionamos 4. exaspera 5. asustan 6. me divierto 7. se preocupa 8. anima 9. sorprende 10. se sientan

D

1. Nos asustas. 2. La tranquilizamos (calmamos). 3. Levanta la mano. 4. Lo animo. 5. Me molestan. 6. Aburren a sus amigos.

E

1. Yo me jacto de mis hijos. 2. Tú te quejas de todo. 3. Nosotros no nos atrevemos a hablar de eso. 4. Pedro y Elena se divorcian por falta de comunicación. 5. Maite y su hermano se desmayan por tener la tensión baja.

F

1. Dicen que Lucía se compromete con Benjamín. / Y parece que Margarita se casa con Leonardo. 2. ¿Se acuerda de la dirección de Armando? / Lo siento. ¡Me olvido de todo! 3. ¿No sabes? Nos instalamos en nuestra casa nueva hoy. / Me alegro de saberlo. 4. ¿Quién se ocupa de los detalles de la reunión? / Yo me ocupo de los informes y Diego se ocupa de los otros documentos. 5. ¿Por qué te despides de todos los invitados? / Es que la fiesta me aburre mucho. ¡Me voy!

G

1. Ud. y Jorge se entienden (se comprenden) muy bien. 2. Micaela y yo nos vemos todos los días. 3. ¿Por qué no nos tuteamos? 4. Los niños se abrazan. 5. ¿Nos ayudamos con el proyecto? 6. Roberto y Alejandra se quieren mucho. 7. Nos conocemos bastante bien. 8. Eunice y su prima (primo) se escriben una vez al año.

H

1. Me pruebo la blusa y la falda. 2. Los niños se quitan los zapatos. 3. María Elena se peina. 4. ¿Te vistes ahora mismo? 5. Nos levantamos a las siete de la mañana todos los días. 6. Se hace tarde. ¡Tienen que apresurarse! 7. Cada vez que Samuel juega al fútbol se lastima el pie. 8. Nos arreglamos y nos vamos.

I

1. Deben darse prisa. 2. ¿Vas a despertarte temprano? 3. Manolo acaba de probarse el traje. 4. Ud. comienza a alimentarse bien. 5. Tratamos de cuidarnos lo más posible. 6. Quieren divertirse mucho en la playa. 7. Tengo que mantenerme en forma. 8. ¿Arturo no puede ponerse en forma? 9. Las chicas empiezan a acatarrarse. 10. Necesitamos relajarnos un poco. 11. ¿Prefieres ducharte por la mañana? 12. Logran instalarse en el condominio.

J

1. Me voy a graduar en junio.   2. Se quieren sentar cerca de nosotros.   3. El niñito se sabe vestir solo.   4. No se deben meter en todo.   5. Me prefiero reunir con Uds. la semana próxima.   6. Nos tenemos que apresurar o perdemos el avión.   7. Se empiezan a reír.   8. ¿Te piensas casar con Federico?   9. Nos esperamos ver pronto.   10. ¿Catalina se vuelve a enamorar?   11. Se acaba de acordar de la fecha.   12. Pablo se logra colocar en una empresa importante.

K

1. hermosamente   2. estupendamente   3. inteligentemente   4. honradamente   5. regularmente   6. alegremente   7. nerviosamente   8. compulsivamente   9. comercialmente   10. tristemente   11. cómodamente   12. fácilmente   13. atentamente   14. arrogantemente   15. asustadamente

L

1. perfecto   2. general   3. cuidadoso   4. reciente   5. último   6. difícil   7. frecuente   8. rotundo   9. pesado   10. frío   11. normal   12. gracioso   13. pobre   14. amable   15. tranquilo

M

1. frecuentemente   2. claramente   3. inteligentemente   4. difícilmente   5. alegremente   6. tranquilamente   7. atentamente   8. cómodamente   9. tristemente   10. amablemente   11. arrogantemente   12. felizmente   13. sinceramente   14. oscuramente   15. ruidosamente

N

1. Tú te cepillas los dientes.   2. Pilar y yo nos lavamos la cabeza.   3. Roberto se afeita.   4. Uds. se secan el pelo.   5. Ignacio se pone la ropa.   6. Yo me paso el hilo dental.   7. Marisol y Julieta se pintan los labios.   8. Ud. se ducha.

O

1. Me emociono mucho al oír música. / Al oír música, me emociono mucho.   2. Mario va a casa al salir de la oficina. / Al salir de la oficina, Mario va a casa.   3. ¿Te duermes en seguida al acostarte? / Al acostarte, ¿te duermes en seguida?   4. Eva se enoja al saber qué pasa. / Al saber qué pasa, Eva se enoja.   5. Uds. se visten al terminar de ducharse. / Al terminar de ducharse, Uds. se visten.   6. Te limpias los dientes al despertarte. / Al despertarte, te limpias los dientes.   7. Los niños se bañan al llegar del parque. / Al llegar del parque, los niños se bañan.   8. ¿Ud. se lava el pelo al levantarse? / Al levantarse, ¿Ud. se lava el pelo?   9. Me divierto mucho al reunirme con mis amigos. / Al reunirme con mis amigos, me divierto mucho.   10. Nos tranquilizamos al ver que todo está bien. / Al ver que todo está bien, nos tranquilizamos.

P

1. de   2. de   3. a   4. en   5. con   6. a   7. En   8. de   9. con   10. de   11. de   12. de   13. de   14. de

Q

1. Leemos el quinto libro.   2. Juego en el octavo partido.   3. Escribo el sexto correo electrónico.   4. Siguen el tercer plan.   5. Es la séptima semana del viaje.   6. Hacen la segunda práctica.   7. Tomas la novena clase a distancia.   8. Se reúnen el primer miércoles del mes.   9. Es la cuarta vez que los visitamos.   10. Es la primera conferencia de la serie.   11. Es el décimo año de la empresa.   12. ¿Conoces a su tercera hija?

R

1. Señora, ¿cómo se llama Ud.? / Me llamo Isabel Ortega Castellanos.   2. ¿Cómo se llama él? / Se llama Antonio Herrera Calderón.   3. Niño, ¿cómo te llamas? / Me llamo Juan Manuel Echevarría.   4. ¿Cómo se llama ella? / Se llama Alicia Marqués Goya.

S

1. se callan   2. se equivoca   3. se mejora   4. aprovecharnos   5. se hace   6. se muere   7. se portan   8. burlarse

T

1. Me llamo Gabriela Torres Ribera. Al despertarme, me cepillo los dientes, me ducho y me lavo el pelo. Después de vestirme, me maquillo (me pinto la cara) y me peino. Mi esposo Fernando se ducha, se afeita y se viste. Después de desayunar, visto a los niños y Fernando los lleva al colegio. Mi esposo y yo nos vamos para la oficina.   2. Me llamo Antonio Lapesa Mondragón. Acabo de graduarme en la universidad y busco trabajo. Soy contador. Espero colocarme en una empresa grande. También acabo de comprometerme. Mi prometida Pilar, que es diseñadora de páginas web, quiere casarse este año pero yo creo que no debemos apresurarnos. Tenemos que trabajar unos años para poder comprar una casa. No nos preocupamos porque nos queremos, nos entendemos y siempre nos ayudamos. Sabemos que vamos a tener éxito.

3. Me llamo Mario Sánchez Vargas. Me acatarro frecuentemente. Hace seis semanas que me siento mal. El médico me dice que estoy bien pero que debo cuidarme mejor. Por eso voy a comenzar a hacer ejercicio. Quiero ponerme en forma. Voy a trotar y levantar pesas. Tengo que dejar de comer comida basura y empezar a alimentarme bien. Sé que debo relajarme más, acostarme más temprano y vivir más tranquilamente. ¡Voy a aburrirme pero voy a sentirme muy bien!

U

Answers will vary.

9 Travel, Likes and Dislikes

A

1. trabajó   2. esperaste   3. comprendimos
4. miré   5. imprimieron   6. llevaron   7. compró
8. comieron   9. viajé   10. debiste   11. corriste
12. aprendí   13. bebió   14. abrimos   15. vendió
16. manejé   17. escribió   18. regresamos
19. viviste   20. tomaron

B

1. Subiste al avión.   2. Prefirió un vuelo directo.
3. Viajamos a Ciudad de Panamá.   4. Fui al aeropuerto en taxi.   5. Hicieron escala en Miami.
6. Saqué mi tarjeta de embarque.   7. Facturaron el equipaje.   8. Volvió de Panamá el domingo.
9. Pagué los billetes en línea.   10. ¿No pudiste encontrar tu maleta?   11. Se abrocharon el cinturón de seguridad.   12. Perdió el vuelo.   13. Llegué a la terminal A.   14. ¡Fue un viaje maravilloso!

C

1. Me mandó un email.   2. Le expliqué mi idea.
3. Nos recordaron la fecha.   4. Les entregó los documentos.   5. Le vendiste tu carro.
6. Te devolvimos el dinero.   7. Le contó la historia.
8. Les enseñaron la casa.

D

1. Ellos nos pidieron un favor.   2. Tú le leíste un libro.   3. Yo les traje el periódico.   4. Nosotros te dijimos lo que pasó.   5. Ud. le explicó el plan.
6. Él me regaló unas flores.   7. Ellas le hicieron una comida muy rica.   8. Uds. les dieron un regalo.

E

1. Tú le entregaste el informe al director.
2. Manolo les mostró su nuevo apartamento a sus amigos.   3. Yo le hice unas preguntas al asesor.
4. Ellos le pidieron la cuenta a la mesera.
5. Daniela les sirvió unas tapas a los invitados.
6. Uds. le dieron el software al programador.
7. Ella le dijo la verdad a su abogada.   8. Tú les

escribiste un email a tus abuelos.   9. Nosotros le vendimos el coche a nuestra vecina.   10. Los profesores les explicaron los problemas a sus estudiantes.

F

1. Me interesan tus ideas.   2. Les encantan estas novelas.   3. Le faltan unas reservaciones.   4. Nos entusiasman los partidos de béisbol.   5. Me gustan estos conciertos.   6. ¿Te caen bien los gerentes?
7. Le quedan unos proyectos.   8. Nos hacen falta otras computadoras.   9. Les fascinan aquellas tiendas de ropa.   10. ¿No te importan sus problemas?

G

1. Nos interesó esa película.   2. Le gustaron los programas.   3. ¿Te cayó mal este tipo?   4. Les hizo falta más dinero.   5. Me encantó la obra de teatro.
6. Nos faltó tiempo para terminar el proyecto.
7. Le quedó el examen de química.   8. Les entusiasmaron las conferencias.

H

1. Me gustó.   2. No le importaron.   3. Les encantó.
4. ¿Te hicieron falta?   5. Les convino.
6. Nos interesó mucho.   7. Les sobraron.
8. Me entusiasmó verlos.   9. Les cayó mal.
10. ¿Le interesó trabajar en Europa?   11. Nos encantó manejar por el desierto.   12. ¿Te importó pasar por el control de seguridad?

I

1. Nos van a interesar esos libros.   2. Le va a hacer falta un mapa.   3. Les va a sobrar comida.
4. Te van a caer bien nuestros amigos.   5. Me va a encantar viajar en tren.   6. No les va a importar llegar tarde.   7. Te va a convenir conocer al director de mercadeo.   8. Le va a tocar jugar pronto.

J

1. creyó   2. construí   3. leyeron   4. distribuimos
5. contó   6. volvieron   7. quise   8. entendimos
9. comenzamos   10. llovió   11. pensaste   12. dije
13. pudieron   14. supe   15. trajimos   16. vino
17. seguiste   18. durmieron   19. estuve   20. dio
21. puse   22. fuimos   23. hiciste   24. fueron
25. pidió   26. hubo   27. conduje   28. tuvieron
29. viste   30. prefirió

K

1. Ya los vio.   2. Ya nos reunimos.   3. Ya lo pidieron.   4. Ya me matriculé.   5. Ya se casó con él.
6. Ya los trajimos.   7. Ya lo comencé.   8. Ya la construyeron.   9. Ya los hice.   10. Ya se puso en contacto conmigo.   11. Ya las siguieron.
12. Ya almorcé.   13. Ya fuimos.   14. Ya lo busqué.
15. Ya lo recogió.

L

1. sonó   2. se asustó   3. se levantó   4. se afeitó
5. se duchó   6. se vistió   7. Se dio   8. Llegó
9. Corrió   10. tuvo

M

1. hice   2. viajamos   3. pasamos   4. tomamos
5. nos quedamos   6. llegamos   7. tuvimos
8. pudimos   9. Fue

N

1. estudiaron   2. se graduaron   3. se colocó
4. empezó   5. se comprometieron   6. se casaron
7. compraron   8. tuvieron

O

1. Les falta un asiento de pasillo.   2. Les quedan
tres asientos de ventana.   3. Le toca a Ud. pasar
por la aduana.   4. No nos conviene hacer escala.
5. Me caen bien estos auxiliares de vuelo.
6. ¿Le hace falta sacar su tarjeta de embarque?
7. ¡A ti te gusta viajar en avión pero a mí me
encanta tomar el tren de alta velocidad!

P

1. cumplió   2. asistí   3. comimos   4. bebimos
5. se alegró   6. traje   7. tuvo   8. se entusiasmó
9. fuimos   10. oímos   11. bailamos   12. nos
divertimos

Q

1. Pudimos recorrer seis países.   2. Por fin supe
su dirección.   3. Tuvo una idea maravillosa.
4. La pasajera no quiso apagar su celular.
5. ¿Pudiste facturar tu equipaje?   6. ¿Cuándo
conociste a los señores Díaz?

R

1. el viaje de negocios   2. el asiento de ventana
3. el auxiliar de vuelo   4. la puerta de embarque
5. el equipaje de mano   6. el control de seguridad
7. el vuelo de conexión   8. el tren de alta velocidad
9. el plan de mercadeo

S

1. Hace cinco años que hicimos un viaje a Chile. /
Fue un vuelo agotador, ¿verdad?   2. El avión
despegó y veinte minutos después me desabroché
el cinturón de seguridad. / Y yo me acomodé en mi
asiento y me dormí inmediatamente.   3. ¿Te gustó
el paisaje del sudoeste? / Sí, me encantó.
Manejamos por el desierto y vimos cactos
impresionantes.   4. ¿Tuvieron que hacer escala? /
No, fue un vuelo directo.   5. ¿Qué hizo cuando
bajó (al bajar) del avión? / Recogí mi equipaje y
pasé por la aduana.   6. ¿Mostraste tu pasaporte en
la puerta de embarque? / No, pero le entregué la
tarjeta de embarque a la señorita.   7. ¿Facturó

su maleta? / No, el auxiliar de vuelo la colocó
en el compartimiento de arriba.   8. ¡Qué
embotellamiento! Vamos a perder nuestro vuelo. /
¡Qué va! Conozco un atajo.

T

Answers will vary.

U

Answers will vary.

10 Childhood, Family History, University

A

1. hablaba   2. comían   3. escribíamos   4. eran
5. creías   6. tenía   7. volvían   8. sabía   9. decías
10. veía   11. venían   12. había   13. tomábamos
14. hacía   15. vivías   16. podía   17. querían
18. pedía   19. iba   20. jugabas   21. subían
22. entendía   23. leíamos   24. dábamos   25. estaba
26. ponía   27. pensaban   28. almorzabas
29. seguía   30. construía

B

1. trabajaban   2. recorrías   3. iba   4. nos
reuníamos   5. Hacía   6. veía   7. eran   8. servían
9. enseñaba   10. había   11. encantaba
12. dábamos   13. querían   14. tomaba
15. pensabas   16. sabía   17. gustaba   18. vestía
19. vivían   20. estábamos

C

1. Yo me reunía con mis amigos todos los
domingos.   2. ¿Uds. iban a la sierra todos los
inviernos?   3. María Elena almorzaba con nosotros
cada semana.   4. Rodrigo y yo asistíamos a un
concierto todas las semanas.   5. ¿No podías hacer
un viaje cada año?   6. Les daba muchos regalos
todos los años.   7. Siempre se divertían mucho
en las fiestas.   8. Los chicos veían ese programa
a menudo.

D

1. los maletines nuestros   2. el cartapacio mío
3. las cámaras suyas   4. el gorro suyo   5. el celular
tuyo   6. el abrigo suyo   7. las tarjetas de crédito
suyas   8. el coche suyo   9. la cartera mía   10. la
pintura nuestra   11. los aretes tuyos   12. la casa de
campo suya

E

1. estos informes tuyos   2. tres amigas suyas
3. un apartamento suyo   4. una idea mía   5. estos
problemas suyos   6. ese coche suyo   7. una
empresa nuestra   8. unos planes suyos   9. este
reloj mío   10. esa cuñada suya

F

1. era   2. íbamos   3. quedaba   4. gustaba
5. preferían   6. encantaban   7. hacía
8. nadábamos   9. nevaba   10. esquiábamos
11. montaba   12. se llamaba   13. fascinaba

G

1. fueron pintados   2. fue prendida   3. fueron
entregadas   4. fue vendido   5. fueron acostados
6. fue servido   7. fueron cultivadas   8. fue fundada
9. fueron discutidos   10. fue subido   11. fueron
despedidos   12. fue cantada

H

1. Los papeles fueron firmados por el director.
2. La teoría fue explicada por la doctora Vega.
3. El informe fue terminado por los asesores.
4. Las fotos fueron tomadas por los turistas
italianos.   5. Mi sitio web fue diseñado por un
amigo mío.   6. El botón fue cosido por Consuelo.
7. Todas las fechas fueron aprendidas por los
estudiantes.   8. Los datos fueron entrados por el
desarrollador de programas.   9. El partido fue
ganado por el equipo peruano.   10. La tele fue
prendida por Guillermo.

I

1. Se visita la zona histórica.   2. Se sacan fotos.
3. Se cultivan verduras.   4. Se hace turismo.
5. Se resuelve el problema.   6. Se oye música.
7. Se realiza el proyecto.   8. Se producen vinos.
9. Se sirven platos vegetarianos.   10. Se ven
mariposas.

J

1. Se navega en la red.   2. Se abre a las nueve
y media.   3. Se vive muy bien en nuestro país.
4. Se habla por celular.   5. Se trabaja de lunes
a jueves.   6. Se sale para el centro.   7. Se sube
en el ascensor.   8. Se llega a la puerta de embarque.
9. Se maneja con cuidado.   10. Se baja en la
escalera mecánica.

K

1. Se puede cambiar el vuelo.   2. Se permite subir
a la pirámide.   3. No se debe comer comida basura.
4. Se necesita apagar el celular.   5. No se puede ver
nada por la niebla.   6. No se permite fumar en
este edificio.   7. Se debe dejar una propina.
8. Se necesita pasar por el control de seguridad.

L

1. Se lo enseñábamos.   2. Te los consigo.   3. Se la
cuenta.   4. Me las trajeron.   5. Se lo entregué.
6. Nos las mostraban.   7. Se los mandabas.   8. Se la
sirvió.   9. No se lo presta.   10. Me las enviaba.

M

1. Sí, me la puse.   2. Sí, se las prueba.   3. Sí, se lo
abrocharon.   4. Sí, se lo corta.   5. Sí, nos los
cepillábamos.   6. Sí, se la maquillan.   7. Sí, se lo
rompió.   8. Sí, me lo sequé.

N

1. conocía / llegaron   2. tenías / te casaste
3. recorríamos / empezó   4. fue / dolía
5. se durmió / escuchaba   6. buscábamos / vimos
7. Eran / regresaron   8. era / llevaron   9. Hacía /
salieron   10. estaban / fundaron   11. comprendía /
explicó   12. dijeron / pensaban   13. hacíamos /
pidieron   14. podía / se rompió   15. nadabas /
sirvieron

O

1. Vamos a vendérsela. / Se la vamos a vender.
2. Acaba de regalárnoslos. / Nos los acaba de
regalar.   3. Voy a decírselo. / Se lo voy a decir.
4. Acabamos de escribírtelo. / Te lo acabamos de
escribir.   5. Van a llevármelas. / Me las van a llevar.
6. Acabas de devolvérsela. / Se la acabas de
devolver.   7. Voy a hacérselos. / Se los voy a hacer.
8. Acaban de dárnoslo. / Nos lo acaban de dar.

P

1. No, pero se lo voy a abrochar pronto. / No, pero
voy a abrochárselo pronto.   2. No, pero se los voy
a limpiar pronto. / No, pero voy a limpiárselos
pronto.   3. No, pero se las voy a poner pronto. /
No, pero voy a ponérselas pronto.   4. No, pero se
los voy a atar pronto. / No, pero voy a atárselos
pronto.   5. No, pero se lo voy a secar pronto. / No,
pero voy a secárselo pronto.   6. No, pero se lo voy
a quitar pronto. / No, pero voy a quitárselo pronto.
7. No, pero se lo voy a cepillar pronto. / No, pero
voy a cepillárselo pronto.   8. No, pero se lo voy a
cortar pronto. / No, pero voy a cortárselo pronto.

Q

1. Quisimos hacer turismo.   2. Supieron su
nacionalidad.   3. ¿El contrato? No quiso dárselo.
4. Yo tenía un plan.   5. ¿Conociste a esos amigos
suyos?   6. No pudo reunirse conmigo.

R

1. Estaba muy nublado cuando llegamos a la playa.
2. Cuando los turistas fueron a ver las pirámides,
hacía mucho calor.   3. Hacía noventa grados
cuando volvió al cafetal.   4. Cuando el avión
despegó, hacía mucho viento.   5. Estaba despejado
cuando empezó la merienda campestre.   6. ¿Llovía
cuando saliste del teatro?   7. Nevaba cuando ella
pasó por la casa.   8. Hacía frío cuando se
despertaron.

S

1. Nos dio hambre.   2. Les dio miedo.   3. Te dio sueño.   4. Le dio vergüenza.   5. Me dio confianza. 6. Le dio calor.   7. Les dio celos.   8. Le dio dolor. 9. Les dio envidia.   10. Nos dio frío.

T

1. La película aburrida le daba sueño.   2. Las canciones nos daban ganas de bailar.   3. Nuestro apoyo les daba confianza.   4. Su amigo guapo le daba celos a su novio.   5. El buen aroma de la sopa me daba hambre.   6. El comportamiento de su niño les daba vergüenza a sus padres.   7. ¿Qué te daba envidia?   8. La lluvia nos daba frío.

U

1. me despertaba   2. me cepillaba   3. me duchaba 4. me maquillaba   5. me vestía   6. desayunaba 7. salía   8. asistía   9. hacía   10. esperaba   11. tenía 12. faltaba   13. trabajaba

V

1. Eran las nueve de la noche cuando ellos volvieron de las pirámides.   2. Eran las siete y media de la mañana cuando tú te levantaste. 3. Era la una de la tarde cuando nosotros fuimos a la merienda campestre.   4. Eran las tres cuarenta y cinco de la tarde cuando los directores de la empresa se reunieron.   5. Eran las cinco de la tarde cuando yo empecé a jugar al tenis.   6. Eran las ocho menos veinte de la noche cuando Uds. llegaron a la finca.   7. Eran casi las once de la noche cuando Ud. terminó de escribir su informe. 8. Eran las diez de la mañana cuando él salió para el cafetal.

W

1. llegaba   2. eran   3. esperaban   4. soñaban 5. tenían   6. trabajaban   7. era   8. sabían   9. vivían 10. daba

X

1. ¿Cuánto tiempo hacía que tú tocabas el piano cuando te dieron una beca? / Hacía ocho años que tocaba el piano.   2. ¿Cuánto tiempo hacía que ella jugaba al golf cuando comenzó a llover? / Hacía dos horas que jugaba al golf.   3. ¿Cuánto tiempo hacía que Uds. esperaban a sus primos cuando llegaron? / Hacía media hora que esperábamos a nuestros primos.   4. ¿Cuánto tiempo hacía que él trabajaba en Chile cuando su empresa lo mandó al Perú? / Hacía cinco meses que trabajaba en Chile.

Y

1. Hacía una hora que yo buscaba al perro. (Yo buscaba al perro hacía una hora.)   2. ¿Desde cuándo cultivaban los agricultores el maíz? 3. ¿Cuánto (tiempo) hacía que te interesaba el arte moderno?   4. Hacía cincuenta años que se producían carros en esta planta. (Se producían carros en esta planta hacía cincuenta años.) 5. Hacíamos ecoturismo desde junio.   6. Hacía muchos años que servían comida sana. (Servían comida sana hacía muchos años.)   7. ¿Cuánto (tiempo) hacía que nevaba?   8. Él asistía a una universidad estatal desde el año pasado.

Z

1. Me dijeron que mi primo se casaba.   2. Nos escribió que iba al extranjero.   3. Me escribieron que disfrutaban de sus vacaciones.   4. Me texteó que estaba en camino.   5. Le dije que la quería mucho.   6. Le pregunté si trabajaba todavía en la base de datos.   7. Me contó que le interesaba estudiar administración de empresas.   8. Nos informó que hacía un estudio de mercado.

AA

1. ¿Las carpetas? Se las devolvimos a ella ayer. 2. ¿El contrato? Se lo mandó a los abogados ayer. 3. ¿El billete? Me lo dieron ayer.   4. ¿Los jardines? Nos los mostró ayer.   5. ¿El paquete? Se lo envolvieron ayer.   6. ¿El dinero? Me lo pidió ayer. 7. ¿Los aretes? Se los regalamos ayer.   8. ¿La cartera? Te la traje ayer.   9. ¿Los documentos? Se los entregué ayer.   10. ¿Las galletas? Se las hice ayer.

BB

Answers will vary.

CC

Answers will vary.

11 Health and Accidents

A

1. iba / pudo   2. pensaban / cambiaron 3. bajaba / subía   4. entró / saludó   5. dijo / quería 6. almorcé / seguí   7. visitábamos / montábamos 8. se levantaron / se arreglaron   9. me desperté / tenía

B

1. Llovía / tuvieron   2. esperábamos / dejó 3. comía / tomaba   4. Estaba / hubo   5. pegó / se pusieron

C

1. Yo era secretario del director ejecutivo hasta que se enfermó.   2. Elena y Mercedes dejaron de trabajar en esa sucursal.   3. El número de teléfono fue cambiado así que no pudimos llamarlos.
4. ¿El gerente trasladó o despidió a Joaquín?
5. Víctor no terminó el informe porque no había suficientes datos.

D

1. ¿Cuánto tiempo hacía que se conocían cuando se comprometieron?   2. Hacía una semana que nos veíamos cuando empezamos a tutearnos.
3. ¿Cuánto tiempo hacía que nos ayudábamos con el proyecto cuando Ud. se mudó?   4. Mientras Lola y Juan se abrazaban y se besaban, el hermanito de Lola empezó a reírse.   5. Se comprendían muy bien hasta que algo pasó.   6. Nos conocimos cuando trabajábamos en una compañía de alta tecnología.

E

1. imprimíamos / dejó   2. leía / oyó   3. veía / vinieron   4. preparaba / tocó   5. jugaban / comenzó

F

1. Me dijeron que su hija iba a graduarse en la universidad.   2. Alonso era solterón hasta que conoció a y se casó con Sofía.   3. Victoria se hizo abogada cuando tenía veintisiete años.
4. Eras muy joven cuando te recibiste de médico.
5. Los gemelos eran superdotados y simpáticos pero también algo presumidos.

G

1. la casona   2. contestón   3. facilón   4. llorón
5. mirón   6. la muchachona   7. matón
8. el martillazo   9. el perrazo   10. el puñetazo
11. los ojazos   12. el catarrazo

H

1. la ropita   2. el dedito   3. la niñita   4. el pajarito
5. la vocecita   6. el chiquito   7. fresquito
8. el jovencito   9. la botellita   10. el calorcito
11. la fiestecita   12. Miguelito   13. poquito
14. la nietecita   15. el abuelito   16. cerquita
17. la cabecita   18. Rodriguito   19. mismito
20. el choquecito   21. el pececito   22. la lucecita
23. la tosecita

I

1. A Juanita le duele el estómago.   2. A Pedro le dolía la espalda.   3. Les duelen las rodillas.
4. A nuestra sobrinita le duele la garganta.
5. Te dolía la cabeza.   6. Al jugador le duelen los tobillos.   7. Al nietecito de Paco le dolía el oído.
8. Les dolían los ojos.

J

1. Se le acabó el filtro solar.   2. Se nos olvidaron las toallas de playa.   3. ¿Se les quedó el repelente contra mosquitos en casa?   4. Se me cayeron los lentes de sol.   5. Se les descompuso el carro.
6. Se te perdieron las gafas oscuras.   7. Se le quebraron los platos.

K

1. Los mosquitos nos comían vivos.   2. ¡Qué picadura! No debes rascártela.   3. Catalina tomaba el sol hasta que una abeja le picó.   4. A Pedro se le perdieron las gafas oscuras (los lentes de sol) en la arena.   5. Se les quedó la tienda de campaña en el campamento.   6. ¡Pobrecita! El champú le entró en los ojos.

L

1. supe / estaba   2. dijeron / iba   3. esperábamos / dio   4. estaba / hizo   5. llevaron / dolía / tenía

M

1. bajábamos / vimos   2. estaba / sonó   3. ardía / apagaron   4. era / estalló

N

1. iba   2. llegó   3. quedaba   4. se acercó   5. oyó
6. vio   7. preguntó   8. pasaba (pasó)   9. dijo
10. cruzaba   11. atropelló   12. atendían   13. tenía

O

Answers will vary.

P

Answers will vary.

Q

Answers will vary.

R

Answers will vary.

12 People: Character and Personality, Societal Problems

A

1. Consuelo es más presumida que Aurora. / Aurora es menos presumida que Consuelo.
2. Nosotros estamos más entusiasmados que Jaime y Federico. / Jaime y Federico están menos entusiasmados que nosotros.   3. La profesora de química es más exigente que el profesor de física. / El profesor de física es menos exigente que la profesora de química.   4. La chaqueta es más cara que los pantalones. / Los pantalones son menos caros que la chaqueta.   5. Yo soy más optimista que tú. / Tú eres menos optimista que yo.
6. El condominio es más moderno que la casa. / La casa es menos moderna que el condominio.

7. Uds. son más corteses que Juan Manuel. /
Juan Manuel es menos cortés que Uds.
8. Los tacos están más ricos que los tamales. /
Los tamales están menos ricos que los tacos.

B

1. Elena es tan caprichosa como Victoria.   2. Pedro
es tan ingenuo como tú.   3. Ellos son tan egoístas
como Rodrigo.   4. Paquita es tan coqueta como
su prima.   5. Los empleados son tan trabajadores
como el director.   6. Uds. están tan estresados
como sus amigos.   7. Ana María es tan calculadora
como su cuñada.   8. Bernardo está tan emocionado
como Beatriz.   9. Nuestros hijos están tan
ocupados como nosotros.   10. Tú eres tan
comprensiva como tus papás.

C

1. Guillermo escuchó más atentamente que
Josefa. / Josefa escuchó menos atentamente que
Guillermo. / Guillermo escuchó tan atentamente
como Josefa.   2. Alberto trabajó más
ambiciosamente que Santiago. / Santiago trabajó
menos ambiciosamente que Alberto. / Alberto
trabajó tan ambiciosamente como Santiago.
3. Uds. fueron de compras más frecuentemente que
nosotros. / Nosotros fuimos de compras menos
frecuentemente que Uds. / Uds. fueron de compras
tan frecuentemente como nosotros.   4. La familia
Suárez vivió más cómodamente que la familia
Morales. / La familia Morales vivió menos
cómodamente que la familia Suárez. / La familia
Suárez vivió tan cómodamente como la familia
Morales.   5. Nosotros manejamos más lentamente
que tú. / Tú manejaste menos lentamente que
nosotros. / Nosotros manejamos tan lentamente
como tú.   6. Antonio se ofendió más fácilmente
que su hermano. / Su hermano se ofendió menos
fácilmente que Antonio. / Antonio se ofendió tan
fácilmente como su hermano.   7. Damián corrió
más rápidamente que Uds. / Uds. corrieron menos
rápidamente que Damián. / Damián corrió tan
rápidamente como Uds.   8. Tú pensaste más
profundamente que yo. / Yo pensé menos
profundamente que tú. / Tú pensaste tan
profundamente como yo.   9. Blanca contestó
más amablemente que Pepe. / Pepe contestó menos
amablemente que Blanca. / Blanca contestó tan
amablemente como Pepe.   10. Ud. reaccionó más
sensiblemente que Daniela. / Daniela reaccionó
menos sensiblemente que Ud. / Ud. reaccionó tan
sensiblemente como Daniela.

D

1. Yo cursaba más materias que tú. / Tú cursabas
menos materias que yo. / Yo cursaba tantas
materias como tú.   2. El niño tenía más hambre
que su hermanita. / Su hermanita tenía menos
hambre que el niño. / El niño tenía tanta hambre
como su hermanita.   3. Uds. compraban más libros
de texto que los otros estudiantes. / Los otros
estudiantes compraban menos libros de texto que
Uds. / Uds. compraban tantos libros de texto como
los otros estudiantes.   4. Eva veía más películas que
María Elena. / María Elena veía menos películas
que Eva. / Eva veía tantas películas como María
Elena.   5. Tú comías más comida chatarra que tus
amigos. / Tus amigos comían menos comida
chatarra que tú. / Tú comías tanta comida chatarra
como tus amigos.   6. Nosotros leíamos más obras
maestras que ellos. / Ellos leían menos obras
maestras que nosotros. / Nosotros leíamos tantas
obras maestras como ellos.   7. Sofía recorría más
países que su marido. / Su marido recorría menos
países que Sofía. / Sofía recorría tantos países como
su marido.   8. Ignacio hacía más ejercicio que
Mateo. / Mateo hacía menos ejercicio que Ignacio. /
Ignacio hacía tanto ejercicio como Mateo.

E

1. La abuela Raquel es la más sensata.   2. El tío
Rodrigo es el más cascarrabias.   3. Los primos
Laura y Martín son los más calculadores.
4. Las nietas Teresita y Paquita son las más
coquetas.   5. La cuñada Lucía es la más
entrometida.   6. Los sobrinos Ramón y Eugenia
son los más tercos.   7. El yerno Manolo es el más
realista.   8. La nuera Montserrat es la más pesada.

F

1. Anita es más presumida que su hermana.
2. Jorge es menos maleducado que sus amigos.
3. Cristóbal estaba tan estresado como tú.
4. Mis hermanos son tan considerados como yo.
5. Matilde es la persona más tímida de su familia.
6. Juanito es el alumno más raro de su clase.

G

1. elegantísima   2. riquísimos   3. larguísimos
4. interesantísimo   5. buenísimas   6. hermosísimos
7. simpatiquísimas   8. facilísimos   9. clarísima
10. ocupadísimos

H

1. Es el mejor libro de nuestra biblioteca.
2. Es la marca más famosa del mercado.
3. Trabajábamos más que nunca.   4. Enrique
viajaba tan frecuentemente como nosotros.

5. El año pasado Perla ganó más de doscientos mil dólares.   6. A Pablo no le quedan más que mil setecientos dólares en su cuenta de ahorros.   7. Nuestro equipo le ganó al otro equipo y con mucho.   8. Ellos compraron tantos bolígrafos y lápices como nosotros.   9. ¿Cree que este gerente es más exigente que el antiguo (el anterior)?   10. ¡Qué va! Es el gerente más indulgente de la empresa.   11. La salud es más importante que nada.   12. Raquel se queja más que nadie.

I

1. Prefiero el marrón, pero me gusta el negro también.   2. Prefiero los de cuentos, pero me gustan los de poesía también.   3. Prefiero la de enfrente, pero me gusta la de al lado también.   4. Prefiero los de arte, pero me gustan los de ciencias también.   5. Prefiero el italiano, pero me gusta el mexicano también.   6. Prefiero los fabricados en los Estados Unidos, pero me gustan los fabricados en el extranjero también.   7. Prefiero la grande, pero me gusta la pequeña también.   8. Prefiero las obligatorias, pero me gustan las optativas también.   9. Prefiero los vegetarianos, pero me gustan los de carne también.   10. Prefiero el de lana, pero me gusta el de algodón también.

J

1. Nuestra calle es más tranquila que la suya (la de ellos).   2. Tu proyecto era tan interesante como el mío.   3. Sus cursos son menos difíciles que los nuestros.   4. Nuestras empresas ganaron tanto dinero como las suyas (las de Ud.).   5. Su equipo juega tan bien como el tuyo.   6. La novia de Ricardo es tan alegre como la suya (la de su hermano).   7. Este celular funcionaba mejor que el suyo (el de Susana).   8. Tus profesores son tan exigentes como los míos.

K

1. Me gusta ésta (esta) más que aquélla (aquella).   2. Me gusta aquél (aquel) más que éste (este).   3. Me gustan ésos (esos) más que éstos (estos).   4. Me gustan éstas (estas) más que aquéllas (aquellas).   5. Me gusta éste (este) más que aquél (aquel).   6. Me gustan éstos (estos) más que ésos (esos).

L

1. Estos cartuchos de tinta cuestan más que esos (ésos/aquellos/aquéllos).   2. Los guantes de seda son más finos que los de cuero.   3. Este abrigo rojo es más largo que ese (ése/aquel/aquél) azul marino.   4. Creo que (Me parece que) conociste tantas ciudades latinoamericanas como nosotros.

M

1. Hay más ruido ambiental que nunca en nuestra sociedad.   2. Esta es la región más contaminada del estado.   3. Hay gente que cree que el reciclaje es más importante que nada.   4. Hay menos crimen en nuestra ciudad que en la suya.   5. Había muchísimo espíritu cívico en el país durante los años cincuenta.   6. Hay más drogadicción que nunca.

N

1. Este apartamento es más amplio que los que vio anteriormente.   2. Aquel condominio es más grande y menos caro que el mío.   3. Esta casa tiene tantos dormitorios como la suya pero tiene menos cuartos de baño que la nuestra.   4. Esta computadora es más potente que la que tenía.   5. La computadora anterior era más fácil de usar que la que tengo ahora.

O

1. lingüística e idiomas   2. Costa Rica u Honduras   3. sensible e ingenua   4. mujeres u hombres   5. pesimista u optimista   6. franceses e italianos   7. este u oeste   8. sinagogas e iglesias   9. oxígeno e hidrógeno   10. libertad e igualdad   11. rinocerontes e hipopótamos   12. escocés u holandés

P

1. No, para ellos, no.   2. No, por Uds., no.   3. No, con ellas, no.   4. No, para ti, no.   5. No, con él, no.   6. No, por ella, no.   7. No, contigo, no.   8. No, contigo, no.

Q

Answers will vary.

R

Answers will vary.

13 Business and the Growth of Cities

A

1. descompuesto   2. escrita   3. caídos   4. roto   5. aumentado   6. hecha   7. vistos   8. leídas   9. muertas   10. llevados

B

1. Carmen está angustiada.   2. Rodrigo y Diego están aburridos.   3. Nosotras estamos emocionadas.   4. Tú estás estresada.   5. Juanita está deprimida.   6. Carlos y Mateo están entusiasmados.   7. Yo estoy preocupado.   8. Esteban y Vera están acatarrados.   9. Ud. está cansada.   10. Fernando está confundido.

C

1. he 2. vuelto 3. oído 4. ha 5. dicho 6. han
7. visto 8. hemos 9. has 10. dado

D

1. Ha cursado dos asignaturas optativas.
2. Han querido visitarnos. 3. Hemos puesto la
mesa. 4. Ha llovido todo el día. 5. Ha sido difícil
adelgazar. 6. Se han incluido los ingresos y los
gastos. 7. He abierto las ventanas. 8. No has visto
a nadie, ¿verdad? 9. Ha habido mucho ajetreo hoy.
10. Hemos estado tan emocionados como Uds.
11. Han tenido que pagar el seguro de salud.
12. ¿Has pedido más vino?

E

1. Yo he escrito los documentos. / Los documentos
están escritos. 2. Nosotros hemos hecho el plan
de negocios. / El plan de negocios está hecho.
3. Ella ha pagado la hipoteca. / La hipoteca está
pagada. 4. Uds. han recibido la invitación. /
La invitación está recibida. 5. Ellos han abierto
las fábricas. / Las fábricas están abiertas. 6. Tú has
facturado el equipaje. / El equipaje está facturado.
7. Él ha alquilado el apartamento. / El apartamento
está alquilado. 8. Ellas han puesto la mesa. /
La mesa está puesta. 9. Ud. ha descargado su
canción favorita. / Su canción favorita está
descargada. 10. Ellos han construido los
rascacielos. / Los rascacielos están construidos.

F

1. El equipo ha hecho el plan de negocios.
2. Alejo y yo hemos elaborado el presupuesto.
3. Los asesores han recogido los datos. 4. El artista
gráfico ha dibujado el logo. 5. Yo he creado
diapositivas en PowerPoint. 6. Tú has mandado
los emails. 7. Uds. se han reunido en la sala de
conferencias. 8. Leonardo ha diseñado el folleto.
9. Claudia y su asistente han leído todos los
documentos. 10. Ud. ha impreso el volante.

G

1. Ya se las he regalado. 2. Ya se lo hemos pedido.
3. Ya se lo ha leído. 4. Ya se lo he dado. 5. Ya las
he llevado. 6. Ya nos lo han dicho. 7. Ya me la ha
prestado. 8. Ya lo hemos hecho.

H

1. Ya les ha dicho lo que oyó. 2. ¿Ya le has dado el
pésame a la viuda de Daniel? 3. ¿El presupuesto?
Se lo hemos elaborado. 4. ¿El contrato? No nos lo
han explicado todavía. 5. ¿La cafetera? No he
tenido tiempo de devolvérsela. 6. ¿Los ingresos
y los gastos? ¿Se los ha mostrado a la contadora?
7. Ha habido mucho ajetreo en la empresa.

I

1. Nos hemos matriculado ya. 2. Se ha graduado
ya. 3. Me la he lavado ya. 4. Se han reunido ya.
5. Me las he probado ya. 6. Se han casado ya.
7. Me he comprometido con él ya. 8. Nos hemos
mudado ya. 9. Se los han cepillado ya. 10. Se la
ha maquillado ya.

J

1. Ya está levantado. 2. Ya estoy enamorada.
3. Ya están acostados. 4. Ya estamos vestidas.
5. Ya estamos bañados. 6. Ya estoy arreglada.
7. Ya están instalados. 8. Ya están divorciados.

K

1. está tumbado 2. están inclinados 3. está
dormido 4. está agachado 5. estamos parados
6. está montada 7. están levantados 8. está
echado

L

1. ¡Cuánto ha crecido la ciudad en los últimos
años! / Y la población ha aumentado muchísimo.
Hay casi cuatro millones de habitantes. 2. Nuestro
pueblecito se ha convertido en una ciudad grande e
importante. / Ya lo creo. Muchos edificios han sido
construidos (se han construido) y poco a poco hay
menos barrios bajos. 3. ¡Han hecho maravillas!
Nuestra ciudad está muy cambiada. / Es verdad.
Pero, ¡qué aglomeración! ¡Qué tráfico! ¡Qué ruido!

M

1. Cuando Ud. compró los cartuchos de tinta, Jorge
ya había impreso las invitaciones. 2. Cuando los
invitados llegaron para cenar, Pepita y Tomás ya
habían puesto la mesa. 3. Cuando despegó el
avión, los pasajeros ya se habían abrochado el
cinturón de seguridad. 4. Cuando nosotros
conocimos a Nora, ella ya se había hecho ingeniera.
5. Cuando Eduardo comenzó a trabajar, sus colegas
ya habían leído los documentos. 6. Cuando
llegaste al cementerio, el entierro ya había tenido
lugar. 7. Cuando sonó el teléfono, tú ya te habías
despertado. 8. Cuando vi a Antonio, su empresa
ya lo había trasladado a otra sucursal. 9. Cuando
Uds. nos dieron la noticia, ya la habíamos oído
del vecino. 10. Cuando Nora regresó a su pueblo
natal, el pueblo ya se había convertido en una
ciudad grande.

N

1. ¿Ya ha elaborado el presupuesto? / Sí, he incluido
ingresos y gastos. 2. ¿Está puesta la mesa? / Sí, y la
cena está servida. 3. Ha sido un día muy difícil. /
¿Por qué lo dices? ¿Has tenido que hacer mucho
trabajo? 4. ¿Nevaba cuando regresaban a casa? /

No, ya habíamos regresado a casa cuando empezó a nevar.   5. Cuando aterrizó el avión, los pasajeros ya habían prendido sus celulares. / Supongo que también habían bajado el equipaje de mano. 6. Cuando llegamos a casa de Mario, la fiesta ya había terminado. / ¿Y nadie se lo había dicho antes? ¡Qué barbaridad!

O

Answers will vary.

P

Answers will vary.

Q

Answers will vary.

14   Directions, Air Travel, Recipes

A

1. Corra el maratón.   2. Maneje con cuidado. 3. Abra las ventanas.   4. Asista al concierto. 5. Cruce la calle.   6. Suba al avión.   7. Coma con nosotros.   8. Siga por el río.   9. Elabore un presupuesto.   10. Lea este libro.   11. Diseñe el sitio web.   12. Vuelva para el viernes.   13. Pida una disculpa.   14. Haga un plan de negocios.

B

1. Beban mucha agua.   2. Trabajen con el equipo. 3. Vivan felizmente.   4. Escriban el email. 5. Conduzcan con cuidado.   6. Aprendan las fechas de memoria.   7. Tomen el tren.   8. Vistan a los niños.   9. Prendan la televisión.   10. Analicen los datos.   11. Cobren el cheque.   12. Compartan sus ideas.   13. Duerman la siesta.   14. Sirvan la comida.

C

1. Lleguen Uds. temprano.   2. Sirva Ud. la cena. 3. Abra Ud. la ventana.   4. Crucen Uds. la calle con cuidado.   5. Mire Ud. la señal de tráfico.   6. Suban Uds. en el ascensor.   7. Guarde Ud. los datos. 8. Elaboren Uds. un presupuesto.

D

1. Guarde los suéteres. / No guarde los suéteres. 2. Vea el programa. / No vea el programa. 3. Estacione en la plaza. / No estacione en la plaza. 4. Añada más sal. / No añada más sal.   5. Cierre la puerta. / No cierre la puerta.   6. Imprima los contratos. / No imprima los contratos.   7. Ponga la mesa. / No ponga la mesa.   8. Pruebe ese plato. / No pruebe ese plato.   9. Descargue el archivo. / No descargue el archivo.   10. Repita las palabras. / No repita las palabras.

E

1. Guarden los suéteres. / No guarden los suéteres. 2. Vean el programa. / No vean el programa. 3. Estacionen en la plaza. / No estacionen en la plaza.   4. Añadan más sal. / No añadan más sal. 5. Cierren la puerta. / No cierren la puerta. 6. Impriman los contratos. / No impriman los contratos.   7. Pongan la mesa. / No pongan la mesa.   8. Prueben ese plato. / No prueben ese plato. 9. Descarguen el archivo. / No descarguen el archivo.   10. Repitan las palabras. / No repitan las palabras.

F

1. Vende el carro. / No vendas el carro.   2. Navega en la web. / No navegues en la web.   3. Sube en el ascensor. / No subas en el ascensor.   4. Sigue por esta calle. / No sigas por esta calle.   5. Haz la maleta. / No hagas la maleta.   6. Piensa en eso. / No pienses en eso.   7. Ven el sábado. / No vengas el sábado.   8. Sal antes de las cuatro. / No salgas antes de las cuatro.   9. Ten prisa. / No tengas prisa. 10. Juega al golf. / No juegues al golf.

G

1. No te preocupes.   2. Vete.   3. La verdad. Dísela. 4. Le debes dinero. Devuélveselo.   5. No seas así. 6. Esta corbata es fea. No te la pongas.   7. No estés enojado (enojada) conmigo. (No te enojes conmigo.)   8. La cena, por favor. Háznosla. 9. Él necesita los auriculares. Dáselos. (A él le hacen falta los auriculares. Dáselos.)   10. Ten paciencia.

H

1. ¿El perro? Mírenlo. / No lo miren.   2. ¿El piano? Tóquelo. / No lo toque.   3. ¿Las revistas? Entréguemelas. / No me las entregue. 4. ¿Los regalos? Escójaselos. / No se los escoja. 5. ¿Las llaves? Búsquenlas. / No las busquen. 6. ¿La noticia? Cuéntesela. / No se la cuente. 7. ¿La idea? Explíquensela. / No se la expliquen. 8. ¿La orquesta? Diríjanosla. / No nos la dirija. 9. ¿La cuenta? Páguensela. / No se la paguen. 10. ¿El partido? Empiécenlo. / No lo empiecen.

I

1. Léalo. / Léanlo. / Léaselo. / Léanselo. 2. Tráigalas. / Tráiganlas. / Tráigaselas. / Tráiganselas.   3. Explíquelo. / Explíquenlo. / Explíqueselo. / Explíquenselo.   4. Dígalo. / Díganlo. / Díganoslo. / Dígannoslo. 5. Muéstrelas. / Muéstrenlas. / Muéstreselas. / Muéstrenselas.   6. Sírvalo. / Sírvanlo. / Sírvanoslo. / Sírvannoslo.   7. Lávese. / Lávense. / Lávese las manos. / Lávense las manos. / Láveselas. /

Lávenselas. 8. Pídalos. / Pídanlos. / Pídaselos. / Pídanselos. 9. Póngase la chaqueta. / Pónganse la chaqueta. / Póngasela. / Pónganselas. 10. Séquese el pelo. / Séquense el pelo. / Séqueselo. / Séquenselo.

J

1. Lleguemos el domingo. / No lleguemos el domingo. 2. Hagamos turismo. / No hagamos turismo. 3. Saquemos el pasaporte. / No saquemos el pasaporte. 4. Demos consejos. / No demos consejos. 5. Vamos al teatro. / No vayamos al teatro. 6. Durmamos la siesta. / No durmamos la siesta. 7. Salgamos esta noche. / No salgamos esta noche. 8. Vengamos en tren. / No vengamos en tren. 9. Pensemos en el futuro. / No pensemos en el futuro. 10. Pidamos un café. / No pidamos un café. 11. Sentémonos en el sofá. / No nos sentemos en el sofá. 12. Quedémonos unos días más. / No nos quedemos unos días más.

K

1. Sí, veámosla. / Sí, vamos a verla.
2. Sí, discutámoslas. / Sí, vamos a discutirlas.
3. Sí, consigámoslos. / Sí, vamos a conseguirlos.
4. Sí, compartámoslos. / Sí, vamos a compartirlos.
5. Sí, pidámoslo. / Sí, vamos a pedirlo.
6. Sí, visitémosla. / Sí, vamos a visitarla.
7. Sí, aparquémoslo. / Sí, vamos a aparcarlo.
8. Sí, traduzcámoslas. / Sí, vamos a traducirlas.
9. Sí, probémonoslos. / Sí, vamos a probárnoslos.
10. Sí, cortémonoslo. / Sí, vamos a cortárnoslo.

L

1. No, no la veamos. 2. No, nos las discutamos.
3. No, no los consigamos. 4. No, no los compartamos. 5. No, no lo pidamos. 6. No, no la visitemos. 7. No, lo aparquemos. 8. No, no las traduzcamos. 9. No, no nos los probemos.
10. No, no nos lo cortemos.

M

1. Paseémonos por el parque. / No nos paseemos por el parque. 2. Casémonos en diciembre. / No nos casemos en diciembre.
3. Pongámonoslos. / No nos los pongamos.
4. Reunámonos el domingo. / No nos reunamos el domingo. 5. Abrochémonoslo. / No nos lo abrochemos. 6. Despertémonos temprano. / No nos despertemos temprano. 7. Lavémonoslas. / No nos las lavemos. 8. Vámonos ahora. / No nos vayamos ahora. 9. Sequémoselo. / No se lo sequemos. 10. Despidámonos de ellos. / No nos despidamos de ellos.

N

1. Sí, entrégueselos. / No, no se los entregue.
2. Sí, muéstreselas. / No, no se las muestre.
3. Sí, pídaselo. / No, no se lo pida. 4. Sí, déselo. / No, no se lo dé. 5. Sí, calcúleselos. / No, no se los calcule. 6. Sí, hágasela. / No, no se la haga.
7. Sí, descríbaselo. / No, no se lo describa.
8. Sí, tráigaselo. / No, no se lo traiga.

O

1. Sí, muéstremelos. 2. Sí, explíquemela.
3. Sí, pónmelo. 4. Sí, házmela.
5. Sí, entréguemelos. 6. Sí, démelas.
7. Sí, préstamelo. 8. Sí, envíemela. 9. Sí, dímelo.
10. Sí, sírvemelas.

P

1. No, no me los muestre. 2. No, no me la explique. 3. No, no me lo pongas. 4. No, no me la hagas. 5. No, no me los entregue. 6. No, no me las dé. 7. No, no me lo prestes. 8. No, no me la envíe. 9. No, no me lo digas. 10. No, no me las sirvas.

Q

1. Sí, léela. 2. No, no la pongas todavía.
3. Sí, sácalos. 4. No, no lo calientes todavía.
5. Sí, bátelas. 6. Sí, échalas. 7. No, no lo añadas todavía. 8. Sí, fríelas. 9. No, no los sirvas todavía.
10. Sí, prepáralo.

R

1. Tranquilízate. 2. No te preocupes.
3. No te vuelvas loca. 4. No te muerdas las uñas.
5. No seas tonta. 6. Ve a la fiesta sin cuidado.
7. No te pongas nerviosa. 8. No te alteres.
9. Sé feliz. 10. Relájate. 11. Disfruta de las festividades. 12. Diviértete mucho.

S

1. Seguir las instrucciones. 2. No pisar el césped.
3. ¡Pintura fresca, no tocar! 4. Agregar una pizca de sal. 5. Lavar y secar las hojas de lechuga.
6. Pulsar el botón. 7. Enjuagar bien el pelo.
8. Introducir la contraseña.

T

1. Tenga la bondad de prestarme los auriculares.
2. Haga el favor de contarme lo ocurrido.
3. Favor de explicárnoslo. 4. Favor de hacer una copia de seguridad. 5. Tenga la bondad de decírmelo. 6. Favor de ayudarme con el abrigo.
7. Haga el favor de llamarme lo antes posible.
8. Tenga la bondad de enviármelas para la semana entrante.

U

Answers will vary.

V

Answers will vary.

W

1. Ase la carne a la parrilla.　2. Remueva la sopa.
3. Mezcle las frutas y las chispas de chocolate.
4. Agregue (Agréguele) jugo de limón al pescado.
5. Enfríe el vino.　6. Sazone con sal y pimienta.
7. Hornee el pan.　8. Pique las cebollas.

X

Answers will vary.

15　Holidays and Celebrations, Planning for the Future

A

1. Entregaré el informe.　2. Venderá su casa.
3. No discutirán ese asunto.　4. Te divertirás
mucho.　5. Dormirá la siesta.　6. Jugaré al tenis.
7. Diseñaremos el sitio web.　8. Elegiré un
nuevo celular.　9. ¿No comerás nada más?
10. Se reunirán en la sala de conferencias.
11. Conseguiré una beca.　12. Hará ochenta grados.

B

1. diré　2. saldrá　3. querrás　4. nos pondremos
5. vendrán　6. tendrán　7. Hará　8. sabremos
9. podrá　10. Habrá

C

1. Los gemelos tendrán siete u ocho años.
2. Sabrás su número de teléfono.　3. Serán las once.
4. Camila querrá ver esta obra de teatro.　5. Su casa
costará una fortuna.　6. Estarán acatarrados.
7. Cristóbal se hará ingeniero.　8. Este anillo valdrá
miles de dólares.　9. Habrá muchos documentos
sobre este tema.　10. Cabrá el equipaje en el
maletero del coche.

D

1. ¿Cuántos años tendrá el señor Durán?　2. Tendrá
cincuenta años.　3. ¿Qué hora será?　4. Serán las
cuatro.　5. ¡Qué traje más elegante! Costará mucho
dinero.　6. No puedo encontrar mi tarjeta de
crédito. ¿Dónde estará?　7. Nevará mañana.
8. Sabrán lo que pasó.

E

1. Daniel y yo elaboraríamos el presupuesto.
2. Uds. aprenderían español en Bogotá.
3. Tú tendrías suerte.　4. Yo no se lo diría a nadie.
5. La cocinera querría añadir más sal.　6. Nosotros
haríamos escala en Miami.　7. Mis colegas
compartirían los gastos.　8. Sus suegros no podrían
visitarlos.　9. Tú saldrías más tarde.　10. Ud. se
mudaría a ese barrio.

F

1. ¿Cuántos años tendría María Elena cuando
terminó la maestría?　2. Tendría veintitrés años
cuando la terminó.　3. ¿Qué hora sería cuando los
señores Fernández llegaron al balneario?　4. Sería
mediodía.　5. ¿Quién tendría la culpa del crimen?
6. Sería el mayordomo.　7. ¿Dónde estarían Uds.
cuando los llamamos?　8. Estaríamos todavía
en la oficina.　9. ¿Qué habría en el paquete?
10. Habría juguetes para los niños.

G

1. A Uds. les gustará esta comida mexicana.
2. A ella le entusiasmará conocer a nuestros amigos.
3. A ti te interesará este proyecto.　4. A mí me
quedarán dos exámenes todavía.　5. A ellos les
faltará dinero.　6. A nosotros nos harán falta más
datos.　7. A Ud. le convendrá encargarse de la
oficina.　8. A él no le importará nada.

H

1. Vamos a asistir al concierto.　2. Voy a salir para
la hacienda.　3. Uds. van a irse pasado mañana.
4. ¿Vas a poder acompañarme a la boda?
5. Va a haber una fiesta de quinceañera para Inés.
6. La fiesta va a ser en el Hotel Palacio.　7. Ellos van
a tener que trabajar.　8. Manuel va a querer esquiar.

I

1. van / iremos　2. hará / hacen　3. pide / pediré
4. volvemos / volveré　5. tomará / toma
6. me paseo / te pasearás　7. almorzaremos /
almuerzan　8. te reúnes / me reuniré

J

1. lloverá　2. llegaremos　3. se pondrá
4. se matriculará　5. entregarán　6. venderán
7. querrás　8. se encargarán

K

1. regresaría　2. se casarían　3. pasaría　4. daría
5. podrían　6. habría　7. encantarían　8. veríamos

L

1. Me gustaría aprender a esquiar.
2. A los niños les entusiasmaría abrir sus regalos.
3. Te interesarían mucho estos museos.
4. ¡Nos encantaría tomar una copa de champaña!
5. A Carlos no le importaría nada.
6. A Ud. le haría falta su pasaporte.
7. Le tocaría a Julia en el juego de mesa.
8. A Uds. les convendría tomar un vuelo sin escala.

M

1. ¿Qué dirá?　2. ¿Qué sabrá?　3. ¿Qué pensará?
(¿Qué creerá?)　4. ¿Qué comprenderá?
(¿Qué entenderá?)　5. ¿Qué se imaginará?
6. ¿Qué supondrá?　7. ¿Qué se preguntará?
8. ¿Qué conjeturará?

N

1. Buenas tardes, señor Díaz. Ud. es uno de los pocos candidatos que hay para este puesto.
2. Mucho gusto, señor. Muchas gracias.
3. Nos gustó su carta de motivación y su currículum vitae es impresionante. Por favor, dígame más de su experiencia profesional.
4. Hacía quince años que trabajaba para mi empresa anterior. Tengo las habilidades requeridas y las habilidades comunicativas muy buenas. Y siempre cumplo con las fechas límite.
5. Ud. tendría que resolver problemas difíciles y mostrar iniciativa.   6. Estoy seguro de que podría. Como gerente y director de proyecto, tuve éxito en todos mis proyectos y me llevé muy bien con mi equipo.   7. Estoy contento de saberlo. El trabajo en equipo es muy importante para nuestra empresa. Gracias, señor Díaz. Estaremos en contacto con Ud.   8. Muchas gracias, señor Torres. Yo estaría muy contento de trabajar con Ud.

O

1. Eva, ¿sabes si Carmen, Daniel y Federico asistirán a la reunión?   2. Carmen y Federico sí estarán pero Daniel me dijo que tendría que ver a un cliente por la tarde. No sabía que habría una reunión hoy.   3. El señor Torres quiere lanzar una campaña publicitaria para anunciar el nuevo producto así que tendremos mucho que hacer.
4. Eladio, tú y yo elaboraremos el presupuesto. Federico hablará del mercadeo de redes y Carmen explicará sus ideas sobre los medios sociales.
5. El señor Torres tendrá muestras del producto y querrá crear un logo y un lema.   6. Creo que los diseñadores se encargarán del diseño gráfico. Mira. El señor Torres acaba de entrar. Empezará la reunión.

P

1. ¡Isabel sí se preocupará!   2. ¡Mis papás sí comprenderán!   3. ¡Tú sí te quejarás!   4. ¡Yo sí se lo diré a todos!   5. ¡Ud. sí se ofenderá!   6. ¡Rodrigo y yo sí nos sorprenderemos!   7. ¡Uds. sí se enojarán!
7. ¡Alfredo sí tendrá la culpa!

Q

Answers will vary.

R

Answers will vary.

S

Answers will vary.

T

1. "Keep your eyes open before marriage and half closed after it."—Benjamin Franklin   2. "Marry an archaeologist. The older you become, the lovelier he'll find you."—Agatha Christie   3. "Marrying for a second time is the triumph of hope over experience."—Samuel Johnson

THE ULTIMATE SPANISH 201

16 Family Relations and Careers

A

1. lleguen   2. te abroches   3. den   4. haya   5. sean
6. diga   7. se enferme   8. compartamos

B

1. vuelven   2. saques   3. haga   4. es   5. paguemos
6. estás   7. me quede   8. tiene   9. guste
10. pierdan

C

1. Pilar, es necesario que la saques.   2. Alonso, es importante que los tomes.   3. Andrés, es útil que lo traigas.   4. Silvia, insisto en que las aprendas de memoria.   5. Gilberto, es imprescindible que la hagas.   6. Flor, es preciso que empieces a escribirla.

D

1. Quiero (Deseo) salir.   2. Esperamos que sea aplicada.   3. Es necesario (Es preciso) tomar apuntes.   4. Es importante que lean mucho.
5. ¿Prefieres comprar los boletos en línea?
6. Será imprescindible que aprendamos todas las fechas.   7. ¡Quieren (Desean) divertirse mucho!
8. Es bueno que se gradúen este año.

E

1. Le aconsejo a Marta que beba mucha agua.
2. Les recomiendo a mis amigos que duerman ocho horas diarias.   3. Le propongo a Pablo que se ponga a dieta.   4. Le digo a Inés que tome vitaminas.
5. Le exijo a mi primo que pierda peso.   6. Les pido a mis papás que hagan ejercicio.   7. Le ruego a mi abuelito que deje de comer comida basura.
8. Insisto en que mis colegas se alimenten bien.

F

1. Papá, no creo que entiendas el problema.
2. Esperamos que Marta logre pescar un marido.
3. Es dudoso que Antonio y Victoria se quieran.
4. Blanca no cree que sus padres conozcan a su novio.   5. Es malo que los familiares no se lleven bien.   6. Los abuelos les dicen a sus nietos que los visiten.   7. Mario le exige a su cuñado que le devuelva el dinero.   8. Cristina insiste en que su suegro pague la boda.

G

1. Es que nosotros somos íntimos amigos.
2. No estoy seguro que ella vaya a la fiesta.
3. Es dudoso que haga buen tiempo mañana.
4. Es cierto que mis primos están de vacaciones.
5. No es evidente que la empresa tenga problemas económicos. 6. No es que tú y yo nos veamos todos los días. 7. Es evidente que Uds. no se ponen de acuerdo. 8. Estamos seguros que él puede diseñar el sitio web.

H

1. Se alegran de que nos quedemos con ellos.
2. Le sorprende que el museo esté cerrado.
3. Tenemos miedo de que gasten demasiado dinero.
4. Siento que te sientas mal. 5. Tememos que el avión no despegue ahora. 6. Les gusta que nos mantengamos en contacto con ellos.

I

1. Le pido a Juan que elabore el presupuesto.
2. Le exijo a Enrique que cree una base de datos.
3. Les digo a mis asistentes que trabajen en equipo.
4. Le mando a Nora que se dedique a los medios sociales. 5. Insisto en que Catalina se encargue de lanzar el nuevo producto. 6. Les digo a los asesores que resuelvan el problema del servicio al cliente.
7. Le aconsejo a Lorena que comience la campaña publicitaria. 8. Les propongo a mis colegas que realicen un plan de investigación global de mercado.

J

1. está 2. apoyemos 3. tienen 4. busques 5. son 6. juegue 7. rompa 8. tengan

K

1. La maestra nos dice que leamos el capítulo siete.
2. Le aconsejo que escriba el informe. / Le aconsejo escribir el informe. 3. Me recomiendan que traiga mi calculador de bolsillo. / Me recomiendan traer mi calculador de bolsillo. 4. Eduardo me dice que él y Lorenzo no se llevan bien. 5. Insisto en que dejes de fumar. 6. Les pido que vengan a nuestra casa. / Les pido venir a nuestra casa. 7. El jefe me exige que entregue el informe para el martes. / El jefe me exige entregar el informe para el martes.
8. Les propongo que asistan a la reunión. / Les propongo asistir a la reunión.

L

1. A sus papás les gusta que Leonor se haga actriz.
2. El abuelo se alegra de que Ramón siga la carrera de ingeniería. 3. La abuela prohíbe que su nieta salga con ese tipo. 4. Los tíos dejan que su hija vaya al extranjero para estudiar inglés. 5. Miguel le aconseja a su hermano que no se comprometa con Lola. 6. Los papás les dicen a sus hijos que sean corteses y amables. 7. Los cuñados hacen que sus hijos se inscriban en la universidad.
8. La familia Gómez espera que todos ellos logren tener salud, felicidad y éxito.

M

1. Es malo que Luisito no les haga caso a sus papás.
2. Es posible que Fernanda se haga arqueóloga.
3. La tía Sara quiere que Juan y Blanca hagan las paces de una vez. 4. Vámonos antes de que se haga tarde. 5. No me parece que esta blusa haga juego con la falda. 6. Le dicen a Arturo que deje de hacer el ridículo. 7. Te aconsejamos que hagas un alto.
8. Esperamos que Lorenzo Olivo haga el papel de Hamlet en esta producción.

N

1. Es bueno que Ud. ahorre dinero.
2. Es imprescindible que ellos se pongan el repelente contra mosquitos. 3. Es urgente que yo salga para el aeropuerto. 4. Es preciso que Uds. promocionen la marca. 5. Es mejor que tú juegues al tenis por la mañana. 6. Es importante que todos nosotros comamos granos integrales. 7. Urge que él vaya al médico. 8. Más vale que Ud. viaje en tren. 9. Hace falta que ella aprenda las fechas de memoria. 10. Es útil que yo actualice los datos.

O

1. Te aconsejo que te cuides mucho. 2. Quiero que salgas con nosotros al teatro. 3. Es necesario que te cortes el pelo. 4. Hace falta que apagues la computadora. 5. Es mejor que vengas a vernos hoy. 6. Insisto en que me hagas caso. 7. Más vale que tengas paciencia. 8. Me alegro de que te diviertas mucho. 9. Te recomiendo que te pruebes el abrigo azul marino. 10. Urge que te aproveches de las ofertas de enero.

P

1. Es poco probable que Pedro consiga el puesto.
2. Es imprescindible que apoyemos a nuestros amigos. 3. Quizás (Tal vez) estos estudiantes extranjeros sean de origen inglés. 4. Es una lástima que Lupe no encuentre sus aretes. 5. Laura y Sergio niegan que se divorcien. 6. Les he dicho a los niños que se laven las manos. 7. Más vale que hagas tu tarea ahora. 8. Es malo que no se pongan en contacto con nosotros más a menudo.

Q

1. Better late than never.   2. It's better to be alone than in bad company.   3. It's better to give than to receive.   4. A bird in the hand is worth two in the bush.   5. It's better to regret what you did rather than what you didn't do.   6. Prevention is better than cure.   7. Better the devil you know than the one you don't.   8. Health is better than wealth.

R

Answers will vary.

S

Answers will vary.

17 Family and Friends

A

1. Él lo oyó ladrando. / Él lo oyó ladrar.
2. Yo la observé cocinando. / Yo la observé cocinar.
3. Ellos las escucharon cantando. / Ellos las escucharon cantar.   4. Uds. los oyeron riendo. / Uds. los oyeron reír.   5. Nosotros los miramos actuando. / Nosotros los miramos actuar.   6. Tú la viste corriendo. / Tú la viste correr.   7. Ud. las observó sonriendo. / Ud. las observó sonreír.
8. Ella los escuchó gritando con alegría. / Ella los escuchó gritar con alegría.   9. Yo lo miré durmiendo. / Yo lo miré dormir.   10. Tú y yo la oímos estornudando. / Tú y yo la oímos estornudar.

B

1. Estamos paseando al perro.   2. Está corriendo el maratón.   3. Están discutiendo por nada.
4. Estoy leyendo una novela distópica.   5. ¿Estás probando la sopa de ajo?   6. Estoy saliendo de la oficina.   7. Está sintiendo muchas emociones.
8. Está envolviendo el regalo de cumpleaños.
9. Estamos abriendo una cuenta de ahorros.
10. ¿Están empezando a grabar la película?
11. Está lloviendo muy fuerte.   12. Estoy oyendo un ruido.

C

1. Yo estaba haciendo unos carritos de plastilina.
2. Uds. estaban saltando a la cuerda.   3. Carlitos estaba aprendiendo el alfabeto.   4. Tú estabas armando un rompecabezas.   5. Clarita estaba vistiendo a su oso de peluche.   6. Paquito y yo estábamos construyendo un castillo medieval de cubos.   7. Marisol estaba leyendo unos cuentos de hadas.   8. Todos nosotros estábamos jugando al escondite.

D

1. Yo estoy abriéndolos. / Yo los estoy abriendo.
2. ¿Uds. estaban esperándolo? / ¿Uds. lo estaban esperando?   3. Nosotros estamos sirviéndosela. /

Nosotros se la estamos sirviendo.   4. Ella estaba quejándose de todo. / Ella se estaba quejando de todo.   5. Yo estoy poniéndomela. / Yo me la estoy poniendo.   6. ¿Ud. estaba leyéndoselo? / ¿Ud. se lo estaba leyendo?   7. Ellos están tranquilizándose. / Ellos se están tranquilizando.   8. Tú estabas diciéndosela. / Tú se la estabas diciendo.   9. Él está probándoselos. / Él se los está probando.   10. Uds. estaban lavándoselas. / Uds. se las estaban lavando.

E

1. Estarán enfermándose.   2. José estará paseando al perro.   3. Luz estará planeando la fiesta de cumpleaños.   4. Estarán divirtiéndose mucho.
5. ¿En qué estarás pensando?   6. Estará durmiendo la siesta.   7. ¿Qué libros estará Ud. leyendo?
8. Ya estará lloviendo.   9. El equipo estará terminando el proyecto.   10. ¡Los chicos estarán volviéndose locos!

F

1. Sí, sigo leyéndolas. / Sí, las sigo leyendo.
2. Sí, sigue corriéndolo. / Sí, lo sigue corriendo.
3. Sí, seguimos pintándolas. / Sí, las seguimos pintando.   4. Sí, sigo enseñándola. / Sí, la sigo enseñando.   5. Sí, sigue ayudándolos. / Sí, los sigue ayudando.   6. Sí, siguen escribiéndolos. / Sí, los siguen escribiendo.   7. Sí, sigo resolviéndolos. / Sí, los sigo resolviendo.   8. Sí, seguimos tomándolas. / Sí, las seguimos tomando.

G

1. Llevamos cinco años viviendo en Panamá.
2. Lleva siete años trabajando de jefe de cocina.
3. Llevo cuatro meses haciéndolas.   4. Llevan una hora jugando al tenis.   5. Lleva dieciocho años dirigiéndola.   6. Llevo ocho meses cocinándolos.
7. Llevo tres días elaborándolo.   8. Llevamos cuarenta minutos imprimiéndolos.

H

1. Estaba nevando cuando llegamos.   2. Jorge sigue trabajando como un burro.   3. ¡Qué aguacero! Estoy mojándome (Me estoy mojando) hasta los huesos.   4. ¡Llevas dos horas probándote zapatos!   5. La niña va aprendiendo a contar.
6. ¿Siguen esperándonos?   7. Estos estudiantes van dominando el español.   8. ¿Qué estarán haciendo nuestros amigos?   9. Estarán asistiendo a un concierto.   10. Estábamos reuniéndonos para hablar del proyecto.

I

1. Mi hermano se ha encargado de crear invitaciones en línea.   2. Mis hermanas han hecho decoraciones con globos y manualidades.
3. Mi papá ha colgado la piñata.   4. Mi mamá

ha preparado una rica torta de chocolate.
5. Yo he pedido un deseo.   6. Yo he soplado las
velas.   7. Los invitados me han regalado unas cosas
muy bonitas.   8. ¡Todos nosotros nos hemos
divertido muchísimo!

J

1. Ya los ha leído.   2. Ya nos hemos reunido.
3. Ya la he visto.   4. Ya los han servido.   5. Ya me lo
he probado.   6. Ya se han matriculado.   7. Ya la he
abierto.   8. Ya nos hemos paseado.

K

1. ¿Es cierto que los recién casados habían vuelto de
la luna de miel?   2. ¿Es cierto que Mario se había
puesto en contacto contigo?   3. ¿Es cierto que nos
habíamos olvidado del cumpleaños del primo?
4. ¿Es cierto que Isabel había dejado plantado a su
novio de tres años?   5. ¿Es cierto que el pueblo
entero había huido del huracán?   6. ¿Es cierto que
tú te habías enterado de la fuga?   7. ¿Es cierto que
Uds. habían visto el estreno de la película?
8. ¿Es cierto que nadie les había dado la buena
noticia a Uds.?

L

1. Las cajas fueron llevadas a la buhardilla por mi
hermano.   2. El préstamo fue pedido por los
señores Ayala.   3. Las copias de seguridad fueron
hechas por estos asistentes.   4. Los entremeses
fueron preparados por la jefa de cocina.
5. Este cuadro fue pintado por un pintor francés.
6. Las chicas del colegio fueron invitadas por la
quinceañera.   7. La consultoría fue abierta por
Octavio y José.   8. La exposición interactiva fue
montada por aquellas directoras.

M

1. Se envían los paquetes.   2. Se buscaban
ingenieros.   3. Se preparó el arroz con pollo.
4. Se debe conocer el museo interactivo.
5. Se elaboró el presupuesto.   6. Se vivía bien en
esta ciudad.   7. Se tendrá que llegar para las nueve.
8. Se han abierto sucursales en el extranjero.
9. Se entra a la galería por aquella puerta.
10. No se podría trabajar los viernes.

N

1. A Marcelo se le perdió la bicicleta.   2. A la
señorita Ortiz se le quedaron los paquetes en el
coche.   3. A Ud. se le acabó la paciencia.
4. A ti se te rompieron las medias.   5. Al mesero
se le cayeron los platos.   6. A mis amigos se les
descompuso la videocámara.   7. A mí se me
ocurrió una idea genial.   8. Al beisbolista se le
quebró el meñique.   9. A nosotros se nos perdieron
las mochilas.   10. A Uds. se les olvidó la
contraseña.

O

1. No, que la organice la planeadora.   2. No, que
lo elabore nuestro colega.   3. No, que se la sirva
la mesera.   4. No, que la creen los analistas.
5. No, que se los envíe el secretario.   6. No, que lo
resuelvan los mediadores.   7. No, que lo empiece el
gerente.   8. No, que se los entreguen las abogadas.

P

1. Que llame a la policía entonces.   2. Que tome
unas aspirinas entonces.   3. Que siga una dieta más
sana entonces.   4. Que rompa el noviazgo entonces.
5. Que se ponga el suéter entonces.   6. Que pidan
un préstamo entonces.   7. Que abran el paraguas
entonces.   8. Que vaya de vacaciones entonces.

Q

1. Carmencita, ¡que no se te caiga ese vaso!
2. Luisito, ¡que no se te rompan los anteojos!
3. Cecilia, ¡que no se te acabe el papel!   4. Martín,
¡que no se te pierda la mochila!   5. Adelita, ¡que
no se te queden los mitones en la sala de clase!
6. Marco, ¡que no se te quiebre la pierna!
7. Miguelito, ¡que no se te ocurra decir tonterías!
8. Rita, ¡que no se te descompongan esos juguetes
electrónicos!

R

1. ¿Está escribiendo los informes?   2. No, ya los he
escrito. Ahora estoy leyéndolos (los estoy leyendo).
3. ¿Por qué te estabas fastidiando (estabas
fastidiándote)?   4. Es que Timoteo estaba haciendo
travesuras.   5. Vamos a cenar muy pronto. Que
Diego se lave las manos.   6. Lo vi lavándoselas.
(Lo vi lavárselas.) (Vi que se las lavaba.) ¡Que se
sirva la cena!   7. Está lloviendo a cántaros y no
tenemos (un) paraguas.   8. Estamos mojándonos
(Nos estamos mojando) hasta los huesos.
9. ¿Cómo se llama la empresa de arquitectura que
diseñó este edificio de apartamentos?   10. Fue
diseñado y construido por Serrano y Asociados.
11. ¡Qué pena! Se nos acabó el aceite de oliva.
12. Y a mí se me olvidó comprarlo.

S

Answers will vary.

T

Answers will vary.

U

Answers will vary.

V

1. "The happiest moments of my life have been the
few which I have spent at home in the bosom of
my family."—Thomas Jefferson   2. "Culture is
transmitted through the family and when this
institution stops working properly, the result is the

decline of the culture."—Mario Vargas Llosa
3. "When I was fourteen, my father was so ignorant I couldn't stand him. But when I got to be twenty-one, I was astonished at how much he had learned in seven years."—Mark Twain 4. "A true friend is someone who takes you by the hand and touches your heart."—Gabriel García Márquez 5. "There's no greater pleasure than finding an old friend, except for making a new one."—Rudyard Kipling

18 Education and Health

A
1. dijéramos 2. dirigiera 3. se hiciera 4. supieran
5. discutiera 6. tuvieran 7. pudiéramos
8. hubiera 9. estuviera 10. leyeras 11. siguieran
12. fuera 13. llegaran 14. nos reuniéramos
15. te probaras 16. se graduaran

B
1. Te pedí que vinieras a vernos más a menudo.
2. Sentíamos que el profesor de física renunciara a su puesto. 3. Se alegraron de que yo diera una conferencia. 4. Era probable que la empresa abriera otras sucursales. 5. ¿Les exigió que empezaran el proyecto esta semana? 6. Esperaba que Uds. se divirtieran mucho en la boda.
7. Le recomendaron que hiciera ejercicio para adelgazar. 8. Te dije que no te enojaras por cada cosa. 9. No nos gustaba que siguieran contando chismes. 10. Les aconsejó que tomaran las cosas con calma.

C
1. Ella esperaba que su hija siguiera sus pasos.
2. Le aconsejaron que se hiciera ingeniero.
3. Me alegré de matricularme en el programa de maestría. 4. ¿Ud. les pidió que actualizaran la base de datos? 5. Era bueno que Uds. solicitaran una beca. 6. Sus padres eran muy comprensivos.
7. ¿Es egresada de la facultad de derecho?
8. Era importante que viéramos el plan de estudios (el currículo). 9. Los egresados de la facultad de ingeniería encontraron buenos puestos después de graduarse. 10. Creemos que va a cursar la licenciatura en química.

D
1. A nuestros hijos les toca el chequeo de rutina.
2. No había vacuna para prevenir la influenza en mil novecientos dieciocho. 3. El doctor Jonas Salk desarrolló una vacuna para prevenir la poliomielitis. 4. Teníamos miedo de que el Covid-19 se propagara por todo el país.
5. Su médico de familia les dijo que no se preocuparan. 6. Los pacientes iban mejorándose.

7. La enfermera le tomó la tensión al paciente y le aplicó la vacuna contra la gripe (la influenza).
8. Era necesario que la médica pusiera a sus pacientes obesos a dieta. 9. El cardiólogo les aconsejó a sus pacientes que hicieran ejercicio y dejaran de fumar. 10. Aunque no tenía síntomas, era posible que fuera portadora del virus.

E
1. enfrente del cual, enfrente del que 2. en la cual, en la que 3. para los cuales, para los que (para quienes) 4. al otro lado del cual, al otro lado del que 5. en medio de la cual, en medio de la que 6. cerca de la cual, cerca de la que 7. a causa de los cuales, a causa de los que 8. según los cuales, según los que 9. después de las cuales, después de las que 10. durante el cual, durante el que

F
1. el río hacia el cual (el que) vamos 2. una enfermedad contra la cual (la que) necesitamos una vacuna 3. la fecha antes de la cual (la que) tenemos que pagar 4. los documentos sobre los cuales (los que) necesito más información
5. la escuela en frente de la cual (la que) hay una tienda de cómputo 6. un barrio en medio del cual (del que) hay un parque 7. un rascacielos encima del cual (del que) hay un restaurante 8. el museo de arte delante del cual (del que) hay dos estatuas

G
1. que sean serios y responsables 2. que tengan mucha experiencia 3. que quieran aprender
4. que se lleven bien con sus colegas 5. que no se quejen por cada cosa 6. que no pierdan el tiempo
7. que no lleguen tarde 8. que sean corteses

H
1. donde Uds. elijan 2. cuando Uds. digan
3. en el restaurante que les guste 4. lo que Uds. deseen 5. a la hora que Uds. quieran 6. con quien (quienes) Uds. prefieran

I
1. sin que nadie nos viera 2. sin que nadie nos preguntara nada 3. sin que nadie nos molestara
4. sin que nadie nos ayudara 5. sin que nadie nos buscara 6. sin que nadie se fijara en nosotros

J
1. con tal (de) que nos cuidemos 2. con tal (de) que usemos desinfectante 3. con tal (de) que evitemos lugares mal ventilados 4. con tal (de) que nos lavemos las manos a menudo 5. con tal (de) que mantengamos una distancia segura entre personas 6. con tal (de) que no nos toquemos la cara

K

1. recibamos   2. termines   3. contestaron
4. entreguen   5. ofrezcan   6. se sentaron   7. vio
8. se hicieron

L

1. para que aprendiera mucho   2. para que no se
aburriera   3. para que pudiera tomar cursos más
rigurosos   4. para que tuviera mejores profesores
5. para que le dieran más tarea   6. para que
estuviera motivado

M

1. Regina esperaba que sus hijos no se aburrieran
en la escuela.   2. Les dije que se quejaran al
director.   3. ¿Les aconsejó que presentaran la
solicitud en línea?   4. Estábamos seguros (de)
que Benjamín iba a asistir a esa escuela pública
subvencionada.   5. Les gustaría que viéramos
su sitio web.   6. Era importante que el nivel
académico fuera altísimo.   7. ¿Qué hicieron para
que su hija sacara buenas notas?   8. No dudábamos
que los padres querían lo mejor para sus hijos.

N

1. Lupe y Ricardo insistían en que sus hijos
asistieran a una escuela privada.   2. Tú le
recomendaste a tu amigo que siguiera una clase
de español en línea.   3. Era bueno que la profesora
de Lucía fuera un buen modelo a seguir.   4. Isabel
prefería que sus papás la educaran en casa.
5. Moisés y yo esperábamos que nuestro hijo
tomara clases de nivel superior.   6. Uds. dudaban
que a Ignacio le conviniera ese plan de estudios.
7. Yo me alegraba de que los estudiantes estuvieran
tan motivados.   8. Era necesario que la secundaria
ofreciera cursos de preparación universitaria.

O

Answers will vary.

P

Answers will vary.

Q

Answers will vary.

R

1. "The work of the teacher doesn't consist so much
in teaching everything that can be learned, as in
inspiring in the student a love and respect for
knowledge."—John Locke   2. "The problem isn't
that Johnny doesn't know how to read. The problem
isn't that Johnny can't think. The problem is that
Johnny doesn't know what it is to think; he confuses
it with feeling."—Thomas Sowell   3. "The future of
children is always today. Tomorrow will be too
late."—Gabriela Mistral   4. "A man can't be taught

anything; he can only be helped to find the answer
within himself."—Galileo Galilei   5. "I hope that
some day the practice of transmitting cowpox to
human beings will become widespread—when that
day arrives, there will no longer be smallpox."
—Edward Jenner   6. "The best doctors in the world
are Doctor Diet, Doctor Rest, and Doctor
Happiness (Cheerfulness)."—Jonathan Swift

19 Theater, Teleworking, and Shopping Online

A

1. Sus hermanas ya se habrán preparado para un
examen.   2. Nosotros ya habremos salido a ver una
obra de teatro.   3. Su mamá ya habrá visto su
telenovela favorita.   4. Tú ya habrás visitado con
los abuelos por videollamada.   5. Su papá ya habrá
teletrabajado con sus colegas.   6. Yo ya habré leído
un mamotreto.   7. Uds. ya habrán echado un
vistazo a unas tiendas virtuales.   8. Ud. ya habrá
disfrutado de happy hour con sus amigos.

B

1. El director ejecutivo habrá preparado el orden
del día.   2. El asistente administrativo les habrá
enviado el enlace a los empleados.   3. Nosotros
habremos decidido nuestra estrategia.
4. Tú habrás leído los documentos pertinentes.
5. Algunos empleados ya habrán hecho el login.
6. Los gerentes se habrán unido a la reunión.
7. Ud. les habrá dado la bienvenida a todos.
8. Yo habré abierto la sesión.

C

1. ¿Qué habrán hecho?   2. Creo que Ana habrá
comprado billetes.   3. Carlos y Raúl habrán asistido
a la junta en línea.   4. Para esa fecha, Felipe y
Susana habrán comenzado a trabajar de forma
remota. (Para esa fecha, Felipe y Susana habrán
comenzado a teletrabajar.)   5. Ya nos habremos
acostumbrado a tomar clases en línea.   6. Tú habrás
perdido una gran oportunidad.   7. Todos nosotros
habremos aprendido a usar la funcionalidad de
compartir pantalla.   8. Muchos teatros habrán
cerrado sus puertas.

D

1. darse prisa   2. Tengo muchas ganas de verlo.
3. un taxi sin pasajeros   4. persona que nos
indica los asientos   5. habrá terminado la obra
6. No tienes por qué preocuparte.   7. No te
preocupes.   8. Por eso no viaja.   9. No puedo
acostumbrarme al teletrabajo.   10. Es que tuve
un sueño intranquilo.

E

1. Carlos habría estudiado para el examen.
2. Yo no lo habría perdido.   3. Su esposa no se habría acostumbrado al teletrabajo.   4. Tú no lo habrías parado.   5. Nosotros lo habríamos paseado.
6. Sus hermanas la habrían visto.   7. Uds. no se los habrían regalado.   8. Yo habría ido a verla.

F

1. ¿Por qué le habría dado él tanto dinero a un revendedor?   2. Habríamos ido al partido contigo.
3. Me habría gustado ver el campeonato.
4. ¿A quién (quiénes) habrías invitado a la fiesta?
5. Yo habría invitado a todos nuestros amigos.
6. Ellos habrían estado más motivados.   7. ¿Quién lo habría creído?   8. Yo habría preferido ver una ópera.

G

1. ¿Qué hora será?   2. Serán las tres.   3. ¿Cuántos años tendrá Carlitos?   4. Tendrá nueve o diez años.
5. Lloverá ahora.   6. ¿Dónde estará mi paraguas?
7. ¿Qué hora sería?   8. Serían las ocho.
9. No contestaron el teléfono. ¿Dónde estarían?
10. Estarían fuera.   11. O estarían ocupados.
12. Tendrían mucho que hacer.

H

1. No habrán terminado su trabajo.   2. Habrán abierto las puertas del teatro.   3. Ya te habrán entregado la mercancía.   4. Diego se habrá comprado un maletín de herramientas.
5. Habrás encontrado el punto de retiro.
6. La devolución del artículo habrá sido fácil.
7. Los billetes habrán costado mucho dinero.
8. Te habrá sido difícil conseguir este trabajo.

I

1. Habrá estudiado mucho.   2. Los gerentes habrán retrasado la función.   3. Se habrán acostado.
4. Se le habrá perdido.   5. Se nos habrá acabado.
6. No habrá hecho la tarea.   7. Los estudiantes se habrán portado mal.   8. Habrán decidido quedarse en casa.

J

1. ¿En qué estará trabajando mi esposo?
2. ¿Qué estarán pensando mis padres?
3. ¿Con quiénes estarán jugando mis hijos?
4. ¿Por qué nos estará llamando la vecina?
5. ¿Por qué estará ladrando tanto el perro de los Huerta?   6. ¿Qué estarán construyendo en la esquina esos obreros?   7. ¿Por dónde estará trotando mi primo?   8. ¿Qué estarán viendo en línea los niños de al lado?

K

1. ¡Lo maravilloso de la comida es el postre!
2. ¡No vas a creer lo felices que somos!   3. Nosotros te habríamos dicho lo antes posible.   4. Lo de los medios sociales es vergonzoso.   5. Lo interesante del espectáculo es la música.   6. Él habría querido gastar lo menos posible.   7. Lo más emocionante del libro es el desenlace.   8. Habremos visto lo bueno, lo malo y lo feo de la situación.

L

1. No creemos que el abogado haya escrito los contratos.   2. Es importante que hayan conocido muchos países europeos.   3. No piensan que te hayas acostumbrado al teletrabajo.   4. Es una lástima que la directora de mercadeo haya perdido esta oportunidad.   5. Sienten que su equipo no haya ganado el campeonato.   6. Me alegro de que los estudiantes hayan estado más motivados.
7. Es mejor que hayas devuelto la mercancía que compraste en línea.   8. No les gusta que las entradas para el espectáculo hayan costado una fortuna.

M

1. Me alegro de que nos hayan invitado a ir al teatro con ellos.   2. Esperamos que la empresa de vanguardia lo haya contratado.   3. ¿Le sorprende que unos empleados hayan perdido la reunión?
4. ¿No hay nadie que haya oído lo que pasó?
5. Es posible que le haya comprado un maletín de herramientas a su hermano.   6. Es bueno que hayas ahorrado tres horas viajando a la oficina.
7. Siente que Uds. no hayan confiado en ella.
8. Dudan que hayamos perdido la fecha límite.

N

1. Ojalá (que) a Uds. les guste esta película india.
2. Ojalá (que) la hayan contratado como directora de mercadeo.   3. Ojalá (que) no te hayas perdido el concierto.   4. Ojalá (que) hayan expandido su mercado internacional.   5. Ojalá (que) nuestro equipo ganara el partido de fútbol.   6. Ojalá (que) la película estuviera doblada.   7. Ojalá (que) pudiéramos asistir al estreno de la obra.   8. Ojalá (que) su empresa de vanguardia tenga mucho éxito. (Ojalá (que) su empresa de vanguardia sea muy exitosa.)

O

Answers will vary.

P

Answers will vary.

Q

Answers will vary.

R

Answers will vary.

S

1. "I never did a day's work in my life. It was all fun."—Thomas Edison   2. "The compensation for work well done is the opportunity to do more work well done."—Jonas Salk   3. "Nobody can get to the top armed with talent alone. God gives talent; work transforms the talent into genius."—Anna Pavlova   4. "To start a business requires two things: innovate a great product and have a supportive team full of determination and enthusiasm."—Elon Musk   5. "Music can name the unnameable and communicate the unknowable."—Leonard Bernstein   6. "The theater cannot disappear because it is the only art where humanity confronts itself."—Arthur Miller   7. "Movies touch our heart, awaken our imagination, and change our way of seeing things. They transport us to other places. They open doors and our minds. Movies are the memories of our lives."—Martin Scorsese

20 The Economy and Politics

A

1. hubieran hecho   2. hubiera decidido
3. hubieran prestado   4. hubieran invitado
5. hubiéramos entendido   6. hubieras caminado
7. hubiera tratado   8. hubieran llegado

B

1. Teníamos miedo de que clausuraran el periódico. / *We were afraid that they would close down the newspaper.*   2. Esperaba que publicaran mi artículo. / *I hoped that they would publish my article.*   3. No creía que asistieran a la junta. / *I didn't think they would attend the meeting.*
4. Fue bueno que se organizara una protesta. / *It was good that people were organizing a protest.*
5. Te aconsejé que no tocaras ese tema. / *I advised you not to bring up that subject.*   6. Preferíamos que nos dejaran en paz. / *We preferred that they leave us alone.*   7. Los estudiantes temían que prohibieran la reunión. / *The students were afraid that they would ban the meeting.*   8. Nadie quería que perdiéramos la libertad de expresión. / *Nobody wanted us to lose our freedom of speech.*

C

1. Era posible que hubieran criticado al gobierno. / *It was possible that they had criticized the government.*   2. Temía que hubieran compartido estos artículos. / *I feared that they had shared these articles.*   3. Esperaba que no hubieras posteado nada ofensivo. / *I was hoping that you hadn't posted anything offensive.*   4. Era dudoso que ella hubiera leído ese periódico. / *It was doubtful that she had read that newspaper.*   5. Era bueno que hubiéramos puesto el periódico estudiantil en línea. / *It was good that we had put the student newspaper online.*
6. No me gustó que la administración hubiera tenido esta estrechez de miras. / *I didn't like that the administration had had this narrow-mindedness.*

D

1. a. No creo que él haga un viaje de negocios.
b. No creo que él haya hecho un viaje de negocios.
c. No creía que él hiciera un viaje de negocios.
d. No creía que él hubiera hecho un viaje de negocios.   2. a. Nos alegramos de que tú estudies música. b. Nos alegramos de que tú hayas estudiado música. c. Nos alegrábamos de que tú estudiaras música. d. Nos alegrábamos de que tú hubieras estudiado música.   3. a. Es probable que los estudiantes conozcan a este profesor. b. Es probable que los estudiantes hayan conocido a este profesor. c. Era probable que los estudiantes conocieran a este profesor. d. Era probable que los estudiantes hubieran conocido a este profesor.   4. a. Esperan que podamos terminar el artículo. b. Esperan que hayamos podido terminar el artículo. c. Esperaban que pudiéramos terminar el artículo. d. Esperaban que hubiéramos podido terminar el artículo.

E

1. Si ella tuviera un título universitario, conseguiría un buen trabajo.   2. Si la universidad respetara la libertad de prensa, los estudiantes no se organizarían.   3. Si el gobierno permitiera diferencias de opinión, nosotros no protestaríamos.
4. Si no postearas temas controvertidos, la administración no te criticaría.   5. Si ellos no compartieran artículos ofensivos en las redes sociales, el director no estaría enojado.   6. Si él no escribiera artículos de blog, no sabríamos lo que piensa.

F

1. Seguiremos como si no hubiera problema.
2. Él pregunta como si le interesara (tuviera interés).   3. No hagas como si no supieras.
4. ¿Por qué camina Ud. como si tuviera dolor?
5. Ellos contestaron como si no hubieran comprendido.   6. Parecía como si ella no se hubiera divertido.   7. Hagamos como si hoy fuera la última vez.   8. Uds. trabajan como si no quisieran terminar el proyecto.

G

1. Hay mucho que queda por hacer.
2. La ciudad tiene que tomar medidas importantes.
3. El desempleo está en aumento por todo el país.
4. Me parte el alma que tengamos que despedirlos.
5. Estamos al borde de un gran avance científico.
6. Me gusta leer los artículos de opinión y los artículos de invitado.   7. ¿Organizan una manifestación? ¿De qué se trata?
8. La Constitución de los Estados Unidos de América garantiza la libertad de prensa y la libertad de asociación.

H

1. hubieras dicho / habría asistido, hubieras dicho / hubiera asistido   2. hubiéramos leído / habríamos comprendido, hubiéramos leído / hubiéramos comprendido   3. habría conocido / hubiera pasado, hubiera conocido / hubiera pasado   4. se hubiera casado / habría tenido, se hubiera casado / hubiera tenido   5. Habría habido / se hubiera vuelto, Hubiera habido / se hubiera vuelto   6. hubiera avisado / habríamos podido, hubiera avisado / hubiéramos podido   7. habría estado / hubieran visitado, hubiera estado / hubieran visitado
8. habrías hecho / hubieran prohibido, hubieras hecho / hubieran prohibido

I

1. respetara   2. se habría disparado (se hubiera disparado)   3. asistirán   4. vivirá   5. hubiera subido   6. supieran   7. se habría convertido (se hubiera convertido)   8. quedaría

J

1. a. Si la ciudad no dicta órdenes de confinamiento, mucha gente se enfermará. b. Si la ciudad no dictara órdenes de confinamiento, mucha gente se enfermaría. c. Si la ciudad no hubiera dictado órdenes de confinamiento, mucha gente se habría (hubiera) enfermado.   2. a. Si el periódico no critica al gobierno, el gobierno no lo cerrará. b. Si el periódico no criticara al gobierno, el gobierno no lo cerraría. c. Si el periódico no hubiera criticado al gobierno, el gobierno no lo habría (hubiera) cerrado.   3. a. Si los precios no suben, no habrá una manifestación. b. Si los precios no subieran, no habría una manifestación. c. Si los precios no hubieran subido, no habría (hubiera) habido una manifestación.   4. a. Si compartes tu artículo en las redes sociales, mucha gente lo leerá. b. Si compartieras tu artículo en las redes sociales, mucha gente lo leería. c. Si hubieras compartido tu artículo en las redes sociales, mucha gente lo habría (hubiera) leído.   5. a. Si todos los restaurantes cierran, será un gran problema para la ciudad.

b. Si todos los restaurantes cerraran, sería un gran problema para la ciudad. c. Si todos los restaurantes hubieran cerrado, habría (hubiera) sido un gran problema para la ciudad.

K

1. Ojalá que sea una manifestación pacífica.
2. Ojalá tuviéramos más poder adquisitivo.
3. Ojalá él no hubiera tocado un tema tan controvertido.   4. Ojalá que todos los ciudadanos comprendan la importancia de la Constitución. (Ojalá que todos los ciudadanos comprendan lo importante que es la Constitución.)   5. Ojalá los chicos no hubieran pasado tanto tiempo en las redes sociales.   6. Ojalá que la profesora dictara una conferencia sobre la política económica.
7. Ojalá las escuelas no cierren por la epidemia.
8. Ojalá que Uds. hayan leído el periódico estudiantil.

L

1. Ojalá (Esperamos) que los conciertos fomenten el turismo.   2. Estos platos segovianos me abren (me están abriendo) el apetito.   3. ¡Esta ciudad es un sueño hecho realidad!   4. Si ellos hubieran hecho un viaje a España, habrían (hubieran) conocido Segovia.   5. Hagamos un brindis (Vamos a hacer un brindis) con este vino tinto de la región.
6. Ojalá hubieras pasado por lo menos un mes en España.   7. Es asombroso que los romanos hayan construido el acueducto sin usar argamasa.
8. Si no hubiera tráfico denso y música a todo volumen, habría (hubiera) menos contaminación medioambiental.

M

Answers will vary.

N

Answers will vary.

O

Answers will vary.

P

Answers will vary.

Q

1. "When governments fear the people, there is liberty. When the people fear the government, there is tyranny."—Thomas Jefferson   2. "Politics is almost as exciting as war, and no less dangerous. In war you can only be killed once, but in politics many times."—Winston Churchill   3. "What amazes me most about the United States isn't so much the impressive size of some businesses as the impressive number of small businesses."—Alexis de Tocqueville   4. "The democratic health of a country

can be measured by evaluating the diversity of opinion, freedom of speech, and the critical spirit of its various media."—Mario Vargas Llosa
5. "In times of universal deceit, telling the truth becomes a revolutionary act."—George Orwell
6. "Many people want the government to protect the consumer. A much more urgent problem is to protect the consumer from the government."—Milton Friedman

21 Building Spanish Vocabulary

A
1. jugar 2. ayudar 3. ensayar 4. emplear
5. aconsejar 6. gobernar 7. caminar 8. dañar
9. volver 10. desarrollar 11. firmar 12. apoyar

B
1. beber 2. contener 3. parar 4. oír 5. partir
6. subir 7. correr 8. herir 9. medir 10. cuidar
11. bajar 12. cruzar

C
1. inspirar 2. computar 3. vacunar 4. decidir
5. televisar 6. funcionar 7. describir
8. modernizar 9. revisar 10. erosionar
11. profesar 12. construir

D
1. resonar 2. perseverar 3. estar 4. sugerir
5. convivir 6. influir 7. referir 8. ignorar
9. conferenciar 10. depender

E
1. agradecer 2. conocer 3. pensar 4. estacionar
5. crecer 6. tratar 7. entender 8. sentir
9. descubrir 10. envejecer

F
1. el paseo 2. el boxeo 3. el empleo 4. el bloqueo
5. el zapateo 6. el bombardeo 7. el escaneo
8. el formateo 9. el fildeo 10. el bateo

G
1. la sopa / *soup bowl* OR *soup tureen*
2. la moneda / *change purse* 3. el perro / *doghouse*
4. la sal / *saltshaker* 5. el pájaro / *birdhouse*
6. el pez / *fishbowl* 7. la llave / *key ring*
8. el billete / *wallet* 9. la arena / *sandbox*
10. el papel / *wastebasket*

H
1. existir 2. dormir 3. fascinar 4. atraer 5. reír
6. creer 7. contribuir 8. nacer 9. correr
10. seguir 11. brillar 12. pertenecer

I
1. olvidadizo 2. asustadizo 3. movediza
4. enamoradizo 5. quebradizas 6. enojadiza

J
1. levadizo 2. desmoronadiza 3. pegadiza
4. corrediza 5. llovediza 6. anegadizo
7. mudadiza 8. huidizo 9. plegadiza

K
1. destrozón 2. mandona 3. contestón 4. abusón
5. preguntona 6. gritón

L
1. bailón 2. peleón 3. regañón 4. juguetona
5. saltón 6. refunfuñona 7. gruñón 8. llorona
9. mandona 10. adulón 11. dormilón
12. respondón

M
1. la palidez 2. la sencillez 3. la naturaleza
4. la timidez 5. la certeza 6. la escasez
7. la franqueza 8. la lindeza 9. la riqueza
10. la vejez 11. la estupidez 12. la sutileza

N
1. mañanero 2. llevadera 3. pasajero
4. azucarera 5. traicionero 6. petroleras
7. banquera 8. ranchera 9. playero 10. bananeras
11. callejeros 12. faldero

O
1. el zapato / *shoemaker* 2. la carne / *butcher*
3. el coche / *driver* 4. la oveja / *sheepdog, shepherd*
5. la costura / *dressmaker* 6. la verdura / *vegetable seller* 7. el camión / *truck driver* 8. la niña / *babysitter, nanny* 9. el mensaje / *messenger*
10. el libro / *bookseller* 11. el banco / *banker*
12. el hotel / *hotel manager*

P
1. a border town 2. a girl with copper-colored hair
3. a sad, gray sky 4. the baby is wearing a onesie
5. pure, untainted prose 6. limestone

Q
1. enfermizo 2. primerizo 3. postizo 4. pajizo
5. rojizo

R
1. el rompecabezas 2. el lavadientes
3. el rompeolas 4. el limpiapipas
5. el cuentakilómetros 6. el espantapájaros
7. el quitanieves 8. el lavacoches 9. el salvavidas
10. el guardarropas 11. el escurreplatos
12. el paraguas 13. el parabrisas
14. el sacacorchos 15. el abrecartas
16. el pararrayos 17. el portaviones
18. el sacapuntas 19. el parachoques
20. el paracaídas

S

1. el banano   2. el naranjo   3. la ciruela
4. el avellano   5. el canelo   6. la castaña
7. la almendra   8. el cerezo   9. la frambuesa
10. el granado

T

1. el higueral   2. el naranjal   3. el cerezal
4. el bananal   5. el duraznal   6. el manzanar
7. el olivar   8. el limonar

U

Answers will vary.

Glossary

The Spanish-English glossary includes the vocabulary used in the text. Numbers after glossary entries refer to the chapter in which the item first appears. Gender is indicated by the definite articles **el, la, los, las**. The following abbreviations are also used.

adj.	adjective	*i.o.*	indirect object	*pl.*	plural
d.o.	direct object	*irreg.*	irregular verb	*p.p.*	past participle
fem.	feminine	*lit.*	literally	*rev. constr.*	reverse construction verb
inf.	infinitive	*masc.*	masculine	*sing.*	singular

Verbs like **ir**, marked "**ir** (*irreg.*)", have multiple irregularities and should be checked in the Verb Charts. Verbs with an irregularity only in the **yo** form of the present tense are marked as in "**conocer** (**yo conozco**)." Remember that irregularities in the **yo** form also appear in the subjunctive.

Verbs with changes in the vowel of the stem are marked as follows: **pensar** (**e > ie**), **volver** (**o > ue**), **pedir** (**e > i**).

Verbs with spelling changes are marked as follows: **buscar** (**c > qu/e**), **llegar** (**g > gu/e**), **abrazar** (**z > c/e**), **escoger** (**g > j/o, a**).

Verbs with both changes in the vowel of the stem and spelling changes are marked as follows: **comenzar** (**e > ie, z > c/e**), **seguir** (**e > i, gu > g/o, a**).

a fin de que *so that* 18
la abeja *bee* 11
abierto *open* 4
el abogado, la abogada *lawyer* 3
abonarse *to subscribe* 19
abrazar (z > c/e) *to hug* 8
el abrigo *overcoat* 2; *coat* 4
abril *April* 5
abrir *to open* 6
abrocharse *to buckle/fasten* 9
 abrocharse el cinturón de seguridad *to fasten one's seatbelt* 9
la abuela *grandmother* 4
el abuelo *grandfather* 4
aburrido *bored, boring* 4
aburrir *to bore (someone)* 8
aburrirse *to get bored, be bored* 8
el abuso *abuse* 12
 abuso de drogas *drug abuse* 12
acá *here* 17
acabar *to finish* 6
 acabar de + *inf.* *to have just (done something)* 6
acabársele a uno *to run out of* 11
académico *academic* 18
acampar *to camp, go camping* 11
acaso *maybe, perhaps* 13
acatarrado *sick with a cold* 4
acatarrarse *to catch a cold* 8
el accidente *accident* 11
el aceite *oil* 1
 aceite de oliva *olive oil* 3
 los aceites de baño *bath oils* 8
la aceituna *olive* 3
la acera *sidewalk* 20

acercarse (a) (c > qu/e) *to come/go closer, approach* 8
el acomodador, la acomodadora *usher* 19
acomodarse *to get comfortable, settle in* 9
acompañar *to accompany, go with* 11
el acondicionador *conditioner* 8
aconsejar *to advise* 16
el acontecimiento *event* 16
acordar (o > ue) en *to agree on* 17
acordarse (de) (o > ue) *to remember* 8
acostado *lying down* 4
acostarse (o > ue) *to go to bed* 8
acostumbrarse a *to get used to* 18
la actitud *attitude* 15
actual *current* 20
actualizar (z > c/e) *to update* 9
actualmente *at present, currently* 13
el acueducto *aqueduct* 20
adaptarse a *to adapt to* 19
adelgazar (z > c/e) *to get thin* 11
además *besides, in addition* 6
adentrarse en *to go into* 18
adiós *goodbye* 1
la administración de empresas *business administration* 2
el administrador, la administradora de bases de datos *database administrator* 3
la admisión *admission* 18
admitir *to admit* 18
adorable *cute, adorable* 11
la aduana *customs* 9
el aduanero *customs inspector* 9
el aeropuerto *airport* 9
afeitarse *to shave* 8
afortunadamente *fortunately* 11

afortunado *fortunate, lucky* 19
afuera *outside* 20
la agenda electrónica *electronic appointment book* 1
el/la agente *agent* 3
agosto *August* 5
agotado *exhausted, wiped out* 9
agotador *exhausting* 9
agotarse *to sell out* 19
agradable *nice, pleasant* 9
el agricultor *farmer* 10
el agua (*fem.*) *water* 3
   agua de colonia *cologne* 8
   agua mineral *mineral water* 3
el aguacate *avocado* 3
el aguacero *downpour* 11
el aguafiestas *wet blanket, party pooper* 8
ahora *now* 4
   ahora mismo *right now* 5
ahorrar *to save* 5
el aire *air* 1
   en el aire *in the air, airborne* 9
el aire acondicionado *air conditioning* 7
el ajetreo *hustle and bustle* 13
el ajo *garlic* 15
al (*contraction*) *to the* 5
   al contrario *on the contrary* 11
   al fondo de *at the back of* 4
   al lado (de) *next to* 4
   al + *inf.* *upon, when* 8
la alarma *alarm* 9
   falsa alarma *false alarm* 11
la albóndiga *meatball* 3
el alcázar *fortress, royal palace* 20
el álgebra *algebra* 18
alegrarse (de) *to be glad, be happy* 8
alegre *cheerful* 4
alejarse (de) *to move away (from)* 8
la alergia *allergy* 11
algo *something* 5
el algodón *cotton* 4
alguien *someone, anyone* 5
alguno, alguna, algunos, algunas *some* 2
la alimentación *food, groceries, foodstuffs* 19
alimentarse *to feed oneself, eat* 8
el alimento *food* 3
los alimentos frescos *fresh food* 3
el alivio *relief* 17
la almohada *pillow* 14
almorzar (o > ue, z > c/e) *to have lunch* 8
el almuerzo *lunch* 5
   tomar el almuerzo *to have lunch* 5
alquilar *to rent* 5
alterado *upset, unnerved* 11
alto *tall* 4; *high* 11
el alza (*fem.*) *rise* 20
amable *kind* 4
amarillo *yellow* 2
ambicioso *ambitious* 12
ambos, ambas *both* 2
la ambulancia *ambulance* 11
el amigo, la amiga *friend* 2
amplio *spacious* 12
el análisis *analysis* 1
   análisis de sangre *blood test* 11
el/la analista *analyst* 3
   analista de seguridad de (la) información
      information security analyst 3

analizar (z > c/e) *to analyze* 13
la anarquía *anarchy* 20
anaranjado *orange* 2
anda (< andar) *come on* 6
el anfitrión, la anfitriona *host* 3
angustiado *distressed* 4
el anillo *ring* 15
   anillo de boda *wedding ring* 15
animado *lively, busy, bustling* 2; *inspired* 19
el animal *animal* 1
animar(se) *to cheer up, feel like doing something* 8
ánimo *cheer up, come on* 17
el ánimo *spirit, encouragement* 17
el aniversario *anniversary* 15
anoche *last night* 9
anteayer *the day before yesterday* 9
los anteojos *eyeglasses* 17
anterior *previous* 12
antes (de) *before* 8
   lo antes posible *as soon as possible* 8
el antibiótico *antibiotic* 11
anticuado *old-fashioned, outdated, antiquated* 18
antiguo *former* 12
antipático *unpleasant* 4
anunciar *to announce* 15
el anuncio *announcement* 7
añadir *to add* 14
el año *year* 6
   el Año Nuevo *New Year's* 15
   el año próximo *next year* 8
   el año que viene *next year* 6
apagar (g > gu/e) *to shut off (appliance)* 9
aparcar (c > qu/e) *to park* 14
el apartamento *apartment* 2
   apartamento de lujo *luxury apartment* 13
apenas *hardly, barely* 13
aplicado *studious* 16
aplicar *to apply, give (an injection)* 18
apoyar *to support* 16
el/la app *app* 18
aprender *to learn* 6
   aprender de memoria *to learn by heart* 16
apresurarse (de) *to hurry* 8
aprovechar *to take advantage of* 6
aquel, aquella, aquellos, aquellas *that, those* 3
aquí *here* 1
el arco *arch* 20
el arete *earring* 1
el armario *closet* 1
el arquitecto *architect* 4
el arquitecto, la arquitecta de red *computer network
      architect* 3
arreglarse *to get ready (clothing, hair)* 8
arrepentirse (e > ie) (de) *to regret (something)* 8
arriba *above, upstairs, overhead* 9
arrogante *arrogant* 4
arrojar *to throw* 20
el arroz *rice* 3
   arroz con pollo *chicken with rice* 3
el arte *art* 1
el artículo *article* 2
   artículo de opinión *opinion piece* 20
el/la artista *artist, performing artist* 3
asado *roasted* 20
el asalto *mugging* 20
el ascensor *elevator* 11
asegurar *to assure* 13

el aseo personal *personal grooming* 8
el asesinato *murder* 20
el asesor, la asesora *consultant* 3
    asesor financiero, asesora financiera *financial advisor* 3
el asiento *seat* 9
    asiento de pasillo *aisle seat* 9
    asiento de ventana *window seat* 9
la asignatura *subject (school), course* 12
    asignatura obligatoria *required course, requirement* 12
    asignatura optativa *elective (course)* 12
el asistente médico, la asistente médica *physician assistant* 3
    asistir a *to attend* 6
    asombroso *amazing* 4
el aspecto negativo *disadvantage, negative aspect* 19
la aspiradora *vacuum cleaner* 17
la aspirina *aspirin* 11
el/la astronauta *astronaut* 18
el asunto *matter* 17
    asustado *scared* 4
    asustar *to frighten/scare (someone)* 8
    asustarse *to get frightened/scared* 8
el atajo *shortcut* 9
    atender (e > ie) *to tend to, look after* 11
    atento *considerate* 4
el aterrizaje *landing (airplane)* 9
    aterrizar (z > c/e) *to land (airplane)* 9
el/la atleta *athlete* 3
el atraco *holdup* 11; *mugging* 20
    atractivo *attractive* 12
    atrapar *to catch* 11
    atrasado *late, behind schedule* 4
    atreverse a *to dare to* 13
    atropellar *to run over* 11
el atún *tuna* 3
los audífonos *hearing aids* 17
    aumentar *to gain* 11; *to increase* 13
    aumentar de peso *to gain weight* 11
el aumento *increase* 20
    aún más *even more* 12
    aun si *even if* 19
los auriculares *earphones, headset* 9
    auténtico *authentic* 3
el autobús *bus* 5
el automóvil *car* 1
la autopista *turnpike* 4
el autor, la autora *author* 12
el auxiliar / la auxiliar de vuelo *flight attendant* 9
el ave *bird, chicken* 3
la avenida *avenue* 2
las aves *poultry* 3
el avión *airplane* 5
    ayer *yesterday* 9
    ayudar *to help* 5
el ayuntamiento *city hall* 20
el azúcar *sugar* 3
    azul *blue* 2

    bailar *to dance* 5
el bailarín, la bailarina *dancer* 3
el baile *dance* 4
    bajar *to go down* 6; *to decrease, diminish* 20
    bajar de peso *to lose weight* 11
    bajar del avión *to get off the airplane* 9
el balón de fútbol *soccer ball* 17

el baloncesto *basketball* 6
    jugar al baloncesto *to play basketball* 6
    bañar(se) *to bathe, take a bath* 8
el banco *bank* 1
la banda *band* 5
el baño *bath* 8
el bar *bar* 1
    barato *inexpensive, cheap* 2
la barbaridad *outrageousness* 13
el barco *boat* 5
el barrio *neighborhood* 2
    barrio bajo *poor neighborhood* 13
la base *base* 1
    base de datos *database* 1
    bastante, bastantes *quite a lot of* (Spanish America); *enough* (Spain) 2
    bastar *to be enough* 20
la basura *garbage* 12
la batata *sweet potato* 3
el batido de fruta *fruit shake* 3
la batidora eléctrica *electric mixer* 17
    batir *to beat* 14
el bautizo *baptism* 13
el bebé *baby* 13
    beber *to drink* 6
la bebida *beverage* 3
    bebida sin alcohol *nonalcoholic beverage* 3
la beca *scholarship* 10
el béisbol *baseball* 6
    jugar al béisbol *to play baseball* 6
las bellas artes *fine arts* 16
    la facultad de bellas artes *School of Fine Arts* 16
la belleza *beauty* 8
    besar *to kiss* 8
la biblioteca *library* 4
la bicicleta *bicycle* 5
    montar en bicicleta *to take a bicycle ride* 5
    bien *well* 4
el billete *ticket, bill (currency)* 1
el billetero *wallet* 1
la biología *biology* 12
el bistec, el biftec *steak* 3
    blanco *white* 2
el bluejean *jeans* 4
la blusa *blouse* 4
la boda *wedding* 4
el boleto *ticket* 9
el bolígrafo *ballpoint pen* 12
la bolsa *bag* 1
el bolso *handbag* 1
el bombero, la bombera *firefighter* 11
la bondad *goodness* 14
    bonito *pretty* 2
el borde *edge* 20
    bordo: a bordo *on board* 9
el bosque nacional *national forest* 5
la botella *bottle* 5
    botella de vino *bottle of wine* 5
el botón (los botones) *button* 17
el brazo *arm* 9
el bricolaje *do-it-yourself (DIY)* 19
el brindis *toast* 15
la broma *joke* 20
    bromear *to joke* 20
    bronceado *tan, suntanned* 14
el bronceador *suntan lotion* 8
    bueno *good* 2

la bufanda *scarf* 4
el bufete *lawyer's office* 5
buscar (c > qu/e) *to look for, seek* 9
el buzón *mailbox, inbox* 10

el caballo *horse* 5
    montar a caballo *to go horseback riding* 5
el cabello *hair* 8
caber (*irreg.*) *to fit* 7
la cabeza *head* 8
la cabra *goat* 10
el cacto *cactus* 9
caer (*irreg.*) *to fall* 7
    caerle a uno (*rev. constr.*) *to like/dislike* (*usually a person*) 9
    caérsele a uno *to drop* 11
el café *café* 1; *coffee* 3
el cafetal *coffee plantation* 10
la cafetera *coffee pot* 13
la caja *box* 1
el cajero automático *ATM* 11
calculador *calculating* 12
la calculadora de bolsillo *pocket calculator* 16
calcular *to calculate* 15
la calefacción *heat* 7
calentar (e > ie) *to heat* 14
la calle *street* 1
calmar(se) *to calm down* 8
la cama *bed* 9
la cámara *camera* 1
cambiar *to change* 9
    cambiar de idea *to change one's mind* 11
caminar *to walk* 5
el camino *path* 9; *way, road* 17
la camisa *shirt* 2
la camiseta *T-shirt* 2
campestre *rural, country* 10
el camping *camping* 5
    hacer camping *to go camping* 5
el campo *field* 4; *country, countryside* 17
    campo de fútbol *soccer field* 4
    campo de fútbol americano *football field* 5
la cancha *field, court* 5
    cancha de baloncesto *basketball court* 5
    cancha de tenis *tennis court* 5
la canción *song* 7
candente *hot/hot-button* 20
cansado *tired* 4
el/la cantante *singer* 3
cantar *to sing* 5
el cántaro *pitcher, jug* 17
la cantidad *quantity* 7
    una cantidad de *a lot of* 7
    una gran cantidad de *a large amount/number of* 10
la capital *capital (city)* 3
el capítulo *chapter* 16
caprichoso *unpredictable* 12
la cara *face* 8
¡caramba! *oh no!, my goodness!* 4
el cardiólogo, la cardióloga *cardiologist* 18
cargar (g > gu/e) *to upload* 5
el cariño *love, affection* 17
    cariño *honey* (term of endearment) 17
    cariñoso *loving, affectionate* 10
la carne *meat* 3
la carne de res, la carne de vaca *beef* 3

la carne roja *red meat* 3
el carnicero, la carnicera *butcher* 3
caro *expensive* 2
la carpeta *folder* 1
el carpintero, la carpintera *carpenter* 3
la carretera *highway, road* 4
el carro *car* 1
la carta *menu* 3
el cartapacio *briefcase* 1
la cartera *wallet; handbag* 1
el cartucho de tinta *ink cartridge* 12
la casa *house* 1
    en casa *at home* 5
    casado (con) *married (to)* 4
    casarse (con) *to get married (to)* 8
    cascarrabias *cantankerous* 12
castigar *to punish* 20
el catarro *cold (health)* 11
la catedral *cathedral* 1
la categoría *category, line of merchandise* 19
católico *Catholic* 4
la cazuela *pot* 13
el CD (cedé) *CD* 1
la cebolla *onion* 3
celebrar *to celebrate* 5
el celular *cell phone* 9
el cementerio *cemetery* 13
cenar *to have dinner* 5
la censura *censorship* 20
el centro *downtown* 1
el centro comercial *shopping center, mall* 1
cepillar(se) *to brush* 8
    cepillarse el pelo / los dientes *to brush one's hair/teeth* 8
el cepillo de dientes *toothbrush* 8
el cepillo para el pelo *hairbrush* 8
cerca (de) *near* 4
el cerdo *pork* 3
la cereza *cherry* 3
cerrado *closed* 4
cerrar (e > ie) *to close* 6
la cerveza *beer* 3
la champaña *champagne* 15
el champú *shampoo* 8
la chaqueta *jacket* 4
chequear *to check* 15
el chequeo *checkup* 11
la chequera *checkbook* 17
la chica *girl* 4
el chico *boy, kid* 4
chiquito *small* 2
el chisme *gossip* 13
chocar (c > qu/e) *to crash* 11
el chocolate *chocolate* 3
    chocolate caliente *hot chocolate* 3
el colesterol *cholesterol* 11
el choque *crash* 11
    choque de carros *car crash* 11
el cibercafé *internet café* 1
el científico, la científica *scientist* 3
cierto *certain* 2
la cifra *figure* 17
el cine *movie theater* 1
el cirujano, la cirujana *surgeon* 18
la cita *appointment* 11
    tener cita con el médico *to have a doctor's appointment* 11

la ciudad *city* 1
la civilización *civilization* 10
el clarinete *clarinet* 5
claro *bright, light* 2; *of course* 1
claro que sí *of course* 1
la clase *class* 1
clase a distancia *internet course* 6
clausurar *to close down* 20
el clavo *nail* 19
el/la cliente *customer* 19
el clima *climate* 1
la clínica *clinic* 18
el club *club* 5
club de jazz *jazz club* 4
el coche *car* 1
la cocina *kitchen; cuisine* 6
cocinar *to cook* 5
el cocinero, la cocinera *cook, chef* 3
el cóctel *cocktail party* 17
la codicia *greed* 20
coger (g > j/o, a) *to take, grab* 9
el colaborador, la colaboradora *co-worker, contributor* 20
el/la colega *colleague* 15
el colegio *high school* 4
colocar (c > qu/e) *to place, put* 9
colocarse (c > qu/e) *to get a job/position* 8
la comedia *comedy* 19
comenzar (i > ie, z > c/e) *to begin* 6
comenzar a + *inf. to begin to (do something)* 6
comer *to eat* 6
comer como un pajarito *to eat like a little bird* 11
comercial *commercial* 2
la comida *food, meal* 3; *dinner* 4
comida basura *junk food* 8
comida orgánica *organic food* 3
comida rápida/chatarra *fast food, junk food* 3
comida vegetariana *vegetarian food* 3
comilón (< comer) *big eater, gluttonous* 11
la comisaría de policía *police station* 15
como *as, like* 6
como de costumbre *as usual* 4
cómo no *of course* 4
¿cómo? *how?, what?* 1
cómodo *comfortable* 1
el compañero, la compañera *friend* 11
compañero de clase *classmate* 11
la compañía *company* 4
el compartimiento de arriba *overhead compartment* 9
compartir *to share* 6
compensar *to make up for* 19
completamente *completely* 2
complicado *complicated* 19
componer (*irreg.*) *to compose* 11
la composición *composition* 12
la compra *purchase* 19
el comprador, la compradora *shopper* 6
comprar *to buy* 5
comprender *to understand* 6
comprensivo *understanding* 12
comprometerse *to get engaged* 8
el compromiso *date, appointment* 16
compulsivo *compulsive* 6
la computación *computer science* 2
la computadora *computer* 1
el cómputo *computation* 1
la tienda de cómputo *computer store* 1

con *with* 3
con tal (de) que + *subjunctive provided that + verb* 18
el concierto *concert* 4
condición: a condición de que *on condition that* 18
el condominio *condominium* 2
conducir (*irreg.*) *to drive* 9
la conferencia *lecture* 4
la confianza *confidence* 20
confiar en *to trust in* 19
el confinamiento *lockdown, confinement* 20
confundido *confused* 17
conmigo *with me* 6
conocer (yo conozco) *to know* 6
el conocimiento *knowledge* 17
conseguir (e > i) *to get* 9
el consejo *piece of advice* 7
dar consejos *to give advice* 7
considerado *considerate* 12
la constitución *constitution* 20
construir *to build* 10
la consulta *doctor's office* 18
el consultor, la consultora *consultant* 17
la consultoría *consulting firm, consultancy* 17
la contabilidad *accounting* 2
el contador, la contadora *accountant* 3
la contaminación del ambiente *environmental pollution* 12
contaminado *polluted* 12
contar (o > ue) *to tell, relate, narrate* 6; contar (o > ue) (con) *to count (on)* 6
contento *happy* 4
contestar *to answer* 13
contigo *with you* 6
contratar *to hire* 19
el contrato *contract* 2
el control de seguridad *security (check)* 9
controvertido *controversial* 20
convencer (yo convenzo) *to convince* 19
convenirle a uno (*rev. constr.*) *to be good/suitable for someone* 9
convertir (e > ie, e > i) *to convert* 13
convertirse (en) *to become* 13
la copa *glass, goblet, drink* 19
coqueta *flirtatious* 12
el corazón *heart* 18
la corbata *necktie* 4
el cordero *lamb* 3
el coronavirus *coronavirus* 18
el correo *mail* 6
correo electrónico *email* 4
cortar *to cut* 8
cortarse el pelo *to cut one's hair* 8
el cortaúñas *nail clippers* 8
cortés *polite* 12
corto *short* 2
la cosa *thing* 8
por cualquier cosa *for every little thing* 8
coser *to sew* 6
la costa *coast, seashore* 6
costar (o > ue) *to cost* 10
costoso *costly, expensive* 13
la costumbre *custom* 15
como de costumbre *as usual* 15
crecer (yo crezco) *to grow* 13
creer *to believe, think* 6

la crema de afeitar *shaving cream* 8
la crema hidratante *moisturizing cream* 8
el crimen *crime* 12
la crisis *crisis* 1
criticar *to criticize* 20
cruzar (z > c/e) *to cross* 14
el cuaderno *notebook* 12
la cuadra *(city) block* 4
  a una cuadra de *one block from* 4
el cuadro *painting, picture* 5
¿cuál? ¿cuáles? *which (one)?, which ones?* 4
cualquiera *any* 2
¿cuánto? ¿cuánta? *how much?* 2
¿cuántos? ¿cuántas? *how many?* 1
el cuarto *room* 1
  cuarto de baño *bathroom* 12
la cuchara *spoon* 13
la cucharita *teaspoon* 13
el cuchillo *knife* 13
el cuello *neck* 11
el cuidado *care* 8
  con cuidado *carefully* 8
  cuidado personal *personal care* 8
  cuidadosamente *carefully* 8
  cuidarse *to take care of oneself* 8
cultivar *to grow, raise* 10
el cumpleaños *birthday* 5
  cumplir *to be/turn ___ years old* 15
  cumplir con *to meet (as a deadline)* 15
la cuñada *sister-in-law* 4
el cuñado *brother-in-law* 4
el cura *priest* 17
la curiosidad *curiosity* 18
el currículo *curriculum* 18
cursar *to take a course, study* 12
cursi *tacky, tasteless* 17
el curso *course (of study)* 12
cuyo *whose* (relative pronoun) 20

la dama de honor *bridesmaid* 17
dañar *to damage, harm* 14
dar *(irreg.)* *to give* 7
  dar a luz *to give birth* 11
  dar consejos *to give advice* 7
  dar pena *to make (someone) feel sad/sorry* 17
  dar el pésame *to express one's sympathy/condolences* 13
  darse prisa *to hurry, be in a hurry* 8
los datos *data* 1
de *of, from* 2
  de nada *you're welcome* 1
  ¿de qué parte? *where?, from which part?* 3
  de repente *suddenly* 11
  de todas formas *anyway* 7
  de vanguardia *leading-edge, innovative* 19
  de veras *really* 3
debajo de *under* 4
deber *should, ought to, must* 6
el deber *duty* 18
debido a *due to* 20
decepcionado *disappointed* 12
decir *(irreg.)* *to say, tell* 7
  ¿cómo se dice? *how do you say?* 7
  decir que sí/no *to say yes/no* 7
dedicarse a *to devote oneself to* 18
el dedo *finger* 11
definitivamente *for good, permanently* 20

dejar *to leave, let* 8
  dejar de + *inf.* *to stop (doing something)* 8
del *(contraction)* *of/from the* 2
delante de *in front of* 4
deletrear *to spell* 10
delgado *thin* 4
delicioso *delicious* 3
el delito *crime* 20
demasiado *too much* 5
denso *dense* 20
el/la dentista *dentist* 3
el departamento *department* 1
el/la dependiente *salesperson* 3
el depilatorio *depilatory, hair remover* 8
el deporte *sport* 1
  hacer deportes *to do/play sports* 5
deprimido *depressed* 4
la derecha *right side* 4
  a la derecha de *to the right of* 4
el derecho *law* 2; *right* 20
  los derechos civiles *civil rights* 20
derecho *straight ahead* 14
desabrocharse *unfasten, unbuckle* 9
  desabrocharse el cinturón de seguridad *to unfasten one's seatbelt* 9
desafiante *challenging* 19
desaparecer *to disappear* 20
el desarrollador / la desarrolladora de programas *software developer* 3
el desarrollador / la desarrolladora de web *web developer* 3
desarrollar *to develop* 18
desayunar *to have breakfast* 8
el desayuno *breakfast* 5
  tomar el desayuno *to have breakfast* 5
descargar (g > gu/e) *to download* 5
descomponérsele a uno *to have something break down* 11
descompuesto *(p.p. descomponer)* *broken, broken down, malfunctioning* 4
el descubrimiento *discovery* 20
descubrir *to discover* 9
desde luego *of course* 10
desear *to want, wish* 6
el desempleo *unemployment* 13
el desfile *parade* 15
el desierto *desert* 9
la desilusión *disappointment* 10
desilusionado *disappointed* 17
desnudarse *to get undressed* 8
desocupado *empty* 17
el desodorante *deodorant* 8
la despedida de soltera *bachelorette party* 17
la despedida de soltero *bachelor party* 17
despedir (e > i) *to fire* 11
despedirse (e > i) (de) *to say goodbye (to)* 8
despegar (g > gu/e) *to take off (airplane)* 9
el despegue *takeoff (airplane)* 9
despejar *to clear (up)* 6
despertarse (e > ie) *to wake up* 8
despistado *absentminded* 12
después *after, afterwards* 5
después (de) *after* 8
el destornillador *screwdriver* 19
destrozado *devastated, heartbroken* 20
el deterioro *damage* 20
detrás de *behind* 4

la deuda *debt* 20
la devolución *return (of merchandise)* 19
devolver (o > ue) *to return, give back* 6
el día *day* 1
   al día siguiente *the next day* 9
   día libre *day off* 4
la diapositiva *slide* 7
dibujar *to draw* 5
diciembre *December* 5
dictar una orden *to issue an order* 20
el diente *tooth* 8
la dieta *diet* 11
   ponerse a dieta *to go on a diet* 11
diferente *different* 2
difícil *difficult* 2
difícilmente *with difficulty* 8
la dificultad *difficulty* 8
   con dificultad *with difficulty* 8
dinámico *dynamic* 19
el dinero *money* 1
Dios mío *my gosh, my goodness* 11
la dirección *address* 4
   dirección electrónica *email address* 6
directo *direct* 9
   el vuelo directo *direct/nonstop flight* 9
el director, la directora *director* 4; *principal (of school)* 18
la disciplina *discipline* 18
el disco compacto *compact disc, CD* 4
la discoteca *discotheque* 5
disculpar *to excuse* 14
discutir *to discuss, argue* 6
el diseñador, la diseñadora de videojuegos *video game designer* 3
diseñar *to design* 5
el disfraz *costume* 17
disfrutar (de) *to enjoy* 5
disminuir (yo disminuyo) *to decrease, decline* 20
disparar *to shoot* 20
dispararse *to go off* (of a gun); *to skyrocket* (of prices) 20
dispensar *to excuse* 14
el disquete *diskette* 12
la distancia *distance* 6
distanciar *to put at a distance, keep away from* 20
el disturbio *disturbance, riot* 20
   los disturbios *unrest* 20
divertido *amusing, entertaining, fun* 3
divertirse (e > ie, e > i) *to have a good time* 8
divorciado *divorced* 4
divorciarse *to get divorced* 8
doblar *to turn* 14
el doctorado *doctorate (PhD)* 18
el documental *documentary* 7
el documento *document, paper* 1
doler (o > ue) *(rev. constr.)* *to hurt, ache; distress* 11
el dolor *pain, ache* 11
   dolor de cabeza/estómago/diente *headache/stomachache/toothache* 11
el domicilio *home* 19
dominar *to master* 6
el domingo *Sunday* 4
¿dónde? *where?* 1
   ¿adónde? *(to) where?* 1
   ¿de dónde? *(from) where?* 1
dormido *sleeping* 4
dormilón (< dormir) *given to sleeping, sleepyhead* 11

dormir (o > ue) *to sleep* 6
dormirse *to go to sleep, fall asleep* 8
el dormitorio *bedroom* 12
la dosis *dose* 18
el drama *drama* 1
la drogadicción *drug addiction* 12
ducharse *to take a shower* 8
la duda *doubt* 13
   no cabe duda *there's no doubt* 13
dudar *to doubt* 16
dudoso *doubtful* 16
los dulces *candy* 3
durar *to last* 17
el durazno *peach* 3
duro *hard, difficult* 13

echar *to throw* 14
la economía *economics* 2
el ecoturismo *ecotourism* 10
el edificio *building* 4
educar en casa *to homeschool* 18
educarse *to be educated* 18
el efecto *effect* 9
   en efecto *exactly* 9
egoísta *selfish* 12
el ejercicio *exercise* 5
   hacer ejercicio *to exercise* 5
el *the* (before a masc. noun) 1
elaborado *fancy* 17
elaborar *to draw up, develop* 13
el/la electricista *electrician* 3
el electrodoméstico *household appliance* 1
la electrónica *electronics* 19
elegante *elegant* 15
elegir (e > i, g > j/o, a) *to choose* 9
el elevador *elevator* 11
eliminar *to eliminate* 20
ellas *they* (fem.) 4
ellos *they* (masc.) 4
el email *email* 13
embarazada *pregnant* 11
   estar embarazada *to be pregnant* 11
embargo: sin embargo *nevertheless, however, still* 20
el embotellamiento *traffic jam* 9
emocionado *excited* 4
emocionarse *to be moved, get excited* 8
empezar (e > ie, z > c/e) *to begin* 6
   empezar a + *inf.* *to begin to (do something)* 6
el empleado, la empleada *employee* 20
emprendedor(a) *enterprising* 4
emprender *to undertake* 20
la empresa *firm, company* 5
el empresario, la empresaria *entrepreneur, businessperson* 19
en *in, at, on* 1
   en absoluto *not at all* 4
   en caso de que *in case* 18
   en efecto *exactly* 8
   en frente *across the street, opposite* 1
   en frente de *opposite, facing* 4
   en punto *on the dot* 4
   en realidad *really, actually* 4
   en seguida *immediately* 7
enamorado *in love* 8
   el Día de los Enamorados *Valentine's Day* 15
enamorarse (de) *to fall in love (with)* 8
encantador(a) *charming* 4

encantarle a uno (*rev. constr.*) *to love something* 9
encargar (g > gu/e) *to order* 5
encargarse (de) (g > gu/e) *to be in charge (of)* 15
la enchilada *enchilada* 3
encima de *on top of* 4
encontrar (o > ue) *to find* 6
encontrarse (o > ue) con *to run into* 17
endeudarse *to go into debt* 20
enérgico *energetic* 19
enero *January* 5
enfadado *angry* 4
enfadar *to make (someone) angry* 8
enfadarse *to get angry* 8
enfermarse *to get sick* 8
la enfermedad *illness* 11
la enfermería *nursing* 2
el enfermero, la enfermera *nurse* 3
el enfermero practicante, la enfermera practicante *nurse practitioner* 3
el enfrentamiento *clash* 20
enfriar *to chill* 17
engañar *to deceive* 12
engordar *to get fat* 11
el enjuague *mouthwash* 8
enojado *angry* 4
enojar *to make (someone) angry* 8
enojarse *to get angry* 8
enorme *huge, enormous* 20
la ensalada *salad* 3
la enseñanza *teaching* 18
enseñar *to show* 10; *to teach* 18
entender (e > ie) *to understand* 6
entenderse (e > ie) *to understand each other, get along* 8
la entereza *integrity* 17
entero *whole, entire* 19
el entierro *funeral, burial* 13
entonces *then* 6
la entrada *ticket* 19
entrar (a/en) *to go in, enter* 6
entre *between* 20
entregar (g > gu/e) *to hand in/over, turn in/over* 9
los entremeses *hors d'oeuvres* 3
entrometido *meddlesome* 12
entusiasmado *enthusiastic* 4
entusiasmarle a uno (*rev. constr.*) *to be/get excited about something* 9
entusiasmarse *to get excited, feel thrilled* 8
enviar (yo envío) *to send* 13
la epidemia *epidemic* 20
la época *time* 10
en aquella época *at that time* 10
el equipaje *luggage* 9
equipaje de mano *carry-on luggage* 9
el equipo *team* 11
equivocarse (c > qu/e) (al) *to be wrong* 11
equivocarse de número *to get the wrong number* 11
la erosión *erosion* 20
las escaleras *stairs* 11
la escalera mecánica *escalator* 11
escaparse *to escape* 11
escoger (g > j/o, a) *to choose* 15
escribir *to write* 6
el escritor, la escritora *writer* 3
escuchar *to listen*
la escuela *school* 4
el escuincle, la escuincla *child, kid, brat* (Mexico) 17

ese, esa, esos, esas *that, those* 3
el esmalte de uñas *nail polish* 8
el espacio exterior *outer space* 18
la espalda *back (anatomy)* 11
espantoso *frightening, dreadful* 18
la especialidad *specialty, special dish* 20
el espectáculo *show* 4
esperar *to hope; to wait for; to expect* 5
el espíritu *spirit* 12
espíritu cívico *civic spirit* 12
espléndido *wonderful, splendid* 9
la esposa *wife* 3
el esposo *husband* 3
esquiar (yo esquío) *to ski* 15
la esquina *street corner* 1
la estabilidad *stability* 20
la estación *station* 4; *season* 5
estación de tren *train station* 4
el estacionamiento *parking lot* 4
estacionar *to park* 14
el estadio *stadium* 5
el estado civil *marital status* 4
estallar *to break out, explode* 11
el estante *shelf* 1
estar (*irreg.*) *to be* 4
estar de acuerdo *to agree* 4
estar de buen/mal humor *to be in a good/bad mood* 4
estar de pie *to be standing* 4
estar de vacaciones *to be on vacation* 4
estar de viaje *to be on a trip* 4
estar de visita *to be visiting* 15
estar frito *to be done for / finished / doomed* 4
estar harto de *to be sick of (something), be fed up with (something)* 18
estar seguro (de que) *to be sure (that)* 4
estatal (*adj.*) *state*
la universidad estatal *state university* 10
el este *east* 9
este, esta, estos, estas *this, these* 3
el/la estilista *hair stylist* 3
el estilo de vida *lifestyle* 11
el estómago *stomach* 11
la estrechez de miras *narrow-mindedness* 20
estrecho de miras *narrow-minded* 20
el estrés *stress* 11
estresado *stressed* 4
estricto *strict* 12
el/la estudiante *student* 3
estudiar *to study* 6
estupendo *terrific, great* 2
el evento *event* 19
exactamente *exactly* 15
el examen *examination, test* 1
exasperar *to exasperate* 8
excelente *excellent* 7
el exceso *excess* 17
exigente *demanding* 12
exigir (g > j/o, a) *to demand* 16
expandir *to expand* 19
la experiencia *experience* 6
el experto *expert* 6
explicar (c > qu/e) *to explain* 9
la exposición *exhibit* 17
exposición de arte *art exhibit* 5
la expresión *expression, self-expression, speech* 20
extenderse (e > ie) a *to extend to, cover* 20

extrañar a *to miss (someone)* 18
extranjero: en el extranjero *abroad* 11

la fábrica *factory* 13
fabuloso *fabulous* 7
fácil *easy* 2
la facilidad *ease, easiness* 8
con facilidad *easily* 8
fácilmente *easily* 8
facturar *to check* 9
facturar el equipaje *to check the luggage* 9
la facultad *school (within a university)* 12
facultad de bellas artes *School of Fine Arts* 16
facultad de ciencias *(school of) sciences* 12
la falda *skirt* 4
falso *two-faced* 12
faltarle a uno (*rev. constr.*) *to be short of something, not have something* 9
la familia *family* 3
familiar (*adj.*) *family* 16
famoso *famous* 4
el farmacéutico, la farmacéutica *pharmacist* 3
la farmacia *drugstore* 1
fastidiado *annoyed* 17
la fatiga *fatigue* 18
el favor *favor* 14
favor de + *inf.* *please* 14
favorito *favorite* 17
febrero *February* 5
la fecha de nacimiento *date of birth* 4
la fecha límite *deadline* 19
las felicidades *congratulations* 8
feliz *happy* 18
feo *ugly, nasty* 2
los fiambres *cold cuts* 17
fiarse de (yo me fío) *to trust* 8
la fiebre *fever* 11
la fiesta *party* 2
fiesta de disfraces *costume party* 17
fijarse (en) *to notice* 8
el film *film* 7
la filosofía *philosophy* 12
el filtro solar *sunblock, sunscreen* 11
el fin de semana *weekend* 6
la finca *farm* 10
fino *of better quality* 12
la física *physics* 12
el físico, la física *physicist* 11
flaco *thin* 4
la flauta *flute* 5
la flor *flower* 1
el/la florista *florist* 3
el folleto *brochure* 2
fomentar *to promote, boost* 20
el fondo *bottom, back* 4
el fontanero, la fontanera *plumber* (Spain) 3
formar parte *to be a part* 19
la fortuna *fortune* 17
la foto *photo* 5
tomar fotos *to take photos* 5
la frecuencia *frequency* 8
con frecuencia *frequently* 8
frecuentemente *frequently* 8
freír (e > i) (yo frío) *to fry* 14
frente a *in front of* 4
la fresa *strawberry* 15
el frijol *bean* 3

el frío *cold (weather)* 6
hace frío *it's cold* 6
frito *fried* 4
la frontera *frontier, border* 18
la fruta *fruit* 3
el fuego *fire* 14
a fuego lento *on a slow flame, over low heat* 14
fuera *out, outside* 5
fuerte *strong, hard* 6
la fuga *elopement* 17
fugarse *to run away; to elope* 17
fumar *to smoke* 10
la función *performance* 19
la funcionalidad *function, feature* 19
funcionar *to work, function* 12
fundar *to found* 10
la furgoneta *van* 9
furioso *furious* 4
el fútbol *soccer* 5
fútbol americano *football* 5
jugar al fútbol *to play soccer* 6
jugar al fútbol americano *to play football* 6

la galería de arte *art gallery* 5
la galleta *cookie* 14
galleta con chispas/pepitas de chocolate *chocolate chip cookie* 3
la gallina *hen, chicken* 10
ganar *to earn* 5; *to win* 11
ganar una fortuna *to make a fortune* 17
ganarse la vida *to earn a living* 16
la ganga *bargain* 6
el garaje *garage* 2
garantizar *to guarantee* 20
la gasolina *gas* 17
la gasolinera *gas station* 4
gastar *to spend* 5
los gastos *expenses* 13
el gato *cat* 4
la gaveta *drawer* 1
el gemelo *twin* 15
generalmente *generally* 8
generoso *generous* 10
la gente *people* 1
buena gente *good person* 16
el/la gerente *manager* 3
gerente de marketing (mercadeo) *marketing manager* 3
gerente de sucursal *branch manager* 11
gerente de ventas *sales manager* 3
el gimnasio *gym* 5
las golosinas *candy, sweets, treats* 3
goloso *sweet-toothed* 3
ser goloso *to have a sweet tooth* 3
gordo *fat* 4
el gorro *cap* 4
grabar *to record* 5
gracias *thank you* 1
muchas gracias *thank you very much* 1
gracioso *funny, witty* 4
el grado *grade* 18
graduarse (yo me gradúo) (en) *to graduate (from)* 8
grande *big* 2
el grano *grain* 10
grano integral *whole grain* 10
la grasa *fat* 11
la gravedad *gravity* 18

la   gripe *flu* 11
      gris *gray* 2
el   grito *shout, scream* 7
      gruñón, gruñona *grouchy, grumpy* 12
el   guante *glove* 4
      guapo *good-looking, handsome (male)* 3
      guardar *to save* 13
el   guardia *guard* 17
      ¡guau! *wow!* 18
la   guerra *war* 11
los   guisantes *peas* 3
la   guitarra *guitar* 5
      gustarle a uno *(rev. constr.) to like* 9
el   gusto *pleasure* 7
         con gusto *gladly* 7

      haber *(irreg.) to have* (auxiliary verb) 7
la   habilidad *ability* 17
la   habitación *room* 2
el   habitante *inhabitant* 13
      hablado *(p.p. hablar) spoken* 6
         el francés hablado *spoken French* 6
      hablar *to speak* 5
      hacer *(irreg.) to do, make* 6
         hace + *expression of time* + que + *verb in present
            tense have/has been doing something* 6
         hace fresco *it's cool* 6
         hace ___ grados *it's ___ degrees* 6
         hacer cola *to stand in line, line up* 7
         hacer lo correcto *to do the right thing* 18
         hacer escala *to make a stopover* 9
         hacer las maletas *to pack* 9
         hacer maravillas *to do wonderful things* 13
         hacer un papel *to play a role/part* 10
         hacer preparativos *to prepare for, get ready* 9
         hacer la tarea *to do homework* 16
         hacer un viaje *to take a trip* 5
         hacerle caso a alguien *to pay attention to
            someone* 16
      hacerse *to become* 11
         se hace tarde *it's getting/growing late* 8
la   hacienda *estate* 15
      haga el favor de *please* 14
el   hambre *hunger* 6
la   hamburguesa *hamburger* 3
      harto: estar harto de *to be sick of (something),
         be fed up with (something)* 18
      hasta *even* 11
      hay *there is, there are* 1
      hay que *one must, one has to* 6
      hecho *done* 4
         hecho a la perfección *perfectly done* 4
         muy hecho *too well done* 4
         poco hecho *underdone* 4
el   hecho *fact* 19
la   heladería *ice cream store* 1
el   helado *ice cream* 1
      helar (e > ie) *to freeze* 6
la   herida *injury, wound* 11
      herido *injured, wounded* 11
la   hermana *sister* 4
el   hermano *brother* 4
      hermoso *beautiful* 2
la   herramienta *tool* 19
la   higiene *hygiene, cleanliness* 20
la   hija *daughter* 4
el   hijo *son* 4

el   hilo dental *dental floss* 8
la   hipoteca *mortgage* 13
la   historia *history* 2; *story* 9
      histórico *historical* 16
la   hoja de afeitar *razor blade* 8
el   hombre *man* 6
         hombre *my friend* (interjection) 17
         hombre de negocios *businessman* 4
la   honradez *honesty, integrity* 17
      honrado *honest* 4
la   hora *time (clock), hour* 4
         a la misma hora *at the same time* 7
         ¿a qué hora? *at what time?* 4
         es hora de *it's time to* 7
         horas libres *free time* 5
         las horas punta *rush hour* 9
         media hora *half an hour* 9
      horrendo *terrible, horrible* 9
      horrible *horrible, terrible* 2
el   hospital *hospital* 1
el   hotel *hotel* 1
el   hotelero, la hotelera *hotel manager* 3
      hoy *today* 4
el   hueso *bone* 17
el   huevo *egg* 3
         huevo revuelto *scrambled egg* 6
      huir de algo *to flee from, run away from* 17

la   idea *idea* 6
         no tener la menor idea *to have no idea at all* 15
el   idioma *language* 1
         idioma extranjero *foreign language* 18
la   iglesia *church* 4
      igual *like, the same* 18
      imaginarse *to imagine* 10
el   imperio *empire* 10
      imponente *impressive, stunning* 20
la   importancia *importance* 16
      importante *important* 2
      importarle a uno *(rev. constr.) to matter to
         someone* 9
      imprescindible *crucial* 16
      impresionante *impressive, awesome* 4
la   impresora *printer* 4
      imprevisto *impromptu, unforeseen, unexpected* 15
      imprimir *to print* 6
los   impuestos *taxes* 13
el   impuntual *latecomer* 19
el   incendio *fire* 11
      incluir (yo incluyo) *to include* 13
      incluso *including* 19
      incómodo *uncomfortable* 18
la   incompetencia *incompetence* 20
la   independencia *independence* 15
         el Día de la Independencia *Independence Day* 15
      indulgente *lenient* 12
la   infección *infection* 11
la   inflación *inflation* 20
      inflexible *rigid, inflexible* 12
la   influencia *influence* 20
la   influenza *influenza* 18
      informar *to inform* 11
el   informe *report* 1
el   ingeniero, la ingeniera *engineer* 3
el   ingenio *ingenuity, resourcefulness* 17
      ingenuo *naïve* 12
los   ingresos *income* 13

inmediatamente *immediately* 14
el/la inmigrante *immigrant* 10
inolvidable *unforgettable* 17
inquieto *worried* 4
insaciable *insatiable* 18
inscribir *to enroll* 18
inscribirse *to register* 8
insistir en *to insist* 16
instalarse *to move in* 8
la inteligencia *intelligence* 17
inteligente *intelligent* 2
la interactividad *interactivity* 17
interactivo *interactive* 17
interesante *interesting* 2
interesarle a uno (*rev. constr.*) *to be interested in something* 9
el interior *interior, inside* 2
interminable *unending* 9
el/la intérprete *performer, interpreter* 3
íntimo *intimate, close* (relationship) 16
la investigación *research* 18
el invierno *winter* 5
la invitación *invitation* 13
el invitado *guest* 7
invitar *to invite* 5
la inyección *injection* 18
el iPod *iPod* 1
ir (*irreg.*) *to go* 5
ir a (+ *inf.*) *to be going to* (do something) 5
ir al campo *to go to the country* 17
ir de compras *to go shopping* 5
irse *to go away* 8
la izquierda *left side* 4
a la izquierda de *to the left of* 4

el jabón *soap* 8
el jamón *ham* 3
el Jánuca *Hanukkah* 15
el jardín *garden, yard* 2
el jardinero, la jardinera *gardener* 3
el jetlag *jet lag* 9
el jogging *jogging* 5
hacer jogging *to jog, go jogging* 5
joven *young* 6
la joya *jewel* 1
la joyería *jewelry store* 1
el joyero, la joyera *jeweler* 3
jubilarse *to retire* (stop working) 11
judío *Jewish* 4
el jueves *Thursday* 4
el jugador, la jugadora *player* 6
jugar (u > ue, g > gu/e) *to play* 6
jugar al baloncesto / béisbol / fútbol / fútbol americano / tenis *to play basketball/baseball/soccer/football/tennis* 6
el jugo *juice* 3
el juguete *toy* 1
la juguetería *toy store* 1
julio *July* 5
junio *June* 5
la junta *meeting* 19
juntos *together* 5
juvenil (*adj.*) *childhood, of early years* 18

el kilómetro *kilometer* 4

la *the* (before a fem. noun) 1
la (*d.o.*) *her, it, you* (informal) 7

el labio *lip* 8
los lácteos *dairy* 3
el lado *side* 4
el ladrón, la ladrona *thief* 11
la lana *wool* 4
el lanzamiento *launch* 18
el lápiz *pencil* 1
lápiz para los labios *lipstick* 8
largo *long* 2
las (*d.o.*) *them, you* (pl.) 7
la lástima *pity, shame* 16
es una lástima que *it's a pity that* 16
latino *Latin*
la lavadora *washing machine* 7
el lavaplatos *dishwasher* 7
lavar(se) *to wash* 8
lavarse el pelo / la cabeza / la cara / las manos / los pies *to wash one's hair/hair/face/hands/feet* 8
le (*i.o.*) *him, her, you* 9
la lealtad *loyalty* 17
la leche *milk* 3
la lechuga *lettuce* 3
leer *to read* 6
la legumbre *vegetable* 3
lejos (de) *far (from)* 4
lentamente *slowly* 10
los lentes *glasses* 11
lentes de contacto *contact lenses* 11
lentes de sol *sunglasses* 11
lento *slow* 14
les (*i.o.*) *them, you* (pl.) 9
levantar *to lift* 5
levantarse *to get up* 8
leve *light, minor* 11
la libertad *freedom, liberty* 20
libertad de expresión *freedom of speech* 20
libre *free* (time) 5
la librería *bookstore* 1
el librero, la librera *bookseller* 3
el libro *book* 1
libro de recetas de cocina *cookbook* 6
libro de texto *textbook* 12
la licencia de conducir *driver's license* 17
la licencia de manejar *driver's license* 15
la licenciatura *bachelor's degree* 18
el líder *leader* 19
la lima de uñas *nail file* 8
lindo *nice, lovely, pretty* (Spanish America) 2
la línea *line* 9
en línea *online* 9
el lío *problem, complication, bit of trouble* 9
lío de tráfico *traffic jam* 10
nada de líos *no problems* 9
listo *ready* 4
la literatura *literature* 18
llamar *to call* 5
llamarse *to be named* 8
la llave *key* 1
llegar (g > gu/e) *to arrive* 5
llevar *to take, carry, wear* 5
lleva más tiempo *it takes longer* 9
llevar a cabo *to conduct, carry out* 19
llevarse bien/mal con *to get along / not get along with* 8
llorón (< llorar) *given to crying, crybaby* 11
llover (o > ue) *to rain* 6

la lluvia *rain* 7
lo (*d.o.*) *him, it, you* (informal) 6
la loción para después del afeitado *aftershave* 8
loco *crazy* 17
el locutor, la locutora *newscaster* 3
lograr *to get, obtain* 6
   lograr + *inf.* *to succeed in (doing something), manage to (do something)* 6
la lonchera *lunch box* 18
los (*d.o.*) *them, you* (pl.) 7
la lucha *fight, struggle* 10
el lugar *place* 1
el lujo *luxury* 13
   el apartamento de lujo *luxury apartment* 13
la luna *moon* 18
el lunes *Monday* 4
la luz *light* 1

la madrastra *stepmother* 4
la madre *mother* 4
madrugar (g > gu/e) *to get up early* 9
la maestría *master's degree* 15
magnífico *great, terrific, magnificent* 2
el maíz *corn* 10
mal *ill, sick* 4
maleducado *rude* 12
la maleta *suitcase* 1
   hacer las maletas *to pack* 5
el maletín *briefcase, attaché case* 1
   maletín de herramientas *tool kit, tool box* 19
malo *bad* 2
la mamá *mother, mom* 4
la mañana *morning* 4
mañana *tomorrow* 5
   pasado mañana *the day after tomorrow* 5
mandar *to send* 13
el mando *control, direction* 17
mandón (< mandar) *bossy* 11
manejar *to drive* 6
la manera *way* 14
el mango *mango* 15
la manifestación *demonstration* 20
el/la manifestante *demonstrator, protester* 20
la mano *hand* 1
mantener (*irreg.*) *to maintain* 8
   mantenerse en contacto *to stay in touch* 8
   mantenerse en forma *to stay in shape* 8
la mantequilla *butter* 3
   mantequilla de cacahuete *peanut butter* 3
la manzana *apple* 3
el mapa *map* 1
el maquillaje *makeup* 8
maquillarse *to put on makeup* 8
la máquina *machine* 9
   máquina (maquinilla) de afeitar *electric razor* 8
   máquina de lavar *washing machine* 17
el mar *sea; seashore* 5
la maravilla *wonder* 20
maravilloso *wonderful, marvelous, terrific* 2
el marcador *marker* 18
mareado *dizzy* 9
el marido *husband* 3
la mariposa *butterfly* 10
los mariscos *shellfish* 3
marrón *brown* 2
el martes *Tuesday* 4
el martillo *hammer* 19

marzo *March* 5
la mascarilla *mask, surgical mask* 18
las matemáticas *math, mathematics* 2
la materia *subject (school)* 12
la matrícula *registration, enrollment* 8
matricularse *to register, enroll* 8
mayo *May* 5
el MBA *Master's in Business Administration* 15
me (*d.o.*) *me* 6
me (*i.o.*) *me* 9
el mecánico, la mecánica *mechanic* 3
la medianoche *midnight* 4
la medicina *medicine* 2
el médico, la médico (la médica) *doctor* 3
la medida *measure, step* 20
medieval *medieval* 9
medio *half* 2
medioambiental *environmental* 20
el mediodía *noon* 4
mejor *better, best* 2
   a lo mejor *maybe* 11
mejorar *to improve* 10
mejorarse *to get better* 8
menos *less* 6
   a menos que *unless* 18
   menos mal *fortunately* 6; *thank goodness* 19
mentiroso *deceitful* 12
el mercadeo *marketing* 9
el mercado *market* 6
la merienda *snack* 5; *afternoon snack* 10
   merienda campestre *picnic* 10
   tomar la merienda *to have a snack* 5
el mes *month* 1
   el mes próximo *next month* 6
la mesa *table* 2
la mesera *waitress* 3
el mesero *waiter* 3
meter *to put in, insert* 6
meterse (en) *to meddle, butt in* 8
el metro *subway* 5
la metrópolis *metropolis, capital (city), major city* 13
mi, mis *my* 2
el microondas *microwave* 7
la miel *honey* 17
el miembro *member* 15
el miércoles *Wednesday* 4
mil (miles) *a thousand (thousands)* 20
la milla *mile* 4
mínimo *minimal, very small* 18
el minuto *minute* 17
mirar *to look at* 5
miserable *paltry, miserable* 10
mismo *same* 2
la mochila *backpack* 1
el mocoso *brat* 17
la moda *fashion, clothing* 19
moderno *modern* 2
modo: de ningún modo *not at all* 7
mojarse *to get wet* 17
molestar *to annoy/bother (someone)* 8
molestarse *to get annoyed* 8
la molestia *bother* 17
molesto *annoyed* 4
el momento *moment* 13
la montaña *mountain* 9
montar *to set up* 19
el montón de *lots of, loads of* 19

el monumento *monument* 4
morado *purple* 2
moreno *dark-haired, dark-skinned* 4
morir (o > ue, o > u) *to die* 6
morirse (o > ue, o > u) *to die* 8
mortal *deadly* 18
el mosquito *mosquito* 11
mostrar (o > ue) *to show* 9
motivado *motivated* 19
el móvil *cell phone* 1
mucho, mucha *much, a lot* 2
   con mucho *to a large degree* 19
muchos, muchas *many, a lot of* 2
mudarse *to move (change residence)* 8
muerto *dead* 13
la mujer *woman, wife* 3
la multa *fine* 20
el mundo *world* 6
la muñeca *doll* 17
la muralla *wall* 10
el museo *museum* 1
   museo de arte *art museum* 1
   museo de ciencias *science museum* 4
la música *music* 2
el musical *musical* 19
el músico, la música *musician* 3
musulmán, musulmana *Muslim* 4
muy *very* 2

el nacimiento *birth* 11
la nacionalidad *nationality* 4
nada *nothing* 5
   nada + *adj. not at all* +adj. 11
   nada más *that's all, nothing else* 5
   ni nada *nor anything* 6
nadar *to swim* 5
nadie *no one, nobody* 5
la naranja *orange* 3
la nariz *nose* 1
la nave espacial *spacecraft, spaceship* 18
navegar (g > gu/e) *to surf* 5
   navegar en la red *to surf the internet* 5
la Navidad *Christmas* 15
necesario *necessary* 16
necesitar *to need* 6
los negocios *business* 9
negro *black* 2
los nervios *nerves* 19
   tener los nervios de punta *to be on edge,*
     be a nervous wreck 19
nervioso *nervous* 4
nevar (e > ie) *to snow* 6
la nevera *refrigerator, fridge* 17
ni *nor, neither* 6
   ni nada *nor anything* 6
la niebla *fog* 10
la nieta *granddaughter* 4
el nieto *grandson* 4
la nieve *snow* 7
la niña *girl* 4
ningún, ninguno, ninguna, ningunos, ningunas
   no, none, not any 2
   a ninguna parte *nowhere* 6
   de ningún modo *not at all* 7
el niño *boy* 4
   niño prodigio *child prodigy* 11
los niños *children* 17

el nivel *level* 18
no *no* 1
   ¿no? *isn't it?* 4
   ¿no sabes? *you know?* (lit., *don't you know?*)
     2
la noche *night* 4
   esta noche *tonight* 5
   la Noche Vieja *New Year's Eve* 15
el nombre *name* 8
el nordeste *northeast* 9
normal *normal, not unusual* 20
normalmente *normally* 8
el noroeste *northwest* 9
el norte *north* 9
nos (*d.o.*) *us* 7
nos (*i.o.*) *us* 9
notar *to notice* 12
la noticia *piece of news* 13
las noticias *news* 7
la novela *novel* 6
la novia *girlfriend, fiancée* 3
noviembre *November* 5
el novio *boyfriend, fiancé* 3
nublado: está nublado *it's cloudy* 7
nuestro, nuestra *our* 2
nuevo *new* 2
la nuez *nut* 3
el número *number* 1
   número de teléfono *telephone number* 4
nunca *never* 9
   como nunca *as never before* 9

la obra *work, play (theater)* 5
   obra de teatro *play* 5
   obra maestra *masterpiece* 12
octubre *October* 5
ocupado *busy* 4
ocuparse de *to take care of* 8
ocurrírsele a alguien *to dawn on someone, think of*
   something 11
odiar *to hate* 19
el oeste *west* 9
ofender *to offend, insult* 8
ofenderse *to get insulted, be offended* 8
ofensivo *offensive* 20
la oferta *sale* 6
   las ofertas de enero *January sales* 6
la oficina *office* 2
   oficina de turismo *tourist office* 1
el/la oficinista *office worker* 3
ofrecer (yo ofrezco) *to offer* 9
el oído *ear (inner)* 11
oiga *say* (lit., *hear, listen*) 1
oír (*irreg.*) *to hear, listen to* 7
   oye *hey, say* 7
ojalá *I hope* 16; *I wish* 18
la ojera *dark circle under the eye* 11
el ojo *eye* 11
olvidadizo *forgetful* 10
olvidarse (de) *to forget* 8
   olvidársele a uno *to forget (something)* 11
la ópera *opera* 19
oponerse (*irreg.*) *to oppose* 16
la oportunidad *opportunity* 19
optimista *optimistic* 12
la orden *order, command* 20
el ordenador *computer* (Spain) 7

el   organizador, la organizadora *organizer* 15
     organizador de bodas *wedding planner* 15
     organizar (z > c/e) *to organize* 9
     orgulloso *proud* 18
el   origen *origin, descent, background* 3
el   oro *gold* 3
la   orquesta *orchestra* 15
     oscuro *dark* 2
el   otoño *fall, autumn* 5
     otro, otra *another, another one* 1
     otra vez *again* 4
la   oveja *sheep* 10

el   padrastro *stepfather* 4
el   padre *father* 4
los   padres *parents* 4
el   padrino *godfather* 17
     padrino de boda *best man* 17
     pagar (g > gu/e) *to pay* 5
la   página *page* 5
     página web *web page* 5
el   país *country* 3
el   paisaje *landscape* 9
el   pájaro *bird* 11
el   pan *bread* 3
     pan comido *piece of cake, easy as pie* 9
     pan integral *whole grain bread* 3
el   panadero, la panadera *baker* 3
la   pantalla *screen* 4
     pantalla táctil *touch screen* 17
el   pantalón *pants* 4
los   pantalones *pants* 2
el   papá *father, dad*
     los papás *parents* 4
la   papa *potato* 3
     papas fritas *French fries* 3
la   papaya *papaya* 15
el   papel *paper* 1
el   paquete *package* 1
     para *for* 1
     estar para + *inf. to be about to (do something)* 6
     para eso fuimos *that's why we went* 9
     para que *so that* 18
     parado *standing* 4
el   paramédico, la paramédica *paramedic* 11
     parar *to hail* (lit., *to stop*) 19
     parecer (yo parezco) *to seem* 7
el/la pariente *relative* 15
el   parque *park* 17
el   parqueo *parking lot* 4
el   parquímetro *parking meter* 6
la   parte *part* 3
el   partido *game* 4
     partido de fútbol *soccer game/match* 19
     pasado (*p.p.* pasar) *passed* 9
     el año pasado *last year* 9
     el mes pasado *last month* 9
     la semana pasada *last week* 9
el   pasajero *passenger* 9
la   pasantía *internship* 10
el   pasaporte *passport* 3
     pasar *to spend* 6; *to pass, come by* 7
     pasar tiempo *to spend time* 19
las   pasas *raisins* 3
la   Pascua *Easter* 15
     Pascua judía *Passover* 15

     pasear *to take for a walk* 5
     pasearse *to stroll, go for a walk* 8
el   paseo *boulevard* 2
el   pasillo *aisle* 9
     el asiento de pasillo *aisle seat* 9
el   paso *step* 18
la   pasta *pasta* 3
la   pasta de dientes *toothpaste* 8
el   pastel *pastry, pie* 3
el   pastor *minister, pastor* 17
la   patata *potato* (Spain) 3
     patinar *to skate* 5
el   patio *yard, patio* 2
el   pavo *turkey* 3
la   paz *peace* 1
el   peatón *pedestrian* 11
     peatonal (*adj.*) *pedestrian* 2
el/la pediatra *pediatrician* 11
     pedir (e > i) *to ask for, order* 6
     pegado *glued, stuck* 19
     peinarse *to comb one's hair* 8
el   peine *comb* 8
la   película *film, movie* 3
el   pelo *hair* 8
la   pelota *ball* 6
la   peluquería *hair salon, barber shop* 1
la   pena *sorrow, pity* 17
     ¡Qué pena! *What a shame!, What a pity!* 19
     pensar (e > ie) *to think* 6
     pensar + *inf. to intend to (do something)* 6
     peor *worse, worst* 2
     pequeño *small* 2
la   pera *pear* 3
     perder (e > ie) *to lose* 9
     perderse *to get lost* 9; *to miss (an event)* 19
     perdérsele *to lose* 11
     perdón *excuse me* 1
     perdonar *to forgive, pardon, excuse* 14
     perezoso *lazy* 12
     perfectamente *very well, great* 4
el   perfume *perfume* 8
el   periódico *newspaper* 2
el/la periodista *journalist* 3
el   período de atención *attention span* 17
el   perito *expert* 19
     permitir *to allow* 16
     pero *but* 2
el   perro *dog* 2
el   perro caliente *hot dog* 3
la   persona *person* 1
la   pesa *weight* 5
     pesado *heavy, boring* 2; *annoying, boring* 7
el   pésame *expression of sympathy/condolences at someone's loss* 13
     dar el pésame *to express one's sympathy/condolences* 13
las   pesas *weights, dumbbells* 5
el   pescado *fish* 3
     pesimista *pessimistic* 12
     pésimo *awful, dreadful* 18
el   peso *weight* 11
     aumentar de peso *to gain weight* 11
     bajar de peso *to lose weight* 11
el   petróleo *oil* 10
el   pez *fish* 1
el   piano *piano* 5

la picadura *bite* (*insect*) 11
   picadura de abeja *bee sting* 11
   picadura de mosquito *mosquito bite* 11
picante *spicy* 3
picar (c > qu/e) *to itch* 11
el pie *foot* 4
   a pie *on foot* 11
la piedra *stone* 20
la piel *skin* 1
la pierna *leg* 11
el pijama *pajamas* 14
la pimienta *pepper* 3
la piña *pineapple* 3
pintar *to paint* 5
pintarse *to put on makeup* 8
   pintarse la cara / los labios / las uñas *to put on makeup / lipstick / nail polish* 8
el pintor, la pintora *painter* 3
la pintura *painting* 9
las pinzas *tweezers* 8
la pirámide *pyramid* 1
la piscina *swimming pool* 5
el piso *floor* 8
la pista *track* 5
la pizza *pizza* 3
la placa *license plate* 14
el plan *plan* 1
   plan de estudios *curriculum* 18
   plan de mercadeo *marketing plan* 9
   plan de negocios *business plan* 13
planear *to plan* 17
el plano *street map* 6
la plataforma *platform* 19
el plátano *banana* 3
el plato *dish* 3
   plato acompañante/adicional *side dish* 3
la playa *beach* 4
la plaza *square* 4
plenamente *fully* 14; *completely, totally* 17
el plomero, la plomera *plumber* 3
la población *population* 13
pobre *poor* 2
   pobre de mí *poor me* 12
la pobreza *poverty* 12
poco *little, not much* 2
   pocos, pocas *few, not many* 2
poder (*irreg.*) *to be able, can* 6
el poder *power* 20
polarizador *polarizing* 20
polémico *contentious* 20
el/la policía *policeman/policewoman* 3
la policía *police* (*force*) 11
el político, la política *politician* 3
el pollo *chicken* 3
la polución *pollution* 12
poner (*irreg.*) *to put; to put/turn on; to show* (*film*) 7
   poner la mesa *to set the table* 13
ponerse *to put on* (*clothing*) 8
   ponerse + *adj.* *to become* 11
   ponerse a + *inf.* *to begin to* (*do something*) 8
   ponerse de pie *to stand up* 9
   ponerse en contacto *to get in touch* 8
   ponerse en forma *to get into shape* 8
popular *popular* 12
la popularidad *popularity* 20

por *for, around, along, on, in the area of* 1
   por añadidura *to top it all off* 17
   por aquí *around here* 1
   por la avenida *along the avenue* 6
   por ciento *percent* 10
   por desgracia *unfortunately* 6
   por dónde *where* 6
   por eso *therefore, that's why* 4
   por favor *please* 1
   por semana *weekly* 5
   por supuesto *of course* 19
positivo *positive* 17
postear *to post* 20
el postre *dessert* 3
potente *powerful* 12
practicar (c > qu/e) *to practice* 5
el precio *price* 13
precisamente *exactly* 5
preciso *necessary* 16
precolombino *pre-Columbian* 10
preferir (e > ie) *to prefer* 6
preguntar *to ask* (*a question*) 13
preguntarse *to wonder* 20
preguntón (< preguntar) *inquisitive, nosey* 11
prender *to turn on* (*appliance*) 9
preocupado *worried* 4
preocuparse *to worry* 8
la preparación universitaria *college prep* 18
preparar *to prepare* 5
   prepararse para la prueba *to prepare for the quiz* 16
la presentación *presentation* 19
la presión *pressure* 11
   presión sanguínea *blood pressure* 11
prestar *to lend* 10
presumido *conceited, full of oneself, arrogant* 11
el presupuesto *budget* 13; *estimate* 17
prevenir *to prevent* 18
la primavera *spring* 5
primero *first* 2
los primeros auxilios *first aid* 11
los primeros intervinientes *first responders* 18
el primo, la prima *cousin* 4
principalmente *mainly* 19
el principio *beginning* 19
privado *private* 10
   la universidad privada *private university* 10
probable *probable* 16
   poco probable *improbable, not likely, unlikely* 16
probar (o > ue) *to try, taste* 6
el problema *problem* 1
producir (*irreg.*) *to produce* 10
el producto *product* 10
la profesión *profession* 4
el profesor, la profesora *professor, teacher* 3
profundamente *deeply* 11
el programa *program* 1
la programación *programming* 5
el programador, la programadora *programmer* 4
programar *to program* 6
prohibir (yo prohíbo) *to forbid, prohibit* 14
los prometidos *the fiancés, engaged couple* 8
pronto *soon* 5
propagar (g > gu/e) *to spread* 18
la propina *tip* (*for service*) 10
proponer (*irreg.*) *to propose* 16
el protector solar *sunscreen* 9
proteger *to protect, shield* 17

protestante *Protestant* 4
protestar contra *to protest against* 20
el proveedor *caterer* 17; *provider* 19
próximo *next* 17
el proyecto *project* 13
la prueba *quiz* 16
publicar *to publish* 20
público (*adj.*) *public* 20
el público *audience* 7
el puente *bridge* 14
la puerta *door, gate* 9
    puerta de embarque *boarding gate* 9
pues *then, well (then)* 3
el puesto *position, job* 10
puesto (*p.p.* poner) *put* 13
pulsar *to press* 17
la pulsera *bracelet* 1
el punto *point* 4
puro *pure, just, nothing but* 13

¿qué? *what?* 1
quebrársele *to break* 11
quedar *to be located (permanent location)* 2
    quedarle a uno (*rev. constr.*) *to have something left* 9; *to fit someone (clothing)* 11
quedarse *to stay, remain* 8
    quedársele *to leave (something) behind* 11
quejarse (de) *to complain (about)* 8
quejumbroso *whiny* 17
la quemadura *burn* 11
    quemadura de sol *sunburn* 11
quemarse *to burn* 14
querer (*irreg.*) *to want* 6; *to love* 10
quererse (*irreg.*) *to love each other* 8
la quesadilla *quesadilla* 3
los quesos *cheeses* 17
la quiebra *bankruptcy* 20
¿quién? ¿quiénes? *who?* 1
    ¿para quién? *for whom?* 1
la química *chemistry* 2
la quinceañera *girl's sweet 15 party; 15-year-old girl* 17
el quiosco *kiosk* 14
quitarse *to take off (clothing)* 9
quizás *perhaps* 11

el rabino *rabbi* 17
la radio *radio* 7
la raqueta de tenis *tennis racket* 6
raro *strange, weird* 4
el rascacielos *skyscraper* 13
rascarse (c > qu/e) *to scratch* 11
el rato *while (period of time)* 5
    ratos libres *free time* 5
reaccionar *to react* 13
la realidad *reality*
realista *realistic* 12
realizar (z > c/e) *to achieve, realize* 10; *to perform* 20
realizarse (z > c/e) *to take place* 15
realmente *really* 2
la rebaja *discount, sale* 19
rebasar *to exceed* 15
el/la recepcionista *receptionist* 3
la receta (de cocina) *recipe* 6
    el libro de recetas de cocina *cookbook* 6
recetar *to prescribe, give a prescription* 11
recibir *to receive* 6
    recibirse de + *profession to get one's* ____ *degree* 11

el reciclaje *recycling* 12
recientemente *recently* 8
recoger (g > j/o, a) *to pick up, gather* 9
recomendar (e > ie) *to recommend* 16
reconocido (*p.p.* reconocer) *recognized* 6
recordar (o > ue) *to remember* 17
recorrer *to travel around, tour* 9
el recuerdo *memory* 9
la red *web, internet* 1; *network* 20
    las redes sociales *social media* 20
reforzar (o > ue) *to strengthen, reinforce* 20
el refresco *soft drink* 3
regalar *to give as a gift* 15
el regalo *gift* 1
regañar *to scold* 17
la región *region* 3
registrarse *to check in* 14
la regla *ruler* 18
regresar *to come/go back, return* 6
regular *so-so* 4
reírse (e > i) (yo me río) (de) *to laugh (at)* 8
la relación *relation, relationship* 16
    las relaciones familiares *family relations* 16
relajarse *to relax* 8
relativamente *relatively* 2
la religión *religion* 4
el reloj *wristwatch* 1
el repelente contra mosquitos *mosquito repellent* 11
repentinamente *suddenly* 17
el rescatador *rescuer* 18
la reservación *reservation* 9
reservar *to reserve* 9
el resfriado *cold (health)* 11
resfriarse (yo me resfrío) *to catch a cold* 8
resistir *to resist* 6
resolver (o > ue) *to solve* 6
respirar *to breathe* 13
la responsabilidad *responsibility* 17
responsable *responsible* 20
la restauración *restoration* 20
el restaurante *restaurant* 1
el resultado *result* 11
retirar *to withdraw* 11
retrasar *to delay* 19
el retraso *delay* 9
reunido *having a meeting* 4
la reunión *meeting* 4
reunirse (yo me reúno) (con) *to get together (with)* 8
el revendedor *scalper* 19
reventar (e > ie) *to explode* 6
revisar *to look over, check, review* 17
la revista *magazine* 2
revuelto (*p.p.* revolver) *scrambled* 6
    el huevo revuelto *scrambled egg* 6
ricachón (< rico) *very rich* 11
rico *delicious* 3; *rich* 11
ridículo *ridiculous* 4
el riesgo *risk* 18
el río *river* 14
el robo *robbery* 20
la rodilla *knee* 11
rogar (o > ue, g > gu/e) *to request* 16
rojo *red* 2
romper *to break, tear* 6
    romper con alguien *to break up with someone* 17
rompérsele *to break* 11
la ropa *clothing* 1

rotundamente *definitely, emphatically* 8
rubio *blond* 4
el ruido *noise* 2
   ruido ambiental *noise pollution* 12
   ruidoso *noisy* 2
la rutina *routine* 8
   rutina diaria *daily routine* 8

el sábado *Saturday* 4
saber (*irreg.*) *to know* 6
   saber + *inf. to know how to (do something)* 6
sabroso *tasty* 3
el sacapuntas *sharpener* 18
sacar (c > qu/e) *to take out, get out* 5
   sacar billetes/boletos *to get tickets* 9
   sacar buenas notas *to get good grades* 16
   sacar provecho de *to benefit from* 18
el sacerdote *priest* 17
la sal *salt* 3
   las sales de baño *bath salts* 8
la sala *room (public), living room* 4
   sala de clase *classroom* 16
   sala de conferencias *conference room* 4
   sala de emergencias *emergency room* 18
   sala de espera *waiting room* 18
   sala de recepción *reception (area)* 15
   sala de urgencias *emergency room* 18
el salario *salary* 13
la salchicha *sausage* 3
salir (yo salgo) *to go out, leave* 2
el salón *ballroom* 15
   salón de belleza *hair salon, beauty salon* 1
la salsa *salsa, sauce* 3
saludar *to say hello, greet, wave* 11
el sándwich *sandwich* 3
la sangre *blood* 11
sano *healthy* 10
el sarpullido *rash* 11
el/la sartén *frying pan* 13
el saxofón *saxophone* 5
el secador de pelo/cabello *hair dryer* 8
la secadora *dryer* 7
secar (c > qu/e) *to dry* 8
   secarse el pelo *to dry one's hair* 8
el secretario, la secretaria *secretary* 3
el secuestrador *kidnapper* 20
la sed *thirst* 6
sediento *thirsty* 20
seguir (e > i, gu > g/o, a) *to follow, continue* 6;
   + -ndo *form (gerund) to keep on (doing*
   something), continue (doing something) 18
la seguridad *security* 9
seguro *sure, certain* 15
   estar seguro de que *to be sure that* 15
el seguro de salud *health insurance* 13
la selva *forest, jungle* 10
el semáforo *traffic light* 14
   el semáforo está en rojo / en verde / en amarillo /
   en naranja *the traffic light is red/green/yellow/*
   yellow 14
la semana *week* 5
   la semana entrante *next week* 6
el semestre *semester* 6
la señal *sign* 14
   señal de tráfico *traffic sign* 14
sencillo *simple* 6
el señor *man, Mr., sir* 1

la señora *woman, Mrs., ma'am* 1
la señorita *young woman, Ms., miss* 1
sensato *sensible* 12
sensible *sensitive* 11
sentado *sitting, seated* 4
sentarse (e > ie) *to sit down* 8
sentimental *sentimental* 15
sentir (e > ie) *to feel* 7
   lo siento *I'm sorry* 7
sentirse (e > ie, e > i) *to feel* 8
   sentirse mareado *to feel dizzy* 9
septiembre *September* 5
ser (*irreg.*) *to be* 1
serio *serious* 12
los servicios de internet *internet services* 19
la servilleta *napkin* 13
servir (e > i) *to serve* 6
sí *yes* 1
la sierra *mountain range, mountains* 15
la siesta *nap* 10
   dormir la siesta *to take a nap* 10
el siglo *century* 20
el sílabo *syllabus* 18
el sillón *armchair* 9
simpático *nice, likeable* 4
simple *simple* 2
sin embargo *nevertheless, however, still* 20
la sinagoga *synagogue* 9
sincero *sincere* 12
el sistema *system* 1
   sistema solar *Solar System* 18
el sitio web *website* 4
sobrarle a uno (*rev. constr.*) *to have more than*
   enough of something 9
sobresaltado *startled* 11
la sobrina *niece* 4
el sobrino *nephew* 4
el socorrista *rescuer* 18
el socorro *help, aid* 17
el sofá *couch* 9
el software *software* 5
el sol *sun* 6
   hace/hay sol *it's sunny* 6
solicitar *to apply for* 15
   solicitar una beca *to apply for a scholarship* 15
la solicitud *application* 18
solo *alone* 17
solterón *confirmed bachelor* 11
el sombrero *hat* 4
sonar (o > ue) *to sound, ring* 11
soñar (con) (o > ue) *to dream (of/about)* 10
el sonido *sound* 7
la sopa *soup* 3
sorprender *to surprise* 16
   sorprenderle a uno (*rev. constr.*) *to surprise* 16
la soya, la soja *soy* 3
su, sus *his, her, your, its, your* (pl.)*, their* 2
el suavizante (para el pelo) *hair conditioner* 8
subir *to go up, take up* 6
   subir al avión *to get on the airplane* 9
subvencionado *subsidized* 18
   la escuela pública subvencionada *charter school*
   18
la sucursal *branch (business)* 11
   el/la gerente de sucursal *branch manager* 11
el sudeste *southeast* 9
la suegra *mother-in-law* 15

el   suegro *father-in-law* 15
el   sueño *dream* 10
la   suerte *luck* 1
       por suerte *luckily* 11
el   suéter *sweater* 4
       suficiente, suficientes *enough* 2
       sufrir de *to have; to suffer from* 18
       sumamente *extremely* 2
       superdotado *very gifted* 11
       superior *advanced* 18
el   supermercado *supermarket* 1
       suponer (*irreg.*) *to suppose* 10
el   sur *south* 9
el   suroeste *southwest* 9
       suscribirse *to subscribe* 8
       suspender *to discontinue, suspend* 10
el   susto *fright* 11

el   taco *taco* 3
       tal vez *perhaps, maybe* 16
el   talento *talent* 17
el   taller mecánico *mechanic's shop* 4
       también *also, too* 1
       tampoco *neither, not either* 4
       tan *so* 4
las   tapas *tapas, hors d'oeuvres* 3
la   taquilla *ticket window* 9
       tardar *to take long* 15
       tardar en hacer algo *to take a long time to do
            something* 15
la   tarde *afternoon* 4
       tarde *late* 5
la   tarjeta *pass, card* 1
       tarjeta de crédito *credit card* 1
       tarjeta de embarque *boarding pass* 1
la   tasa *rate* 20
el   taxi *taxi cab* 4
el/la taxista *taxi driver* 3
la   taza *cup* 13
       te (*d.o.*) *you* (informal) 6
       te (*i.o.*) *you* (informal) 9
el   té *tea* 3
el   teatro *theater* 1
el   técnico, la técnica *technician* 4
la   tele *TV* 7
el   teléfono *telephone* 1
       teléfono celular *cell phone* 1
la   telenovela *TV serial drama* 7
el   teletrabajo *teleworking* 19
la   televisión *television* 4
el   televisor *TV set* 4
el   telón (del teatro) *(theater) curtain* 19
el   tema *topic* 1
       temer *to fear* 16
la   temperatura *temperature* 6
       temprano *early* 5
el   tenedor *fork* 13
       tener (*irreg.*) *to have* 6
       tener calor *to be warm* 7
       tener celos *to be jealous* 7
       tener frío *to be cold* 7
       tener ganas de + *inf. to feel like (doing
            something)* 6
       tener hambre *to be hungry* 7
       tener lugar *to take place* 13
       tener un niño *to have a child* 11
       tener que + *inf. to have to (do something)* 7

       tener sed *to be thirsty* 6
       tenga la bondad de + *inf. please* 14
el   tenis *tennis* 6
       jugar al tenis *to play tennis* 6
la   tentación *temptation* 6
       resistir a la tentación *to resist temptation* 6
       terco *stubborn* 12
la   terminal *terminal (airport)* 9
       terminar *to finish* 6
la   ternera *veal* 3
el/la terrorista *terrorist* 20
la   tía *aunt* 4
el   tiempo *time* 6; *weather* 6
los   tiempos que corren *nowadays* 16
la   tienda *store* 1
       tienda de campaña *tent* 11
       tienda de cómputo *computer store* 1
       tienda de deportes *sporting goods store* 1
       tienda de electrodomésticos *appliance store* 1
       tienda de ropa *clothing store* 1
       tienda de zapatos *shoe store* 1
       tienda por departamentos *department store* 1
la   tierra *land, ground* 9
       en la tierra *on the ground, landed* 9
       tomar tierra *to touch down (airplane)* 9
la   Tierra *Earth* 18
las   tijeras *pair of scissors* 18
el   timbre *doorbell* 7
       tímido *shy* 12
el   tinte para el cabello *hair coloring* 8
el   tío *uncle* 4
el   tipo *guy* 4
el   tobillo *ankle* 11
       tocar (c > qu/e) *to play (a musical instrument)* 5;
            to touch 9
       tocar un tema *to bring up a subject* 20
       tocarle a uno (*rev. constr.*) *to be one's turn* 15
el   tocino *bacon* 3
       todo, toda, todos, todas *all, the whole* 2
       todo el, toda la, todos los, todas las *all, every* 3
       todo el día *all day* 4
       tomar *to take; to drink* 5
       tomar el almuerzo/desayuno *to have lunch/
            breakfast* 5
       tomar apuntes *to take notes* 16
       tomar una copa *to have a drink* 5
       tomar (clases) en línea *to take (classes) online* 18
       tomar el sol *to sunbathe* 11
       tomar tierra *to touch down (airplane)* 9
el   tomate *tomato* 3
       tonto *silly, stupid* 4
la   tormenta *storm* 10
el   tornillo *screw* 19
la   torre *tower* 1
la   torta *cake* 3
la   tortilla *tortilla (Mexico), omelet (Spain)* 3
la   tos *cough* 1
       trabajador(a) *hardworking* 4
       trabajar *to work* 1
       trabajar de + *profession to work as a +
            profession* 17
el   trabajo *work, job* 4
       tradicional *traditional* 20
       traducir (*irreg.*) *to translate* 7
       traer (*irreg.*) *to bring, have with one* 7
el   tráfico *traffic* 11
la   tragedia *tragedy* 19

el traje *suit* 4
el trámite *step* 9
   hacer los trámites *to make arrangements* 9
   tranquilizarse (z > c/e) *to calm down, stop worrying* 8
   tranquilo *quiet* 2
   transitado *heavily trafficked* 2
el tranvía *trolley* 1
   trasladar *to transfer* 11
   tratar de + *inf. to try to (do something)* 6
   través: a través de *by means of, through* 9
las travesuras *pranks, mischief* 17
   tremendo *awful* 11
el tren *train* 1
   tren de alta velocidad *high-speed train* 9
   triste *sad* 4
   triunfar *to succeed* 10
el triunfo *triumph, success* 10
   tronar (o > ue) *to thunder* 6
   tropical *tropical* 10
   trotar *to jog* 5
   tu, tus *your* (informal) 2
   tumbado *lying* 4
el turismo *sightseeing* 5; *tourism* 20
   hacer el turismo *to go sightseeing* 5

el/la uberista *Uber driver* 3
   últimamente *lately* 8
   último *last* 12
   un *a, an* (before a masc. noun) 1
   un poco *a little* 4
   una *a, an* (before a fem. noun) 1
la uña *nail* 8
   único *only* 2
la universidad *university* 4
   universidad estatal *state university* 10
   universidad privada *private university* 10
el universo *universe* 18
   uno *one* 1
   urgente *urgent* 16
   urgir (g > j/o, a) *to be urgent/pressing* 16
   usar *to use* 6
   usted (Ud.) *you* (formal sing.) 3
   ustedes (Uds.) *you* (pl.)
   útil *useful* 2
los útiles escolares *school supplies* 18
la uva *grape* 15
las uvas pasas *raisins* 3

la vaca *cow* 10
las vacaciones *vacation* 4
   ir de vacaciones *to go on vacation* 5
la vacuna *vaccine* 18
la vacunación *vaccination* 18
   vale *okay* 20
   valer (*irreg.*) *to be worth, cost* 7
el valor *value* 15
   vanguardia: de vanguardia *leading-edge, innovative* 19
   varios, varias *several* 2
el vaso *glass* 13
el vecino, la vecina *neighbor* 6
   vegetariano *vegetarian* 5
la velocidad *speed* 9
el velorio *wake* 13
   vender *to sell* 6

   venir (*irreg.*) *to come* 7
la ventaja *advantage* 19
la ventana *window* 9
   el asiento de ventana *window seat* 9
   ver (*irreg.*) *to see* 7
el verano *summer* 5
la verdad *truth* 1
   de verdad *really* 18
   ¿verdad? *right?, isn't it?, don't you?* 4
   verdaderamente *really* 2
   verde *green* 2
las verduras *greens, green vegetables* 3
   verter (e > ie) *to pour* 17
el vestido *dress* 4
   vestirse (e > i) *to dress, get dressed* 8
el veterinario *veterinarian* 18
la vez *time, occasion* 1
   la última vez *the last time* 9
   una vez *once* 9
   viajar *to travel* 5
el viaje *trip* 4; *commute* 19
   hacer un viaje *to take a trip* 5
   viaje de negocios *business trip* 6
las vibraciones *vibrations* 20
la víctima *victim* 11
la vida *life* 10
el video *video* 7
el videojuego *video game* 14
la videollamada *videochat* 17
   viejo *old* 2
el viento *wind* 6
   hace viento *it's windy* 6
el viernes *Friday* 4
el vino *wine* 3
   violeta *purple* 2
el violín *violin* 5
la visita *visitor* 15
   estar de visita *to be visiting* 15
   visitar *to visit* 5
la vitamina *vitamin* 11
la viuda *widow* 13
el viudo *widower* 13
la vivienda *housing, housing unit, dwelling* 13
   vivir *to live* 6
   vivo *alive* 11
   volver (o > ue) *to return, go back* 6
   volver a + *inf. to (do something) again* 11
   volverse (o > ue) + *adj. to go/become* + adj. 17
la voz *voice* 1
el vuelo *flight* 9
   vuelo de conexión *connecting flight* 9
   vuelo directo *direct/nonstop flight* 9
   vuestro, vuestra *your* (Spain) 2

   y *and* 1
   ya *already* 4
   ya no *no more, no longer* 6
   yo *I* 3
el yoga *yoga* 5
   hacer yoga *to do yoga* 5

la zanahoria *carrot* 3
la zapatería *shoe store* 1
el zapato *shoe* 1
la zona *area* 2
el zoológico *zoo* 4

Index